PROGRAM FLOW ANALYSIS:
Theory and Applications

D0208260

PROGRAM FLOW ANALYSIS: THEORY AND APPLICATIONS

Steven S. Muchnick

University of California
Berkeley, California

University of Kansas
Lawrence, Kansas

Neil D. Jones

Aarhus University
Aarhus, Denmark

University of Kansas
Lawrence, Kansas

Prentice-Hall, Inc., Englewood Cliffs, New Jersey 07632

Library of Congress Cataloging in Publication Data

Main entry under title:

Program flow analysis.

   (Prentice-Hall software series)
   Bibliography: p.
   Includes index.
   1. Electronic digital computers—Programming.
I. Muchnick, Steven S., 1945– II. Jones, Neil D.
III. Series.
QA76.P75118   001.64'2   80-22759
ISBN 0-13-729681-9

Editorial/Production Supervision
  and Interior Design by KATHRYN GOLLIN MARSHAK
Cover Design by EDSAL ENTERPRISES
Manufacturing Buyer: JOYCE LEVATINO

© **1981 by Prentice-Hall, Inc., Englewood Cliffs, New Jersey 07632**

Printed in the United States of America

10 9 8 7 6 5 4 3 2 1

Prentice-Hall International, Inc., *London*
Prentice-Hall of Australia Pty. Limited, *Sydney*
Prentice-Hall of Canada, Ltd., *Toronto*
Prentice-Hall of India Private Limited, *New Delhi*
Prentice-Hall of Japan, Inc., *Tokyo*
Prentice-Hall of Southeast Asia Pte. Ltd., *Singapore*
Whitehall Books Limited, *Wellington, New Zealand*

Contributing Authors

F. E. ALLEN
*IBM Thomas J. Watson
Research Center
Yorktown Heights, New York*

LORI A. CLARKE
*University of Massachusetts
Amherst, Massachusetts*

JOHN COCKE
*IBM Thomas J. Watson
Research Center
Yorktown Heights, New York*

PATRICK COUSOT
*Scientific and Medical
University of Grenoble
Grenoble, France*

VERONIQUE DONZEAU-GOUGE
*INRIA LABORIA
Rocquencourt, France*

NEIL D. JONES
*University of Kansas
Lawrence, Kansas*

KEN KENNEDY
*Rice University
Houston, Texas*

ETIENNE MOREL
*CII—Honeywell Bull
Louveciennes, France*

STEVEN S. MUCHNICK
*University of Kansas
Lawrence, Kansas*

LEON OSTERWEIL
University of Colorado
Boulder, Colorado

AMIR PNUELI
University of Pennsylvania
Philadelphia, Pennsylvania
Tel Aviv University
Tel Aviv, Israel

CLAUDE RENVOISE
CII—Honeywell Bull
Louveciennes, France

DEBRA J. RICHARDSON
University of Massachusetts
Amherst, Massachusetts

BARRY K. ROSEN
IBM Thomas J. Watson
Research Center
Yorktown Heights, New York

MICHA SHARIR
New York University
New York, New York

REINHARD WILHELM
Technical University of Munich
Munich, West Germany

Contents

**Chapter 5   GLOBAL FLOW ANALYSIS AND OPTIMIZATION
IN THE MUG2 COMPILER GENERATING
SYSTEM   132**

REINHARD WILHELM

**Chapter 6   INTERPROCEDURAL ELIMINATION
OF PARTIAL REDUNDANCIES   160**

ETIENNE MOREL
CLAUDE RENVOISE

**Chapter 11   DENOTATIONAL DEFINITION OF PROPERTIES
OF PROGRAM COMPUTATIONS   343**

VERONIQUE DONZEAU-GOUGE

**Chapter 12   COMPLEXITY OF FLOW ANALYSIS, INDUCTIVE
ASSERTION SYNTHESIS, AND A LANGUAGE
DUE TO DIJKSTRA   380**

NEIL D. JONES
STEVEN S. MUCHNICK

Preface

Flow analysis is a tool for discovering properties of the run-time behavior of a program without actually running it. The properties discovered usually apply to all possible sequences of control and data flow, and so give global information impossible to obtain by individual runs or by inspection of only a part of the program. Frequently flow analysis can be viewed as executing the program in parallel over a symbolic, much-simplified version of its real data domain and hence is known alternately by the names *symbolic execution* or *abstract interpretation*. The information obtained from flow analysis can be used to drive the optimization phase of a compiler, to generate invariant assertions for program verification, to improve software reliability by aiding the generation of program documentation and automation of a large part of the debugging process, and to direct the actions of a content- and goal-oriented program development system.

. The purpose of this volume is to present a series of tutorial and research papers on the applications of flow analysis, as well as its methods and underlying theory. It is intended to enable the reader to determine whether flow analysis methods are applicable to problems he or she is concerned with and to provide guidance in carrying out such applications. The timing of this book has been determined by the emergence of flow analysis as a technique with applications outside of compiling. As few as three years ago a book on flow analysis would have been concerned entirely with low-level optimizations in compilers. These techniques are now recognized as being of much wider utility, and occasionally are taught in undergraduate compiler construction courses. Five or six years from now flow analysis may be as commonplace as automatic generation of parsers is now. At present, however, and for the next few years this is an area which will continue to grow rapidly both in its applications and in the firmness of its foundations.

The book is divided into four sections. The first introduces program flow analysis, the second and third concern applications to program optimization and to software engineering, respectively, and the fourth provides some theoretical underpinnings. Each section is introduced by a short overview of its subject area.

The first section contains two chapters, one by Kennedy and the other by Rosen. The Kennedy chapter surveys methods for performing data flow analysis in compilers. It concerns efficient algorithms for various types of flow analysis and some of the optimizations which can be based on the information obtained from the analysis. Rosen's chapter introduces a general theory of data flow analysis, emphasizing both principles and pitfalls. His starting point is the conception of numerical degrees of availability of an expression value, in contrast to the usual yes/no answer.

The second section contains five applications of flow analysis to program optimization. The chapter by Allen, Cocke, and Kennedy develops a general framework and a new algorithm for operator strength reduction, used to implement induction variables efficiently. The next chapter, by Jones and Muchnick, presents two models for analyzing data structures which together can be the basis for a quite sophisticated storage reclamation system for dynamic data structures in a language such as LISP, Pascal, or PL/I. Wilhelm describes in the following chapter a compiler generating system called MUG2 which makes extensive use of global flow analysis in the optimizing phases of the compilers it produces. Morel and Renvoise extend methods due to the same authors for eliminating redundant code within a procedure to global (interprocedural) redundant code elimination. The last chapter, by Sharir and Pnueli, develops two powerful techniques for interprocedural flow analysis.

The third section contains two chapters on applications of flow analysis to software engineering. The chapter by Osterweil presents a powerful methodology for program testing which depends in large part on flow-analytic methods. The other, by Clarke and Richardson, discusses three approaches to symbolic evaluation of programs and their application to program testing and (partial) verification.

The final section presents three aspects of the theoretical underpinnings of flow analysis. The first, by Patrick Cousot, defines systems of exact and approximate semantic equations associated with programs and elucidates their properties. Cousot relates them to program correctness, error detection (and hence debugging), and preexecution analysis. The next, by Veronique Donzeau-Gouge, shows how to derive flow analysis information from the denotational semantics of Scott and Strachey by considering nonstandard interpretations of the data domains. The final chapter, by Jones and Muchnick, obtains bounds on the computational complexity of two different types of flow analysis, and relates this to the complexity of program verification and of checking type consistency in a programming language proposed by Dijkstra.

Thus the book spans the gamut from highly theoretical foundations to thoroughly practical reporting of system developers' experience, and from surveys of existing work to frontier-level research. It is hoped the reader will find much here to interest him or her and will not neglect either end of this spectrum, as much is to be gained from a solid grounding in both theory and practice.

The book is intended for graduate students in computer science and their teachers, as well as for practitioners in the field. It will serve the needs of those requiring a survey of current research in the field or guidance in developing practical applications of data flow analysis methods, as it includes papers which represent the state of the art in both areas.

We would like to thank the contributing authors for their efforts and patience; Susan Walker, Deena Kerbow, and Linda McClain for typing much of the manuscript; and Deena Kerbow and Nuzhat Haneef for unifying the bibliography.

STEVEN S. MUCHNICK
Berkeley, California

NEIL D. JONES
Aarhus, Denmark

PROGRAM FLOW ANALYSIS:
Theory and Applications

Part I

INTRODUCTION TO PROGRAM FLOW ANALYSIS

Program flow analysis originated as a technique to statically determine properties of programs to be exploited in the optimization phase of a compiler,† and so it is appropriate that we begin this volume with two papers which survey this area. The first, by Kenneth Kennedy, discusses some of the properties flow analysis can discover, shows how to formulate them in a flow-analytic framework, and gives a series of algorithms for performing the resulting analyses. It presents an excellent, practically oriented introduction to the subject. The second chapter, by Barry Rosen, introduces the theory of data flow analysis by showing how to cast a specific problem, determining degrees of availability of complex expression values, in a general theoretical framework. It pays particular attention to possible theoretical pitfalls, especially those resulting from making design decisions too early in the specification of a problem or its solution method. Thus the first of these chapters will provide a broad overview of the capabilities of flow analysis in compiling

†According to Hecht [Hech 77], it was probably first used by Vyssotsky as long ago as 1961 as part of a compile-time diagnostic facility for a Bell Laboratories IBM 7090 FORTRAN II compiler.

and specific approaches to its immediate use in practical situations, while the other will prepare the reader to design flow-analytic approaches to as yet unexplored problems.

But flow analysis is a method with much wider applicability than just to optimization in compilers. It can, for example, be used to generate invariant assertions for program verifiers [Cous77c], to provide semantic content for a goal-oriented program development system [RicC76, Hewi75], and to improve software reliability by aiding in debugging and the production of documentation as discussed in Part III.

In its most general form, it is a method for finitely describing what a program does to its data. The resulting description may be either exact, as in the case of generating inductive assertions, or approximate, as in determining expression availability, deducing data types of variables, and most other applications. Whereas actual execution of a program produces the sequence of states the data and control pass through, flow analysis produces instead a so-called static semantics: for each possible point of control in the program, it gives a finite description of the set of data states the program could be in when execution passes through that point. For example, consider the program below. Let $\perp$ represent the undefined value, n the value input

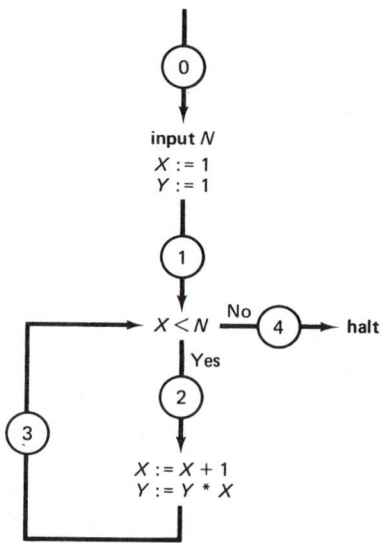

for N and $\langle N, X, Y \rangle$ the values of the three variables, respectively. Then any possible computation could be represented by a sequence as follows:

Control state   Data state

$$
\begin{array}{ll}
\textcircled{0} & \langle \bot, \bot, \bot \rangle \\
\textcircled{1} & \langle n, 1, 1 \rangle \\
\left. \begin{array}{l} \textcircled{2} \\ \textcircled{3} \end{array} \right. & \left. \begin{array}{l} \langle n, i, i! \rangle \\ \langle n, i + 1, (i + 1)! \rangle \end{array} \right\} i = 1, 2, \ldots, n - 1 \\
\textcircled{4} & \langle n, \max(1, n), (\max(1, n))! \rangle
\end{array}
$$

The corresponding static semantics would describe the set of all possible computations by means of a function F from program points to sets of triples of values given by

$$
\begin{aligned}
F(\textcircled{0}) &= \{\langle \bot, \bot, \bot \rangle\} \\
F(\textcircled{1}) &= \{\langle n, 1, 1 \rangle \,|\, n \in N\} \\
F(\textcircled{2}) &= \{\langle n, i, i! \rangle \,|\, i < n\} \\
F(\textcircled{3}) &= \{\langle n, i + 1, (i + 1)! \rangle \,|\, i < n\} \\
F(\textcircled{4}) &= \{\langle n, n, n! \rangle \,|\, n \in N\}
\end{aligned}
$$

Data flow properties can then be viewed as approximate descriptions of the static semantics—approximate in the sense that they do not provide full information, not in the sense that they may be incorrect. An instance of such a property is the statement that the value of each variable is positive whenever it is defined [Sint72], and may easily be derived from this program by the rule of signs. Instead of executing the program over the integers, we execute it over the abstract data domain $\{\bot, \text{negative}, \text{zero}, \text{positive}, \top\}$, where $\top$ represents unknown sign; instead of interpreting $X := Y * X$ as multiplication, we interpret it as asserting that the product of two positive numbers is positive, and so on. Since we cannot decide whether $X < N$ in this model if we merely know that the values of both are positive, we assume both outcomes are possible. In this way we obtain information which is useful and which applies to all possible executions of the program for any input values. Further, it can be obtained without actually executing the program for any real data at all.

We leave the description of appropriate methods for data flow analysis to the first chapter.

Chapter 1

A Survey
of Data Flow
Analysis Techniques

Ken Kennedy

1-1. INTRODUCTION

High-level programming languages are valuable programming tools because they permit the specification of algorithms in notations more natural for expressing the abstract concepts involved. Thus, freed from attending to numerous machine-dependent implementation details, the programmer can produce correct, reliable code more easily. Why then aren't such languages universally used for programming? The usual answer is that the resulting programs are inefficient. That is, the code generated by a high-level language is less efficient than the code a good assembly language programmer would write. The problem is that the generality of programming languages, the very generality which is such a desirable aid to algorithm specification, prevents the programmer from making use of specific machine features to improve the efficiency of the code. Unfortunately, compilers for these languages fail to take up enough of the slack. Since a major aim of programming languages is to encourage programming at a more abstract level, there must be an improvement in the efficiency of object programs produced by compilers. This is the goal of compiler optimization.

Note that optimization is not intended to compensate for poor programming, but rather to reduce the inefficiencies in code to within "reasonable" bounds—to a point where the advantages of high-level language programming outweigh any remaining efficiency penalties. For some languages, optimizing compilers might well be expected to produce code for inner loops that would be competitive with loops hand-coded by assembly language programmers.

This last goal is difficult to achieve because high-level languages, if they are to be usable, must include general-purpose features flexible enough to serve many different applications. It is not enough to merely include a grab bag of specialized features because programmers would find such a grab bag difficult to learn and use. The assembly language expert can write efficient code because he or she knows the specific purpose to which each data structure in a particular program will be put; therefore the language expert can choose for each structure the machine realization that will be most efficient. By contrast, the high-level language programmer must use one of the general-purpose data structures provided by the language. In the absence of better information, the compiler generates code for accesses to these structures which will be correct for any legal application. Thus it is unable to take advantage of any efficient shortcuts which the specific problem at hand might allow. If the compiler is to compete with assembly language coding, it must be able to determine enough of the nature of the program being compiled to safely take those shortcuts; in other words, it must be able to perform some kind of global program analysis.

As an example, consider run-time subscript range checking. It is desirable to capture all attempts to reference outside the limits of an array because out-of-bounds references are the sources of many subtle errors. Unfortunately, range checks are expensive and can result in a significant speed degradation. Optimization offers a viable alternative to the common but questionable practice of eliminating all range checks: global program analysis can show that many range checks are superfluous, while others may be safely moved to less frequently executed code [Harr77a, Suzu77]. The result will be more efficient programs without the cost of compromised reliability.

There is a widely held notion that optimization is intended to compensate for bad programming. Nothing could be further from the truth. In fact, no currently known technique can compensate for the main component of bad programming: a poor choice of algorithm. Instead, optimization encourages *good* programming by making high-level languages more attractive and by taking care of small matters of efficiency so the programmer is free to concentrate on the essence of the problem.

A variety of code improvement transformations have been proposed in the literature; I won't attempt to discuss them all since they are covered in two important compendia: The Allen-Cocke catalogue [Alle72a] and the "Irvine Catalogue" [Stan76]. But as background for the discussion of analysis methods, I will mention the most prominent techniques. First, two transformations are fundamental to optimization in straight-line code.

(a) *Redundant subexpression elimination* [Cock70a, Fong77]. If two instructions that both compute the expression $A * B$ are separated by code which contains no store into either A or B, then the second instruction can be eliminated if the result of the first is saved.

(b) *Constant folding* [Cock70b]. If all the inputs to an instruction are constants whose values are known, the result of the instruction can be computed at compile time and the instruction replaced by a "load" of the constant value.

In simple loops, two more transformations can lead to significant improvements.

(c) *Code motion* [Cock70a, Cock70b]. Instructions that depend only upon variables whose values do not change in a loop may be moved out of the loop, improving performance by reducing the instructions' frequency of execution.

(d) *Strength reduction* [Alle69, Cock77, Fong76, Paig77, Alle79]. Instructions that depend on the loop induction variable cannot be moved out of the loop, but sometimes they can be replaced by less expensive instructions. For example, in the loop

$$I := 1;$$
while $I < 100$ **do**

$$\cdot$$
$$\cdot$$

$$A := I * 5;$$

$$\cdot$$

$$\cdot$$

$$I := I + 1$$
od

the value of $I * 5$ can be saved in a temporary T whose value is incremented by 5 on each iteration; $I * 5$ can then be replaced by a load from T as shown below.

$$I := 1;$$
$$T := 5;$$
while $I < 100$ **do**

$$\cdot$$

$$\cdot$$

$$A := T;$$

$$\cdot$$

$$\cdot$$

$$I := I + 1;$$
$$T := T + 5$$

od

In effect, the multiplication has been replaced by an addition.

Automatic introduction of instructions at new positions in a program (à la code motion) gives rise to two important questions. First, the *safety* question asks whether the new instruction can cause an error interrupt that would not have occurred in the original program. This problem can be illustrated by the example in Fig. 1-1. It is easy to see that if a computation of

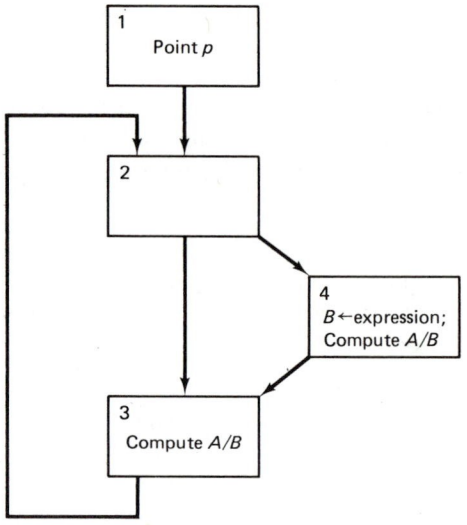

Figure 1-1   Safety example

A/B is inserted at point p in block 1, the computation in block 3 becomes redundant and can be eliminated. But what if the purpose of the branch from block 2 to block 3 is to prevent an attempt to divide by zero? Moving A/B to block 1 might well introduce an error interrupt that the programmer has been careful to avoid.

The question of *profitability* asks whether we are really moving code to a region of less frequent execution. Most compilers assume that code inside a loop is executed more often than code outside the loop, but this assumption could be wrong if there are several alternative branches within the loop. It is possible to do a fairly complete job of frequency estimation [Cock76], but few compilers make the attempt since it is not known whether the benefits will justify the cost.

Both "constant folding" and "redundant subexpression elimination," introduced earlier as local optimizations, can be applied on a global scale as well. Complementing these are two new global optimizations that "clean up" after other transformations.

(e) *Variable folding* [Lowr69]. Instructions of the form $A := B$ will become useless if B can be substituted for subsequent uses of A.

(f) *Dead code elimination* [Kenn75c]. If transformations like variable folding are successful, there will be many instructions whose results are never used. Dead code elimination detects and deletes such instructions.

An extremely important class of transformations is intended to improve the efficiency of procedure invocation.

(g) *Procedure integration* [Alle72a]. Under certain circumstances, a procedure call can be replaced by the body of the procedure being called (open linkage); in other cases the overhead associated with standard calling sequences, parameters, and global variables can be reduced by compiling the procedure with the calling program (semiopen linkage).

Procedure integration is an extremely important optimization because procedure calls, desirable from the point of view of programming methodology, are often unbelievably inefficient in nonoptimizing compilers. Thus good modular programming is penalized rather than rewarded by most compilers.

The last three optimizations are classified as "machine-dependent" because they aim to increase efficiency by taking advantage of special features of the target machine.

(h) *Register allocation* [Beat74]. This optimization seeks to eliminate load and store instructions by assigning variables to CPU registers whenever possible.

(i) *Instruction scheduling* [Seth70, Beat72]. The proper arrangement of instructions often leads to improved performance. Different machines give rise to different scheduling criteria: on a machine with pipelined arithmetic units the goal is to achieve maximum parallelism, while on simpler machines the goal is to minimize register usage.

(j) *Detection of parallelism* [Schn75]. For vector machines it is desirable to detect inherently parallel operations and code them as vector instructions.

This list is by no means complete, but it gives the flavor of some typical optimizing transformations. For those interested in reading further, an excellent introductory treatment of optimization appears in [Aho77], and Knuth's famous empirical study [Knut71] demonstrates the utility of various optimization techniques.

1-2. OPTIMIZATION IN BASIC BLOCKS

One of the first steps in analyzing a program for the purpose of code improvement is to subdivide the program into *basic blocks*, which are simply sequences of consecutive instructions that are always executed from start to finish. In other words, a basic block may only be entered at the first instruction and left at the last. Fig. 1-2 shows how a PL/I program would be parti-

```
REPT:   GET LIST(A,B,C);   1
        IF A = 0   THEN  STOP;   2
        DISC = B*B − 4.0*A*C;   3
        IF DISC > = 0  THEN DO;
              DROOT = SQRT(DISC);                4
              R1 = (−B + DROOT)/(2.0*A);
              R2 = (−B − DROOT)/(2.0*A);
              END;
        ELSE DO;
              DROOT = SQRT(−DISC);   5
              R1 = −B/(2.0*A);
              R2 = DROOT/(2.0*A);
              END;
        PUT DATA(DISC,R1,R2);   6
        GO TO REPT;
```

Figure 1-2 A PL/I program fragment partitioned into basic blocks

tioned into basic blocks. Of course, in a compiler the partitioning is usually performed on some intermediate code representation of the program.

The subdivision process itself is fairly straightforward. I present a method adapted from [Aho77] that identifies a set of *leader instructions*, instructions which begin basic blocks, and then constructs a block by appending to its leader all subsequent instructions up to, but not including, the next leader. The algorithm is informally specified in an Algol-like high-level language which admits set theoretic notation.

Algorithm BB: Basic Block Partition

Input: A program PROG in which instructions are numbered in sequence from 1 to |PROG|. INST(i) denotes the ith instruction.

Output:
1. The set LEADERS of initial block instructions.
2. $\forall x \in$ LEADERS, the set BLOCK(x) of all instructions in the block beginning at x.

Method:

```
begin
    LEADERS := {1}; ¢ first instruction in PROG ¢
    for i := 1 to |PROG| do
        if INST(i) is a branch
            then add the index of each potential target to LEADERS
        fi
    od;
    TODO := LEADERS;
    while TODO ≠ φ do
        x := element of TODO with smallest index;
        TODO := TODO − {x};
        BLOCK(x) := {x};
        for i := x + 1 to {PROG} while i ∉ LEADERS do
            BLOCK(x) := BLOCK(x) ∪ {i}
        od
    od
end
```

Once the program is subdivided into blocks, each block can be optimized using local techniques. In this section I will describe the *value numbering* scheme of Cocke and Schwartz [Cock70b], which performs redundant expression elimination and constant folding in straight-line code. As a side effect, the method can also compute some of the information used by the global analysis methods treated later.

Suppose the source language version of a basic block under consideration is as follows:

$$A := 4$$
$$K := I * J + 5$$
$$L := 5 * A * K$$
$$M := I$$
$$B := M * J + I * A$$

This might be transformed into the intermediate code in Table 1-1.

Table 1-1. Intermediate code example.

$T1: A := C4$	$T5: C5 * A$	$T9: M * J$
$T2: I * J$	$T6: T5 * K$	$T10: I * A$
$T3: T2 + C5$	$T7: L := T6$	$T11: T9 + T10$
$T4: K := T3$	$T8: M := I$	$T12: B := T11$

Each triple in this code represents a simple operation; operands may be variables, constants (e.g., $C4$), or the results of previous operations (e.g., $T2$).

The main data structure of the *value numbering* method is a hash-coded *table of available expressions* which is used to help uncover redundant subexpressions. As each triple is treated in sequence from the start of a block, the table is searched for a previous instance of the same expression. If a match is found, the new triple may be eliminated if all subsequent references to it are replaced by references to the previous triple.

For the method to work, there must be some way to determine when two operands are identical. This is provided by a system of *value numbers* in which each distinct value created or used within the block receives a unique identifying number. Two entities have the same value number only if, based upon information from the block alone, their values are provably identical. For example, after scanning the first instruction in Table 1-1,

$$T1: \ A := C4$$

variable A and constant $C4$ would have the same value number. The "current" value number associated with a variable (or constant) is kept in the symbol table entry for that variable; the value number for the result of a triple is kept in the table of available computations and as an auxiliary field of the triple itself. The hash function for entry to the available expression table is based on the value numbers of the operands and a special code for the operator.

Constant folding is handled via an auxiliary bit in each symbol table entry, indicating whether the current value is a constant, and a bit in each triple, indicating whether the result is a constant. Also required is a table of constants, indexed by value number, which contains the actual run-time values of constants.

Algorithm VN, presented in a high-level mixture of English and Algol, embodies the ideas discussed so far. Note that an instruction is assumed to be the value of a structured variable with an operator field OP, some auxiliary information, and two operands L and R (left and right, respectively).

Algorithm VN: Value Numbering in a Basic Block

Input:
1. A basic block of triples.
2. A symbol table SYMTAB.

Output: An improved basic block, after redundant subexpression elimination and constant folding.

Intermediate:
1. Table of available expressions AVAILTAB.
2. Table of constants CONSTVAL.

Method:

```
begin
    while there is another instruction do
        INSTR := the next instruction;
        OPERATOR := OP of INSTR;
        if OPERATOR = store then
            find r, the value number of R of INSTR
                (this may assign a new value number);
            if r represents a constant value then
                so indicate in the SYMTAB entry for L of INSTR
            fi
        else ¢ an expression ¢
            find value numbers l,r for L of INSTR and R of INSTR
                (this may assign new value numbers);
            if l and r represent constant values then
                compute the value x of the result by applying OPERA-
                    TOR to CONSTVAL(l) and CONSTVAL(r);
                enter the new constant x in CONSTVAL, assigning a new
                    value number in the process;
                delete INSTR
            else ¢ check for availability ¢
                look up the triple ⟨l,operator,r⟩ in AVAILTAB, setting
                    FOUND := true if successful;
                if FOUND then
                    record the fact that any reference to this triple is to be
                        subsumed by a reference to the previous one (a
                        pointer to which is contained in AVAIL);
                    delete INSTR;
                else ¢ not available ¢
                    enter ⟨l,operator,r⟩ in AVAILTAB, assigning a new
                        value number to the result
                fi
            fi
        fi
    od
end
```

Consider the application of this algorithm to the example intermediate code from Table 1-1.

In processing triples 1 through 4, nothing unusual takes place. Value numbers are assigned to variables A, I, J, and K and to constants $C4$ and $C5$. The results of triples $T2$ and $T3$ are recorded as available. The information collected up to this point is displayed in Fig. 1-3.

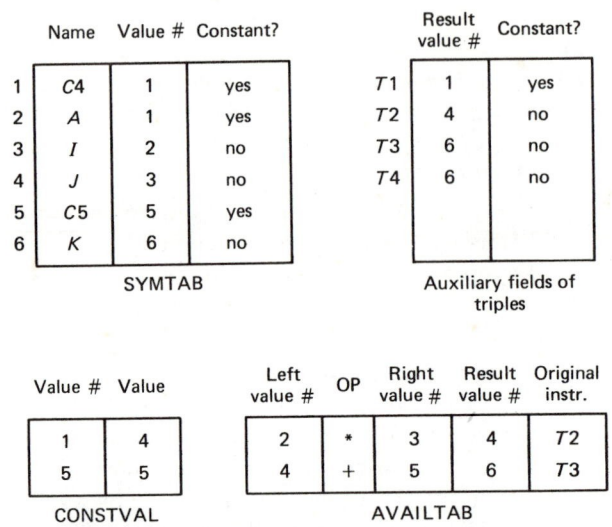

Figure 1-3 Information collected up to instruction 5

At instruction 5, the algorithm looks up $C5$ and A and discovers that they are both constant. The resulting $C20$ may be computed from values in CONSTVAL; it receives a new value number (7) and is recorded in CONSTVAL. Finally, triple 5 is deleted. In the next step, triple 6 will be modified to use $C20$ in place of $T5$.

Figure 1-4 displays the information collected by the algorithm up to instruction 9. At this point it discovers that operands M and J have value numbers 2 and 3, respectively, and that there is a previous computation ($T2$) of the product of these values. Therefore triple 9 can be deleted and subsequent references to it replaced by references to $T2$. The final optimized code is shown in Table 1-2.

Table 1-2 Final optimized code

$T1: A := C4$	$T6: C20 * K$	$T10: I * A$
$T2: I * J$	$T7: L := T6$	$T11: T2 + T10$
$T3: T2 + C5$	$T8: M := I$	$T12: B := T11$
$T4: K := T3$		

It is especially interesting that instruction 9 is discovered to be identical to $I * J$ even though an alias is used for I.

The method I have described is an elementary prototype of more sophisticated versions which can also handle array references and structured variables [Cock70b, Aho77, Kenn78].

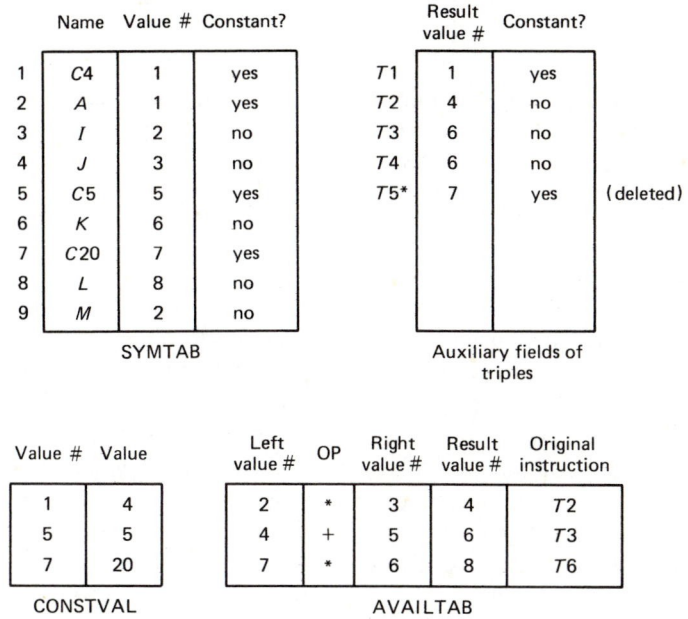

Figure 1-4 Information collected up to instruction 9

An important side effect of this or any other basic block analysis routine is that it can be modified to compute certain sets which are useful in determining global information. For example, the final version of the available computations table can be used to determine the set of expressions which are "available on exit" from the block. In the next section we turn to the problem of performing global analysis once we have such sets for each basic block.

1-3. GLOBAL DATA FLOW ANALYSIS

While analysis within basic blocks can lead to substantial improvements in a program, larger gains may be achieved by going a step further and gathering information on a global scale. For example, suppose the expression $A * B$ in block b is not eliminated by local methods; that is, there is no earlier computation of $A * B$ in b. Suppose also that neither A nor B is redefined in b prior to the computation of $A * B$. If we can prove that, no matter what control path is to be taken at run-time, $A * B$ will always be computed before control reaches b, then we can still eliminate the computation in b. Establishing facts like this requires an analysis of control flow in the program that is thorough enough to yield useful information about data relationships.

In essence, the problem is this: Given control flow structure, we must discern the nature of the data flow (which definitions of program quantities can affect which uses) within the program. The questions about data flow fall into two classes:

1. Those which, given a point in the program, ask what can happen before control reaches that point (i.e., what definitions can affect computations at that point);

2. Those which, given a point in the program, ask what can happen after control leaves that point (i.e., what uses can be affected by computations at that point).

Class 1 problems are usually called *forward flow* problems, while class 2 problems are *backward flow* problems. The gathering of information to solve problems of either class is accomplished in two phases. Once the program is subdivided into basic blocks, possible block-to-block transfers are noted and program loops are found. This phase is known as *control flow analysis*. Next the information about how uses and definitions relate to one another is gleaned in the *global data flow analysis* phase. The construction of data flow information is difficult because most nontrivial programs have complex control flow graphs; nevertheless, a number of solution methods exist. In this chapter I shall outline a few of the most important.

The control flow of a program may be represented as a directed graph $G = (N, E, n_0)$ where N is the set of nodes, E is the set of edges, and n_0 is the program entry node. In this model, nodes represent basic blocks and edges represent possible block-to-block transfers. Figure 1-5 shows the control flow graph corresponding to the PL/I program in Fig. 1-2.

Two special notations will be used frequently in discussing control flow

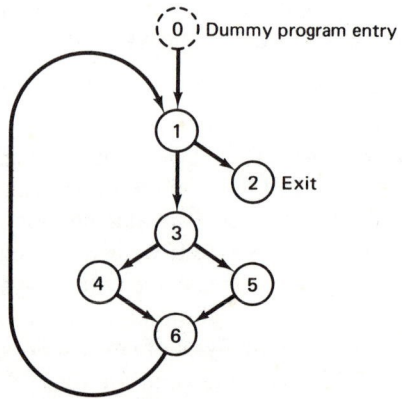

Figure 1-5   Control flow graph for Fig. 1-2

graphs. The *successor set* $S(x)$ for a node x is defined as

$$S(x) = \{y \in N \,|\, (x, y) \in E\}$$

and the *predecessor set* $P(x)$ is

$$P(x) = \{y \in N \,|\, (y, x) \in E\}$$

A *simple path* in G is a sequence of nodes $(n_1, n_2, \ldots, n_k)$ such that all nodes are distinct and $(n_i, n_{i+1}) \in E$, $1 \leq i < k$. A *simple cycle* is a simple path except that $n_1 = n_k$.

We shall use as examples two problems which are typical of class 1 and 2 data flow problems.

(a) *Available expression analysis.* We say that an expression is *defined* at a point if the value of that expression is computed there. An expression is said to be *killed* by a redefinition of one of its argument variables. In these terms an expression is *available* at point p in G if every path leading to p contains a prior definition of that expression which is not subsequently killed. Let AVAIL(b) be the set of expressions available on entry to block b. We define a system of equations for AVAIL(b), $b \in N$, in terms of sets which can be computed from local information. Let NKILL(b) be the set of expressions which are not killed in block b and DEF(b) be the set of expressions which are defined in b without being subsequently killed in b, i.e., the set of expressions which are always available on exit from b. These definitions lead directly to the system of equations:

$$\text{AVAIL}(b) = \bigcap_{x \in P(b)} (\text{DEF}(x) \cup (\text{AVAIL}(x) \cap \text{NKILL}(x))) \qquad (1\text{-}1)$$

Solution of this system will provide the desired global information.

(b) *Live variable analysis.* A path in $G = (N, E, n_0)$ is said to be *X-clear* if that path contains no assignment to the variable X. The variable X is *live* at point p in G if there exists an X-clear path from p to a use of X. Let LIVE(b) be the set of variables which are live on entry to block b. Once again we seek a system of equations for the live sets in terms of local sets. Let IN(b) be the set of variables which are live on entry to b because of a use within b, and let THRU(b) be the set of variables which are redefined in b. The following system of equations is the result:

$$\text{LIVE}(b) = \text{IN}(b) \cup \bigcup_{x \in S(b)} (\text{THRU}(b) \cap \text{LIVE}(x)) \qquad (1\text{-}2)$$

Similar equation systems can be developed for most data flow analysis problems. In fact, Kildall [Kild73], Kam and Ullman [Kam76], Graham and Wegman [Grah76], and Tarjan [Tarj75b] all formalized their treatment of data flow analysis by providing axioms for "acceptable" equation systems, thus unifying their methods. To show that a particular problem can be handled by a standard algorithm, one need only show that the sets of quantities and rules for combining the sets at control flow junctions satisfy the required axioms. This approach simplifies the discussion of data flow methods. Curiously, it has also contributed to the classification of the algorithms by ranges of applicability [Kam76, Fong77]. Fast solution methods to these problems have taken a number of forms. Nine such methods are surveyed here, four in detail.

1-3.1. Iterative Techniques

Perhaps the simplest approach to data flow analysis is to iterate through the nodes of the graph applying the appropriate equations until no changes take place. Such a method has been studied by Hecht and Ullman [Hech76, Ullm73] and subsequently by Kennedy [Kenn76]. Here is the iterative algorithm for live variable analysis.

Algorithm IT: Iterative Live Analysis

Input: IN(b), THRU(b), $\forall b \in N$.
Output: LIVE(b), $\forall b \in N$.
Method:

> **begin**
>   **for all** $b \in N$ **do** LIVE(b) := IN(b) **od**;
>   *change* := **true**;
>   **while** *change* **do**
>   *change* := **false**;
>   **for all** $b \in N$ **do**
>   oldlive := LIVE(b);
>   LIVE(b) := IN(b) $\cup \bigcup\limits_{x \in S(b)}$ (THRU(b) $\cap$ LIVE(x));
>   **if** LIVE(b) $\neq$ oldlive **then** change := **true fi**
>   **od**
>   **od**
> **end**

If $n = |N|$, this algorithm requires $O(n^2)$ extended (or "bit vector") steps for the entire computation. Kildall [Kild73] has described a very general form of the iterative algorithm using lattice theory, while Kam and Ullman [Kam76] have shown that there exist optimization problems for which the iterative algorithm does not converge rapidly—for example, constant propagation.

1-3.2. Nested Strongly Connected Regions

A somewhat structured approach to data flow is based upon the loop organization in the program. This method proceeds from local to global analysis by first extending data flow information to inner loops, then effectively collapsing these loops to single nodes before continuing to the next level. Many optimizations such as code motion can be performed in stages using this method with code being "bubbled" outward to less frequently executed regions. This is the technique originally used by Allen [Alle69]. The difficulty is that it is not always easy to find a suitable collection of nested strongly connected regions. The accepted way of locating such a collection was first devised by Earnest, Balke, and Anderson [Earn72]; it involves the application of two ordering algorithms on the nodes of the control flow graph. Earnest [Earn74] continued this work by presenting a number of optimization algorithms which used nested regions. Beatty [Beat74] has developed an elegant register assignment algorithm using this method.

1-3.3. Interval Analysis

A simpler way to partition the control flow graph into regions was developed by Cocke and Allen [Alle70, Alle71, Cock70a, Alle76]. An *interval* in G is defined to be a set I of blocks with the following properties:

1. There is a node $h \in I$, called the *head* of I, which is contained in every control flow from a block outside I to a block within I; i.e., I is a single-entry region.

2. I is connected. (This property is trivial if G is connected.)

3. $I - \{h\}$ is cycle-free; i.e., all cycles within I must contain h.

Given a node h in some graph G, the following algorithm, due to Allen and Cocke [Alle76], constructs MAXI(h), the maximal interval with head h. In presenting the algorithm, I use the notation $S[M]$, where M is a set of nodes, to mean

$$\bigcup_{x \in M} S(x)$$

that is, the set of successors of nodes in M.

Algorithm MI: Maximum Interval Construction.

Input: The specified head h.
Output: MAXI(h).
Method:

```
begin
    I := {h};
    while ∃ x ∈ (S[i] − I) such that P(x) ⊂ I
        do
            I := I ∪ {x̃}
        od;
    MAXI(h) := I
end
```

As we shall see, the order in which Algorithm MI adds nodes to an interval I is important, so it is usually given a name: *interval order*. Interval order is a total ordering on I which preserves the partial order generated by the subgraph $I - \{h\}$. The significance is that if nodes of I are processed in interval order, a particular node $x(\neq h)$ will be treated only after every node in $P(x)$ has been processed. Similarly, if I is processed in *reverse interval order*, every node in $S(x) \cap I$ will be treated before x is. These order-of-processing observations are crucial to data flow algorithms based on intervals.

Using Algorithm MI as a subprogram, the following algorithm, also due to Allen and Cocke [Alle76], partitions a flow graph into a set of disjoint intervals. Algorithm IP is based upon the observation that any node which is the successor of some node in interval I, but which is not in I itself, must be the head of some other interval J.

Algorithm IP : Interval Partition.

Input: A flow graph $G = (N, E, n_0)$.
Output: A set INTS(G) of disjoint intervals which form a partition of G.
Auxiliary:
  A set H of potential interval heads.
  A set DONE of heads for which intervals have been computed.
Method:

> **begin** ¢ the program entry n_0 is a head ¢
> $\quad H := \{n_0\};$
> $\quad \text{DONE} := \phi;$
> **while** $H \neq \phi$ **do**
> $\quad\quad x := $ an arbitrary node in H;
> $\quad\quad$ find MAXI(x) using Algorithm MI;
> $\quad\quad$ INTS(G) := INTS(G) $\cup$ {MAXI(x)};
> $\quad\quad$ ¢ add new heads ¢
> $\quad\quad\quad H := H \cup (S[\text{MAXI}(x)] - \text{MAXI}(x) - \text{DONE})$
> $\quad$ **od**
> **end**

As an example, consider the flow graph displayed in Fig. 1-6. When Algorithm IP is applied to this graph, it identifies nodes 1, 2, and 5 as interval heads; the corresponding intervals are $\{1\}$, $\{2, 3, 4\}$ and $\{5, 6, 7\}$.

For a given flow graph G, the *derived flow graph* $I(G)$ is defined as follows:

1. The nodes of $I(G)$ are the intervals in INTS(G).

2. If J, K are two intervals, there is an edge from J to K in $I(G)$ if and only if there exist nodes $n_J \in J$ and $n_K \in K$ such that n_K is a successor of n_J in G. Note that n_K must be the head of K.

3. The initial node of $I(G)$ is MAXI(n_0).

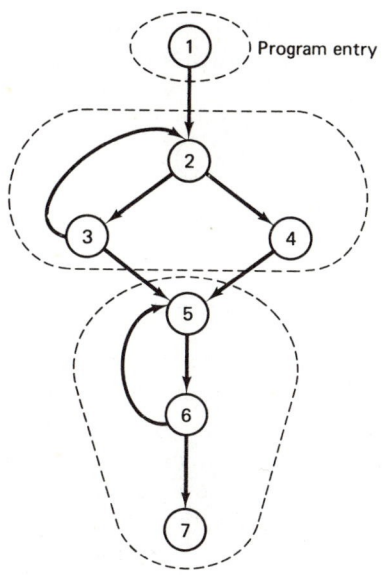

Figure 1-6 A flow graph with intervals

The sequence $(G_0, G_1, \ldots, G_m)$ is called the *derived sequence* for G if $G = G_0$, $G_{i+1} = I(G_i)$, $G_{m-1} \neq G_m$, and $I(G_m) = G_m$. G_i is called the *derived graph of order i* and G_m is the *limit flow graph* of G. A flow graph is said to be *reducible* if and only if its limit flow graph is the trivial flow graph, a single node with no edge; otherwise, the flow graph is *nonreducible* [Alle70, Alle76, Cock70b].

Figure 1-7 shows the rest of the derived sequence for the example in Fig. 1-6.

In this example, the graph is reducible; however, that will not always be

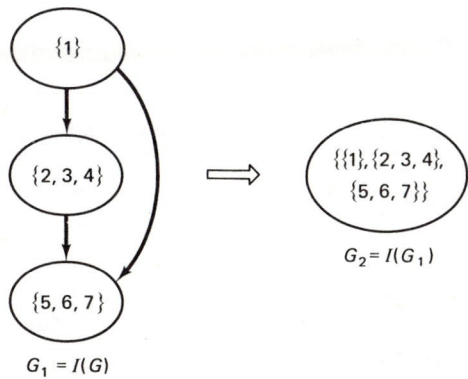

Figure 1-7 Derived sequence for Fig. 1-6

the case, as Fig. 1-8 demonstrates. If we apply Algorithm IP to this graph, the result will be the same graph—each node is an interval unto itself.

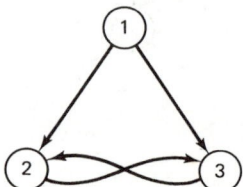

Figure 1-8   A nonreducible graph

As it happens, the data flow analysis algorithms based on intervals work only for reducible graphs, so nonreducibility could present a serious obstacle. However, we are able to ignore this problem for two reasons. First, three empirical studies have shown that flow graphs arising from actual computer programs are almost always reducible, i.e., more than 95% of the time [Alle72, Knut71, Kenn77]. Second, any nonreducible graph can be transformed to a reducible one by a process known as *node splitting* [Cock70b]. Figure 1-9 shows a split version of Fig. 1-8; the new graph, semantically identical to the old one, has been made reducible through the use of an exact copy of node 3.

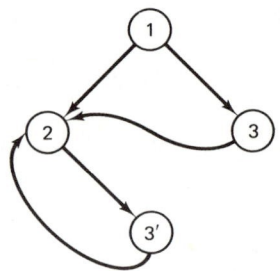

Figure 1-9   Split version of Fig. 1-8

Thus, secure in the knowledge that node splitting can always be applied in those rare cases where a graph fails to reduce, we can concentrate on finding fast data flow algorithms for reducible flow graphs.

Like all approaches which are based upon a program's control flow structure, the interval partition gives rise to a two-pass algorithm for data flow analysis. I will discuss the method as it applies to live analysis, treating each pass separately.

(a) *Pass 1: local to global.* During the first pass, local quantities IN and THRU are computed for larger and larger regions of the program. The heart of this pass is Algorithm I1 below, which computes IN and THRU for an interval from their values for blocks in the interval. Note that a second parameter has been added to THRU to indicate a particular successor; this permits handling of THRU for composite regions like intervals.

Algorithm I1 : Interval Pass 1.

> *Input:*
> 1. An interval I.
> 2. $IN(x)$, $\forall x \in I$; $THRU(x, y)$, $\forall x \in I$, $\forall y \in S(x)$.
> *Output:* $IN(I)$; $THRU(I, J)$, $\forall J \in S(I)$.
> *Auxiliary:* For each $x \in I$, $PATH(x)$, the set of variables A for which there is a clear path (not containing a store into A) from the entry of I to the entry of x.
> *Method:*

> > **begin**
> > $IN(I) := IN(h)$;
> > $PATH(h) := \Omega$ ¢ $\Omega = $ set of all variables ¢
> >   **for all** $x \in I - \{h\}$ in interval order **do**
> > $PATH(x) := \bigcup_{x \in P(x)} (PATH(y) \cap THRU(y,x))$;
> > $IN(I) := IN(I) \cup (PATH(x) \cap IN(x))$
> >   **od**;
> >   ¢ let h_J denote the head of J ¢
> >   **for** J such that $h_J \in S[I]$ **do**
> > $THRU(I,J) := \bigcup_{y \in P(h_J) \cap I} (PATH(y) \cap THRU(y,h_J))$
> >   **od**
> > **end**

If $G_0, G_1, \ldots, G_m$ is the derived sequence (where $G_0 = G$), pass 1 consists of applying Algorithm I1 to each interval in G_0, then to each interval in G_1, and so on until it has been applied to the single interval in G_{m-1}. At this point, IN and THRU sets will have been computed for each node in the derived sequence of graphs.

(b) *Pass 2: global to local.* During the second pass, LIVE is computed for smaller and smaller regions of the program. Let x^* denote the single node in G_m. Pass 2 begins with the assignment

$$LIVE(x^*) := IN(x^*)$$

This is clearly correct since x^* has no successors. The remainder of the pass consists of repeated application of Algorithm I2, which computes LIVE sets for each node in an interval I, given correct live sets for the entry to I and to each successor J of I. This precondition is assured by the order in which I2 is applied: first to the interval x^*, then to each interval in G_{m-2}, and so on (backwards through the derived sequence) until LIVE sets have been computed for every node in the original graph G.

The algorithm itself is based on the observation that if nodes of $I - \{h\}$ are treated in *reverse* interval order, the live analysis equation (1-2) can always be applied because the correct LIVE set for each successor of a given node $x \in I - \{h\}$ will have been previously computed. To see this, suppose we are processing nodes of $I - \{h\}$ and we arrive at node x. A successor y of x can be one of three things:

1. y is another node in $I - \{h\}$, in which case LIVE(y) has already been computed because nodes are being treated in reverse interval order,

2. y is the head of I, in which case LIVE(I) can be used for LIVE(y),

3. y is the head of some successor interval J, in which case LIVE(J) can be used.

Algorithm I2 is a direct encoding of these insights.

Algorithm I2: Interval Pass 2.

Input:
    1. An interval I with head h.
    2. IN(x), $\forall x \in I$; THRU(x, y), $\forall x \in I$, $\forall y \in S(x)$.
    3. LIVE(I); LIVE(J), $\forall J \in S(I)$.
Output: LIVE(x), $\forall x \in I$.
Method:

```
begin
    LIVE(h) := LIVE(I);
    for all J ∈ S(I) do
        LIVE(head of J) := LIVE(J)
    od
    for all x ∈ I - {h} in reverse interval order do
        LIVE(x) := IN(x) ∪ ⋃ (THRU(x,y) ∩ LIVE(y))
                              y∈S(x)
    od
end
```

Although interval analysis has been shown to require fewer bit vector operations than the iterative method in many cases [Kenn76], it is still $O(n^2)$ in the worst case, and in practical implementations the elegantly simple iterative method may prove faster. The main advantage of the interval approach is that it constructs a representation of the program control flow structure which can be used for other optimizations [Cock70a]. Allen, Cocke, Schwartz, Kennedy, Aho, and Ullman [Alle70, Cock70a, Alle76, Cock70b, Kenn71a, Kenn76, Aho73] have applied interval analysis in the solution of data flow problems. Allen and Cocke [Alle70, Cock70a] first used intervals to solve class 1 (forward) problems, while Kennedy [Kenn71, Kenn76] indicated the interval solution for class 2 (backward) problems.

1-3.4. $T1$-$T2$ Analysis

In search of better theoretical results and faster algorithms, Ullman [Ullm73] introduced two transformations on program graphs. Transformation $T1$ collapses a self-loop to a single node, while transformation $T2$ collapses a sequence of two nodes to a single node if the second has the first as its only predecessor. When $T1$ and $T2$ are repeatedly applied to a control flow graph, the graph is often reduced to a single node. Hecht and Ullman [Hech72] have shown that the reducible flow graphs in the $T1$-$T2$ sense are exactly the interval-reducible graphs. This result has led to a number of useful characterizations of flow graph reducibility [Hech72, Hech74].

$T1$-$T2$ analysis also allowed Ullman [Ullm73] to design an algorithm which uses balanced "3-2" trees to perform available expression computation in $O(n \log n)$ extended steps. Ullman's method can be extended to many other class 1 problems; however it is not known whether it can be adapted to class 2 problems.

1-3.5. Node Listings

A variation of the iterative method for data flow analysis builds an intermediate representation of the control flow called a *node listing* [Kenn75b], which is then used to solve the data flow equations. I here describe the node listing method for live analysis.

In the solution of the live analysis problem we are concerned with how operations in one block can effect "liveness" on entry to another. Thus we are interested in propagating information from every block in the program to every other block. Thus it is natural to consider the paths along which this information is propagated. A *node listing* for control flow graph $G = (N, E, n_0)$ is defined to be a sequence

$$l = (n_1, n_2, \ldots, n_m)$$

of nodes from N (nodes may be repeated) such that every simple path in G is a subsequence of l. That is, if

$$(x_1, x_2, \ldots, x_k)$$

is a simple path in G, then there exist indices

$$j_1, j_2, \ldots, j_k$$

such that $j_i < j_{i+1}$, $1 \leq i < k$, and $x_i = n_{j_i}$, $1 \leq i \leq k$.

For any control flow graph there exists a node listing of length $\leq n^2$ where $n = |N|$ since

$$l = (n_1, n_2, \ldots, n_n, n_1, n_2, \ldots, n_n, \ldots, n_1, \ldots, n_n)$$

with n repetitions of $(n_1, \ldots, n_n)$ is certainly such a listing. A node listing is *minimal* if there is no shorter listing for G.

The utility of this concept is demonstrated by the following algorithm which, given a node listing, computes the live sets in a manner similar to the Hecht-Ullman iterative method.

Algorithm NL: Node Listing Live Analysis.

Input: IN(b), THRU(b), $\forall b \in N$.
Output: LIVE(b), $\forall b \in N$.
Method:

```
begin
    for all b ∈ N do LIVE(b) := IN(b) od;
    for i := |nodelist| to 1 by −1 do
        b := nodelist[i];
        LIVE(b) := IN(b) ∪  ⋃  (THRU(b) ∩ LIVE(x))
                             x∈S(b)
    od
end
```

The node listing concept is introduced in [Kenn75b]; in [Aho76] Aho and Ullman show that for reducible flow graphs an $O(n \log n)$ length node listing can be found in $O(n \log n)$ time. Combining this method with Algorithm NL produces an $O(n \log n)$ algorithm to solve either class 1 or class 2 data flow problems. Markowsky and Tarjan [Mark75] have shown that $O(n \log n)$ is a lower bound of the node listing algorithm; i.e., no better worst-case bound can be found, although there are linear listings for a large class of graphs [Kenn75b].

1-3.6. Path Compression

Another $O(n \log n)$ data flow analysis algorithm was discovered by Graham and Wegman [Grah76]. It is based on three transformations which are similar to Ullman's $T1$ and $T2$. The Graham-Wegman transformations are depicted in Fig. 1-10. Transformation T_1 removes a self loop; T_2 compresses a two-step path to a one-step path, eliminating the middle node whenever it has no other successors (T_2b); T_3 eliminates a successor of the entry

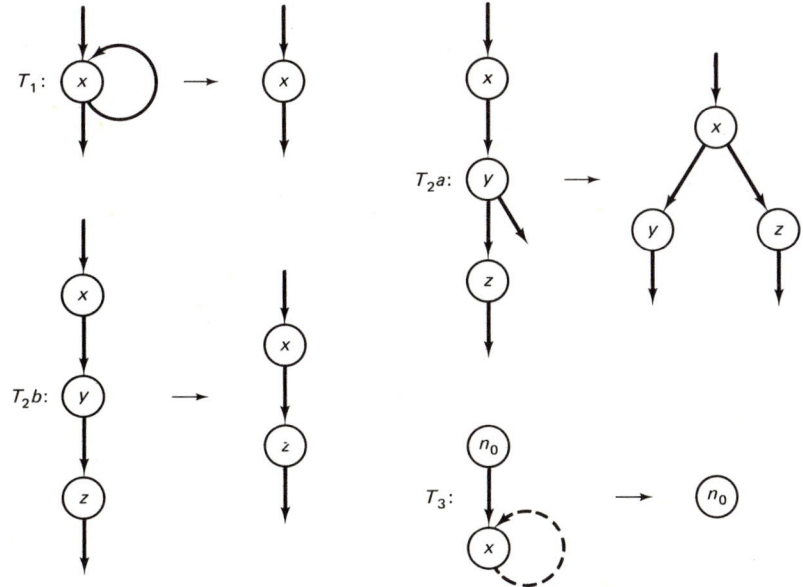

Figure 1-10 Graham-Wegman path compression transformations

node that has no successors of its own. For technical reasons, application of T_1 requires that the node with the loop have a unique predecessor. An example reduction using these transformations is shown in Fig. 1-11. Graham and Wegman have shown that any graph reducible in the interval sense will be reduced by T_1-T_3.

Data flow analysis using the path compression transformations is similar to interval analysis. The method I present here differs from the one originally published by Graham and Wegman in that it easily handles backward as well as forward analysis.

Given a flow graph, the first step is to construct a "parse," i.e., a list of transformations which will reduce the graph to a single node. The complexity analysis is very sensitive to the order in which transformations are applied. Graham and Wegman use a clever algorithm to choose a parse that reduces loops from the inside out and minimizes the number of T_2 transformations. Since T_2 transformations are the most expensive, this strategy achieves a good time bound.

Once available, the parse is employed in a two-pass algorithm which computes IN and THRU for composite regions of increasing size in a pass through the reduction sequence, then computes LIVE for each node as it appears in the reverse reduction sequence (or *production* sequence). This process is embodied in Algorithm P2, which applies a set of associated computations at each reduction or production. Each transformation in the

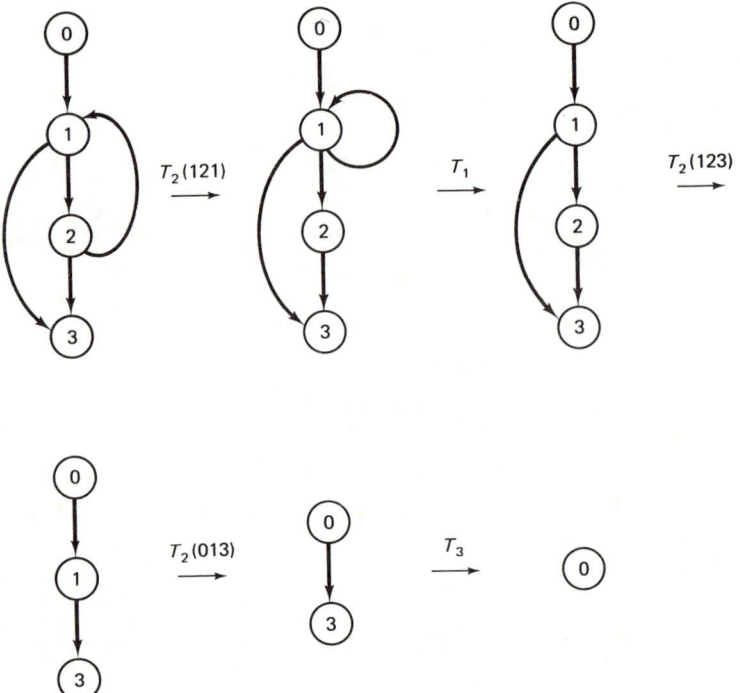

Figure 1-11 Sample Graham-Wegman reduction

parse is really a pair $\langle t, \eta \rangle$, where t is a transformation number and η is a mapping from the nodes in the production to nodes of the graph being reduced; in other words, η specifies the region of application for transformation t. Such a pair is called a *transformation instance*.

Algorithm P2: Two-pass Live Flow Analysis

Input:
1. A graph $G = (N, E, n_0)$.
2. IN(x), $\forall x \in N$; THRU(x, y), $\forall x \in N$, $\forall y \in S(x)$.
3. A list PARSE, consisting of transformation instances $\langle t, \eta \rangle$ which reduce G.

Output: LIVE(x), $\forall x \in N$.

Method:

> **begin**
>   ¢ pass 1 ¢
>   **for** $i := 1$ **to** $|$PARSE$|$ **do**
> $\langle t, \eta \rangle :=$ PARSE$[i]$;
>   apply the reduction computations associated with t to the
>   nodes specified by η.

```
od;
LIVE(n₀) := IN(n₀);
¢ pass 2 ¢
for i := |PARSE| to 1 by −1 do
    ⟨t,η⟩ := PARSE[i];
        apply the production computations associated with t to the
        nodes specified by η.
    od
end
```

All that remains is to specify the computations associated with each transformation. Figure 1-12 shows the computations of IN and THRU performed during the reduction pass. Note that path compression emphasizes edges rather than nodes, so the THRU sets being constructed are for composite edges. For notational convenience, we define THRU of a nonexistent edge to be the empty set. Figure 1-13 shows the production computations; an initial LIVE set for each node is determined when the node first appears as the result of some production. This live set is then revised as new exit edges are added by T_2a productions.

In practice, path compression is very fast indeed; in fact, it operates in linear time for an extremely large subclass of the reducible flow graphs. Its only disadvantage is that, although classified as a "structured" method, the structure it uncovers seems unnatural because it is based on edges rather than nodes. Nevertheless, path compression is an excellent algorithm from both the theoretical and practical standpoints.

1-3.7. Balanced Path Compression

In 1975, Tarjan devised an algorithm [Tarj75a] which combined elements of the node listing approach with a stronger form of path compression using a balanced tree data structure he had introduced in [Tarj75b]. The result is a very fast algorithm with running time $O(n\alpha(n, n))$, where α is related to a functional inverse of Ackermann's function. Thus for all practical purposes the algorithm is asymptotically linear; unfortunately it seems very complex, so until there is some experience with an implementation, one cannot tell whether it is suitable for inclusion in a compiler. Tarjan's algorithm can be used to solve a variety of class 1 problems, but it is not yet clear that it can be adapted to class 2 problems.

1-3.8. Graph Grammars

In an attempt to further simplify the problem of data flow analysis, Farrow, Kennedy, and Zucconi [Farr76] studied further restrictions on the class of acceptable graphs, restrictions stronger than the traditional notion of

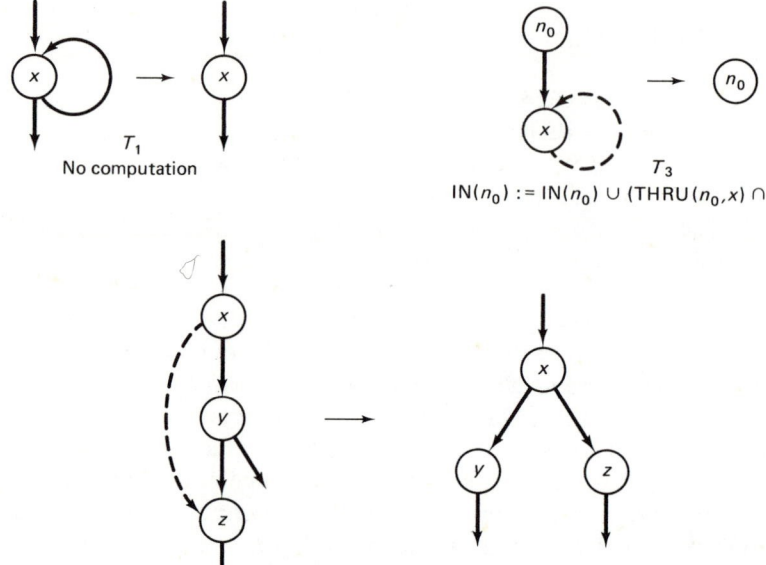

$$T_1$$
No computation

$$T_3$$
$$IN(n_0) := IN(n_0) \cup (THRU(n_0, x) \cap IN(x))$$

$$T_2 a$$
$$THRU(x, z) := THRU(x, z) \cup (THRU(x, y) \cap THRU(y, z))$$

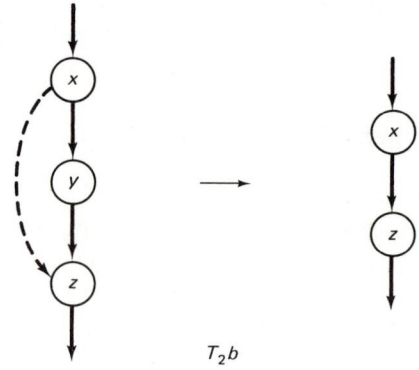

$$T_2 b$$
$$IN(x) := IN(x) \cup (THRU(x, y) \cap IN(y))$$
$$THRU(x, z) := THRU(x, z) \cup (THRU(x, y) \cap THRU(y, z))$$

Figure 1-12 Reduction computations

reducibility. They introduced the *Semi-Structured Flow Graph* (SSFG) grammar, depicted informally in Fig. 1-14, and studied the class of flow graphs generated by that grammar. The set of rules in Fig. 1-12 was chosen because it seems to include most of the control structures proposed as extensions of the basic Böhm and Jacopini set for structured programming [Böhm66]. For example, the SSFG grammar can generate the double-exit

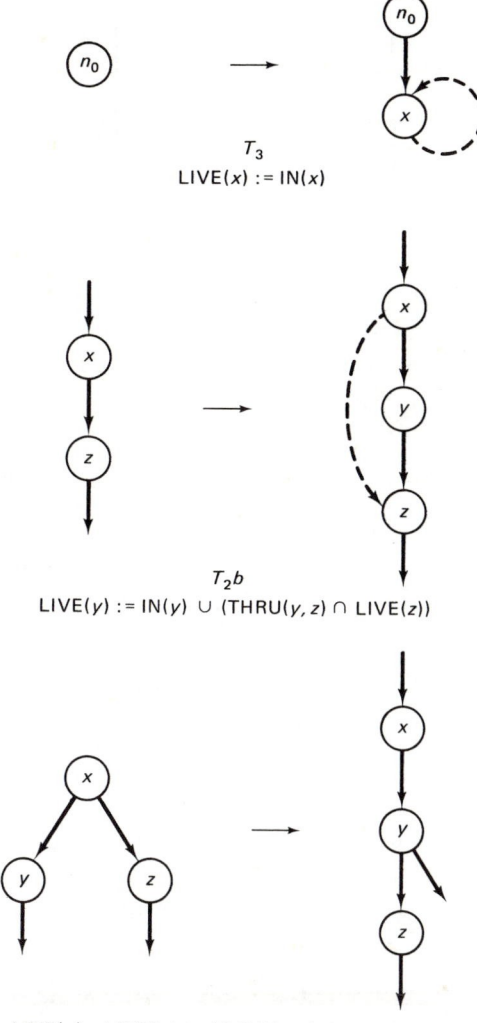

$$T_3$$
$$\text{LIVE}(x) := \text{IN}(x)$$

$$T_2b$$
$$\text{LIVE}(y) := \text{IN}(y) \cup (\text{THRU}(y, z) \cap \text{LIVE}(z))$$

$$\text{LIVE}(y) = \text{LIVE}(y) \cup (\text{THRU}(y, z) \cap \text{LIVE}(z))$$

Figure 1-13 Production computations

loop used by Ashcroft and Manna [Ashc71] to demonstrate a limitation of the Böhm-Jacopini control structures (see Fig. 1-15).

The major problem with using SSFG or any other graph grammar for data flow analysis is that of *graph parsing*, constructing a parse for an arbitrary graph. For the SSFG rules, an important step toward the fast parsing algorithm was a proof that corresponding SSFG reductions can be applied in any order without affecting the result. In other words, reducibility of a given graph is not sensitive to the order in which reductions are applied. Farrow,

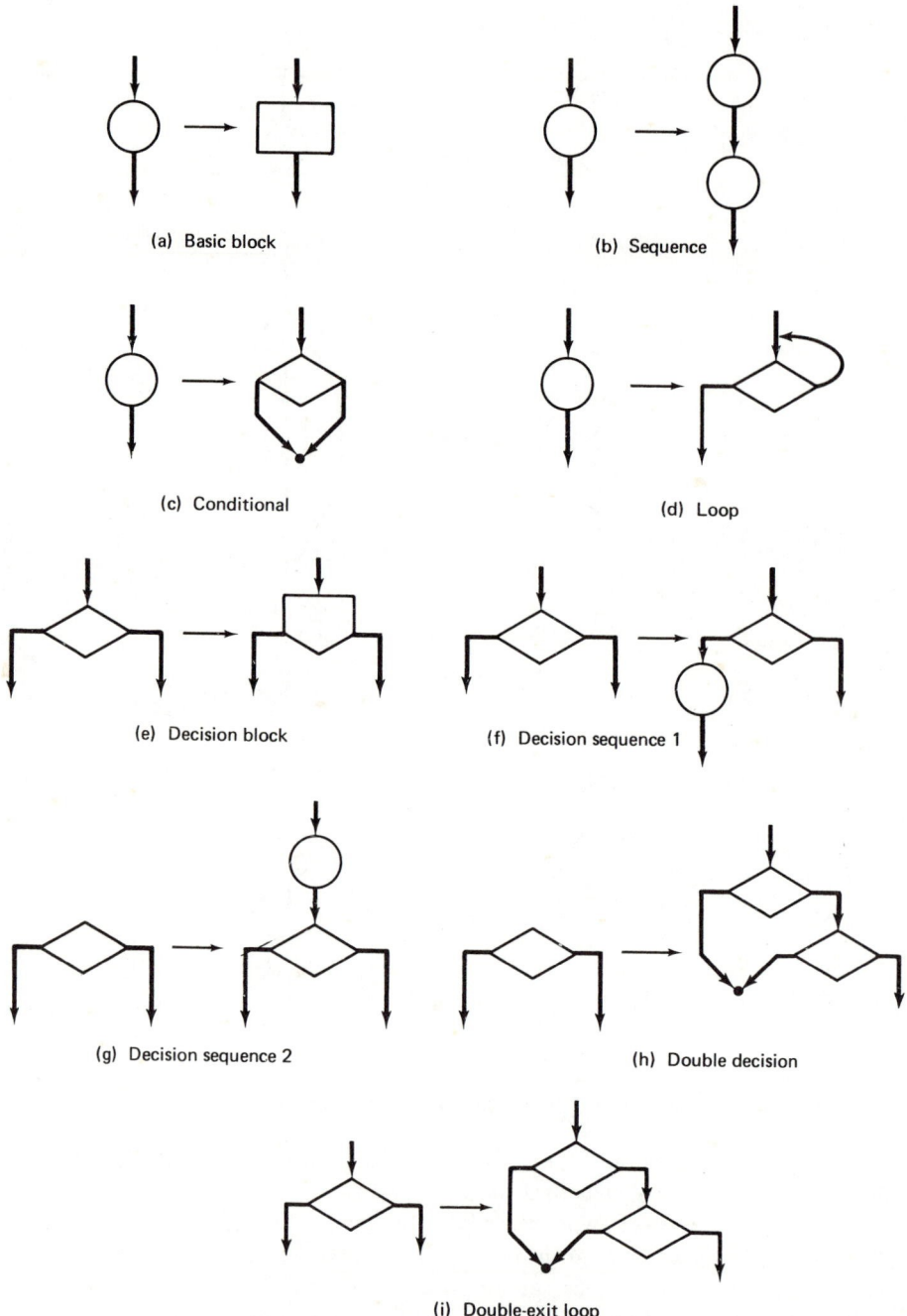

(a) Basic block

(b) Sequence

(c) Conditional

(d) Loop

(e) Decision block

(f) Decision sequence 1

(g) Decision sequence 2

(h) Double decision

(i) Double-exit loop

Figure 1-14 SSFG grammar

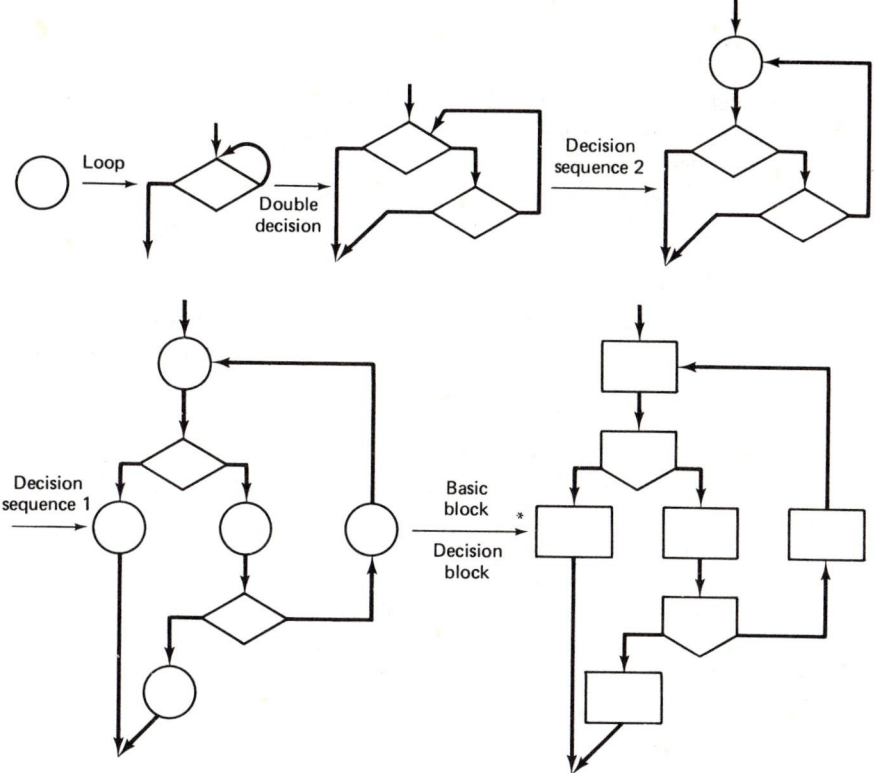

Figure 1-15 Derivation of the Ashcroft-Manna counterexample

Kennedy, and Zucconi established this result by proving, via a long graphical argument, that the SSFG reductions have the *Finite Church-Rosser* property [Aho72, Seth74]. As a result of this property, they were able to devise a parsing algorithm which applies reductions in a disciplined way and avoids wandering around the graph.

I present the parsing algorithm in two parts. First, Algorithm CO (collapse) finds all the reductions which apply at a particular node x. If it discovers at least one reduction, it sets a success flag to **true** and returns the reduction list.

Algorithm CO: Collapse

Input: A graph Γ and a node x in Γ.
Output:
1. A flag *SUCCESS* indicating whether or not a reduction has been found.

2. A list of reductions P_x (possibly empty).

3. A modified graph Γ'.

Method:

```
begin Px := ε; SUCCESS := false;
    reducing := true; Γ' := Γ;
    while reducing do
        for each production P in GSSFG do
            if right-hand-side(P) is isomorphic to a region R in Γ'
            headed by x
            then
                apply P⁻¹ to reduce R to a single node x', forming a new
                version of Γ'; add the production P to Px along with some
                auxiliary information;
                x := x';
                SUCCESS := true;
                goto reduced
            fi
        od;
        reducing := false;
    reduced:
        skip
    od
end
```

The SSFG parsing algorithm assumes a list L of nodes of the program in *straight order*, a fairly obvious order for nodes of the flow graph [Earn72, Hech75], and produces a parse P_r. The basic scheme is to take each node from L in sequence and try a collapse. Whenever a collapse succeeds, the algorithm backs up to a predecessor, indicated by a "link," to try further collapses; otherwise it moves on to the next node on L. This disciplined backup is the key to a linear time bound.

Algorithm PA: SSFG Parse

Input:

1. A graph Γ.

2. A list L of nodes of Γ in straight order.

Output:

1. A list P_r of reductions.

2. An answer to the question, "Is Γ in the language generated by G_{SSFG}?"

Method:

```
begin
    L := the list of unvisited nodes (straight order);
    x := the entry of Γ;
    P_Γ := ε;
    remove x from L;
    while x ≠ null do
        perform a collapse at node x;
        ¢ collapse produces Γ', P_x, and the flag SUCCESS ¢
        make x the unique linked predecessor of all unvisited succes-
            sors of x in Γ';
        append P_x to P_Γ;
        Γ := Γ';
        if SUCCESS ¢ at least one reduction ¢
            and x is linked to a predecessor
        then x := linked predecessor of x
        elif L = ε then x := null
        else x := hd L; L := tl L
        fi
    od;
    if Γ is now a single computation node
    then the graph is SSFG and P_x is a valid parse
    else the graph is not SSFG
    fi
end
```

The operation of this algorithm is demonstrated by the example in Fig. 1-16. In this figure, links are indicated by dotted lines. Nodes are numbered in straight order. The steps are as follows:

1. An unsuccessful collapse is attempted at node 1. A link to 1 is inserted in 2.

2. A collapse at node 2 discovers a "decision sequence 1" involving node 4. Links to 2 are inserted in nodes 3 and 10 [Fig. 1-16(b)].

3. A backup leads to another unsuccessful collapse at 1.

4. A collapse at node 3 discovers a long sequence of reductions: two "decision sequence 1" reductions [Fig. 1-16(c)], a "double-exit loop" and a "decision sequence 1" [Fig. 1-16(d)], a "conditional" and a "decision sequence 2" [Fig. 1-16(e)]. A link to 3 is inserted in 10, but *not* in 2 (it has been visited).

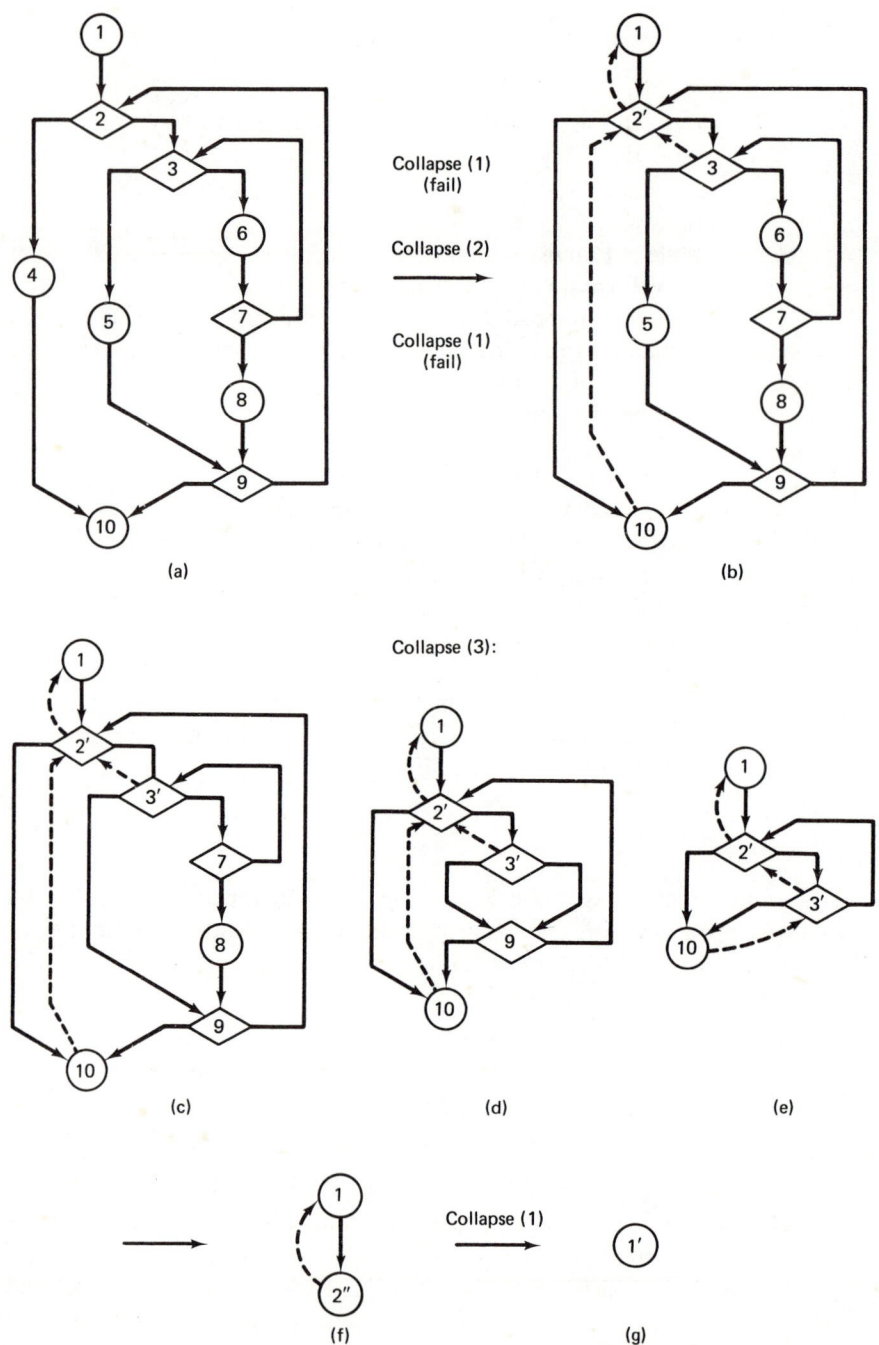

Figure 1-16 An example parse

5. After a backup, a collapse at node 2 discovers a "double-exit loop," a "conditional," and a "sequence" [Fig. 1-16(f)].

6. After one more backup, a collapse at node 1 produces the final "sequence" reduction.

It has been shown that this algorithm, in time linear in the number of blocks in the original program, either produces a parse for Γ or reports that Γ is not reducible. If the graph is reducible, the length of its parse must also be linear in the size of the original graph.

With the parse in hand, we can apply the same two-pass algorithm used by path compression (Algorithm P2) to perform data flow analysis. Space does not permit me to specify the computations associated with each of the nine transformations in the SSFG grammar; instead, I have selected two rules, "sequence" and "double-exit loop," as examples. Reduction computations for these rules are shown in Fig. 1-17 and production computations in Fig.

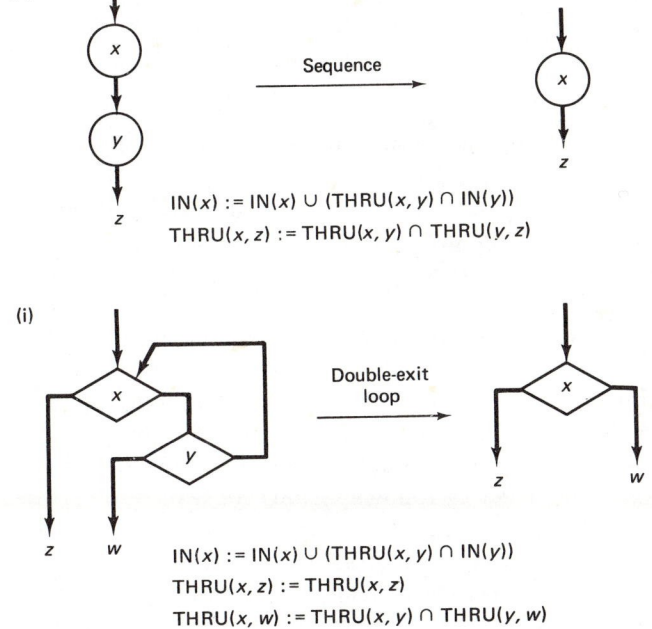

(b) Sequence

$$IN(x) := IN(x) \cup (THRU(x, y) \cap IN(y))$$
$$THRU(x, z) := THRU(x, y) \cap THRU(y, z).$$

(i) Double-exit loop

$$IN(x) := IN(x) \cup (THRU(x, y) \cap IN(y))$$
$$THRU(x, z) := THRU(x, z)$$
$$THRU(x, w) := THRU(x, y) \cap THRU(y, w)$$

Figure 1-17 Sample reduction computations

1-18. As with path compression, a correct LIVE set is determined for each node when it first appears as the result of some production. Since there is a fixed number of operations associated with each transformation in the parse, the linear parse length implies that the entire computation takes linear time.

An important byproduct of the method is the parse itself, which can be

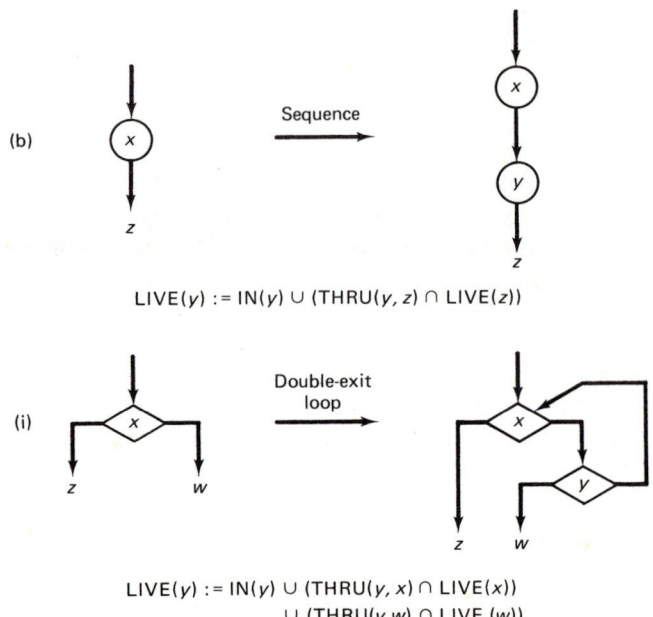

$$\text{LIVE}(y) := \text{IN}(y) \cup (\text{THRU}(y, z) \cap \text{LIVE}(z))$$

$$\text{LIVE}(y) := \text{IN}(y) \cup (\text{THRU}(y, x) \cap \text{LIVE}(x))$$
$$\cup (\text{THRU}(y,w) \cap \text{LIVE}(w))$$

Figure 1-18 Sample production computations

used for many different data flow problems and which provides a convenient representation of the structure of the program. Because it uncovers loops and other control constructs, this representation can be used to perform optimizations like code motion and strength reduction. The structure discovered by the SSFG parse is more natural than that discovered by the interval method or the Graham-Wegman technique, because the SSFG grammar is based upon control structures arising from good programming practice.

The main drawback of the graph grammar approach is its limited range of applicability. In order to find out how much of a drawback that is, Kennedy and Zucconi conducted a followup study in which they analyzed 500 FORTRAN subroutines taken from running programs used by several departments in the School of Natural Sciences at Rice University. All these programs were written before the emphasis on structured programming, yet 94% were Cocke-Allen–reducible and, of these, 88% were SSFG–reducible. In other words, 88% of the programs for which most other methods work can be reduced and hence analyzed by the SSFG method [Kenn77].

As a final note I would point out that the Graham-Wegman algorithm is also linear on all the SSFG-reducible graphs. It is gratifying to observe that well-structured programs can produce benefits other than the obvious ones—e.g., faster compilation speeds. In a sense, programs that are easier for humans to understand are also easier for compilers to understand.

1-3.9. High-Level Data Flow Analysis

The methods surveyed thus far are designed to work with a low-level version of the program. One might well ask if it is possible to perform the same analysis on a high-level representation such as the parse tree. The answer is yes. This approach, often called *high-level data flow analysis*, is similar to the graph grammar method, except no complicated graph-parsing algorithm is required. For simplicity, I will illustrate the method by considering a language which contains no *escape* or *goto* statements. Consider the simple grammar fragment below.

$\langle program \rangle ::= \textbf{begin} \langle statement \rangle \textbf{end}$

$\langle statement \rangle ::= \langle assignment \rangle$

$\langle statement \rangle ::= \langle statement \rangle; \langle statement \rangle$

$\langle statement \rangle ::= \textbf{if} \langle condition \rangle \textbf{then} \langle statement \rangle \textbf{else} \langle statement \rangle \textbf{fi}$

$\langle statement \rangle ::= \textbf{while} \langle condition \rangle \textbf{do} \langle statement \rangle \textbf{od}$

Although this grammar is clearly ambiguous, we can nevertheless write a parser which resolves the ambiguity in some sensible way, say by grouping from left to right.

The parse tree for a program generated by this grammar will have a $\langle program \rangle$ node as its root and a number of $\langle statement \rangle$ nodes as nonterminals in the tree. Data flow analysis can be applied to such a tree in the familiar two-pass fashion. The first pass propagates IN and THRU sets associated with $\langle statement \rangle$ nonterminals up toward the root; the second pass propagates LIVE sets down toward the leaves. To specify the entire procedure within this framework, one need only specify the computations that can occur at each $\langle statement \rangle$ node: for pass 1, how to compute IN and THRU for a $\langle statement \rangle$ given IN and THRU for its parts, and for pass 2, how to compute LIVE for subparts of a $\langle statement \rangle$ given LIVE for the $\langle statement \rangle$ along with IN and THRU for the parts, as determined on pass 1. These specifications must be given for each rule of the grammar.

As an illustration, consider the computations associated with the sample grammar given earlier. For compactness, I will specify these computations using the shorthand notations S for $\langle statement \rangle$, C for $\langle condition \rangle$, P for $\langle program \rangle$, and A for $\langle assignment \rangle$; I will use subscripts to distinguish different occurrences of the same nonterminal in a single rule. Each nonterminal S will have a number of associated *attributes*: IN, THRU, LIVE, and LIVEOUT (the set of variables live on exit) for the region that S represents. The specification is completed by associating with each rule of the grammar *semantic equations*, which show how to compute the various attributes. To apply the semantic equations at a particular node while traversing the parse tree, set up a correspondence between the node and its sons on the one hand

and the nonterminals of the production that applies at the node on the other. Then the semantic equations associated with the rule can be used to compute attributes for the tree nodes.

Here is the complete specification for the sample grammar.

1. $P ::= $ **begin** S **end**

   ¢ no computations on pass 1 ¢
   ¢ pass 2 computations ¢
   $\text{LIVE}(S) := \text{IN}(S);$
   $\text{LIVEOUT}(S) := \phi;$

2. $S ::= A$

   ¢ pass 1 ¢
   $\text{IN}(S) := \text{IN}(A);$
   $\text{THRU}(S) := \text{THRU}(A);$
   ¢ pass 2 ¢
   $\text{LIVE}(A) := \text{IN}(A) \cup (\text{THRU}(A) \cap \text{LIVEOUT}(S));$

3. $S_0 ::= S_1 ; S_2$

   ¢ pass 1 ¢
   $\text{IN}(S_0) := \text{IN}(S_1) \cup (\text{THRU}(S_1) \cap \text{IN}(S_2));$
   $\text{THRU}(S_0) := \text{THRU}(S_1) \cap \text{THRU}(S_2);$
   ¢ pass 2 ¢
   $\text{LIVEOUT}(S_2) := \text{LIVEOUT}(S_0);$
   $\text{LIVE}(S_2) := \text{IN}(S_2) \cup (\text{THRU}(S_2) \cap \text{LIVEOUT}(S_2));$
   $\text{LIVEOUT}(S_1) := \text{LIVE}(S_2);$
   $\text{LIVE}(S_1) := \text{IN}(S_1) \cup (\text{THRU}(S_1) \cap \text{LIVEOUT}(S_1));$

4. $S_0 ::= $ **if** C **then** S_1 **else** S_2 **fi**

   ¢ pass 1 ¢
   $\text{IN}(S_0) := \text{IN}(C) \cup (\text{THRU}(C) \cap (\text{IN}(S_1) \cup \text{IN}(S_2)));$
   $\text{THRU}(S_0) := \text{THRU}(C) \cap (\text{THRU}(S_1) \cup \text{THRU}(S_2));$
   ¢ pass 2 ¢
   $\text{LIVEOUT}(S_1) := \text{LIVEOUT}(S_2) := \text{LIVEOUT}(S_0);$
   $\text{LIVE}(S_1) := \text{IN}(S_1) \cup (\text{THRU}(S_1) \cap \text{LIVEOUT}(S_1));$
   $\text{LIVE}(S_2) := \text{IN}(S_2) \cup (\text{THRU}(S_2) \cap \text{LIVEOUT}(S_2));$
   $\text{LIVEOUT}(C) := \text{LIVE}(S_1) \cup \text{LIVE}(S_2);$
   $\text{LIVE}(C) := \text{IN}(C) \cup (\text{THRU}(C) \cap \text{LIVEOUT}(C));$

5. $S_0 ::= $ **while** C **do** S_1 **od**

   ¢ pass 1 ¢
   $\text{IN}(S_0) := \text{IN}(C) \cup (\text{THRU}(C) \cap \text{IN}(S_1));$
   $\text{THRU}(S_0) := \text{THRU}(C);$
   ¢ pass 2 ¢

$$\text{LIVEOUT}(C) := \text{LIVEOUT}(S_0) \cup \text{IN}(S_1)$$
$$\cup (\text{THRU}(S_1) \cap \text{IN}(C));$$
$$\text{LIVE}(C) := \text{IN}(C) \cup (\text{THRU}(C) \cap \text{IN}(C));$$
$$\text{LIVEOUT}(S_1) := \text{LIVE}(C);$$
$$\text{LIVE}(S_1) := \text{IN}(S_1) \cup (\text{THRU}(S_1) \cap \text{LIVEOUT}(S_1));$$

The high-level approach, described here via an *attributed grammar* [Knut68], has several advantages. First, because the computations at each node of the parse tree are selected from a finite set and because the tree is traversed exactly twice, the total amount of processing is linear in the number of nodes of the parse tree. However, the constant of proportionality depends on the richness of the set of control structures—the richer the language, the more complex the data flow analysis.

Second, the method lends itself to convenient updating of data flow when sections of the parse tree are modified by optimization. If the leaf of some subtree is changed, new values of IN and THRU can be propagated upward to the first nonterminal where these sets are unchanged; then the computation of modified LIVE sets can be propagated back toward the leaves. This process limits the updating in response to a change to the region where the change actually makes a difference.

Finally, the first pass of high-level analysis can be performed as a part of the parse itself. Whenever a composite control structure is recognized, the IN and THRU sets for the region it represents are computed from IN and THRU for its parts according to the semantic equations above.

Various formulations of high-level data flow analysis have been proposed [Wulf75, Neel75, Jaza75b]. Particularly notable is its use in the BLISS/11 compiler at Carnegie-Mellon [Wulf75]. The name "high-level data flow analysis" was coined by Rosen in his detailed treatment of the method [Rose77]. Rosen's approach generalizes to more complicated control structures by using flexible semantic equations that can be applied in different situations.

1-3.10. Summary Table

Table 1-3 summarizes the characteristics of the algorithms I have described. The column labeled "Speed" shows the asymptotic complexity of each method. In the "Simple" column, "S" indicates an easy-to-program method, "C" indicates a complicated method, and "M" indicates average difficulty. A "yes" under "Structure" says that the method uses a model of the program loop structure in its computation, i.e., that the algorithm attempts to discover the structure of the program. A "yes" in the "Both ways" column indicates that the algorithm works in the given time on both forward and backward data flow problems. The last column shows the class of graphs for which each algorithm was analyzed (in most cases this is also the class to which the algorithm is applicable).

Table 1-3   Summary of data flow methods

Method	Speed	Simple ?	Structure ?	Both ways ?	Graph class
Iterative	n^2	S	no	yes	all
Interval	n^2	M	yes	yes	reducible
Bal. tree	$n \log n$	C	yes	no	reducible
Path comp.	$n \log n$	M	semi	yes	reducible
Node list	$n \log n$	M	no	yes	reducible
Bal. path	$n\alpha(n, n)$	C	no	?	reducible
Grammar	n	M	yes	yes	L(grammar)
High-level	n	S	yes	yes	parse trees

1-3.11. Interprocedural Analysis

The foregoing material has said nothing about the effect of procedure calls on data flow analysis. Usually calls within blocks are treated as complex instructions which may affect the values of many variables. It is the function of *interprocedural data flow analysis* [Alle74] to construct *summary information* for a procedure: which variables are used and which are redefined as the result of a call. For example, interprocedural analysis might construct IN and THRU sets for the procedure call to support live analysis.

Interprocedural analysis is important because, in its absence, extremely conservative assumptions must be made. For example, in live analysis, it must be assumed that a procedure uses every variable it has access to; in availability analysis it must be assumed that it kills every expression it can and defines no new ones. Broad assumptions like these quickly dilute the power of data flow analysis.

Interprocedural analysis is a complex process, particularly for languages with complex scoping rules [Bart78]. It usually entails constructing a call graph and summary information for a single activation of each procedure in the graph, then taking a transitive closure on the graph. Since it is treated elsewhere in this volume, I will not discuss it in detail, but the reader should be aware that it is an essential part of any system for global data flow analysis.

1-4. USE-DEFINITION CHAINS

For data flow analysis problems which are more complex than the ones examined previously, data interconnections may be expressed in a pure form which directly links instructions that produce values to instructions that use them. These links are called *use-definition chains*. For the purposes of this exposition, I will assume that these chains are realized in the following forms:

1. For each instruction i and input variable V, $DEFS(V, i)$ is the set of instructions which may be the most recent defining instructions for V at run time. In other words, $DEFS(V, i)$ contains the set of instructions which may compute the value of V used by i.

2. For each instruction i and output variable V, $USES(V, i)$ is the set of instructions which may use the value of V computed by i at run time. These sets are related as follows:

$$x \in DEFS(A,y) \equiv y \in USES(A,x).$$

I will postpone, for the moment, a discussion of how use-definition chains are used in favor of a discussion of how to compute the sets DEFS and USES. Suppose we are considering an instruction y and an input variable A. If there is a defining instruction x earlier in the same block, then this is the only possible member of $DEFS(A, y)$. Otherwise, we must discover which instructions in the program compute values that can "reach" the beginning of the block; every such instruction that has A as its output variable should be in $DEFS(A, y)$. Thus the problem is reduced to computing, for each block b in the program, the set $REACHES(b)$ of pointers to instructions that compute values which are available on entry to b. Let $DEFOUT(y, x)$ be the set of instructions in block y which produce values that are still available on entry to successor x, and let $NKILL(y, x)$ be the set of instructions whose output variables are not redefined in passing through block y to block x. Then the following system of equations holds.

$$\left.\begin{aligned} REACHES(n_0) &= \phi \\ REACHES(x) &= \bigcup_{y \in P(x)} (DEFOUT(y, x) \cup (REACHES(y) \\ &\qquad \cap NKILL(y, x))) \end{aligned}\right\} \quad (1\text{-}3)$$

This is exactly the kind of system which can be solved by any of the data flow analysis methods described in Section 1-3.

Once DEFS is available, USES can be produced by simple inversion. The informal algorithm below can be used for this purpose.

Algorithm US: USES Computation

Input: DEFS.
Output: USES.
Method:

    begin
        $USES(*) := \phi$;

```
for each instruction i in the program do
  for each input variable A of instruction i do
    for each instruction j in DEFS(A,i) do
      USES(output(j),j) := USES(output(j),j) ∪ {i}
    od
  od
od
end
```

To illustrate the usefulness of these chains, I present an application to dead code elimination. The usual method for eliminating dead code is to first find and mark all instructions which are "useful" in some sense. This is done by starting with a set of *critical instructions*, instructions which are useful by definition. For example, you might declare all output instructions to be critical. Once every instruction in the critical set is marked, the method proceeds to mark any instruction that defines a variable used by at least one marked instruction, continuing until no more instructions can be marked. The use-definition chains help in the location of instructions which can compute some input of a marked instruction. To manage the process, Algorithm MK below uses a workpile of instructions ready to be marked.

Algorithm MK: Mark Useful Instructions

Input:
  1. Use-definition chains, DEFS(v, i).
  2. Set of critical instructions CRIT.
Output: For each instruction i, MARK(i) = true iff i is useful.
Method:

```
begin
  MARK(*) := false;
  PILE := CRIT;
  while PILE ≠ φ do
    x := an arbitrary element of PILE;
    PILE := PILE − {x};
    MARK(x) := true;
    for each y ∈ DEFS(A,x) do
      if ¬MARK(y) then
        PILE := PILE ∪ {y}
      fi
    od
  od
end
```

All that remains after application of the marking algorithm is to remove any unmarked instructions as useless.

While Algorithm MK demonstrates a fairly powerful application of use-definition chains, it only uses chains in one direction. We shall next consider the problem of global constant folding, whose solution requires simultaneous use of chains in both directions. This is because each constant instruction discovered may lead to more folding at the use points of its output variables, and testing an instruction for constant inputs implies an examination of the defining points of those inputs. Put another way, each time an instruction is replaced by a constant, the folding algorithm must recheck all uses of its output variable to see if the using instruction might also be eliminated. Such a check necessarily involves looking at other definitions which can reach the use. The situation is depicted in Fig. 1-19.

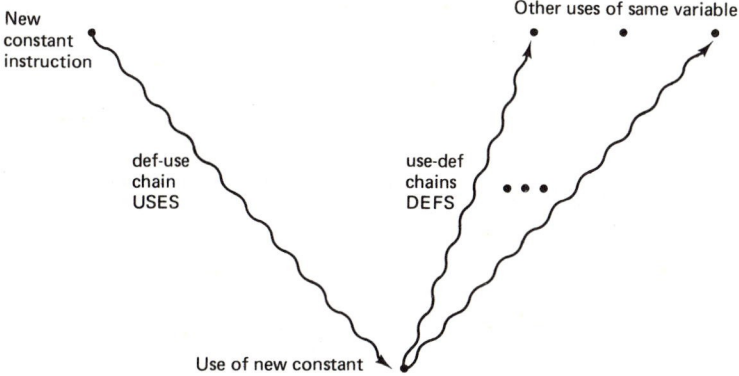

Figure 1-19 The need for two types of chains in constant folding

The method implied by the above observation is realized in Algorithm CP. Like Algorithm MK, it uses a workpile to control iterations. A number of set-theoretic notations are used in the informal specification; these have the obvious meanings. The algorithm also uses a subroutine COMPUTE to evaluate constant instructions.

Algorithm CP: Constant Propagation

Input:

1. A program PROG containing instructions of the usual type.
2. A flag $CONST(a, i)$ for each instruction i and input or output variable A of i. Initially, $CONST(A, i)$ is **true** only if A represents a constant denotation.
3. The chains USES and DEFS.

Output:
1. The modified CONST flags.
2. The mapping VAL(A, i) which provides the run-time constant value of variable A at instruction i; VAL(A, i) is defined only if CONST(A, i) is **true**.

Method:

```
begin ¢ start with the trivially constant instructions ¢
    PILE := {x ∈ PROG|(∀A ∈ inputs(x)|CONST(A,x))};
    while PILE ≠ φ do
        x := an arbitrary element of PILE;
        PILE := PILE − {x};
        B := output(x);
        for each i ∈ USES(B,x) do
            ¢ check for constant inputs ¢
            conB := true;
            for each y ∈ DEFS(B, i) − {x} while conB do
                if CONST(B,y) and VAL(B,y) = VAL(B,x)
                    then conB := true
                    else conB := false
                fi
            od;
            ¢ test the exit condition ¢
            if conB then
                CONST(B,i) := true;
                VAL(B,i) := VAL(B,x);
                ¢ is the instruction now constant? ¢
                if (∀A ∈ inputs(i)|CONST(A,i)) then
                    C := output(i);
                    CONST(C,i) := true;
                    VAL(C, i) := COMPUTE(i);
                    PILE := PILE ∪ {i}
                fi
            fi
        od
    od
end
```

Although termination and correctness of Algorithm CP are subtle, the interested reader will not find it difficult to establish them. The algorithm is interesting because it serves as a model for many other optimization algorithms. One such will be seen in Section 1-6.

1-5. SYMBOLIC INTERPRETATION

The analysis methods presented so far can only solve restricted classes of data flow problems. The algorithms of Section 1-3 work only for problems which ask whether or not a single event may (or must) have happened before control reaches some point (in the forward case) or may happen later (in the backward case). They are not effective for questions about *sequences* of events along control flow paths. Use-definition chain methods are more general, but they too can be imprecise because information is gathered by jumping between uses and definitions rather than by following individual execution paths [Kapl78b].

The most precise method for gathering global data flow information is *symbolic interpretation* [Wegb75, King76]. As implied by the name, symbolic interpretation entails executing the program with symbolic values for all variables whose values are indeterminate at compile time. For example, if the value of N in a given FORTRAN program is always 5 but the value of M is read in as data, M would be assigned a symbolic value α. Then after executing the statement

$$L = N*M$$

L will have the (partially) symbolic value 5α.

It should be easy to see that the value numbering method of Section 1-2 is just symbolic interpretation restricted to straight-line code. As in value numbering, the compiler can uncover useful facts about the relationships among values of program variables at point p by executing the program symbolically up to that point. But there is, of course, a hitch. At conditional transfers of control, the truth value of the condition may depend on symbolic values; that is, it may not be possible to determine at compile time which way control will go at run time. In such cases, interpretation must proceed down *both* paths. But this leads to problems at points where control paths join. If X has value α on one path and β on another, its value after they join must be expressed as "either α or β." In loops, value conjunctions of arbitrary length can be built, as the example in Fig. 1-20 shows.

Suppose we assign X the value α at block 1; then interpreting around the loop shows that its value at block 2 can be either α or 5α. Another interpretation adds 25α to the list of alternatives. Clearly, there are infinitely many possible values. Since symbolic interpretation attempts to prove everything it can about a program, it terminates only when it has enumerated all possible values of the properties it is keeping track of, so interpretation would not terminate on this example.

The problem is solved by restricting the application of symbolic interpretation to determining properties from a *well-founded property set* [Wegb75]. Simply put, if we take two properties from a well-founded set, their conjunc-

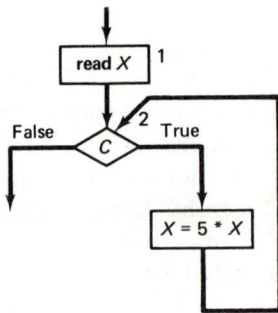

Figure 1-20 A loop for symbolic interpretation

tion ("either property α or property β") can be approximated by another property in the set, say γ; furthermore, after finitely many such approximations a limiting property will be reached. For example, suppose we are optimizing a language in which variables may dynamically take on values of three different types: *real*, *integer*, and *character*. Suppose also that the special atomic type *undefined* is used for uninitialized variables. By adding three more types—*number*, *atom*, and *inconsistent*—we can characterize our knowledge of variable types with the well-founded property set shown in Fig. 1-21.

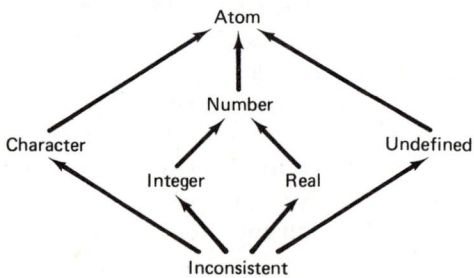

Figure 1-21 A well-founded property set for variable types

In this diagram, arcs lead from more specific to less specific information. To determine the result of a disjunction of two distinct types, locate the types in the diagram and find the first type which can be reached from both by following arrows. Thus the disjunction "*real* or *integer*" yields *number*, while "*real* or *undefined*" yields *atom*.

Since the disjunction of a type with itself produces the same type, a stable upper bound must be reached in this set after at most three distinct disjunctions. Thus a symbolic interpreter which terminates only when a steady state is reached will always terminate using this set. In general, symbolic interpretation is guaranteed to terminate when determining properties from a well-founded set on a finite program [Wegb75].

To convey the flavor of this method, I will include an adaptation of Wegbreit's simplest interpretation scheme. (More complicated versions, which unroll loops, will not be described.) First we assume a very simple model in which there are only two types of statements, *simple* and *conditional*. A simple statement x has a single successor given by $next(x)$, while a conditional y has two successors: $next_T(y)$, taken when the condition is true, and $next_F(y)$, taken when it is false.

Assume we are dealing with a well-founded property set $\mathbf{P}$ which has a property conjunction or *join* operation $\vee$ such that, for $p_1, p_2 \in \mathbf{P}, p_1 \vee p_2$ is the approximation of "either p_1 or p_2." Furthermore, assume there is a *least general property*, denoted by $\mathbf{0}$, such that for any property $p \in \mathbf{P}$, $p \vee \mathbf{0} = p$. In Fig. 1-20, "type = *inconsistent*" is $\mathbf{0}$.

Finally, the execution of an elementary statement may change the property which holds after that statement. Let $outprop(x, p)$ be the property which holds after simple statement x is executed, given that property p holds initially. Similar functions $outprop_T(x, p)$ and $outprop_F(x, p)$ give the resultant properties on the true and false branches, respectively, of a conditional.

Algorithm SI: Symbolic Interpretation

Input:
1. A program PROG consisting of instructions with successor fields *next* or $next_T$ and $next_F$.
2. A well-formed property set $\mathbf{P}$ with join operation $\vee$ and minimal element $\mathbf{0}$.
3. The semantic mappings *outprop*, $outprop_T$, and $outprop_F$.

Output: For each statement $x \in \mathbf{P}$, PROP[x], the most specific property provably true on entry to x (within the given framework).

Method:

```
begin
  for each x ∈ PROG do
    PROP[x] := 0
  od;
  let x₀ := the program entry statement;
  PILE := {⟨x₀,0⟩};
  while PILE ≠ ϕ do
    let z be an arbitrary element in PILE;
    PILE := PILE − {z};
    ⟨x,p⟩ := z;
    oldp := PROP[x];
    PROP[x] := PROP[x] ∨ p;
```

```
        while x ≠ exit statement and oldp ≠ PROP[x] do
            if x is a simple statement then
                p := outprop(x,PROP[x]);
                x := next[x];
            else ¢ a conditional; save the false branch ¢
                yF := nextF[x];
                PILE := PILE ∪ {⟨yF,outpropF(x,PROP[x])⟩};
                ¢ follow the true branch ¢
                p := outpropT(x,PROP[x]);
                x := nextT[x]
            fi;
            oldp := PROP[x];
            PROP[x] := PROP[x] ∨ p
        od
    od
end
```

Using the well-foundedness of **P**, it is not too difficult to show that this algorithm terminates. Some unnecessary iterations can be avoided by using a more sophisticated structure for PILE so that the two pairs $\langle x, p_1 \rangle$ and $\langle x, p_2 \rangle$ are automatically combined into $\langle x, p_1 \vee p_2 \rangle$ when the second is added to a PILE already occupied by the first. The more complicated versions of Algorithm SI that unroll loops for more precision are straightforward extensions [Wegb75, King76].

If symbolic interpretation is so good, why isn't it used exclusively? The main reason is efficiency. Most problems involve property sets much richer than the one in Fig. 1-20. For example, instead of specifying the type of a single variable, a property might specify the types of *all* program variables. Such property sets give rise to numerous iterations before a steady state is reached. Thus symbolic interpretation is rarely used in compilers. However its suitability for complex problems makes it an important tool for optimization research and program verification [King76, Cous77a, Suzu77, Cous78].

1-6. OPTIMIZATION OF VERY-HIGH-LEVEL LANGUAGES

I shall conclude this survey with a discussion of some current work on optimization for very-high-level languages, focusing on the SETL project at New York University. SETL is a language based on the theory of sets [Schw75d, Kenn75a]. It has a standard set of fundamental data types (real, integer, character, bit, and strings of characters or bits) along with two structured types (sets and tuples). It derives its power from its fundamental view of data as sets and mappings (sets of ordered pairs). An introductory treatment of the language may be found in [Kenn75a].

The SETL implementation identifies two classes of objects, *long* and *short*. Both items use a *root word* for their representation. As shown in Fig. 1-22, the first few bits of the root word identify the object type and the rest are used for actual data, in the case of a short object, or control information and a pointer in the case of a long object. A long object's data is contained in an extended *representing block* stored elsewhere and pointed to by the root word.

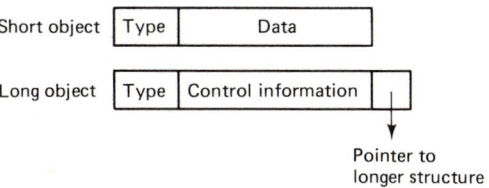

Figure 1-22 Object representation in SETL

Currently, SETL uses representing blocks organized as arrays for tuples and hash tables for sets. Individual entries in these blocks are root words for the individual members.

The general unoptimized implementation scheme is as follows. Code is translated into a series of calls to SETL run-time library routines. Each routine implements one SETL primitive in its most general form. In particular, since SETL does not have type declarations, type tests must be made at run time. Consider the primitive

$$s_1 \text{ eq } s_2$$

which tests for equality between objects of any type. Even after it is discovered that s_1 and s_2 are both sets, the test is a complex one involving another primitive, the membership test $\in$

$$s_1 \text{ eq } s_2 \equiv (\forall x \in s_1 \,|\, x \in s_2) \,\&\, (\forall y \in s_2 \,|\, y \in s_1)$$

The strategy of the SETL optimizer is to use special knowledge of the program, gleaned through global analysis, to replace as many expensive library calls as possible by in-line *code stubs*, which assume the most common case and test for exceptions, calling the library only when necessary. As an example, consider the expression $x + y$. In the general case, x and y could be sets, integers, tuples, reals, strings, etc. But suppose a global analysis of types determines that x and y are both integers; then the situation is greatly simplified, although we still don't know whether they are long or short integers (long integers require multiword storage). The code stub assumes, as the most likely case, that both are short integers. It then has the following flavor.

Stub: add x and y as short integers;
execute a fast test for overflow or type error;
if test positive then call library routine
else record results **fi**

Thus with the aid of global type analysis, the optimizer is able to effect a substantial efficiency gain.

This example leads us naturally to consider the nature of global type analysis. Type analysis was the subject of Tenenbaum's Ph.D. thesis [Tene74b] and has been subsequently studied by Jones and Muchnick [Jone76] and Kaplan and Ullman [Kapl77a]. The first step in type analysis is to define an *algebra of type symbols* which is built up from:

1. A number of *atomic type symbols*:

    I (integer), R (real), UD (undefined), NS (set of arbitrary elements), G (general), Z (error), etc.

2. Alternation of types:

    $$t = t_1 | t_2 | \ldots | t_k$$

3. Set formation:

    $$t = \{t_1\}$$

4. Tuple formation (fixed length):

    $$t = \langle t_1, t_2, \ldots, t_k \rangle$$

5. Tuple formation (indefinite length):

    $$t = [t_1]$$

Next we define the rules for determining the output type of an operation given the input types. This is encoded in a transition function F which, for each operation op and input types $t_1, t_2, \ldots, t_n$ of the operands, produces

$$t_0 = F_{op}(t_1, t_2, \ldots, t_n)$$

where t_0 is the output type (or at least the best approximation to it within the algebra). Finally an operation $\bigvee$, which allows alternation of types at merging paths, is defined; i.e.,

$$t = \bigvee_{i=1}^{k} t_i$$

is the type of an object which has types $t_1, \ldots, t_k$ on k merging paths.

With these definitions, global type determination can be carried out by a direct analog of the use-definition chain algorithm for constant propagation. Although this is the same problem we solved by symbolic interpretation in the last section, use-definition chains permit a more efficient implementation. The workpile is initialized to a set of instructions with clearly defined (or constant) types. Thereafter an instruction is examined whenever a refinement of one of its input types is detected.

Algorithm TA: Type Analysis

Input:
1. A program PROG.
2. A mapping TYPE, such that TYPE(A, x) is the best initial estimate of the type of variable A at x (for most variables this is 'UD').
3. The sets DEFS and USES.

Output: For each instruction x and input or output variable A, TYPE(A, x), a conservative approximation to the most specific type information provably true at x.

Method:

```
begin
    PILE := {x ∈ PROG | (∀ A ∈ inputs(x) | TYPE(a,x) ≠ 'UD')};
    while PILE ≠ φ do
        x := an arbitrary element in PILE;
        PILE := PILE − {x};
        B := output(x);
        for each i ∈ USES(b,x) do
            ¢ recompute type ¢
            oldtype := TYPE(b,i);
            TYPE(B,i) :=      ⋁       TYPE(B,y);
                          y∈DEFS(B,i)
            if TYPE(B,i) ≠ oldtype then
                ¢ a type refinement ¢
                TYPE(output(i),i) := F_{op(i)} applied to the input types of i;
                PILE := PILE ∪ {i}
            fi
        od
    od
end
```

In his dissertation, Tenenbaum showed how the above type analysis could be enhanced by a backward pass which elicits type information from uses and propagates it back to definition points [Tene74b]. Kaplan and Ullman extended this idea to incorporate multiple passes in both directions [Kapl77a]. It is clear that symbolic interpretation could also be used for type analysis to produce more specific results. I will not have space to treat the numerous other SETL optimizations here. I refer the interested reader to a series of papers [Schw74a, Schw75a, Schw75b, Schw75c, Dewa77] which lay out most of the methods used by that project; several of these involve automatic or semiautomatic data structure choice. A number of papers treat further SETL optimizations [Fong76, Paig77, Fong77]. In general, the optimization of very-high-level languages should prove a fruitful area for new research and for further application of established techniques.

ACKNOWLEDGMENT

I am grateful to Barry Rosen for several suggestions which substantially improved this chapter.

Chapter 2

Degrees of Availability as an Introduction to the General Theory of Data Flow Analysis

Barry K. Rosen

2-1. INTRODUCTION

The question of whether the value of an expression is available at a given point in a program is usually answered YES or NO, but very-high-level languages pose availability questions that require more subtle answers. Fong [Fong77] associates two availability bits with each expression at each point in the program: AVAIL for availability in the traditional sense and IAVAIL for availability in a new, weaker sense. The new information can be exploited by an optimizing compiler, bit it is rather difficult to obtain. The bit IAVAIL falls outside the more or less standard algebraic framework for data flow analysis. For programs with "reducible" graphs it can be found by adapting the AVAIL algorithm from [Ullm73] in the way explained in [Fong77]. One of our purposes here is to show that the *practical need* which motivates the introduction of IAVAIL can be met within the more or less standard framework. By seeking more information than is sought in [Fong77], we derive two advantages. First, there are many known algorithms that can be applied, including algorithms that are simpler or more widely applicable than that of [Ullm73]. Second, the additional information is directly useful in optimization. Instead of asking *whether* an expression is available, we ask *how* available it is. Numerical degrees of availability replace the traditional YES/NO bits.

The usual way to relate programs to control flow graphs is reviewed in Section 2-2. This is not always the best way, but it is familiar and can be described briefly. In Section 2-3, the motivation for IAVAIL is reviewed, with particular attention to the distinction between a practical need for information and the precise mathematical question that attempts to model that need. Careful modeling leads naturally to some key ideas from the general theory of data flow analysis. Presenting the ideas in this way may counteract the unfortunate impression (which seems to be rather widespread) that the general theory is a recondite mathematical topic of marginal practical interest. On the contrary, thorough analysis is one of the central issues in designing compilers that generate good code. Available theory is relevant, which is not to say that applications are easy. Some of the pitfalls are discussed in Section 2-4. Analysis is but a means to the end of generating good code. The actual uses of data flow information have not yet been studied with the same mathematical thoroughness that has been applied to analysis itself. Some of the issues are considered in Section 2-5. Finally, Section 2-6 compares two fundamentally different strategies, usually known as *iteration* and *elimination*, in data flow algorithms.

This chapter emphasizes principles and pitfalls while using a minimum of mathematical machinery. The goal is a view of the forest despite all the trees. Many of the trees are already examined in more conventionally structured introductions to data flow analysis, such as [Aho77, Hech77] or Chapter 1 in this volume. The trees examined here were chosen in part because conventional introductions avoid them and in part because they are interesting specimens that the author knows well. After reading this chapter one should consult conventional introductions and the cited research literature. This route into the data flow forest is particularly suitable for two related purposes. First, one may wish to apply the existing theory in new ways. Second, one may wish to add to the theory in ways that will be useful in new applications.

A small amount of standard mathematical notation will be used, as when $\{0, 1\}$ denotes the set containing just the two numbers 0 and 1, while $[0, 1]$ denotes $\{x \,|\, 0 \le x \le 1\}$ (the set of all numbers x with $0 \le x \le 1$). A *map* (or *function*) f consists of three sets: a set A of possible *arguments*, a set V of possible *values*, and a set f_{pairs} of ordered pairs (a, v) with a in A and v in V. Given any one choice of a in A, there must be exactly one v in V such that (a, v) is in f_{pairs}. We write $f(a)$ for the value of f at a (i.e., the unique v such that (a, v) is in f_{pairs}), and we write $f \colon A \longrightarrow V$ to indicate that f is a map with argument set A and value set V. We also say that f is a map *from A to V*. For example, squaring of numbers in $[0, 1]$ defines a map SQUARE: $[0, 1] \longrightarrow [0, 1]$ with SQUARE(0.3) = 0.09. Given two maps $f \colon A \longrightarrow V$ and $f' \colon A' \longrightarrow V'$ such that $V = A'$, we have another map $(f' \circ f) \colon A \longrightarrow V'$ with

$(f' \circ f)(a) = f'(f(a))$ for each a in A. A good way to pronounce the symbol $\circ$ is to say *after*. It is easy to see that $(g \circ (f' \circ f)) = ((g \circ f') \circ f)$ whenever either side of the equation makes sense, so we will just write $g \circ f' \circ f$ by analogy with $b \times a' \times a$ for numbers. Of special interest is the case where $A = V$, so that we can consider $f \circ f$, $f \circ f \circ f$, and so on. By analogy with $\times$ as an operation on numbers, we write f^k for $k = 2$, 3, and so on. Of course f^1 is just f itself. Finally, f^0 is the *identity map* $\mathbf{1}: A \longrightarrow A$ with $\mathbf{1}(a) = a$ for all a. Strictly speaking, we should write $\mathbf{1}_A$ because each set has its own identity map.

A (finite) graph G consists of two (finite) sets NODES and ARCS (whose members are called *nodes* and *arcs*) and two maps $\mathbf{s}: \text{ARCS} \longrightarrow \text{NODES}$ and $\mathbf{t}: \text{ARCS} \longrightarrow \text{NODES}$ (called the *source* and *target* maps). We draw pictures of graphs by drawing boxes, circles, ovals, or whatever else is convenient for the nodes. For an arc c with source $\mathbf{s}(c)$ and target $\mathbf{t}(c)$, we draw an arrow from the picture of $\mathbf{s}(c)$ to the picture of $\mathbf{t}(c)$. An arc is said to run *from* its source *to* its target. In the literature, arcs are also called *edges* or sometimes *links*, while nodes are also called *vertices*. An arc from node n to node p is often defined to be the ordered pair (n, p). Under our definition this corresponds to adding an assumption: If arcs c and d have $\mathbf{s}(c) = \mathbf{s}(d)$ and $\mathbf{t}(c) = \mathbf{t}(d)$, then $c = d$. It is good mathematical practice to refrain from assuming things until one has a use for them, so we will allow the possibility of arcs $c \neq d$ with the same source and target. This does happen in data flow analysis. Two arcs with the same source and target are easy to draw: just draw two arrows from one picture of a node to another. A *path* in a graph is a sequence $\mathbf{c} = (c_1, \ldots, c_k)$ of arcs such that the target of c_k is also the source of c_{k+1} whenever $1 \leq k < K$. The null sequence (with $K = 0$) is trivially counted as a path. Like an arc, a nonnull path may be said to have a *source* (the source of its first arc) and a *target* (the target of its last arc). Like an arc, a nonnull path runs *from* its source *to* its target. The null path runs from any node to itself. A nonnull path from a node to itself is a *cycle*.

Trees include nonnull sequences but allow for more possibilities. Consider a sequence $\mathbf{x} = (x_1, \ldots, x_K)$ of items (not necessarily arcs in a graph). Given an integer k such that x_k appears in $\mathbf{x}$, either x_k is the last item or there is a unique next item x_{k+1}. A tree is like a nonnull sequence, but next items are no longer unique. Instead, a tree can *branch* to several "next" items after x_k. The first item in a tree is the *root*. The various "next" items after an item are its *sons*. An item with no sons is a *leaf*. For each tree we have a graph whose nodes are the items. For each son p of an item n there is an arc from n to p. There is a unique path from the root to any item in the tree. The items encountered on this path form a sequence. There is no need to distinguish between a tree that has just one leaf and the corresponding sequence (root, $\ldots$, leaf). A tree with several leaves defines a sequence for each leaf, and the tree itself is a compact way to display the similarities among these sequences.

2-2. REVIEW OF USUAL CONTROL FLOW GRAPH

We suppose that programs consist of *instructions* whose possible effects are known. Instructions are rather small, in that they fetch the values of a few variables and then change the values of a few variables to certain functions of the fetched values. All fetching precedes all changing. (This need not be literally true, but it needs to be adequate as a description of the net effect of executing instructions.) Values of variables, however, may be large objects like files and arrays. A program has *entry* instructions that may have control initially and it has *exit* instructions that stop execution and return control to the environment running the program. Instructions other than exit instructions can pass control within the program, both by explicitly naming successors and by appearing immediately ahead of them in a listing of the whole program. One could let nodes be instructions and arcs be control flow relations among instructions. This would be a special case of the usual graph. In the most general form of the usual graph, nodes are *extended basic blocks* (or just *blocks* for short) of instructions. To avoid having large graphs for programs of practical interest, it is usually considered advisable to have many instructions in a block. On the other hand, we want the control flow within each block to be very simple. Using extended basic blocks is one way to accomplish this. Each block is a tree of instructions, such that control can only enter the tree at the root. Each entry instruction is the root of a block, and blocks rooted in this way are the *entry blocks*. The tree leaves in a block are of two kinds: exit instructions and instructions that pass control within the program (either back to the root of the same block or to the root of another block). Each leaf that is not an exit instruction thus defines an arc in the graph for each way it can pass control. This arc runs *from* the block containing the leaf *to* the block whose root receives control. In particular, there may be an arc from a block to itself and there may be more than one arc from block n to block p. Many authors only allow a tree with one leaf to serve as a block (a *basic block* in contrast with our *extended* basic block). Extended basic blocks have sometimes been used, as in [Kenn76, Schn73]. The main advantage of trees with more than one leaf is that we get smaller graphs because the nodes are larger blocks. The main disadvantage is that trees are more complicated than sequences.

Figure 2-1 shows the graph for an example program, with each node shown as a box around the corresponding tree of instructions. The example program gets integers Q from an input file IN. The number of zeroes in IN is accumulated in COUNT. The nonzero input values are accumulated alternately in sets A and B, with a boolean variables SWITCH to control the alternation. With the exit instruction 920 placed in a block by itself for later convenience, the graph has three nodes and five arcs. Had we used only basic

```
901  enter
902  COUNT ← 0
903  A ← ∅
904  B ← ∅
905  SWITCH ← false
906  X ← A ∪ B
907  goto 919 if empty (IN)
908  get Q from IN
909  goto 917 if Q = 0
910  goto 914 if SWITCH
911  A ← A ∪ {Q}
912  SWITCH ← true
913  goto 906
914  B ← B ∪ {Q}
915  SWITCH ← false
916  goto 906
917  COUNT ← COUNT + 1
918  goto 906
919  put (A, B, X, COUNT) into OUT
920  exit
```

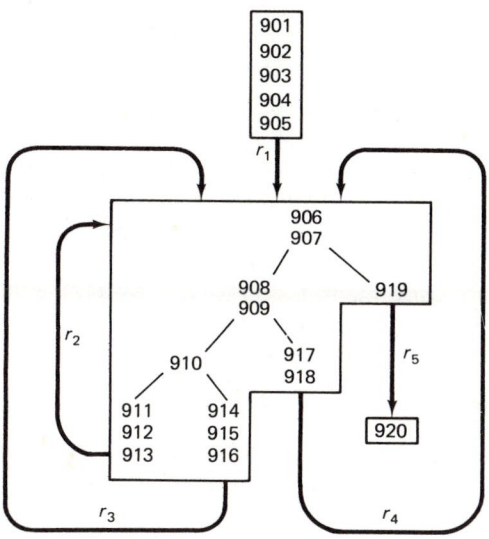

Figure 2-1 Control flow graph for an example program with 20 instructions. The empty set ϕ has nothing in it.

blocks rather than extended basic blocks, nine nodes and eleven arcs would have been needed.

With blocks for nodes and arcs as defined above, we have a graph that is generally a good deal smaller than the program itself but implicitly contains all the control flow information. For each arc c we have a sequence $\tau(c)$ of instructions: look at the block n that c runs out of, look at the leaf in the tree that adds c to the graph, and list the instructions on the unique path from root to leaf. For example, $c = r_5$ in Fig. 2-1 defines the sequence $\tau(r_5) = (906, 907, 919)$. The sequence $\tau(c)$ is an *instruction path*: any sequence of instructions such that control can pass along it. Instruction paths are related to paths in the graph, even when they are not of the form $\tau(c)$. If an instruction path α begins at an entry instruction, then it has the form $\pi \cdot \phi$ (where $\cdot$ is concatenation). The path π may be null. If not null, it ends at a nonexit leaf in a block and has the form $\tau(c_1) \cdot \tau(c_2) \cdot \ldots \cdot \tau(c_K)$ for some nonnull path $(c_1, \ldots, c_K)$ in the graph. The path ϕ is entirely within one block, running from the root to the last instruction in α. (This discussion may sound a little stilted. One must be careful in relating instruction paths to paths in the graph if one wants to *apply* the theory correctly, without missing or doubling instructions at roots or leaves in blocks.) For example, let $\alpha = (901, \ldots, 905, 906, \ldots, 913, 906, 907)$ in Fig. 2-1. Then $\alpha = \pi \cdot \phi$ with $\pi = \tau(r_1) \cdot \tau(r_2)$ and $\phi = (906, 907)$. From now on the variable α will range over the instruction paths that start with entry instructions. If we say "for each α," then we are really saying "for each instruction path α starting with an entry instruction."

A very special case of the usual control flow graph can be obtained by letting each block contain just one instruction. This is simple but misses the point of blocking. The opposite extreme is to let each block be as large as possible, subject to the requirement of being a tree entered only at the root. Because real languages have many instruction types with special properties, a mixed strategy is generally preferable. Certain special instructions that need special attention are given blocks by themselves, but blocks are otherwise as large as is possible or convenient. For present purposes it will suffice to isolate exit instructions in their own blocks, and even this will not be necessary until idleness of variables is studied in Section 2-5.

2-3. AVAILABILITY

During a computation, an expression **R** is *available* at an instruction if it has previously been computed and has suffered no subsequent change in value, where an expression is considered to have changed in value whenever any of the variables involved in it has changed its value. (To simplify analysis we do not attempt to detect situations where one change promptly cancels the effect of another change, at least for the present.) If an instruction θ computes $\mathbf{R}$ even though $\mathbf{R}$ is available, this seems rather wasteful. When $\mathbf{R}$ was computed before, we should have saved the result for θ to fetch rather than recompute. (We assume that saving and then fetching is cheaper than recomputing. Of course this is not always true.) In deciding whether to replace θ by a similar instruction that fetches an old value of $\mathbf{R}$, a compiler has to consider the safety of this change for all computations. For each path α to θ that might arise in a computation, the compiler might check that, indeed, there is a previous instruction v that computes $\mathbf{R}$, such that neither v nor any instruction between v and θ can possibly change $\mathbf{R}$. (To avoid undecidabilities, the compiler can deal with any recursive set of paths that includes all those that are really possible at run time.) In many programs the relevant set of paths α is astronomically large if finite at all, so direct enumeration is inappropriate. Even so, the bit $\text{AVAIL}(\theta)$ in $\{0, 1\}$ can be effectively computed for each instruction θ, with $\text{AVAIL}(\theta) = 1$ if $\mathbf{R}$ is available at θ along each path α to θ.

In the early optimizing compilers that first motivated the theory of data flow analysis, an expression $\mathbf{R}$ almost always had the form $A \ \square \ B$ for scalar variables A, B and an arithmetic operator $\square$. For such expressions the choice between recomputing and storing/fetching can be difficult. More recently, it has been noticed that the $A \ \square \ B$ syntax is irrelevant to data flow analysis. An *expression* could be almost anything that appears in a program and incurs computational costs whenever it is encountered at run time. Something like "the result of sorting the file EMPLOYEES on the value of the AGE field of each record" (expressed in various ways by various languages) could be an expression for our purposes. Such an expression has the advantage that fetching is definitely cheaper than recomputing so long as there are enough disk tracks or tape drives to keep the sorted file ready for reading. (Here to "fetch" is simply to put the reading cursor at the start of the file.) It has the disadvantage that notations for file handling are not as standardized and concise as notations for scalar arithmetic. For our purposes it is helpful to consider expressions using set-valued variables and operations on sets. Like arithmetic, set theory has a standard and concise notation. Like files, the values of set variables and expressions are often *large* objects that change in *small* steps. Only one operation on sets will be necessary for the present: $A \cup B$ is the set consisting of everything in A together with everything in B.

An instruction that can change $\mathbf{R}$ is usually said to "kill" the availability of $\mathbf{R}$, while one that computes $\mathbf{R}$ without also changing $\mathbf{R}$ is said to "generate" the availability of $\mathbf{R}$. Given an instruction θ and an instruction path α to θ, we say that $\mathbf{R}$ is available at θ along α provided that some instruction v which generates $\mathbf{R}$ is strictly before θ and is not followed by any instructions which kill $\mathbf{R}$ and are strictly before θ. Let $\text{AVAIL}(\theta)$ in $\{0, 1\}$ be 1 if $\mathbf{R}$ is available at θ along each path α to θ. For numerical expressions with only scalar variables, this single bit of information is appropriate for modeling the practical question of availability. But suppose **R** has the form $A \cup B$, where A and B are set variables. An assignment such as $A \leftarrow C$ certainly kills availability of **R**, as does $A \leftarrow A \cup \{x\}$. But the second assignment has an additional property. The new value of **R** can be found from the old one by performing the operation $\ldots \cup \{x\}$, and this is much cheaper than recomputing $A \cup B$. Performing $\ldots \cup \{x\}$ after fetching the old value is not the same as merely fetching the old value, but it has the same practical significance. When the value of **R** is wanted, we can find it by using results of old computations rather than by computing from scratch. The set union and difference examples are considered in detail in [Fong77], while heuristics for a broad class of examples are outlined in [Paig77]. Among the instructions that kill the availability of **R**, instructions such that the new value may be easily found from the old one are said to "only incidentally kill" it in [Fong77]. Drawing the same distinctions with smoother English, we divide the instructions that can change **R** into two classes. Only those that can change **R** radically enough to require a new computation will now be said to *kill* the availability of **R**. An instruction that can change **R**, but only in such a way that the new value can be found cheaply from the old one, will be said to *wound* the availability of **R**. One could distinguish various degrees of severity of wounds. (Grisly words like "kill" and "wound" are objectionable, but the killing metaphor is too standardized to change. Since we have to tolerate "kill" already, we may as well use clear words like "wound" rather than grotesque phrases like "only incidentally kill.") Given an instruction θ and an instruction path α to θ, we say that E is *partially available* at θ along α provided that some instruction ν which generates **R** is strictly before θ and is not followed by any instructions which kill **R** (in the new narrower sense) and are strictly before θ. Between ν and θ the availability of **R** may be wounded, but each wound can be healed. The bit IAVAIL(θ) [Fong77, p. 51] is 1 if **R** is partially available along each path α to θ and there is a bound on the number of wounds that **R** might suffer between a generating instruction and θ. This boundedness requirement puts the IAVAIL bit outside the more or less standard framework [Fong77, Fig. 3].

Before attempting to compute IAVAIL bits in a nonstandard way, let us consider whether they really tell us what we need to know for optimization. After 1000 wounds **R** will still be partially available, but recomputation will be cheaper than the total cost of healing all wounds if **R** is $A \cup B$ with A and B declared to have at most 256 members. We want to know how often **R** may have been wounded, not just whether it is partially available. To keep as close to the old set $\{0, 1\}$ of AVAIL values as possible, we can use the interval $[0, 1]$ of numbers. Just after a generating instruction, **R** has a *degree* of availability of 1. Just after a killing instruction, **R** has a degree of availability of 0. A wounding instruction multiplies the previous degree of availability by some w with $0 < w < 1$. (A good way to choose w is to let $w = 2^{-h}$, where h is an estimate of the cost of healing the wound.) Thus an instruction ψ has an effect $\text{CHA}(\psi): [0, 1] \to [0, 1]$ on the degree of availability. If there is no change, then $\text{CHA}(\psi)$ is the identity map. If ψ generates (kills) $\mathbf{R}$, then $\text{CHA}(\psi)$ is constant with value 1 (respectively, 0). Otherwise ψ wounds $\mathbf{R}$ and $\text{CHA}(\psi)$ is multiplication by w for some w with $0 < w < 1$. (With $w = 2^{-h}$ it would be convenient to replace multiplication by addition of exponents.)

Given an instruction θ and an instruction path α to θ, we now have a degree of availability of $\mathbf{R}$ at θ along α. Let $\text{DAVAIL}(\theta)$ in the interval $[0, 1]$ be the *greatest lower bound* of the set of all degrees of availability of $\mathbf{R}$ at θ along α, as various paths α are considered. It can be shown that $\text{DAVAIL}(\theta) > 0$ for exactly those instructions θ with $\text{IAVAIL}(\theta) = 1$, so no information is lost when we consider DAVAIL rather than IAVAIL. Much information is gained, since the numerical value of DAVAIL can be compared with estimates of the cost of recomputing $\mathbf{R}$ in deciding whether optimizations that exploit partial availability are likely to be profitable. Another advantage of DAVAIL is that it can be found within the standard framework, as we will show below. This claim may sound paradoxical: DAVAIL includes the information in IAVAIL, which falls outside the framework. The difficulties with boundedness summarized in [Fong77, Fig. 3] only arise *after* a design decision has been made: the data flow information for $\mathbf{R}$ at each point in the program is to be a single bit. This design decision is part of the modeling process that links a practical concern with partial availability to the mathematical theory of data flow analysis. By considering DAVAIL, we decide otherwise, so the consequences of the single-bit decision do not necessarily befall us.

Recall that control flow can be summarized by a graph whose nodes are blocks, and that blocks are trees of instructions. For each node n let θ_n be the instruction at the root of n. Define I mapping the set of nodes into $[0, 1]$ by

$$I(n) = \text{DAVAIL}(\theta_n) \qquad (2\text{-}1)$$

so that I holds part of the information in DAVAIL. The rest of the information can easily be recovered from I and *local* analysis that stays within a single block. Given an instruction ψ, let n be the block containing ψ. Then $\text{DAVAIL}(\psi)$ can be computed from $I(n)$ by inspecting the instructions along the path from θ_n to ψ in the block. We propagate $I(n)$ to ψ, changing the number appropriately in light of what the successive instructions do. (If $\psi \neq \theta_n$ and there are k instructions before ψ on the path, then there are k changes.) The main advantage of I over DAVAIL is that it is smaller: programs tend to have many instructions in each block.

Let $L = L_{\text{DAVAIL}}$ be $[0, 1]$ with only certain properties of the usual order relation $\leq$ considered. Specifically, $\leq$ is reflexive, antisymmetric, and transitive. Whenever a relation $\leq$ on a set L has these properties, we say that L is a *partially ordered set*. In this context a *lower bound* for a subset X of L is any λ in L such that $\lambda \leq \xi$ for all ξ in X. A *greatest* lower bound γ has $\lambda \leq \gamma$ for all lower bounds λ. If X has a greatest lower bound, then it has only one of them. For our $L = L_{\text{DAVAIL}}$, any subset X of L does have a greatest lower bound **glb** X. One more twist brings DAVAIL squarely into the world of known analysis algorithms. For each arc c we have a map $F_c : L \longrightarrow L$ defined by $F_c = \text{CHA}(\theta_K) \circ \text{CHA}(\theta_{K-1}) \circ \ldots \circ \text{CHA}(\theta_1)$, where $(\theta_1, \ldots, \theta_K)$ is the instruction path from root to leaf in the block that adds c to the graph and $\text{CHA}(\theta)$ is the effect of θ on the degree of availability of **R**. For any path $\mathbf{c} = (c_1, \ldots, c_K)$ there is a sequence $(f_1, \ldots, f_K)$ of maps with $f_k = F_d$ for $d = c_k$. Let $F_{\mathbf{c}} = f_K \circ f_{K-1} \circ \ldots \circ f_1$. In particular, if $\mathbf{c}$ is null, than $F_{\mathbf{c}}$ is the identity map $\mathbf{1}_L$. The usual assumption that **R** is not available at the start can be represented by $E:$ ENTRY NODES $\longrightarrow [0, 1]$ with $E(m) = 0$ for each entry node m. Then (2-1) is equivalent to

$$I(n) = \textbf{glb}\{F_{\mathbf{c}}E(m) \mid m \text{ is an entry node and } \mathbf{c} \text{ is a path from } m \text{ to } n\} \quad (2\text{-}2)$$

where $F_{\mathbf{c}}(E(m))$ is written as $F_{\mathbf{c}}E(m)$ to avoid having so many parentheses. (We will often omit parentheses in this way.) The advantage of Eq. (2-2) is that it applies to many data flow questions about programs, not just to DAVAIL or to questions with answers in $[0, 1]$. To study (2-2) we need a partially ordered set L with greatest lower bounds, so that the **glb** notation makes sense. We need a graph with $F_c : L \longrightarrow L$ assigned to each arc c, such that F_c is *isotone:* if $\xi \leq \eta$ then $F_c \xi \leq F_c \eta$. We need designated entry nodes and entry information $E(m)$ in L for each entry node m. (In our treatment of DAVAIL and in much of the literature $E(m)$ is taken to be **glb** L, the smallest thing in L. This is often inappropriate, especially in the interprocedural analysis discussed in Section 2-4.) Given all this, no matter how L and so on were obtained, we can *define* $I:$ NODES $\longrightarrow L$ by Eq. (2-2) and then inquire how to *compute* it. The available algorithms vary in what they assume about the graph or about the maps F_c. In our example, all ξ, η in L have

$$F_c(\textbf{glb}\{\xi, \eta\}) = \textbf{glb}\{F_c\xi, F_c\eta\} \quad (2\text{-}3)$$

Indeed, any nonempty subset X of L, even an infinite subset, has

$$F_c(\textbf{glb } X) = \textbf{glb}\{F_c\xi \mid \xi \in X\} \quad (2\text{-}4)$$

For DAVAIL and for any other problem satisfying (2-4) one can compute I defined by (2-2) by a method that converges but may not terminate. (This may sound paradoxical, but it is really commonplace. Consider $\pi = 3.14159\ldots$ in numerical analysis.) The computation begins with the guess

$$I_0(n) = (\textbf{if } n \text{ is an entry node \textbf{then} } E(m) \textbf{ else } \top)$$

where $\top = \mathbf{glb}\ \varnothing$ is the maximum element of L. In our example $\top = 1$. Whenever there is an arc c running from a node n to a node p such that n is reachable by a path from an entry node and the current guess fails to have $I_k(p) \leq F_c I_k(n)$, the next guess I_{k+1} will have $I_{k+1}(p) = \mathbf{glb}\{I_k(p), F_c I_k(n)\}$. If possible, the guess is corrected until it stabilizes, at which point I_k is demonstrably equal to I defined by (2-2). What if it never stabilizes? Then we go on forever, with the understanding that each arc c is to be examined infinitely often. The limit $I_\omega = \mathbf{glb}\{I_k \,|\, k = 0, 1, 2, \ldots\}$ is demonstrably equal to I defined by (2-2). There are several variations on this *iterative* algorithm in the literature, depending on how one organizes the scan for places where corrections are needed. See Section 2-6 for details. In studying such algorithms it is usual to assume that L is *well-founded:* there are no infinite chains $\xi_0 > \xi_1 > \xi_2 > \ldots$ in L. Unlike our own L_{DAVAIL}, most of the semilattices that do arise in data flow analysis are well-founded. For these semilattices the sequence of guesses is certain to stabilize in finitely many steps.

Also available are *elimination* algorithms, which have a number of advantages over iteration (to be sketched in Section 2-6). One advantage of elimination is that we can sometimes find I in finitely many steps even when L is not well-founded. Degrees of availability is a case in point. Instead of assuming well-foundedness, elimination algorithms assume that each map F_c belongs to a set M of maps that is closed under certain operations on maps from L to L, and that good algorithms to perform the operations are available. For all $f, g \in M$, the *composition* $f \circ g$ (with $\circ$ as usual) and the *pointwise glb* with $(\mathbf{glb}\{f, g\})(\xi) = \mathbf{glb}\{f(\xi), g(\xi)\}$ are in M. Moreover, M is *rapid*. The general definition in [Rose78b] is complicated by the need to avoid assuming (2-4) throughout the theory. When (2-4) holds, rapidity may be defined quite simply. Given $f \in M$, can we find

$$f^* = \mathbf{glb}\{f^k \,|\, k = 0, 1, 2, \ldots\} \tag{2-5}$$

in a finite number of steps, independent of the choice of f? (The composition and pointwise glb operations count as single steps.) If so, and if M is closed under this operation, then M is rapid. The following lemma will help us show that M is indeed rapid when degrees of availability are sought. Rapidity lets us apply elimination methods to this problem, so that exact answers are obtained after finitely many steps despite the presence of infinite descending chains.

Lemma. [G. Markowsky]. For each ξ in $L_{\text{DAVAIL}} = L$ let $K\xi$ be the constant map $(K\xi)(\eta) = \xi$ and let $T\xi$ be the multiplication map $(T\xi)(\eta) = \xi\eta$. Let M be the smallest set of maps on L including each $K\xi$ and $T\xi$ but also closed under composition and pointwise glb. For each $f \in M$ there is a unique ξ in L such that either $f = K\xi$ or there is a unique ρ in L with $f = \mathbf{glb}\{K\xi, T\rho\}$.

Proof. The claim is true of each $K\xi$ and $T\xi$. We must show that it will also be true of $f \circ g$ and $\mathbf{glb}\{f, g\}$ if it is true of f and g. For $f \circ g$ the only nontrivial case is when $f = \mathbf{glb}\{K\xi, T\rho\}$ and $g = \mathbf{glb}\{K\eta, T\sigma\}$. Abbreviating $\mathbf{glb}\{x, y\}$ to $x \wedge y$, we calculate:

$$f \circ g = (K\xi \circ K\eta) \wedge (K\xi \circ T\sigma) \wedge (T\rho \circ K\eta) \wedge (T\rho \circ T\sigma)$$
$$= K\xi \wedge K\xi \wedge K(\rho\eta) \wedge T(\rho\sigma)$$
$$= K\zeta \wedge T\tau \text{ for } \zeta = \xi \wedge \rho\eta \text{ and } \tau = \rho\sigma$$

For $f \wedge g$ in this case we get $(K\xi \wedge T\rho) \wedge (K\eta \wedge T\sigma) = K\zeta \wedge T\tau$ for $\zeta = \xi \wedge \eta$ and $\tau = \rho \wedge \sigma$. The other cases are similar but a little simpler, and uniqueness is easily checked. ■

Theorem.   For M as in the Lemma, M is rapid.

Proof.   Any member f of M may be represented by a triple (const?, ξ, ρ), where the bit const? tells whether f is constant (in which case $f = K\xi$) or not constant (in which case $f = K\xi \wedge T\rho$). If $f = K\xi$, then $f^* = K\xi \wedge T\rho$ for $\rho = 1$. If $f = K\xi \wedge T\rho$ for $\rho = 1$, then $f = (K\xi)^*$ and so $f^* = (K\xi)^{**} = (K\xi)^* = f$. Finally, suppose $f = K\xi \wedge T\rho$ for $\rho < 1$. Each positive k has $f^k = K\eta \wedge T\sigma$ for $\eta = \xi\rho^{k-1}$ and $\sigma = \rho^k$, so $f^*\zeta \le \rho^k$ for all k and $f^* = K0$. In all cases we can find f^* quickly from f, and M is closed under this operation. ■

2-4.   PITFALLS

In Eq. (2-2) and accompanying remarks we outlined the more or less standard algebraic framework for modern data flow analysis. The details vary as one moves through the literature. Like most pioneers, the pioneers in this area made some choices that seemed good at the time (or were not even recognized to be *choices*) but that eventually proved otherwise. For example, consider the choice of whether local information should be associated with arcs or nodes. Some authors associate $F_c: L \longrightarrow L$ with each arc c, as we did, while others associate $F_n: L \longrightarrow L$ with each node n. Using nodes in the theory precludes applications to compilers that build text blocks with more than one leaf in each tree, unless one obscures the applications with extra nodes. Using nodes also precludes any natural formulation of certain elimination algorithms. By themselves, variations like arcs/nodes in placing local information are only minor nuisances. The number of such variations is large enough that thoughtful comparative reading is difficult. Serious misunderstandings have occurred, as when [Hech77, p.161] and [Kam77, p.305] claim that [Grah76] is restricted to problems that satisfy Eq. (2-3). Before applying any particular paper to any particular problem, one must check whether that paper's presuppositions hold (or can be obtained by some sleight of hand). This is not as easy as it should be: presuppositions are sometimes tacit or even contrary to what is explicitly assumed. For example, many authors assume that at most one arc can run from n to p. [There is only one ordered pair (n, p), and arcs are often defined to be ordered pairs.] As is noted in [Rose77b], some of these authors then present algorithms that often *need* more than one arc from n to p if they are to perform correctly. With due regard for the variations and minor mistakes, we can say there *is* a standard general framework adequate for most of the static analysis problems in compiling. Well, almost adequate. The local information we presuppose is simply not there in some cases, as when instructions may be procedure calls. This leads to *interprocedural* analysis wherein the local information for a call within a procedure is derived from an analysis of the called procedure. The early history of this topic is reviewed in [Rose79], which is the first rigorous mathematical treatment. With care, we can obtain local information specific to each call without the overhead of a separate analysis of the called procedure for each call. In addition to the works cited by [Rose79], the reader should consult [Bann79] and Chapter 7 for a well-rounded picture of work on interprocedural data flow. Note that [Bann79, Rose79] and their references all deal with specific kinds of local information. Under Eq. (2-3) and the assumption that our rapid set M of maps is itself well-founded (where $f \leq g$ if $f(\xi) \leq g(\xi)$ for all ξ), it is possible to generalize [Rose79], provided we ignore a pitfall that is usually also ignored in intraprocedural analysis. (Such a generalization is part of what the "functional approach" in Chapter 7 accomplishes.)

The final pitfall is the profound difference between real programming languages and the toy languages customarily used to illustrate the theory. In toy languages the relation between syntax and semantics is so transparent that one may acquire a false sense of security and some very bad habits. An assignment instruction $A \leftarrow B + C$ in a toy language may be said to "define" A and no other variables, while it "uses" B, C and no other variables. In a real language the three variables can refer to overlapping storage, as when A, B are subscripted rather than simple variables. Whether A and B do overlap depends on subscript values. In compilers like FORTRAN H [Lowr69] this problem is avoided by simply giving up: optimization is restricted to simple variables. Even simple variables can overlap, as when A is a formal parameter and B is a global variable that may have been passed to A by reference. In this case the semantics of $A \leftarrow B + C$ are not what an isolated syntactic analysis suggests. Again, conservative compilers simply give up. Reference parameters have been justly criticized by researchers in language design and program verification, but the fact that distinct names may overlap in storage is unlikely to be exorcised by language design alone. Subscripted variables are probably here to stay. More generally, what instructions mean varies with the environment in which they are executed.

Syntactic analysis of isolated instructions can only serve the purposes of semantic analysis when we either work with toy languages or work with real ones in an extremely conservative way. Language design decisions affect the combinatorics of the gap between syntax and semantics. There is no evidence that good language design alone can eliminate the gap.

2-5. USING DATA FLOW INFORMATION

Suppose the expression **R** has a fairly high degree of availability at some instruction where the value of **R** is wanted. We would like to replace evaluation of **R** by a fetch from a variable V_R whose job it is to hold this value. Prior computations of **R** may need to be changed so as to make sure that V_R does its job. Consideration of one of the simpler ways to exploit availability information is very instructive and soon leads to difficult questions in compiler design. Suppose that all the instructions generating the availability of **R** have the form (vbl) $\leftarrow$ **R** for some variable (vbl). The fact that **R** is available at an instruction θ will not be helpful to us if **R** can be generated by $X \leftarrow$ **R** along one instruction path to θ but by $Y \leftarrow$ **R** along another. At θ we will not know whether to look in X or in Y for **R**. Worse still, an intervening $X \leftarrow 0$ after $X \leftarrow$ **R** would leave **R** available (if $X \leftarrow$ **R** generates **R** then X does not occur in **R**), but not *in* X. After finding that there is indeed some availability to exploit, we can introduce a *new* variable V_R and replace each instruction (vbl) $\leftarrow$ **R** by the corresponding sequence of instructions ($V_R \leftarrow$ **R**, (vbl) $\leftarrow V_R$). This is not so inefficient as it looks, for reasons that will emerge shortly. For the moment, the introduction of V_R is just a simple way to make sure that the value of **R** will be available in V_R whenever it is available at all.

Unfortunately, **R** may have been wounded a few times after the last time it was fully available. At compile time we do not even know which sequence of wounds needs to be healed. One way to solve this problem is to heal the wounds as fast as they occur. For example, suppose that **R** is $A \cup B$. Immediately after an assignment $A \leftarrow A \cup \{x\}$ has wounded **R**, we can insert a new assignment $V_R \leftarrow V_R \cup \{x\}$ to heal the wound. When this has been done often enough, the transformed program will be such that **R** is fully available (and in V_R) at any instruction where we want to replace computation by fetching.

The scheme sketched above is simple and obviously correct. An "optimized" program does the same thing as the original program, but some computations of **R** have been replaced by fetches from V_R. Even under our working assumption that such fetches are significantly cheaper than recomputations, it is possible that the "optimized" program runs slower than the original on many inputs. There may be instruction paths along which availability of R is generated, then various wounds are inflicted and healed, and then a branch instruction occurs. If control flows one way (call it "left"), then no instructions that use V_R (having formerly computed R) are encountered. If control flows the other way (call it "right"), then such an instruction is encountered. When control flows right, we save time by fetching rather than recomputing. By requiring all nonzero degrees of availability to be rather close to 1 before any attempt will be made to exploit availability of R, we can ensure that this savings is large enough to balance the (estimated) costs of all healings. But when control flows left, we incur the costs of healing to no purpose. Whether there is a net gain on the average depends on how often control flows right rather than left. Once again, an apparently YES/NO question turns on numbers. Now the numbers are the probabilities of branching right or left.

There is one situation where the costs of healing can be avoided without knowledge of probabilities. Suppose V_R has been used (apart from healing) for the last time in a program, and then one of the variables in R is changed. This wounds the availability of R, and so our simple scheme would have us heal the wound by assigning to V_R. But this variable will never do any useful work. Before healing a wound, we should ask whether V_R might later be used. If we can be sure that V_R will never again be used, then we can avoid the expense of healing. A variable that will never again be used is *idle*, while a variable that is not idle is *busy*. A busy variable may or may not be used, depending on which control path is followed in the future. (The idle/busy distinction is also drawn with the words "dead" and "live" in the literature.) Idleness of variables is very much like availability of expressions, but now information flows *backwards*. Any variable that is strictly local to the program being analyzed is idle after each exit instruction. If control can flow directly from an instruction θ to an instruction ψ, any variable that is idle after ψ and not used by ψ will also be idle after θ, at least insofar as instruction paths where ψ follows θ are concerned. If other instructions can follow θ, then only the variables idle after θ for all paths from θ to exit instructions should be considered idle after θ without mention of ψ. Proceeding as at the start of Section 2-3, we consider a variable V and a bit $\text{IDLE}_{\text{after}}(\theta)$ for each instruction θ, telling whether V is idle after θ. This global bit is determined by local information encountered along paths. An instruction ψ *idles* V if either ψ is an exit instruction and V is strictly local to the program or ψ is certain to change the value of V. Idling V is analogous to computing R in availability analysis. Using V, on the other hand, is analogous to changing R. Along an instruction path β from θ to an exit instruction, V is idle after θ if there is a subsequent instruction ν that idles V, such that neither ν nor any instruction between θ and ν can possibly use V. If θ is an exit instruction, then $\text{IDLE}_{\text{after}}(\theta)$ is 1 if θ idles V. If θ is not an exit instruction, then $\text{IDLE}_{\text{after}}(\theta)$ is 1 if V is idle after θ along each instruction path β from θ to an exit instruction.

As with (degrees of) availability, we would like to deal with a graph that has many instructions for each node and to recover idleness information for instructions from idleness information for nodes. To proceed exactly as in Eq. (2-1) and the accompanying remarks, we would like to have the information $I(n)$ associated with a node n be $\text{IDLE}_{\text{after}}(\theta_n)$ for θ_n, the root of the tree of instructions defining n. This will work fine if we build a graph in the manner of Section 2-2 but with backwards flow throughout: each block is a tree of instructions such that control can only *leave* the tree at the root, and so on. Constructing two graphs for one program is rather a nuisance, so it is usual to study problems like idleness with the same graph used to study availability. Because the usual class of control flow graphs is not symmetrical when flow is reversed, it is helpful to consider information a little different from idleness *after* an instruction. Let $\text{IDLE}_{\text{before}}(\theta)$ be 1 if both of the following conditions hold:

$$\theta \text{ cannot possibly use } V \tag{2-6a}$$

$$\theta \text{ idles } V \text{ or } \text{IDLE}_{\text{after}}(\theta) = 1 \tag{2-6b}$$

If θ is not an exit instruction, it is easy to show that V is idle after θ if, and only if, V is idle before any instruction ψ that can receive control from θ. Thus we can recover $\text{IDLE}_{\text{after}}$ from $\text{IDLE}_{\text{before}}$. Moreover, $\text{IDLE}_{\text{before}}$ is directly useful. At the start of a series of computations involving V we may fetch V into a register R and then operate with R instead of V to save time. The permanent storage for V will have outdated information after a change in the contents of R, but this will do no harm as long as as we continue to look in R whenever we want the value of V. Before freeing R for some other purpose, we should store R into V. Now suppose we need a register to perform an instruction θ and that V is idle before θ. The code to perform θ can use R *without* first storing R into V: it is safe to leave outdated information in an idle variable.

Since $\text{IDLE}_{\text{before}}$ determines $\text{IDLE}_{\text{after}}$ and is useful anyway, we can relate it rather than $\text{IDLE}_{\text{after}}$ to the forward-flowing graph used for availability computations. The obvious analog of Eq. (2-1) is

$$I'(n) = \text{IDLE}_{\text{before}}(\theta_n) \tag{2-7}$$

As noted at the end of Section 2-2, we may assume that exit instructions are in blocks by themselves. A graph node with arcs running from it has no exit instructions. A graph node without such arcs is a block consisting of a single exit instruction. For each such *exit node* p let $E'(p)$ in $\{0, 1\}$ be 1 if the variable V is strictly local to the program. For each nonexit instruction θ let $\text{CHA}'(\theta)$:

$\{0, 1\} \rightarrow \{0, 1\}$ be the effect of θ on idleness information. If θ can possibly use V, then $CHA'(\theta)$ is constant with value 0. If θ cannot possibly use V but is certain to change V, then $CHA'(\theta)$ is constant with value 1. Otherwise, if θ cannot possibly use V and is not certain to change V, then $CHA'(\theta)$ is the identity map $\mathbf{1}$. For each arc c we have a map $F'_c: \{0, 1\} \rightarrow \{0, 1\}$ defined by $F'_c = CHA'(\theta_1) \circ CHA'(\theta_2) \circ \ldots \circ CHA'(\theta_K)$, where $(\theta_1, \ldots, \theta_K)$ is the instruction path from root to leaf in the block that adds c to the graph. For any path $\mathbf{c} = (c_1, \ldots, c_K)$ there is a sequence $(f_1, \ldots, f_K)$ of maps, with $f_K = F'_d$ for $d = c_k$. Let $F'_c = f_1 \circ f_2 \circ \ldots \circ f_K$. As with Eqs. (2-1) and (2-2), we find that Eq. (2-7) is equivalent to

$$I'(n) = \mathbf{glb}\{F'_c E'(p) \,|\, p \text{ is an exit node and } \mathbf{c} \text{ is a path from } n \text{ to } p\} \qquad (2-8)$$

The mathematics of finding I' defined by Eq. (2-8) is clearly much the same as the mathematics of finding I defined by Eq. (2-2).

With I' and thus $\text{IDLE}_{\text{after}}$ in hand, we can improve upon the most straightforward use of V_R to avoid computing $\mathbf{R}$ when it has a high degree of availability. One approach is to retain the simple scheme but to clean up later. In general, an instruction θ whose *only* effect is to change a variable V that is idle after θ is said to be a *useless* instruction. Such an instruction can be removed from the program. After optimizing according to our simple scheme, we can remove wound-healing instructions that are useless. (To avoid self-fulfilling prophecy in the analysis, a wound-healing instruction itself should not be taken as a possible use of V_R.) As in [Lowr69], we can also replace any two variables that are never simultaneously busy by a single variable. Even if the original program presents few opportunities for such cleaning up, simple versions of many optimizations will create them. Instead of trying to be extremely clever in each of many optimizations (thereby committing ourselves to writing and maintaining a very complicated compiler), we can perform each primary optimization in a rather simple way, then optimize away the minor inefficiencies with secondary cleanup optimizations. The net effect of doing a dozen things in extremely clever ways can be obtained by doing two dozen things in straightforward ways. The latter strategy should enhance the reliability and maintainability of ambitious optimizing compilers. This attitude is widespread in much recent compiler research, especially [Cart77, Harr77b, Knut74, Love77].

Cleaning up after an optimization is an example of a more general effect that can be called the *Pick and Shovel Principle*. With both a pick and a shovel, a person can accomplish vastly more in the way of digging than is possible with either tool alone. The pick loosens dirt for removal by the shovel, which exposes more dirt for loosening by the pick. An ambitious but reliable compiler can proceed in the same fashion, using simple tools to make opportunities for each other. The compiler can detect and exploit opportunities created by its own actions. There are two major design difficulties ignored in the analogy between compiling and digging.

First, the number of simple tools in a compiler is greater than two. In what order should tools be used? From a theoretical point of view this problem is almost entirely open, though much folklore exists. The small amount of relevant literature includes results to the effect that certain optimizations of straight-line code can be done in any convenient order without changing the ultimate results [Aho72] add abstract conditions (on families of transformations of arbitrary "objects") that suffice for such order-independent behavior [Huet77, Seth74]. There are also brief, informal discussions of reasonable ways to proceed, as in [Aho77, Sec. 14.9].

Second, where should tools be used? Applying one tool to optimize one place in the program may create an opportunity for another tool elsewhere. How can the good news travel? The good news that a certain file has been sorted on a certain key (perhaps as a byproduct of another operation) should travel to any place in the program where this knowledge can be exploited, but there is no need to send the news everywhere in an elaborate computation that never refers to the file. This second problem has recently begun to attract theoretical attention. Traditionally, data flow algorithms were written so as to read in a graph with local information in M assigned to each arc (or to each node). The algorithms halted with global information assigned to each node. Only the initial analysis in a pick and shovel compiler has this form. Thereafter, we are confronted by a small change in a previously analyzed program. We want to *update* the results of analysis to reflect the change. To analyze the changed program by an ordinary algorithm would be inefficient. Unchanged parts of a large program would be reanalyzed, and information would be propagated everywhere rather than just where it is wanted. The importance of updating without a whole new analysis was recognized in [Rose77c] and led to the general algorithm of [Rose78b]. The formal presentation is in the traditional style, but ease of updating was more prominent than traditional considerations in the design of the algorithm. The distinction between *exhaustive* analysis of the entire program and *demand* analysis that assigns accurate current information to specified parts of the program was drawn in [Babi78b], which modifies the exhaustive algorithm from [Babi78a] to a demand-driven form. The algorithm of [Rose78b] can also be converted to demand-driven form, the main requirement being that certain intermediate results should be stored for future reference. A clever programmer might try to impose an updating capability and analysis on demand when implementing an ordinary algorithm, but major surgery would be required. In the history of medicine, surgery did come before scientific understanding. Routinely successful surgery did not. The only currently available basis for understanding demand analysis of programs written in real high-level languages is provided by [Rose78b]. Even there the theorems only deal with the costs of traditional exhaustive analysis. A great deal remains to be done.

2-6. ITERATION AND ELIMINATION

The following algorithm is essentially that of [Kild73], restated in current notation with members of M assigned to arcs rather than nodes. The input includes a graph G with a set $\mathbf{N}_G$ of nodes and a set $\mathbf{A}_G$ of arcs. An arc c runs from its source $\mathbf{s}_G c$ to its target $\mathbf{t}_G c$. The input includes F assigning F_c in M to each c in $\mathbf{A}_G$. There is also a set $\mathbf{E} \subseteq \mathbf{N}_G$ of designated entry nodes and entry information $E(m)$ in L for each m in $\mathbf{E}$. Knowing what is true at entry nodes at the time of entrance, we want to determine what is true at all nodes at all times. The quadruple $(G, F, \mathbf{E}, E)$ is called a *global flow problem*. The algorithm is called *BASICITER* here because it is the basic iterative algorithm. The underlying similarity of iterative algorithms is well known, but it is not well known that natural optimizations of the other common iterative algorithms are essentially derivable from BASICITER by implementing the crucial data structure in ways not considered in [Kild73]. Following [Holl78], we will show how to obtain a natural optimization of Algorithm MK in [Kam76] from BASICITER. This particular optimization is not new [Hech75, p.531], but there seems to be little appreciation of the ease with which various good iterations are *derivable* from BASICITER.

> BASICITER: **begin declare** P $= (G, F, \mathbf{E}, E)$ global flow problem with L well-founded;
>   **declare** $I: \mathbf{N}_G \longrightarrow L$;   #This will be the output. #
>   **declare** W subset of $\mathbf{N}_G$;   #A subset of $\mathbf{A}_G$ could also be used. #
>   #The major differences among iterative algorithms are   #
>   #differences in how operations on W are performed. #
>   **declare** n, p nodes in G;   **declare** c arc in G;   **declare** y in L;
>   **get** P;
>   **for all** n **in** $\mathbf{N}_G$ **do**
>   **if** $n \in \mathbf{E}$ **then** $I(n) \longleftarrow E(n)$ **else** $I(n) \longleftarrow \top_L$;
> $W \longleftarrow \mathbf{E}$;
>   **while** $W \neq \emptyset$ **do**
>   [**take** n **from** W;
>   #This chooses v from W, by means deliberately left open. #
>   #The net effect is the same as that of $n \longleftarrow v$ and
> $W \longleftarrow W - \{v\}$. #
>   **for all** c **in** $\{c \in \mathbf{A}_G \,|\, \mathbf{s}_G c = n\}$ **do**
>   [$p \longleftarrow \mathbf{t}_G c$; $y \longleftarrow F_c I(n)$;

```
            if ¬(I(p) ≤ y) then
               [ I(p) ← glb{I(p),y};
                  if (p is not already in W) then give p to W
                  #Giving is the opposite of taking.   #
               ]
         ]
      ];
      put I
end
```

There are many ways to implement the *worklist* W of nodes. As [Kild73] notes, we could use a pushdown stack. For testing whether a node is in the stack, we might allow reading into the stack without popping, but it would be better to store a bit with each node that tells whether the node is already on the stack. Then **give** could be implemented by pushing onto the stack and turning on the bit for the node given to W. A queue could be used instead of a stack. Algorithm MK in [Kam76] is a different iteration that avoids an explicit worklist by listing the nodes in a special order called *rPostorder* (and useful for other purposes too) and then running over all the nodes repeatedly until the guess stabilizes. By choosing the implementation of the worklist carefully, we can obtain the advantages of rPostorder in BASICITER while avoiding certain duplications of effort that occur in Algorithm MK. Deliberately confusing nodes n with their positions 1, 2, 3, . . . in the rPostorder listing, we can write $n \leftarrow n + 1$ with the understanding that this really means going on to the next node in the sequence. "Adding 1" to the last node returns us to the first node. Now W can be implemented as an array of bits, with **take** n **from** W implemented as

$$[\text{while } \neg W[n] \text{ do } n \leftarrow n + 1; \; W[n] \leftarrow \text{false}]$$

Of course we need to add $n \leftarrow 1$ to the initialization of W. Maintaining a count of the number of **true** bits in W as an array would be convenient for the test whether $W \neq \varnothing$ as a set. For relatively simple problems like availability of expressions the experience with BASICITER and rPostorder has been quite good [Holl78, More79]. The number of times that nodes are taken from the worklist is usually no more than $3|\mathbf{N}_G|$, where $|\mathbf{N}_G|$ is the number of nodes.

Also available are *elimination* algorithms, which have a number of advantages over iteration. The major disadvantage is that they are more complicated and various. It is easy to explain detailed iterative algorithms by writing BASICITER at a very high level, then implementing the worklist in various ways. Elimination algorithms need to be understood individually, but there is a broad strategy that partially fulfills the unifying role of BASICITER for iteration. Certain pairs of nodes are given special attention and certain sets of paths between these nodes are given special attention. Given a triple (n, Π, p), where Π is a special set of paths from n to p, we find a member of M that summarizes all possible transformations of data flow information that can take place when control flows from n to p along one of the paths in Π. For each path $\mathbf{c}$ in Π we already have $F_\mathbf{c}$ in M. When Eq. (2-4) holds for all F_c in M, the desired summary is defined to be

$$g = \mathbf{glb}\{F_\mathbf{c} \mid \mathbf{c} \in \Pi\}$$

When Eq. (2-4) is not assumed, we must seek a subtler kind of summary to avoid undecidabilities [Kam77, Thm. 7]. In any case, the summary g of (n, Π, p) is accurate enough that we can forget the complexity of Π and imagine a single arc d from n to p with $F_d = g$. A solution to the original problem can be found quickly from a solution to the simpler problem. A sufficiently long sequence of such reductions leads from the original problem to a problem so trivial that even a computer can solve it by inspection, and then we follow the sequence of reductions backwards towards the original problem to obtain a solution.

Why should we go to all this trouble? One reason has already been noted. The partially ordered set L may not be well-founded, as happens with L_{DAVAIL}. There are also cases where L is well-founded, but the lengths of descending chains can be impractically large. A chain of the form $\xi_0 > \xi_1 > \ldots > \xi_{\text{MAXINT}}$, where MAXINT is the largest integer representable in a given computer's fixed-point arithmetic, may as well be infinite. There is also a sense in which the worst-case time bounds for iteration are intrinsically worse than those for the fastest known elimination method [Tarj76]. Another time bound comparison [Kenn76] studies the constants behind O expressions for worst-case bounds, with results that cannot be summarized so briefly. Sharpness of data flow information is another consideration. In contexts where Eq. (2-3) fails it is known that I_{ideal} defined by Eq. (2-2) is too much to ask for [Kam77, Thm. 7]. In these contexts iteration algorithms all find the same information I_{iter} with $I_{\text{iter}}(n) \leq I_{\text{ideal}}(n)$ for all n. Elimination algorithms do not all find the same information, but they all have $I_{\text{iter}}(n) \leq I_{\text{elim}}(n) \leq I_{\text{ideal}}(n)$. The elimination algorithms in [Grah76, Rose78b, Tarj75b] sometimes have $I_{\text{iter}}(n) < I_{\text{elim}}(n)$, so that more information is obtained. Interval analysis [Alle76, Kenn71a] has only been formulated in contexts where Eq. (2-3) holds, but it is easy to generalize this elimination method to show the same behavior. Other elimination methods that formally presuppose Eq. (2-3) are probably amenable to generalization as well, though with [Babi78a, Ullm73] there would be more verifications to be made.

An important but frequently overlooked advantage to elimination is that the summary information itself is useful for many purposes beyond obtaining I_{elim} in an exhaustive analysis. Diagnostic applications are sketched in [Rose77a, Sec. 6]. For demand analysis with updating it is very helpful to have summarized the effects of large parts of a program. Summaries of unchanged parts remain valid when the program changes. Good news can be sent from here to there by applying summaries. Of course the choice of *which* triples (n, Π, p) to summarize will influence the utility of an elimination algorithm for diagnostic or demand analysis purposes. Before choosing triples one must choose a graph. The usual graph representation reviewed in Section 2-2 is not the only one. For diagnostics and for demand analysis of programs written in high-level languages, it is not the best one. There is no simple correspondence between source syntax and the result of translating into lower-level instructions and then blocking the instructions together. Program changes ripple through the usual representation in complicated ways. Data flow information is tied to a lower-level translation of the program rather than the program itself, and this makes it very difficult to compose detailed but intelligible diagnostics. A high-level graph representation is contrasted with the usual one in [Rose77a]. A general elimination algorithm that exploits the regularities in well-written programs is presented in [Rose78b]. Because it is syntax-directed and chooses triples (n, Π, p) that arise naturally, the algorithm of [Rose78b] is particularly adaptable for diagnostics and analysis on demand. The other elimination algorithms are all more adaptable than iteration for these purposes, but the degree of adaptability varies.

ACKNOWLEDGMENTS

Helpful comments on this chapter were received from H. Ehrig, D. Kozen, and J. Staples, as well as from the editors.

Part II

APPLICATIONS
TO PROGRAM OPTIMIZATION

The purpose of a compiler is to translate source programs which specify computations to be carried out by a (usually fictitious) machine into equivalent object programs which can be carried out by another (usually real) machine. A number of efficient methods have been devised to perform such translations; however the object programs usually produced by a straightforward compilation algorithm are blatantly inefficient. Thus a compiler often has one or more "optimization" phases which successively transform the object program into more efficient equivalent versions.

Actually "improvement" would be a better term than "optimization," since a truly optimal (i.e., best) version is generally impossible to obtain, for both practical and theoretical reasons. Practically, the number of programs equivalent to a given one is enormous, if not infinite; theoretically, deciding equivalence is an intractable or unsolvable problem (depending on the formulation used). Further, there may not even be a "best" program equivalent to a given one: by the Blum Speedup Theorem [Hart71], for some programs there is an infinite sequence of equivalent programs, each much faster than the previous one on all but a finite number of inputs.

Consequently we study only transformations which preserve equivalence and (usually) increase run-time efficiency. These transformations can vary widely in their applicability, complexity, and effect. The simplest are probably the *peephole optimizations* [Aho77] which operate on short sequences of intermediate or object code. A trivial example is the elimination of the STORE instruction in the following sequence:

$$
\text{LOAD} \quad \text{REG,LOC}
$$
$$
\text{STORE} \quad \text{REG,LOC}
$$

Somewhat more complex are the transformations which can be applied wherever a particular syntactic pattern is recognized, possibly using information from the symbol table. These include many expression optimizations, replacing a procedure with only a single call by inline code and eliminating tail-recursive procedure calls [Stee76].

The most complex and important transformations are those which require information about a program's possible dynamic behavior to determine their applicability. Examples include moving code out of loops, operator strength reduction, and constant folding. Thus we require a method which can efficiently obtain information which is valid for all possible executions of the program. Such methods are generally described as *data flow–analytic*.

The actual and potential uses of data flow analysis in compilers have increased tremendously in sophistication since its inception. From the work of Vyssotsky mentioned in the introduction to Part I, it has grown through the formulation of intraprocedural bit-vector problems such as those discussed in Section 1-1 and the development of iterative and elimination algorithms, to methods for interprocedural analysis as in Chapters 6 and 7 and the relational methods of Chapters 4 and 12. In this part of the book, the reader will find five research contributions in this area. Chapter 3, by Allen, Cocke, and Kennedy, discusses a new approach to an old highly practical problem, reduction of operator strength. Chapter 4, by Jones and Muchnick, presents two approaches to determining properties of dynamic data structures. It provides a basis for optimizing storage management by determining the shapes of structures and their sharing and cyclic properties. Chapter 5, by Wilhelm, shows how to incorporate flow analysis into a compiler generator, making possible the automatic generation of multipass optimizing compilers. Chapter 6 extends earlier work of its authors, Morel and Renvoise, to do interprocedural elimination of partially redundant computations. It thus subsumes earlier algorithms for elimination of redundant computations and extraction of loop-invariant computations and extends them to interprocedural applicability. Chapter 7, by Sharir and Pnueli, presents two quite general approaches to interprocedural flow analysis which provide significantly sharper information than previous methods.

Chapter 3

Reduction
of Operator Strength†

F. E. Allen
John Cocke
Ken Kennedy

3-1. INTRODUCTION

Subscript computations involving loop induction variables are used in high-level language programs to iteratively reference elements of vectors, arrays, structures, etc. The following FORTRAN program fragment is an example.

DIMENSION $A(10,10)$, $B(10,10)$, $C(10,10)$

. . .

DO 10 $J = 1,10$

. . .

$A(I,J) = B(I,J) * C(I,J)$

. . .

10   CONTINUE

Many machines have index registers for use in referencing data and fast instructions for incrementing or decrementing these index registers. An optimizing compiler must transform the subscript calculations in the source program into instructions utilizing index registers.

†The research reported in this chapter was partially supported by the National Science Foundation under grant GJ-40585.

The strength reduction optimization transformation is so named because it is intended to replace certain operations by faster ones. A multiplication involving a loop induction variable can sometimes be transformed into an index register increment.

Consider an internal form of the FORTRAN program in which the redundant subscript calculations have already been eliminated. (Remember FORTRAN stores arrays columnwise.)

$$J = 1$$
$$\text{LOOP:} \quad t_1 = J * 10$$
$$t_2 = I + t_1$$
$$t_3 = \textbf{indexedload}(B, t_2)$$
$$t_4 = \textbf{indexedload}(C, t_2)$$
$$t_5 = t_3 * t_4$$
$$\textbf{indexedstore}(A, t_2, t_5)$$
$$\cdot$$
$$\cdot$$
$$\cdot$$
$$J = J + 1$$
$$\textbf{if } J \leq 100 \textbf{ then go to } \text{LOOP}$$

The loop as it now stands can be further improved by applying a method due to Babbage [Gold72] based on the observation that multiplication is merely a series of additions. Making use of this, Babbage was able to design a machine which mechanically printed out values of a polynomial on a sequence of equidistant argument values. The most powerful operation employed was addition.

It is possible to apply the same technique to eliminate the multiplication $J * 10$. Suppose we know the value of $J * 10$; the value of $(J + 1) * 10$ can then be obtained by a simple application of the distributive law:

$$(J + 1) * 10 = J * 10 + 10$$

Thus, if we maintain the value of $J * 10$ in a temporary location throughout the loop, we can always calculate its next value by a simple addition. Applying this observation, we may transform our example loop to:

$$J = 1$$
$$t_0 = 10 \qquad\qquad\qquad (t_0 \text{ holds the value } J * 10)$$
$$\cdot$$
$$\cdot$$
$$\cdot$$
$$\text{LOOP:} \qquad\quad \cdot$$
$$t_1 = t_0 \qquad\qquad\qquad \text{(multiplication replaced by copy)}$$
$$t_2 = I + t_1$$
$$t_3 = \textbf{indexedload}(B, t_2)$$
$$t_4 = \textbf{indexedload}(C, t_2)$$
$$t_5 = t_3 * t_4$$

$$\textbf{indexedstore}(A, t_2, t_5)$$

$$\vdots$$

$$J = J + 1$$
$$t_0 = t_0 + 10 \qquad \text{(new value of } J * 10)$$
$$\textbf{if } J \leq 100 \textbf{ then go to } \text{LOOP}$$

In this version, we have replaced a multiplication by a copy and an addition. On many machines, the time required by these two operations is less than the time required to perform a multiplication. We have therefore achieved an efficiency gain within the loop.

This technique, *reduction of operator strength*, is particularly important in a language like FORTRAN because the programmer has no way to avoid subscript calculations if multidimensional arrays are used.

A related improvement can be obtained by noting that the temporary t_2 contains the value of $J * 10 + I$ throughout the loop. By reducing this addition, we may eliminate all references to t_0 and t_1 within the loop. Once again, the reduction is based on the distributive law

$$(J + 1) * 10 + I = (J * 10 + I) + 10$$

The resulting code is significantly simplified.

$$J = 1$$
$$t_2 = 10 + I$$

$$\vdots$$

LOOP:

$$t_3 = \textbf{indexedload}(B, t_2)$$
$$t_4 = \textbf{indexedload}(C, t_2)$$
$$t_5 = t_3 * t_4$$
$$\textbf{indexedstore}(A, t_2, t_5)$$

$$\vdots$$

$$J = J + 1$$
$$t_2 = t_2 + 10$$
$$\textbf{if } J \leq 100 \textbf{ then go to } \text{LOOP}$$

A final improvement can be achieved in the case that J is never used after loop exit, which is common for FORTRAN DO-variables. The only remaining use of J within the loop is in the loop-ending test. However, $J \leq 100$ if and only if $J * 10 + I \leq 1000 + I$. This fact allows us to test t_2 rather than J, and the increment of J can be deleted.

$$t_2 = 10 + I$$
$$t_6 = 1000 + I$$

.

.

LOOP: .

$$t_3 = \textbf{indexedload}(B, t_2)$$
$$t_4 = \textbf{indexedload}(C, t_2)$$
$$t_5 = t_3 * t_4$$
$$\textbf{indexedstore}(A, t_2, t_5)$$

.

.

$$t_2 = t_2 + 10$$
if $t_2 \le t_6$ **then go to** LOOP

The code which results from these transformations approaches the limit of efficiency for this particular computation.

In this paper we investigate reduction of operator strength with the aim of automating this process for reasonably general cases. Section 3-2 contains a catalog of the types of strength reduction which might be considered. In Section 3-3 gathering of required preliminary information is discussed. The algorithm itself appears in Section 3-4, while Section 3-5 covers the methods of code "cleanup" subsequent to strength reduction.

3-2. CANDIDATES FOR STRENGTH REDUCTION

In this section we consider a number of specific strength reductions, many of which have been previously cataloged by Allen [Alle69] and Schwartz [Schw74b]. Suppose that we have selected a strongly connected region for consideration and that a previous common subexpression elimination and code motion pass has identified the set $\{a, b, c, d, e\}$ of *region constants*, i.e., variables which are not modified within the region. An important first task is to identify the set of *induction variables* $\{i, j, k, l, m\}$ within the region. This is the maximal set of variables which are defined within the region only by simple instructions of the form:

$$i = j \pm k$$
$$i = \pm j$$

where j and k are either region constants or induction variables. Algorithms for doing this are presented in [Alle69, Cock70b, Cock77]. Note that under this definition the FORTRAN DO-variable is always an induction variable and that this makes variables such as I and J induction variables in the program segment in Fig. 3-1, unlike some less inclusive definitions of induction variables [Aho77].

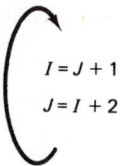

$$I = J + 1$$
$$J = I + 2$$

Figure 3-1

We shall use x, y, and z to denote real variables and t_i to denote compiler-generated temporaries. The following strength reductions are possible.

1. Multiplication of an induction variable by a region constant can always be reduced to additions. For example, Fig. 3-2(a) becomes Fig. 3-2(b),

(a)   (b)

Figure 3-2

where $a * b$ is a region constant and may be computed outside the loop.

2. Multiplication of one induction variable by another can always be reduced to additions [see Fig. 3-3(a) which reduces to Fig. 3-3(b)].

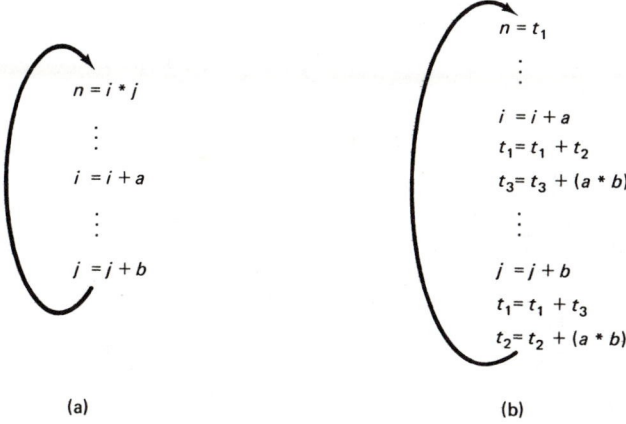

(a)   (b)

Figure 3-3

In the reduced version of this example, t_1 contains $(i * j)$, t_2 contains $(j * a)$, and t_3 contains $(i * b)$. With this in mind it is easy to see the motivation for the new transformations:

$$(i + a) * j = i * j + j * a$$
$$(j + b) * i = i * j + i * b$$

3. Multiplication of an induction variable by itself can be reduced to additions. See Fig. 3-4(a), which reduces to Fig. 3-4(b), where t_1 contains $(i * i)$ and t_2 contains $(2 * a * i + a * a)$.

$$(i + a) * (i + a) = (i * i) + (2 * a * i + a * a)$$

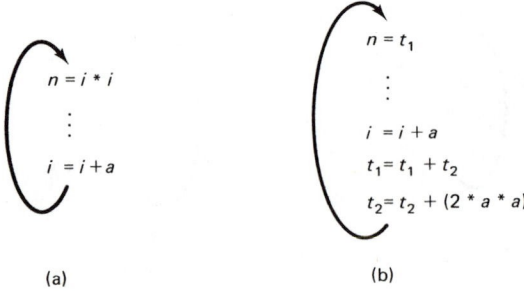

(a)   (b)

Figure 3-4

4. Integer division of an induction variable by a region constant may be reduced to additions, subtractions, and branches, as shown in Fig. 3-5, where t_1 contains the value (i / a) and t_2 contains the value $(i \bmod a)$.

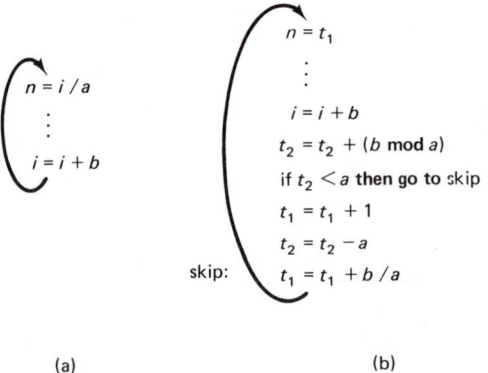

(a)   (b)

Figure 3-5

5. The integer modulo function may be similarly reduced, as shown in Fig. 3-6.

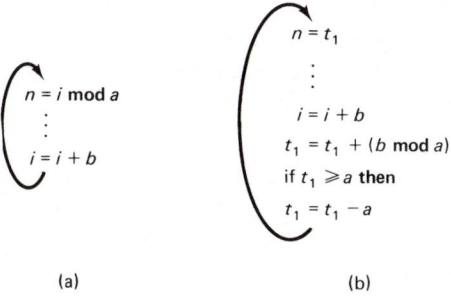

(a) (b)

Figure 3-6

6. Exponentiation to an induction variable may be reduced to multiplications (see Fig. 3-7).

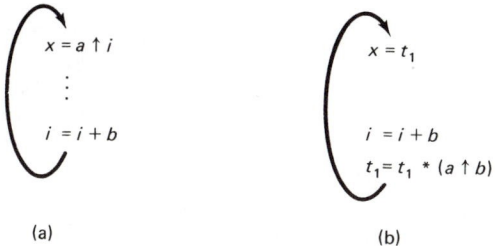

(a) (b)

Figure 3-7

7. Integer addition may be usefully reduced if such reduction permits other reductions or code elimination. For example, suppose the only uses of i and j are in the computation of n. Then Fig. 3-8

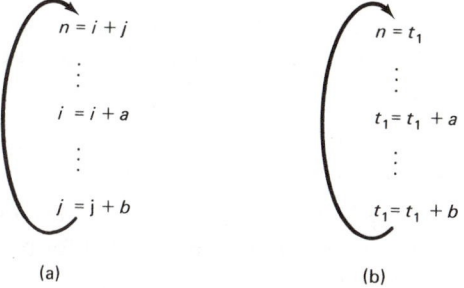

(a) (b)

Figure 3-8

shows such a reduction. This set of reductions, appropriately expanded to include corresponding cases for real variables, represents the standard set of "reasonable" transformations. However, the concept may be generalized to a number of startling cases.

8. General order n polynomials in induction variables can always be reduced to additions, because $p(i + c) = p(i) + p_1(i)$ where p_1 is of order $n - 1$ or less.

9. The computation of many trigonometric functions at a series of equidistant points may be reduced to multiplications and additions. See Fig. 3-9, where tsinx holds the value of $sin(x)$, tcosx the value of $cos(x)$, tsinΔx the value of $sin(\Delta x)$, and tcosΔx the value of $cos(\Delta x)$. The latter two are loop constants.

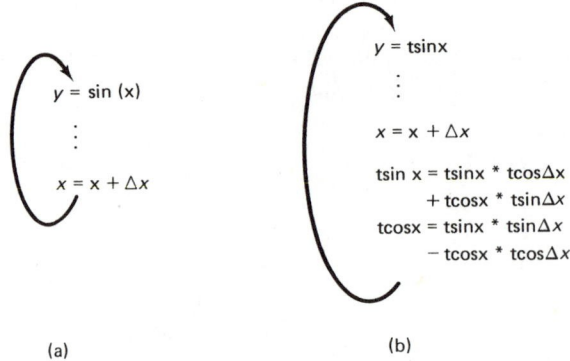

(a)

(b)

Figure 3-9

10. The iterative computation of a continuous differentiable function at points x, $x + \Delta x$, $x + 2\,\Delta x$, etc., may be replaced by a quadratic interpolation.

Very-high-level languages, such as the set-oriented language SETL, offer other opportunities for strength reduction [Earl74, Fong76, Paig77, Schw77b] which can result in very substantial improvements in execution time.

In general, reduction of operator strength within a strongly connected region may be described as follows:

Suppose an operation $y = f(x_1, \ldots, x_j, \ldots, x_n)$ occurs in the region and we wish to move it out.

However, this motion is not possible because redefinitions of the arguments of f exist in the region which have the form

$$x_j = h_j(x_1, \ldots, x_n)$$

It is known that identities of the form

$$f(x_1, \ldots, x_{j-1}, h_j(x_1, \ldots, x_n), x_{j+1}, \ldots, x_n)$$
$$= g_j(x_1, \ldots, x_n, f(x_1, \ldots, x_j, \ldots, x_n))$$

hold; i.e., the new value of f after x_j is modified can be expressed as a function of the old value. Furthermore, the functions g_j are less expensive to compute than the function f.

Then we may reduce f by

1. Introducing a new variable t.
2. Replacing $y = f(x_1, \ldots, x_n)$ by $y = t$.
3. Replacing each redefinition

$$x_j = h_j(x_1, \ldots, x_n)$$

   by the pair of statements

$$x_j = h_j(x_1, \ldots, x_n)$$
$$t = g_j(x_1, \ldots, x_n, t)$$

4. Placing the instruction

$$t = f(x_1, \ldots, x_n)$$

   prior to region entry.

A general strength reduction algorithm would need to have a large number of mathematical identities at hand in order to do a complete job. Also in the case where general expressions are being inserted, the problem of "safety" may be introduced. For example, an error interrupt might be raised by the inserted code, particularly the insertion of $t = f(x_1, \ldots, x_n)$ prior to region entry. This may need to be protected by a conditional so it is executed exactly when the region is entered. For these reasons, reductions in most actual compilers are restricted to the simpler cases [(1) to (7)]. In the remainder of this paper we concentrate on cases (1), (2), and (7) (multiplication of an induction variable by another induction variable or by a constant and addition of induction variables). The reader should not find it difficult to generalize these methods.

3-3. USE-DEFINITION CHAINS

Our method for performing reduction in strength will involve moving a subexpression, say $i * j$, from its original location to the definition points which can effect it. A subexpression is said to be *defined* at point p if any of its argument variables receives a new value at that point; p is then said to be a *definition point* for the expression. Given a particular evaluation of sub-expression $e(i, j)$ at q, the set of *definition points which can affect* that evaluation is the set of definition points P such that there is a control flow path from $p \in P$ to q which contains no other definition of the data item defined at p.

Since we will be attempting to reduce expressions involving induction variables, the points at which induction variables are assigned values are the definition points for expressions of interest. Let $IV = \{i, j, k, \ldots\}$ be the set of induction variables for a given strongly connected region. The set of *IV-points* for the region is the set of instructions which assign a value to some member of IV. If CAND is the set of candidate expressions, the *CAND-points* are those instructions which evaluate a candidate for reduction. We will call p a *critical point* if it is either an IV-point or a CAND-point.

For each CAND-point p we wish to know which IV-points are definitions affecting the expression at p. This is not particularly difficult to determine, but the problem is a bit more subtle. Once our algorithm moves an expression to a definition point, it will transform that expression to another one with different arguments and mark the new one as a candidate for reduction. Therefore points which are initially IV-points may also become CAND-points during the reduction process, and it is not easy to determine which expressions will become candidates at which points. We therefore require at each critical point the set of definition points for every possible subexpression involving induction variables. This may seem like a great many; however, three observations allow us to limit the total number of expressions to be considered.

1. The operation (addition, multiplication, etc.) is unimportant in determining definition points. Therefore we need only compute these points for each pair of possible arguments (i, j) of a sub-expression.

2. Since there are no definition points for region constants within the strongly connected region, the set of definition points for (i, a), where a is a constant, is exactly the same as the set for (i, i).

3. Order of expression arguments is unimportant in determining definition points, so we may assign a canonical ordering to the elements of IV, say $(i_1, i_2, \ldots, i_m)$, and only consider the pairs (i_j, i_k) such that $j \leq k$. In other words we make use of the fact that the definition points for (i_k, i_j) are precisely the definition points for (i_j, i_k).

Under the above restrictions, we need only consider $n(n + 1)/2$ expression forms, where $n = |IV|$.

In short, we must determine at each critical point p, the set of definition points for expressions involving the canonical argument pairs (i_j, i_k). We may view this as computing a set $defs(p)$ of tuples of the form

$$((i, j), \text{def}_1, \text{def}_2, \ldots, \text{def}_m)$$

where (i, j) is a canonical pair and $\{\text{def}_i, 1 \leq i \leq m\}$ is the set of definition points for an expression of the form $i \ op \ j$ (or $j \ op \ i$) which might appear at p.

The *defs* sets are a form of data flow information usually called *use-definition chains*. Such information can be computed in any of a number of standard ways [Kenn74, Kenn71b], and we shall not treat their computation here. The usefulness of use-definition chains arises from our ability to compute them in a prepass over the region, allowing us to avoid further control flow analysis during strength reduction.

3-4. THE ALGORITHM

Several methods for performing strength reduction have appeared in the literature [Alle69, Cock77]. In [Cock77] a scheme based on "hashed temporaries" is outlined. This method has the disadvantage that more temporaries are generated than are really needed, making code cleanup time-consuming. The algorithm proposed here avoids these difficulties through the use of the modified use-definition chains discussed in Section 3-3.

We assume that there exists a mapping from each possible expression involving induction variables and region constants to an appropriate unique temporary name. Such a mapping can be implemented via a hashing scheme as in [Cock77]. We denote the temporary for $i * j$ by $t(i * j)$.

Suppose we have chosen a list of candidates for reduction and organized this list as a queue. We then choose a candidate from the queue, say

$$x = i * j$$

which appears at point p.

We replace this instruction (see Fig. 3-10) by

$$x = t(i * j)$$

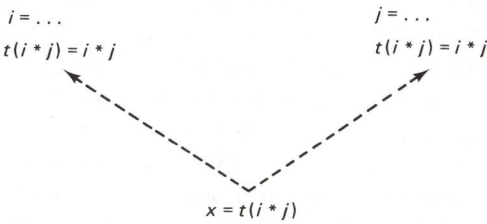

Figure 3-10

and insert

$$t(i * j) = i * j$$

after each definition point for *i op j* which reaches *p*; i.e., we search *defs*(*p*) for the list of definition points corresponding to (i, j) and insert $t(i * j) = i * j$ at each of these points (immediately following the defining instruction). Next we transform the sequence of instructions at these definition points according to the following rules which are based on the form of the defining instruction.

1. If $i = k$, where k is an induction variable or a region constant, the value k is folded into the expression for $t(i * j)$ to yield the sequence

    $$i = k$$

    $$t(i * j) = k * j$$

    Since $i = k$ is not a definition point for $k * j$, we may add $t(i * j) = k * j$ to the list of reduction candidates.

2. If $i = l + k$, where l is an induction variable and k is another induction variable or a region constant, then the sequence

    $$i = l + k$$

    $$t(i * j) = i * j$$

    may be transformed to

    $$t(l * j) = l * j$$

    $$t(k * j) = k * j$$

    $$t(i * j) = t(l * j) + t(k * j)$$

    $$i = l + k$$

    Finally, the instructions

    $$t(l * j) = l * j$$

    $$t(k * j) = k * j$$

    are added to the list of reduction candidates.

Note here that new reduction candidates will have the appropriate use-definition information available because use-definition chains for all possible expressions have been computed for each critical point.

During the reduction process, many new instructions will be inserted in the vicinity of each critical point; thus it is convenient to view these instructions as the result of partial expansion of a macro appearing at that critical point. We therefore treat all these instructions as if they were located at the same place. The partial expansion at critical point *p* is called the *macro block* for *p*.

If the reduction process is to halt, there must be some way to recognize when insertions are superfluous. The following method will suffice. Suppose our next step is to insert $t(i * j) = i * j$ in the macro block associated with $i = l + k$. Before the insertion is performed, we search that block for an assignment to $t(i * j)$. If such an assignment is found, the insertion is not performed and no new candidate is added to the candidate list.

Let us now turn to some examples of this process. Consider the loop shown in Fig. 3-11.

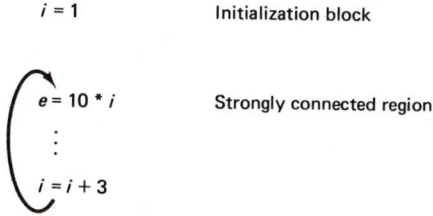

$i = 1$ Initialization block

$e = 10 * i$ Strongly connected region

$i = i + 3$

Figure 3-11

Note that the expression $10 * i$ has defining points $i = 1$ in the region initialization block (called the *prolog*) and $i = i + 3$ in the region itself. The first stage of insertions and transformations will change this to Fig. 3-12.

$i = 1$
$t(i * 10) = 10$

$e = t(i * 10)$

$t(i * 10) = i * 10$
$t(i * 10) = t(i * 10) + 30$
$i = i + 3$

Figure 3-12

The only new candidate created during this stage is $t(i * 10) = i * 10$. In the second stage, all definition points already have an assignment to $t(i * 10)$, so no new insertions are performed. Also, the superfluous instruction $t(i * 10) = t(i * 10)$ need not be retained, so the final version is as shown in Fig. 3-13. For simplicity, we have taken the liberty of replacing $t(3 * 10)$ by the constant 30 in the above example. We shall continue to perform such obvious simplifications in the remaining examples.

$$i = 1$$
$$t(i * 10) = 10$$

$$e = t(i * 10)$$
$$\vdots$$
$$t(i * 10) = t(i * 10) + 30$$
$$i = i + 3$$

Figure 3-13

A second example introduces some subtleties of this problem (see Fig. 3-14).

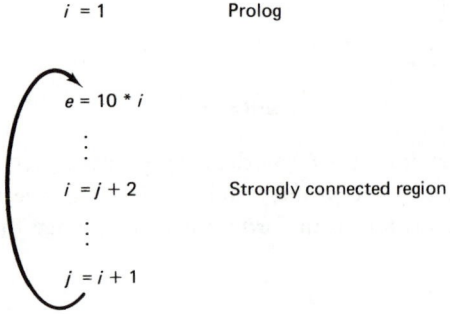

$$i = 1 \qquad \text{Prolog}$$

$$e = 10 * i$$
$$\vdots$$
$$i = j + 2 \qquad \text{Strongly connected region}$$
$$\vdots$$
$$j = i + 1$$

Figure 3-14

As before, our candidate is $i * 10$. The first stage of insertion and substitution produces the program shown in Fig. 3-15.

$$i = 1$$
$$t(i * 10) = 10$$

$$e = t(i * 10)$$
$$\vdots$$
$$t(j * 10) = j * 10$$
$$t(i * 10) = t(j * 10) + 20$$
$$i = j + 2$$
$$\vdots$$
$$j = i + 1$$

Figure 3-15

The new candidate for reduction is $j * 10$. We eliminate the instruction $t(j * 10) = j * 10$ and insert the same instruction in the prolog (all induction variables are assumed to be defined in the prolog) and at the definition $j = i + 1$. Transformation yields Fig. 3-16.

$i = 1$
$t(i * 10) = 10$
$t(j * 10) = j * 10$

$e = t(i * 10)$

$\vdots$

$t(i * 10) = t(j * 10) + 20$
$i = j + 2$

$\vdots$

$t(i * 10) = i * 10$
$t(j * 10) = t(i * 10) + 10$
$j = i + 1$

Figure 3-16

On the next step, the instruction $t(i * 10) = i * 10$ will be deleted and moved to each defining point. However, all such points already have an assignment to $t(i * 10)$: therefore, the algorithm halts with the final result shown in Fig. 3-17.

$i = 1$
$t(i * 10) = 10$
$t(j * 10) = j * 10$

$e = t(i * 10)$

$\vdots$

$t(i * 10) = t(j * 10) + 20$
$i = j + 2$

$\vdots$

$t(j * 10) = t(i * 10) + 10$
$j = i + 1$

Figure 3-17

Before proceeding to a more complex example, we consider an important special case. Suppose our candidate expression is $i * i$ and we move $t(i * i) = i * i$ to a definition point of the form $i = i + a$. Then the following macro block must result.

$$t(i * a) = i * a$$
$$t(2 * i * a) = 2 * t(i * a)$$
$$t(a * a) = a * a$$
$$t(2 * i * a + a * a) = t(2 * i * a) + t(a * a)$$
$$t(i * i) = t(i * i) + t(2 * i * a + a * a)$$
$$i = i + a$$

If the operation in the second instruction is to be further reduced, $t(i * a)$ must itself be an induction variable, which will be the case after $i * a$ has been completely reduced. Our only problem then is to find use-definition chains for $2 * t(i * a)$; but these are exactly the same as chains for an operation $i \text{ op } a$. On the other hand, we may not wish to reduce this expression since it can be immediately replaced by a shift or an add

$$t(2 * i * a) = t(i * a) + t(i * a)$$

Consider the example loop shown in Fig. 3-18. The first stage transforms this into the code shown in Fig. 3-19. Reducing $i * 3$ yields Fig. 3-20, and reducing $2 * t(i * 3)$ yields Fig. 3-21. The initialization and increment of

$$i = 1$$

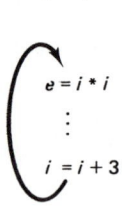

$$e = i * i$$
$$\vdots$$
$$i = i + 3$$

Figure 3-18

$t(i * 3)$ may now be deleted since $t(i * 3)$ is no longer used (in fact, these deletions are performed by a subsequent "dead computation elimination" pass [Kenn73a]).

Suppose that we continue with this example by reducing the *addition* $t(i * 6 + 9) = t(i * 6) + 9$. We then get the code in Fig. 3-22, which after dead code elimination becomes the code in Fig. 3-23.

The example above leads us to seek conditions under which it is profitable to reduce additions. In this case, $t(i * 6 + 9)$ is defined as the sum of an induction variable $t(i * 6)$ and a region constant 9. The induction variable

$$i = 1$$
$$t(i * i) = 1$$

$$e = t(i * i)$$
$$\vdots$$

$$t(i * 3) = i * 3$$
$$t(i * 6) = 2 * t(i * 3)$$
$$t(i * 6 + 9) = t(i * 6) + 9$$
$$t(i * i) = t(i * i) + t(i * 6 + 9)$$
$$i = i + 3$$

Figure 3-19

$$i = 1$$
$$t(i * i) = 1$$
$$t(i * 3) = 3$$

$$e = t(i * i)$$
$$\vdots$$

$$t(i * 6) = 2 * t(i * 3)$$
$$t(i * 6 + 9) = t(i * 6) + 9$$
$$t(i * i) = t(i * i) + t(i * 6 + 9)$$
$$t(i * 3) = t(i * 3) + 9$$
$$i = i + 3$$

Figure 3-20

$$i = 1$$
$$t(i * i) = 1$$
$$t(i * 3) = 3$$
$$t(i * 6) = 6$$

$$e = t(i * i)$$
$$\vdots$$

$$t(i * 6 + 9) = t(i * 6) + 9$$
$$t(i * i) = t(i * i) + t(i * 6 + 9)$$
$$t(i * 6) = t(i * 6) + 18$$
$$t(i * 3) = t(t * 3) + 9$$
$$i = i + 3$$

Figure 3-21

$$i = 1$$
$$t(i * 1) = 1$$
$$t(i * 6) = 6$$
$$t(i * 6 + 9) = 15$$

$$e = t(i * i)$$
$$\vdots$$

$$t(i * i) = t(i * i) + t(i * 6 + 9)$$
$$t(i * 6 + 9) = t(i * 6 + 9) + 18$$
$$t(i * 6) = t(i * 6) + 18$$
$$i = i + 3$$

Figure 3-22

$$i = 1$$
$$t(i * i) = 1$$
$$t(i * 6 + 9) = 15$$

$$e = t(i * i)$$
$$\vdots$$

$$t(i * i) = t(i * i) + t(i * 6 + 9)$$
$$t(i * 6 + 9) = t(i * 6 + 9) + 18$$
$$i = i + 3$$

Figure 3-23

was incremented over the loop and its only purpose was to compute $t(i * 6 + 9)$; thus it was profitable to replace all increments of $t(i * 6)$ by direct increments of $t(i * 6 + 9)$, allowing the deletion of all references to $t(i * 6)$.

This situation should arise frequently, particularly when we have additions of *created* induction variables such as $t(i * a)$. We therefore propose to reduce all additions of created induction variables in the hope of eliminating more dead code in a later pass. The following example shows how this might work: Starting with the code in Fig. 3-24, reduction of $k * 10$ yields Fig. 3-25 and reduction of $i * 10$ and $j * 10$ yields Fig. 3-26. Next we attempt to reduce the expression $t(k * 10) = t(i * 10) + t(j + 10)$. This done, we can eliminate all references to $t(i * 10)$ and $t(j * 10)$ since their only use is in the computation of $t(k * 10)$. The result is shown in Fig. 3-27. Later, variable subsumption optimization [Kenn73b] will pave the way for further code

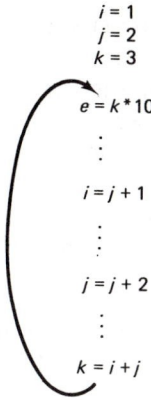

$$i = 1$$
$$j = 2$$
$$k = 3$$

$$e = k * 10$$

$$\vdots$$

$$i = j + 1$$

$$\vdots$$

$$j = j + 2$$

$$\vdots$$

$$k = i + j$$

Figure 3-24

$$i = 1$$
$$j = 2$$
$$k = 3$$
$$t(k * 10) = 30$$

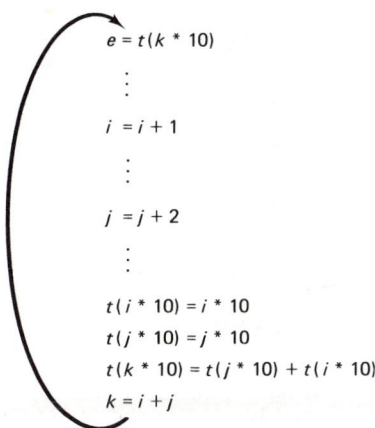

$$e = t(k * 10)$$

$$\vdots$$

$$i = i + 1$$

$$\vdots$$

$$j = j + 2$$

$$\vdots$$

$$t(i * 10) = i * 10$$
$$t(j * 10) = j * 10$$
$$t(k * 10) = t(j * 10) + t(i * 10)$$
$$k = i + j$$

Figure 3-25

reduction. For example, it could be recognized that $t(k * 10)$ and $t(i * 10 + j * 10)$ may occupy the same memory location.

We now summarize these considerations in an informal algorithm.

Algorithm R: Reduction of Operator Strength

Input: A strongly connected region and its prolog.

Output: An equivalent strongly connected region with multiplications of induction variables eliminated.

$i = 1$

$t(i * 10) = 10$

$j = 2$

$t(j * 10) = 20$

$k = 3$

$t(k * 10) = 30$

$e = t(k * 10)$

⋮

$t(i * 10) = t(i * 10) + 10$

$i = i + 1$

⋮

$t(j * 10) = t(j * 10) + 20$

$j = j + 2$

⋮

$t(k * 10) = t(i * 10) + t(j * 10)$

$k = i + 1$

Figure 3-26

$i = 1$

$j = 2$

$t(i * 10 + j * 10) = 30$

$k = 3$

$t(k * 10) = 30$

$e = t(k * 10)$

⋮

$t(i * 10 + j * 10) = t(i * 10 + j * 10) + 10$

$i = i + 1$

⋮

$t(i * 10 + j * 10) = t(i * 10 + j * 10) + 20$

$j = j + 2$

⋮

$t(k * 10) = t(i * 10 + j * 10)$

$k = i + j$

Figure 3-27

Intermediate:

1. Use-definition information described in Section 3-3.
2. The set $IV = \{i, j, k, \ldots\}$ of induction variables for the region.
3. The set $RC = \{a, b, c, \ldots\}$ of region constants.
4. A mapping t of symbolic expressions to temporary names $i * j \longrightarrow t(i * j)$.
5. A list L of candidate instructions.
6. A set CP of critical points.

Method:

R1. Determine the sets IV and RC by any standard method.

R2. Select the initial set of candidates for reduction, i.e., instructions which evaluate expressions $i * x$ where $i \in IV$, $x \in IV \cup RC$. Put these candidates on the list L.

R3. Compute the set CP of critical points and the sets $defs(p) \; \forall p \in CP$.

R4. Select the first candidate $e = i * x$ ($i \in IV$, $x \in IV \cup RC$) and remove it from L.

R5. If the candidate instruction is of the form $t(i * x) = i * x$, delete it from the region; otherwise, replace it with $e = t(i * x)$.

R6. For each definition point p of $i * x$ (found by consulting the use-definition chains) do the following:

    R6a. If $t(i * x)$ already has an assignment in the macro block for p, do nothing (i.e., go to the next point).

    R6b. If p is a point in the region prolog, insert $t(i * x) = i * x$ at the end of that prolog and continue. (Obvious constant folding might be performed.)

    R6c. If the definition is of the form $i = k$, insert $t(i * x) = i * x$ after the definition and transform the sequence to

$$t(i * x) = k * x$$
$$i = k$$

    Then add $t(i * x) = k * x$ to the candidate list L.

    R6d. If the definition is of the form $i = k + l$ and $x \neq i$ then insert $t(i * x) = i * x$ and transform to

$$t(k * x) = k * x$$
$$t(l * x) = l * x$$
$$t(i * x) = t(k * x) + t(l * x)$$
$$i = k + l$$

    Add the first two instructions to L.

R6e.   If $x = i$ and the definition is $i = k + l$, then insert and transform to

$$t(k * k) = k * k$$
$$t(l * l) = l * l$$
$$t(l * k) = l * k$$
$$t(2 * l * k) = 2 * t(l * k)$$
$$t(2 * l * k + l * l) = t(2 + l * k) + t(l * l)$$
$$i = k + l$$

Obvious simplifications in the above sequence should be made when $l \in$ RC. Add the first four instructions to L.

R7.   Add all additions of temporary names (induced during strength reduction) to the candidate list L.

R8.   If $L \neq \phi$, go to R3; otherwise, halt.

Execution of the above algorithm will eliminate *all* multiplications of induction variables by other induction variables and region constants. In the process, a new class of induction variables—the induced temporaries—will be created. If the algorithm is then reapplied, all polynomials of order 3 in induction variables will be reduced. In general, by applying the algorithm repeatedly until some predetermined stopping point or until no reduction candidates remain, all polynomials in induction variables can be reduced to additions. To see why this is so, consider what a typical compiler would do with the polynomial

$$i^3 + 3i^2 - 10$$

where i is an induction variable. A reasonable sequence of code would be

$$t_1 = i * i$$
$$t_2 = 3 * t_1$$
$$t_3 = i * t_1$$
$$t_4 = t_2 + t_3$$
$$t_5 = t_4 - 10$$

If this code were found in a region to which strength reduction is being applied, the first invocation of Algorithm R would reduce $i * i$, allowing t_1 to become an induction variable; the second invocation would reduce $3 * t_1$ and $i * t_1$, eliminating all multiplications in the region.

Of course, multiple invocations of Algorithm R would increase the need for an effective code cleanup involving variable subsumption [Kenn73b] and dead code elimination [Kenn73a].

3-5. LINEAR FUNCTION TEST REPLACEMENT

If the dead code elimination pass of our optimizer is to be effective, we must cause as many instructions as possible to become useless. After reduction in strength, it frequently happens that the only uses of induction variables are in "test" instructions of the form

if $i \leq c$ **then go to** loop

where c is a region constant. If we can achieve the effect of this test without using i, we will be able to eliminate all modifications of i within the region (assuming i is dead on exit from the region). Note that

$$i \leq c \text{ iff } t(a * i + b) \leq t(a * c + b)$$

where a and b are other region constants. Hence, we can replace the test of i with a test of one of the induced temporaries known to contain a linear function of i throughout the region. Naturally $t(c * a + b) = c * a + b$ must be inserted in the prolog if this is to work. Once this is done, instructions involving i will be deleted by the dead code eliminator whenever i is dead on exit from the region.

3-6. SUMMARY AND CONCLUSIONS

We have presented a somewhat general method for performing strength reduction in strongly connected regions and have investigated the implications of this optimization. The technique is based upon the use of data flow information in the form of use-definition chains within the region. The algorithm presented removes all multiplications of induction variables by region constants or other induction variables; however it can be iteratively applied to eliminate arbitrary polynomials in induction variables. Reduction of additions and linear function test replacement are two methods which will allow later optimization passes to more completely eliminate useless code.

ACKNOWLEDGMENT

The authors wish to thank Jack Schwartz of New York University for providing us with many insights on the nature of strength reduction.

Chapter 4

Flow Analysis
and Optimization
of LISP-like Structures[†]

Neil D. Jones
Steven S. Muchnick

4-1. INTRODUCTION

In [Jone76] the authors introduced the concept of binding time optimization and presented a series of data flow–analytic methods for determining some of the binding time characteristics of programs. In this paper we extend that work by providing methods for determining the class of shapes which an unbounded data object may assume during execution of a LISP-like program, and we describe a number of uses to which that information may be put to improve storage allocation in compilers and interpreters for advanced programming languages.

We are concerned chiefly with finding, for each program point and variable, a finite description of a set of graphs which includes all values the variable could assume at that point during the execution of a program. If this set is small or regular in structure, this information can then be used to optimize the program's execution, mainly by use of more efficient storage allocation schemes.

[†]The research reported in this chapter was partially supported by the National Science Foundation under grant MCS76–80269.

In the first part we show how to construct from a program a tree grammar whose nonterminals generate the desired sets of graphs, which in this case will all be trees. The tree grammars are of a more general form than is usually studied [Enge75, That73], and so we show that such a grammar may be converted to the usual form. The resulting tree grammar could naturally be viewed as a recursive type definition [Hoar75] of the values the variables may assume. Further, standard algorithms may be employed to test for infiniteness, emptiness, or linearity of the tree structure.

In the second part selective updating is allowed, so an alternate semantics is introduced which more closely resembles traditional LISP implementations, and which is equivalent to the tree model for programs which do not use selective updating. In this model data objects are directed graphs. We devise a finite approximation method which provides enough information to detect cell sharing and cyclic structures whenever they can possibly occur. This information can be used to recognize when the use of garbage collection or of reference counts may be avoided.

The work reported in the second part of this paper extends that of Schwartz [Schw75b, Schw75c] and Cousot and Cousot [Cous77f]. They have developed methods for determining whether the values of two or more variables share cells; we provide information on the detailed structure of what is shared. The ability to detect cycles is also new. It also extends the work of Kaplan [Kapl78b], who distinguishes only binary relations among the variables of a program, does not handle cycles, and does not distinguish selectors (so that his analysis applies to nodes representing sets rather than ordered tuples).

4-2. PROGRAMS WITH TREELIKE DATA

In the first part of this paper, we shall carry out our analyses on a simple programming language called SL (structure language) whose syntax is as follows:

$$\text{program} \longrightarrow \{[\text{label}:] \text{stmt}\}^+$$

stmt $\longrightarrow$ assign | if | goto

assign $\longrightarrow$ var := exp | var := **input** | **output** := exp

if $\longrightarrow$ **if** test goto

test $\longrightarrow$ **atom** exp | **null** exp | var $\{=|\neq\}$ var

goto $\longrightarrow$ **goto** label

exp $\longrightarrow$ atom | var | var.sel | **cons** (exp $\{, \text{exp}\}^*$)

We assume that instances of the syntactic classes var, sel, atom, and label are members, respectively, of the sets Var, Sel, Atom, and Label which are pairwise disjoint.

4-2.1. Informal Discussion

The language SL closely resembles LISP with the PROG feature but without functions or p-lists, and extended to allow arbitrary numbers of selectors. See Reynolds [Reyn68] for methods to handle recursively defined functions.†

The semantics of SL are essentially those of LISP, with two minor exceptions: the customary uses of NIL (a special atom in LISP) must be done via the empty or undefined data structure $\perp$; and any attempt to apply a selector (e.g., CAR, CDR) to an atom or $\perp$ will result in program abortion instead of being "undefined."

In LISP without selective updating operations it is natural to view the value of a variable as a tree without regard to cells, pointers, etc. Each internal node will have an edge labeled s leading to a subtree, for each s in the set of selectors Sel $= \{sel_1, \ldots, sel_m\}$. If $T_1, \ldots, T_m$ are trees, $\mathbf{cons}(T_1, \ldots, T_m)$ denotes the tree consisting of a root node, with edges labeled $sel_1, \ldots, sel_m$ leading to the roots of $T_1, \ldots, T_m$, respectively. If T has this structure, then $T.sel_i$ denotes the subtree T_i.

All trees in examples in this paper will use the fixed set of selectors Sel $= \{hd, tl\}$. Trees will be given pictorially with the root at the top, leaves at the bottom, and atoms labeling the leaves. Selectors may be omitted for convenience, in which case the edge directed southwest (southeast) from a node goes to the "hd" subtree ("tl" subtree).

4-2.2. Semantics of SL

The value of an atom is an element of the set ATOM and is given by the function α: Atom $\longrightarrow$ ATOM. We assume that atoms are otherwise unspecified simple data objects: numbers, bounded-length character strings, booleans, etc.

Trees are defined formally by the sequences of labels encountered on paths from the root to the leaves. Such a sequence is written as $s_1.s_2.\ldots.s_n.a$ where $n \geq 0, s_1, \ldots, s_n \in$ Sel and $a \in$ ATOM. The set of all such label sequences is naturally described by Sel* $\times$ ATOM.

By definition a *tree* is a finite subset T of Sel* $\times$ ATOM such that if

---

†Reynold's work came to our attention after this development was completed. He treats a subset of LISP with recursive function calls and without sequential execution. It seems clear that the two methods could be combined.

$s_1. \ldots .s_n.a \in T$, then $s_1. \ldots .s_n.s_1'. \ldots .s_p'.b \in T$ only if $p = 0$ and $a = b$. The null tree $T = \varnothing$ is written as $\perp$ (read "bottom").

The definition allows trees with "missing branches" such as {hd.1, tl.hd.2}. In diagrams the missing branches will be drawn, and their leaves labeled with $\perp$. Some examples are shown in Fig. 4-1.

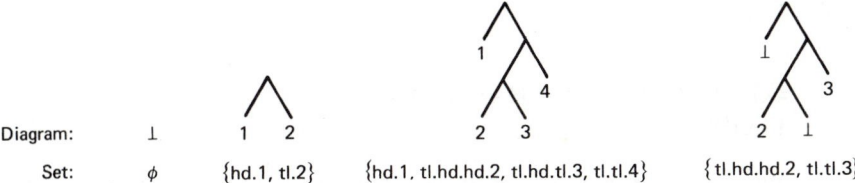

Diagram: $\perp$ 1   2   2   3   2 $\perp$

Set: ϕ {hd.1, tl.2}   {hd.1, tl.hd.hd.2, tl.hd.tl.3, tl.tl.4}   {tl.hd.hd.2, tl.tl.3}

Figure 4-1

By definition if $T, T_1, \ldots, T_m$ are trees and $s \in$ Sel, then

$$T.s = \{t_1 \ldots t_n.\text{atom} \mid s.t_1 \ldots t_n.\text{atom} \in T\}$$

and

$$\mathbf{cons}(T_1, \ldots, T_m) = \bigcup_{i=1}^{m} \{\text{sel}_i.t_1 \ldots t_n.\text{atom} \mid t_1 \ldots t_n.\text{atom} \in T_i\}$$

Note that this definition implies $\perp.s = \text{atom}.s = \perp$. The definitions are naturally extended as follows: Let $A, B_1, \ldots, B_m$ be sets of trees. Then

$$A.s = \{T.s \mid T \in A - \mathbf{ATOM} - \{\perp\}\}$$

$$\mathbf{cons}(B_1, \ldots, B_m) = \{\mathbf{cons}(T_1, \ldots, T_m) \mid T_1 \in B_1, \ldots, T_m \in B_m\}$$

Following the style of denotational semantics [Miln76, Stoy77], we define the meanings of the various constructs in terms of the domains $\mathbf{ATOM}$, $\mathbf{VAL} = 2^{\text{Sel}^* \times \text{ATOM}}$, and $\mathbf{STORE} = [\text{Var} \to \mathbf{VAL}]$ (a store $\sigma \in \mathbf{STORE}$ is a function mapping each variable to its current value). We only define the meanings of expression evaluation and assignment statement execution. The other features of SL can be formally defined by well-known means, including continuations.

$\mathcal{E}: \text{Exp} \to \mathbf{STORE} \to \mathbf{VAL}$ is a partial function given by:

$$\mathcal{E}[\![\text{atom}]\!]\, \sigma = \{\mathcal{a}[\![\text{atom}]\!]\}$$

$$\mathcal{E}[\![\text{var}]\!]\, \sigma = \sigma(\text{var})$$

$$\mathcal{E}[\![\text{var}.s]\!]\, \sigma = \sigma(\text{var}).s$$

$$\mathcal{E}[\![\mathbf{cons}(e_1, \ldots, e_m)]\!]\, \sigma = \mathbf{cons}(\mathcal{E}[\![e_1]\!]\, \sigma, \ldots, \mathcal{E}[\![e_m]\!]\, \sigma)$$

$\mathcal{a}\mathcal{S}: \text{Assign} \to \mathbf{STORE} \to \mathbf{STORE}$ is given by

$$\mathcal{a}\mathcal{S}[\![\text{var} := \text{exp}]\!]\, \sigma = \lambda x \in \text{Var}.\ (\textbf{if } x = \text{var } \textbf{then } \mathcal{E}[\![\text{exp}]\!]\sigma \textbf{ else } \sigma(x))$$

Execution of a statement and the whole program will be aborted if:

1. An expression which must be evaluated is undefined.

2. An if statement compares two values either of which is a nonempty, nonatomic tree.

3. A nonempty, nonatomic tree is read by a statement "var := **input**".

Note that point 2 implies that these tests model EQ in LISP, rather than EQUAL.

4-3.   STRUCTURE SHAPES AND DATA FLOW EQUATIONS

We now show how to construct a system of forward data flow equations from a program. Let X be a program variable in Var, and I a program point. The system will then have a variable $F(I, X)$. The least-fixed-point solution of the system will associate with $F(I, X)$ a set of tree shapes which includes all possible shapes that X could have at point I in any possible execution of the program.

The set of shapes is defined simply by:

$$\text{Shape} = 2^{\text{Sel}^* \times \{\text{O}\}}$$

That is, we have replaced all elements of **ATOM** by the symbol ○ which represents an arbitrary atom. Next, we form the lattice 2^{Shape} of all subsets of **Shape**, with the usual subset ordering. The variables in the equation system will have elements of 2^{Shape} as values.

As in [Jone76] we first convert an SL program to a flowchart and annotate it with program points in the set $\mathcal{PP} = \{0, 1, \ldots, n\}$, one for each arc in the flowchart. Consider the flowchart segments of Fig. 4-2.

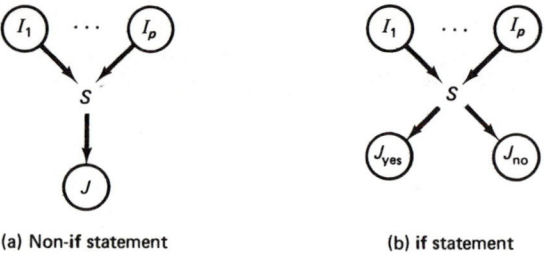

(a) Non-if statement   (b) if statement

Figure 4-2

The equations are formed as follows:

Form of S	Equation
$X := $ atom or $X := $ **input**	$F(J, X) = \{\text{O}\}$
$X := Y$	$F(J, X) = F(I_1, Y) \cup \ldots \cup F(I_p, Y)$

$$X := Y.s \qquad F(J, X) = F(I_1, Y).s \cup \ldots \cup F(I_p, Y).s$$

$$X := \mathbf{cons}(Y_1, \ldots, Y_m) \qquad F(J, X) = \bigcup_{i=1}^{p} \mathbf{cons}(F(I_i, Y_1), \ldots, F(I_i, Y_m))$$

if atom X
$$\begin{cases} F(J_{\text{yes}}, X) = \bigcup_{i=1}^{p} F(I_i, X) \cap \{\circ\} \\ F(J_{\text{no}}, X) = \bigcup_{i=1}^{p} F(I_i, X) - \{\circ\} \end{cases}$$

if null X
$$\begin{cases} F(J_{\text{yes}}, X) = \bigcup_{i=1}^{p} F(I_i, X) \cap \{\bot\} \\ F(J_{\text{no}}, X) = \bigcup_{i=1}^{p} F(I_i, X) - \{\bot\} \end{cases}$$

if $X = Y$ or
if $X \neq Y$
$$\begin{cases} F(J_{\text{yes}}, X) = \bigcup_{i=1}^{p} F(I_i, X) \cap \{\circ, \bot\} \\ F(J_{\text{no}}, X) = \bigcup_{i=1}^{p} (F(I_i, X) \cap F(I_i, Y)) \cap \{\circ, \bot\} \end{cases}$$

other
$$F(J, X) = F(I_1, X) \cup \ldots \cup F(I_p, X)$$

Finally, the equation

$$F(I_0, X) = \{\bot\}$$

is included for the initial program point I_0 and each variable X.

Note that the only way in which statements constrain the shapes of values flowing to them is through the possibilities for abortion of execution. Taking these constraints into account through backward flow analysis, as discussed in our work [Jone76] or Kaplan and Ullman's work [Kapl78a], could provide more specific information about shapes. However, we ignore this possibility for the present since the extension is straightforward.

To obtain the maximal information available from forward flow analysis about the program's data values, the $F(I, X)$ sets should be as small as possible, as long as they include every value which may be computed. It is for this reason that the sets $\{\circ\}$, $\{\bot\}$, and $\{\circ, \bot\}$ appear in the equations—to conclude as much as possible from the program's assumed correctness.

4-4. SOLVING THE FLOW EQUATIONS

There are at least two methods available to solve the data flow equations. One is iteration in either its regular or chaotic form (see [Jone76] and [Cous77c]) starting with every $F(I, X) = \emptyset$. It should be clear that the functions involved are all continuous, so solutions always exist.

This method is appropriate if the solution is finite. Unfortunately this is not generally the case for the systems under consideration here. Instead, we shall introduce here a method based on regular tree grammars which handles the finite and infinite cases equally well. The objective is to obtain a regular tree grammar such that the language it generates is a safe approximation to the minimal fixed point of the system of flow equations. This is useful, since tree grammars are a well-understood extension of regular string grammars; consequently, existing algorithms can be used to test for finiteness, linearity, etc.

The approach is to regard each data flow equation as a production in an extended regular tree grammar, which is then transformed into an ordinary tree grammar.

4-4.1. Tree Grammars

A *regular tree grammar* (see, for example, [Enge75] or [That73]) is a grammar $G = \langle N, \Sigma, P, S \rangle$ with N a finite set of nonterminal symbols, Σ a ranked alphabet of terminal symbols such that $N \cap \Sigma = \varnothing$, $S \in N$ the initial nonterminal, and P a finite set of productions of the form $A \longrightarrow t$ where $A \in N$ and $t \in T_\Sigma(N)$. Here $T_\Sigma(N)$ is defined by

1. $N \cup \Sigma_0 \subseteq T_\Sigma(N)$.
2. If $k \geq 1$, $a \in \Sigma_k$, and $T_1, \ldots, T_k \in T_\Sigma(N)$, then $a[T_1, \ldots, T_k] \in T_\Sigma(N)$.
3. Nothing else is in $T_\Sigma(N)$.

Note that the linear representation $a[T_1, \ldots, T_k]$ in item 2 corresponds to the tree shown in Fig. 4-3.

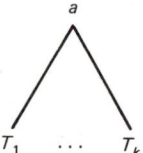

Figure 4-3

In order to describe our edge-labeled trees by tree grammars, we choose $k = m$ and $\Sigma_0 = \text{ATOM} \cup \{\perp\}$, $\Sigma_1 = \text{Sel}$, $\Sigma_2 = \ldots = \Sigma_{m-1} = \varnothing$, $\Sigma_m = \{\theta\}$. If T is a tree as used in our description of SL, the corresponding element $\mathcal{R}(T)$ of $T_\Sigma(N)$ is recursively defined by the equations in Fig. 4-4.

For example, we have the equation shown in Fig. 4-5.

We assume the semantics of a regular tree grammar is defined by least-fixed points, in the same manner as was done by Ginsburg [Gins66] for context-free grammars. That is, nonterminals are interpreted as sets of trees, and the productions are viewed as a system of set equations. It should be clear that this gives the same generated set $L(G)$ as the usual tree-rewriting semantics since the analogy between regular tree grammars and context-free grammars is very close.

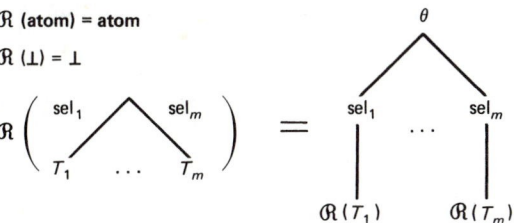

$$\Re \text{ (atom)} = \text{atom}$$

$$\Re (\perp) = \perp$$

Figure 4-4

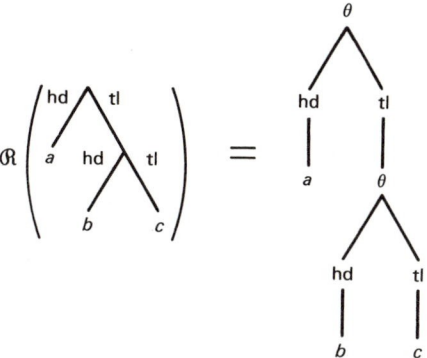

Figure 4-5

We will also write tree productions in the SL notation for convenience. This does no harm since it is easily seen that $T_1 \Rightarrow T_2$ by production $A \rightarrow T_3$ iff $\Re(T_1) \Rightarrow \Re(T_2)$ by $A \rightarrow \Re(T_3)$. For example, the natural interpretation of $A \rightarrow \bigwedge_{B \ \ C}$ is that for all $T_b \in B$, $T_c \in C$, the tree $\bigwedge_{T_b \ \ T_c}$ is in A. Translating into T_Σ terminology, the production is as shown in Fig. 4-6(a) and means that if $\Re(T_b) \in B$, $\Re(T_c) \in C$, then the tree in Fig. 4-6(b) is in A.

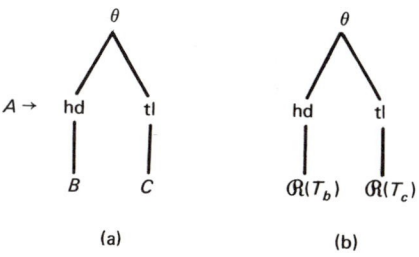

Figure 4-6

Having shown the connection to ordinary tree grammars, we now proceed to assume that all grammars are expressed and interpreted in terms of SL trees.

Definition. An *extended regular tree grammar* is a quadruple $G = \langle N, \Sigma, P, S \rangle$ where N, Σ, P, and S are as above, except that P is now allowed to contain productions of the form $A \longrightarrow B.s$ where $s \in \text{Sel}$.

The semantics of such a production in terms of sets is simply the assertion that $B.s \subseteq A$. For example the three productions in Fig. 4-7(a) would correspond to the set equation in Fig. 4-7(b).

$$A \rightarrow B, \quad A \rightarrow \overset{\text{hd} \quad \text{tl}}{\underset{C \qquad C}{\bigwedge}} \quad A \rightarrow A.\text{tl}$$

(a)

$$A = B \ \cup \ \left\{ \overset{\text{hd} \quad \text{tl}}{\underset{T_1 \qquad T_2}{\bigwedge}} \ \middle| \ T_1, T_2 \in C \right\} \ \cup \ \left\{ T_2 \ \middle| \ \overset{\text{hd} \quad \text{tl}}{\underset{T_1 \qquad T_2}{\bigwedge}} \ \text{is in } A \text{ for some } T_1 \right\}$$

(b)

Figure 4-7

The new production type clearly gives rise to a continuous function, so the solution of the extended regular tree grammar may be found, as before, by least fixed points.

Examining the flow equations, we see that they are nearly in the extended tree grammar form except for restrictions involving $\bigcirc$ and $\bot$. Referring to Fig. 4-2(a), let I be any of the $I_1, \ldots, I_p$ preceding S; then the construction of the grammar can now be expressed by Fig. 4-8.

S	Production
$X := Y$	$F(J, X) \rightarrow F(I, Y)$
$X := \text{atom or } X := \text{input}$	$F(J, X) \rightarrow \bigcirc$
$X := Y.s$	$F(J, X) \rightarrow F(I, Y).s$
$X := \text{cons}(Y_1, \ldots, Y_m)$	$F(J, X) \rightarrow \overset{\displaystyle \bigwedge}{\quad F(I, Y_1) \quad F(I, Y_m)}$
otherwise	$F(J, X) \rightarrow F(I, X)$

Figure 4-8

4-4.1.1. *An example*

Consider the program in Fig. 4-9 which builds a linear tree X from input items, and then transfers them to Y so they appear in the original order.

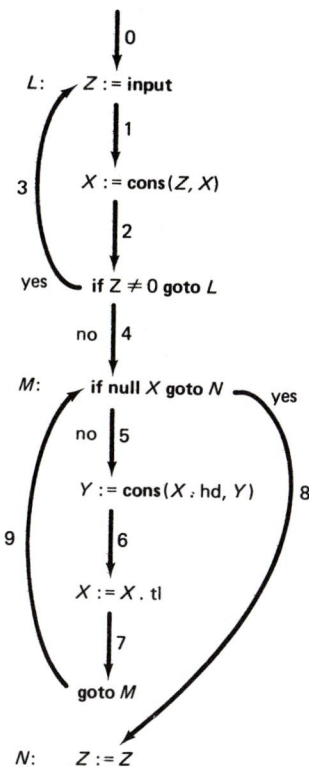

Figure 4-9

The productions obtained from this are shown in Fig. 4-10. Simplifying them by compressing chains of productions and renaming, we get Fig. 4-11. The solutions are shown in Fig. 4-12. Note that the right linearity or finiteness of each variable's values is evident.

Theorem. If $G = \langle N, \Sigma, P, S \rangle$ is an extended regular tree grammar, there is an ordinary regular tree grammar $G' = \langle N, \Sigma, P', S \rangle$ with $L(G) = L(G')$.

Proof. We first give the construction, which uses Büchi's method of "derived rules" [Büch64]. Define the relation $\triangleright$ on $N \cup \Sigma_0$ to be the smallest reflexive, transitive relation such that

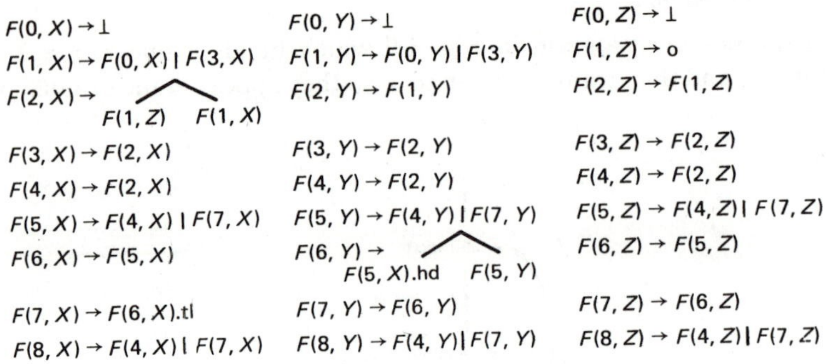

$F(0, X) \to \bot$ $F(0, Y) \to \bot$ $F(0, Z) \to \bot$

$F(1, X) \to F(0, X) \,|\, F(3, X)$ $F(1, Y) \to F(0, Y) \,|\, F(3, Y)$ $F(1, Z) \to o$

$F(2, X) \to$ [tree: $F(1, Z)$, $F(1, X)$] $F(2, Y) \to F(1, Y)$ $F(2, Z) \to F(1, Z)$

$F(3, X) \to F(2, X)$ $F(3, Y) \to F(2, Y)$ $F(3, Z) \to F(2, Z)$

$F(4, X) \to F(2, X)$ $F(4, Y) \to F(2, Y)$ $F(4, Z) \to F(2, Z)$

$F(5, X) \to F(4, X) \,|\, F(7, X)$ $F(5, Y) \to F(4, Y) \,|\, F(7, Y)$ $F(5, Z) \to F(4, Z) \,|\, F(7, Z)$

$F(6, X) \to F(5, X)$ $F(6, Y) \to$ [tree: $F(5, X)$.hd, $F(5, Y)$] $F(6, Z) \to F(5, Z)$

$F(7, X) \to F(6, X)$.tl $F(7, Y) \to F(6, Y)$ $F(7, Z) \to F(6, Z)$

$F(8, X) \to F(4, X) \,|\, F(7, X)$ $F(8, Y) \to F(4, Y) \,|\, F(7, Y)$ $F(8, Z) \to F(4, Z) \,|\, F(7, Z)$

Figure 4-10

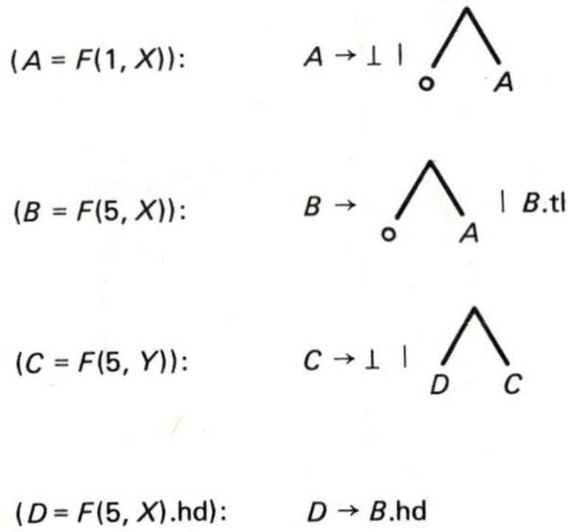

$(A = F(1, X))$: $A \to \bot \,|\,$ [tree: o, A]

$(B = F(5, X))$: $B \to$ [tree: o, A] $|\, B$.tl

$(C = F(5, Y))$: $C \to \bot \,|\,$ [tree: D, C]

$(D = F(5, X)$.hd$)$: $D \to B$.hd

Figure 4-11

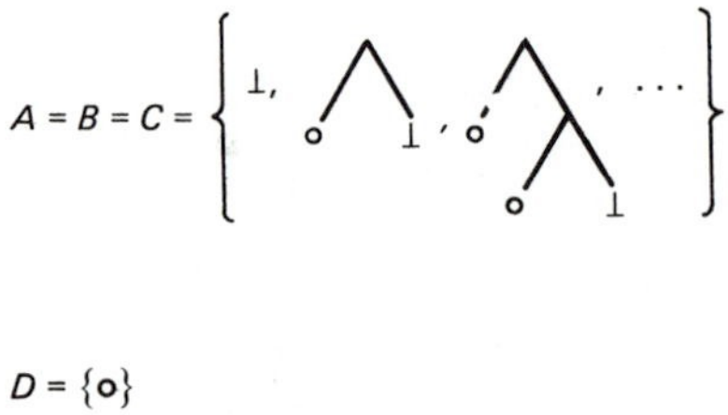

$$A = B = C = \left\{ \bot, \; [\text{tree}], \; [\text{tree}], \; \ldots \right\}$$

$D = \{o\}$

Figure 4-12

1. $A \longrightarrow X$ implies $A \rhd X$.

2. $A \longrightarrow B.\text{sel}_i$, $B \rhd C$,   and $C \longrightarrow \mathbf{cons}(T_1, \ldots, T_i, \ldots, T_m)$ imply $A \rhd T_i$, provided $T_1, \ldots, T_m$ all derive nonempty sets of terminal trees.

Now define $G'' = \langle N, \Sigma, P'', S \rangle$, where
$$P'' = P \cup \{A \longrightarrow X \,|\, A \in N \text{ and } A \rhd X\}$$

and

$$P' = P'' - \{A \longrightarrow B.s \in P\}$$

For the proof, first note that $A \rhd X$ implies $A \supseteq X$. Thus $L(G) = L(G'') \supseteq L(G')$.

To prove the converse we show that $L(G'') \subseteq L(G')$. Let $T_0 \in L(G'')$. This statement must be verifiable from the productions or equations by a sequence of statements, each of one of the following forms:

1. a is in A since $A \longrightarrow a$ is in P'' and $a \in \Sigma_0$.

2. T is in A since $A \longrightarrow B$ is in P'' and T is in B.

3. $\mathbf{cons}(T_1, \ldots, T_m)$ is in A since $A \longrightarrow \mathbf{cons}(X_1, \ldots, X_m)$ is in P and T_i is in X_i for $i = 1, \ldots, m$.

4. T_i is in A since $A \longrightarrow B.\mathbf{sel}_i$ and $\mathbf{cons}(X_1, \ldots, X_m)$ is in B and T_i is in X_i for $i = 1, \ldots, m$.

The last statement of the sequence must begin "T_0 is in S," and each substatement "T is in B" must begin some preceding line.

Such a verification may naturally be represented by a deduction tree $\mathfrak{D}$ whose internal nodes are labeled with pairs (A, T), where T is a tree and T is an element of A. The root of $\mathfrak{D}$ is labeled (S, T_0), and each internal node's presence must be justifiable by (1), (2), (3), or (4) above.

Now we show how to transform $\mathfrak{D}$ into a deduction tree using only (1), (2), and (3), thus showing that $T_0 \in L(G')$. It suffices to show how to remove any node justified by (4).

Now let node n be a lowest node justified by (4), and let it have label (A, T_i). Then $\mathfrak{D}$ must locally have the form shown in Fig. 4-13.

Now $B \rhd C$ (see Remark below) so $A \rhd C_i$, and $A \longrightarrow C_i$ is in P'. Thus this segment of the deduction tree could be replaced by Fig. 4-14.

> *Remark:* The first time this process is applied, there must be a chain of productions $B = B_1 \longrightarrow B_2 \longrightarrow \ldots \longrightarrow B_n = C$, so $B \rhd C$. In the transformed tree, $A \rhd C_i$. This implies that if at any stage of transformation a local form as above occurs, there is a chain from B to C with either $B_i \longrightarrow B_{i+1}$ or $B_i \rhd B_{i+1}$. Consequently $B \rhd C$. ∎

4-4.1.2. The example revisited

Elimination of productions with selectors on the right proceeds as follows:

1. $A \rhd \bot$ and $C \rhd \bot$ follow from the productions.

2. $B \rhd A$ follows from $B \longrightarrow B.\mathbf{tl}$, $B \rhd B$, and $B \longrightarrow \mathbf{cons}(\bigcirc, A)$.

3. $D \rhd \bigcirc$ follows from $D \longrightarrow B.\mathbf{hd}$ and $B \longrightarrow \mathbf{cons}(\bigcirc, \bot)$.

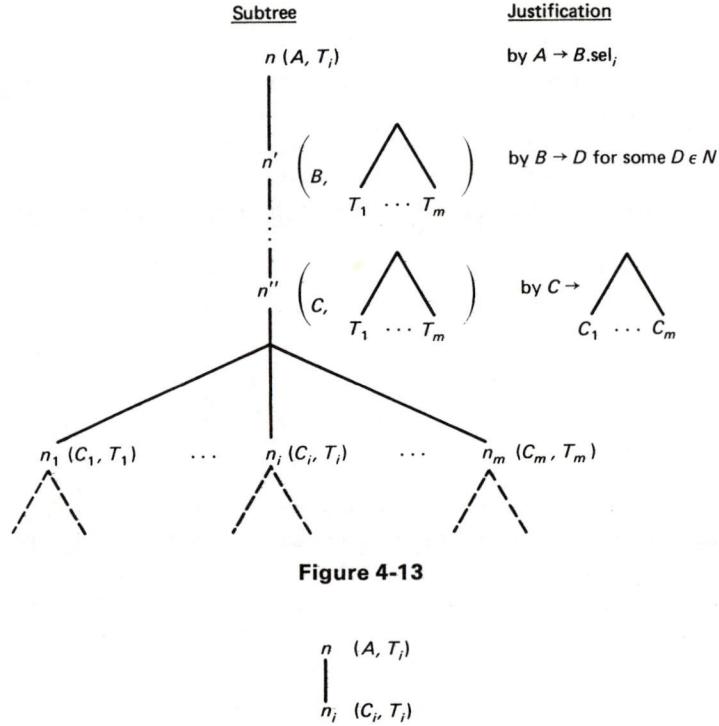

Figure 4-13

$$
\begin{array}{l}
n \quad (A, T_i) \\
| \\
n_i \quad (C_i, T_i)
\end{array}
$$

Figure 4-14

The revised grammar has the productions shown in Fig. 4-15, and it is easily checked that it has the same solution as the grammar with selectors on the right.

This method does not yield a perfect solution, for two reasons. First, the flow analysis method associates with each node and each variable a regular set of values. While this makes grammatical analysis possible, it can

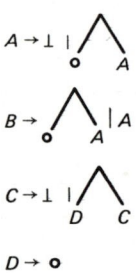

Figure 4-15

lose some information, as in the following example:

$$X := 1;$$
$$L: \quad X := \mathbf{cons}(X,X);$$
$$\mathbf{if} \sim \mathbf{goto}\ L$$

The values X may actually have at L are the complete binary trees of heights $0, 1, 2, \dots$. However the method above leads to the productions shown in Fig. 4-16, which have *all* binary trees as solution.

Figure 4-16

The second reason is the restrictions concerning $\bigcirc$ and $\perp$ in the flow equations which were ignored in constructing the productions. We conjecture that these restrictions do not destroy the regularity of the solutions, although they may increase the complexity of obtaining them.

4-5. RELATING THE TREE GRAMMARS TO STORAGE ALLOCATION

A simple and fairly efficient implementation of SL may be organized as follows. Each internal node is represented by a record with fields $s_1, \dots, s_m$, one for each selector in Sel. Any nonatomic tree is identified by a pointer to the record for its root node. Each program variable is bound to a *root word*, contained in a fixed run-time location, whose content is a pointer to the root record of its current value (or the value itself if atomic). Thus an assignment $X := Y$ merely copies one root word into another: $X := Y.s$ copies the s field of Y's root record into X's root word, and $X := \mathbf{cons}(Y_1, \dots, Y_m)$ makes the root word of X point to a newly allocated record whose fields $s_1, \dots, s_m$ are initialized to the values of $Y_1, \dots, Y_m$.

This method involves only a bounded amount of work for each statement type, and provides maximal natural storage sharing; that is all that can be achieved without the use of a hashing cons [Goto74]. There are some obvious inefficiencies common to LISP-like languages which are amenable to data flow analysis.

We now briefly discuss those which can be handled by use of the tree grammars just presented. The main tool used is the fact that familiar context-free grammar algorithms generalize directly to tree grammars. In particular, infiniteness is easily decidable.

1. Let X be a variable, and consider $V(X) = \bigcup_{I \in \wp \wp} F(I, X)$, i.e. our upper bound on the set of values X may assume during execution.

   (a) If $V(X)$ contains at most one shape other than $\perp$, a fixed location may be assigned to the root word of X, so its subfields may be addressed directly without need for the root word.

   (b) If $V(X)$ is finite, a storage area for X may be allocated statically for X before execution. This area need not participate in storage reclamation activities.

   (c) Now consider $V(X).sel_i$. If this is empty, no record within a value of X needs to contain an sel_i field; if it is finite, a fixed area may be assigned to sel_i.

2. Let statement $X := Y.s$ be preceded by program point I. If $\bigcirc$ or $\perp$ is in $F(I, Y)$, a run-time error is possible; if $F(I, Y) \subseteq \{\bigcirc, \perp\}$, a run-time error will definitely occur.

More will be said about optimization of LISP-like programs in the second part of this paper, particularly concerning storage reclamation by reference counts and garbage collection, and the use of CDR-coding [Bake78] will be discussed.

4-6. ELIMINATION OF REFERENCE COUNTS AND GARBAGE COLLECTION

In the remainder of this paper we assume an implementation like that described in the last section; in addition we extend the language (to a more powerful version called SUSL) by the addition of selective updating, in a manner similar to RPLACA and RPLACD in LISP.

Two standard methods for storage management are the use of reference counts and garbage collection. Garbage collection is the more powerful method, but the collection process is quite expensive and, in its classical forms, disruptive to the computation, especially in interactive and real-time contexts. When cyclic data structures cannot occur, as in SL, the method of reference counting may be used. However, this method requires both space overhead to store the counts and time to update them.

In this part of the paper we describe a method to reduce both types of overhead, often to zero, by a preexecution program analysis. The analysis constructs finite approximations to the actual run-time data structures which may occur, and is guaranteed to detect cyclic structures and nodes with reference counts greater than one, if they can possibly exist. In this way, run-time data cells may be put into three classes:

1. Those whose reference counts never exceed one. These may be returned to free storage as soon as pointers to them are destroyed. No reference counts need be maintained.

2. Those which may not appear in cycles, but whose reference counts may exceed one. These may be allocated with reference count fields which are maintained during execution.

3. Other cells, which may appear in cycles. The overhead of reference counts may be avoided at the expense of using garbage collection.

In Clark and Green [ClaS77] it is observed that only 2 to 8 % of LISP cells are ever pointed to more than once, so this optimization should result in substantial savings. Further, our method for detecting opportunities for optimization appears to be significantly more general than that of Barth [Bart77b].

Before proceeding to give an alternate semantics for SL based on the ideas sketched above and presenting methods for analyzing its storage allocation properties, we shall extend the language to include selective updating in a manner which models the functions RPLACA and RPLACD in LISP and assignment to records with pointers in languages such as Pascal and PL/I. The new operation is written as $X.s := Y$, and its intended effect is to replace the s-labeled edge from the root of X by an edge leading to the root node of Y. This selective updating operation makes it possible to create cyclic structures, as shown in Fig. 4-17, where performing $X.hd := X$ on the structure

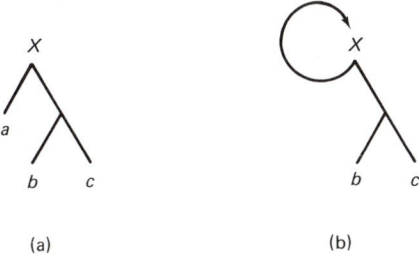

(a)   (b)

Figure 4-17

in (a) results in that shown in (b). Thus the language with selective updating is more powerful than that without it. We call the language with selective updating SUSL (selective updating structure language).

We now give a semantics for SUSL which incorporates within it an alternate semantics for SL equivalent to that in Section 4-2 and based on the implementation ideas in Section 4-5. To do this we first redefine the STORE to consist of all directed graphs of the following sort:

1. Each internal node has one son for each selector in Sel.
2. Each leaf is labeled with an atom or $\perp$ (the null tree).
3. Each variable in Var labels one and only one node.
4. Each node is accessible from a variable-labeled node.
5. Each node is a member of a universal set **NODE** of nodes.

For example, the graph in Fig. 4-18(a) is a store corresponding to the values of X, Y, and Z in Fig. 4-18(b).

The following auxiliary function is used in the semantic definition:

$$node: \quad \text{Var} \longrightarrow \text{STORE} \longrightarrow \text{NODE}$$

$$node\ v\sigma = \text{the node in } \sigma \text{ labeled } v$$

In the example in Fig. 4-18(a), *node* $Z\sigma$ is the upper-rightmost node.

The effect of the assignment statement is a function

$$\mathcal{A}\mathcal{S}: \quad \text{Assign} \longrightarrow \text{STORE} \longrightarrow \text{STORE}$$

defined below. In general, $\mathcal{A}\mathcal{S}[\![S]\!]\sigma$ is found by modifying σ (unless S aborts), as described in the following table. Afterwards, all nodes which are inaccessible from variables are removed from the new σ.

Form of S	$\mathcal{A}\mathcal{S}[\![S]\!]\sigma$
var := atom	add a new leaf node labeled $\mathcal{A}$(atom); move var to the new node
var_1 := var_2	move var_1 to label *node* $var_2\sigma$
var_0 := **cons**($var_1, \ldots, var_m$)	make a new node n and move var_0 to label it; for $i = 1, \ldots, m$, add an sel_i edge from n to *node* $var_i\sigma$
var_1 := var_2.sel	**if** *node* $var_2\sigma$ has an sel descendant n **then** move var_1 to node n **else** $\mathcal{A}\mathcal{S}[\![S]\!]\sigma$ is undefined
var_1.sel := var_2	**if** *node* $var_1\sigma$ has an sel edge from it **then** replace it by an sel edge leading to *node* $var_2\sigma$ **else** $\mathcal{A}\mathcal{S}[\![S]\!]\sigma$ is undefined

Execution is aborted in exactly the same situations as in the semantics of SL given above.

Let σ be an acyclic **STORE** graph and X a variable occurring in σ. Define *tree* $X\sigma$ to be the tree which results from performing node splitting on the directed acyclic graph comprising all nodes and edges reachable from

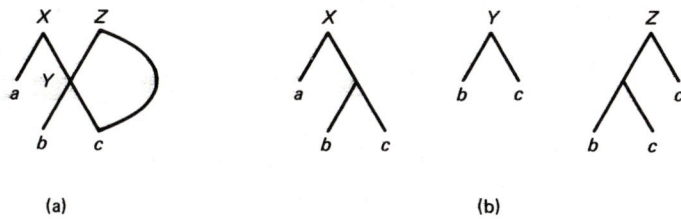

(a)   (b)

Figure 4-18

node $X\sigma$. For example if σ is as shown in Fig. 4-18(a), then *tree* $Z\sigma$ is the tree labeled Z shown in Fig. 4-18(b). Then we have the following theorem:

> **Theorem.** Let assign be any SL assignment statement (or, equivalently, any SUSL assignment statement other than a selective-updating operation) and σ an acyclic SUSL store with variables $X_1, \ldots, X_n$. Then
>
> $$\mathcal{C}\!S_{\text{SL}}[\![\text{assign}]\!] \{X_1 \rightarrow tree\ X_1\sigma, \ldots, X_n \rightarrow tree\ X_n\sigma\}$$
> $$= \{X_1 \rightarrow tree\ X_1(\mathcal{C}\!S_{\text{SUSL}}[\![\text{assign}]\!]\sigma), \ldots,$$
> $$X_n \rightarrow tree\ X_n(\mathcal{C}\!S_{\text{SUSL}}[\![\text{assign}]\!]\sigma)\}$$
>
> where $\{a_1 \rightarrow b_1, \ldots, a_n \rightarrow b_n\}$ denotes the finite function $f\colon \{a_1, \ldots, a_n\} \rightarrow \{b_1, \ldots, b_n\}$ satisfying $f(a_i) = b_i$ for $i = 1, \ldots, n$.

Thus the two languages are semantically equivalent if we ignore the selective-updating operation. We omit the proof of this since it just amounts to showing that the usual LISP implementation strategy is valid.

Define a node in a **STORE** graph to be *shared* if there are two or more distinct paths from variables (or possibly from the same variable) to the node, and to be *cyclic* if it is contained within a cycle in the graph.

4-7. MODELING THE SHARING SEMANTICS

As is usual in flow analysis, our approach is to define a system which is finite and whose solution in effect symbolically executes the program in parallel over all possible execution paths. The structures just described may grow unboundedly in two ways: they can grow in depth (i.e., path length from a variable to a leaf), and there may be an unbounded number of inaccessible (garbage) nodes. To remedy this we discard inaccessible nodes, and consider only bounded approximations to the graphs (annotated with sharing and circularity information to aid in the reference count analysis).

Define a directed graph to be *k-limited* if each node is accessible from a known node labeled with a variable by a selector-labeled path of length $\leq$ k. Then the flow analysis lattice **Share** is the set of all sets of directed k-limited graphs of the following form:

1. Each variable $X \in$ Var labels one node, denoted *node(X)*, and each node may be labeled by one or more variables.

2. There are two sorts of nodes: *unknown*, labeled ?, and *known*, not labeled ?.

3. Unknown nodes may be labeled with either of the following (as well as a ?):

       s   indicating that the unknown structure represented by the node may contain sharing

       c   indicating that the unknown structure may contain a cycle

4. Each leaf is labeled with ○ (indicating an atom), ⊥ (indicating the null tree), or ? and possibly *s* or *c*.

5. Each known node has one outgoing solid edge $\xrightarrow{\text{sel}}$ for each sel $\in$ Sel.

6. Each unknown node may have any number of outgoing, unlabeled dotted edges - - -➤, each going to a different node.

The lattice operations are set union (join) and intersection (meet). An unknown node represents a set of nodes whose internal structure is not represented in the k-limited approximation.

Given a fixed set of selectors and a fixed set of variables, the number of k-limited graphs with no inaccessible nodes is clearly finite. As an example of a k-limited graph, consider the 3-limited graph in Fig. 4-19.

A node in a **Share** graph is defined to be *shared* if there are two or more

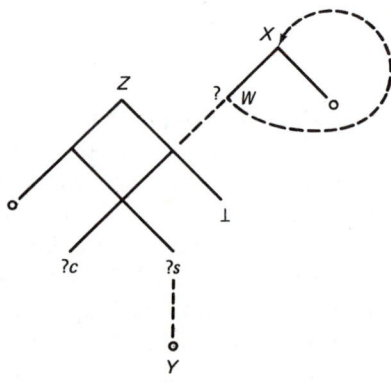

Figure 4-19

distinct paths from variables (or possibly the same variable) to the node, or if it is accessible from a node labeled s, or if it is itself labeled c. It is *cyclic* if it is included in an explicit cycle or labeled c.

4-8. CONSTRUCTING THE DATA FLOW EQUATIONS

Our approach is to associate with each program point I a set of k-limited graphs $F(I)$, each graph modeling a store resulting from one or more execution paths. Consider the flowchart segments of Fig. 4-20.

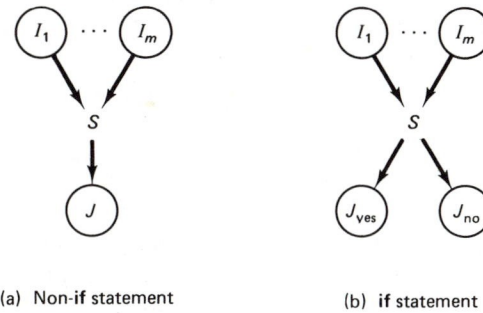

(a) Non-if statement   (b) if statement

Figure 4-20

The equations are formed as follows, where

$$D = F(I_1) \cup \ldots \cup F(I_m)$$

The functions *clean* and *next* are defined below.

Form of S	Equation
assignment	$F(J) = clean(next[\![S]\!]D)$
if atom var	$\begin{cases} F(J_{yes}) = \{\bar{y} \in D \,|\, node\ \text{var}\ \bar{y}\ \text{is labeled}\ \bigcirc\ \text{or}\ ?\} \\ F(J_{no}) = \{\bar{y} \in D \,|\, node\ \text{var}\ \bar{y}\ \text{is unknown, or is known} \\ \qquad\qquad \text{and not labeled}\ \bigcirc\} \end{cases}$
if null var	$\begin{cases} F(J_{yes}) = \{\bar{y} \in D \,|\, node\ \text{var}\ \bar{y}\ \text{is labeled}\ \bot\ \text{or}\ ?\} \\ F(J_{no}) = \{\bar{y} \in D \,|\, node\ \text{var}\ \bar{y}\ \text{is unknown, or is known} \\ \qquad\qquad \text{and not labeled}\ \bot\} \end{cases}$
if $\text{var}_1 = \text{var}_2$ **if** $\text{var}_1 \neq \text{var}_2$	$\begin{cases} F(J_{yes}) = F(J_{no}) = \{\bar{y} \in D \,|\, node\ \text{var}_1\ \bar{y}\ \text{and}\ node\ \text{var}_2\ \bar{y} \\ \qquad\qquad \text{are both labeled}\ \bigcirc\ \text{or both labeled}\ \bot\} \end{cases}$
other	$F(J) = D = F(I_1) \cup \ldots \cup F(I_m)$

To define *clean* and *next*, let XShare be the set of all sets of graphs satisfying conditions (1) through (6) of the definition of Share; however, they need not be k-limited. The functionalities are now *next*: Assign $\longrightarrow$ Share $\longrightarrow$ XShare and *clean*: XShare $\longrightarrow$ Share. The idea is that *next* applies the statement, and *clean* makes the resulting graph(s) k-limited.

The function *node* can be carried over to the graphs in Share and XShare naturally.

We now explain how to compute *next* $[\![S]\!]\,\bar{\sigma}$ for an assignment statement S and set of graphs $\bar{\sigma}$. First,

$$next\ [\![S]\!]\ \bar{\sigma} = \bigcup_{\bar{\gamma} \in \bar{\sigma}} next\ [\![S]\!]\ \{\bar{\gamma}\}$$

If $\{\bar{\gamma}\} \in$ Share, *next* $[\![S]\!]\,\{\bar{\gamma}\}$ will normally consist of one graph, obtained by modifying $\bar{\gamma}$ as described in the table below. However *next* $[\![S]\!]\,\{\bar{\gamma}\}$ will be empty if S aborts, and may have more than one element if a variable is moved to a descendant of an unknown node.

Form of S	*next* $[\![S]\!]\,\{\bar{\gamma}\}$
var := atom or var := **input**	add a new leaf labeled $\bigcirc$ to $\bar{\gamma}$; move var to the new node
$var_1 := var_2$	move var_1 to label *node* $var_2\bar{\gamma}$
$var_0 := \mathbf{cons}(var_1, \ldots, var_m)$	make a new node n and move var_0 to label it; for $i = 1, \ldots, m$ add an sel_i edge from n to *node* $var_i\bar{\gamma}$

$var_1.sel := var_2$	**case**
	    node $var_1\bar{\gamma}$ has an sel edge: replace it
	        by an sel edge leading to *node* $var_2\bar{\gamma}$
	    node $var_1\bar{\gamma}$ is labeled $\bigcirc$ or $\perp$:
	        next $[\![S]\!]\,\{\bar{\gamma}\} = \varnothing$
	    node $var_1\bar{\gamma}$ is unknown:
	        Add an edge $\dashrightarrow$ from *node* $var_1\bar{\gamma}$ to
	        node $var_2\bar{\gamma}$ (if not present)
	endcase

$var_1 := var_2.sel$	**case**
	    node $var_2\bar{\gamma}$ has an sel descendant n:
	        move var_1 to node n
	    node $var_2\bar{\gamma}$ is known but has label $\bigcirc$ or
	        $\perp$: *next* $[\![S]\!]\,\{\bar{\gamma}\} = \varnothing$
	    node $var_2\bar{\gamma}$ is unknown with immediate
	        descendants $n_1, \ldots, n_r$:
	        next $[\![S]\!]\,\{\bar{\gamma}\} = \{\bar{\gamma}_0, \bar{\gamma}_1, \ldots, \bar{\gamma}_2\}$
	        where: $\bar{\gamma}_1, \ldots, \bar{\gamma}_r$ are $\bar{\gamma}$ with var_1
	        moved to nodes $n_1, \ldots, n_r$; and $\bar{\gamma}_0$ is
	        $\bar{\gamma}$ with var_1 moved to *node* $var_2\bar{\gamma}$
	endcase

In Fig. 4-21 we illustrate *next* $[\![S]\!] \bar{\sigma}$ for several statements S, where $\bar{\sigma}$ contains only the single 3-limited graph of Fig. 4-19.

The purpose of the function *clean* is to restore the k-limited character of the graphs in *next* $[\![S]\!] \bar{\sigma}$. We first define

$$\mathbf{C}(\bar{\gamma}) = \{n \in \bar{\gamma} \mid \text{node } n \text{ is not accessible from any known, variable-labeled node by a path of length } k - 1 \text{ or less}\}$$

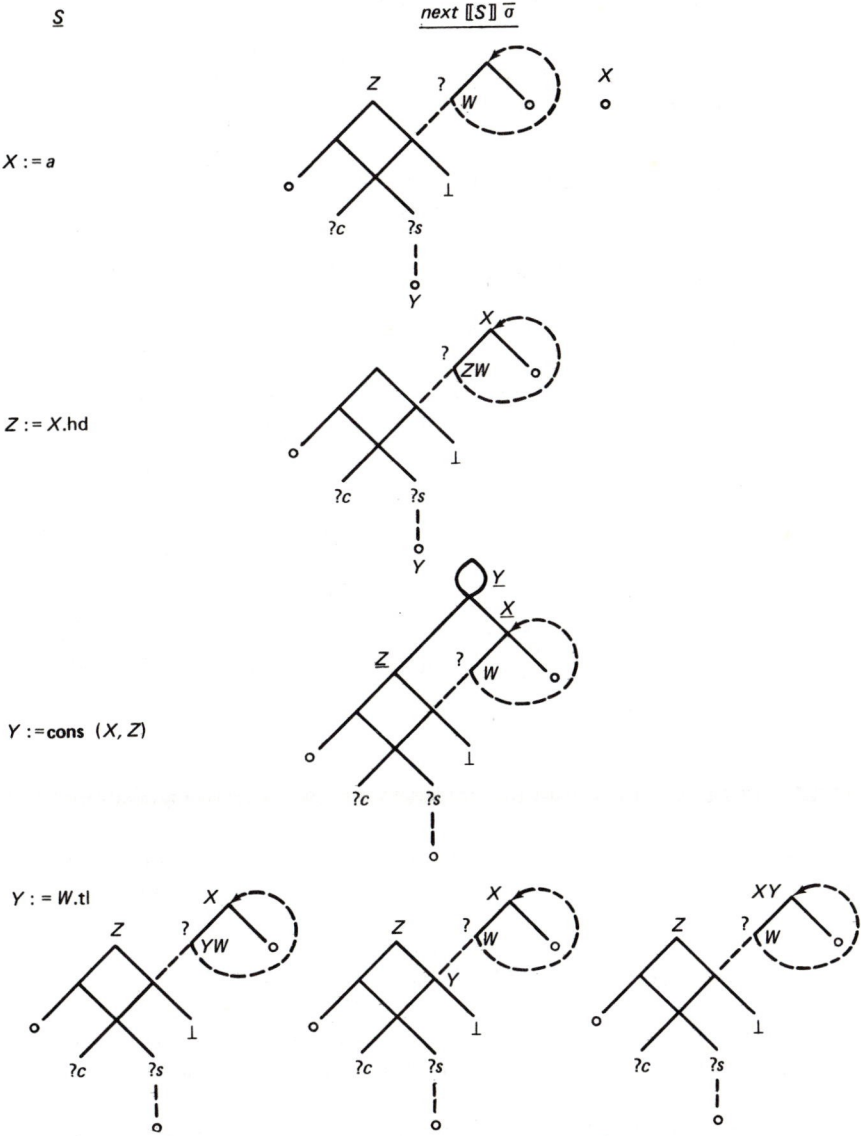

Figure 4-21

Now *clean* $\bar{\sigma}$ is the set of k-limited graphs resulting from applying the following transformation to each graph $\bar{\gamma}$ in $\bar{\sigma}$:

1. Remove all nodes which are inaccessible from variables.

2. Partition $\mathbf{C}(\bar{\gamma})$ into strongly connected components $C_1, C_2, \ldots$

3. **for** each C_i **do**
   if C_i contains at least one edge
   then coalesce C_i into a single unknown node, labeled c

4. Let the resulting graph be called $\bar{\gamma}'$. Partition $\mathbf{C}(\bar{\gamma}')$ into undirected connected components $C'_1, C'_2, \ldots$

5. **for** each C'_i **do**
   if C'_i contains more than one node
   then coalesce C'_i into a single unknown node $\bar{n}$;
       if C'_i contains a node labeled c
       then label $\bar{n}$ with c
       else if C'_i contains a shared node or a node labeled s
           then label $\bar{n}$ with s

The "coalescing" operation above is done by merging the nodes of C into a single node $\bar{n}$, preserving incoming and outgoing edges, and variable labels within C. More precisely,

1. Create a new node $\bar{n}$.

2. Label it with ? and with all variables labeling nodes in C.

3. Redirect any edge coming into C to point to $\bar{n}$.

4. Replace any edge coming out of C by a dotted edge $--->$ to the same endpoint, provided such an edge does not already exist.

5. Delete all nodes of C and edges between them.

As an example of *clean*, suppose we start with the graph in Fig. 4-22. Steps (1) through (5) result in the graphs in Fig. 4-22(b) to (f), assuming the resulting graph is to be 2-limited.

Note that our comments about backward flow analysis in Section 4-3 apply here as well.

4-9. SOLUTION OF THE FLOW EQUATIONS

Note that Share is finite. It is not hard to see that $F(\ )$ is monotonic, so the minimal-fixed-point solution may be obtained by regular or chaotic iteration.

As an example of the kind of information that can be obtained from the

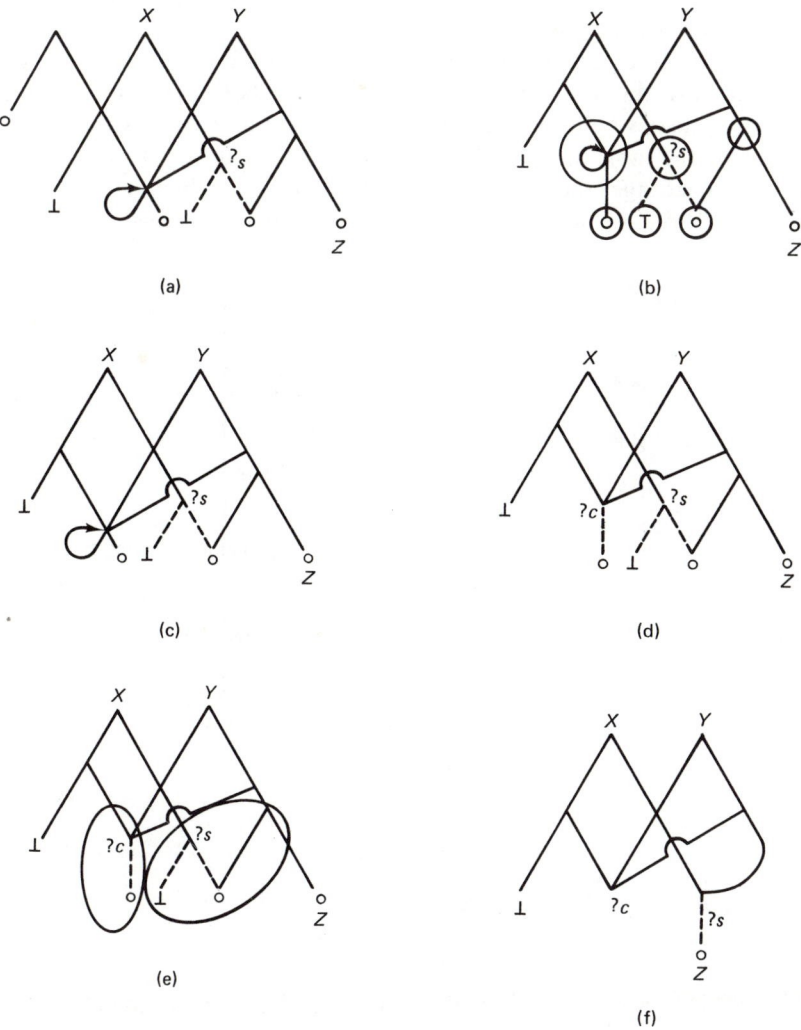

(a)

(b)

(c)

(d)

(e)

(f)

Figure 4-22

equations, suppose no node accessible from *node Xσ* in any Share graph in the solution is in a cycle or labeled c. Then no node accessible from X in any computation can be part of a cycle, so the descendants of X need not be managed by garbage collection. Similar remarks apply to sharing: a non-shared node can be deallocated as soon as any reference to it is destroyed.

Theorems establishing these facts will be proved in the next section. First we give an example of the flow equations and their solution, using again the program in Fig. 4-9. For illustrative purposes we compress this program a bit and insert a few program points to obtain the flowchart and forward flow equations in Fig. 4-23.

To solve the equations we proceed by the method of chaotic iterations, iterating $F(1)$ to stability and then in turn iterating $F(2)$, $F(3)$, and $F(4)$ until the whole system stabilizes. The solution for $F(1)$ and $F(2)$ with $k = 2$ is indicated by the table in Fig. 4-24. No shared or cyclic structures occur, so the simplest storage allocation method may be used. Further, $X := X.\text{tl}$ frees one cell which can be used immediately by the $Y := \mathbf{cons}(X.\text{hd}, Y)$.

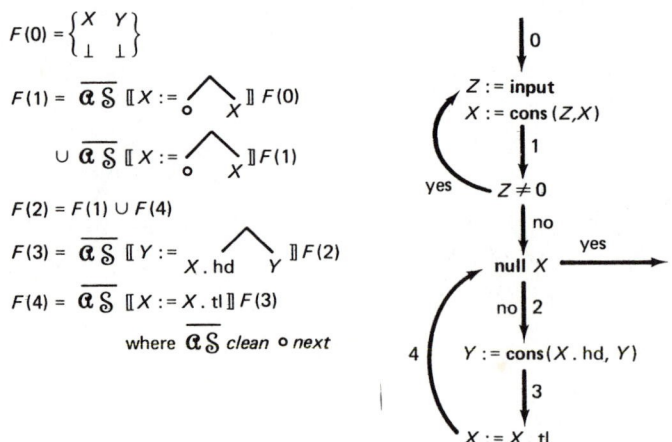

Figure 4-23

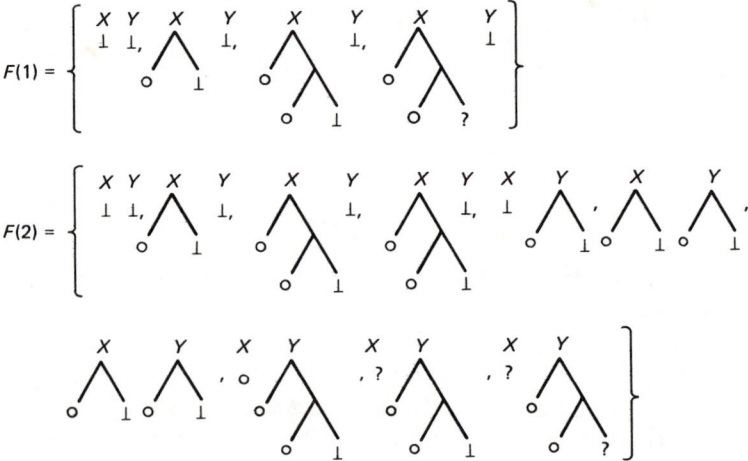

Figure 4-24

4-10. THEOREMS ON DETECTION OF SHARING AND CYCLES

We show in this section that the Share model is capable of detecting any sharing or cycling which may occur in the data structures of an SUSL program. Of course, since the model is finite and based on conservative assumptions, it may also indicate the possibility of sharing or cycling where none occurs in the actual program.

To state the results we first need to define a compatibility relation between STORE and Share graphs which will embody the intuitive notion that, if a STORE σ results from an SUSL computation leading to program point I, then the set of Share graphs $F(I)$ contains a graph $\bar{y}$ representing σ. For example, for the STORE graph in Fig. 4-25(a), the Share graph in Fig. 4-25(b) is compatible, while that in Fig. 4-25(c) is not.

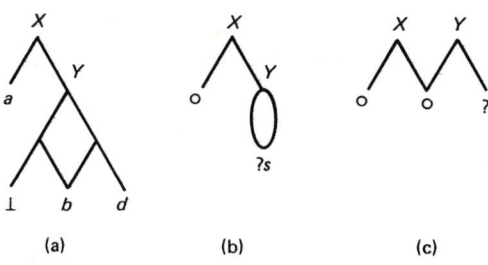

(a) (b) (c)

Figure 4-25

Let $nodes(\sigma)$ be the set of nodes in graph σ. By definition an *admissible node correspondence* from σ to $\bar{y}$ is any function $\Gamma: nodes(\sigma) \longrightarrow nodes(\bar{y})$ such that:

1. $\Gamma(node\ X\sigma) = node\ X\bar{y}$ for all $X \in$ Var.
2. Let there be an edge in σ from n to n_1 with selector label sel. Then:
   (a) If $\Gamma(n)$ is known, there is an sel-labeled edge in $\bar{y}$ from $\Gamma(n)$ to $\Gamma(n_1)$.
   (b) If $\Gamma(n)$ is unknown, either $\Gamma(n) = \Gamma(n_1)$ or there is a dotted edge from $\Gamma(n)$ to $\Gamma(n_1)$.

Further, σ and $\bar{y}$ are *compatible* (written $\sigma \sim \bar{y}$) iff:

1. There is an admissible node correspondence Γ from σ to $\bar{y}$.
2. If node n is shared in σ then either $\Gamma(n)$ is shared in $\bar{y}$ or $\Gamma(n)$ is accessible in $\bar{y}$ from a node labeled s or c.

127

3. If node n is contained in a cycle in σ then either $\Gamma(n)$ is contained in a cycle in $\bar{\gamma}$ or $\Gamma(n)$ is labeled c.

Thus it is easy to see that the graph in Fig. 4-25(c) is not compatible with that in Fig. 4-25(a) because, among other reasons, the tail descendant of *node $X\sigma$* is *node $Y\sigma$*, while the tail descendant of *node $X\bar{\gamma}$* is not *node $Y\bar{\gamma}$*.

We next show that the transition functions $\mathcal{AS}(\ )$ and $\overline{\mathcal{AS}}(\ )$ preserve compatibility.

Theorem.   Let assign be an SUSL assignment statement, σ a STORE graph and $\bar{\gamma}$ a Share graph such that $\sigma \sim \bar{\gamma}$. Then there exists $\bar{\gamma}'' \in \overline{\mathcal{AS}}[\![\text{assign}]\!] \{\bar{\gamma}\}$ such that $\mathcal{AS}[\![\text{assign}]\!]\, \sigma \sim \bar{\gamma}''$.

Proof.   The proof compares the effects of $\mathcal{AS}$, *next* and *clean* on σ and $\bar{\gamma}$, by an enumeration of cases, to show that the diagram in Fig. 4-26 commutes.

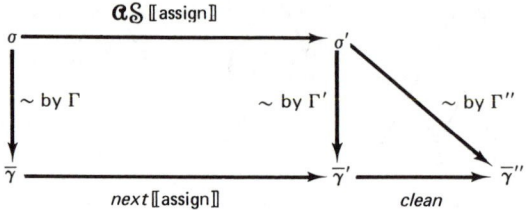

Figure 4-26

In the diagram $\sigma' = \mathcal{AS}[\![\text{assign}]\!]\, \sigma$, Γ is the admissible node correspondence given by $\sigma \sim \bar{\gamma}$, $\bar{\gamma}'$ is a graph in *next* $[\![\text{assign}]\!] \{\bar{\gamma}\}$, $\bar{\gamma}'' = $ *clean* $\bar{\gamma}'$, and Γ' and Γ'' are defined below.

Now *next* $[\![\text{assign}]\!] \{\bar{\gamma}\}$ is a singleton in nearly all cases, uniquely defining $\bar{\gamma}'$. The only exception occurs when assign has the form $\text{var}_1 := \text{var}_2.\text{sel}$ and *node* $\text{var}_2\bar{\gamma}$ is unknown. In this case *next* $[\![\text{assign}]\!] \{\bar{\gamma}\}$ is a set $\{\bar{\gamma}_0, \ldots, \bar{\gamma}_r\}$. Let n be the sel descendant of *node* $\text{var}_2\sigma$. Γ is admissible, so $\Gamma(n) = $ *node* $\text{var}_2\bar{\gamma}_i$ for some $\bar{\gamma}_i$ in $\{\bar{\gamma}_0, \ldots, \bar{\gamma}_r\}$, which we choose to be $\bar{\gamma}'$.

If $\mathcal{AS}$ does not create new nodes or edges, Γ' may be chosen identical to Γ, restricted to the nodes in σ'. Admissibility is trivial. If a new node is created by $\mathcal{AS}$, one is also created by *next*, and they naturally correspond in Γ'. If new edges are created by **cons** in σ', the same new edges appear in $\bar{\gamma}'$, so admissibility is preserved. Finally, if $\mathcal{AS}$ creates a new edge in σ' by an assignment $\text{var}_1.\text{sel} := \text{var}_2$, then *next* creates a new edge in $\bar{\gamma}'$, which satisfies the admissibility condition.

Thus we have constructed an admissible node correspondence Γ' between σ' and $\bar{\gamma}' \in$ *next* [[assign]] $\{\bar{\gamma}\}$ from the admissible node correspondence Γ between σ and $\bar{\gamma}$. To see that σ' is compatible with $\bar{\gamma}'$, note that by admissibility any path in σ' corresponds to some path in $\bar{\gamma}'$. Thus any new shared nodes or cycles in σ' correspond to shared nodes or cycles in $\bar{\gamma}'$. Further, the labels c and s in $\bar{\gamma}$ are left unchanged in $\bar{\gamma}'$, unless they become inaccessible.

Now we define $\bar{\gamma}'' = clean(\bar{\gamma}')$ and $\Gamma'': nodes(\sigma') \longrightarrow nodes(\bar{\gamma}'')$ from Γ' by setting $\Gamma''(n) = \Gamma'(n)$ if $\Gamma'(n)$ was not coalesced in constructing $\bar{\gamma}''$ from $\bar{\gamma}'$ and $\Gamma''(n) = \bar{n}$ if $\Gamma'(n)$ was coalesced into $\bar{n}$. It remains to check that the conditions of compatibility are satisfied between σ' and $\bar{\gamma}''$.

To see $\Gamma''(node\ X\sigma') = node\ X\bar{\sigma}''$, first suppose $\Gamma'(node\ X\sigma')$ was not coalesced in forming $\bar{\gamma}''$. Then by admissibility of Γ', $\Gamma''(node\ X\sigma')$ $= \Gamma'(node\ X\sigma') = node\ X\bar{\gamma}' = node\ X\bar{\gamma}''$. If $\Gamma'(node\ X\sigma')$ was coalesced into $\bar{n}$, then $\Gamma''(node\ X\sigma') = \bar{n}$. Since X labeled $\Gamma'(node\ X\sigma')$, it also labels $\bar{n}$ as required.

Now suppose an edge exists in σ' from n to n_1, labeled sel, and consider $\Gamma''(n)$ and $\Gamma''(n_1)$. If $\Gamma(n)$ was not coalesced, then admissibility of Γ' implies an edge exists from $\Gamma'(n)$ to $\Gamma'(n_1)$, or $\Gamma'(n)$ and $\Gamma'(n_1)$ are the same unknown node. Such an edge or identity is preserved by *clean*. Now if $\Gamma'(n)$ was coalesced into $\bar{n}$, either it was coalesced into $\Gamma'(n)$ or it was not. If so, then $\Gamma''(n) = \Gamma''(n_1)$, satisfying the admissibility condition; if not, then by definition of the coalescence operation there will be an edge from $\Gamma''(n)$ to $\Gamma''(n_1)$.

Consequently Γ'' is an admissible node correspondence between σ' and $\bar{\gamma}''$. To see compatibility, suppose node n is shared in σ'. If $\Gamma'(n)$ is accessible from a node labeled s or c in $\bar{\gamma}'$, the same is true in $\bar{\gamma}''$ since *clean* does not remove s or c labels or destroy connectivity. Suppose now n is explicitly shared in σ', so two distinct paths to n from one or two variables exist in σ', and that $\Gamma''(n)$ is not accessible from any node labeled s or c. Then by admissibility of Γ', two distinct paths p_1 and p_2 to $\Gamma'(n)$ exist in $\bar{\gamma}'$. Consider the corresponding image paths $clean(p_1)$ and $clean(p_2)$. If $clean(p_1) \neq clean(p_2)$, then $\Gamma''(n)$ is shared in $\bar{\gamma}''$. If $clean(p_1) = clean(p_2)$, there must be nodes $\bar{n}_1$ in p_1 and $\bar{n}_2$ in p_2 whose successors are the same shared node; call it $\bar{n}_3$. Now $\Gamma''(\bar{n}_1) = \Gamma''(\bar{n}_2)$, so by definition of *clean*, $\bar{n}_1$ and $\bar{n}_2$ belong to the same connected component C of $\bar{\gamma}$. If $\bar{n}_3$ is in C, $\bar{n}_3$ is shared so $\Gamma''(\bar{n}_3)$ will be labeled s or c, a contradiction. If $\bar{n}_3$ is not in C and C is a strongly connected component, $\Gamma''(\bar{n}_1)$ will be labeled c, a similar contradiction. Finally if $\bar{n}_3$ is not in C and C is an undirected connected component, $\bar{n}_3$ is not in $\mathbf{C}(\bar{\gamma})$ from the definition of *clean*. Thus there is a path from some *node*

$X\bar{\gamma}'$ to $\bar{n}_3$ of length k or less. This path, if continued through $\bar{n}_3$ to $\Gamma'(n)$, is distinct from p_1, and its image will be distinct from $clean(p_1)$, satisfying the second compatibility condition.

Now suppose node n is in a cyclic path $n = n_1, n_2, \ldots, n_r = n$ in σ'. By admissibility of Γ'', if at least two n_i's are distinct, $\Gamma''(n_1), \ldots,$ $\Gamma''(n_r)$ is a cycle in $\bar{\gamma}''$. If $\Gamma''(n_i) = \Gamma''(n)$ for all i, then either $\Gamma'(n_i) = \Gamma'(n)$ for all i, in which case the third compatibility condition is satisfied, or $\Gamma'(n_1), \ldots, \Gamma'(n_r)$ forms a cycle in $\bar{\gamma}$. In this case these nodes form part of a strongly connected component, so $\Gamma''(n)$ will be labeled c in $\bar{\gamma}''$ as required. ∎

To relate the above theorem to the identification of situations where storage management methods that are simpler and more efficient than garbage collection can be used, we first define *graph $X\bar{\gamma}$* for a variable X and a Share graph $\bar{\gamma}$ to be the subgraph of $\bar{\gamma}$ comprising all nodes reachable from *node $X\bar{\gamma}$* and all edges between them. We then have the following two corollaries:

Corollary. If *graph $X\bar{\gamma}$* contains no shared nodes for all $\bar{\gamma} \in F(I)$ for all program points I, then variable X requires neither reference counting nor garbage collection; i.e., any node reachable from the root of X may be deallocated immediately when a reference to it is removed.

Proof. By the theorem, all sharing which can occur in the STORE semantics is recognized in the compatible Share graphs. If no node in *graph $X\bar{\gamma}$* is ever shared in any possible $\bar{\gamma}$, then nodes reachable from X can never be shared. ∎

Corollary. If *graph $X\bar{\gamma}$* contains no cyclic nodes for all $\bar{\gamma} \in F(I)$ for all I, then variable X requires no garbage collection; i.e., management of storage for nodes reachable from the root of X may be done by reference counting.

Proof. Similar to that for preceding corollary. ∎

The above results are global in two respects: they concern the behavior of a variable throughout the execution of a program, and they concern all nodes reachable from it. The information present in the $F(I)$ is sufficient, however, to obtain results which are local in both senses. This could be applied to make very efficient use of a dynamic storage management system in which cells are divided into three types: those which are immediately deallocated, those which are reference-counted, and those which are garbage-collected. Then a particular cell which can be identified as never being shared in the future can be allocated as the first type, one which may be shared but will never be cyclic as the second type, and the remainder as the last type. We leave the detailed development and analysis of this approach to later work.

It should be noted in closing that Baker [Bake78] has studied the situation in which reference counting is an appropriate method for dynamic storage management. His findings indicate that our intended use is an appropriate one.

Chapter 5

Global Flow Analysis
and Optimization
in the MUG2
Compiler Generating System

Reinhard Wilhelm

5-1. INTRODUCTION

The state of the art and future trends in compilation are heavily influenced by two types of developments: the design of new programming languages, offering new problems to the compiler writer, and the developing theory of compilation, in particular the growing field of formal methods for the description of programming languages and compilers. Progress in the area of formal description of compilation, especially of semantic analysis, code optimization, and code generation will produce more powerful compiler generating systems.

This paper presents one such advanced system, MUG2, designed and currently being implemented at the Technical University of Munich. MUG2 is unique among compiler generating systems in that it offers description tools and generators for multipass semantic analysis, code optimization, and code generation [Ganz77]. In this paper, the description tools for the first two of these tasks, namely *modified attribute grammars* [Ganz74] and *attributed transformational grammars* [Wilh74] are used to describe global data flow analysis and two optimization algorithms for a small language.

Besides demonstrating the capabilities of these description tools, the example is of interest by itself, since it shows the cooperation of several compiler passes. In the first pass described, which might be any of several semantic analysis passes, global data flow information is collected in attributes associated with nodes in the program tree. The first optimization pass, which performs constant propagation and folding, makes use of this global data flow information in transforming the program. Data flow information might be invalid after this transformation. But our example shows that it can be updated for use in further optimization passes. The second optimization pass moves invariant computations out of loops. This pass also both exploits and updates data flow information.

It is important to note that there are no inherent inefficiencies connected to the use of MUG2 description mechanisms and that a uniform mechanism can be used to describe both the first evaluation of data flow information and the necessary reevaluations after optimizing transformations.

The compiler described is for a small language called BJ, containing only sequential flow, conditional statements, and while-loops [Böhm66]. The mechanisms can easily be extended to handle other one-entry, one-exit statements. Flow analysis information for BJ programs can efficiently be gathered from a tree-structured representation, and other syntax-directed methods can be chosen for the tasks in mind.

As our example concentrates on global data flow problems, we devote the first section to high-level data flow analysis [Rose77c], although simplified for our small language.

Section 5-2 gives an overview of MUG2 and its description tools. Examples for the more unconventional description tools are given.

In Sections 5-3 through 5-6, we work through the description of three optimization passes for BJ programs. The syntactic structure of BJ programs and their intermediate representation are described by means of a string-to-tree grammar in Section 5-3. High-level flow analysis for BJ programs is described using modified attribute grammars in Section 5-4. Attributed transformational grammars are employed to specify how the flow information collected is used and updated in a constant propagation pass and an invariant code motion pass in Sections 5-5 and 5-6.

The modified attribute grammar mechanism allows controlled use of global variables, which is a necessity for the generation of efficient compilers. This capability is exploited in the description of global flow analysis for the language BJ extended by a **leave**-statement in Section 5-7.

Global data flow analysis, as described for BJ, is an adaptation of the high-level flow analysis method of Rosen [Rose77c]. Conventional flow analysis techniques [Ullm75] work on an intermediate text representation of a program with expressions decomposed into sequences of binary and unary operations and with the control structure of the program translated into an explicit branching structure. Data flow analysis is driven by this branching structure, the control flow graph. In contrast to this, Rosen makes use of the semantics of the control constructs, as far as their effect on data flow is concerned. These effects can be described at language definition time and hence used in generating a compiler.

For our example, we only need the idea behind this approach, not the full formalism.

The flow information which we want to compute consists of three fundamental flow bits for each statement α and each variable x in a program.

$mod(\alpha, x) = 1$ iff the value of x may be *modified* by the execution of statement α; 0 otherwise

$use(\alpha, x) = 1$ iff the value possessed by x upon entry to α may be *used* when statement α is executed; 0 otherwise

$pre(\alpha, x) = 1$ iff the value of x may be *preserved* when statement α is executed; 0 otherwise

The definition of these flow bits is given in an inductive way. First, they are defined for simple statements (in BJ, the assignment statement); then computation rules are given that compute the flow bits associated with a structured statement based upon the flow bits already computed for its constituents. We use bit vectors to collect each of the three flow bits for all program variables.

5-2.   THE DESCRIPTION TOOLS OF MUG2

MUG2 supports the automatic generation of optimizing multipass compilers. Its description tools and generators for lexical and syntactical analysis are the same as in MUG1 [Wilh76]. In addition, MUG2 offers description tools and generators for tree generation, multipass semantic analysis, optimizing program tree transformations, and code generation.

Compilers having several passes require an intermediate form for source programs. In a compiler, a formal specification of this form is the basis for the description of the compiler subtasks. A treelike structure, similar to that of a parse tree, constitutes a natural intermediate form because of the following:

1. The result of syntactic analysis is a parse tree.

2. Semantic analysis relates semantic information with constructs of the program corresponding to nodes in the tree.

3. Optimizations of the program can be conceived as transformations of the tree.

4. Code can be generated during a tree traversal.

An abstract syntax tree variously decorated with semantic information during different compiler phases, i.e. an *attributed program tree,* appears to be a suitable intermediate form and is, therefore, used in MUG2-generated compilers. Consequently, MUG2-generated compilers work as follows (Fig. 5-1): A control module first makes the parser direct the first pass, during which, in an interleaved fashion, the source program is lexically and syntactically analyzed, the (still attribute-free) program tree constructed, and the first attribute evaluation pass carried out. Then the control module activates

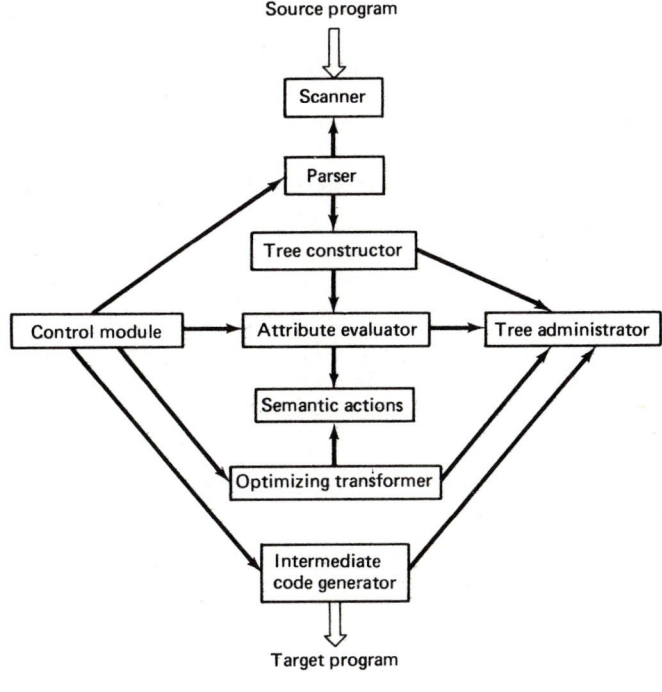

Figure 5-1

the attribute evaluator, optimizing transformer and code generator modules for further evaluation passes which perform code optimization and emit code, respectively.

All the modules will be automatically generated except for the tree administrator, which realizes the abstract data type "attributed program tree." The tools for the description of the different compiler subtasks are listed in Fig. 5-2.

We will now give a brief overview of these description tools. Since all these formalisms deal with trees, we will first informally introduce the most

Compiler subtask	Description tool	References
Lexical analysis	Regular expressions	[Ganz76]
Syntax analysis and construction of the attribute-free program tree	String-to-tree grammar	[Gieg79]
Semantic analysis	Modified attribute grammar	[Ganz74, Gieg79]
Optimizing transformations	Attributed transformational grammar	[Wilh74, Wilh75]
Generation of intermediate code	Code functions	[Ripk75]

Figure 5-2

important concepts related to the generation, attribution, and transformation of trees.

(Attribute-free) trees, as used in MUG2, are rooted, ordered, and labeled. Each node in a tree is labeled with a symbol from a finite alphabet σ of *operators*. An operator $\circ \in \sigma$ has a fixed arity $g(\circ) \geq 0$. The notation $\circ.i$ for $0 \leq i \leq g(\circ)$ is used to denote the *i*th *operand* of $\circ$. Parameter symbols from another alphabet X disjoint from σ may label leaves of trees. A tree possibly having parameter nodes is called a *template*; a tree with only operator nodes is called an *operator tree*. By substituting operator trees for all parameter nodes in a template, we construct an *instance* of the template. A template is said to *match* all its instances. The tree σ in Fig. 5-3 is an instance of the template τ. Let A be a finite set of *attributes*. A subset of A is associated with each operator $\circ$.

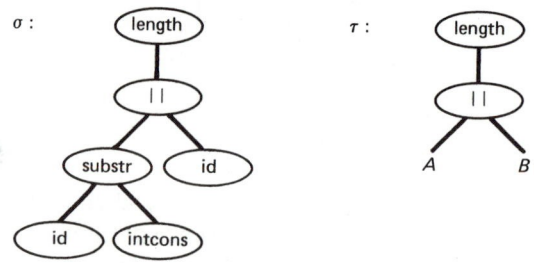

Figure 5-3

We will now informally introduce three of the above-mentioned description tools, namely string-to-tree grammars, modified attribute grammars, and attributed transformational grammars. For each we will pick some examples from our compiler description in Sections 5-3 through 5-6. If the context is unclear, the reader is asked to patiently await later illumination.

5-2.1. String-to-Tree Grammars

A string-to-tree grammar for a language L defines the (context-free) syntactic structure and intermediate tree form of L-programs. Each production of the grammar consists of a string part, which is a context-free production, followed by the symbol $\Longrightarrow$, followed by the tree part, which is a template. Labels in the tree part can correspond to symbols in the right-hand side of the string part in either of the following ways:

1. A parameter may correspond to a nonterminal with an identical name.

Example. See Fig. 5-4(a).
The tree to be generated for PROGRAM is a tree with root labeled prog and a single son, the tree for STATS.

2. A parameter may correspond to a nonterminal, and an operator label to a terminal, by a position prefix indicating the position of the syntactic symbol in the string part.

Example. See Fig. 5-4(b).

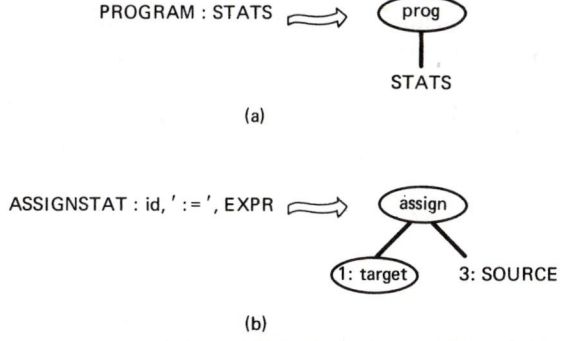

(a)

(b)

Figure 5-4

The operator "target" is introduced as a new label for identifiers on the left-hand side of assignments. The name SOURCE is introduced for expressions on the right-hand sides of assignments. From now on we can separate identifiers and expressions in the context of assignments from those occurring in other contexts.

An empty tree part indicates that the tree to be generated for the left-hand side nonterminal of the string part is the one generated for the right-hand side (which must be unambiguous!).

Example.

STAT : ASSIGNSTAT

The tree for STAT is identical to the tree for ASSIGNSTAT. Nonterminals in the string part and parameters in the tree part are written in capital letters; terminals in the string part and operators in the tree part are written in lower-case letters.

5-2.2. Modified Attribute Grammars

In MUG2, modified attribute grammars [Ganz74] are used to describe the association of static semantic information with nodes in the program tree. Hence, attribute computation rules are not based on the context-free grammar of a language, but on the tree parts of the string-to-tree grammar.

Attributes may be inherited or derived (synthesized) as in [Knut68]. For each *derived* attribute d and each operator $\circ$ possessing d, there must be an evaluation rule defining the value of d at any node n labeled with $\circ$ in terms of the values of its inherited attributes and the values of derived attributes of its operands.

For each *inherited* attribute i and for each operator $\circ$ possessing i, there must be an evaluation rule defining the value of i at any node n labeled with $\circ$ in terms of its own inherited attributes, inherited attributes of its father, and derived attributes of its brothers. Attribute evaluation must be subdivided into passes by the user of MUG2. This contrasts with the conventional attribute grammar approach, where the compiler generating system has to find an appropriate attribute evaluation strategy (cf. [Gieg78] for an overview of various approaches). In the light of the inherent inefficiencies of the problems connected with the conventional approach (cf. [Jaza75a]), the MUG2 approach seems to be more practical.

Each evaluation pass is realized as a left-to-right (or right-to-left) depth-first tree traversal. In our example we will have only left-to-right passes.

Before descending to a node-bearing operator $\circ$, all its inherited attributes from this pass are evaluated according to the evaluation rules. When ascending to a node-bearing operator $\circ$, all its derived attributes belonging to this pass are evaluated according to the evaluation rules.

Operators with (some) identical attribute evaluation rules may be grouped into classes to reduce size and redundancy of a description.

Example.

opclass ops = plus, equal;

For each attribute a declaration has to be given. It contains a specification of the direction (inherited/derived), type, identification, and transfer operators, i.e., node labels at which the value of an attribute is expected in later passes.

The attribute declaration

derived bitvector use **attached to** id, const, ops,
assign, if, while, sep;

declares the derived bit-vector attribute "use" for global flow analysis. Values of this attribute have to be stored at any node labeled with one of the operators given in the declaration.

Now we will explain a few attribute evaluation rules.

use **of** const := **0** ;

Since no variable is used here, an all-zero use-bit vector is associated with a const node.

use **of** id := *init-to-one*(idno **of** id);

Clearly, this is a *use* of a variable.

Note: Identifiers on the left-hand side of assignments will appear with label target and not with label id according to the string-to-tree grammar for BJ.

use **of** ops := use **of** ops.1 **or** use **of** ops.2;

The set of variables *used* in a composed expression is the union of the sets of variables from the two subexpressions.

use **of** sep := use **of** sep.STATS **or**
(use **of** sep.STAT **and** pre **of** sep.STATS);

A *separator* denotes sequential flow between a statement list and a statement. The set of variables, which may be used in the composed statement list, is equal to the set of variables which may be used in the component statement list plus those variables which may be used in the component statement and possibly preserved in the component statement list.

cvalue **of** const := lexsem **of** const;

idno **of** id := lexsem **of** id;

idno **of** target := lexsem **of** target;

Lexsem is a standard attribute set by the lexical analyzer. It can be thought of as containing the value of an integer constant or a unique number for an identifier, respectively.

To eliminate many identity attribute computation functions, the user may specify *transfer intervals*. These are regions of the attributed program tree where an attribute does not change its value. Therefore, inherited (derived) attributes are transferred unchanged top-down (bottom-up) from one end of the region to the other.

i-mod **of** while := mod **of** while;

i-mod **in** [while **downto** while[**unchanged** ;

Modify information about a while loop is propagated top-down to anywhere in the loop, excluding inner loops.

5-2.3.   Attributed Transformational Grammars (AT-Grammars)

Since programs are represented as attributed trees in MUG2-generated compilers, optimizing transformations are realized by tree transformations. These can be described by AT-grammars [Wilh74], a formal concept based upon the transformational grammars of deRemer [DeRe74] and the subtree replacement systems of Rosen [Rose73]. These formalisms were extended to allow the formulation of applicability restrictions beyond the purely syntactic match. Predicates on attributes are used for that purpose. In addition, the application of a transformation rule may cause reevaluation of attributes.

For an informal introduction to this mechanism we need the following concepts. A *transformation rule* (T-rule) p is a pair of tree templates (s, t), written as $s \Rightarrow t$, such that all parameters occurring in t also occur in s. s is called the *input template* of p, It(p); t is called the *output template* of p, Ot(p). An instance of the T-rule $s \Rightarrow t$ is obtained by consistent replacement of the parameter nodes in s and t by operator trees, i.e., replacement of all nodes in s and t which have the same parameter label by the same operator tree. The instances of s and t thus obtained are called *corresponding*. A T-rule is *applicable* to a tree t if its input template matches a subtree of t. The *application* of this T-rule p means the replacement of the subtree matched by It(p) by the corresponding instance of Ot(p).

In order to describe the transformation of attributed program trees, we associate predicates P on attributes of the input template and functions F from attributes of the input template to attributes of the output template with the T-rules. The predicates allow the formulation of the enabling conditions of the transformations, and the functions allow recomputation of attributes for further optimization or code generation.

An attributed transformation rule (AT-rule) is written $s \overset{P}{\underset{F}{\Rightarrow}} t$. Such an *AT-rule is applicable* to a tree r if s matches a subtree of r and if P applied to the attributes of this subtree evaluates to *true*. The application of that rule consists of the application of $s \Rightarrow t$ and the recomputation of attribute values for the transformed subtree. For this recomputation, one can use functions explicitly associated with the AT-rule and functions used in previous passes for the definition of attribute evaluation of labels occurring in the output template.

The following examples are taken from the constant propagation pass, described later on. The AT-rule shown in Fig. 5-5(a) describes the compile-time evaluation of constant expressions. No enabling condition is given. The value resulting from the addition is associated with the newly created const node, and an all-zero use bit vector is appended to the node as updated

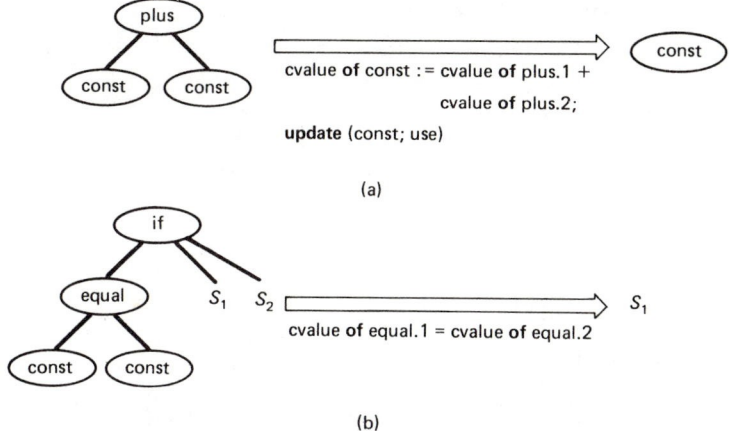

Figure 5-5

flow information, using an evaluation rule from a previous pass. Our second example, shown in Fig. 5-5(b), concerns comparisons between constant operands, which clearly can be evaluated at compile time, allowing the conditional to be replaced by either its true part or false part at compile time. The correct selection is formulated in the enabling predicate.

5-3. THE STRING-TO-TREE GRAMMAR FOR BJ

See Fig. 5-6.

5-4. GLOBAL DATA FLOW ANALYSIS FOR BJ

The following modified attribute grammar describes how fundamental data flow information about BJ programs is collected in the bit vectors use, mod, and pre associated with nodes in the program tree.

0 denotes the all-zero bit vector

1 denotes the all-one bit vector

or denotes the logical or operation

and denotes the logical and operation

Names of semantic functions in attribute definitions are printed in italics. For the first pass we need the following semantic functions:

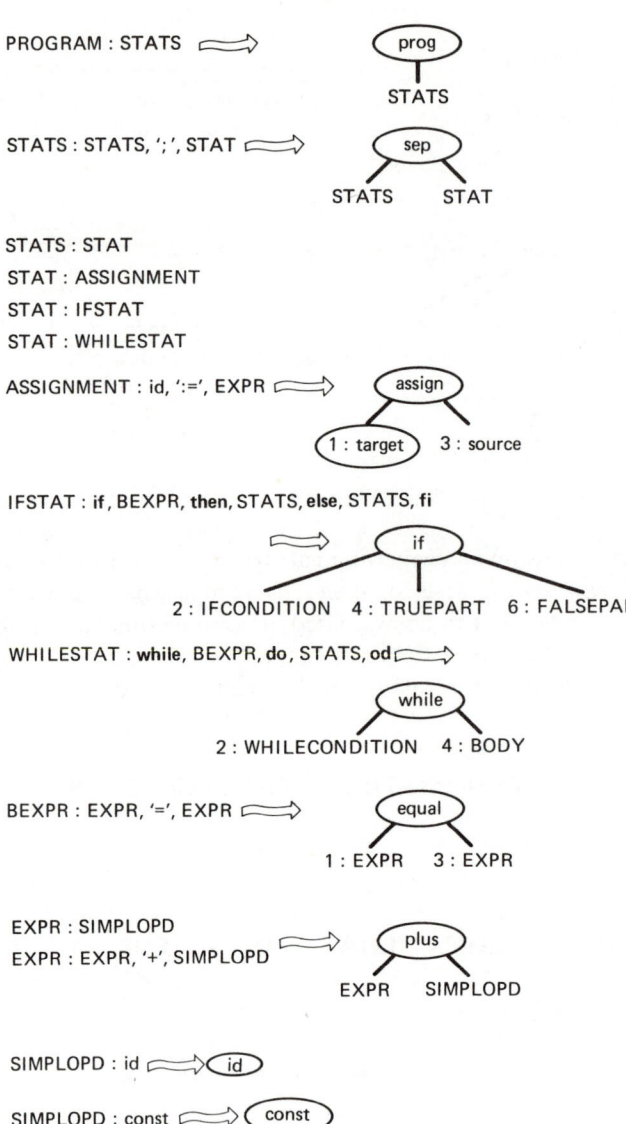

Figure 5-6

```
function init-to-one(int pos) returns bitvector:
  begin
    bitvector a init 0;
    a[pos] := 1;
    a
  end;
```

```
function init-to-zero(int pos) returns bitvector:
  begin
    bitvector b init 1;
    b[pos] := 0;
    b
  end;

pass collecting global data flow information;
  opclass ops = plus, equal;
  derived bitvector mod, pre attached to
    assign, if, while, sep;
  derived bitvector use attached to id, const, ops,
    assign, if, while, sep;
  derived int cvalue attached to const;
  derived int idno attached to id, target;

use of const := 0;
use of id     := init-to-one(idno of id);
use of ops    := use of ops.1 or use of ops.2;

use of assign   := use of SOURCE;
mod of assign := init-to-one(idno of target);
pre of assign   := init-to-zero(idno of target);

use of sep  := use of sep.STATS or
                 (use of sep.STAT and pre of sep.STATS);
mod of sep := mod of sep.STATS or mod of sep.STAT;
pre of sep  := pre of sep.STATS and pre of sep.STAT;

use of if  := use of IFCONDITION or
                 use of TRUEPART or use of FALSEPART;
mod of if := mod of TRUEPART or mod of FALSEPART;
pre of if  := pre of TRUEPART or pre of FALSEPART;

use of while   := use of WHILECONDITION or
                    use of BODY;
mod of while := mod of BODY;
pre of while   := 1;

cvalue of const := lexsem of const;
idno of id       := lexsem of id;
idno of target   := lexsem of target;

ssap;
```

The attribute evaluation pass just described produces general-purpose flow information which can be beneficially used by a variety of optimizations.

5-5. CONSTANT PROPAGATION FOR BJ PROGRAMS

In many optimizing compilers, constant propagation is only done inside blocks of straight-line code. There is a compile-time efficiency argument for this. If a pool of variables *assumed* to be constant at a certain point in the program is carried around the control flow graph, iteration will be needed for any cycle in the graph (cf. [Kild73]). This iteration will stop when the pool is stable. At that time, the pool will only contain variables which are *known* to be constant at the nodes in the cycle; see Fig. 5-7 for an example.

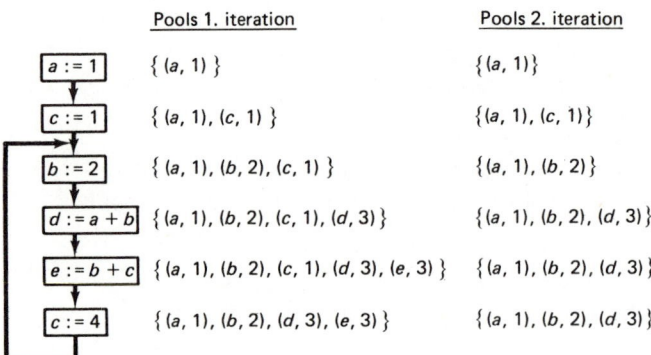

Figure 5-7

BJ contains while-loops, for which iteration would be required when using the conventional approach. But we can benefit from the flow information computed in the first pass.

We have recorded the set of variables which may be modified inside the loop in the mod bit vector of a while node. These variables may be eliminated from the pool of available constant variables when we start processing the loop. This guarantees that stable pools will result after only one iteration. Thus, constant propagation may be performed in one pass.

After applying transformations, we often can make use of the semantic functions from the first pass to update flow information. We note this by **update**(label; attributelist) or **update**(attributelist).

The following functions are used to compute attribute values in the constant propagation pass (the corresponding transformations are shown in Fig. 5-8):

mode pool = **list of** (**int** idno, cvalue);

mode pool-entry = **struct**(**int** idnumber, value);

function *is-element*(**int** idno; **pool** p) **returns bool**:

co checks, whether a pair with first component idno
is in pool p or not;

function *find*(**int** idno; **pool** p) **returns int**:
co returns the cvalue for idno from pool p;

function *intersect*(**pool** p_1, p_2) **returns pool**:
co returns a pool containing those pairs that occur identically in both
input pools p_1 and p_2;

function *insert*(**pool** p; **int** idno, cval) **returns pool**:
co inserts a new pair (idno, cval) into the pool p, replacing a pair
with the same idno if it exists;

function *delete*(**pool** p; **int** idno) **returns pool**:
co deletes the pair with first component idno, if it exists;

function *not-mod-vars*(**pool** p; **bitvector** m) **returns pool**:
co eliminates all pairs (idno, cvalue) from pool p for which m[idno]
$= 1$ holds;

pass constant propagation;
inherited pool i-pool;
derived pool d-pool;
attributes
expected idno **at** id, target,
        cvalue **at** const,
        mod, use **at** while, if, sep;
updated use;

i-pool **of** prog.1   := **empty-list**;
i-pool **of** sep.STATS := i-pool **of** sep;
i-pool **of** sep.STAT := d-pool **of** sep.STATS;
d-pool **of** sep   := d-pool **of** sep.STAT;

i-pool **of** IFCONDITION := i-pool **of** if;
i-pool **of** TRUEPART   := i-pool **of** if;
i-pool **of** FALSEPART := i-pool **of** if;
d-pool **of** if   := *intersect*(d-pool **of** TRUEPART,
                           d-pool **of** FALSEPART)

i-pool **of** WHILECONDITION := *not-mod-vars*(i-pool **of** while,
                                 mod **of** while);
i-pool **of** BODY   := *not-mod-vars*(i-pool **of** while,
                                 mod **of** while);
d-pool **of** while   := *not-mod-vars*(i-pool **of** while,
                                 mod **of** while);

i-pool **of** SOURCE := i-pool **of** assign;
i-pool **of** ops.1   := i-pool **of** ops;
i-pool **of** ops.2   := i-pool **of** ops;

Transformations

$C1$:

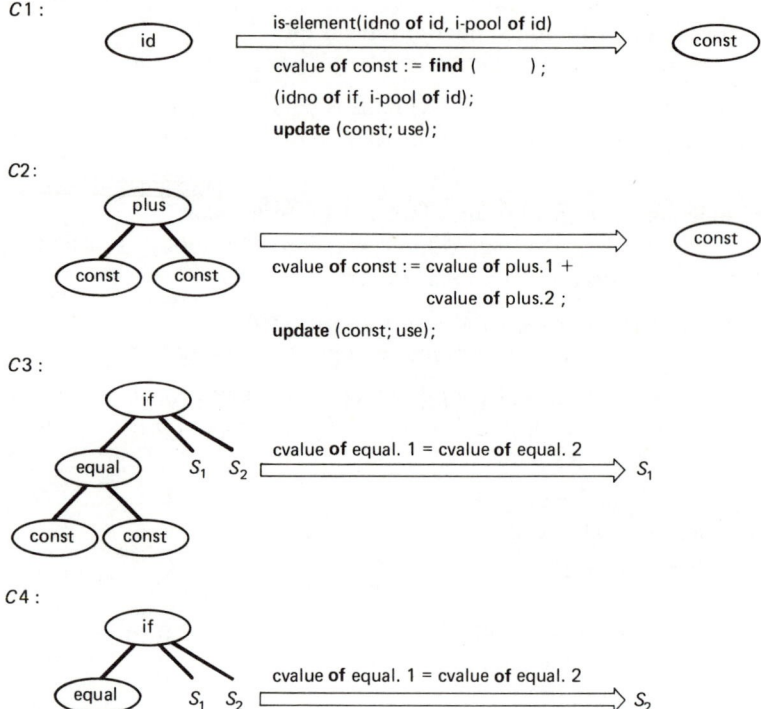

$C2$:

$C3$:

$C4$:

co application of $C3$ or $C4$ will probably make flow information above the if-node
invalid. One could argue that the pre and mod bit vectors should be updated.
This is not done here, since there is reason to believe that the applicability
of these rules signals a logical error by the programmer. In consequence one
might not detect all possible optimizations, but what is more important, one
will not make any incorrect ones;

$C5$:

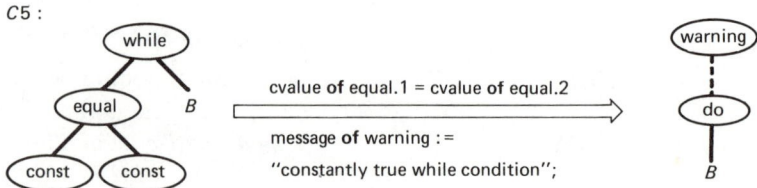

Figure 5-8

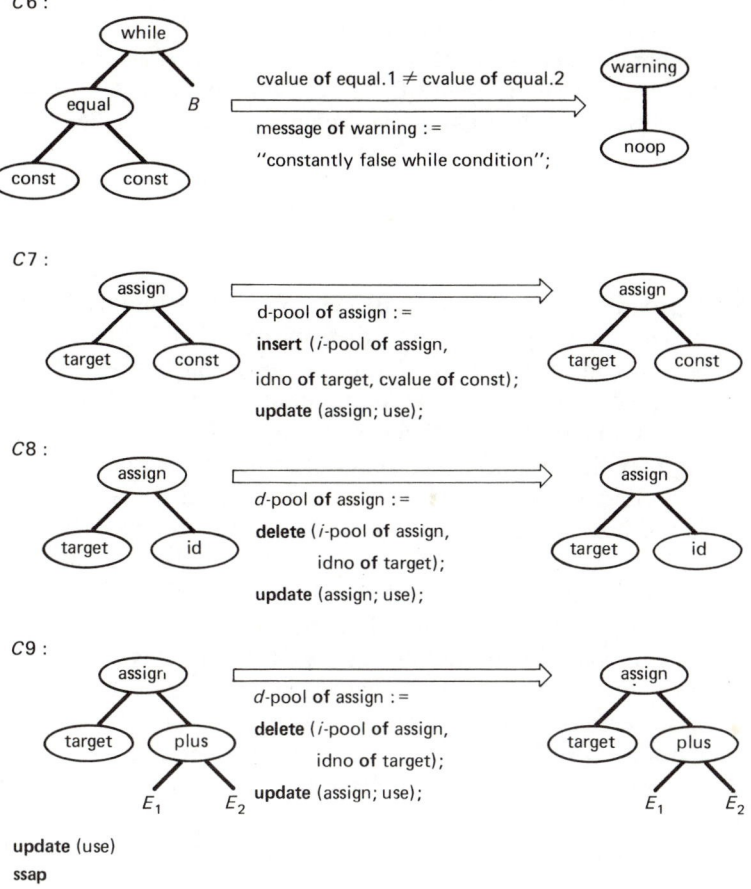

Figure 5-8 (cont.)

This pass will be realized in a depth-first, left-to-right tree traversal, starting at the root and returning to it. The transformation rules will be tried in a monotonic bottom-up way. Hence, rule C1 will always be applied before rule C8, making sure that all possible optimizations will be done.

5-6. MOVING INVARIANT EXPRESSIONS OUT OF WHILE-LOOPS

In this pass, the optimizing compiler will exploit the computed global data flow information to find arithmetic expressions in loops which are invariant under execution of the loop body. An expression is invariant if none of the variables occurring in the expression can be modified by execution of the loop. Information about which variables can be modified is available in the mod bit vector at the while node. But we need this information at any arithmetic operator subject to this optimization. Hence, we will carry this information in an attribute i-mod from any while node to all the nodes in the loop condition and the loop body, excluding inner loops. See Fig. 5-9.

5-7. GLOBAL FLOW ANALYSIS FOR BJ + leave

The programming language BLISS [Wulf71] contains a powerful **leave**-statement, allowing multilevel exit from nested statements. If we add such a **leave**-statement to BJ, we no longer have only one-entry, one-exit statements in BJ programs. There is no limit to the depth of statement nesting, and a statement can contain exits to any enclosing labeled statement. This means that flow information about statements can only be stored in stack-type attributes. This would be very space-inefficient. A less expensive solution is the use of global stacks or tables for this purpose. The MUG2 description tool for semantic analysis allows the controlled use of global variables. A compound statement with heading "**at** ○ **entry**" is to be executed every time the attribute evaluator descends to a node with operator ○. Similarly, a compound with heading "**at** ○ **exit**" is to be executed when the attribute evaluator leaves a subtree with root operator ○. Circular dependencies between local attributes of an operator ○ and global attributes, evaluated upon entry or exit to ○-nodes, will be detected by the system. Global data flow analysis for BJ + **leave** is used as an example of this feature. See Fig. 5-10.

We will first explain the purpose of the attributes used in the flow analysis pass.

The *derived* attribute leftbyleave of a statement indicates whether it can only be left by a **leave** statement.

The *inherited* attribute level of a statement counts the depth of nesting of enclosing labeled statements (cf. Fig. 5-11).

In the *derived* attribute leftlevels of a statement we record those enclosing statements to which the statement contains a **leave** statement (cf. Fig. 5-12).

The *derived* bit vectors d-mod, d-pre, and d-use of a statement contain the flow information about "regular" paths (not terminating with a **leave**-statement) through the statement.

The *inherited* bit vector i-mod, i-pre, and i-use of a statement contain flow information about all paths from the entrance of the innermost enclosing labeled statement to the statement itself (cf. Fig. 5-13).

In case the enclosing labeled statement is a loop, we must take into account also the paths which reach the statement under consideration after

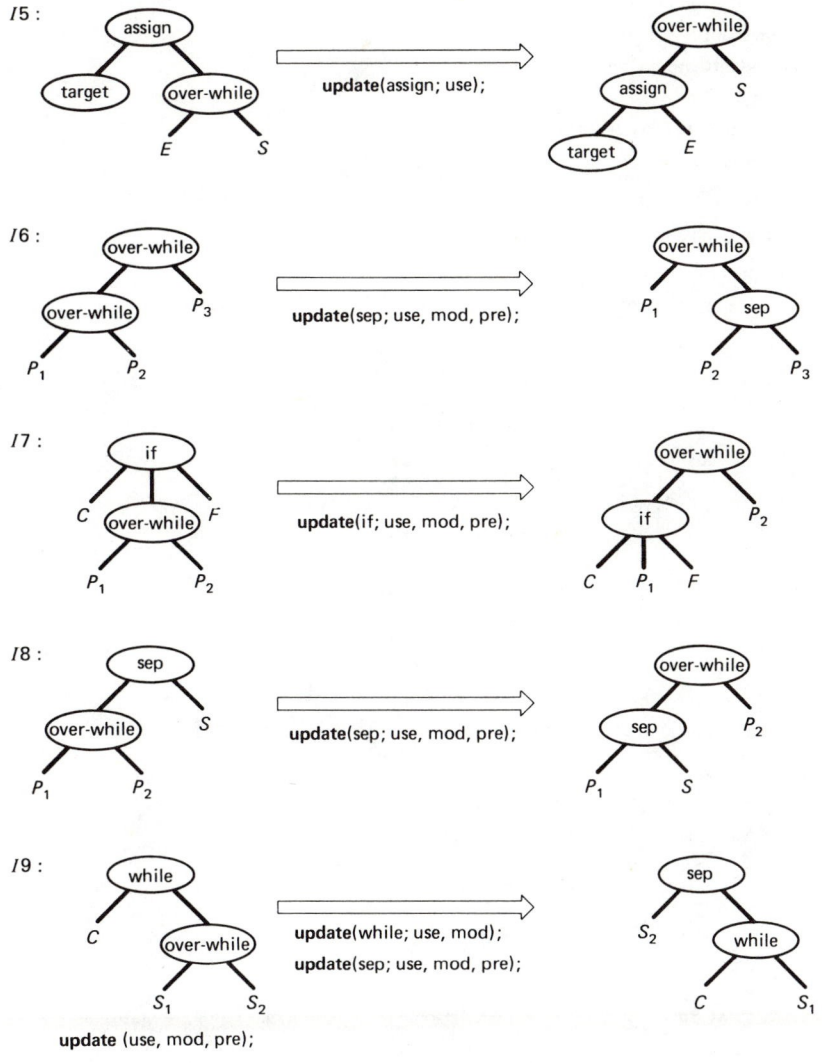

I5 :   **update**(assign; use);

I6 :   **update**(sep; use, mod, pre);

I7 :   **update**(if; use, mod, pre);

I8 :   **update**(sep; use, mod, pre);

I9 :   **update**(while; use, mod);   **update**(sep; use, mod, pre);

update (use, mod, pre);

co this set of rules is incomplete, since for rules *I2, I3, I4, I7, I8,* and *I9*
the corresponding rules with the over-while node at other sons are left out
for space reasons;

ssap;

Figure 5-9

149

pass invariant code motion,

inherited bitvector *i*-mod;

attributes

expected use **at** plus; mod **at** while;

updated use, mod, pre;

i-mod **of** prog. 1 : = **1**;

i-mod **in** [prog **downto** while[**unchanged**;

co no attempt should be made to move expressions
    out of the main program;

i-mod **of** while : = mod **of** while;

i-mod **in** [while **downto** while[**unchanged**;

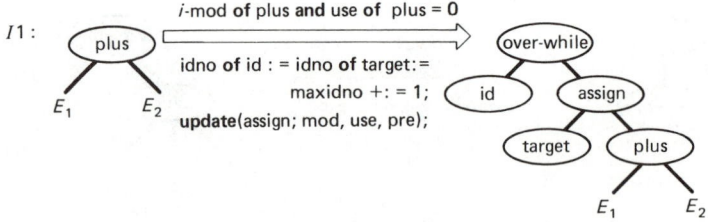

co an invariant expression is found and assigned to a newly created temporary
    variable. This assignment will be moved upwards out of the loop, while the
    id node — a use of this variable — will stay at this place;

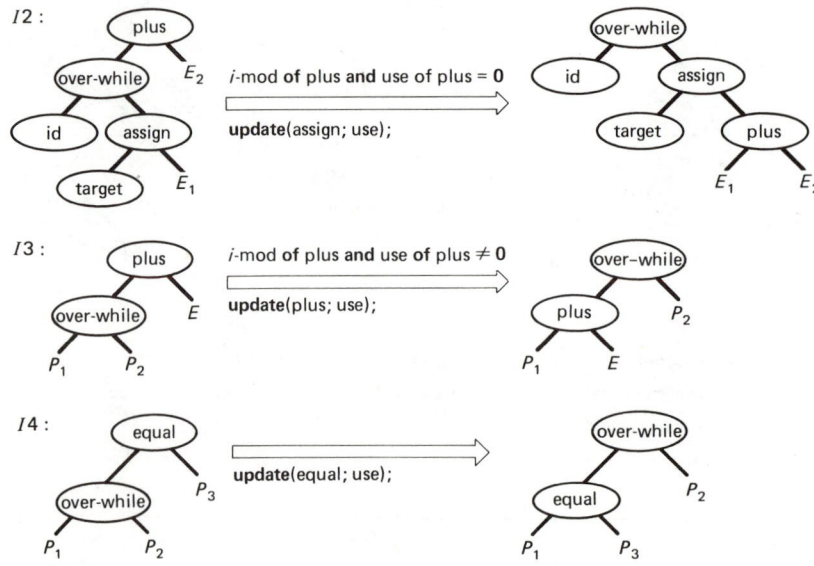

Figure 5-9 (cont.)

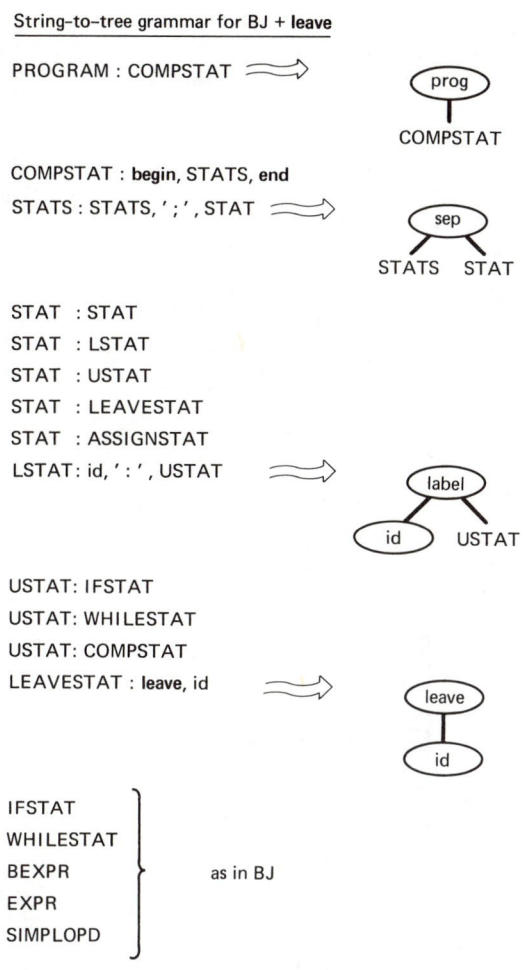

String-to-tree grammar for BJ + **leave**

PROGRAM : COMPSTAT

COMPSTAT : **begin**, STATS, **end**
STATS : STATS, ' ; ' , STAT

STAT : STAT
STAT : LSTAT
STAT : USTAT
STAT : LEAVESTAT
STAT : ASSIGNSTAT
LSTAT : id, ' : ' , USTAT

USTAT : IFSTAT
USTAT : WHILESTAT
USTAT : COMPSTAT
LEAVESTAT : **leave**, id

IFSTAT
WHILESTAT
BEXPR   as in BJ
EXPR
SIMPLOPD

Figure 5-10

at least one execution of the loop body (cf. Fig. 5-14). The flow information in the inherited bit vectors is used if a path is found to end with a **leave** statement. At this time the collected information will be or-ed to that entry in the global tables modstack, prestack, usestack which corresponds to the enclosing statement terminated by the **leave** statement (cf. Fig. 5-15).

Since we have only recorded the information about paths starting at the innermost enclosing labeled statement and through the eventual innermost loop, we have to or the information about paths outside this enclosing statement into these global tables every time we have completely analyzed another enclosing labeled statement or loop, respectively. We record data flow infor-

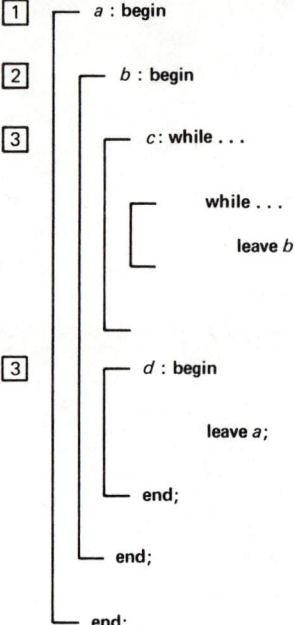

Figure 5-11

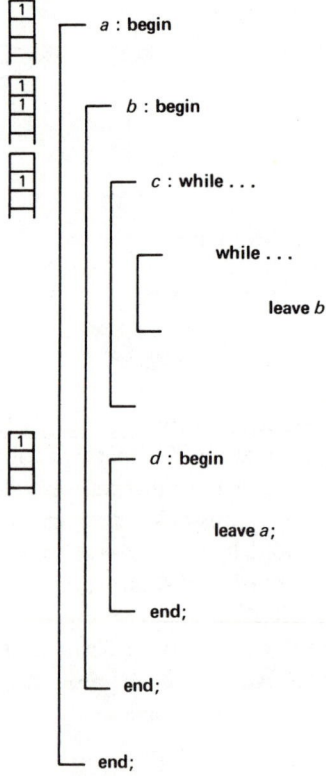

Figure 5-12

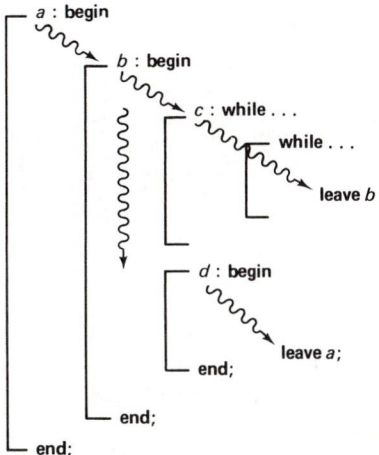

Figure 5-13

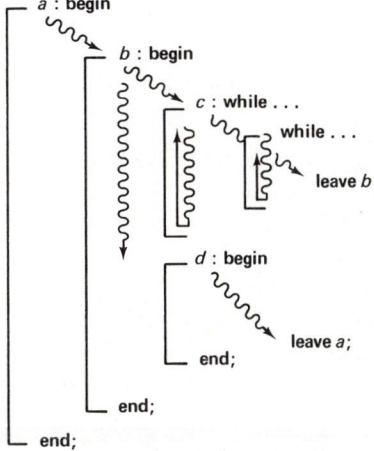

Figure 5-14

mation about regular paths through statements in local attributes as in the BJ case, while we record data flow information about paths ending with a **leave** in the corresponding entries of the three global tables modstack, prestack and usestack.

When a labeled statement is completely analyzed, the information in the d-mod, d-pre, and d-use attributes is or-ed together with the information in the entries of the three global tables corresponding to this labeled statement (the tables are indexed by the level of nesting).

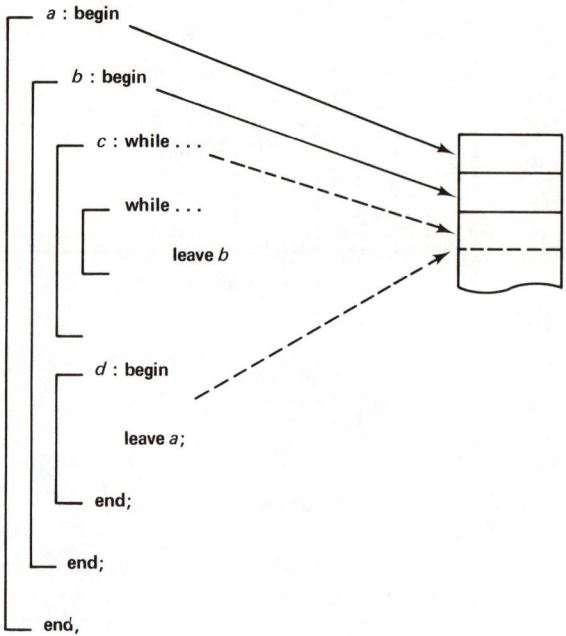

Figure 5-15

pass collecting global data flow information;
   opclass ops = plus, equal;
   derived bool leftbyleave;
   inherited int llevel;
   derived bitvector leftlevels;
   derived bitvector d-mod, d-pre **attached to**
     if, while, sep, assign;
   derived bitvector d-use **attached to** id, const, ops,
     assign, if, while, sep;
   inherited bitvector i-mod, i-use, i-pre;
   derived int idno **attached to** id, target, label;
   derived int cvalue **attached to** const;

   global table of int level;
   global table of bitvector usestack, modstack, prestack;

   leftbyleave **of** leave := **true**;
   leftbyleave **of** assign := **false**;
   leftbyleave **of** if   := leftbyleave **of** if.2 **and**
                            leftbyleave **of** if.3;
   leftbyleave **of** while := **false**;

leftbyleave **of** sep $\quad$:= leftbyleave **of** sep.1 **or**
$\qquad$ leftbyleave **of** sep.2;
leftbyleave **of** label $\quad$:= **if** leftlevels **of** label.2 [llevel **of** label.2] = 1
$\qquad$ **then false**
$\qquad$ **else** leftbyleave **of** label.2
$\qquad$ **fi**;

llevel **of** program := **0**;
llevel **in** [program **downto** label] **unchanged**;
llevel **of** label.2 := llevel **of** label + 1;
llevel **in**]label **downto** label] **unchanged**;

leftlevels **of** leave $\quad$:= init-to-one (level [idno **of** leave.1]);
leftlevels **of** assign := **0**;
leftlevels **of** if $\qquad$:= leftlevels **of** if.2 **or**
$\qquad$ leftlevels **of** if.3;
leftlevels **of** while $\quad$:= leftlevels **of** while.2;
leftlevels **of** sep $\qquad$:= leftlevels **of** sep.1 **or**
$\qquad$ leftlevels **of** sep.2;
leftlevels **of** label $\quad$:= clear (leftlevels **of** label.2,
$\qquad$ llevel **of** label.2);

$\left.\begin{array}{l} d\text{-use} \\ d\text{-mod} \\ d\text{-pre} \end{array}\right\}$ **of** assign, while, if $\left.\vphantom{\begin{array}{l} a \\ b \end{array}}\right\}$ as in BJ
d-use **of** id, const, ops $\left.\vphantom{\begin{array}{l} a \end{array}}\right)$

d-mod **of** sep := **if** leftbyleave **of** sep.1 **or**
$\qquad$ leftbyleave **of** sep.2
$\qquad$ **then 0**
$\qquad$ **else** d-mod **of** sep.1 **or** d-mod **of** sep.2
$\qquad$ **fi**;

d-use **of** sep := **if** leftbyleave **of** sep.1 **or**
$\qquad$ leftbyleave **of** sep.2
$\qquad$ **then 0**
$\qquad$ **else** d-use **of** sep.1 **or** (d-use **of** sep.2 **and** d-pre **of** sep.1)
$\qquad$ **fi**;

d-pre **of** sep := **if** leftbyleave **of** sep.1 **or**
$\qquad$ leftbyleave **of** sep.2
$\qquad$ **then 0**
$\qquad$ **else** d-pre **of** sep.1 **or** d-pre **of** sep.2
$\qquad$ **fi**;

d-mod **of** label := d-mod **of** label.2 **or**
$\qquad$ modstack [level [idno **of** label.1]];

d-use **of** label := *d*-use **of** label.2 **or**
                              usestack [level [idno **of** label.1]];
d-pre **of** label := *d*-pre **of** label.2 **or**
                              prestack [level [idno **of** label.1]];

at leave **exit**
begin usestack [level [idno **of** leave.1]] :=
        usestack [level [idno **of** leave.1]] **or**
        i-use **of** leave;
     prestack [. . .] := . . .
     modstack [. . .] := . . .
end;

at label **entry**
begin
     level [idno **of** label.1] := llevel **of** label + 1;
     usestack [llevel **of** label + 1] := **0**;
     modstack [llevel **of** label + 1] := **0**;
     prestack [llevel **of** label + 1] := **0**;
end;

at label **exit**
begin
for lev **from** 1 **to** llevel **of** label + 1 **do**
     if leftlevels [lev] = 1
     then
        usestack [lev] := usestack [lev] **or** *i*-use **of** label;
        modstack [lev] := modstack [lev] **or** *i*-mod **of** label;
        prestack [lev] := prestack [lev] **or** *i*-pre **of** label;
     fi
end;

at while **exit**
for lev **from** 1 **to** llevel **of** while **do**
     if leftlevel [lev] = 1
     then
        usestack [lev] := usestack [lev] **or** *d*-use **of** while;
        modstack [lev] := modstack [lev] **or** *d*-mod **of** while;
     fi
i-mod **of** program.1 := **0**;
i-use **of** program.1 := **0**;
i-pre **of** program.1 := **1**;

i-mod **of** label.2 := **0**;
i-use **of** label.2 := **0**;
i-pre **of** label.2 := **1**;

i-mod **of** sep.1 := i-mod **of** sep;
i-use **of** sep.1 := i-use **of** sep;
i-pre **of** sep.1 := i-pre **of** sep;

i-mod **of** sep.2 := **if** leftbyleave **of** sep.1
  then 0
  else d-mod **of** sep.1 **vel**
    i-mod **of** sep
  fi;

i-use **of** sep.2 := **if** leftbyleave **of** sep.1
  then 0
  else d-use **of** sep.1 **vel**
    l-use **of** sep.1
  fi;

i-pre **of** sep.2 := **if** leftbyleave **of** sep.1
  then 0
  else d-pre **of** sep.1 **et**
    i-pre **of** sep.1
  fi;

i-mod ⎫
i-use ⎬ for if and while are trivial!
i-sep ⎭

As an example of the above, we study the intercommunication between attributes and global variables with the program of Fig. 5-16. Only the computation of the d-mod attribute of the statement labeled a is shown.

```
begin
  x := ...
a: while ... do
     y := ... ;
   b: while ... do
        if ...
        then z := ... ;
          leave a
        else x := ...
        fi
      od
   od
end
```

Figure 5-16

If the while-statement is executed, variable y is modified in any case and x may be modified on a path through loop b ending with a "normal" exit from loop b or on a path ending with a **leave** (after more than one execution of the loop).

Variable z may only be modified on a path through loops a and b ending with a **leave**.

The program tree of the example program is depicted in Fig. 5-17. The values of the d-mod attributes and the global mod-stack are those computed when attribute evaluation returns to the root; mod information about paths ending with leave is recorded in mod-stack, and mod information about paths with "normal" exit is recorded in the attribute d-mod.

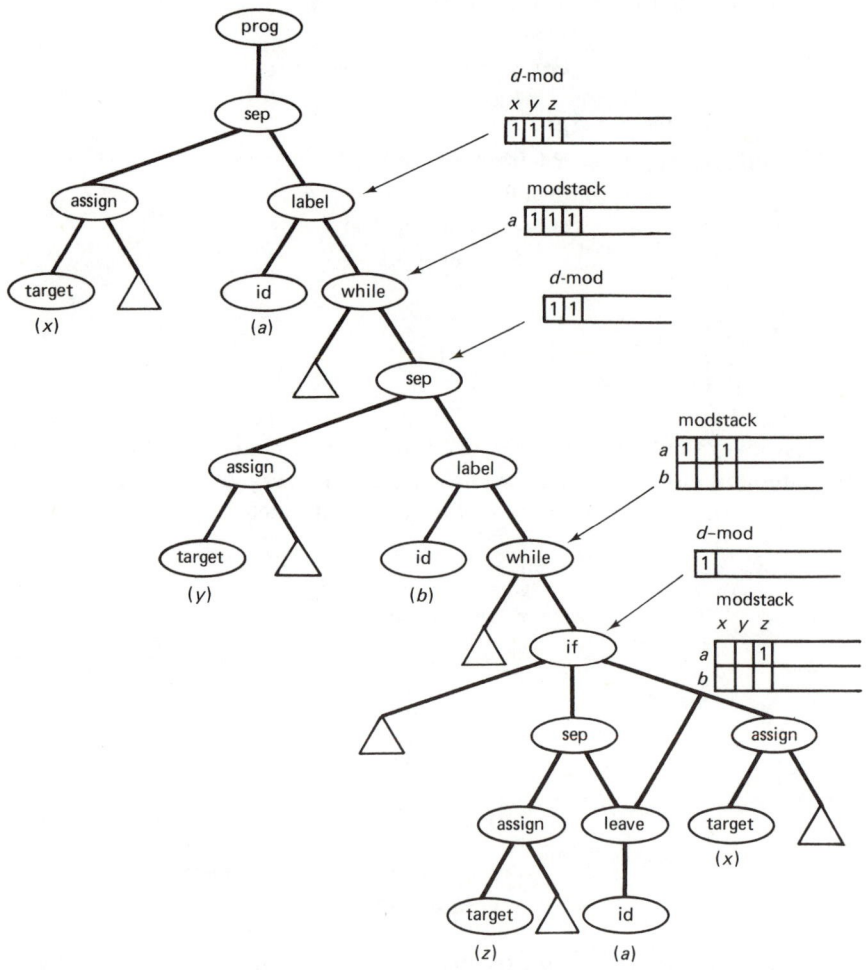

Figure 5-17

5-8. CONCLUSION

The power of the description tools of the compiler generating system MUG2 was demonstrated by completely describing three compiler passes, namely global data flow analysis, constant propagation and folding, and invariant code motion from while loops. All three passes were guided by the parse tree. It cannot be expected that optimization for languages allowing unrestricted flow of control can be described so elegantly by these mechanisms. Extending the tools will allow us to exploit the very well developed theory of compiler code optimization in compiler generating systems.

ACKNOWLEDGMENTS

I would like to thank Robert Giegerich for essential comments to different versions of this paper, Reiner Güttler for preparing the figures, and Mrs. E. Quitsch for typing the final version.

Chapter 6

Interprocedural Elimination of Partial Redundancies

Etienne Morel
Claude Renvoise

6-1. INTRODUCTION

Program optimization techniques are indispensable in compilers to allow programmers to concentrate on the logical level of problems, paying particular attention to readability and reliability, and leaving the task of producing efficient programs to automatic transformations. Even though automatic transformation of a bad algorithm into a good one is far from being achieved, numerous techniques exist to automatically increase the quality of the code produced by compilers.

This chapter focuses on global optimization, i.e., on transformations which can only be performed by taking into account information gathered in large sections and possibly the whole of a program. Two techniques of global optimization have been widely presented: elimination of redundant computations and extraction of invariant computations from loops. Both aim to decrease the number of computations performed at run time by a program. Another technique has been presented in [More79] which includes both of these techniques: elimination of partially redundant computations. A partially redundant computation is a computation performed twice on a given execution path without any modification of its operands in between. It is clear from this definition that a redundant computation and a computation invariant in a loop are particular cases of partially redundant computations. An algorithm which eliminates partial redundancies then eliminates both of these inefficiencies at the same time. Such an algorithm is presented in [More79]. It eliminates redundancies and moves each expression directly to the entrance of the outermost loop in which it is invariant. Based on a boolean formulation, it simultaneously processes all the expressions of a program. Moreover, it can be applied to any program graph and treats all the implicit or explicit loops of the program at the same time without previous collection of information on the shape of the program graph.

This algorithm is powerful enough to simultaneously process a set of procedures compiled together, but in this case, pessimistic assumptions must be made on the effect of a procedure call, even if the procedure is local to the compiled unit. Better optimization can be obtained by separately treating each procedure of the compiled unit in a way which benefits from the presence of a called procedure. This is done by collecting the information needed for the application of the algorithm to a given procedure from the entire set of procedures which are present. Such collection is currently referred to as *interprocedural data flow analysis.*

Data flow analysis includes all the techniques which try to collect at compile time information about the dynamic behavior of programs. Such interprocedural analyses have already been presented for collecting information about modification and use of variables [Alle74] and which are powerful enough to deal with reference parameters and recursive procedures [Bart78]. The information we require to perform a more sophisticated data flow analysis is more complex. A basis for such analysis has been presented in [More74] for the interprocedural elimination of redundant computations.

This paper consists of two major parts. In the first, we present an original method for performing interprocedural data flow analysis which can be applied to a wide class of problems where information must be propagated across procedure calls. In the second part, we present an extension of the basic algorithm which uses the result of this interprocedural analysis to allow computations to be moved across procedure boundaries. We prove that this algorithm is correct and efficient. Implementation aspects are discussed in the last section.

Preliminary definitions. The optimizations described in this paper are applied to a program representation obtained by decomposition of the source text into elementary commands associated with a directed graph. All assignment statements of the source text are split into evaluation of the right-hand side, followed by assignment of the result to the left-hand side. Moreover, if necessary, expressions are split into binary operations.

The nodes of the graph represent basic blocks. A basic block is a maximal sequence of elementary commands with a single entry point and a single exit point. There is an arc in the graph from the exit point of i to the entry point of j if block j can be executed immediately after block i. The sets of predecessors and successors of block i are denoted Pred(i) and Succ(i), respectively. The set of all the blocks of the program is denoted B. Paths are taken to be sequences of arcs.

Each procedure in the unit to be compiled has a single entry block and a single return block. If this is not naturally satisfied, an empty block is introduced as predecessor of the several entry blocks of the procedure; similarly, an empty block can be introduced as successor of the several return blocks of a procedure. For a given procedure, the entry block will be denoted e and the return block will be denoted r. The entry of the entry block and the exit of the return block will be referred to as the entry and exit points of the procedure, respectively. For practical reasons, the return block contains only the return instruction.

For solution of the systems of equations in Section 6-2, every node must have at least one successor and one predecessor. For this purpose, a unique fictitious node denoted f is introduced in the graph as predecessor of the entry blocks and successor of the return blocks of all the local procedures. This fictitious node f does not belong to the set of basic blocks B nor to any procedure. In the treatment of a given procedure, it will be used to summarize information associated with the various program points where this procedure is called.

A special block is generated in the program graph of a procedure for each procedure call. Such a block, containing only the call to a procedure P, is termed a *call block* of P. The set of all the call blocks of a given procedure P will be denoted Caller(P).

In figures, basic blocks will be represented by circles, and call blocks will be represented by squares.

6-2. COMPUTATION OF DATA FLOW INFORMATION

The first level of data flow information is the determination of the contents of the basic blocks of the program in a form suitable for global data flow analysis. The contents of the blocks can be represented by boolean variables associated with each expression and each block. They are termed *local*. The second level is the determination of the interactions of instructions located in different blocks of a given procedure. It is also represented by boolean variables, which are termed *global*. Finally, the behavior of an entire procedure with respect to its environment can be represented by boolean variables.

6-2.1 Local boolean variables

This information is computed by a simple scan over the contents of a basic block. The variables are up-transparency, down-transparency, local availability, and local anticipability.

Up-transparency UTRANSP. A block is said to be *up-transparent* for an expression if the block does not contain any modification of the operands of the expression, or if the first modification of an operand of the expression occurring in the block is preceded by a computation of the expression.

Down-transparency DTRANSP. A block is said to be *down-transparent* for an expression if the block does not contain any modification of the operands of the expression, or if the last modification of an operand of the expression occurring in the block is followed by a computation of the expression.

Local availability CMOP. An expression is said to be *locally available* in a block i if there is at least one computation of the expression in the block i, and if the commands appearing in the block after the last computation of the expression do not modify its operands.

Local anticipability ANTLOC. An expression may be *locally anticipated* in a block i if there is at least one computation of the expression in block i, and if the commands appearing in the block before the first computation of the expression do not modify its operands.

Two other local boolean variables are introduced for interprocedural data flow analysis purposes. They are PTRANSP (partial transparency) and PCOMP (partial computation). For a basic block, let us assume for the moment that PCOMP = COMP and PTRANSP = DTRANSP.

6-2.2 Global boolean properties

One of the goals of optimization is to try to eliminate unnecessary computations. This can be done at a local level by a simple scan over each basic block. A computation is deleted if it already appears in the block and if its operands have not been modified since the previous computation. Similarly, at a global level, a computation which can be locally anticipated in a block can be deleted if it already occurs on every path leading to this block, and if for each of these paths, no instruction between the last occurrence of this computation and the entry of the block modifies any of its operands. Such a situation can be detected by computing for the whole program the "availability" of the expressions at entry to each block.

Some other expression computations are also unnecessary, but cannot be easily deleted. This is the case for an expression which can be locally anticipated in a block, and which has already been computed on some but not all of the paths leading to this block without subsequent modification of its operands. Thus on some paths, the computation is redundant, but on the other paths, it is required. Such situations can be detected by computing for the whole program the "partial availability" of the expressions on entry to each block.

Optimization may also include moving computations from one program point to another. This can only be done if it is safe and efficient. Safety and efficiency both obey the same rule: *never insert a computation on a path from the entry point where it was not present.* Availability of an expression at a point ensures that it has already been computed before this point. Similarly, "anticipability" of an expression at a given point ensures that the expression is computed on every path starting from this point and that the parts of paths going from this point to the computations do not modify the operands of the expression.

These properties apply to all program points and are defined whether the expression occurs at the point or not. In practice, we will concentrate on points which are block entries or exits.

For the sake of clarity, only one expression will be considered and subscripts will be used to index the set B. We will use AVIN_i, ANTIN_i, PAVIN_i to denote respectively the global availability, anticipability, and partial availability of the expression on entry to the block i; similarly we will use AVOUT_i, ANTOUT_i, PAVOUT_i to denote the same properties on exit from the block i. The relations between global and local properties for all blocks of the graph are expressed in the form of systems of boolean equations. Boolean conjunctions are denoted $\cdot$ and $\prod$; similarly $+$ and $\sum$ are used for boolean disjunctions. The operator for boolean negation is denoted $\neg$. In a boolean expression, "$+$" has lower precedence than "$\cdot$". FALSE and TRUE will be represented by 0 and 1, respectively.

Availability System. An expression is available on entry to a block if it is available on exit from each predecessor of the block. An expression is available on exit from a block if it is locally available or if it is available on entry to the block and down-transparent in this block:

$$\text{AVOUT}_i = \text{COMP}_i + \text{DTRANSP}_i \cdot \text{AVIN}_i$$
$$\text{AVIN}_i = \prod_{j \in \text{Pred}(i)} \text{AVOUT}_j \qquad \left. \begin{array}{c} \\ \\ \end{array} \right\} \text{ for } i \in B \qquad (6\text{-}1)$$

Anticipability system. An expression may be anticipated on exit from a block if it can be anticipated on entry to each successor of the block:

$$ANTIN_i = ANTLOC_i +$$
$$UTRANSP_i \cdot ANTOUT_i \quad \text{for } i \in B$$
$$ANTOUT_i = \prod_{j \in Succ(i)} ANTIN_j$$
(6-2)

Partial availability system. An expression is partially available on entry to a block if it is partially available on exit from at least one predecessor of the block:

$$PAVOUT_i = PCOMP_i + PTRANSP_i \cdot PAVIN_i$$
$$PAVIN_i = \sum_{j \in Pred(i)} PAVOUT_j \quad \text{for } i \in B$$
(6-3)

Solution of boolean systems. All these systems can be solved for all the expressions at the same time by iteration, starting from a given value for the unknowns. This value is TRUE for systems involving the conjunction operator $\prod$ and FALSE for systems involving the disjunction operator $\sum$. In both cases, the convergence of this iterative approach to the optimal solution is assured, and the number of iterations is small (three in most cases for structured programs). All this is detailed in [More74] or [Huan75].

6-2.3. Representation of procedure calls

The computation of global boolean properties in a procedure is based on the knowledge of local boolean properties for all its blocks. When a procedure includes calls to other procedures, the behavior of such calls must be reflected in the local boolean properties of the blocks which contain these calls.

For languages where every procedure is separately compiled and cannot contain other procedures (for example FORTRAN), a procedure call must be assumed to modify all nonlocal variables, and this is reflected in the coefficients of the blocks which contain calls. For these blocks, the value of ANTLOC, COMP, and PCOMP are set to FALSE for all the expressions. UTRANSP, DTRANSP, and PTRANSP are set to FALSE for nonlocal variables, and to TRUE for local variables.

In other cases, the "call graph" of the compiled unit is built, where (1) the nodes of the graph are the procedures local to the compiled unit, and (2) there is an edge from node A to node B if procedure A contains a call (or several calls) to procedure B.

In Section 6-2.3.1, we present the computation of the boolean properties reflecting the behavior of a procedure. In Section 6-2.3.2, we explain the mechanisms used for propagation of procedure behavior through cycle-free call graphs. In Section 6-2.3.3, we present the problems and solutions connected with cycles in call graphs, i.e., the presence of recursive calls. In order to separate the problems, the reader will assume in the following that all variables are global and accessible by all procedures. The refinements introduced by scope rules will be discussed in Section 6-2.3.4.

6-2.3.1. *Boolean properties associated with a procedure*

For a normal block, the static order and the dynamic order of the instructions are the same. The influence of such a block on its environment can easily be detected and represented by its local boolean properties UTRANSP, DTRANSP, ANTLOC, and COMP. The influence of a call block is the influence of the whole procedure it represents. Although a procedure can be seen as a single-entry, single-exit set of instructions, its influence cannot be computed by a single scan over its body, because the static and dynamic instruction orders can be different. Boolean variables UTRANSP, DTRANSP, ANTLOC, and COMP can be associated with a procedure with the same meaning as for a normal block, but are computed by solving boolean systems over the whole body of the procedure. In the following, we assume that the procedure does not contain any call blocks. The value of all the boolean variables associated with each of its blocks can then be obtained by a simple scan of the contents of the blocks.

Local availability.   Let us consider Eq. (6-1) for availability for a given block i:

$$AVOUT_i = COMP_i + DTRANSP_i \cdot AVIN_i$$

It implies: $COMP_i = TRUE$ iff $AVOUT_i = true$ when $AVIN_i = false$. The COMP coefficient of a block i can then be seen as the value of $AVOUT_i$ when $AVIN_i = false$, and this is directly applicable to the detection of the COMP coefficient associated with a procedure.

Let B' be the set of basic blocks of the procedure and e and r its entry and return blocks, respectively. Initial values are given by:

$$AVOUT_r^0 = false$$

$$AVOUT_i^0 = AVIN_i^0 = true \text{ for all blocks} \qquad \text{(system with } \textstyle\prod \text{ operator)}$$

The following system of equations is then computed iteratively over the procedure:

$$\left. \begin{aligned} AVOUT_i^0 &= COMP_i + DTRANSP_i \cdot AVIN_i^0 \\ AVIN_i^0 &= \prod_{j \in Pred(i)} AVOUT_j \end{aligned} \quad \text{for } i \in B' \right\} \qquad (6\text{-}4)$$

When the system has converged, the COMP coefficient for the procedure is set equal to $AVOUT_r^0$. As for a normal block, this local availability of an expression in a procedure indicates that the expression is computed on all the paths going from its entry to its exit point without subsequent modification of its operands.

Down-transparency. As for local availability, the equation

$$AVOUT_i = COMP_i + DTRANSP_i \cdot AVIN_i$$

implies: $DTRANSP_i = true$ iff $AVOUT_i = true$ when $AVIN_i = true$ (since by definition $COMP_i = true$ implies $DTRANSP_i = true$). The DTRANSP coefficient of a block i is the value of $AVOUT_i$ when $AVIN_i = true$. To compute the DTRANSP coefficient of a procedure, the equation system (6-5) is then solved iteratively over the blocks of the procedure with the following initial values:

$$AVOUT_f^1 = true$$

$$AVOUT_i^1 = AVIN_i^1 = true \text{ for all blocks} \qquad \text{(system with } \prod \text{ operator)}$$

$$\left.\begin{array}{l} AVOUT_i^1 = COMP_i + DTRANSP_i \cdot AVIN_i^1 \\ AVIN_i^1 = \displaystyle\prod_{j \in \mathbf{Pred}(i)} AVOUT_j^1 \qquad \text{otherwise} \end{array} \quad \text{for } i \in B' \right\} \qquad (6\text{-}5)$$

When the system has converged, the DTRANSP coefficient of the procedure is set equal to $AVOUT_i^1$. As for a normal block, down-transparency of an expression in a procedure indicates that, for every path going from its entry to its exit, either the path does not modify the operands of the expression or the last such modification made on the path is followed by a computation of the expression.

Up-transparency. Similar reasoning can be applied to computing UTRANSP. The equation

$$ANTIN_i = ANTLOC_i + UTRANSP_i \cdot ANTOUT_i$$

implies: $UTRANSP_i = true$ iff $ANTIN_i = true$ when $ANTOUT_i = true$ (since by definition, $ANTLOC_i = true$ implies $UTRANSP_i = true$). The UTRANSP coefficient of a block i can be seen as the value of $ANTIN_i$ when $ANTOUT_i = true$. To compute the UTRANSP coefficient for a procedure, the system of equations (6-6) is solved iteratively over the blocks of the procedure with the following initial values:

$$ANTIN_f^1 = true$$

$$ANTIN_i^1 = ANTOUT_i^1 = true \text{ for all blocks} \qquad \text{(system with } \prod \text{ operator)}$$

$$\left.\begin{array}{l} ANTIN_i^1 = ANTLOC_i + UTRANSP_i \cdot ANTOUT_i^1 \\ ANTOUT_i^1 = \displaystyle\prod_{j \in \mathbf{Succ}(i)} ANTIN_j^1 \end{array} \quad \text{for } i \in B' \right\} \qquad (6\text{-}6)$$

When the system has converged, the UTRANSP coefficient of the procedure is set equal to $ANTIN_e^1$. As for a normal block, up-transparency of an expression in a procedure indicates that, for every path from its entry to its exit, either the path does not modify the operands of the expression or the first modification made on the path is preceded by a computation of the expression.

Local anticipability. Local anticipability of an expression in a basic block indicates that if a computation of this expression is inserted as the first instruction of this block, there exists a computation of the same expression in the block which becomes redundant and hence can be deleted. Local anticipability of an expression in a procedure has the same significance. For procedures, this requires that (1) there must exist a computation of this expression on every path starting from the entry block, and (2) these computations must be suppressible if a new computation of this expression is inserted as the first instruction of the entry block.

The availability of an expression on entry to every block of a procedure when the expression is available on entry to the procedure has already been computed in system (6-5), giving $AVIN_i^1$ for every block. This information is reused to compute a modified anticipability system derived from system (6-2).

System (6-7) is iteratively solved with the initial values:

$$ANTIN'_f = false$$

$$ANTIN'_i = ANTOUT'_i = true \text{ for every } i \in B' \quad \text{(system with } \textstyle\prod \text{ operator)}$$

$$\left. \begin{aligned} ANTIN'_i &= (ANTLOC_i + UTRANSP_i \\ &\quad \cdot ANTOUT'_i) \cdot AVIN_i^1 \qquad \text{for } i \in B' \\ ANTOUT'_i &= \prod_{j \in Succ(i)} ANTIN'_j \end{aligned} \right\} \qquad (6\text{-}7)$$

Lemma. If $ANTIN'_e = true$, a computation of the expression becomes redundant on every path starting from the entry point if a new computation of this expression is inserted as the first instruction of this entry block.

Proof. Comparison between systems (6-2) and (6-7) obviously implies that $ANTIN'_i \leq ANTIN_i$ for every $i \in B$. $ANTIN'_e = true$ then implies $ANTIN_e = true$. This implies that there exists a computation of the expression on every path starting from the entry point and the first such computation done on every path is accessible from the entry point through a modification-free path. Assume that such a computation located in a block k will not become redundant. This implies $ANTLOC_k \cdot AVIN_k^1 = false$, and since $ANTLOC_k = true$, this implies $AVIN_k^1 = false$ and then $ANTIN'_k = false$. Let $[e, b_1, b_2, \ldots, b_n, k]$ be a path going from the entry point to k. As all the blocks of this path are modification-free $(UTRANSP = true)$ and computation-free

(ANTLOC $= false$) for the expression, application of (6-7) yields

$$\text{ANTIN}'_k = false \Rightarrow \text{ANTOUT}'_{b_n} = false \Rightarrow \text{ANTIN}'_{b_n} = false \Rightarrow$$
$$\ldots \Rightarrow \text{ANTOUT}'_e \Rightarrow \text{ANTIN}'_e = false$$

and we are led to a contradiction on the value of ANTIN'_e. ∎

When system (6-7) has converged, the ANTLOC coefficient of the procedure is set equal to ANTIN'_e.

Partial transparency (PTRANSP) and partial computation (PCOMP). These coefficients are specific to the representation of procedures. A procedure is partially transparent for an expression if there is at least one path going from its entry point to its exit point where either there is no modification of the operands of the expression, or the last such modification is followed by a computation of the expression. Similarly, an expression is partially computed in a procedure if there exists at least one path going from its entry point to its exit point which includes a computation of the expression not followed by a modification of any of its operands. As for local availability and down-transparency which are computed by solving the same system (6-1) with different initial values for the entry block [giving systems (6-4) and (6-5)], PCOMP and PTRANSP are computed by solving the system (6-3) of partial availability with different initial values for the fictitious block:

1. $\text{PAVOUT}^0_f = false$

$$\left.\begin{aligned}\text{PAVOUT}^0_i &= \text{PCOMP}_i + \\ &\quad \text{PTRANSP}_i \cdot \text{PAVIN}^0_i \qquad \text{for } i \in B' \\ \text{PAVIN}^0_i &= \sum_{j \in \text{Pred}(i)} \text{PAVOUT}^0_j\end{aligned}\right\} \qquad (6\text{-}8)$$

2. $\text{PAVOUT}^1_f = true$

$$\left.\begin{aligned}\text{PAVOUT}^1_i &= \text{PCOMP}_i + \\ &\quad \text{PTRANSP}_i \cdot \text{PAVIN}^1_i \qquad \text{for } i \in B' \\ \text{PAVIN}^1_i &= \sum_{j \in \text{Pred}(i)} \text{PAVOUT}^1_j\end{aligned}\right\} \qquad (6\text{-}9)$$

These systems involve the disjunction operator $\sum$; the initial value is thus FALSE for all the unknowns. After solution of these systems, PCOMP of the procedure is set equal to PAVOUT^0_f and PTRANSP of the procedure is set equal to PAVOUT^1_f.

6-2.3.2. *Propagation of information in a cycle-free call graph*

By solving the boolean systems presented in Section 6-2.3.1 over the blocks of a procedure, one obtains boolean variables which represent the influence of a call of this procedure on the set of expressions to be optimized. These boolean variables associated with a whole procedure P are similar to those associated to a single block and are used to set values for the local boolean variables associated with the call blocks of P. In order to compute the behavior of a procedure, the values of local boolean variables associated with each of its blocks must be known. If this procedure does not contain call blocks of other procedures, the values of all the local boolean variables can be obtained by a single scan of the blocks. But if the procedure contains call blocks, the behavior of the called procedures must be known to set values of the local boolean variables of these call blocks. This implies an order of treatment of procedures compiled together: called procedures must be treated before their callers.

For a call to a procedure external to the compiled unit, the most pessimistic behavior must be assumed, i.e.,

$$COMP = PCOMP = ANTLOC = UTRANSP$$
$$= DTRANSP = PTRANSP = \textit{false}$$

In practice, this pessimistic assumption can be improved by use of scope rules (cf. Section 6-2.3.4). For procedure calls local to the compilation unit when the call graph is cycle-free, we may topologically sort this graph, and give a number to each procedure so that a procedure has a number greater than that of any of its callers. Treating the procedures in decreasing numerical order ensures that if a procedure P contains a call to a procedure Q, the values of the boolean variables associated with the call block of Q in P have already been computed, and this allows a correct computation of the boolean variables representing the procedure P.

This can be represented by the following algorithm, expressed in a pseudo programming language:

```
Procedure data-flow-analysis;
    Type proc-info = Record
        ANTLOC, COMP, PCOMP, UTRANSP, DTRANSP,
        PTRANSP: boolean;
    End;
    BEHAVIOR: array [1..Max-number-of-proc] of proc-info;
Begin
    Apply topological sort to the call graph;
    For each procedure P, in decreasing order do
        For every block i in P do
            if i is a call block to an external procedure then
                set all local boolean variables to false
```

> **elsif** i is a call block of a local procedure Q **then**
> > set local boolean variables from BEHAVIOR[Q]
> **else**
> > scan the block to compute local boolean variables
> **end**
> **Repeat;**
> Solve systems (6-4), (6-5), (6-6), (6-7), (6-8), (6-9);
> Set BEHAVIOR[P] to the results of the preceding systems;
> **Repeat**
End

> *Note:* This is described for one expression, but in practice all the expressions are treated simultaneously, and information such as ANTLOC, COMP, etc., are not boolean variables, but sets of boolean variables.

6-2.3.3. *Treatment of recursive procedure calls*

The method presented in Section 6-2.3.2 allows an easy computation of the behavior of all local procedures because an order can be defined on the call graph which allows a single-pass processing. In the presence of recursive calls, a single pass can no longer be used since the computation of the behavior of a procedure P requires the previous determination of the local boolean variables associated with each of its blocks, and one (or more) of these blocks can be a call block to P itself. The same problem arises when cycles in the call graph contain several nodes, i.e., several procedures.

In these cases, behavior of procedures can be computed iteratively over the call graph. This algorithm is not presented here for the following two reasons. First, this chapter is not meant to be seen as a theoretical paper on data flow analysis, but a practical paper on program optimization. Data flow analysis is only a tool to compute information to be used by the optimization process presented in Section 6-3. This optimization process can perform interprocedural elimination of partial redundancies in a single pass over each procedure when there are no recursive calls, i.e., when the call graph is cycle-free. But iterative computation of behavior of procedures in cyclic call graphs implies that the optimization process must be applied iteratively, and this can lead to a very expensive algorithm. This is further discussed in Section 6-4. Moreover, proof that this iterative data flow analysis terminates and gives correct results is too long to be presented here.

So, in practice, the call graph is made cycle-free by deleting the edges corresponding to recursive calls, and the method presented in Section 6-2.3.2 can then be applied. The loss of information implied by this destruction of edges is limited to a subset of the call blocks of a recursive procedure.

Example.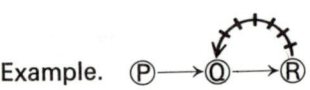

There are two call blocks for Q: one in P, the other in R. The deleted edge is the edge corresponding to the recursive call of Q located in R. The order of treatment implied by the topological sort is then R, Q, P. When treating R, all the local boolean variables associated with the call block of Q are initialized with *false* (as for a call to an external procedure). But when treating P, the call block of Q located in P can be initialized with more precise behavior of Q, since Q has already been treated.

In practice, this is done automatically by applying the procedure *data-flow-analysis* as presented in Section 6-2.3.2 to such artificially cycle-free graphs, in addition initializing the array BEHAVIOR to *false* for all boolean variables of all procedures. So, if a call block for Q is considered before Q has been treated, its local variables are automatically set to *false*. Elsewhere, values actually representing Q are used.

6-2.3.4. *Utilization of scope rules*

All block-structured languages contain scope rules which tell the compiler the set of program points where a variable can be legally accessed. This information is very helpful for optimization purposes, especially for setting transparency values associated with call blocks.

When a procedure is called, only variables which can legally be accessed by this procedure can be modified. Moreover, we are only interested in modification of variables external to a procedure since inner variables of a procedure cannot be accessed outside it, and thus cannot appear as operands of an expression outside the procedure. The first of these two points leads to the following obvious rule for setting the DTRANSP, UTRANSP, and PTRANSP variables associated with the call block of an external procedure:

> **Rule.**   For each expression of the module, if none of its operands can be accessed by the called procedure, DTRANSP = UTRANSP = PTRANSP = *true*; otherwise DTRANSP = UTRANSP = PTRANSP = *false*.

The second point leads to the following rule for setting the transparency variables associated with a recursive call to a local procedure (cf. Section 6-2.3.2):

> **Rule.**   For each expression in a module, if all its operands are local to the called procedure, DTRANSP = UTRANSP = PTRANSP = *true*; otherwise DTRANSP = UTRANSP = PTRANSP = *false*.

This rule is based on the fact that a recursive call to a procedure creates a new incarnation of its local variables.

Example.

$$\textbf{Procedure } P;$$
$$A, B, I: \textbf{integer};$$

begin
$\quad I := A + B;$
$\quad \quad \textbf{call } P;$
$\quad A := A + B$
end

The expression $A + B$ is said to be transparent in the call block of P because the recursive call of P will modify another incarnation of A. The second computation of $A + B$ will then be found to be redundant.

The boolean variables associated with the nonrecursive call blocks of a local procedure can be updated by simply copying the boolean variables representing the behavior of the procedure without making any scope test on the operands of the expressions. This may introduce meaningless information (operands of an expression which are thought to be modified at a point where they are not even accessible) but leads to no error for correct programs if scope rules are respected.

6-3. INTERPROCEDURAL ELIMINATION OF PARTIAL REDUNDANCIES

Elimination of partial redundancies can be seen as an upward movement of computations along the paths where their value is not available, to points where the computations can be inserted in a secure and efficient way. For a redundant computation, this movement is null since the value of the expression is available on all paths. For an invariant computation in a loop, it is moved up to the entry point of the loop since that is the first point where it may appear in a secure and efficient way. In a loop-by-loop treatment, a computation may be moved several times. In our algorithm, code motion is viewed as the elimination of computations which become redundant after new computations have been inserted. The algorithm detects the optimal places where new computations may be inserted, and the places where partially redundant computations may be suppressed; this is done simultaneously for all the expressions in a program.

In Section 6-3.1, we recall the basis of this algorithm. In Section 6-3.2, we present the application of this algorithm to interprocedural optimization. The proof that this application is correct and leads to optimization is given in Section 6-3.3. An example is detailed in Section 6-3.4.

6-3.1. Elimination of partial redundancies in a procedure

We first recall the algorithm presented in [More79]. The principle of the algorithm is to introduce new computations of the expression at program points chosen so that partially redundant computations become redundant and hence can be deleted. The algorithm is here assumed to be applied to a single procedure. For reasons of simplicity, only one expression is considered. The steps of the algorithm are as follows:

1. Solution of the boolean systems for availability, anticipability, and partial availability.

2. Determination of predecessors of blocks containing partial redundancies in which a new computation may be introduced. This involves the computation of the boolean properties PPIN and PPOUT (placement possible on entry and placement possible on exit).

3. Determination of the subset comprising those blocks on exit from which a computation must be inserted. These blocks satisfy the boolean property INSERT.

4. Determination of the blocks containing suppressible partial redundancies. These blocks satisfy the boolean property SUPPRESS.

5. Insertion of new computations at the exits from those blocks satisfying INSERT = *true* and suppression of the partially redundant computations in the blocks which satisfy SUPPRESS = *true*.

Computation of global properties. Treating each procedure separately implies that the expression is neither available nor partially available on entry to the procedure. Similarly, it is not anticipable on exit from the procedure. These pessimistic assumptions are introduced into the boolean systems through the fictitious node of the graph by setting:

$$\text{AVOUT}_f = \text{PAVOUT}_f = \text{ANTIN}_f = false$$

The systems (6-1), (6-2), and (6-3) are then solved for the procedure's blocks giving the availability, anticipability, and partial availability of the expression on entry to and exit from every block of the procedure.

Determination of PPIN and PPOUT. For the sake of clarity, an artificial constant term denoted CONST is introduced in the definition of

PPIN. $CONST_i$ is defined for every block i as

$$ANTIN_i \cdot [PAVIN_i + (\neg ANTLOC_i) \cdot DTRANSP_i]$$

This constant term is TRUE for blocks containing a partial redundancy and for empty blocks where the expression can be anticipated. (A block is "empty" for an expression if it neither computes nor modifies the expression.) The following system is then solved with the fictitious block being initialized with $PPIN_f = PPOUT_f = AVOUT_f = false$:

$$\left. \begin{aligned} PPIN_i &= CONST_i \cdot \prod_{j \in Pred(i)} (PPOUT_j + AVOUT_j) \\ &\quad \cdot (ANTLOC_i + DTRANSP_i \cdot PPOUT_i) \qquad \text{for } i \in B \\ PPOUT_i &= \prod_{k \in Succ(i)} PPIN_k \end{aligned} \right\} \quad (6\text{-}10)$$

This is a system of boolean equations involving the conjunction operator Π. The desired solution is the largest one, and thus it can be solved by iteration, starting with *true*s for all the unknowns.

Determination of INSERT and SUPPRESS. For each block i of the program, $INSERT_i$ and $SUPPRESS_i$ are respectively computed by:

$$INSERT_i = PPOUT_i \cdot \neg AVOUT_i \cdot (\neg PPIN_i + \neg DTRANSP_i)$$

$$SUPPRESS_i = ANTLOC_i \cdot PPIN_i$$

Insertion and suppression of computations. At the end of the algorithm, new computations are inserted at exits from blocks satisfying $INSERT = true$. Then the first computations of the expression in the blocks which satisfy $SUPPRESS = true$ are redundant and may be deleted.

Proof of the basic algorithm. The correctness of this algorithm is established by the following lemmas and theorems whose proofs can be found in [More79]. Some similar proofs will be developed in the next section to demonstrate the correctness of the interprocedural elimination of partial redundancies.

Lemma 1. After insertion of the new computations on exit from blocks satisfying $INSERT = true$, the new availability value on entry to any block for which $PPIN_i = true$ will be $AVIN'_i = true$.

Theorem 1. After insertion of the new computations at the exits of blocks for which $INSERT = true$, the first computation of the expression in any block i satisfying $SUPPRESS_i = true$ becomes redundant.

Lemma 2. Let i be a block satisfying $INSERT_i = true$. Every path starting from the exit of i includes a computation which will be deleted.

Lemma 3.   Let i be a block satisfying $\text{INSERT}_i = true$. The paths starting from the exit of i cannot encounter another block satisfying INSERT $= true$ before encountering a block satisfying SUPPRESS $= true$.

Theorem 2.   At the end of the transformation, no path of the graph contains more computations of the expression than it contained before.

6-3.2.   Application of the algorithm to a set of procedures

In Section 6-2.2 an order has been defined for computing the behavior of all the local procedures. This was done by processing a procedure before all the other procedures which call it. On the other hand, partial redundancies are eliminated by applying the algorithm given at the beginning of Section 6-3.1 to each procedure, with each procedure treated after the procedures which call it. This treatment order, called descending order, is natural since:

1.   Availability and partial availability of the expression on entry to a procedure P can be exactly known, since their values depend only on the values of the same properties on entry to the call blocks of P.

2.   Advantage can be taken of optimizations made in the procedures which call P.

3.   To guarantee the efficiency of a transformation performed in a caller of P, it may be necessary to eliminate computations located in P.

In applying the basic algorithm to a given procedure P, the relationships between P and the procedures which call it are taken into account by the following initialization rules:

Rule 1.   If there exists a call block of P for which SUPPRESS $= true$, an occurrence of the expression must be introduced on entry to all the call blocks of P for which AVIN $+$ PPIN $= false$. The ANTLOC values associated with these blocks are set to $true$.

Proof.   Assume that a call block of P belonging to a procedure Q satisfies SUPPRESS $= true$. Effectiveness of the algorithm applied to Q is guaranteed only if the suppressions indicated by the algorithm are performed. A call block does not contain computation. But SUPPRESS $= true$ implies ANTLOC $= true$, and for a call block of P, according to the definition of 6-2.3.1, this implies that a computation of the expression will be deleted on every path going from the entry to the exit of P if the value of the expression is available on entry to P. The suppression of all these computations is sufficient to establish correctness of the transformations made in Q. Since the availability of the expression on entry to P equals the boolean product of the availability of the expression on entry to all the call blocks of P, these suppressions will occur if the availability of the expression is artificially created at entry to the call blocks where it is not already satisfied, i.e., by insertion of computations. Moreover, such insertions are legal since the entries to these call blocks satisfy ANTLOC = *true*, which implies ANTIN = *true*. Proof that these insertions do not create new partial redundancies is obvious and is left to the reader. ∎

Rule 2. The value of the availability and partial availability of an expression on entry to a procedure P is taken into account by setting the values associated with the fictitious block to the following:

$$\text{AVOUT}_f = \left[\prod_{i \in \text{Caller}(P)} (\text{AVIN}_i + \text{PPIN}_i) \right] + \sum_{i \in \text{Caller}(P)} \text{SUPPRESS}_i$$

$$\text{PAVOUT}_f = \text{AVOUT}_f + \sum_{i \in \text{Caller}(P)} \text{PAVIN}_i$$

Rule 3. An occurrence of the expression is introduced in the return block of a procedure P if all its call blocks satisfy INSERT = *true*. In this case, the ANTLOC value of the return block is set to *true*, and the INSERT values of the call blocks are set to *false*. In all cases, ANTIN_f is set to *false*.

The application of this rule obviously leads to a space optimization since several insertions are replaced by a single one. Moreover, the inserted computation may be found to be partially redundant during the optimization of P, and can then be moved to a more optimal place.

As above, the same algorithm treats naturally cycle-free call graphs and call graphs with recursive calls for which edges corresponding to recursive calls have been deleted in order to make them cycle-free. In the first case, all the procedures containing a call block of P have been treated before P is treated, and all the values for AVIN, PPIN and SUPPRESS are known for all these call blocks of P, allowing an exact determination of the context on entry and on exit of the procedure by application of the three initialization rules. In the second case, pessimistic values are attributed to the recursive call blocks of P located in not-yet-treated procedures by setting AVIN = PPIN = SUPPRESS = *false* for all of them, and the application of the initialization rules when treating P then delivers a suboptimal context. In the presence of this suboptimal context, partially redundant computations are sometimes maintained in P or its callers.

The descending order of processing in Fig. 6-1 is Q, P, R. When processing P, Rule 2 gives $\text{AVOUT}_f = \textit{false}$ since R has not yet been processed, and nothing is modified in P (Fig. 6-1). Using the real value of AVOUT_f (which is *true*) would lead to the detection of a redundant computation in P (Fig. 6-2).

In Fig. 6-3, the descending order of processing is Q, P, R. While processing Q, a partial redundancy is eliminated by inserting a computation of $a + b$ on exit from the call block of P. When processing P, Rule 3 says that

Example 1:

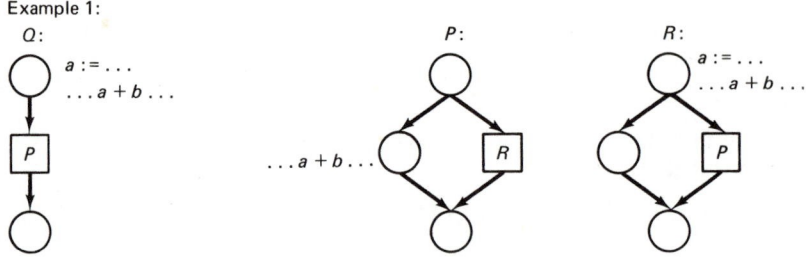

Figure 6-1

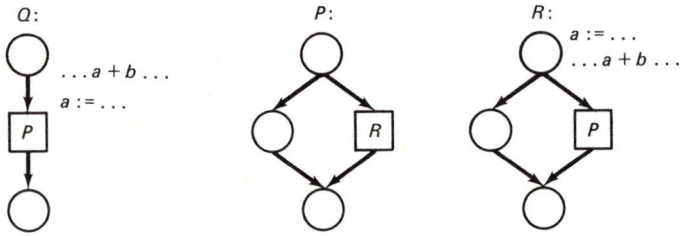

Figure 6-2

Example 2:

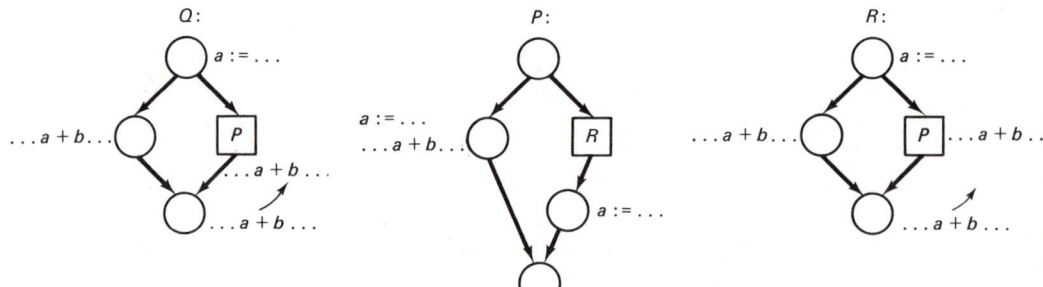

Figure 6-3

no computation need be inserted on exit from P since R has not yet been processed. Treatment of R is similar to that of Q. The optimal program is shown in Fig. 6-4, where the two computations to be inserted on exit from the call blocks of P are merged into a single one at the exit of the return block of P and suppressed later as partially redundant.

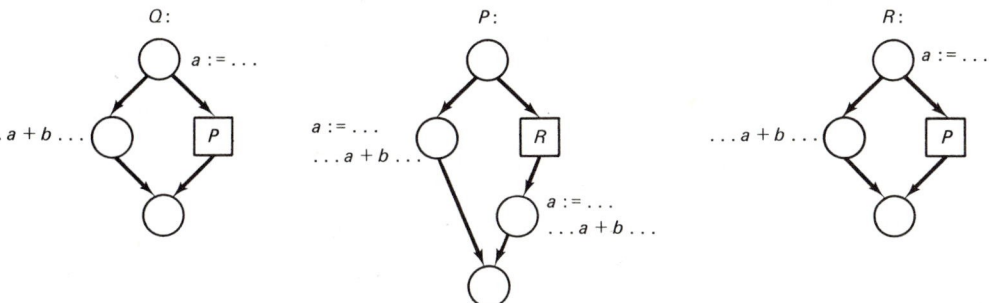

Figure 6-4

In both cases, optimal results could be obtained by iteration of the descending phase. This is further discussed in Section 6-4.

For a procedure which can be called by procedures external to the compilation unit, namely its entry procedures, all these three rules are replaced by $\text{AVOUT}_f = \text{PAVOUT}_f = \text{ANTIN}_f = \textit{false}$ without any inserting of computations. Elimination of interprocedural partial redundancies is then performed by the following algorithm:

Procedure partial-redundancies-elimination;

Begin
  For each procedure P, in increasing order, **do**
    ⌐Apply initialization rules;
    Solve systems (6-1), (6-2), (6-3);
  Ⓐ Compute PPIN and PPOUT for all blocks of P with system
    (6-10);
    ⌊Compute INSERT and SUPPRESS for all blocks of P
  Repeat;
  For each block i in B **do**
    Insert and suppress computations according to the values of
      INSERT_i and SUPPRESS_i
  Repeat
End

Part Ⓐ of this algorithm will be referred to later as *treatment of P*.

6-3.3. Proof of the effectiveness of the algorithm

The proof that the transformation is correct and profitable is similar to that of the basic algorithm.

Lemma 4. After insertion of the new computations on exit from blocks satisfying INSERT = *true*, the new value of the availability on entry to any block for which $PPIN_i = true$ will be $AVIN_i' = true$.

Preliminary definition.   A path going from the exit of a block i to the entry of a block j is denoted $]i, j[$. Note that i and j do not belong to $]i, j[$. The path $]i, j[$ is a single edge if $j \in Succ(i)$, and it then contains no block. This is an *empty path* for an expression if the local boolean properties for the blocks belonging to this path are DTRANSP = *true* and COMP = ANTLOC = *false*.

Proof.   Let i be a block satisfying $PPIN_i = true$ and let us assume that $AVIN_i' = false$. This can occur only if there exist:

1.   A block k such that $AVOUT_k = INSERT_k = DTRANSP_k = false$ (or if k is the fictitious block, $AVOUT_k = false$)

and

2.   An empty path $]k, i[$ such that $INSERT_m = false$ for any block m belonging to $]k, i[$

Intuitively, the path $]k, i[$ contains no computation, and none will be inserted on it. Thus $AVOUT_k' = false$, and this influence propagates through $]k, i[$, causing $AVOUT_m' = false$ for every block m belonging to $]k, i[$ and thus $AVIN_i' = false$. $AVOUT_k = INSERT_k = DTRANSP_k = false$ implies $PPOUT_k = false$. (If k is the fictitious block, $PPOUT_k = false$ by definition.)

Let j be the successor of k in $]k, i[$. Now $PPOUT_k = AVOUT_k = false$ implies $PPIN_j = false$. If $j = i$, we are led to a contradiction on the value of $PPIN_i$, else $PPIN_j = AVOUT_j = INSERT_j = false$ implies $PPOUT_j = false$. The same reasoning could then be applied to the block j and, by following the path from k towards i, we conclude that $PPOUT = AVOUT = false$ for the predecessor of i in $]k, i[$. Then $PPIN_i = false$, and we are led to a contradiction.   ∎

Lemma 5. After insertion of the new computations at the exits of the blocks where INSERT = *true*, a redundant computation can be deleted on every path starting from the entries of the blocks where SUPPRESS = *true*.

Proof. These blocks obviously satisfy $\text{PPIN}_i = true$. According to Lemma 4, the new value of the availability is $\text{AVIN}'_i = true$. Since the insertion of new computations cannot change the value of ANTLOC_i, we will have $\text{ANTLOC}_i \cdot \text{AVIN}'_i = true$ and hence a redundancy. If i is not a call block, a redundant computation is located in the block and can be deleted. If i is a call block of a procedure P, initialization rule 1 ensures that the expression will become available on entry to P. Moreover, the definition of ANTLOC for a procedure P ensures that if $\text{ANTLOC}_p = true$, a computation of the expression will become redundant on every path starting from the entry of P if the expression is made available to P. These redundancies will be detected while processing P, since decreasing order ensures that P will be treated after the procedures which call it. ■

Lemma 6. Let i be a block satisfying $\text{INSERT}_i = true$. Every path starting from the exit of i includes a block verifying $\text{SUPPRESS} = true$.

Proof. $\text{INSERT}_i = true$ implies $\text{PPOUT}_i = true$ and thus $\text{ANTIN}_j = true$ for each $j \in \text{Succ}(i)$. Hence, every path starting from the exit of i contains a block satisfying $\text{ANTLOC} = true$. It now suffices to prove that these blocks satisfy $\text{PPIN} = true$, since $\text{SUPPRESS} = \text{ANTLOC} \cdot \text{PPIN}$.

Let j be one of these blocks, and let us assume that $\text{PPIN}_j = \text{FALSE}$. Since the computation located in j has created the anticipability of the expression on exit from i, there exists an empty path $]i, j[$.

$\text{PPIN}_j = false$ implies $\text{PPOUT} = false$ for every predecessor block of j. Let k be a predecessor of j in $]i, j[$. If $k = i$, we are led to a contradiction on the value of PPOUT_i, else $\text{PPOUT}_k = false$, $\text{DTRANSP}_k = true$, and $\text{ANTLOC}_k = false$ imply $\text{PPIN}_k = false$. The same reasoning could then be applied to the block k, and by following $]i, j[$ in the reverse order, we conclude that $\text{PPIN} = false$ for the successor of i in $]i, j[$. Then $\text{PPOUT}_i = false$, and we are led to a contradiction; so PPIN_j must be *true*. ■

Lemma 7. Let i be a block satisfying $\text{INSERT}_i = true$. The paths starting from the exit of i cannot encounter another block satisfying $\text{INSERT} = true$ before encountering one satisfying $\text{SUPPRESS} = true$.

Proof. According to Lemma 6 every path starting from the exit of i encounters a block satisfying $\text{SUPPRESS} = true$, and this path is an empty path. Let j be one of these blocks and $]i, j[$ be the empty path.

Let k be a block of $]i, j[$ such that $\text{INSERT}_k = true$. Since $\text{INSERT}_k = \text{PPOUT}_k \cdot \neg\text{AVOUT}_k \cdot (\neg\text{PPIN}_k + \neg\text{DTRANSP}_k)$, $\text{INSERT}_k = true$ and $\text{DTRANSP}_k = true$ imply $\text{PPIN}_k = false$. The proof of Lemma 6 shows that the value $\text{PPIN}_j = false$ of a given block j propagates upwards through an empty path $]i, j[$ causing $\text{PPIN} = false$ for all the blocks of this path and finally $\text{PPOUT}_i = false$. In the present lemma, $\text{PPIN}_k = false$ causes $\text{PPOUT}_i = false$ through $]i, k[$. This implies $\text{INSERT}_i = false$ and we are led to a contradiction. ∎

Theorem 4.   At the end of the transformation, no path of the graph contains more computations of the expression than it contained before.

Proof.   This is clear from Lemmas 5, 6, and 7. ∎

6-3.4.   Example

The optimization process is now detailed on the following program (Fig. 6-5) composed of a procedure P which contains two calls to a local procedure Q, which contains a call to an external procedure R which can

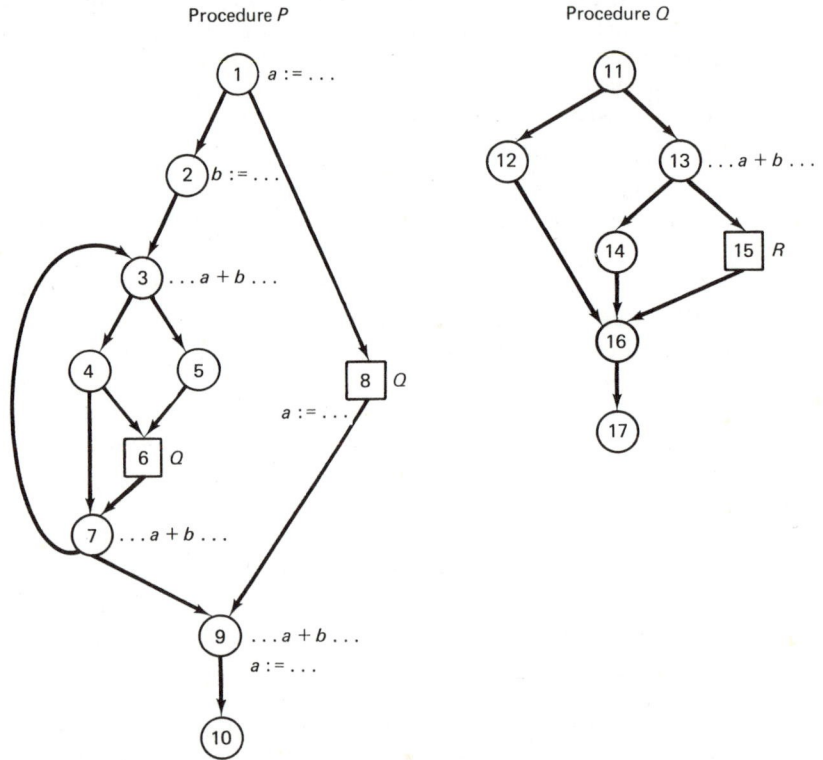

Figure 6-5

modify the variables of the expression $a + b$. This program contains 17 blocks, three of them being call blocks (6, 8, 15). The expression $a + b$ is computed in blocks 3, 7, 9, 13. One of its operands is modified in blocks 1, 2, 5, 9. All the computations are partially redundant. Local boolean properties for normal blocks:

> ANTLOC is *true* for nodes 3, 7, 9, 13; *false* elsewhere.
>
> COMP and PCOMP are *true* for nodes 3, 7, 13; *false* elsewhere.
>
> UTRANSP is *false* for nodes 1, 2, 5; *true* elsewhere.
>
> DTRANSP and PTRANSP are *false* for nodes 1, 2, 5, 9; *true* elsewhere.

The local properties associated with call block 15 are ANTLOC = COMP = PCOMP = UTRANSP = DTRANSP = PTRANSP = *false*, since the procedure R is external.

The local properties representing the behavior of Q are:

$$\text{ANTLOC}_Q = \text{false} \qquad \text{COMP}_Q = \text{false} \qquad \text{PCOMP}_Q = \text{true}$$
$$\text{UTRANSP}_Q = \text{true} \qquad \text{DTRANSP}_Q = \text{false} \qquad \text{PTRANSP}_Q = \text{true}$$

These values computed in the ascending phase are reproduced in the local boolean values associated with blocks 6 and 8 which call Q.

Treatment of P in the descending phase. P is the root of the call graph. The expression is assumed to be unavailable on entry to and not anticipable on exit from return block 10.

    (a) *Global boolean properties (obtained by resolution of boolean systems).*

> ANTIN is *false* for nodes 1, 2, 5, 10; *true* elsewhere.
>
> AVOUT is *true* for nodes 3, 4, 7; *false* elsewhere.
>
> PAVIN is *false* for nodes 1, 2, 8, 10; *true* elsewhere.

    (b) *Values of* PPIN *and* PPOUT *(obtained by resolution of boolean systems).*

> PPIN is *false* for nodes 1, 2, 4, 5, 6, 8; *true* elsewhere.
>
> PPOUT is *false* for nodes 1, 3, 4, 5, 9, 10; *true* elsewhere.

    (c) *Computation of* INSERT *and* SUPPRESS.

> INSERT is *true* for nodes 2, 6, 8; *false* elsewhere.
>
> SUPPRESS is *true* for nodes 3, 7, 9; *false* elsewhere.

Treatment of Q in the descending phase. No call block of Q satisfies SUPPRESS = *true*. Thus rule 1 is not applied. On the other hand, all of them satisfy INSERT $= true$. An occurrence of the expression is introduced in return block 17, and $ANTLOC_{17}$ becomes *true*. $INSERT_6$ and $INSERT_8$ become *false*.

(a) *Global boolean properties.*
The initialization rules give $AVOUT_f = ANTIN_f = false$; $PAVOUT_f = true$.

ANTIN is *false* for node 15; *true* elsewhere.

AVOUT is *true* for nodes 13, 14; FALSE elsewhere.

PAVIN is *true* for all nodes.

(b) *Values of* PPIN, PPOUT.
PPIN is *false* for nodes 11, 15; *true* elsewhere.

PPOUT is *false* for node 13; *true* elsewhere.

(c) *Computation of* INSERT *and* SUPPRESS.
INSERT is *true* for nodes 11, 15; *false* elsewhere.

SUPPRESS is *true* for nodes 13, 17; *false* elsewhere.

Insertion and suppression of computations in the program text at the end of the algorithm lead to the following optimized program (Fig. 6-6):

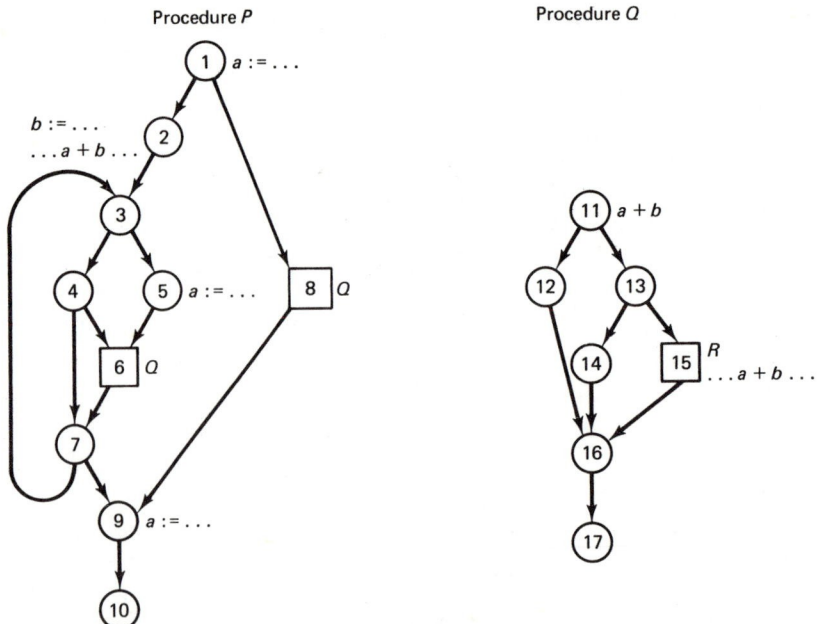

Figure 6-6

The optimization process has decreased by one or two the number of computations of $a + b$ performed at every iteration of the loop 3–7.

6-4. ITERATIVE APPLICATION OF THE OPTIMIZATION PROCESS

Careful examination of Fig. 6-6 shows that the computation in block 11 is still partially redundant when iterating in the loop. Reapplication of the ascending and descending phases of the algorithm would lead to a better optimization. The computation of all the boolean values needed by both phases is left to the reader as an exercise. The final program in Fig. 6-7 is the optimal program:

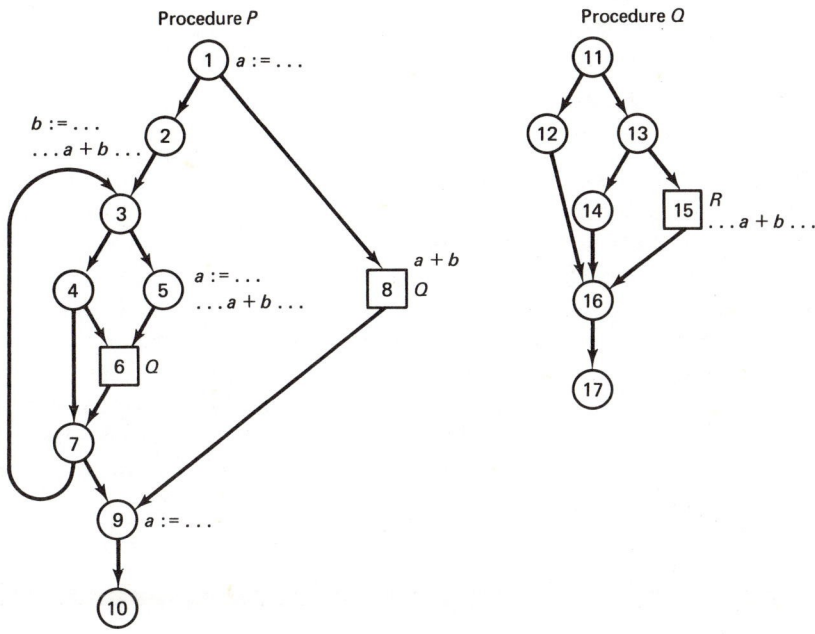

Figure 6-7

In this program most of the paths of the loop are free from computation of $a + b$. The computation is only performed after the possible modifications of its operands. Three cases must be considered for the iterative application of the algorithm:

(a) *The initial call graph is cycle-free.* In this case, exact data flow analysis has been performed in the ascending phase. Partial redundancies left by the descending phase, as in the example in Section 6-3.4, are due to the fact that when processing a procedure P, a computation cannot be moved beyond a call block where DTRANSP = *false* (6 and 8 in the example) and is inserted at exit from these call blocks. When treating the called procedure, insertion of a computation in its return block (17 in the example) may be eliminated as partially redundant, and, after this optimization, the called procedure may satisfy ANTLOC = *true* even though it satisfied ANTLOC = *false* before. This can create new partial redundancies in the callers if at least one of its call blocks satisfies PAVIN = *true* (e.g., block 6 in the example).

In practice, after a given application of the algorithm, the program may be further optimized if at least one procedure P satisfies the following criteria:

1. $\displaystyle\prod_{i \in \text{Caller}(P)} \text{INSERT}_i = true$

2. $\text{ANTLOC}_p = false$

3. $\text{UTRANSP}_p = true$

4. $\displaystyle\sum_{i \in \text{Caller}(P)} \text{PAVIN}_i = true$

In this case, some partial redundancies may remain in the program. New application of the algorithm gives a new value of ANTLOC_p. If it is *true* as in the example of Section 6-3.4, the descending phase is applied again.

Two remarks must be made about this iterative application. First, no guarantee can be given that a reapplication of the algorithm leads to a better program: it may remain unchanged. But in this case the remaining partially redundant computations cannot be eliminated in an efficient and safe manner by a simple code motion. Creation of new blocks or dynamic frequencies of paths must be used (see [More79]). The second remark is that every iteration of the algorithm leaves the program correct, and the iteration can be stopped after any number of applications.

(b) *The call graph has been made cycle-free by deletion of edges.* Since the call graph is cycle-free, the same reasoning as in (a) can be applied for iterating the process, and as in (a), it can be arbitrarily stopped after any number of iterations. In addition to iterating both ascending and descending phases, optimization may be improved by iterating the descending phase at each step to avoid the pessimism of the initialization rules applied to recursively called procedures. In this case, values of AVIN, PPIN, and SUPPRESS for all the recursive call blocks are kept from one iteration to the next. At the first iteration, their values are initialized to *false*, but in later iterations a more precise value may become available. Initialization rules then give a more precise context on entry to and on exit from the recursively called procedures, and some new optimizations can then be performed. This is illustrated in Figs. 6-1 through 6-4. This iteration can also be stopped after an arbitrary number of steps since at the end of each step effectiveness of the transformation is assured.

Nevertheless, pessimistic assumptions made for the recursive call blocks in the data flow analysis phase can sometimes prevent this doubly iterative process from reaching the optimal result.

(c) *The call graph is not cycle-free.* We assume here that an exact data flow analysis has been made in the presence of recursive calls. The proofs presented in Section 6-3.3 to demonstrate the effectiveness of the optimization process are strongly based on the fact that a called procedure is processed after all its callers. This is particularly important in Lemma 5. If a call block of P satisfies SUPPRESS $= true$, the body of P contains computations which may have to be deleted by subsequent processing of P, so P may have to be processed again. Moreover, this new processing of P may cause SUPPRESS $= true$ for a call block of Q in P, and then Q may have to be treated again, etc.

This iteration obviously ends, but its main disadvantage is that it cannot be stopped for reasons of time before its natural end because, while the effectiveness of the optimization is assured at the end of the iteration, it is not at the end of a given step. For this reason, exact data flow analysis in the presence of recursive procedure calls can lead to a very expensive algorithm.

6-5. IMPLEMENTATION

Practical experiments on global optimization have shown that a significant amount of the time spent in a global optimizer is devoted to the recognition of common subexpressions and to determination of the effect of each assignment on every expression. When using a boolean formulation as presented here, another part of the time is spent scanning the contents of the basic blocks in order to compute the local boolean values associated with each expression in each block. Only a small amount of time is spent solving the systems of boolean equations. This is natural since the number of iterations needed for the solution of a given system is small and nearly independent of the size of the program. For structured programs written in a PASCAL-like goto-free language, it has never exceeded 4. Moreover, the set of values of a given property, e.g., COMP, for all the expressions and all the blocks is implemented as a bit matrix. Parallel resolution of a given system for all the expressions at once is then made by performing AND and OR operations over whole matrices, and this can be cheaply realized on most hardware with AND and OR machine instructions. Experimental comparisons between the algorithm for elimination of partial redundancies and some other techniques for performing similar optimizations are presented in

[More79]. It emerges from these comparisons that this algorithm is very fast when applied separately to each procedure. For interprocedural application, the only added task is the solution of systems in the data flow analysis phase, and this is known to be fast. Although this extended algorithm has not yet been implemented, it can reasonably be assumed to be efficient.

6-6.   CONCLUSION

An algorithm for interprocedural optimization has been presented. It is applied to a set of procedures compiled together and which call each other. It is based on the algorithm presented in [More79] for elimination of partial redundancies in a procedure. The interprocedural application is performed by a two-pass mechanism. The information on each procedure for the application of the basic algorithm is computed by a preliminary data flow analysis phase. This phase, which requires a particular processing order on the set of procedures, gives for each procedure P information which represents the impact of a call of P on the environment at the calling point. The second phase suppresses partial redundancies by treating the procedures individually in reverse calling order, reflecting in the treatment of a called procedure the information gathered during the treatment of its callers.

In some cases, optimization can be improved by iterating part or all of this process. The algorithm can be used for recursive procedures, but in this case, some approximations are made in the data flow analysis phase in order to avoid unpredictable costs in the algorithm. As presented here, the algorithm runs in time linear in the size of the program. Implementation of the basic algorithm has been shown to be efficient and well within the state of the art of actual compilers. The same claims seem to be applicable to its interprocedural extension.

Chapter 7

Two Approaches
to Interprocedural
Data Flow Analysis[†]

Micha Sharir
Amir Pnueli

―――――――◆――◆―――――――

7-1. INTRODUCTION

Under the general heading of program analysis we can find today two disciplines which, even though they have similar aims, differ in the means and tools they apply to the task of analysis. The first is the discipline of *program verification*. This is usually presented as the process of finding invariants of the program, or in other words fully characterizing the behavior of the program, discovering all the properties of all possible executions [Mann74, Cous77e]. As such, it is extremely ambitious and hence a priori doomed to failure on theoretical grounds for all but the most restricted program models.

The second discipline falling under the name of *program analysis* is the more pragmatically oriented data flow analysis. Associated with optimizing compilers, this methodology is very much concerned with questions of effectiveness and efficiency, in particular the trade-off between effort invested and the increment in the quality of produced code gained. Quite understandably,

†The work of the first author was partially supported by the National Science Foundation under grant MCS76–00116 and the United States Department of Energy under grant EY-76-C-02-3077.

its objectives are more modest. The reduced ambitiousness is expressed in not trying to extract *all* properties of the program but concentrating on several simple, well-defined properties such as the availability of expressions, the types and attributes of dynamic values, the constancy of variables, etc.

A basic technique used to analyze procedureless programs (or single procedures) is to transform them into flow graphs [Alle69] and assume that all paths in the graphs can represent actual executions of the program. This model does not describe the "true" run-time situation correctly, and in fact most of the graph paths are not feasible, i.e., do not represent possible executions of the program. However, this model is widely adopted for two main reasons:

1. Its relatively simple structure enables us to develop a comprehensive analytic theory, to construct simple algorithms which perform the required program analysis, and to investigate general properties of these algorithms in detail (cf. [Hech77, Aho77] or Chapter 1 for recent surveys of the subject).

2. Isolation of feasible paths from nonfeasible ones is known to be an undecidable problem, closely related to the Turing machine halting problem.

This classical technique faces significant problems in the presence of procedures. These problems reflect the dependence of individual interprocedural branches upon each other during program execution, a dependence which is known at compile time and is essentially independent of any computation performed during execution. Interprocedural branching is thus much easier to analyze than intraprocedural branches, which usually depend on the values assumed by various program variables. It is therefore very tempting to exploit our special knowledge of this branching pattern in program analysis, thereby tracing the program flow in a more accurate manner.

Interprocedural flow cannot be treated as a simple extension of the intraprocedural flow, but calls for a more complicated model whose mathematical properties require special analysis. In addition, many programming languages include features such as procedure variables and parameter passing by reference or by name [Aho77] which complicate the analysis of interprocedural flow.

It is therefore not surprising that interprocedural analysis has been neglected in much research on date flow analysis. Most of the recent literature on this subject virtually ignores any interprocedural aspect of the analysis, or splits the interprocedural analysis into a preliminary analysis phase which gathers overestimated information about the properties of each procedure in a program and which is followed by an intraprocedural analysis of each procedure, suppressing any interprocedural transfer of control and using instead the previously collected, overestimated information to deduce the effects of procedure calls on the program behavior [Alle74]. These approaches use a relatively simple model of the program at the expense of some information loss, arguing that such a loss is intrinsic anyway even in a purely intra-procedural model.

However, there is a growing feeling among researchers that more importance should be given to interprocedural analysis, especially in deeper analyses with more ambitious goals, where avoidance of flow overestimation is likely to be significant in improving the results of the analysis. This is true in particular for analyses related to program verification, in which area several recent papers, notably [DeBa75, Grei75, Hare76, Gall78, Cous77e] have already addressed this issue.

Recently, however, the interest in more accurate interprocedural data flow analysis has increased considerably, and new approaches to the problem appear in several recent works by Rosen [Rose79], Barth [Bart77a], Lomet [Lome75], and others. All these works attempt to generalize, achieve more accurate information than, or be more pragmatic than the traditional methods mentioned earlier. However, none of these methods achieves complete generality. They are all interested in gathering only *local* effects of procedure calls, are limited to simple bit-vector data flow problems, and do not view interprocedural analysis as an integral part of the global data flow analysis, but rather as a preliminary phase, completely independent from the actual program analysis phase. For example, they all ignore the problem of computing data at procedure entries interprocedurally, and are therefore forced to make worst-case assumptions about these values. However, they all can handle recursion. Rosen's work [Rose79] also handles reference parameters and derives "sharpest" static information, at the cost of a rather complex algorithm.

In this paper we introduce two new techniques for performing interprocedural data flow analysis. These techniques are almost generally applicable; they derive the sharpest static information, they integrate interprocedural analysis with intraprocedural analysis, and they handle recursion properly. These two approaches use two somewhat different graph models for the program being analyzed. The first approach, which we term the *functional approach*, views procedures as collections of structured program blocks and aims to establish input-output relations for each such block. One then interprets procedure calls as "super operations" whose effect on the program status can be computed using those relations. This approach relates rather closely to most of the known techniques dealing with interprocedural flow, such as the "worst-case assumptions," mixed with processing of procedures in "inverse invocation order" [Alle74], Rosen's "indirect arcs" method [Rose79], inline expansion of procedures [Alle77], and most of the known interprocedural techniques for program verification [Grei75, Gall78,

Hare76, Cous77e]. Our version of this first technique has the advantage of being rather simple to define and implement (potentially admitting rather efficient implementations for several important special cases), as well as the other advantages mentioned above.

Our second technique, which we term the *call-strings approach*, is somewhat orthogonal to the first approach. This second technique blends interprocedural flow analysis with the analysis of intraprocedural flow, and in effect turns a whole program into a single flow graph. However, as information is propagated through this graph, it is "tagged" with an encoded history of the procedure calls encountered during propagation. In this way we make interprocedural flow explicit, which enables us to determine, whenever we encounter a procedure return, what part of the information at hand can validly be propagated through this return, and what part has a conflicting call history that bars such propagation.

Surprisingly enough, very few techniques using this kind of logic have been suggested up to now. We may note in this connection that a crude approach, but one using similar logic, would be one in which procedure calls and returns are interpreted as ordinary branch instructions. Even though the possibility of such an approach has been suggested occasionally in the literature, it has never been considered seriously as an alternative interprocedural analysis method. A related approach to program verification has been investigated by de Bakker and Meertens [DeBa75], but, again, this has been quite an isolated attempt and one with rather discouraging results, which we believe to be due mainly to the ambitious nature of the analyses considered. There is some resemblance, though, between this second approach and the inline expansion method [Alle77] (see Section 7-4 for details).

We shall show that an appropriate sophistication of this approach is in fact quite adequate for data flow analysis, and gives results quite comparable with those of the functional approach. This latter approach also has the merit that it can easily be transformed into an approximative approach, in which some details of interprocedural flow are lost, but in which the relevant algorithms become much less expensive.

A problem faced by any interprocedural analysis is the possible presence of recursive procedures. The presence of such procedures causes interprocedural flow to become much more complex than it is in the nonrecursive case, mainly because the length of a sequence of nested calls can be arbitrarily large. Concerning our approaches in this case, we will show that they always converge in the nonrecursive case, but may fail to yield an effective solution of several data flow problems (such as constant propagation) for recursive programs. It will also be seen that much more advanced techniques are needed if we are to cope fully with recursion for such problems.

We note that it is always possible to transform a program with procedures into a procedureless program by converting procedure calls and returns into ordinary branch instructions, monitored by an explicit stack. If we do this and simply subject the resulting program to intraprocedural analysis, then we are in effect ignoring all the delicate properties of the interprocedural flow and thus inevitably overestimating flow. This simple observation shows that the attempt to perform more accurate interprocedural analysis can be viewed as a first (and relatively easy) step toward accurate analysis of more sophisticated properties of programs than are caught by classical global analysis.

This chapter is organized as follows: Section 7-2 contains preliminary notations and terminology. Section 7-3 presents the functional approach, first in abstract, definitional terms, and then shows that it can be effectively implemented for data flow problems which possess a finite semilattice of possible data values and sketches an algorithm for that purpose. We also discuss several cases in which unusually efficient implementation is possible. (These cases include many of those considered in classical data flow analyses.) Section 7-4 presents the call-strings approach in abstract, definitional terms showing that it also yields the solution we desire, though in a manner which is not necessarily effective in the most general case. In Section 7-5 we show that this latter approach can be effectively implemented if the semilattice of relevant data values is finite and investigate some of the efficiency parameters of such an implementation. Section 7-6 presents a variant of the call-strings approach which aims at a relatively simple, but only approximative, implementation of interprocedural data flow analysis. Section 7-7 is a concluding section in which some further directions of research are suggested and discussed.

We would like to express our gratitude to Jacob T. Schwartz for encouragement and many helpful suggestions and comments concerning this research, and to Barry K. Rosen for careful reviewing and helpful comments on this manuscript.

7-2. NOTATIONS AND TERMINOLOGY

In this section we will review various basic notations and terminology used in intraprocedural analysis, which will be referred to and modified subsequently. The literature on data flow analysis is by now quite extensive, and we refer the reader to [Hech77], [Aho77], or Chapter 1, three excellent recent introductory expositions of that subject.

To analyze a program consisting of several subprocedures, each subprocedure p, including the main program, is first divided into *basic blocks*. An (extended) basic block is a maximal single-entry multiexit sequence of code. For convenience, we will assume that each procedure call constitutes a single-instruction block. We also assume that each subprocedure p has a unique exit block, denoted by e_p, which is also assumed to be a single-instruction block, and that p has a unique entry (root) block, denoted by r_p.

Assume for the moment that p contains no procedure calls. Then the *flow graph* G_p of p is a rooted directed graph whose nodes are the basic blocks of p, whose root is r_p, and which contains an edge (m, n) for each direct transfer of control from the basic block m to (the start of) the basic block n, effected by some branch instruction. The presence of calls in p induces several possible interprocedural extensions of the flow graph, which will be discussed in the next section.

Let G be any rooted directed graph. G is denoted by a triplet (N, E, r), where N is the set of its nodes, E the set of edges, and r its root. A *path* p in G is a sequence of nodes in N $(n_1, n_2, \ldots, n_k)$ such that for each $1 \leq j < k$, $(n_j, n_{j+1}) \in E$. p is said to lead from n_1 (its initial node) to n_k (its terminal node). p can be also represented as the corresponding sequence of edges $((n_1, n_2), \ldots, (n_{k-1}, n_k))$. The *length* of p is defined as the number of edges along p ($k - 1$ in the above notation). For each pair of nodes $m, n \in N$ we define $\text{path}_G (m, n)$ as the set of all paths in G leading from m to n.

We assume that the program to be analyzed is written in a programming language with the following semantic properties: Procedure parameters are transferred by value, rather than by reference or by name (so that we can, and will, ignore the problem of "aliasing" discussed by Rosen [Rose79]), and there are no procedure variables or external procedures. We also assume that the program has been translated into intermediate-level code in which the transfer of values between actual arguments and formal parameters of a procedure is explicit in the code and is accomplished by argument-transmitting assignments, inserted before and after procedure calls. Because of this last assumption, formal parameters can be treated in the same way as other global variables. (For simplicity, we ignore here some aspects of recursive value stacking, which gives these "assignments" extra flavor. For example, a formal parameter of a recursive procedure p will have the same value after the "epilog" of a recursive call in p to p as the value it had before the call. Such considerations can be incorporated into our techniques, but will not be discussed in this paper. The reader may find it helpful to think of our model as allowing only parameterless procedures, in which case the above problems do not exist.) All these assumptions are made in order to simplify our treatment and are rather reasonable. If the first two assumptions are not satisfied, then things become much more complicated, though not beyond control. The third assumption is rather arbitrary but most convenient. (In [Cous77e], e.g., the converse assumption is made, namely that global variables are passed between procedures as parameters, an assumption which we believe to be less favorable technically.)

A *global data flow framework* is defined to be a pair (L, F), where L

is a semilattice of data or attribute information and F is a space of functions acting on L (and describing a possible way in which data may propagate along program flow paths). Let $\wedge$ denote the semilattice operation of L (called a *meet*), which is assumed to be idempotent, associative, and commutative. We assume that L contains a smallest element, denoted by 0, usually signifying null (worst-case) information (see below), and also a largest element Ω, corresponding to "undefined" information (see Section 7-3 for more details). F is assumed to be closed under functional composition and meet, to contain an identity map, and to be *monotone*, i.e., to be such that for each $f \in F$, $x, y \in L$, $x \le y$ implies $f(x) \le f(y)$. L is also assumed to be *bounded*, i.e., not to contain any infinite decreasing sequence of distinct elements. (L, F) is called a *distributive* framework if, for each $f \in F$ and $x, y \in L$, $f(x \wedge y) = f(x) \wedge f(y)$. We also assume that F contains a constant map f_Ω, which maps each $x \in L$ to Ω. This map corresponds to impossible propagation (see below).

Given a global data flow framework (L, F) and a flow graph G, we associate with each edge (m, n) of G a propagation function $f_{(m, n)} \in F$, which represents the change of relevant data attributes as control passes from the start of m, through m, to the start of n. (Recall that a basic block may have more than one exit, so that $f_{(m, n)}$ must depend on n as well as m.)

Once the set $S = \{f_{(m, n)} : (m, n) \in E\}$ is given, we can define a (graph-dependent) space F of propagation functions as the smallest set of functions acting in L which contains S, f_Ω and the identity map $\mathbf{id}_L$, and which is closed under functional composition and meet. It is clear that this F is monotone iff S is monotone, and that F is distributive iff S is distributive.

Once F is defined, we can formulate the following general set of data propagation equations, where, for each $n \in N$, x_n denotes the data available at the start of n:

$$x_r = 0$$

$$x_n = \bigwedge_{(m, n) \in E} f_{(m, n)}(x_m) \qquad n \in N - \{r\} \tag{7-1}$$

These equations describe attribute propagation "locally." That is, they show the relation between attributes collected at adjacent basic blocks, starting with null information at the program entry.

The solutions of these equations approximate the following abstractly defined function known as the *meet-over-all-paths* solution to a data flow problem

$$y_n = \bigwedge \{f_p(0) : p \in \text{path}_G(r, n)\} \qquad n \in N \tag{7-2}$$

Here we define $f_p = f_{(n_{k-1}, n_k)} \circ f_{(n_{k-2}, n_{k-1})} \circ \cdots \circ f_{(n_1, n_2)}$ for each path $p = (n_1, n_2, \ldots, n_k)$. If p is null, then f_p is defined to be the identity map on L.

Many algorithms which solve the system of equations (7-1) are known by now. These algorithms fall into two main categories: (1) iterative algorithms, which use only functional applications [Kild73, Hech75, Kam76, Hech77, Tarj76], and (2) elimination algorithms, which use functional compositions and meets [Alle76, Grah76, Tarj75b]. These elimination algorithms require some additional properties of F to allow elimination of program loops, a process which may require a computation of an infinite meet in F, unless such properties are assumed. Most of the algorithms in both categories yield the maximum fixed-point solution to Eqs. (7-1), which does coincide with the solution (7-2) provided that the data flow framework in question is distributive [Kild73], but which may fail to do so if the framework is only monotone [Kam77]. However, even in this latter case we still have $x_n \leq y_n$ for all $n \in N$; i.e., obtain an underestimated solution, which is always a safe one [Hech77]. In what follows, we will assume some basic knowledge of these classical data flow algorithms.

7-3.   THE FUNCTIONAL APPROACH
TO INTERPROCEDURAL ANALYSIS

In this section we present our first approach to interprocedural analysis. This approach treats each procedure as a structure of blocks and establishes relations between attribute data at its entry and related data at *any* of its nodes. Using these relations, attribute data is propagated directly through each procedure call.

We prepare for our description by giving some definitions and making some observations concerning the interprocedural nature of general programs. Let us first introduce the notion of an *interprocedural flow graph* of a computer program containing several procedures. We can consider two alternative representations of such a graph G. In the first representation, we have $G = \bigcup \{G_p : p$ is a procedure in the program$\}$, where, for each p, $G_p = (N_p, E_p, r_p)$, and where r_p is the entry block of p, N_p is the set of all basic blocks within p, and $E_p = E_p^0 \cup E_p^1$ is the set of edges of G_p. An edge $(m, n) \in E_p^0$ iff there can be a direct transfer of control from m to n (via a "go-to" or "if" statement, and $(m, n) \in E_p^1$ iff m is a call block and n is the block immediately following that call.

Thus this representation, which is the one to be used explicitly in our first approach, separates the flow graphs of individual procedures from each other.

A second representation, denoted by G^*, is defined as follows: $G^* = (N^*, E^*, r_1)$, where $N^* = \bigcup_p N_p$, and $E^* = E^0 \cup E^1$, where $E^0 = \bigcup_p E_p^0$ and an edge $(m, n) \in E^1$ iff either m is a call block and n is the entry block of the called procedure [in which case (m, n) is called a *call edge*], or if m is an exit block of some procedure p and n is a block immediately following a call to p [in which case (m, n) is called a *return edge*]. The call edge (m, r_p) and a return edge (e_q, n) are said to *correspond* to each other if $p = q$ and $(m, n) \in E_s^1$, for some procedure s. Here r_1 is the entry block of the main program, sometimes also denoted as r_{main}. Of course, not all paths through G^* are (even statically) feasible, in the sense of representing potentially valid execution paths, since the definition of G^* ignores the special nature of procedure calls and returns. For each $n \in N^*$ we define $IVP(r_1, n)$ as the set of all interprocedurally valid paths in G^* which lead from r_1 to n. A path $q \in path_{G^*}(r_1, n)$ is in $IVP(r_1, n)$ iff the sequence of all edges in q which are in E^1, which we will write as q_1 or $q|_{E^1}$, is *proper* in the following recursive sense:

1. A tuple q_1 which contains no return edges is proper.
2. If q_1 contains return edges, and i is the smallest index in q_1 such that $q_1(i)$ is a return edge, then q_1 is proper if $i > 1$ and $q_1(i - 1)$ is a call edge corresponding to the return edge $q_1(i)$, and after deleting those two components from q_1, the remaining tuple is also proper.

Remark: It is interesting to note that the set of all proper tuples over E^1, as well as $\bigcup_n IVP(r_1, n)$, can be generated by a context-free grammar (but not by a regular grammar), in contrast with the set of all possible paths in G^*, which is regular.

For each procedure p and each $n \in N_p$, we also define $IVP_0(r_p, n)$ as the set of all interprocedurally valid paths q in G^* from r_p to n such that each procedure call in q is completed by a subsequent corresponding return edge in q. More precisely, a path $q \in path_{G^*}(r_p, n)$ is in $IVP_0(r_p, n)$ iff $q_1 = q|_{E^1}$ is *complete*, in the following recursive sense.

1. The null tuple is complete.
2. A tuple q_1 is complete if it is either a concatenation of two complete tuples, or else it starts with a call edge, terminates with the corresponding return edge, and the rest of its components constitute a complete tuple.

Example 1.

Main program	*Procedure p*
read a, b;	**if** $a = 0$ **then return**;
$t := a * b$;	**else**
call p;	$\quad a := a - 1$;
$t := a * b$;	$\quad$ **call** p;
print t;	$\quad t := a * b$
stop;	**endif**;
end	**return**;
	end

This program is transformed into the interprocedural flow graph in Fig. 7-1, which includes both edges of $\bigcup_p E_p$ and of E^* (where solid arrows denote intraprocedural edges, dotted arrows denote edges in $\bigcup_p E_p^1$, and dashed arrows denote interprocedural edges, i.e., edges in E^1):

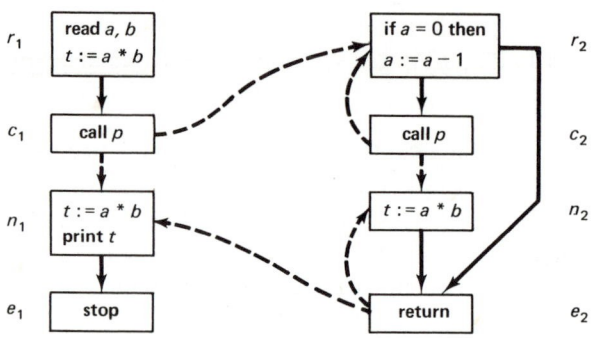

Figure 7-1

The following path q_1 in G^* is an interprocedurally valid path throughout the program [i.e., $q_1 \in \text{IVP}(r_1, e_1)$]: $q_1 = (r_1, c_1, r_2, c_2, r_2, e_2, n_2, e_2, n_1, e_1)$; however, the path $q_2 = (r_1, c_1, r_2, c_2, r_2, e_2, n_1, e_1)$ is not, since $q_2|_{E^1} \equiv ((c_1, r_2), (c_2, r_2), (e_2, n_1))$ is not proper, as can be easily checked. Similarly the path $q_3 = (r_2, c_2, r_2, e_2, n_2)$ is in $\text{IVP}_0(r_2, n_2)$, whereas $q_4 = (r_2, c_2, r_2, c_2, e_2, n_2)$ is not. Heuristically, q_3 reaches n_2 in the same incarnation of p in which it has started, but q_4 reaches n_2 in another incarnation which has been invoked by the initial one.

The notions introduced above appear in the following Path Decomposition Lemma:

Lemma 7-3.1. Let $n \in N^*$ and $q \in \text{IVP}(r_1, n)$. Then there exist procedures $p_1, p_2, \ldots, p_j$, where p_1 is the main program and p_j the procedure containing n, and calls $c_1, \ldots, c_{j-1}$ such that for each $i < j$ c_i is in p_i and calls p_{i+1}, and q can be represented as

$$q = q_1 \| (c_1, r_{p_2}) \| q_2 \| \ldots \| (c_{j-1}, r_{p_j}) \| q_j \qquad (7\text{-}3)$$

where for each $i < j$, $q_i \in \text{IVP}_0(r_{p_i}, c_i)$ and $q_j \in \text{IVP}_0(r_{p_j}, n)$. Conversely, any path which admits such a decomposition is in $\text{IVP}(r_1, n)$. Moreover, this decomposition is unique.

Proof. Let $q^* = q|_{E^1}$. If q^* is empty, then it is also complete, so that $q \in \text{IVP}_0(r_1, n)$, and we have the trivial decomposition $q = q$ with $j = 1$ (n must belong to the main program in this case).

Otherwise, in view of the definition of a proper E^1-tuple, and by making repeated deletions of adjacent call edges and corresponding return edges, we can reduce q^* to a tuple q^{**} which is either a null tuple or a nonempty tuple containing only call edges. Let $j = $ length of $q^{**} + 1$. If $j = 1$, i.e., if q^{**} is empty, it is readily seen that q^* is complete and that n belongs to the main program, and we have again the trivial decomposition $q = q$.

If $j > 1$, let $c_i = q^{**}(i)(1)$, $i = 1, \ldots, j - 1$, and put $p_1 = $ main program, $p_{i+1} = $ the procedure called from c_i, $i = 1, \ldots, j - 1$. In view of the way in which q^{**} was obtained from q, it follows that c_i is in p_i for each $i < j$. Let $m_0 = 1$ and m_i be the original index of $q^{**}(i)$ in q, $i = 1, \ldots, j - 1$. Then we have the decomposition $q = q_1 \| (c_1, r_{p_2}) \| q_2 \ldots \| (c_{j-1}, r_{p_j}) \| q_j$ where $q_i = q(m_{i-1} + 1 : m_i - 1)$, $i = 1, \ldots, j - 1$, and $q_j = q(m_{j-1} + 1 :)$.† It is easily verified that $q_i |_{E^1}$ is complete for each $i \leq j$, and therefore $q_i \in \text{IVP}_0(r_{p_i}, c_i)$ for $i < j$ and $q_j \in \text{IVP}_0(r_{p_j}, n)$.

The proof of the converse assertion is simpler, and follows directly from the definitions of IVP and IVP_0.

The uniqueness of this decomposition is also easy to establish, since $c_1, \ldots, c_{j-1}$ are precisely all the calls along q which are not subsequently completed, and it is fairly obvious from the definitions that these calls and their positions in q are unique, which immediately implies the uniqueness of the whole decomposition. ∎

We can now describe our "functional" approach to interprocedural analysis. Let (L, F) be a distributive data flow framework for G. In the first phase of the functional approach we take F as the direct basis for our analysis. More precisely, for each procedure p and each $n \in N_p$, we define an element $\phi_{(r_p, n)} \in F$ which describes the manner in which attributes in L are propagated from the start of r_p to the start of n along paths in $\text{IVP}_0(r_p, n)$. These functions must satisfy the following (nonlinear) equations, whose heuristic meaning should be self-explanatory: For each $(m, n) \in E^0$, let $f_{(m, n)} \in F$ denote the associated propagation effect. Then

$$\phi_{(r_p, r_p)} \leq \mathbf{id}_L \qquad \text{for each procedure } p$$

$$\phi_{(r_p, n)} = \bigwedge_{(m, n) \in E_p} (h_{(m, n)} \circ \phi_{(r_p, m)}) \qquad \text{for each } n \in N_p \tag{7-4}$$

where

$$h_{(m, n)} = \begin{cases} f_{(m, n)} & \text{if } (m, n) \in E_p^0 \\ \phi_{(r_q, e_q)} & \text{if } (m, n) \in E_p^1 \text{ and } m \text{ calls procedure } q \end{cases}$$

---

†For any tuple or string a, $a(i : j)$ denotes its subpart from the ith component to the jth one, inclusive; $a(i :)$ denotes the subpart of a from the ith component to its end.

This set of equations possesses a maximum fixed-point solution defined as follows: Let F be ordered by writing $g_1 \geq g_2$ for $g_1, g_2 \in F$ iff $g_1(x) \geq g_2(x)$ for all $x \in L$.

Start by putting

$$\phi^0_{(r_p, r_p)} = \mathbf{id}_L \qquad \text{for each procedure } p$$

$$\phi^0_{(r_p, n)} = f_\Omega \qquad \text{for each } n \in N_p - \{r_p\}$$

and then apply Eqs. (7-4) iteratively in a round-robin fashion to obtain new approximations to the ϕ's. (This can be done using iterations of either the Gauss-Seidel type or the Jacobi type, though the former is a better approach.) Let $\phi^i_{(r_p, n)}$ denote the ith approximation computed in this manner. Since $\phi^0_{(r_p, n)} \geq \phi^1_{(r_p, n)}$ for all p, n, it follows inductively that $\phi^i_{(r_p, n)} \geq \phi^{i+1}_{(r_p, n)}$ for each p, n and $i \geq 0$.

A problem which arises here is that F need not in general be a bounded semilattice, even if L is bounded. If L is finite, then F must be finite and therefore bounded, but if L is not finite, F need not in general be bounded.

Nevertheless, even if the sequence $\{\phi^i_{(r_p, n)}\}_{j \geq 0}$ is infinite for some p, n, we still can define its limit, denoted by $\phi_{(r_p, n)}$, as follows: For each $x \in L$, the sequence $\{\phi^i_{(r_p, n)}(x)\}_{j \geq 0}$ is decreasing in L, and since L is bounded, it must be finite, and we define $\phi_{(r_p, n)}(x)$ as its limit. [To ensure that $\phi_{(r_p, n)} \in F$ we must impose another condition upon F, namely: for each decreasing sequence $\{g_i\}_{i>0}$ of functions in F, the limit defined as above is also in F. However, since we will assume that L is finite (so that F is bounded) in any practical application of this approach, we introduce this condition only temporarily, for the sake of the following abstract reasoning. Thus, the above process defines a solution also in F.] Thus, the above process defines a solution $\{\phi_{(r_p, n)}\}_{p, n}$ to Eqs. (7-4), though not necessarily effectively. It is easy to check that the limiting functions defined by the iterative process that we have described are indeed a solution, and that in fact they are the maximal fixed-point solution of (7-4).

Having obtained this solution, we can use it to compute a solution to our data flow problem. For each basic block n let $x_n \in L$ denote the information available at the start of n. Then we have the following set of equations:

$$x_{r_{\text{main}}} = 0 \in L \qquad \qquad (7\text{-}5a)$$

$$x_{r_p} = \bigwedge \{\phi_{(r_q, c)}(x_{r_q}): q \text{ is a procedure and} \atop c \text{ is a call to } p \text{ in } q\} \qquad \text{for each procedure } p \quad (7\text{-}5b)$$

$$x_n = \phi_{(r_p, n)}(x_{r_p}) \qquad \text{for each procedure } p, \text{ and } n \in N_p - \{r_p\} \qquad (7\text{-}5c)$$

These equations can be (effectively) solved by a standard iterative algorithm, which yields the maximal fixed-point solution of (7-5).

We illustrate the above procedure for solution of Eqs. (7-4) and (7-5) by applying it to Example 1 introduced earlier, in which we suppose that available expressions analysis is to be performed. Our interprocedural analysis will show that $a * b$ is available upon exit from the recursive procedure p, so that its second computation in the main program is redundant and can therefore be eliminated. (Some traditional interprocedural methods will fail to detect this fact, since the expression $a * b$ is killed in p.) For simplicity we will only show that part of the analysis which pertains directly to the single expression $a * b$. Assuming this simplification, $L = \{0, 1, \Omega\}$, where 1 indicates that $a * b$ is available and 0 that it is not, and F contains precisely four functions [recall that $f(\Omega) = \Omega$ always]; the "constant" functions **0** and **1**, $\mathbf{id}_L$ and f_Ω. With these notations, Eqs. (7-4) read

$$\phi_{(r_1, r_1)} = \mathbf{id}$$

$$\phi_{(r_1, c_1)} = \mathbf{1} \circ \phi_{(r_1, r_1)}$$

$$\phi_{(r_1, n_1)} = \phi_{(r_2, e_2)} \circ \phi_{(r_1, c_1)}$$

$$\phi_{(r_1, e_1)} = \mathbf{1} \circ \phi_{(r_1, n_1)}$$

$$\phi_{(r_2, r_2)} = \mathbf{id}$$

$$\phi_{(r_2, c_2)} = \mathbf{0} \circ \phi_{(r_2, r_2)}$$

$$\phi_{(r_2, n_2)} = \phi_{(r_2, e_2)} \circ \phi_{(r_2, c_2)}$$

$$\phi_{(r_2, e_2)} = [\mathbf{id} \circ \phi_{(r_2, r_2)}] \wedge [\mathbf{1} \circ \phi_{(r_2, n_2)}]$$

Table 7-1 summarizes the iterative solution of these equations:

Table 7-1

Function	Initial value	After one iteration	After two iterations	After three iterations
$\phi_{(r_1, r_1)}$	id	id	id	id
$\phi_{(r_1, c_1)}$	f_Ω	1	1	1
$\phi_{(r_1, n_1)}$	f_Ω	f_Ω	1	1
$\phi_{(r_1, e_1)}$	f_Ω	f_Ω	1	1
$\phi_{(r_2, r_2)}$	id	id	id	id
$\phi_{(r_2, c_2)}$	f_Ω	0	0	0
$\phi_{(r_2, n_2)}$	f_Ω	f_Ω	0	0
$\phi_{(r_2, e_2)}$	f_Ω	id	id	id

Thus, the first stage of our solution stabilizes after three iterations. Next we solve Eqs. (7-5), which read as follows:

$$x_{r_1} = 0$$

$$x_{r_2} = \phi_{(r_1, c_1)}(x_{r_1}) \wedge \phi_{(r_2, c_2)}(x_{r_2})$$

$$= \mathbf{1}(x_{r_1}) \wedge \mathbf{0}(x_{r_2})$$

For these equations we see after two iterations that

$$x_{r_1} = x_{r_2} = 0$$

from which, using (7-5c), we obtain the complete solution

$$x_{r_1} = x_{r_2} = x_{c_2} = x_{n_2} = x_{e_2} = 0$$

$$x_{c_1} = x_{n_1} = x_{e_1} = 1$$

i.e., $a * b$ is available at the start of n_1, which is what we wanted to show.

Next we shall analyze the properties of the solution of Eqs. (7-4) and (7-5) as defined above. As in intraprocedural analysis our main objective is to show that this solution coincides with the meet-over-all-paths solution defined (in the interprocedural case) as follows:

$$\psi_n = \bigwedge \{ f_q : q \in \text{IVP}(r_{\text{main}}, n) \} \in F \qquad \text{for each } n \in N^* \qquad (7\text{-}6)$$

$$y_n = \psi_n(0) \qquad \text{for each } n \in N^* \qquad \begin{matrix} \text{(this is the meet-over-} \\ \text{all-paths solution)} \end{matrix} \qquad (7\text{-}7)$$

Lemma 7-3.2.   Let $n \in N_p$ for some procedure p. Then

$$\phi_{(r_p, n)} = \bigwedge \{ f_q : q \in \text{IVP}_0(r_p, n) \}$$

Proof.   We first prove, by induction on i, that for all $i \geq 0$

$$\phi^i_{(r_p, n)} \geq \bigwedge \{ f_q : q \in \text{IVP}_0(r_p, n) \}$$

Indeed, for $i = 0$, if $n = r_p$ then $\phi^0_{(r_p, r_p)} = \text{id}_L = f_{q_0}$, where $q_0 \in \text{IVP}_0(r_p, r_p)$ is the empty path from r_p to r_p, so that $\phi^0_{(r_p, r_p)} \geq \bigwedge \{ f_q : q \in \text{IVP}_0(r_p, r_p) \}$. If $n \neq r_p$ then $\phi^0_{(r_p, n)} = f_\Omega \geq f$ for all $f \in F$. Thus the assertion is true for $i = 0$.

Suppose that it is true for some i. For either kind of iterative computation of the functions ϕ^{i+1} using Eqs. (7-4) we have

$$\phi^{i+1}_{(r_p, n)} \geq \bigwedge_{(m, n) \in E_p} (h_{(m, n)} \circ \phi^i_{(r_p, m)})$$

$$\geq \bigwedge_{(m, n) \in E_p} (h_{(m, n)} \circ \bigwedge \{ f_q : q \in \text{IVP}_0(r_p, m) \})$$

for each procedure p and $n \in N_p - \{ r_p \}$. (Note here that if $n = r_p$, then $\phi^{i+1}_{(r_p, n)} = \phi^i_{(r_p, n)} = \phi^0_{(r_p, n)} \geq \{ f_q : q \in \text{IVP}_0(r_p, n) \}$. Our chain of equalities and inequalities then continues.)

$$= \bigwedge_{(m, n) \in E_p^0} (f_{(m, n)} \circ \bigwedge \{ f_q : q \in \text{IVP}_0(r_p, m) \}) \wedge$$

$$\bigwedge_{\substack{(m, n) \in E_p^1 \\ m \text{ calls } p'}} (\phi_{(r_{p'}, e_{p'})} \circ \bigwedge \{ f_q : q \in \text{IVP}_0(r_p, m) \})$$

$$\geq \bigwedge_{(m, n) \in E_p^0} (\bigwedge \{ f_{q \| (m, n)} : q \in \text{IVP}_0(r_p, m) \}) \wedge$$

$$\bigwedge_{\substack{(m, n) \in E_p^1 \\ m \text{ calls } p'}} (\bigwedge \{ f_{q'} : q' \in \text{IVP}_0(r_{p'}, e_{p'}) \} \circ \bigwedge \{ f_q : q \in \text{IVP}_0(r_p, m) \})$$

$$= \bigwedge_{(m, n) \in E_p^0} (\bigwedge \{ f_{q \| (m, n)} : q \in \text{IVP}_0(r_p, m) \}) \wedge$$

$$\bigwedge_{\substack{(m, n) \in E_p^1 \\ m \text{ calls } p'}} (\bigwedge \{ f_{q \| (m, r_{p'}) \| q' \| (e_{p'}, n)} : q \in \text{IVP}_0(r_p, m), q' \in \text{IVP}_0(r_{p'}, e_{p'}) \})$$

It is easily checked that for each function f_{q_1} appearing in the last right-hand side, $q_1 \in \text{IVP}_0(r_p, n)$. Hence, this last right-hand side must be

$$\geq \{f_q : q \in \text{IVP}_0(r_p, n)\}$$

The same inequality is then seen to apply to the limit function $\phi_{(r_p, n)}$ as well.

To prove the inequality in the other direction, we will show that for each $q \in \text{IVP}_0(r_p, n)$, $f_q \geq \phi_{(r_p, n)}$. This will be proven by induction on the length of q. If this length is 0, then n must be equal to r_p and $f_q = \phi_{(r_p, r_p)} = \text{id}_L$. Suppose that the assertion is true for all p, n and all $q \in \text{IVP}_0(r_p, n)$ whose length is $\leq k$, and let there be given p, n, q such that the length of q is $k + 1$. Let (m, n) be the last edge in q, so that we can write $q = q_1 \| (m, n)$.

If $(m, n) \in E_p^0$, then $q_1 \in \text{IVP}_0(r_p, m)$ and its length is $\leq k$. Therefore $f_{q_1} \geq \phi_{(r_p, m)}$ and by (7-4) we have

$$f_q = f_{(m, n)} \circ f_{q_1} \geq h_{(m, n)} \circ \phi_{(r_p, m)} \geq \phi_{(r_p, n)}$$

If $(m, n) \in E^1$, then $m = e_{p'}$ for some procedure p'. It is easily seen from the definition of IVP_0, that q can be decomposed as $q_1 \| (m_1, r_{p'}) \| q_2 \| (e_{p'}, n)$, such that $(m_1, n) \in E_p^1$, $q_1 \in \text{IVP}_0(r_p, m_1)$, $q_2 \in \text{IVP}_0(r_{p'}, e_{p'})$. Since $f_{(m_1, r_{p'})} = f_{(e_{p'}, n)} = \text{id}_L$ (since m_1 and $e_{p'}$ are single instruction blocks, containing only an interprocedural branch instruction), we have

$$f_q = f_{q_2} \circ f_{q_1}$$

But both q_1 and q_2 have length $\leq k$, so that by Eq. (7-4) and the induction hypothesis, we obtain

$$f_q \geq \phi_{(r_{p'}, e_{p'})} \circ \phi_{(r_p, m_1)} = h_{(m_1, n)} \circ \phi_{(r_p, m_1)} \geq \phi_{(r_p, n)}$$

This proves our assertion, from which the lemma follows immediately. ∎

Let us now define, for each basic block n,

$$\chi_n = \bigwedge \{\phi_{(r_{p_j}, n)} \circ \phi_{(r_{p_{j-1}}, c_{j-1})} \circ \cdots \circ \phi_{(r_{p_1}, c_1)} : \qquad (7\text{-}8)$$

$p_1 = $ main program, p_j is the procedure containing n,

and for each $i < j$, c_j is a call to p_{i+1} from $p_i\}$

$$z_n = \chi_n(0) \qquad (7\text{-}9)$$

Theorem 7-3.3. $\psi_n = \chi_n$ for each $n \in N^*$.

Proof. Let $q \in \text{IVP}(r_{\text{main}}, n)$. By Lemma 7-3.1, q admits a decomposition $q = q_1 \| (c_1, r_{p_2}) \| q_2 \| \ldots \| (c_{j-1}, r_{p_j}) \| q_j$ as in Eq. (7-3); i.e., there exist procedures $p_1 = $ main program, $p_2, \ldots, p_j = $ the procedure containing n, and calls $c_1, \ldots, c_{j-1}$ such that for each $i < j$, c_i is a call to p_{i+1} from p_i, and $q_i \in \text{IVP}_0(r_{p_i}, c_i)$, and also $q_j \in \text{IVP}_0(r_{p_j}, n)$.

Thus, by Lemma 7-3.2, we have

$$f_q = f_{q_j} \circ f_{q_{j-1}} \circ \cdots \circ f_{q_1} \geq \phi_{(r_{p_j}, n)} \circ \phi_{(r_{p_{j-1}}, c_{j-1})} \circ \cdots \circ \phi_{(r_{p_1}, c_1)} \geq \chi_n$$

Hence, $\psi_n \geq \chi_n$.

Conversely, let $p_1, \ldots, p_j, c_1, \ldots, c_{j-1}$ be as in Eq. (7-8). By Lemma 7-3.2 we have

$$\phi_{(r_{p_j}, n)} \circ \phi_{(r_{p_{j-1}}, c_{j-1})} \circ \cdots \circ \phi_{(r_{p_1}, c_1)}$$

$$= \bigwedge \{ f_{q_j} \circ f_{q_{j-1}} \circ \cdots \circ f_{q_1} : q_i \in \mathrm{IVP}_0(r_{p_i}, c_i)$$

$$\text{for each } i < j \text{ and } q_j \in \mathrm{IVP}_0(r_{p_j}, n) \}$$

$$= \{ f_{q_1 \| (c_1, r_{p_2}) \| q_2 \ldots \| (c_{j-1}, r_{p_j}) \| q_j} : \text{same as above} \}$$

By Lemma 7-3.1, each concatenated path in the last set expression belongs to $\mathrm{IVP}(r_{\mathrm{main}}, n)$. Thus, the last expression is

$$\geq \bigwedge \{ f_q : q \in \mathrm{IVP}(r_{\mathrm{main}}, n) \} = \psi_n$$

Therefore $\chi_n \geq \psi_n$ so that χ_n and ψ_n are equal for each $n \in N^*$. ∎

We can now prove our main result:

Theorem 7-3.4.   For each basic block $n \in N^*$, $x_n = y_n = z_n$.

Proof.   It is immediate from Theorem 7-3.3 that $y_n = z_n$ for each $n \in N^*$. We claim that $x_{r_p} = z_{r_p}$ for all procedures p in the program. By Eqs. (7-5c), (7-8), and (7-9) this will imply that $x_n = z_n$ for all n.

To prove our claim, we define a new flow graph $G_c = (N_c, E_c, r_1)$, where N_c is the set of all entry blocks and call blocks in the program. $E_c = E_c^0 \cup E_c^1$ is the set of edges of G_c. An edge $(m, n) \in E_c^0$ iff m is the entry node of some procedure p and n is a call within p. Moreover, $(m, n) \in E_c^1$ iff m is a call to some procedure p and n is the entry of p. As before, r_1 is the entry block of the main program. We now define a data flow problem for G_c by associating a data-propagating map $g_{(m,n)} \in F$ with each $(m, n) \in E_c$, in such a way that

$$g_{(m,n)} = \begin{cases} \phi_{(m,n)} & \text{if } (m, n) \in E_c^0 \\ \mathrm{id}_L & \text{if } (m, n) \in E_c^1 \end{cases}$$

It is clear that Eqs. (7-5a) and (7-5b) are equivalent to the iterative equations for the new data flow problem. On the other hand, Eqs. (7-8) and (7-9) define the meet-over-all paths solution for the same problem, if we substitute only entry blocks or call blocks for n. Since F is assumed to be distributive, it follows by Kildall's Theorem [Kild73], that $x_{r_p} = z_{r_p}$ for each procedure p, and this completes the proof of our theorem. ∎

It is now time to discuss the pragmatic problems that will affect attempts to use the functional approach to interprocedural analysis that we have sketched. The main problem is, obviously, how to compute the ϕ's effectively if L is not finite (or if F is not bounded). As examples below will show, in the most general case the functional approach does not and cannot yield an effective algorithm for solving Eqs. (7-4) and (7-5). Moreover, even if the iterative computation of the ϕ's converges, we must still face the problem of space needed to represent these functions. Since the functional method that we have outlined manipulates the ϕ's directly, instead of just applying them to elements of L, it can increase the space required for data flow analysis if L is finite, and may even fail to give finite representation to the ϕ's if L is infinite. We note here that our functional approach belongs to the class of elimination algorithms for solving data flow problems (a class of methods which includes the interval-oriented algorithms of Cocke and Allen [Alle76], and Tarjan's fast elimination algorithms [Tarj75b]), since it uses functional compositions and meets in addition to functional applications. All such elimination algorithms face similar problems, and in practical terms are therefore limited to cases in which the elements of F possess some compact and simple representation, in which meets and compositions of elements of F can be easily calculated, and in which F is a bounded semilattice (or else relevant infinite meets in F are easy to calculate). This family of cases includes the classical "bit-vector" data flow problems (e.g., analysis for available expressions, use-definition chaining, cf. [Hech77]).

It is interesting to ask whether it is possible to modify the functional approach so that it avoids explicit functional compositions and meets, and thus becomes an *iterative* approach. This is possible if L is finite, and an implementation having this property will be sketched below.

The following example will illustrate some of the pragmatic problems noted above, and also some potential advantages of the functional approach over any iterative variant of it. Suppose that we want to perform constant propagation (see, e.g., [Hech77] for a description of the standard framework used in this analysis). Consider the following code:

Example 2.

Main program	*Procedure p*
$A := 0;$	**if** cond **then**
call $P;$	$\quad A := A + 1;$
print $A;$	$\quad$ **call** $p;$
end	$\quad A := A - 1$
	endif;
	return;
	end

If we do not allow symbolic representation of the ϕ's, then, in any iterative approach, we shall have to compute $\phi_{(r_p, e_p)}(\{(A, 0)\})$, for which we need to compute (for the second level of recursion) $\phi_{(r_p, e_p)}(\{(A, 1)\})$, etc., computing $\phi_{(r_p, e_p)}(\{(A, k)\})$ for all integers $k \geq 0$. Thus, an iterative approach would diverge in this example.

However, if symbolic or some other compact representation of the ϕ's is possible, then it can be advantageous to manipulate these functions directly, without applying them to elements of L till their final values have been obtained. This can give us an overall description of their behavior, allowing them to be calculated in relatively few iterations. For example, in the example shown above, it is easily checked that $\phi_{(r_p, e_p)}$ is found to be $\mathbf{id}_L$ after two iterations.

However, convergence of the purely functional approach is not ensured in general. To see this, consider the following slight modification of the preceding example.

Example 3.

Main program	Procedure p
$A := 0;$	**if** cond **then**
call $p;$	$A := A + 2 + \text{sign}(A - 100);$
print $A;$	**call** $p;$
end	$A := A - 1;$
	endif
	return;
	end

It is fairly easy to check that the purely functional approach (which uses symbolic representation of the ϕ's) will diverge if negative integers are included in the program domain. Intuitively, this is due to the fact that it takes more than $100 + k$ iterations through Eqs. (7-4) to detect that $\phi_{(r_p, e_p)}(\{(A, -k)\}) = \varnothing$ for all $k \geq 0$.

Remark: The data flow framework required for constant propagation is in general not distributive. However, it can be shown that the standard framework for constant propagation becomes distributive if the program contains only one single variable and each propagation between adjacent basic blocks either sets the value of that variable to some constant, or calculates the output value of the variable from its input value in a one-to-one manner, as in the above examples.

These examples indicate that if L is not finite, divergence can actually occur. If L is infinite but F is bounded, then a symbolic functional approach would converge, whereas an iterative approach could still diverge if infinite space were needed to represent the ϕ's. Moreover, we have at present no simple criterion which guarantees that F is bounded in cases in which L is infinite. For these reasons, we will henceforth assume that L is a finite semilattice. We can then summarize our results up to this point as follows:

> **Corollary 7-3.5.** If (L, F) is a distributive data flow framework and the semilattice L is finite, then the iterative solution of Eqs. (7-4) converges and, together with Eqs. (7-5), yields the meet-over-all-inter-procedurally-valid-paths solution (7-7).

Next we shall sketch an algorithm which implements the functional approach for general frameworks with a finite semilattice L. We do not assume that any compact representation for elements of F is available, nor that their compositions and meets are easy to calculate, but instead give a purely iterative representation to the functional approach, which avoids all functional compositions and meets and also computes the ϕ's only for values which reach some relevant procedure entry during propagation.

Our algorithm is workpile-driven. The functions ϕ are represented by a two-dimensional partially defined map PHI: $N^* \times L \rightarrow L$, so that for each $n \in N^*$, $x \in L$, PHI(n, x) represents $\phi_{(r_p, n)}(x)$, where p is the procedure containing n. The substeps of the algorithm are as follows:

1. Initialize WORK $:= \{(r_1, 0)\}$, PHI$(r_1, 0) := 0$. [WORK is a subset of $N^* \times L$, containing pairs (n, x) for which PHI(n, x) has been changed and its new value has not yet been propagated to successor blocks of n.]

2. While WORK $\neq \varnothing$, remove an element (n, x) from WORK, and let $y = $ PHI(n, x).

   (a) If n is a call block in a procedure q, calling a procedure p, then

      (i) If $z = $ PHI(e_p, y) is defined, let m be the unique block such that $(n, m) \in E_q^1$, and *propagate* (x, z) to m. [By this we mean: assign PHI$(m, x) := $ PHI$(m, x) \wedge z$, where undefined PHI(m, x) is interpreted as Ω; if the value of PHI(m, x) has changed, add (m, x) to WORK.]

      (ii) Otherwise, propagate (y, y) to r_p. This will trigger propagation through p, which will later trigger propagation to the block following n in q (see below).

   (b) If n is the exit block of some procedure p, i.e., $n = e_p$, find all pairs (m, u) such that m is a block following some call c to p, and PHI$(c, u) = x$, and for each such pair propagate (u, y) to m.

(c)   If n is any other block in some procedure p, then, for each $m \in E_p^0 - \{n\}$, propagate $(x, f_{(n,m)}(y))$ to m.

3.   Repeat step (2) till $\text{WORK} = \varnothing$. When this happens, PHI represents the desired ϕ functions, computed only for "relevant" data values, from which the x solution can be readily computed as follows:

$$x_n = \bigwedge_{a \in L} \text{PHI}(n, a) \qquad \text{for each } n \in N^*$$

Step (3) thus implies that in the implementation we have sketched separate analysis to compute the x solution is unnecessary.

We omit analysis of the above algorithm, which in many ways would resemble an analysis of the abstract approach. However, so as not to avoid the issue of the correctness of our algorithm, we outline a proof of its total correctness, details of which can be readily filled in by the reader. The proof consists of several steps:

1.   The algorithm terminates if L is finite, since each element (n, x) of $N^* \times L$ (which is a finite set) is added to WORK only a finite number of times, because the values assumed by $\text{PHI}(n, x)$ upon successive insertions constitute a strictly decreasing sequence in L, which must of course be finite.

2.   We claim that for each $n \in N^*$,

$$x_n \leq \bigwedge_{a \in L} \text{PHI}(n, a) \tag{7-10}$$

To prove this claim, we show, using induction on the sequence of steps executed by the algorithm, that at the end of the ith step, $x_n \leq \bigwedge_{a \in L} \text{PHI}^i(n, a)$, for each $n \in N^*$, $a \in L$, where PHI^i denotes the value of PHI at the end of the ith step. In executing the ith step, we propagate some pair $(a, b) \in L \times L$ to some $n \in N^*$. By examining all possible cases, it is easy to show, using the induction hypothesis, that $x_n \leq b$, from which (7-10) follows immediately.

3.   In order to prove the converse inequality, it is sufficient, by Theorem 7-3.4, to show that for each $n \in N^*$ and $q \in \text{IVP}(r_1, n)$, $f_q(0) \geq \bigwedge_{a \in L} \text{PHI}(n, a)$. To do this, we first need the following assertion:

Assertion.   Let p be a procedure, $n \in N_p$ and $a \in L$ for which $\text{PHI}(n, a)$ has been computed by our algorithm. Then, for each path $q \in \text{IVP}_0(r_p, n), f_{\hat{q}}(a) \geq \text{PHI}(n, a)$.

Proof.   We proceed by induction on the length of q. This is trivial if the length $= 0$. Suppose that it is true for all p, n, a, and q with length less than some $k > 0$, and let $q \in \text{IVP}_0(r_p, n)$ be of length k.

Write $q = \hat{q} \,\|\, (m, n)$ and observe that either $(m, n) \in E^0$, in which case

$$f_q(a) = f_{(m,n)}(f_{\hat{q}}(a)) \geq f_{(m,n)}(\mathrm{PHI}(m, a)) \geq \mathrm{PHI}(n, a)$$

(the last inequality follows from the structure of our algorithm), or (m, n) is a return edge, in which case q can be written as $\hat{q}_1 \,\|\, (c, r_{p'}) \,\|\, \hat{q}_2 \,\|\, (m, n)$, where $\hat{q}_1 \in \mathrm{IVP}_0(r_p, c)$, $\hat{q}_2 \in \mathrm{IVP}_0(r_{p'}, m)$, and we have

$$f_q(a) = f_{\hat{q}_2}(f_{\hat{q}_1}(a)) \geq f_{\hat{q}_2}(\mathrm{PHI}(c, a)) \geq \mathrm{PHI}(m, \mathrm{PHI}(c, a)) \geq \mathrm{PHI}(n, a)$$

4. Now let q be any path in $\mathrm{IVP}(r_1, n)$. Decompose q as in (7-3), $q = q_1 \,\|\, (c_1, r_{p_2}) \,\|\, \dots \,\|\, (c_j, r_{p_{j+1}}) \,\|\, q_{j+1}$. Then, using the monotonicity of F, we have

$$f_{q_1}(0) \geq \mathrm{PHI}(c_1, 0) = a_1$$

$$f_{q_2}(f_{q_1}(0)) \geq f_{q_2}(a_1) \geq \mathrm{PHI}(c_2, a_1) = a_2$$

[This is because our algorithm will propagate (a_1, a_1) to r_{p_2}, so that $\mathrm{PHI}(c_2, a_1)$ will eventually have been computed.] Continuing in this manner, we obtain $f_q(0) \geq \mathrm{PHI}(n, a_j)$, which proves (3). This completes the proof of the total correctness of our algorithm. ∎

Example 4. Consider Example 1 given above. The steps taken by our iterative algorithm are summarized in Table 7-2 [where, for notational convenience, we represent PHI as a set of triplets, so that it contains (a, b, c) iff $\mathrm{PHI}(a, b) = c$]:

Table 7-2

	Initially		$(r_1, 0, 0)$	$\{(r_1, 0)\}$
Propagate	From	To	Entries added to PHI	WORK
$(0, 1)$	r_1	c_1	$(c_1, 0, 1)$	$\{(c_1, 0)\}$
$(1, 1)$	c_1	r_2	$(r_2, 1, 1)$	$\{(r_2, 1)\}$
$(1, 0)$	r_2	c_2	$(c_2, 1, 0)$	$\{(c_2, 1)\}$
$(1, 1)$	r_2	e_2	$(e_2, 1, 1)$	$\{(c_2, 1), (e_2, 1)\}$
$(0, 0)$	c_2	r_2	$(r_2, 0, 0)$	$\{(e_2, 1), (r_2, 0)\}$
$(0, 1)$	e_2	n_1	$(n_1, 0, 1)$	$\{(r_2, 0), (n_1, 0)\}$
$(0, 0)$	r_2	c_2	$(c_2, 0, 0)$	$\{(n_1, 0), (c_2, 0)\}$
$(0, 0)$	r_2	e_2	$(e_2, 0, 0)$	$\{(n_1, 0), (c_2, 0), (e_2, 0)\}$
$(0, 1)$	n_1	e_1	$(e_1, 0, 1)$	$\{(c_2, 0), (e_2, 0), (e_1, 0)\}$
$(0, 0)$	c_2	n_2	$(n_2, 0, 0)$	$\{(e_2, 0), (e_1, 0), (n_2, 0)\}$
$(1, 0)$	e_2	n_2	$(n_2, 1, 0)$	$\{(e_1, 0), (n_2, 0), (n_2, 1)\}$
$(0, 0)$	e_2	n_2	—	$\{(e_1, 0), (n_2, 0), (n_2, 1)\}$
—	e_1	—	—	$\{(n_2, 0), (n_2, 1)\}$
$(0, 1)$	n_2	e_2	—	$\{(n_2, 1)\}$
$(1, 1)$	n_2	e_2	—	$\varnothing$

Finally we compute the x solution of Eqs. (7-4) and (7-5) in step (3) of our iterative algorithm as follows:

$$x_{r_1} = \text{PHI}(r_1, 0) = 0$$
$$x_{c_1} = \text{PHI}(c_1, 0) = 1$$
$$x_{n_1} = \text{PHI}(n_1, 0) = 1$$
$$x_{e_1} = \text{PHI}(e_1, 0) = 1$$
$$x_{r_2} = \text{PHI}(r_2, 0) \wedge \text{PHI}(r_2, 1) = 0$$
$$x_{c_2} = \text{PHI}(c_2, 0) \wedge \text{PHI}(c_2, 1) = 0$$
$$x_{n_2} = \text{PHI}(n_2, 0) \wedge \text{PHI}(n_2, 1) = 0$$
$$x_{e_2} = \text{PHI}(e_2, 0) \wedge \text{PHI}(e_2, 1) = 0$$

Remark: In our treatment of the functional approach, we have deliberately avoided the issue of its efficient and pragmatic implementation for special simple frameworks in which elimination is feasible. For example, the iterative solution of Eqs. (7-4) may not be the best approach and could be replaced, e.g., by interval-based analysis [Alle76]. Also one might benefit from processing procedures in some useful order, as in [Alle74]. In this chapter we have preferred to emphasize the general approach and its analysis and general applicability. Details of an efficient, pragmatic, and interval-based implementation will be discussed in a subsequent paper.

7-4.   THE CALL-STRING APPROACH TO INTERPROCEDURAL ANALYSIS

We now describe a second approach to interprocedural analysis. This approach views procedure calls and returns in much the same way as any other transfer of control, but takes care to avoid propagation along interprocedurally invalid paths. This is achieved by tagging propagated data with an encoded history of procedure calls along which that data has propagated. This contrasts with the idea of tagging it by the lattice value attained on entrance to the most recent procedure, as in the functional approach. In our second approach, this "propagation history" is updated whenever a call or a return is encountered during propagation. This makes interprocedural flow explicit and increases the accuracy of propagated information. Moreover, by passing to approximate, but simpler, encodings of the call history, we are able to derive approximate, underestimated information for any data flow analysis, which should nevertheless remain more accurate than that derived by ignoring all interprocedural constraints on the propagation. The fact that this second approach allows us to perform approximate data flow analysis even in cases in which convergence of a full analysis is not ensured or when the space requirements of a full analysis is prohibitive gives this second approach real advantages.

We will first describe our second approach in a somewhat abstract manner. We will then suggest several modifications which yield relatively efficient convergent algorithms for many important cases.

As before, we suppose that we are given an interprocedural flow graph G, but this time we make an explicit use of the second representation $G^* = (N^*, E^*, r_1)$ of G. That is, we blend all procedures in G into one flow graph, but distinguish between intraprocedural and interprocedural edges.

Definition. A *call string* γ is a tuple of call blocks $c_1, c_2, \ldots, c_j$ in N^* for which there exists an execution path $q \in \text{IVP}(r_1, n)$, terminating at some $n \in N^*$, such that the decomposition (7-3) of q has the form $q_1 \| (c_1, r_{p_2}) \| q_2 \| \ldots \| (c_j, r_{p_{j+1}}) \| q_{j+1}$ where $q_i \in \text{IVP}_0(r_{p_i}, c_i)$ for each $i \leq j$ and $q_{j+1} \in \text{IVP}_0(r_{p_{j+1}}, n)$. To show the relation between q and γ we introduce a map CM such that $\text{CM}(q) = \gamma$. By the uniqueness of the decomposition (7-3) (cf. Lemma 7-3.1) this map is single-valued. γ can be thought of as the contents of a stack containing the locations of all call instructions which have not yet been completed.

Example 5. In Example 1 of Section 7-3 the following call strings are possible:

$$\lambda\text{—the null call string, } (c_1), (c_1 c_2), (c_1 c_2 c_2), \text{ etc.}$$

However, for each n in the main program and each $q \in \text{IVP}(r_1, n)$, $\text{CM}(q) = \lambda$; no other call strings can "tag" such paths. All the other call strings "tag" paths leading to nodes in the procedure p, and indicate all possible calling sequences (i.e., contents of a stack of all uncompleted calls at some point of the program's execution) that can materialize as execution advances to p.

Let Γ denote the space of all call strings γ corresponding (in the above sense) to interprocedurally valid paths in G^*. Note that if G^* is nonrecursive, then Γ is finite; otherwise Γ will be infinite, and as we shall soon see, this can cause difficulties for our approach.

Let (L, F) be the data flow framework under consideration. We define a new framework (L^*, F^*), which reflects the interprocedural constraints in G^* in an implicit manner, as follows: $L^* = L^\Gamma$, i.e., L^* is the space of all maps from Γ into L. Since we assume that L contains a largest "undefined" element Ω, we can identify L^* with the space of all partially defined maps from Γ into $L - \{\Omega\}$. If Γ is finite, then the representation of L^* as a space of partially defined maps is certainly more efficient, but for abstract purposes the first representation is more convenient. (In examples below, however, we will use partial map representation for elements of L^*.) If $\xi \in L^*$ and $\gamma \in \Gamma$, then heuristically $\xi(\gamma)$ denotes that part of the propagated data which has been propagated along execution paths in $\text{CM}^{-1}\{\gamma\}$.

If we define a meet operation in L^* as a pointwise meet on Γ, i.e., if for $\xi_1, \xi_2 \in L^*$, $\gamma \in \Gamma$, we define $(\xi_1 \wedge \xi_2)(\gamma) = \xi_1(\gamma) \wedge \xi_2(\gamma)$, then L^* becomes a semilattice. The smallest element in L^* is 0^*, where $0^*(\gamma) = 0$ for each $\gamma \in \Gamma$. The largest element in L^* is Ω^*, where $\Omega^*(\gamma) = \Omega$ for each $\gamma \in \Gamma$. Note that unless Γ is finite, L^* need not be bounded. However, if $\xi_1 \geq \xi_2 \geq \ldots \geq \xi_n \geq \ldots$ is an infinite decreasing chain in L^*, its limit is well-defined and can be computed as follows: For each $\gamma \in \Gamma$, the chain $\xi_1(\gamma) \geq \xi_2(\gamma) \geq \ldots$ must be finite (since L is bounded). Define $(\lim \xi_n)(\gamma)$ as the final value of that chain. Obviously $\lim \xi_n = \bigwedge_n \xi_n$ and in the same manner it can be shown that $\bigwedge_n \xi_n$ exists for any sequence $\{\xi_i\}_{i \geq 1}$ in L^*.

In order to describe F^*, we first need to define a certain operation in Γ.

Definition. $\circ : \Gamma \times E^* \to \Gamma$ is a partially defined binary operation such that for each $\gamma \in \Gamma$ and $(m, n) \in E^*$ such that $CM^{-1}\{\gamma\} \cap IVP(r_1, m) \neq \varnothing$ we have

$$\gamma \circ (m, n) = \begin{cases} \gamma & \text{if } (m, n) \in E^0 \\ \gamma \,\|\, [m] & \text{if } (m, n) \text{ is a call edge in } E^1 \\ & \text{(i.e., if } m \text{ is a call block)} \\ \gamma(1 : \#\gamma - 1) & \text{(i.e., } \gamma \text{ without its last component)} \\ & \text{if } (m, n) \text{ is a return edge in } E^1 \text{ such} \\ & \text{that } \gamma(\#\gamma) \text{ is its corresponding call edge} \end{cases}$$

in all other cases, $\gamma \circ (m, n)$ is undefined. Here $\#\gamma$ denotes the length of γ.

The following lemma can be proved in an obvious and straightforward way.

Lemma 7-4.1.   Let $\gamma \in \Gamma$, $(m, n) \in E^*$, $q \in IVP(r_1, m)$ such that $CM(q) = \gamma$. Then $\gamma_1 = \gamma \circ (m, n)$ is defined iff $q_1 = q \,\|\, (m, n)$ is in $IVP(r_1, n)$, in which case $CM(q_1) = \gamma_1$.

The operation $\circ$ defines the manner in which call strings are updated as data is propagated along an edge of the flow graph. Loosely put, the above lemma states that path incrementation is transformed into $\circ$ by the "homomorphism" CM.

Example 6.   In Example 1 of Section 7-3, we have

$$\lambda \circ (c_1, r_2) = (c_1)$$
$$(c_1) \circ (c_2, r_2) = (c_1 c_2)$$
$$(c_1 c_2) \circ (e_2, n_2) = (c_1)$$

and

$$(c_1 c_2) \circ (e_2, n_1)$$

is undefined, indicating that after p had called itself once, the return from p must be to the block following c_2 in p; it is illegal to return then to the main program.

Next, let $(m, n) \in E^*$, and let $f_{(m,n)} \in F$ be the data propagation map associated with (m, n). Note that by our assumptions $f_{(m,n)} = \mathbf{id}_L$ if $(m, n) \in E^1$, since in these cases m is a block containing only a jump which in itself does not affect data attributes. Define $f^*_{(m,n)} : L^* \longrightarrow L^*$ as follows: For each $\xi \in L^*$, $\gamma \in \Gamma$,

$$f^*_{(m,n)}(\xi)(\gamma) = \begin{cases} f_{(m,n)}(\xi(\gamma_1)) & \text{if there exists (a necessarily unique)} \\ & \gamma_1 \text{ such that } \gamma_1 \circ (m, n) = \gamma \\ \Omega & \text{otherwise} \end{cases}$$

The intuitive interpretation of this formula is as follows: $f^*_{(m,n)}(\xi)$ represents information at the start of n which is obtained by propagation of the information ξ, known at the start of m, along the edge (m, n). For each $\gamma_1 \in \Gamma$ for which $\xi(\gamma_1)$ is defined, we propagate $\xi(\gamma_1)$, the γ_1-selected data available at the start of m, to the start of n in standard intraprocedural fashion (that is, using $f_{(m,n)}$). However, this propagated data is now associated not with γ_1 but with $\gamma_1 \circ (m, n)$, which "tags" the set of paths obtained by concatenating (m, n) to all paths which are "tagged" by γ_1, which lead to m, and along which $\xi(\gamma_1)$ has been propagated. If $\gamma_1 \circ (m, n)$ is undefined, then, by Lemma 7-4.1, $\xi(\gamma_1)$ should not be propagated through (m, n) since no path which leads to m and is tagged by γ_1 can be concatenated with (m, n) in an interprocedurally valid manner. In this case, we simply discard $f_{(m,n)}(\xi(\gamma_1))$, as indicated by the above formula.

Example 7.   In Example 1 of Section 7-3, let $\xi_0 = \{(\lambda, 1)\} \in L^*$. Then (for notational convenience, call strings are written without enclosing parentheses): $\xi_1 = f^*_{(c_1, r_2)}(\xi_0) = \{(c_1, 1)\}$, since $\lambda \circ (c_1, r_2) = c_1$ and ξ_0 is defined only at λ. Note that $f_{(c_1, r_2)} = \mathbf{id}$, as is the case for all interprocedural jumps.

$$\xi_2 = f^*_{(r_2, c_2)}(\xi_1) = \{(c_1, f_{(r_2, c_2)}(1))\} = \{(c_1, 0)\}$$

This edge is intraprocedural, so that call strings need not be modified.

$$\xi_3 = f^*_{(c_2, r_2)}(\xi_2) = \{(c_1 c_2, 0)\}$$
$$\xi_4 = f^*_{(r_2, e_2)}(\xi_3) = \{(c_1 c_2, 0)\}$$
$$\xi_5 = f^*_{(e_2, n_2)}(\xi_4) = \{(c_1, 0)\}$$

[But note that, e.g., $f^*_{(e_2, n_1)}(\xi_4) =$ totally undefined map (Ω^*) in L^*, since the only $\gamma_1 \in \Gamma$ for which $\gamma_1 \circ (e_2, n_1)$ is defined is the string c_1, but $\xi_4(c_1)$ is undefined.]

$$\xi_6 = f^*_{(n_2, e_2)}(\xi_5) = \{(c_1, 1)\}$$
$$\xi_7 = f^*_{(e_2, n_1)}(\xi_6) = \{(\lambda, 1)\} \qquad \text{(compare with } f^*_{(e_2, n_1)}(\xi_4) \text{!)}$$

To summarize, we have traced one possible interprocedurally valid path from c_1 to n_1, starting with the information that $a * b$ is available at c_1 and obtaining the fact that it is still available at n_1 (considering just this path, of course). An attempt to return to the main program prematurely resulted in completely discarding the information.

F^* is now defined as the smallest subset of maps acting in L^* which contains $\{f^*_{(m,n)} : (m, n) \in E^*\}$ and the identity map in L^* and which is closed under functional composition and meet.

Lemma 7-4.2.

1. If F is monotone in L, then F^* is monotone in L^*.

2. If F is distributive in L, then F^* is distributive in L^*.

3. If F is distributive in L, then for each $(m, n) \in E$, $f^*_{(m,n)}$ is *continuous* in L^*, that is, $f^*_{(m,n)}(\bigwedge_k \xi_k) = \bigwedge_k f^*_{(m,n)}(\xi_k)$, for each collection $\{\xi_k\}_{k \geq 1} \subseteq L^*$.

Proof. It is easily seen that it is sufficient to prove (1) or (2) for the set $\{f^*_{(m,n)} : (m, n) \in E^*\}$, and this is straightforward from the definitions.

To prove (3), note that for each $\gamma \in \Gamma$ for which there exists $\gamma_1 \in \Gamma$ such that $\gamma_1 \circ (m, n) = \gamma$ we have

$$f^*_{(m,n)}\left(\bigwedge_{k \geq 1} \xi_k\right)(\gamma) = f_{(m,n)}\left(\bigwedge_{k \geq 1} \xi_k(\gamma_1)\right)$$

But since L is bounded, there exists $k_0(\gamma_1)$ such that the last expression equals $f_{(m,n)}\left(\bigwedge_{1 \leq k \leq k_0(\gamma_1)} \xi_k(\gamma_1)\right)$, which in turn, by the distributivity of $f_{(m,n)}$, equals

$$\bigwedge_{1 \leq k \leq k_0(\gamma_1)} f_{(m,n)}(\xi_k(\gamma_1)) = \bigwedge_{1 \leq k \leq k_0(\gamma_1)} f^*_{(m,n)}(\xi_k)(\gamma) \geq \left(\bigwedge_{k \geq 1} f^*_{(m,n)}(\xi_k)\right)(\gamma)$$

Thus $f^*_{(m,n)}\left(\bigwedge_{k \geq 1} \xi_k\right) \geq \bigwedge_{k \geq 1} f^*_{(m,n)}(\xi_k)$. The converse inequality is immediate from the monotonicity of $f^*_{(m,n)}$. ∎

> *Remark:* Note that interprocedural, as distinct from intraprocedural, data flow frameworks depend heavily on the flow graph (Γ itself may vary from one flow graph to another). Thus, for example, there is no simple way to obtain F^* directly from F without any reference to the flow graph. This will not create any problems in the sequel, and we argue that even in the intraprocedural case it is a better practice to regard data flow frameworks as graph-dependent.

We can now define a data flow problem for G^*, using the new framework (L^*, F^*), in which we seek the maximal fixed-point solution of the following equations in L^*:

$$x_{r_1}^* = \{(\lambda, 0)\} \qquad \text{where } \lambda \text{ is the null call string}$$

$$x_n^* = \bigwedge_{(m,n) \in E^*} f_{(m,n)}^*(x_m^*) \qquad n \in N^* - \{r_1\} \tag{7-11}$$

We can show the existence of a solution to these equations in the following manner: Let $x_{r_1}^{*(0)} = \{(\lambda, 0)\}, x_n^{*(0)} = \Omega^*$ for all $n \in N^* - \{r_1\}$. Then apply Eqs. (7-11) iteratively to obtain new approximations to the x^*'s. Let $x_n^{*(i)}$ denote the ith approximation computed in this manner.

Since $x_n^{*(0)} \geq x_n^{*(1)}$ for all $n \in N^*$, it follows inductively, from the monotonicity of $f_{(m,n)}^*$ for each $(m, n) \in E^*$, that $x_n^{*(i)} \geq x_n^{*(i+1)}$ for all $i \geq 0$, $n \in N^*$. Thus, for each $n \in N^*$, $\{x_n^{*(i)}\}_{i \geq 0}$ is a decreasing chain in L^*, having a limit, and we define $x_n^* = \lim_i x_n^{*(i)}$. It is rather straightforward to show that $\{x_n^*\}_{n \in N^*}$ is indeed a solution to (7-11) and that in fact it is the maximal fixed-point solution of (7-11).

Having defined this solution, we will want to convert its values to values in L, because L^* has been introduced only as an auxiliary semilattice, and our aim is really to obtain data in L for each basic block. Since there is no longer a need to split the data at node n into parts depending on the interprocedural flow leading to n, we can combine these parts together, i.e., take their meet. For each $n \in N^*$, we can then simply define

$$x_n' = \bigwedge_{\gamma \in \Gamma} x_n^*(\gamma) \tag{7-12}$$

A detailed example of applying this technique to our running example (Example 1 of Section 7-3) will be given in the next section.

In justifying the approach that we have just outlined, our first step is to prove that x_n' coincides with the meet-over-all-interprocedurally-valid-paths solution y_n defined in the preceding section. This can be shown as follows:

Definition. Let $\text{path}_{G^*}(r_1, n)$ denote the set of all execution paths (whether interprocedurally valid or not) leading from r_1 to $n \in N^*$. For each $p = (r_1, s_2, \ldots, s_k, n) \in \text{path}_{G^*}(r_1, n)$ define $f_p^* = f_{(s_k, n)}^* \circ f_{(s_{k-1}, s_k)}^* \circ \ldots \circ f_{(r_1, s_2)}^*$. For each $n \in N^*$ define $y_n^* = \bigwedge \{f_p^*(x_{r_1}^*): p \in \text{path}_{G^*}(r_1, n)\}$.

Since $\text{path}_{G^*}(r_1, n)$ is at most countable, this (possibly infinite) meet in L^* is well defined.

Theorem 7-4.3. If (L, F) is a distributive data flow framework, then, for each $n \in N^*$, $x_n^* = y_n^*$.

Proof. The proof follows (it is quite similar to the proof of an analogous theorem of Kildall for a bounded semilattice [Kild73]):

1. Let $n \in N^*$ and $p \equiv (r_1, s_2, \ldots, s_k, n) \in \text{path}_{G^*}(r_1, n)$. By (7-11) we have

$$x_{s_2}^* \leq f_{(r_1, s_2)}^*(x_{r_1}^*)$$
$$x_{s_3}^* \leq f_{(s_2, s_3)}^*(x_{s_2}^*)$$
$$.$$
$$.$$
$$.$$
$$x_n^* \leq f_{(s_k, n)}^*(x_{s_k}^*)$$

Combining all these inequalities, and using the monotonicity of the f^*'s, we obtain $x_n^* \leq f_p^*(x_{r_1}^*)$, and therefore $x_n^* \leq y_n^*$.

2. Conversely, we will prove by induction on i that

$$x_n^{*(i)} \geq y_n^* \qquad \text{for all } i \geq 0, \, n \in N^*$$

Indeed, let $i = 0$. If $n \neq r_1$, then $x_n^{*(0)} = \Omega^* \geq y_n^*$. On the other hand, the null execution path $p_0 \in \text{path}_{G^*}(r_1, r_1)$, so that $y_{r_1}^* \leq f_{p_0}^*(x_{r_1}^*) = x_{r_1}^* = x_{r_1}^{*(0)}$. Thus the assertion is true for $i = 0$. Suppose that it is true for some $i \geq 0$. Then $x_{r_1}^{*(i+1)} = x_{r_1}^{*(i)} \geq y_{r_1}^*$, and for each $n \in N^* - \{r_1\}$ we have

$$x_n^{*(i+1)} = \bigwedge_{(m,n) \in E^*} f_{(m,n)}^*(x_m^{*(i)}) \geq \bigwedge_{(m,n) \in E^*} f_{(m,n)}^*(y_m^*)$$

by the induction hypothesis.

We now need the following:

Lemma 7-4.4. For each $(m, n) \in E^*, f_{(m,n)}^*(y_m^*) \geq y_n^*$.

Proof. Since $f_{(m,n)}^*$ is distributive and continuous on L^* (Lemma 7-4.2), we have

$$f_{(m,n)}^*(y_m^*) = f_{(m,n)}^*(\bigwedge \{f_p^*(x_{r_1}^*); p \in \text{path}_{G^*}(r_1, m)\})$$
$$= \bigwedge \{f_{(m,n)}^*(f_p^*(x_{r_1}^*)): p \in \text{path}_{G^*}(r_1, m)\}$$
$$\geq \bigwedge \{f_q^*(x_{r_1}^*): q \in \text{path}_{G^*}(r_1, n)\} = y_n^* \quad \blacksquare$$

Now returning to Theorem 7-4.3, it follows by Lemma 7-4.4 that $x_n^{*(i+1)} \geq \bigwedge_{(m,n) \in E^*} y_n^* = y_n^*$ (each $n \in N^*$ is assumed to have predecessors). Hence assertion (2) is established, and it follows that for each $n \in N^*$, $x_n^* = \lim_i x_n^{*(i)} = \bigwedge_{i \geq 1} x_n^{*(i)} \geq y_n^*$, so that $x_n^* = y_n^*$. $\quad \blacksquare$

Lemma 7-4.5. Let $n \in N^*$, $p = (r_1, s_1, \ldots, s_k, n) \in \text{path}_{G^*}(r_1, n)$ and $\gamma \in \Gamma$. Then $f_p^*(x_{r_1}^*)(\gamma)$ is defined iff $p \in \text{IVP}(r_1, n)$ and $\text{CM}(p) = \gamma$. If this is the case, then $f_p^*(x_{r_1}^*)(\gamma) = f_p(0)$.

Proof. The proof is by induction on $l(p)$, the length of p (i.e., the number of edges in p). If p is the null path, then n must be equal to r_1. Moreover, $CM(p) = \lambda$, $p \in IVP(r_1, r_1)$ and $f_p^*(x_{r_1}^*) = x_{p_1}^*$ is defined only at λ and equals $0 = f_p(0)$. Thus our assertion is true if $l(p) = 0$.

Suppose that this assertion is true for all $n \in N^*$ and $p \in$ path$_{G^*}$ (r_1, n) such that $l(p) < \lambda$. Let $n \in N^*$ and $p = (r_1, s_2, \ldots, s_k, n)$ be a path of length k in path$_{G^*}$ (r_1, n). Let $p_1 = (r_1, s_2, \ldots, s_k)$. By definition, for each $\gamma \in \Gamma$ we have

$$f_p^*(x_{r_1}^*)(\gamma) = f_{(s_k,n)}^*[f_{p_1}^*(x_{r_1}^*)](\gamma)$$

$$= \begin{cases} f_{(s_k,n)}[f_{p_1}^*(x_{r_1}^*)(\gamma_1)] & \text{if there exists } \gamma_1 \in \Gamma \text{ such that} \\ & \gamma_1 \circ (s_k, n) = \gamma \\ \Omega & \text{otherwise} \end{cases}$$

Thus $f_p^*(x_{r_1}^*)(\gamma)$ is defined iff there exists $\gamma_1 \in \Gamma$ such that $\gamma_1 \circ (m, n) = \gamma$ and $f_{p_1}^*(x_{r_1}^*)(\gamma_1)$ is defined. By our inductive hypothesis, this is the case iff $p_1 \in IVP(r_1, s_k)$, $CM(p_1) = \gamma_1$ and $\gamma_1 \circ (s_k, n) = \gamma$. By Lemma 7-4.1, these last conditions are equivalent to $p \in IVP(r_1, n)$ and $CM(p) = \gamma$.

If this is the case, then again, by our inductive hypothesis, $f_{p_1}^*(x_{r_1}^*)(\gamma_1) = f_{p_1}(0)$ and so

$$f_p^*(x_{r_1}^*)(\gamma) = f_{(s_k,n)}[f_{p_1}(0)] = f_p(0) \quad \blacksquare$$

Now we can prove the main result of this section:

Theorem 7-4.6. For each $n \in N^*$, $x_n' = y_n$.

Proof. Let $\gamma \in \Gamma$. By Theorem 7-4.3,

$$x_n^*(\gamma) = \{f_p^*(x_{r_1}^*)(\gamma) : p \in \text{path}_{G^*} (r_1, n)\}$$

and by Lemma 7-4.5,

$$= \bigwedge \{f_p(0) : p \in IVP(r_1, n) \text{ such that } CM(p) = \gamma\}$$

Thus, by (7-12),

$$x_n' = \bigwedge_{\gamma \in \Gamma} x_n^*(\gamma) = \bigwedge \{f_p(0) : p \in IVP(r_1, n)\} = y_n \quad \blacksquare$$

Corollary 7-4.7. If the flow graph G^* is nonrecursive, then the iterative solution of Eqs. (7-11) that we have described will converge and yield the desired meet-over-all-interprocedurally-valid-paths solution of these equations.

Proof. Convergence is assured since Γ is finite, and hence L^* is bounded. Thus (L^*, F^*) is a distributive data flow framework, and by standard arguments the iterative solution of (7-11) must converge

[Kild73, Hech77]. Therefore, Theorem 7-4.6 implies that the limiting solution coincides with the meet-over-all-paths solution. ■

The call-strings approach is of questionable feasibility if Γ is infinite, i.e., if G^* contains recursive procedures. Moreover, as for the functional approach, it is rather hopeless to convert it into an effective algorithm for handling the most general cases of certain data flow problems such as constant propagation. However, as we shall see in the following section, a fairly practical variant of the call-strings approach can be devised for data flow frameworks with a finite semilattice L.

Let us also observe the similarity between the call-string approach and the inline expansion method (discussed, e.g., in [Alle77]). Indeed, tagging data by call strings amounts essentially to creating virtual copies of each procedure, one copy for each possible calling sequence reaching that procedure. Indeed let $\gamma = c_1 c_2 \ldots c_j \in \Gamma$. Then, if c_j calls procedure p from procedure p', we can substitute the virtual copy of p corresponding to γ at the place of c_j in the virtual copy of p' corresponding to $\gamma' = c_1 c_2 \ldots c_{j-1}$. Doing so, c_j and the return from p become no-ops, and we get a full inline expansion of procedures.

7-5. DATA FLOW ANALYSES USING A FINITE SEMILATTICE

Let (L, F) be a distributive data flow framework such that L is finite. As we have seen, the functional approach described in Section 7-3 converges for such a framework. We will show in this section that it is also possible to construct a call-strings algorithm which converges for these frameworks. As noted in the previous section, convergence is ensured if Γ is finite. The idea behind our modified approach is to replace Γ by some finite subset Γ_0 and allow propagation only through interprocedurally valid paths which are mapped into elements of Γ_0. Such an approach is not generally feasible because it can lead to an overestimated (and unsafe) solution, since it does not trace information along all possible paths. However, using the finiteness of L, we will show that Γ_0 can be chosen in such a way that no information gets lost and the algorithm produces the same solution as defined in Section 7-4.

We begin to describe our approach without fully specifying Γ_0. Later we will show how Γ_0 should depend on L in order to guarantee the above solution.

Definitions.

1. Let Γ_0 be some finite subset of Γ with the property that if $\gamma \in \Gamma_0$ and γ_1 is an initial subtuple of γ, then $\gamma_1 \in \Gamma_0$ too.

2. For each $n \in N^*$, let $\text{IVP}'(r_1, n)$ denote the set of all $q \in \text{IVP}(r_1, n)$ such that for each initial subpath q_1 of q (including q), $\text{CM}(q_1) \in \Gamma_0$.

3. We also modify the $\circ$ operation so that it acts in Γ_0 rather than in Γ, as follows: If $\gamma \in \Gamma_0$, $(m, n) \in E^*$ such that there exists $q \in \text{IVP}'(r_1, m)$ where $\text{CM}(q) = \gamma$, then

$$\gamma \circ (m, n) = \begin{cases} \gamma & \text{if } (m, n) \in E^0 \\ \gamma \,||\, [m] & \text{if } (m, n) \text{ is a call edge in } E^1 \text{ and} \\ & \gamma \,||\, [m] \in \Gamma_0 \\ \gamma(1 : \#\gamma - 1) & \text{if } (m, n) \text{ is a return edge in } E^1 \text{ and} \\ & \gamma(\#\gamma) \text{ is the call block preceding } n \\ \text{undefined} & \text{in all other cases} \end{cases}$$

The only difference between this definition of $\circ$ and the previous one is that it will not add a call block m to a call string γ unless the resulting string is in Γ_0. When this is not the case, information tagged by γ will be lost when propagating through (m, n), unless it is also tagged by some other call string to which m can be concatenated.

The following lemma is analogous to Lemma 7-4.1:

Lemma 7-5.1. Let $\gamma \in \Gamma_0$, $(m, n) \in E^*$, $q \in \text{IVP}'(r_1, m)$ such that $\text{CM}(q) = \gamma$. Then $\gamma_1 = \gamma \circ (m, n)$ is defined iff $q_1 = q \,||\, (m, n)$ is in $\text{IVP}'(r_1, n)$, in which case $\text{CM}(q_1) = \gamma_1$.

We now define a data flow framework (L^*, F^*) in much the same way as in Section 7-4, but replace Γ by Γ_0. This leads to a bounded semilattice $L^* = L^{\Gamma_0}$ and to a distributive data flow framework (L^*, F^*).

Hence, Eqs. (7-11) come to be effectively solvable by any standard iterative algorithm which yields their maximal fixed-point solution. To this solution we will want to apply the following final calculation, which is a variant of (7-12):

$$x_n'' = \bigwedge_{\gamma \in \Gamma_0} x_n^*(\gamma) \tag{7-13}$$

Careful scrutiny of the analysis of the previous section reveals that the only place where the nature of Γ_0 and the operation $\circ$ are referred to is in Lemma 7-4.1, and it is easily seen that if we replace Γ and $\circ$ by Γ_0 and the modified $\circ$, throughout the previous analysis, and also replace $\text{IVP}(r_1, n)$ by $\text{IVP}'(r_1, n)$ for all $n \in N^*$, then by proofs completely analogous to those presented in Section 7-4 (but with one notable difference, i.e., that there is now no need to worry about continuity of F^* or infinite meets in L^*, since L^* is now known to be bounded) we obtain the following:

Theorem 7-5.2. For each $n \in N^*$

$$x_n'' = y_n'' \equiv \bigwedge \{f_p(0): p \in \text{IVP}'(r_1, n)\}$$

Up to this point, our suggested modifications have been quite general and do not impose any particular requirements upon L or upon Γ_0. On the other hand, Theorem 7-5.2 implies that x_n'' is an overestimated solution, and as such is useless for purposes of our analysis, as it can yield unsafe information (e.g., it may suggest that an expression is available whereas it may actually be unavailable), unless we can show that x_n'' coincides with the meet-over-all-interprocedurally-valid-paths solution of the attribute propagation equations which concern us. As will be shown below, this is indeed the case if L is finite.

Definition. Let $M \geq 0$ be an integer. Define Γ_M as the (finite) set of all call strings whose lengths do not exceed M. Γ_M obviously satisfies the conditions of part (1) of the previous definition.

Lemma 7-5.3. Let (L, F) be a data flow framework with L a finite semilattice, and let $M = K(|L| + 1)^2$, where K is the number of call blocks in the program being analyzed and $|L|$ is the cardinality of L. Let $\Gamma_0 = \Gamma_M$. Then, for each $n \in N^*$ and each execution path $q \in \text{IVP}(r_1, n)$ there exists another path $q' \in \text{IVP}'(r_1, n)$ such that $f_q(0) = f_{q'}(0)$.

Proof. By induction on the length of q. If the length is 0, then $n = r_1$ and q is the null execution path, which belongs to both $\text{IVP}(r_1, r_1)$ and $\text{IVP}'(r_1, r_1)$, so that our assertion is obviously true in this case.

Suppose that the lemma is true for all paths whose length is less than some $k \geq 1$, and let $n \in N^*$, $q \in \text{IVP}(r_1, n)$ be a path of length k. If $q \in \text{IVP}'(r_1, n)$ then there is nothing to prove, so assume that this is not the case, and let q_0 be the shortest initial subpath of q such that $\text{CM}(q_0) \notin \Gamma_0$. Then q_0 can be decomposed according to Eq. (7-3) as follows:

$$q_0 = q_1 \| (c_1, r_{p_2}) \| q_2 \| \ldots \| (c_j, r_{p_{j+1}}) \| q_{j+1}$$

Hence $j > M$. Next, consider the sequence $\{(c_i, \alpha_i, \beta_i)\}_{i=1}^{j}$, where, for each $i \leq j$, $\alpha_i = f_{q_i} \circ f_{q_{i-1}} \circ \ldots \circ f_{q_1}(0)$, and β_i is either Ω if the call at c_i is not completed in q (this call is certainly not completed in q_0), or $f_{\hat{q}_i}(0)$ if the call at c_i is completed in q, and $\hat{q}_i$ is the initial subpath of q ending at the return which completes the call. Thus, for each call, the sequence records the calling block, the value propagated along this path up to the call, and the value propagated up to the corresponding return, if it materializes. The number of distinct elements of such a sequence is at most $K(|L| + 1)^2 = M$ (we do not count Ω as an element of L; if we did, then the bound can be reduced to $K|L|^2$). Since $j > M$, this sequence must contain at least two identical components (c_a, α_a, β_a) and (c_b, α_b, β_b), where $a < b \leq j$.

Now, if $\beta_a = \beta_b = \Omega$, then neither of the calls c_a, c_b is completed in q. If we rewrite q as

$$q = q'_1 \| (c_a, r_{p_{a+1}}) \| q'_2 \| (c_b, r_{p_{b+1}}) \| q'_3$$

then it is easily seen that the shorter path $\hat{q} = q'_1 \| (c_a, r_{p_{a+1}}) \| q'_3$ is also in $\mathrm{IVP}(r_1, n)$. Moreover

$$\alpha_a = f_{q_1'}(0) = \alpha_b = f_{q_2'} \circ f_{q_1'}(0)$$

so that

$$f_q(0) = f_{q_3'} \circ f_{q_2'} \circ f_{q_1'}(0) = f_{q_3'} \circ f_{q_1'}(0) = f_{\hat{q}}(0)$$

By our induction hypothesis there exists $\hat{q}' \in \mathrm{IVP}'(r_1, n)$ such that $f_{\hat{q}'}(0) = f_{\hat{q}}(0) = f_q(0)$, which proves the lemma for q.

On the other hand, if $\beta_a = \beta_b \neq \Omega$, then it follows that both calls c_a and c_b are completed in q, with c_b necessarily completed first. Thus we can write

$$q = q'_1 \| (c_a, r_{p_{a+1}}) \| q'_2 \| (c_b, r_{p_{b+1}}) \| q'_3 \| (e_{p_{b+1}}, n_b) \| q'_4 \| (e_{p_{a+1}}, n_a) \| q'_5$$

where $n_a = n_b$ is the block immediately following c_a. Again it follows that $\hat{q} = q'_1 \| (c_a, r_{p_{a+1}}) \| q'_3 \| (e_{p_{a+1}}) \| q'_5$ is in $\mathrm{IVP}(r_1, n)$. Moreover

$$\alpha_a = f_{q_1'}(0) = \alpha_b = f_{q_2'} \circ f_{q_1'}(0)$$
$$\beta_a = f_{q_4'} \circ f_{q_3'} \circ f_{q_2'} \circ f_{q_1'}(0) = \beta_b = f_{q_3'} \circ f_{q_2'} \circ f_{q_1'}(0)$$

from which one easily obtains $f_q(0) = f_{\hat{q}}(0)$, and the proof can now continue exactly as before. ∎

The main result of this section now follows immediately:

Theorem 7-5.4. Let (L, F) be a distributive data flow framework with a finite semilattice L, and let $\Gamma_0 = \Gamma_M$, with M as defined above. Then, for each $n \in N^*$, $x''_n = y_n$. That is, the modified algorithm described at the beginning of the present section yields a valid interprocedural solution.

Proof. Since $\mathrm{IVP}'(r_1, n) \subset \mathrm{IVP}(r_1, n)$ we have $x''_n \geq y_n$. On the other hand, let $q \in \mathrm{IVP}(r_1, n)$. By Lemma 7-5.3 there exists $q' \in \mathrm{IVP}'(r_1, n)$ such that $f_q(0) = f_{q'}(0) \geq \bigwedge \{f_p(0): p \in \mathrm{IVP}'(r_1, n)\} = x''_n$. Hence $y_n = \bigwedge \{f_q(0): q \in \mathrm{IVP}(r_1, n)\} \geq x''_n$. ∎

Remark: Note that in Lemma 7-5.3 and Theorem 7-5.4, K can be replaced by the maximal number K' of distinct calls in any sequence of nested calls in the program being analyzed. In most cases this gives a significant improvement of the bound on M appearing in those two results.

We have now shown that finite data flow frameworks are solvable by a modified call-strings approach. However, the size of Γ_0 can be expected to be large enough to make this approach as impractical as the corresponding functional approach. But in several special cases we can reduce the size of Γ_0 still further. The following definition is taken from [Rose78b], rewritten in our notation:

Definition. A data flow framework (L, F) is called *decomposable* if there exists a finite set A and a collection of data flow frameworks $\{(L_\alpha, F_\alpha)\}_{\alpha \in A}$, such that

1. $L = \prod_{\alpha \in A} L_\alpha$, ordered in a pointwise manner induced by the individual orders in each L_α.

2. $F \subseteq \sum_{\alpha \in A} F_\alpha$. That is, for each $f \in F$ there exists a collection $\{f^\alpha\}_{\alpha \in A}$ where $f^\alpha \in F$ for each $\alpha \in A$, such that for each $x = (x_\alpha)_{\alpha \in A} \in L$ we have

$$f(x) = (f^\alpha(x_\alpha))_{\alpha \in A}$$

In the cases covered by this definition we can split our data flow framework into a finite number of "independent" frameworks, each inducing a separate data flow problem, and obtain the solution to the original problem simply by grouping all the individual solutions together.

For example, the standard framework (L, F) for available expressions analysis is decomposable into subframeworks each of which is a framework for the availability of a single expression. Formally, let A be the set of all program expressions. For each $\alpha \in A$ let $L = \{0, 1\}$ where 1 indicates that α is available and 0 that it is not. Then $\{0, 1\}^A$ is isomorphic with L (which is more conveniently represented as the power set of A). It is easily checked that each $f \in F$ can be decomposed as $\sum_{\alpha \in A} f^\alpha$, where for each $\alpha \in A$, $f^\alpha \in F_\alpha$, and is either the constant $\mathbf{0}$ if α can be killed by the propagation step described by f, is the constant $\mathbf{1}$ if α is unconditionally generated by that propagation step, and is the identity map in all other cases. The frameworks used for use-definition chaining and live variables have analogous decompositions.

A straightforward modification of Lemma 7-5.3, applied to each (L_α, F_α) separately yields the following improved result for decomposable frameworks:

Theorem 7-5.5. Let (L, F) be a decomposable distributive data flow framework with a finite semilattice. Define $M = K \cdot \max_{\alpha \in A} (|L_\alpha| + 1)^2$ and let $\Gamma_0 = \Gamma_M$. Then, for each $n \in N^*$, $y_n'' = y_n$.

In the special case of available expressions analysis this is certainly an improvement of Theorem 7-5.4, since it reduces the bound on the length of permissible call strings from $K \cdot O(4^{|A|})$ to $9K$. For this analysis we can do even better since available expression analysis has the property appearing in the following definition.

Definition. A decomposable data flow framework (L, F) is called *1-related* if, for each $\alpha \in A$, F_α consists only of constant functions and identity functions.

This property is characteristic of situations in which there exists at most one point along each path which can affect the data being propagated. Indeed, consider a framework having this property; let $\alpha \in A$ and let $p = (s_1, s_2, \ldots, s_k)$ be an execution path. Let $j \leq k$ be the largest index such that $f_{(s_{j-1}, s_j)}^\alpha$ is a constant function. Then clearly $f_p^\alpha = f_{(s_{j-1}, s_j)}^\alpha$ and is therefore also a constant. Hence in this case the effect of propagation in L_α through p is independent of the initial data and is determined by the edge (s_{j-1}, s_j) alone. If no such j exists, then $f_p = \text{id}|_{L_\alpha}$, in which case no point along p affects the final data.

Note also that since each F_α is assumed to be closed under functional meet, it follows that if (L, F) is 1-related then the only constant functions that F_α can contain are $\mathbf{0}$ (the smallest element in L_α) and $\mathbf{1}$ (the largest element). Hence we can assume, with no loss of generality, that L_α is the trivial lattice $\{0, 1\}$ for each $\alpha \in A$. All the classical data flow analyses mentioned above have 1-related frameworks. It is therefore easily seen that, under these assumptions, 1-related frameworks are those having a semilattice of effective height 1 [Rose78b, Section 7].

For frameworks having the 1-related property it is easy to replace an execution path q by a shorter subpath $\hat{q}$ such that $f_{\hat{q}}^\alpha(0) = f_q^\alpha(0)$ for some $\alpha \in A$. Indeed, to obtain such a $\hat{q}$ we have only to ensure that $\hat{q}$ is also interprocedurally valid and that the last edge (s, s') in q for which $f_{(s, s')}$ is constant belongs to $\hat{q}$. This observation allows us to restrict the length of permissible call strings still further. The following can then be shown:

Theorem 7-5.6. Let (L, F) be a 1-related distributive data flow framework. Put $\Gamma_0 = \Gamma_{3K}$. Then, for each $n \in N^*$, $x_n'' = y_n$.

The analysis developed in this section and the previous one can be modified to deal with nondistributive data flow problems. In the nondistributive case, Theorems 7-4.6 and 7-5.2 guarantee only inequalities of the form

$x'_n \leq y_n$ (resp. $x''_n \leq y''_n$) for all $n \in N^*$. The arguments in this section show that under appropriate conditions $y''_n = y_n$ for each $n \in N^*$, so that assuming these conditions Theorems 7-5.4, 7-5.5, 7-5.6 all yield the inequalities $x''_n \leq y_n$ for each $n \in N^*$. Thus, in the nondistributive case, our approach leads to an underestimated solution, as is the case for intraprocedural iterative algorithms for nondistributive frameworks [Kam77].

Example 8.   We return to Example 1 studied in Section 7-3. Since available expressions analysis uses a 1-related framework, and since the flow graph appearing in that example satisfies $K = K' = 2$, we can take $\Gamma_0 = \Gamma_6$, and apply Kildall's iterative algorithm [Kild73] to solve Eqs. (7-11). Table 7-3 summarizes the steps which are then performed (for notational convenience call strings are written without enclosing parentheses):

Table 7-3

Propagate			Workpile of nodes from which further propagation is required
From	To	Updated x^* value	
(initially)		$x^*_{r_1} = \{(\lambda, 0)\}$	$\{r_1\}$
r_1	c_1	$x^*_{c_1} = \{(\lambda, 1)\}$	$\{c_1\}$
c_1	r_2	$x^*_{r_2} = \{(c_1, 1)\}$	$\{r_2\}$
r_2	c_2	$x^*_{c_2} = \{(c_1, 0)\}$	$\{c_2\}$
r_2	e_2	$x^*_{e_2} = \{(c_1, 1)\}$	$\{c_2, e_2\}$
c_2	r_2	$x^*_{r_2} = \{(c_1, 1), (c_1 c_2, 0)\}$	$\{e_2, r_2\}$
e_2	n_2	$x^*_{n_2} = \Omega^*$(unchanged)	$\{r_2\}$
e_2	n_1	$x^*_{n_1} = \{(\lambda, 1)\}$	$\{r_2, n_1\}$
r_2	c_2	$x^*_{c_2} = \{(c_1, 0), (c_1 c_2, 0)\}$	$\{n_1, c_2\}$
r_2	e_2	$x^*_{e_2} = \{(c_1, 1), (c_1 c_2, 0)\}$	$\{n_1, c_2, e_2\}$
n_1	e_1	$x^*_{e_1} = \{(\lambda, 1)\}$	$\{c_2, e_2, e_1\}$
c_2	r_2	$x^*_{r_2} = \{(c_1, 1), (c_1 c_2, 0), (c_1 c_2 c_2, 0)\}$	$\{e_2, e_1, r_2\}$
e_2	n_2	$x^*_{n_2} = \{(c_1, 0)\}$	$\{e_1, r_2, n_2\}$
e_2	n_1	—	$\{e_1, r_2, n_2\}$
e_1	—	—	$\{r_2, n_2\}$
		$\cdots$	

The next steps of the algorithm update $x^*_{r_2}$, $x^*_{c_2}$, $x^*_{n_2}$, $x^*_{e_2}$ in similar fashion, adding new entries with increasingly longer call strings, up to a string $c_1 c_2 c_2 c_2 c_2 c_2$, but none of $x^*_{r_1}$, $x^*_{c_1}$, or $x^*_{e_1}$ is ever modified. Final x^* values for the blocks appearing in our example are:

$$x^*_{r_2} = x^*_{e_2} = \{(c_1, 1), (c_1 c_2, 0), (c_1 c_2 c_2, 0), \ldots, (c_1 c_2 c_2 c_2 c_2 c_2, 0)\}$$

$$x^*_{c_2} = \{(c_1, 0), (c_1 c_2, 0), \ldots, (c_1 c_2 c_2 c_2 c_2 c_2, 0)\}$$

$$x^*_{n_2} = \{(c_1, 0), (c_1 c_2, 0), \ldots, (c_1 c_2 c_2 c_2 c_2 c_2, 0)\} \qquad (\neq x^*_{c_2}, \text{ by the way})$$

An x'' solution can now easily be computed; of course, this is identical to the solutions obtained by previous methods.

Note that in this example there was no need to maintain call strings of length up to 6 (length 2 would have sufficed). However, to derive correct information in the example depicted as Fig. 7-2, we need call strings in which one call appears three times.

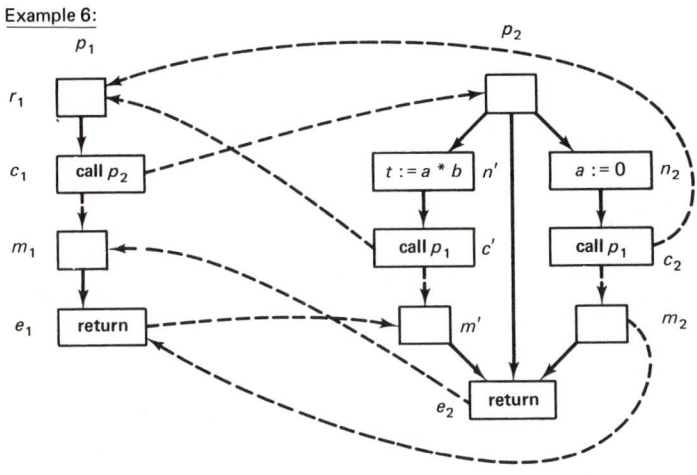

Figure 7-2

The shortest path in Fig. 7-2 showing that $a * b$ is *not* available at m' is $q = (r_1, c_1, r_2, n', c', r_1, c_1, r_2, n_2, c_2, r_1, c_1, r_2, e_2, m_1, e_1, m_2, e_2, m_1, e_1, m')$, in which c_1 appears three times before any of the calls in q is completed.

It is an interesting and challenging problem to find, for a given flow graph, by some preliminary analysis, an optimal set Γ_0 of call strings needed to perform some particular interprocedural data flow analysis without losing information.

7-6. AN APPROXIMATIVE CALL-STRING APPROACH

In this section we present a modification of the call-string approach developed in Section 7-4, which yields a convergent algorithm for any data flow analysis, even though this algorithm may in general fail to produce precisely the desired (meet-over-all-interprocedurally-valid-paths) solution. However, the output of the algorithm to be presented will always be an underestimated (and hence safe) solution. This compromise, which is useful even when L is finite, can make the call-string approach much more efficient.

Moreover, if L is infinite, or if F is not bounded or does not admit compact representation, then this modified approach is one of the very few ways to perform interprocedural analysis that we know of.

Three things should be kept in mind when evaluating any approximative approach to an interprocedural data flow problem: (1) Even in intraprocedural analysis, a meet-over-all-paths solution is itself an underestimation to the "true" run-time situation, since many of the static execution paths which enter into such an analysis may not be executable; (2) many data flow analyses whose semilattices L are not finite are also not distributive [Kam77, Shar78a], so that even the intraprocedural iterative solution of the data flow equations may underestimate the meet-over-all-paths solution; and (3) in nondistributive cases, the meet-over-all-paths solution may not be calculable (cf. [Hech77] for details).

By analyzing the abstract approach presented in Section 7-4, we can easily see that the convergence (and efficiency) of the call-strings approach depends primarily on Γ. Convergence can be ensured in general only if Γ is finite; and the smaller Γ is, the less complex the algorithm becomes. This observation motivates the approach that we propose in this section, whose general outline is as follows.

Choose some finite (preferably rather small) set $\hat{\Gamma}$ which is closed under a binary operation $*$ and has a left identity with respect to this operation. (We suggest that in practice $*$ be associative and noncommutative, but the general description given below will not assume this.) As in Section 7-4, let Γ denote the set of all call strings. Choose an "encoding" map σ which maps each call block to some element of $\hat{\Gamma}$. Using $*$, we can extend σ to Γ by putting $\sigma(\gamma) = \sigma(c_1) * \sigma(c_2) * \ldots * \sigma(c_j)$ (computed left to right) for each $\gamma = (c_1, c_2, \ldots, c_j) \in \Gamma$. We also define $\sigma(\lambda)$ to be w, the left-identity of $\hat{\Gamma}$.

Let (L, F) be any (not necessarily distributive) data flow framework. We will define a modified data flow framework (L^*, F^*) in essentially the same way as we did in Section 7-4, but with some differences reflecting the nature of the approximative approach, as detailed below.

L^* is defined as $L^{\hat{\Gamma}}$. All the observations made in Section 7-4 concerning L^* still apply, only now L^* is bounded since $\hat{\Gamma}$ has been assumed to be finite.

As before, in order to define F^*, we first define an updating operation between encoded call strings and edges in E^*. This updating operation is now more complex than that defined earlier, and need not be one-to-one and single-valued any more. It is therefore best described by assigning to each edge $(m, n) \in E^*$ a relation $R_{(m,n)}$ in $\hat{\Gamma}$. Essentially, $R_{(m,n)}$ is the identity relation for each $(m, n) \in E^0$ and for each call edge (m, n) and its corresponding return edge (m', n') we have $R_{(m',n')} = R_{(m,n)}^{-1}$. Then a path $(n_1, n_2, \ldots, n_k)$ will be considered to be *acceptable* if and only if $R_{(n_1,n_2)} \circ R_{(n_2,n_3)} \circ \ldots \circ R_{(n_{k-1},n_k)} \neq \emptyset$. To make these relations bear some meaningful relationship to the updating map $\circ$ defined in Section 7-4, we first define for each $(m, n) \in$

E^* a relation $I_{(m,n)}$ in Γ, so that for each $\gamma_1, \gamma_2 \in \Gamma$, $\gamma_1 I_{(m,n)}\gamma_2$ iff $\gamma_2 = \gamma_1 \circ (m, n)$, and then require the relation $\sigma \circ R_{(m,n)} \circ \sigma^{-1}$ to contain the relation $I_{(m,n)}$. This condition will guarantee that every interprocedurally valid path is also acceptable by our encoding scheme, but not necessarily vice versa.

To make the above ideas more precise, we suggest the following construction to obtain such suitable relations:

Definition. For each procedure p in the program being analyzed, define $\mathrm{ECS}(p) = \{\sigma(\mathrm{CM}(q)): q \in \mathrm{IVP}(r_1, r_p)\}$. This is the set of all encoded call strings which result from interprocedurally valid paths reaching the entry of p.

These sets can be calculated by a rather simple preliminary analysis based upon the following set of equations (where *main* denotes the main program, which is assumed to be nonrecursive):

$$\mathrm{ECS}(\mathit{main}) = \{w\}$$

$$\mathrm{ECS}(p) = \{\alpha * \sigma(c): c \text{ is a call to } p \text{ from some procedure } p' \qquad (7\text{-}14)$$
$$\text{and } \alpha \in \mathrm{ECS}(p')\} \qquad \text{for } p \neq \mathit{main}$$

After initializing each $\mathrm{ECS}(p)$ to $\varnothing$, for all $p \neq \mathit{main}$, these equations can be solved iteratively in a fairly standard way. (The iterative solution will converge because $\hat{\Gamma}$ is finite.) It is a simple matter to prove that the iterative solution yields the sets $\mathrm{ECS}(p)$ defined above.

Using the sets ECS, we now define the following objects: for each $n \in N^*$, a set of *interprocedurally acceptable* paths leading from the main entry to n, denoted by $\mathrm{IAP}(r_1, n)$; a modified set-valued map $\widehat{\mathrm{CM}}$ from $\bigcup_{n \in N^*} \mathrm{IAP}(r_1, n)$ to $2^{\hat{f}}$; and a modified relation-valued map $R: E^* \longrightarrow 2^{\hat{f} \times \hat{f}}$. For each $(m, n) \in E^*$, $R_{(m,n)}$ is a relation in $\hat{\Gamma}$, so that for each $\alpha, \beta \in \hat{\Gamma}$ we have

$$\alpha R_{(m,n)} \beta \text{ iff } \begin{cases} \alpha = \beta \in \mathrm{ECS}(p) & \text{if } (m, n) \in E_p^0 \text{ for some} \\ & \text{procedure } p \\[1em] \alpha \in \mathrm{ECS}(p) \text{ and } \beta = \alpha * \sigma(m) & \text{if } (m, n) \text{ is a call edge from} \\ & \text{procedure } p \\[1em] \beta \in \mathrm{ECS}(p) \text{ and } \alpha = \beta * \sigma(c) & \text{if } (m, n) \text{ is a return edge} \\ & \text{corresponding to a call edge} \\ & \text{from a call block } c \text{ in} \\ & \text{procedure } p \end{cases}$$

Using these relations, we define the map $\widehat{\mathrm{CM}}$, so that for each $n \in N^*$ and each path $q \in \mathrm{path}_{G^*}(r_1, n)$ of the form $(r_1, s_2, s_3, \ldots, s_{k-1}, n)$ we have

$$\widehat{\mathrm{CM}}(q) = R_{(r_1, s_2)} \circ R_{(s_2, s_3)} \circ \ldots \circ R_{(s_{k-1}, n)}\{w\}$$

Finally, for each $n \in N^*$ we define

$$\text{IAP}(r_1, n) = \{q \in \text{path}_{G^*}(r_1, n): \widehat{\text{CM}}(q) \neq \varnothing\}$$

The intuitive meaning of these concepts can be explained as follows: Since we have decided to record the actual call string by a homomorphism CM of paths into a finite set $\widehat{\Gamma}$, it is inevitable that we will also admit paths which are not in $\text{IVP}(r_1, n)$. Thus $\text{IAP}(r_1, n) \supseteq \text{IVP}(r_1, n)$ and will also contain paths which the encoding CM cannot distinguish from valid IVP paths. In particular, some returns to other than their originating calls will have to be admitted.

Having defined IAP, $\widehat{\text{CM}}$, and R, we next define F^* in essentially the same manner as in Section 7-4. Specifically, for each $(m, n) \in E^*$ we define $f^*_{(m,n)}: L^* \to L^*$ as follows: For each $\xi \in L^*$, $\alpha \in \widehat{\Gamma}$

$$f^*_{(m,n)}(\xi)(\alpha) = \bigwedge \{f_{(m,n)}(\xi(\alpha_1)): \alpha_1 R_{(m,n)} \alpha\}$$

where, by definition, an empty meet yields Ω.

F^* is now constructed from the functions $f^*_{(m,n)}$ exactly as before. The heuristic significance of this definition is the same as in Section 7-4, only now the "tag" updating which occurs when propagation takes place along an interprocedural edge involves less extensive and less precise information. The modified updating operation that has just been defined can be both one-to-many and many-to-one, possibilities which are both reflected in the above formula. It is easy to verify that both monotonicity and distributivity are preserved as we pass from (L, F) to (L^*, F^*).

Next we associate with (L^*, F^*) the data flow problem of determining the maximal fixed-point solution of the equations

$$
\begin{aligned}
x^*_{r_1} &= \{(w, 0)\} \\
x^*_n &= \bigwedge_{(m,n) \in E^*} f^*_{(m,n)}(x^*_m) \qquad n \in N^* - \{r_1\}
\end{aligned}
\qquad (7\text{-}15)
$$

As previously, a solution of these equations can be obtained by standard iterative techniques. Once this solution has been obtained, we make the following final calculation:

$$\hat{x}_n = \bigwedge_{\alpha \in \hat{\Gamma}} x^*_n(\alpha) \qquad (7\text{-}16)$$

The techniques of Section 7-4 can now be applied to analyze the procedure just described. Theorem 7-4.3 retains its validity, if restated as follows:

Theorem 7-6.2.

1. If (L, F) is distributive, then, for each $n \in N^*$, $x^*_n = y^*_n \equiv \bigwedge \{f^*_p(x^*_{r_1}): p \in \text{path}_{G^*}(r_1, n)\}$.

2. If (L, F) is monotone, then, for each $n \in N^*$, $x^*_n \leq y^*_n$.

Instead of Lemma 7-4.5, the following variant applies:

Lemma 7-6.3. Let $n \in N^*$, $p \in \text{path}_{G^*}(r_1, n)$ and $\alpha \in \hat{\Gamma}$. Then $f_p^*(x_{r_1}^*)(\alpha)$ is defined iff $\alpha \in \hat{\text{CM}}(p)$, in which case $f_p^*(x_{r_1}^*)(\alpha) = f_p(0)$.

Proof. By induction on the length of p. The assertion is obvious if p is the null execution path. Suppose that it is true for all paths with length $<k$ and let $p = (r_1, s_2, \ldots, s_k, n) \in \text{path}_{G^*}(r_1, n)$ be a path of length k. Let $p_1 = (r_1, s_2, \ldots, s_k)$. Then for each $\alpha \in \hat{\Gamma}$ we have

$$f_p^*(x_{r_1}^*)(\alpha) = f_{(s_k, n)}^*[f_{p_1}^*(x_{r_1}^*)](\alpha)$$
$$= \bigwedge \{f_{(s_k, n)}[f_{p_1}^*(x_{r_1}^*)(\alpha_1)]: \alpha_1 R_{(s_k, n)}\alpha\}$$

Thus $f_p^*(x_{r_1}^*)(\alpha)$ is defined iff there exists $\alpha_1 \in \hat{\Gamma}$ such that $\alpha_1 R_{(s_k, n)}\alpha$ and $f_{p_1}^*(x_{r_1})(\alpha_1)$ is defined. By inductive hypothesis, this is true iff there exists $\alpha_1 \in \hat{\text{CM}}(p_1)$ and $\alpha_1 R_{(s_k, n)}\alpha$, and, by the definition of $R_{(s_k, n)}$ and $\hat{\text{CM}}$, this last assertion is true iff $\alpha \in \hat{\text{CM}}(p)$. Hence, applying the inductive hypothesis again, $f_{p_1}^*(x_{r_1}^*)(\alpha_1) = f_{p_1}(0)$, for all α_1 appearing in the above meet, so that this meet equals $f_{(s_k, n)}[f_{p_1}(0)] = f_p(0)$. ∎

> *Remark:* As previously noted, and can be seen, e.g., from the proof of the last lemma, use of an encoding scheme creates chances for propagation through paths which are not interprocedurally valid. However, our lemma shows that even if an execution path q is encoded by more than one element of Γ, all these "tags" are associated with the same information, namely $f_q(0)$. Thus information is propagated correctly along each path, only more paths are now acceptable for that propagation. These observations will be made more precise in what follows.

Lemma 7-6.4. For each $n \in N^*$, $\text{IVP}(r_1, n) \subseteq \text{IAP}(r_1, n)$.

Proof. Let $q \in \text{IVP}(r_1, n)$ for some $n \in N^*$. We will show, by induction on the length of q, that $\sigma(\text{CM}(q)) \in \hat{\text{CM}}(q)$, so that, by Lemma 7-6.1, $q \in \text{IAP}(r_1, n)$.

Our assertion is obvious if q is the null execution path. Suppose it is true for all paths whose length is less than some $k \geq 0$, and let $n \in N^*$, $q \in \text{IVP}(r_1, n)$ whose length is k. Write $q = q_1 \| (m, n)$. By inductive hypothesis, $\sigma(\text{CM}(q_1)) \in \hat{\text{CM}}(q_1)$. Now, three cases are possible:

1. $(m, n) \in E^0$. In this case $\hat{\text{CM}}(q) = \hat{\text{CM}}(q_1)$ and $\text{CM}(q) = \text{CM}(q_1)$ so that $\sigma(\text{CM}(q)) \in \hat{\text{CM}}(q)$.

2. (m, n) is a call edge. Then, by definition, $\hat{\text{CM}}(q)$ contains $\sigma(\text{CM}(q_1)) * \sigma(m) = \sigma(\text{CM}(q))$.

3. (m, n) is a return edge. Let (c', r_p) denote the corresponding call edge. Since $q \in \text{IVP}(r_1, n)$, q can be decomposed as $q' \| (c', r_p) \| q'' \| (m, n)$, where $q' \in \text{IVP}(r_1, c')$ and $q'' \in \text{IVP}_0(r_p, m)$. It is evident from the definitions of the quantities involved that that $\text{CM}(q) = \text{CM}(q')$ and that $\text{CM}(q_1) = \text{CM}(q') \| (c')$. Hence $\sigma(\text{CM}(q_1)) = \sigma(\text{CM}(q)) * \sigma(c')$. It thus follows that $\sigma(\text{CM}(q))$ is a member of the set $\{\beta \in \text{ECS}(p) \mid \beta * \sigma(c') = \sigma(\text{CM}(q_1))\}$ which, by definition, is a subset of $\widehat{\text{CM}}(q)$. ■

We can now state an analog of Theorem 7-4.6:

Theorem 7-6.5.

1. If (L, F) is a distributive data flow framework, then, for each $n \in N^*$
    $$\hat{x}_n = \bigwedge \{f_p(0) : p \in \text{IAP}(r_1, n)\} \leq y_n$$
2. If (L, F) is only monotone, then, for each $n \in N^*$
    $$\hat{x}_n \leq \bigwedge \{f_p(0) : p \in \text{IAP}(r_1, n)\} \leq y_n$$

Proof.

1. Let $\alpha \in \widehat{\Gamma}$. By Theorem 7-6.2 and Lemmas 7-6.1 and 7-6.3, we have
    $$x_n^*(\alpha) = \bigwedge \{f_p^*(x_{r_1}^*)(\alpha) : p \in \text{path}_{G^*}(r_1, n)\}$$
    $$= \bigwedge \{f_p(0) : p \in \text{IAP}(r_1, n), \alpha \in \widehat{\text{CM}}(p)\}$$
    Thus, by Eq. (7-16)
    $$\hat{x}_n = \bigwedge_{\alpha \in \widehat{\Gamma}} x_n^*(\alpha) = \bigwedge \{f_p(0) : p \in \text{IAP}(r_1, n)\}$$
    By Lemma 7-6.4, this is
    $$\leq \bigwedge \{f_p(0) : p \in \text{IVP}(r_1, n)\} = y_n$$
    proving (1).
2. Can be proved in a manner completely analogous to the proof of (1), using part (2) of Theorem 7-6.2. ■

Thus $\{\hat{x}_n\}_{n \in N^*}$ is an underestimation of the meet-over-all-paths solution $\{y_n\}_{n \in N^*}$. The degree of underestimation depends on the deviation of $\text{IAP}(r_1, n)$ from $\text{IVP}(r_1, n)$, and this deviation is in turn determined by the choice of $\widehat{\Gamma}$, $*$, and σ. The most extreme underestimation results if we let $\text{IAP}(r_1, n) = \text{path}_{G^*}(r_1, n)$ for all $n \in N^*$, i.e., define $\widehat{\Gamma} = \{w\}$, $w * w = w$, and let σ map all calls to w. If we do this, then the resulting problem is essentially equivalent to a purely intraprocedural analysis, in which procedure calls and returns are interpreted as mere branch instructions.

Another more interesting encoding scheme is as follows. Choose some integer $k > 1$, and let $\hat{\Gamma}$ be the ring of residue classes modulo k. Let $m > 1$ be another integer. For each $\alpha_1, \alpha_2 \in \hat{\Gamma}$, define $\alpha_1 * \alpha_2 = m \cdot \alpha_1 + \alpha_2 (\mod k)$. Let σ be any map which maps call blocks to values between 0 and $m - 1$ (preferably in a one-to-one way). In this scheme, call strings are mapped into a base m representation modulo k of some encoding of their call blocks. Note that if $k = \infty$, i.e., if we operate with integers rather than in modular arithmetic, then $\hat{\Gamma}$ and Γ are isomorphic, with $\mathbf{b}$ corresponding to concatenation. If $k = m^j$, for some $j \geq 1$, and σ is one-to-one and does not map any call block to 0, then the encoding scheme just proposed can roughly be described as follows: Keep only the last j calls within each call string. As long as the length of a call string is less than j, update it as in Section 7-4, However, if q is a call string of length j, then, when appending to it a call edge, discard the first component of q and add the new call block to its end. When appending a return edge, check if it matches the last call in q, and, if it does, delete this call from q and add to its start all possible call blocks which call the procedure containing the first call in q. This approximation may be termed a *call-string suffix approximation*.

At present we do not have available a comprehensive theory of the proper choice of an encoding scheme. Appropriate choice of such a scheme may depend on the program being analyzed, and reflects the trade-off between tolerable complexity of the interprocedural analysis and some desired level of accuracy.

7-7. CONCLUSION

In this chapter we have studied in some detail two basic approaches to interprocedural analysis of rather general data flow problems. We have seen that by requiring the associated semilattice L to be finite, both approaches yield convergent algorithms which produce the "sharpest" interprocedural information, in a natural sense.

The main concern has been to introduce a comprehensive theory of interprocedural data flow analysis for general frameworks. Subsequent research in this area should address itself to more pragmatic issues that arise when trying to implement our approaches. Some of these issues are:

(a) *Pragmatic implementation of the functional approach for bit-vector problems.* These data flow frameworks are amenable to elimination techniques, which are more efficient than iterative techniques. However, our basic way of solving Eqs. (7-4) is iterative in nature and hence is not optimal for these problems. One would mainly like to come up with an algorithm which incorporates standard intraprocedural elimination techniques, such as interval analysis, in a modular manner, which will enable us to implement the functional approach as an extension of already existing intraprocedural algorithms rather than as a completely different algorithm.

In addition, one might wish to study the efficiency of such an implementation, bearing in mind that recursion is a somewhat rare phenomenon in actual programs, and that co-recursion is much rarer. This issue is closely related to Allen's approach of processing procedures in "inverse invocation order" (see also [Rose79] for a similar observation). However, careful refinement of this method is required to handle recursion. Additional gain might be achieved by processing "offline" parts of the flow graph which are call-free, so that one does not have to repeat all the intraprocedural processing whenever an interprocedural effect is propagated. One possible approach to this problem, which, however, is probably not the best possible one for implementation, is indicated in [Rose79, Section 8].

(b) *Pragmatic implementation of more complex interprocedural data flow problems.* If the relevant framework is not amenable to elimination, then the functional approach may be inadequate for such a problem. Moreover, some commonly occurring complex data flow problems, such as constant propagation [Hech77], type analysis [Tene74b, Jone76], value flow [Schw75b] or range analysis [Harr77a], are usually solved by algorithms which make use of the *use-definition map* [Alle69] in a way which propagates information only to points where it is actually needed. As indicated in [Shar77], interprocedural extension of such algorithms calls for some proper interprocedural extension of the use-definition map itself. It seems that such an extension can be based on the call-strings approach (or the approximative call-strings approach), but exact details have yet to be worked out.

(c) *Extending our approaches to handle reference parameters.* Here the problem of "aliasing" (i.e., temporary equivalence of two program variables during a procedure call) arises, which complicates matters considerably if "sharpest" information is still to be obtained. Major work in this area has been done by Rosen [Rose79].

(d) *Extending the ideas of the call-strings approach methods which take into account more semantic restrictions on the execution flow.* Thus only flow paths which satisfy such restrictions would be traced during analysis. The call-return pattern of interprocedural flow is but one such possible restriction (though a very important one). For example, one might also keep track of the values of boolean flags which control intraprocedural branches. Current research in such directions by Holley and Rosen at IBM seems quite promising. (We are indebted to Barry K. Rosen for some stimulating discussion concerning the above-mentioned research.)

The present chapter has been motivated by the research on the design and implementation of an optimizing compiler for the SETL programming language at Courant Institute, New York University. SETL is a very-high-level language [Schw75d] which fits into our interprocedural model; i.e., parameters are called by value and no procedure variables are allowed. Active research is now under way to implement the approaches suggested in this chapter in the optimizer of our system, as discussed in (a) and (b) above.

Part III

APPLICATIONS
TO SOFTWARE ENGINEERING

The potential impact of data flow analysis and other closely related tools, such as symbolic execution, on software engineering is only now beginning to be realized, at least in part because software engineering is itself a relatively young discipline. It is becoming clear that they can be beneficial in program development, debugging, verification, and documentation. This part of the book includes two chapters: one which surveys this area and one which presents some of the methods in detail.

In the area of program development, current efforts to create artificially intelligent programmer's apprentices [Hewi75,RicC76] have as one of their major problems the conceptualization and representation of a program's or program segment's actions. Data flow analysis and symbolic execution are major tools in this area because they provide information about all possible executions of the code at once. The apprentice can use these tools to obtain a description of a program segment's actions and can then compare it with a specification of the programmer's intention to determine the validity of the code or can combine it with similarly obtained descriptions of other segments to obtain higher-level descriptions of larger program segments. This process may ultimately result in the program's being verified, but is more likely during program development to reveal its internal errors, interfacing errors, and

235

shortcomings and to do so in a way which helps to pinpoint their sources. This methodology holds particular promise in the organization of large systems from separately written modules, since the task of testing compatibility of module specifications and interfaces is essentially a flow-analytic one. At a more concrete level, flow analysis has been used in a content-oriented LISP editing system [BroA78] which checks context consistency as it modifies program text.

Applications to debugging are discussed at length in the next two chapters, so we shall not discuss them here. The uses of these tools in verification and documentation are closely related to those described above for program development. Indeed, essentially similar methods can generate invariant assertions for verification [Cous77c] or a description of the action of a program segment which can be augmented with programmer-generated prose to create adequate documentation.

Chapter 8

Using Data Flow Tools in Software Engineering†

Leon Osterweil

8-1. INTRODUCTION

Software engineering is a discipline which has recently been experiencing a period of considerable but unstructured growth. It now shows signs of embarking upon a phase of coordination and consolidation. There has been a large amount of work devoted to the development of software engineering tools. This seems to be particularly promising work, as tools are vehicles for capturing software engineering concepts in a way which is tangible and useful to software practitioners. Through well-implemented tools, desirable policies can be promulgated and enforced throughout a project, in a way which increases the coordination and efficiency of that project.

In the past, the quality of tools produced has been spotty. Worse, however, the goals of most tools and the domains of their efficacy have rarely been clearly enunciated. As a consequence, it has been difficult for the community of software practitioners to select tools appropriate for facilitating work on the specific tasks comprising their software development activities.

†The research reported in this chapter was partially supported by the National Science Foundation under grant MCS77–02194 and the United States Army Research Office under grant DAAG29–78–G–0046.

Thus specification of the goals and domains of efficacy of a tool should be an important part of its documentation. The availability of such specifications should enable practitioners to intelligently select and configure a set of tools into an environment capable of supporting specific software production activities.

In this chapter we propose a generic configuration of tool capabilities. We categorize many of the available tools into a few broad classes, and show how these classes have properties which are nicely complementary. We hypothesize that testing, documentation, and verification are three of the most important software production activities and suggest that these activities can be nicely supported by different configurations of representatives of these few tool classes.

8-2.   CLASS ONE: DYNAMIC TESTING AND ANALYSIS TOOLS

The terms *dynamic testing* and *dynamic analysis*, as used here, are intended to describe most of the systems known as execution monitors, software monitors, and dynamic debugging systems ([Balz69, Fair75, Stuc75, Gris70]).

In dynamic testing systems, a comprehensive record of a single execution of a program is built. This record—the execution history—is usually obtained by instrumenting the source program with code whose purpose is to capture information about the progress of execution. Most such systems implant monitoring code after each statement of the program. This code captures such information as the number of the statement just executed, the names of variables whose values have been altered by executing the statement, the new values of these variables, and the outcomes of any tests performed by the statement. The execution history is saved in a file so that it can later be perused by the tester. This perusal is usually facilitated by the production of summary tables and statistics such as statement execution frequency histograms and variable evolution trees.

Despite the existence of such tables and statistics, it is often quite difficult for a human tester to detect the source or even the presence of errors in the execution. Hence, many dynamic testing systems also monitor each statement execution, checking for such error conditions as division by zero and out-of-bounds array references. The monitors implanted are usually programmed to automatically issue error messages immediately upon detecting such conditions in order to avoid having the errors concealed by the bulk of a large execution history.

Some of this can be exemplified with the aid of a simple-minded program. Figure 8-1 shows a program whose purpose is to produce the areas of rectangles and triangles having integer dimensions, when the dimensions are

```
 1          PROCEDURE AREAS;
 2          DECLARE REAL A(20, 20, 2), INTEGER P1, P2, P3;
 3              PROCEDURE INIT (H, B);
 4              DECLARE INTEGER H, B, I, J, K, REAL XK;
 5              IF H > 20 THEN ERROR STOP;
 6              IF B > 20 THEN ERROR STOP;
 7              DO FOR I = 1 TO H;
 8                  A(I, 1, 1) = I;
 9                  DO FOR J = 2 TO B;
10                      A(I, J, 1) = A(I, J − 1, 1) + I;
11                      END;
12                  END;
13              K = 2;
14              XK = 2.0;
15              DO FOR I = 1 TO H;
16                  DO FOR J = 1 TO B;
17                      A(I, J, K) = A(I, J, K − 1) / XK;
18                      END;
19                  END;
20              END;
21          PROCEDURE LOOKUP (I, J, K);
22          DECLARE INTEGER I, J, K;
23          CASE;
24,25           K = 1:  PRINT "AREA OF" I, J "RECTANGLE IS" A(I, J, K);
26,27           K = 2:  PRINT "AREA OF" I, J "TRIANGLE IS" A(I, J, K);
28,29           ELSE:   PRINT "PARAMETER ERROR:  K = " K;
30              END;
31          END;
32          CALL INIT (20, 20);
33          LOOP FOREVER;
34              READ P1, P2, P3;
35              IF P3 = 0 THEN STOP;
36                      ELSE CALL LOOKUP (P1, P2, P3);
37              END;
38          END;
```

Figure 8-1 An example program

given as input. The program, a procedure called *areas*, is divided into two major functional portions. One function, implemented by procedure *lookup*, returns the area of the triangle or rectangle by using a table lookup. The two dimensions input for the object are used as the first two indices into the table, a three-dimensional array, A. If the area of a rectangle is desired, the value 1 must be input with the dimensions, while a 2 indicates the area of a triangle is desired. A value 0 causes the lookup loop to terminate. The value 1 or 2 is used as the third index of array A.

Array A is initialized by the second functional portion of the program, which is implemented by the procedure *init*. This procedure initializes A in a somewhat indirect way, perhaps motivated by an interest in eliminating the need for multiplications.

In Fig. 8-2 we see the same program augmented by the code necessary to monitor for two types of errors: division by zero and out-of-bounds array

```
1       PROCEDURE AREAS;
2       DECLARE REAL A(20, 20, 2), INTEGER P1, P2, P3;
3           PROCEDURE INIT (H, B);
4           DECLARE INTEGER H, B, I, J, K, REAL XK;
5           IF H > 20 THEN ERROR STOP;
6           IF B > 20 THEN ERROR STOP;
7           DO FOR I = 1 TO H;
E1              IF ~ (1 <= I <= 20) THEN SUBSCRIPT RANGE ERROR;
E2              IF ~ (1 <= 1 <= 20) THEN SUBSCRIPT RANGE ERROR;
E3              IF ~ (1 <= 1 <= 2) THEN SUBSCRIPT RANGE ERROR;
8               A(I, 1, 1) = I;
9               DO FOR J = 2 TO B;
E4                  IF ~ (1 <= I <= 20) THEN SUBSCRIPT RANGE ERROR;
E5                  IF ~ (1 <= J <= 20) THEN SUBSCRIPT RANGE ERROR;
E6                  IF ~ (1 <= 1 <= 2) THEN SUBSCRIPT RANGE ERROR;
E7                  IF ~ (1 <= I <= 20) THEN SUBSCRIPT RANGE ERROR;
E8                  IF ~ (1 <= J − 1 <= 20) THEN SUBSCRIPT RANGE ERROR;
E9                  IF ~ (1 <= 1 <= 2) THEN SUBSCRIPT RANGE ERROR;
10                  A(I, J, 1) = A(I, J − 1, 1) + I;
11                  END;
12              END;
13          K = 2;
14          XK = 2.0;
15          DO FOR I = 1 TO H;
16              DO FOR J = 1 TO B;
E10                 IF ~ (1 <= I <= 20) THEN SUBSCRIPT RANGE ERROR;
E11                 IF ~ (1 <= J <= 20) THEN SUBSCRIPT RANGE ERROR;
E12                 IF ~ (1 <= K <= 2) THEN SUBSCRIPT RANGE ERROR;
E13                 IF ~ (1 <= I <= 20) THEN SUBSCRIPT RANGE ERROR;
E14                 IF ~ (1 <= J <= 20) THEN SUBSCRIPT RANGE ERROR;
E15                 IF ~ (1 <= K − 1 <= 2) THEN SUBSCRIPT RANGE ERROR;
E16                 IF XK = 0 THEN ZERODIVIDE ERROR;
17                  A(I, J, K) = A(I, J, K − 1) / XK;
18                  END;
19              END;
20          END;
21      PROCEDURE LOOKUP (I, J, K);
22      DECLARE INTEGER I, J, K;
23      CASE;
24          K = 1:
E17             IF ~ (1 <= I <= 20) THEN SUBSCRIPT RANGE ERROR;
E18             IF ~ (1 <= J <= 20) THEN SUBSCRIPT RANGE ERROR;
E19             IF ~ (1 <= K <= 2) THEN SUBSCRIPT RANGE ERROR;
25              PRINT "AREA OF" I, J "RECTANGLE IS" A(I, J, K);
26          K = 2:
E20             IF ~ (1 <= I <= 20) THEN SUBSCRIPT RANGE ERROR;
E21             IF ~ (1 <= J <= 20) THEN SUBSCRIPT RANGE ERROR;
E22             IF ~ (1 <= K <= 2) THEN SUBSCRIPT RANGE ERROR;
27              PRINT "AREA OF" I, J "TRIANGLE IS" A(I, J, K);
28,29       ELSE:  PRINT "PARAMETER ERROR: K = " K;
30          END;
31      END;
```

Figure 8-2 The program of Fig. 8-1, with probes for zero-divide and subscript range errors inserted

The probes shown are those which would be inserted by a naive dynamic test tool and have statement numbers preceded by the letter "E".

```
32        CALL INIT (20, 20);
33        LOOP FOREVER;
34           READ P1, P2, P3;
35           IF P3 = 0 THEN STOP;
36                       ELSE CALL LOOKUP (P1, P2, P3);
37           END;
38        END;
```

Figure 8-2   (cont.)

reference. This monitor-augmented program is typical of the code which would be generated automatically by a straightforward dynamic testing tool. The monitors are positioned so as to assure that an occurrence of either of the two errors will be detected immediately before it would occur in the actual execution of the program. To a human observer it is obvious that many of these probes are redundant. We shall be very much concerned with studying the forms of automated analysis necessary to suppress such probes.

Some systems [Fair75, Stuc75] additionally allow the human program tester to create his own monitors and direct their implantation anywhere within the program.

The greatest power of these systems is derived from the possibility of using them to determine whether a program's execution is proceeding as intended. The intent of the program is captured by assertions about the desired and correct relation among values of program variables. These assertions may be specified to be of local or global validity. The dynamic testing system creates and places monitors as necessary to determine whether the program is behaving in accordance with its asserted intent as execution proceeds.

Figure 8-3 shows how the example program might be annotated with assertions. These assertions are designed to capture the intent of the program and explicitly state certain nontrivial error conditions to which this program seems particularly vulnerable. Figure 8-4 shows how the code of Fig. 8-1 might be augmented in order to test dynamically for adherence to or violation of the assertions shown in Fig. 8-3. It should be clear from this example that dynamic assertion verification offers the possibility of very meaningful and powerful testing. With this technique, the tester can in a convenient notation specify the precise desired functional behavior of the program (presumably by drawing upon the program's design and requirements specifications). Every execution is then tirelessly monitored for adherence to these specifications. This sort of testing obviously can focus on the most meaningful aspects of the program far more sharply than the more mechanical approaches involving monitoring only for violations of certain standard conditions such as division by zero or array bounds violation.

The previous paragraphs should make it clear that dynamic testing systems have strong error detection and exploration capabilities. They excel at

```
1          PROCEDURE AREAS;
2          DECLARE REAL A(20, 20, 2), INTEGER P1, P2, P3;
3              PROCEDURE INIT (H, B);
A1             ASSERT NO SIDE EFFECTS;
4              DECLARE INTEGER H, B, I, J, K, REAL XK;
5              IF H > 20 THEN ERROR STOP;
6              IF B > 20 THEN ERROR STOP;
7              DO FOR I = 1 TO H;
8                  A(I, 1, 1) = I;
9                  DO FOR J = 2 TO B;
10                     A(I, J, 1) = A(I, J − 1, 1) + I;
A2                     ASSERT A(I, J, 1) = I * J;
11                     END;
12                 END;
13             K = 2;
14             XK = 2.0;
15             DO FOR I = 1 TO H;
16                 DO FOR J = 1 TO B;
17                     A(I, J, K) = A(I, J, K − 1) / XK;
A3                     ASSERT A(I, J, 2) = 0.5 * A(I, J, 1);
18                     END;
19                 END;
20             END;
21             PROCEDURE LOOKUP (I, J, K);
A4             ASSERT NO SIDE EFFECTS;
22             DECLARE INTEGER I, J, K;
A5             ASSERT 1 <= I <= 20;
A6             ASSERT 1 <= J <= 20;
23             CASE;
24,25              K = 1:  PRINT "AREA OF" I, J "RECTANGLE IS" A(I, J, K);
26,27              K = 2:  PRINT "AREA OF" I, J "TRIANGLE IS" A (I, J, K);
28,29              ELSE:  PRINT "PARAMETER ERROR:  K = " K;
30                 END;
31             END;
32         CALL INIT (20, 20);
33         LOOP FOREVER;
34             READ P1, P2, P3;
35             IF P3 = 0 THEN STOP;
36                     ELSE CALL LOOKUP (P1, P2, P3);
37             END;
38         END;
```

Figure 8-3   The program of Fig. 8-1 as it might be augmented by
assertions capturing the intent of the code

detecting errors during the execution of a program and at tracing these errors
to their sources. It should be observed, however, that this information is
obtained only as a result of an execution occurring in response to actual program input data. The generation of this input data is the responsibility of the
tester and in many cases involves significant effort and insight into the program. In addition, as Figs. 8-2 and 8-4 show, the instrumentation code
required in order to do error monitoring is often quite large, sometimes
increasing both the size and execution time of the subject program several

```
1        PROCEDURE AREAS;
2        DECLARE REAL A(20, 20, 2), INTEGER P1, P2, P3;
3           PROCEDURE INIT (H, B);
4           DECLARE INTEGER H, B, I, J, K, REAL XK;
P1,1        DECLARE INTEGER HTEMP, BTEMP;
P1,2        HTEMP = H;
P1,3        BTEMP = B;
5           IF H > 20 THEN ERROR STOP;
6           IF B > 20 THEN ERROR STOP;
7           DO FOR I = 1 TO H;
8              A(I, 1, 1) = I;
9              DO FOR J = 2 TO B;
10                A(I, J, 1) = A(I, J − 1, 1) + I
P2,1              IF A(I, J, 1) ≠ I ∗ J THEN PRINT "ASSERTION VIOLATION
11                END;                     AFTER STATEMENT 10" A(I, J, 1), I, J;
12             END;
13          K = 2;
14          XK = 2.0;
15          DO FOR I = 1 TO H;
16             DO FOR J = 1 TO B;
17                A(I, J, K) = A(I, J, K − 1) / XK;
P3,1              IF A(I, J, 2) ≠ 0.5 ∗ A(I, J, 1) THEN PRINT "ASSERTION
                                           VIOLATION AFTER
                                           STATEMENT 17" A(I, J, 2),
18                END;                     I, J;
19             END;
P1,4        IF H ≠ HTEMP THEN PRINT "SIDE EFFECTS VIOLATION FOR H" H,
                           HTEMP;
P1,5        IF B ≠ BTEMP THEN PRINT "SIDE EFFECTS VIOLATION FOR B" B,
                           BTEMP;
20          END;
21       PROCEDURE LOOKUP (I, J, K);
22       DECLARE INTEGER I, J, K;
P4,1     DECLARE INTEGER ITEMP, JTEMP, KTEMP;
P4,2     ITEMP = I;
P4,3     JTEMP = J;
P4,4     KTEMP = K;
P5,1     IF ∼ (1 <= I <= 20) THEN PRINT "ASSERTION VIOLATION AFTER
                           STATEMENT 22" I;
P6,1     IF ∼ (1 <= J <= 20) THEN PRINT "ASSERTION VIOLATION AFTER
                           STATEMENT 22" J;
23       CASE;
24,25       K = 1: PRINT "AREA OF" I, J "RECTANGLE IS" A(I, J, K);
26,27       K = 2: PRINT "AREA OF" I, J "TRIANGLE IS" A(I, J, K);
28,29       ELSE: PRINT "PARAMETER ERROR:  K = " K;
30       END;
```

Figure 8-4 The program of Fig. 8-1 as it might be augmented by probes inserted by an assertion-checking tool in response to the assertions shown in Fig. 8-3

The inserted probes are denoted by line numbers beginning with P. Line number P*i,j* is attached to the jth statement generated as a result of assertion A*i* in Fig. 8-3.

```
P4,5        IF I ≠ ITEMP THEN PRINT "SIDE EFFECTS VIOLATION FOR I" I,
                          ITEMP;
P4,6        IF J ≠ JTEMP THEN PRINT "SIDE EFFECTS VIOLATION FOR J" J,
                          JTEMP;
P4,7        IF K ≠ KTEMP THEN PRINT "SIDE EFFECTS VIOLATION FOR K" K,
                          KTEMP;
31          END;
32      CALL INIT (20, 20);
33      LOOP FOREVER;
34          READ P1, P2, P3;
35          IF P3 = 0 THEN STOP;
36                      ELSE CALL LOOKUP (P1, P2, P3);
37          END;
38      END;
```

Figure 8-4   (cont.)

times over. Perhaps more important, however, is the fact that dynamic testing systems are capable of examining only a single execution of a program, and the results obtained are not applicable to any other execution of the program. Hence, the nonoccurrence of errors in a given execution does not guarantee their absence in the program itself.

From the preceding discussion it can be seen that dynamic testing is a powerful technique for detecting the presence of errors. Hence it is a powerful testing technique. Because its results are applicable only to a single execution, it cannot be used to effectively demonstrate the absence of errors. Thus, it is not an appropriate technique for verification (i.e., the process of showing that a program necessarily behaves as intended). Furthermore, although the assertions used for dynamic verification may themselves be valuable documentation of intent, dynamic testing does not itself create useful documentation of the program. Finally it is important to observe that the benefits of dynamic testing can only be derived as the result of heavy expenditures of memory and execution time.

8-3.   CLASS TWO: STATIC ANALYSIS TOOLS

In the category of static analysis tools, we include all programs and systems which infer results about the nature of a program from consideration and analysis of a complete model of some aspect of the program. An important characteristic of such tools is that they do not necessitate execution of the subject program, yet infer results applicable to all possible executions.

A very straightforward example of such a tool is a syntax analyzer. At the end of a syntax scan it is possible to infer that the program is free of syntactic errors.

A more interesting example is a tool such as FACES [Rama75] or RXVP [Mill74] which performs a variety of more sophisticated error scans.

These tools both, for example, perform a scan to determine whether all procedure invocations are correctly matched to the corresponding declarations. The lengths of corresponding argument and parameter lists are compared, and the corresponding individual parameters and arguments are also compared for type and dimensionality agreement. By comparing every procedure invocation with its corresponding declaration in this way, it is possible to assure that the program is free of any possibility of such a mismatch error. Note that this analysis requires no program execution, yet it produces a result applicable to all possible executions. This sort of analysis, requiring a comparison of combinations of statements, can also be used to demonstrate that a program is free of such defects as illegal type conversions, confusion of array dimensionality, superfluous labels, and missing or uninvoked procedures.

Data flow analysis is a still more sophisticated form of static analysis which is based upon consideration of sequences of events occurring along the various execution paths through a program. As such it is capable of more powerful analytic results than combinational scans such as those just described. The DAVE system [Oste76, Fosd76] is a good example of such a tool. This system examines all paths originating from the start of a FORTRAN program and is capable of determining that no path, when executed, will cause a reference to an uninitialized variable. DAVE also examines all paths originating from a variable definition and is capable of determining whether or not there is a subsequent reference to the variable. A definition not subsequently referenced is called a "dead" definition. Hence DAVE is also capable of showing that a FORTRAN program is free of dead variable definitions.

Data flow analysis is based upon examination of a flow graph model of the subject program. The flow graph of each program unit is created, and its nodes are annotated with descriptions of the uses of all variables at all nodes. Nodes representing procedure invocations cannot be annotated in this way immediately. Figure 8-5 shows the collection of three annotated flow graphs which would be created to represent the variable usage by the statements of the example program of Fig. 8-1. Procedures such as *init* and *lookup* which invoke no others are completely annotated. For such procedures a data flow analyzer like DAVE would determine the presence or absence of uninitialized variable references and dead variable definitions. This can be done by using data flow analysis algorithms such as LIVE and AVAIL [Hech75] to efficiently determine the usage patterns of the program variables along the paths leading into or out of a program node.

The precise functioning of the algorithms can be stated as follows. Suppose either of two events **ref** or **def**† can happen to a program variable,

---

†The two events are usually given as **gen** and **kill**. For the sake of clarity, we prefer to use **ref** and **def**.

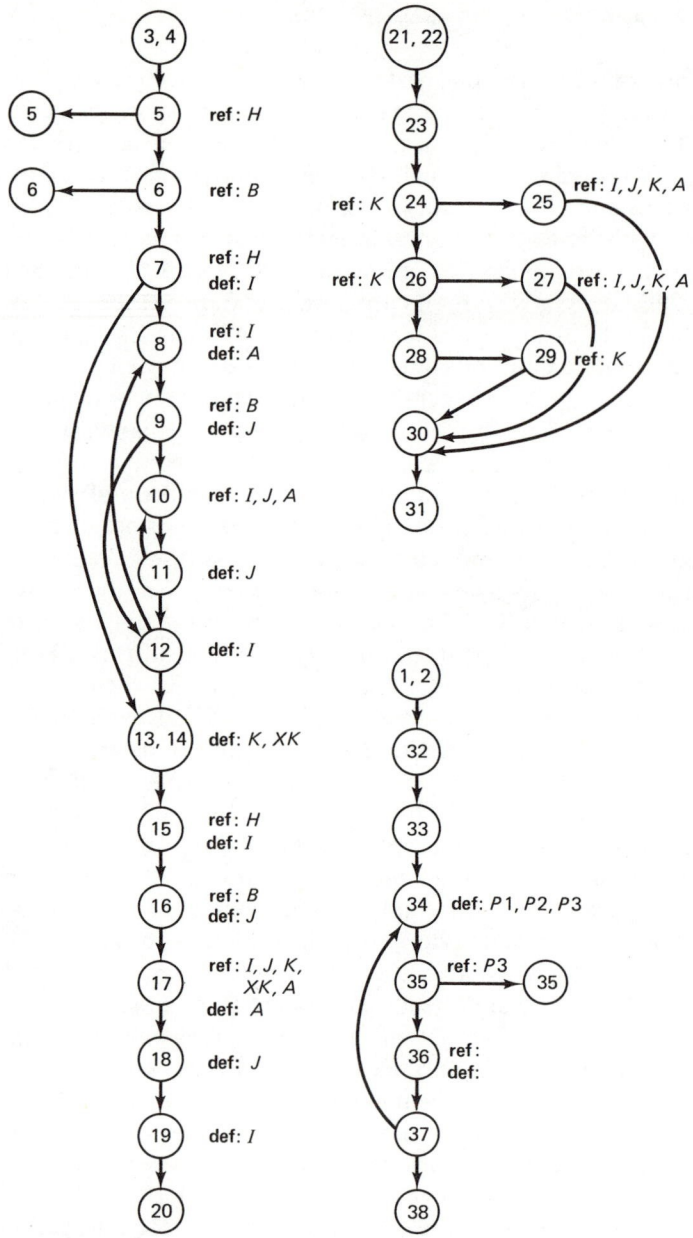

Figure 8-5 The flow graphs of the three procedures in the example program of Fig. 8-1

The node numbers are derived from Fig. 8-1. For each node, the program variables which are defined there and those referenced there are listed. Note that node 36 represents a procedure invocation with variables as arguments. Thus the **ref** and **def** lists cannot be completed.

say x, at a program node. The algorithms determine the functions LIVE {program nodes} $\longrightarrow$ {**T**, **F**} and AVAIL: {program nodes} $\longrightarrow$ {**T**, **F**} for the nodes of the graph, where these functions are defined as follows:

If n is an arbitrary program node, then LIVE$(n) = $ **T** (and we say "x is *live* at n") if and only if there exists a path p, from the node n to another node n' such that x is **ref** at n' and x is not **def** at any node of p between n and n'. Otherwise LIVE$(n) = $ **F**.

If n is an arbitrary program node, then AVAIL$(n) = $ **T** (and we say "x is *available* at n") if and only if for each path p, from the program start node s to n there is a node n' between s and n such that x is **def** at n', and x is not **ref** at any node between n' and n. Otherwise AVAIL$(n) = $ **F**.

From these definitions, it is seen that if a variable x is live at the program start node then an uninitialized reference to x is possible along some path. On the other hand if x is not live at the start node, then x cannot be referenced before definition for any program execution. Similarly, suppose n is a node at which x is **def**. Then if x is live at n, there must be a path from n to a node at which x is **ref**. If x is not live at n, then n represents a dead definition of x.

From this it should be apparent that a live analysis for each variable in a program is capable of determining the presence or absence of these two types of errors in the program. ([Fosd76] shows that avail can be used to determine important variations and subcases of these errors.) This analysis of all variables can be carried out in parallel by the algorithms described in [Hech75] in time which can ordinarily be counted on to be linear in the number of graph nodes for usual program flowgraphs.

The reader should verify that none of the variables local to procedures *init* and *lookup*, represented by the graphs in Fig. 8-5, is live at the procedure start nodes. Moreover, there are no local variables which are both **def** and not live at any node. Hence there are no uninitialized variable reference or dead definition errors for these variables in these procedures. It is important, however, to observe that if, for example, the variable XK were misspelled in statement 14, or if statement 14 were omitted, then XK would be live at node 3. This would correctly diagnose the consequent uninitialized reference at statement 17.

The analysis of the main procedure of Fig. 8-5 can be completed after the **ref** and **def** usage of P1, P2, and P3 in statement 36 is determined. This is accomplished by observing how procedure *lookup* uses its parameters. First, a linear scan of the **def** lists for *lookup*'s nodes is used to ascertain which parameters are **def** for *lookup*. Next the results of a live scan are examined. If a parameter Pi is live at node 21, then Pi is **ref** for procedure *lookup*. These annotations are then transferred position-by-position from the parameter list in statement 21 to the argument list in statement 36. In this way, it is determined that P1, P2, and P3 are all **ref** at node 36 and none of these arguments is **def**.

Having done this, it is possible to complete the data flow analysis of the main program, as described above.

In summary we have seen that static analysis can be used to determine the presence or absence of certain classes of errors and to produce certain kinds of program documentation. Hence it is useful as an adjunct to a testing procedure and offers weak verification capabilities. It is also useful in supplying limited forms of documentation (e.g., the input/output behavior of a procedure's parameters and global variables). There is currently ongoing research which indicates that static analysis, particularly data flow analysis, can be used to both verify and test for wider classes of errors, as well as to produce additional forms of documentation (e.g., [Tayl79]).

Of particular interest to us here is the possibility of using static data flow analysis to suppress certain of the probes generated by dynamic verification tools as part of a comprehensive test procedure. As noted earlier, many of these probes generated by dynamic test aids are redundant. Their presence adds to the size and execution time of a test run, yet has no diagnostic value. Hence an automatic procedure which removes them makes testing more efficient. It also serves to focus attention on the importance of exercising the remaining probes. Sometimes it is possible to remove all the probes generated by an assertion or a single error criterion. In this case, it has been de facto demonstrated that the error being tested for cannot occur, and this aspect of the program's behavior has been verified. This perspective shows how testing and verification activities can be coordinated with each other.

For a specific example of this, let us examine the program in Fig. 8-2. We will demonstrate how the three static analysis approaches—line-by-line, combinational, and data flow—can remove progressively more error probes. It is perhaps illuminating to observe that what is being contemplated here is actually code optimization in the classical sense (e.g., see [Alle76, Scha73]). We are attempting to identify and remove redundant code in some cases and to move code to more advantageous positions in other cases. Even the techniques employed are derived directly from optimization techniques.

A straightforward line-by-line scan of the program in Fig. 8-2 will suffice to remove several test probes. Clearly the inequality tests in statements E2, E3, E6, and E9 must always be true. Hence no more sophisticated analysis is needed to justify the removal of these probes.

A combinational examination of contiguous sequences of tests can eliminate other probes. For example, E4 and E7 contain identical tests, without any intervening flow of control or test variable alteration. Hence one of the tests can be removed. Similarly, either E10 or E13 can be removed, and either E11 or E14 can be removed. This sort of probe removal is based upon analysis that is quite similar to "peephole optimization" [Scha73].

Additional probe removal can be justified by data flow analysis arguments. Suppose the flow graph of the program in Fig. 8-5 were created and annotated as follows. Each node has a **def** list consisting of the range test occurring at that node. The **ref** list at a node consists of all tests referring to variables altered by a definition at this node. Thus for example we would say that $(1 \leq J \leq 20)$ is **def** at E5 and E11, and that $(1 \leq J \leq 20)$ is **def** at E1 and at E4. We would also say that $(1 \leq J \leq 20)$ and $(1 \leq J - 1 \leq 20)$ are **ref** at 9 and 11. More details of this annotation scheme can be found in [Oste77] and [Boll79].

Based upon these conventions, we conclude that if a particular test predicate P is both **def** and available at a particular node n, then the test at node n is redundant. This analysis could be used to remove the test probes at E4 and E7, as well as the probes at E19 and E22. It should be noted that this analysis is more powerful than the combinational analysis outlined above and thus capable of justifying the removal of the probes named earlier.

Static analysis can also be used to justify the deletion of certain probes inserted in response to assertions. Note that assertion A1 in Fig. 8-3 expands to probes P1,1; P1,2; P1,3; P1,4; and P1,5. Assertion A4 also expands to five probes in the program in Fig. 8-4. All these probes could be avoided if a static scan were used first to determine which (if any) of the procedure parameters were used as outputs (**def**s) by the procedure.

In this case static analysis can be used to remove all probes resulting from an assertion. Hence verification of the assertion can be achieved. On the other hand, we saw that many, but not all, of the subscript range checking probes can be removed by static analysis. We shall show shortly that some additional probes can be removed by using symbolic execution and constraint solving.

We have thus shown that there are significant assertion types and error categories which can be completely verified through static analysis. It seems important to determine which other assertion types and error categories give rise to probes which can be partially or totally removed by static analysis. This is currently an open research area. It is clear, however, that assertions of functional equality such as A2 and A3 are beyond easy verification by static analysis. Furthermore the removal of subscript range test probes involving functions of test variables (e.g., $1 \leq J - 1 \leq 20$ in E8) seems to require either a set of special-case static analyses or a different, more general form of analysis. We discuss such a different type of analysis next.

8-4. CLASS THREE: SYMBOLIC EXECUTION TOOLS

By symbolic execution, we mean the process of computing the values of a program's variables as functions which represent the sequence of operations carried out as execution is traced along a specific path through the program. If the path symbolically executed is a path from a procedure start node to an output statement, then the symbolic execution will show the functions by which all the output values are computed. The only unknowns in these functions will be the input values (both procedure parameters and read-in values).

Thus, for example, suppose we symbolically execute the path 1, 2, 32, 3, 4, 5, 6, 7, 8, 9, 10, 11, 10, 11 in the program shown in Fig. 8-1. At node 8 the value of I will be "1", and the value of $A(1, 1, 1)$ will also be "1". After node 10 has been executed the first time, the value of J will be "2" and $A(1, 2, 1)$ will be "1 + 1". The next time node 10 is symbolically executed, J will be "3" and $A(1, 3, 1)$ will be "1 + 1 + 1". If the path 8, 9, 10, 11, 10 is symbolically executed, then when node 8 is reached the value of I will be an unknown and hence represented by "I". The value of $A(I, 1, 1)$ will likewise be represented by "I". When node 10 is reached for the first time, J will receive the value "2" and $A(I, 2, 1)$ will receive the value "$I + I$". Similarly, the next time node 10 is reached, J will receive the value "3" and $A(I, 3, 1)$ will receive the value "$I + I + I$".

A small number of symbolic execution tools have been built [Howd78, King76, ClaL76a]. These tools mechanize the creation of the formulas and maintain incremental symbol tables. They employ formula simplification heuristics in an attempt to forestall the growth in size of the generated formulas and foster recognition of the underlying functional relations. (It should be noted, however, that these simplifiers do not take roundoff error into account and, therefore, may misrepresent the actual function computed by a sequence of floating-point computations.) Hence a symbolic execution tool would report the value of $A(I, 3, 1)$ after two iterations of the loop at node 9 to be "$3 * I$".

The foregoing discussion strongly indicates that symbolic execution is an excellent technique for documenting a program. Symbolic traces provide documentation of the actual functioning of a program along any specific path. In order to use symbolic execution as a technique for testing and verification, however, it is necessary to augment the technique with a constraint-solving capability.

In order to clarify this, let us begin by observing that the above-described functional behavior occurs only when the given path is executed. In general, however, a given program can execute an (often infinite) variety of paths, depending upon the program's input values. The conditions under which a given path is executed can often be determined by symbolic execution and constraint solution. Consider the program given in Fig. 8-1, as represented by the flow graph in Fig. 8-5. Each edge of the flow graph can be labeled by a predicate describing the conditions under which the edge will be traversed. Thus, for example, the edge (7, 8) is labeled "$H \geq 1$", the edge (9, 10) is labeled "$B \geq 2$", (5, 6) is labeled "$H \geq 20$", and edge (11, 10) is labeled "$J \leq B$" (note that node 11 is assumed to represent the loop incrementation and termination test operations). Sequential control flow edges such as $(8, 9)$ and $(10, 11)$ are labeled by the predicate "true". Now clearly a given path will be executed if and only if all of the predicates attached to all its edges are satisfied. Unfortunately a simple textual scan will express these constraints only in terms of the variables within the statements. Thus the constraints will in general not show their underlying interrelations. If the constraints are expressed in terms of the formulas derived through symbolic execution of the path, then a set of constraints all expressed in terms of the program's input values is obtained. Any solution of this set of constraints is a set of input values sufficient to force execution of the given path.

Thus, for example, the nontrivial constraints arising from the path 3, 4, 5, 6, 7, 8, 9, 10, 11, 10, 11 are:

$$H < 20 \quad \text{from } (5, 6)$$
$$B < 20 \quad \text{from } (6, 7)$$
$$H > 1 \quad \text{from } (7, 8)$$
$$B \geq 2 \quad \text{from } (9, 10)$$
$$3 \leq B \quad \text{from } (11, 10)$$

From this we infer that this path will be executed if and only if $3 \leq B \leq 20$ and $1 \leq H \leq 20$. Hence argument values in these ranges will force execution of the specified path.

If we were to symbolically execute the path 1, 2, 32, 3, 4, 5, 6, 7, 8, 9, 10, 11, 10, 11, then the constraints would be:

$$3 \leq 20 \leq 20$$
$$1 \leq 20 \leq 20$$

These are all satisfied; hence we can infer that the path will always be executed.

It is important to observe that some constraint systems are unsatisfiable, indicating that the path spawning them is unexecutable. We shall make important use of this shortly. No less important is the observation that the problem of determining a solution to an arbitrary system of constraints is in general unsolvable. Hence we must not expect that this potentially useful capability can be infallibly implemented.

Experimentation has indicated, however, that for an important class of programs the constraints actually generated are quite tractable [ClaL76a].

Testing and verification capabilities can be achieved by attempting to solve constraints embodying error conditions and statements of intent. Thus, for example, if we create a predicate constraining the subscript I to be "$I < 1$" at statement 8, we are specifying an out-of-bounds array reference error. This constraint is clearly inconsistent with the constraint "$I \geq 1$" attached to edge $(7, 8)$. Hence it is impossible for the first array subscript at statement 8 to be less than the lower bound. Hence we have shown that one of the tests generated in Fig. 8-2 is superfluous. A symbolic execution of a path from node 1 through node 8 will similarly show that testing I against 20 is superfluous for that path. The dynamic test for that error condition can be safely removed if it is shown that all paths through node 8 must create constraints inconsistent with "$I \geq 20$." In this example that is the case because procedure *init* does not alter the value of H and *init* is always invoked with $H = 20$. These facts can be inferred from static analysis. Hence a combination of static analysis, symbolic execution, and constraint solution can be used to eliminate statement E1 of Fig. 8-2. Similar arguments can be used to eliminate statements E4, E7, E5, E8, E10, E11, E12, E13, E14, E15, E19, and E22.

Statements E8 and E15 are particularly interesting. It could be argued that static analysis is sufficient to eliminate these subscript-checking probes as well. The subscripts being checked here, however, are functions of program variables. Surely static analysis rules could be devised for each of these situations, but other rules would have to be devised for other common occurrences. The result would be an inelegant mass of special procedures. A symbolic trace, on the other hand, easily shows all functional relations and readily expresses the needed range-checking tests directly in terms of the input values. Thus the symbolic execution/constraint-solving approach provides an elegant technique which avoids the need for the inelegant special-cases approach.

It is important to note that we have analytically justified the removal of virtually all subscript-checking probes from the program in Fig. 8-2. In particular, all probes inserted to check the subscripts of statements 8, 10, and 17 can be removed. Hence we have verified that these statements reference array A correctly.

Although statement E16 is a probe for a different error (division by zero), it should be apparent that the analytic technique just described can be used to show that the test in E16 is also unnecessary. This error condition is expressed as the constraint "$XK = 0$." This will be inconsistent with any constraint set arising from symbolic execution of a path through node 14. Yet static analysis will show that node 14 must always be executed prior to node E16. Hence it is verified that the division in statement 18 is always well defined.

Probes E17, E18, E20, and E21 cannot be removed, however. In fact, symbolic execution of a path such as 34, 35, 36, 21, 22, 23, 24, 25 yields only the following constraints:†

$$③ \neq 0 \qquad \text{from edge (35, 36)}$$

$$③ = 1 \qquad \text{from edge (24, 25)}$$

†The notation $Ⓘ$ should be read as "the $Ⓘ$th value taken as input, to this path." Hence in this case $③$ means "the third value read in."

Thus clearly when statement 25 is encountered, ③ is constrained to be 1, but ① and ② are subject to no constraints. An out-of-bounds subscript error at statement 25 could be simulated by any of the constraints $I < 1$, $I > 20$, $J < 1$, or $J > 20$. After symbolic execution these become ① < 1, ① > 20, ② < 1, and ② > 20. None of these is inconsistent with the constraints generated by consideration of path edges. Hence a solution such as

$$① = 0$$
$$② = 21$$
$$③ = 1$$

can clearly force an array reference error at statement 25. Thus we see that the symbolic execution/constraint-solving technique is a powerful testing aid. It should be noted that the ATTEST system [ClaL76a] implements most of the capabilities just described.

Perhaps the most important use of symbolic execution/constraint solution is for verifying assertions of functional relations between program variables. At the end of the previous section it was noted that verification of assertions such as A2, A3, A5, and A6 is beyond the power of the static analyzers presented there. We saw that static analysis is quite adept at inferring all the possible sequences of events which might arise during execution of a program, and that by comparing these with specifications of correct and incorrect sequences, testing and verification capabilities are obtained. When the statements of correct behavior are couched as predicates involving program variables, however, symbolic execution/constraint solution is most useful. This is not surprising, as symbolic execution is a technique for tracing and manipulating the functional relations between program variables.

We have already discussed the fact that the subscript references at statements 25 and 27 may cause array bounds violations. This was determined by using symbolic execution/constraint solution to demonstrate that probes P5,1 and P6,1 are not inconsistent with path-induced constraints. Thus they cannot safely be removed, and assertions A5 and A6 cannot be verified.

On the other hand, these techniques can help verify the correctness of assertions A2 and A3. By using symbolic execution for the path 10, 11, 10, we obtain the relation

$$A(I, J, 1) = A(I, J - 1, 1) + I$$

Viewing this as a recurrence relation whose initial condition is given by

$$A(I, 1, 1) = I$$

we can obtain the analytic solution

$$A(I, J, 1) = J * I$$

from the theory of finite difference equations. This relation is exactly the one asserted by A2. Hence this assertion is analytically verified and need not be checked dynamically. Clearly this capability rested heavily upon being able to draw on results from finite mathematics. Cheatham has created a tool with impressive inferential capabilities of this sort [Chea78], although the problem of determining the closed form of a recurrence is in general intractable. Also required here is the ability to recognize when two formulas are equivalent. This problem is likewise intractable in general.

Additional pitfalls of demonstrating functional equivalence are demonstrated by assertion A3. Here we easily see that symbolic execution will establish that after statement 17

$$A(I, J, 2) = A(I, J, 1) / 2.0$$

This is mathematically equivalent to the equation

$$A(I, J, 2) = 0.5 * A(I, J, 1)$$

and is readily recognized as being equivalent. Because of the peculiarities of floating-point hardware, however, the two formulas

$$A(I, J, 1) / 2.0 \text{ and } 0.5 * A(I, J, 1)$$

will often evaluate to different values. Hence the results of symbolic verification and dynamic verification may differ.

Despite these various limitations, we are encouraged to believe that symbolic execution/constraint solution can be used to yield impressive documentation, testing, and verification capabilities. Perhaps these limitations can be put in better perspective by observing that symbolic execution and constraint solution are the basic techniques used in formal verification or so-called "proof of correctness" [Elsp72, Lond75, Hant76]. In formal verification the intent of a program must be captured totally by assertions imbedded according to the dictates of a criterion such as Floyd's method of inductive assertions [Floy67]. The correctness verification is established by symbolically executing all code sequences lying between consecutive assertions and showing that the results obtained are consistent with the bounding assertions. The consistency demonstration is generally attempted by using predicate calculus theorem provers rather than constraint solvers as discussed here. It is crucial to observe, however, that these theorem provers are subject to the same theoretical limitations discussed earlier. The undecidability of the first-order predicate calculus makes it impossible to be sure whether a statement is valid or not. Hence we cannot be guaranteed an answer to the question of whether a symbolic execution will yield results consistent with its bounding assertions. Furthermore the symbolic execution may make simplifications and transformations of real formulas which do not recreate the functioning of floating-point hardware. These and similar limitations of formal verification have long been acknowledged. Yet formal verification is rightly regarded as a useful technique, capable of increasing one's confidence in the functional soundness of a program. This is exactly the sense in which the symbolic execution/constraint solution technique just discussed should be considered worthwhile.

In fact, this technique is of greater worth to a practitioner than formal verification, because of its flexibility. As already observed, formal verification requires a complete, exhaustive statement of a program's intent. The technique just described focuses on attempting to justify or disprove the validity of individual assertions. This gives the practitioner the ability to probe various individual aspects of a program as he or she may desire. From this perspective we view formal verification as the logical, orderly culmination of a process of verifying progressively more complete assertion sets. This culmination is rarely reached because of its prohibitive costs.

8-5. A STRATEGY FOR INTEGRATING TOOL CAPABILITIES

In this section we propose some ways in which the preceding classes of tools can be combined to address important software implementation objectives. It seems that in creating software the overriding goal is to create a product which demonstrably meets its current objectives and shows promise of being adaptable to meet foreseeable changes in the objectives. Much research and experimentation has been devoted to studying how to achieve this goal, and much is yet to be understood. From this past work, however, certain basic needs can be clearly discussed.

Perhaps the foremost lesson learned is that software production, especially on a multiyear, multiperson scale, is a costly, complex activity requiring effective management [BroJ78, Blac77]. Such effective management can only be achieved if there is sufficient visibility of the details of the activity. This visibility enables managers and programmers alike to decide whether the project is on the way to achieving its goals, and if not, what remedial action should be taken. Hence it seems that chief among the capabilities essential in guiding a software project to success are the ability to monitor its status and to determine whether the behavior of the evolving product is deviating from that intended. Visibility is provided by adequate documentation made centrally available by project personnel to each other and to management. Clearly it is our thesis that this process can be substantially facilitated by tools. Determining whether or not a software product is meeting its objective is clearly the goal of the testing and verification processes, which, as the preceding sections suggest, can be viewed as closely coordinated activities. Here too, our thesis is that tools can be of significant help. Moreover, as the preceding sections suggest, documentation can be viewed at least in part as an activity which is preparatory to testing and verification.

A possible diagram of this view of the software production activity is shown in Fig. 8-6. From this diagram it is clear that the activity should be greatly facilitated by automated aids to documentation, testing, and verification. The preceding sections have provided a basis for seeing how such auto-

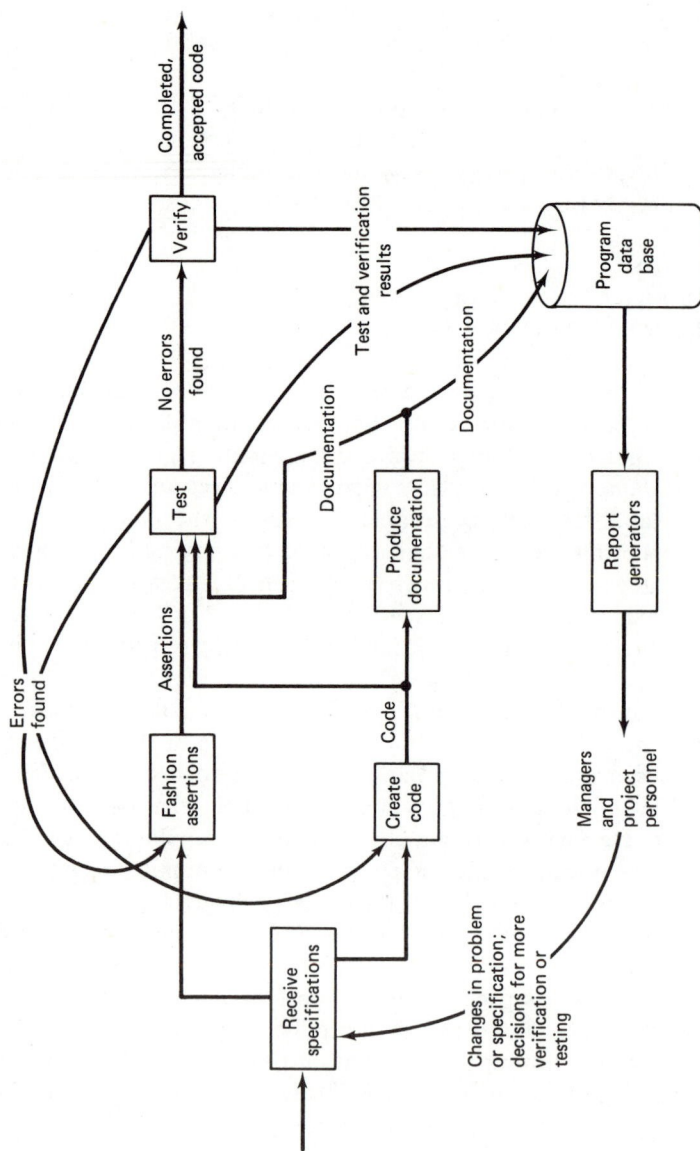

Figure 8-6 Suggested flow of information and processing activities in a software production project

mated aids can be fashioned from a coalition of static analysis, symbolic execution, and dynamic testing aids. We now propose some details.

Complete program documentation must fully describe the structure and functioning of the program. Clearly such documentation must describe a wide variety of aspects of the program. At present it seems that certain parts of this description must be supplied by humans. The previous sections of the paper have shown, however, that some documentation can be generated by tools. This documentation is, moreover, probably more reliably and cheaply done by such tools. In addition, if some documentation is done by tools, the remaining documentation is likely to be done more carefully by humans, thereby suggesting the possibility of greater quality and reliability.

Earlier sections of this chapter suggest that static analysis tools should first be used to create such documentation as cross-reference tables, variable evolution trees and input/output descriptions of individual variables and procedures. Symbolic execution tools should be used next to create descriptions of the functional effects of executing various paths through the code. With constraint solution, a complete input/output characterization of the code can be obtained. Performance characteristics can be measured and documented with the aid of a dynamic testing tool. It is proposed that all this documentation be stored in a central data base, forming a skeleton of the complete documentation. Editors and interactive systems might be used to gather from humans such things as text descriptions of variables and procedures.

Each of the three tool classes produces a different kind of documentation. The types of documentation are only loosely related; hence the order of application of the tools can be dictated by the importance of each to the particular project. It is important to be aware, however, that static analysis is relatively inexpensive, symbolic execution is relatively expensive, constraint solution is usually quite expensive, and dynamic testing can be quite expensive, if extensive elaborate test runs are done.

In a tool-assisted testing activity, the order of application of the tools is important. We have seen that tools can be used to focus the testing effort on paths and situations which appear to be more error-prone. This is done by elimination of probes which were created to test for common programming errors and for adherence to explicit assertions. We saw that many probes can be removed by application of progressively stronger (and more costly) static analysis. Some remaining probes may be removed as a result of symbolic execution/constraint solution. We saw that these probes are likely to be the more substantive ones, monitoring for adherence to asserted functional intent. Their removal constitutes significant verification, but it can be expected that the cost of this will be relatively high. Hence symbolic execution should probably be employed cautiously or not at all *as a test aid.*

Finally a dynamic test tool should be used to gather definite information about the existence and sources of error in the program. As already noted, testing can only show the presence of error for a test case, and even a simple program may have an infinite number of possible test cases. Hence the tool-aided procedure just outlined has added importance in that it helps suggest test cases—namely those designed to exercise probes not analytically removed.

We have seen that testing and verification can be closely related activities. It is important to remember, however, that they do differ, most noticeably in their goals and placement in the software production process. Testing is the process of looking for errors. It should be viewed as an activity which occurs frequently during code production. Verification is the process of demonstrating the absence of errors. As such it should not be undertaken until and unless testing has failed to uncover errors. Thus it is a less frequent, more critical process, usually warranting greater expense and thoroughness. Our earlier discussion has shown specific ways in which partial verification can be obtained as outgrowths of testing activities. We have also seen, however, that some activities provide good verification results but are likely to be relatively costly. Because verification is a less frequent, more critical activity, the extra cost may well be warranted.

A verification activity should start out like the testing activity just described. The first step is to suppress error testing probes and probes resulting from assertions. Static analysis can be used to suppress some probes, but the most significant probes probably can be removed only by symbolic execution. Verification is achieved on an assertion-by-assertion basis only when all probes generated by a single assertion have been removed. In this way stronger, more complete verification can be obtained incrementally for incremental cost and effort. Complete formal verification can be attempted, if desired, as the culmination of this process.

A final word should be said about the need for both verification and testing. It has been observed that testing cannot demonstrate the absence of errors. Hence verification should be attempted. We have also observed that the verification process has its own risks. The most important risk is that a verification attempt may end inconclusively because of failure to determine the consistency of constraints or the truth of a statement. As already noted, this does not necessarily signify the falsity of the assertion, just that the verification attempt ended inconclusively. Another important risk is that the verification may be successful but may rely implicitly upon false assumptions about the semantics of language constructs. As an example of this, we saw that symbolic executors generally make incorrect simplifying assumptions about the functioning of floating-point hardware. As a result even a complete formal verification of program correctness may not completely rule out the possibility of an execution-time error. Hence it seems that both testing and verification should be considered techniques for raising the confidence of project personnel in the software product. Each is capable of bolstering confidence in its own way, and neither should be employed to the exclusion of the other.

8-6. SOFTWARE LIFECYCLE CONSIDERATIONS

The previous sections of this paper have established the importance of having assertions to represent the intent of a program to be documented, tested, and verified. While the importance of assertions has been established, the source of the assertions has not been discussed. In this section we propose that the assertions reasonably and naturally originate in the early requirements and design phases of the software production process. We also propose that the testing, verification, and documentation techniques already described are at least partially applicable to these earlier phases.

Figure 8-7 is a diagrammatic view of how the software production and maintenance process might be divided into phases. It is an adaptation of the "waterfall chart" [ReiD75] which has become widely accepted as a model of those activities. The primary goal of these models is to divide software production and maintenance into definable phases and monitoring points. This division should lead to better-defined criteria for judging the quality and completeness of work in progress. We shall show how this process also produces assertions and how tools can assist in the process.

The requirements definition phase of this process is the phase during which the basic needs of the software project are enunciated. These needs are to be expressed as precisely and completely as possible, but in such a manner as to not suggest or bias an algorithmic solution. One of the most effective ways to do this is to specify the required functional and performance characteristics of the proposed program. Such a specification need not and should not suggest how the functions are to be computed. It should, from the perspective of this paper, be viewed as asserting the intent which the eventual program must satisfy. Hence the eventual code assertions must be directly traceable back to this original statement of intent. We shall explore potential mechanisms for doing this shortly.

The preliminary design phase is characterized by the process of exploring possible strategies for building an algorithmic solution which satisfies the requirements specification. During this phase, processing modules and data abstractions are defined and algorithmic processes employing them are fashioned. Preliminary designs are generally hierarchical, showing, when complete, how the principal components of the algorithmic solution are decomposed into successively more detailed specifications of data and processing. In practice, such a decomposition process invariably leads to greater understanding of the problem and consequent changes in requirements.

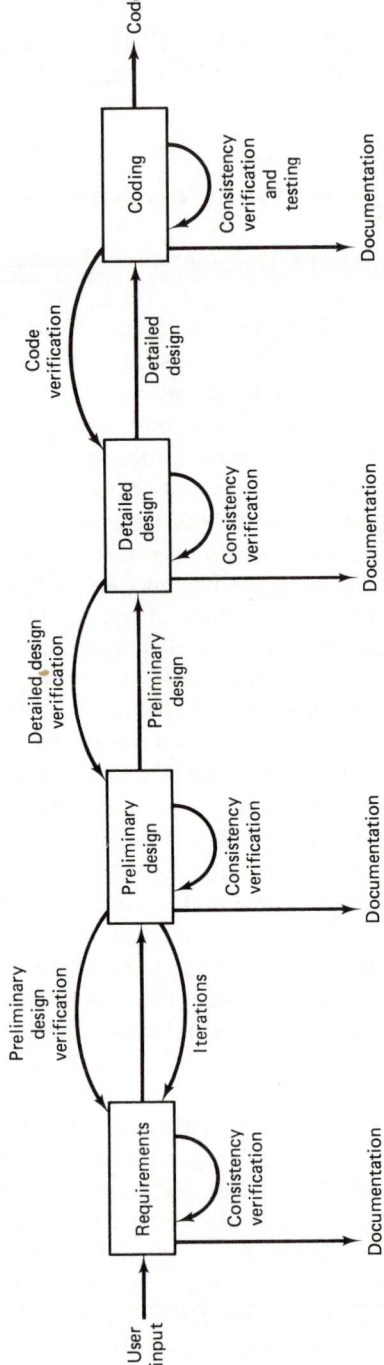

Figure 8-7 A view of the software production process

Hence the requirements and preliminary design activities should be viewed as iterative and intertwined. Together they should be considered to be the process of gaining understanding of the nature of the problem and an acceptable approach to its solution.

From the point of view of this paper, preliminary design is important because it specifies the required functional behavior (assertions) which apply to the various components of the solution. Hence this phase begins the process of attaching successively more detailed assertions to successively smaller algorithmic units. This process should terminate with the construction of code corresponding to very detailed assertions.

The detailed design phase is the phase during which the outline of the solution, established during preliminary design, is elaborated down to the level of actual specifications for code. Detailed design should not be viewed as merely an extension of the preliminary design activity. At the start of detailed design it is necessary for the designers to reorient their thinking from a problem-understanding orientation to a software construction orientation. This is a crucial phase of the software production process, during which the solution elements proposed during preliminary design must be grouped and reorganized into modules and data abstractions [Parn72, Lisk75]. This reorganization should be guided by the desire to clearly capture independent solution concepts in code and to use standard interfaces to conceal the details of their implementation. The module specifications are statements of the functional behavior required to realize the various design concepts. Hence they are assertions. The hierarchical decompositions of the high-level modular assertions analogously become assertions specifying the behavior of the sub-modules comprising higher-level modules. The detailed design process terminates with the creation of specifications (assertions) such as those shown in Fig. 8-3, which are so detailed that they can be met with just a few lines of code each.

As already noted, one of the primary reasons for following this phased approach to software construction is that it affords obvious opportunities for observing and evaluating progress at intermediate stages. Extensive reviews may be conducted at the conclusion of each phase. One of the primary goals of such reviews is to establish whether the work completed during that phase meets the objectives enunciated at the conclusion of the previous phase. Hence each review can quite reasonably be viewed as a testing and verification procedure, using the output of the previous phase as the statement of intent.

These reviews are currently based upon documentation and analysis done primarily by humans. It is our contention that they can be heavily supported by tools and techniques like those described earlier in this paper. In order to do this, the requirements and design specifications must be stated in terms of a rigorous formalism. Some such formalisms have already been devised. Pseudo-code languages and design representation languages such as CLU [Lisk77] are examples of rigorous formalisms for expressing detailed design. Clearly they can be parsed and subjected to certain types of semantic analysis. Virtually all forms of static analysis and symbolic execution can be carried out on them. Hence documentation can be automatically produced and some verification automatically obtained. If the detailed design and preliminary design are both complete and rigorous enough, it is possible to obtain formal verification that the detailed design meets its preliminary design objectives.

It is perhaps more surprising to note that such capabilities can reasonably be expected for requirements and preliminary design specifications. Here again the prerequisite is rigor in the specification. A number of rigorous specification methodologies have been proposed (e.g., SAMM [Step78], SADT [Ross77], PSL/PSA [Teic77]). All seem to be based upon a graphical representation of the requirements and/or preliminary design.

The SREM methodology [Alfo77] is the most interesting as it is handsomely supported by the RSL/REVS family of tools [Bell77]. RSL is a language which is used to capture a requirements/preliminary design specification and recast it into a set of objects and relations stored in a centralized data base. The contents of the data base can be (and are) looked upon as a collection of annotated graphs, modeling the problem and its proposed solution. The REVS system of analytic tools examines the data base and produces documentation, analysis, and limited forms of verification. Each processing element in the design has as part of its specification its input/output behavior and a functional description which may be stated as an algorithmic graph structure. Hence input/output behavior can be automatically documented and verified for consistency. Symbolic execution traces can be created as documentation and for the purposes of verification. It is important to note that since SREM captures both the requirements and preliminary design in a natural intertwined fashion, verification of internal consistency is tantamount to a verification that preliminary design meets requirements.

We finally are able to see where the program assertions originate. The functional descriptions attached to the various processing elements of an RSL-like specification are the initial program assertions. If the specification technique represents the hierarchical decomposition of these elements, then at each decomposition level functional descriptions are attached to the processing elements. As these descriptions become more algorithmic, the possibility of rigorous and automatic verification increases. By the beginning of detailed design they have evolved into rigorous module specifications, and are certainly a suitable basis for the automatic verification approaches described earlier.

Some of the documentation, verification, and testing techniques described earlier in connection with code analysis have been applied to requirements and design representations. It remains to be demonstrated that the methodology outlined in Section 8-5 and its implementation by the tools proposed can be applied equally well to requirements and design. This would establish the feasibility of a single analytic methodology and tool configuration for application to all phases of the software production process.

8-7. ACKNOWLEDGMENTS

The author wishes to thank the National Science Foundation and the U.S. Army Research Office for their support of the research activities from which most of the ideas expressed here have originated. Much valuable insight was also gained while the author was on leave of absence from the University of Colorado Department of Computer Science, and employed by the Space and Military Applications Division of Boeing Computer Services Company. The ideas expressed here have been shaped by stimulating conversations with Les Wade, John Brown, Leon Stucki, Lori Clarke, Bill Howden, Bill Riddle, Dick Taylor, Larry Peters and many others. Finally, the author wishes to thank Harriet Ortiz, Mildred Farnsworth, and Arlene Hunter for their obliging willingness to type the manuscript and editors Steve Muchnick and Neil Jones for their patience.

Chapter 9

Symbolic Evaluation Methods for Program Analysis[†]

Lori A. Clarke
Debra J. Richardson

9-1. INTRODUCTION

Symbolic evaluation is a data flow analysis method that analyzes program behavior by monitoring the manipulations performed on the input data. Symbolic evaluation methods represent computations as algebraic expressions over the input data and thus maintain the relationship between the input data and the resulting values. Normal execution computes numerical values but often loses information about the way in which the numerical values were derived. An incorrect numerical result usually does not uniquely determine the location of a miscalculation. A large part of the debugging process is concerned with isolating an erroneous calculation that resulted in a wrong numerical value. Symbolic evaluation methods can be used to aid in debugging as well as in several other types of program analysis.

There are three basic methods of symbolic evaluation: symbolic execution, global symbolic evaluation, and dynamic symbolic evaluation. Symbolic execution is a path-oriented evaluation method that analyzes input data

†The research reported here was partially supported by the National Science Foundation under grant MCS77–02101 and the United States Air Force Office of Scientific Research under grant AFOSR 77–3287.

dependencies for a path. Global symbolic evaluation represents all possible data dependencies at any point in a program. Dynamic symbolic evaluation produces a trace of the data dependencies for particular input data.

In this chapter we first introduce a formal notation to concisely represent each of the three methods of symbolic evaluation. Each method is then explained, and examples of the three methods are given to demonstrate their corresponding strengths and weaknesses. Also, several applications of each method are discussed. Symbolic execution is the best known of the three techniques, so it is described first and in more detail than the other two methods. Several different implementation techniques of symbolic execution systems are compared. The other symbolic evaluation methods are then described and compared to symbolic execution.

9-2. FUNCTIONAL NOTATION

In this section we introduce some basic notation that will be used in formalizing the results of each of the three methods of symbolic evaluation.

Data flow analysis methods typically represent a program by a directed graph describing the possible flow of control through the program. The nodes in the graph, $\{n_1, n_2, \ldots, n_q\}$, represent statements. Each edge is specified by an ordered pair of nodes (n_i, n_j) that indicates that a possible transfer of control exists from n_i to n_j. Associated with each transfer of control are conditions under which such a transfer occurs. The branch predicate that governs traversal of the edge (n_i, n_j) is denoted by $bp(n_i, n_j)$. For a sequential transfer of control, the branch predicate has the constant value true. For a binary condition following the node n_i and preceding nodes n_j and n_k, the branch predicate for one edge (n_i, n_j) is the complement of the branch predicate for the other edge (n_i, n_k); thus, $bp(n_i, n_j) = \sim bp(n_i, n_k)$. Some conditional statements, such as computed **go to** or **case** statements, may have more than two successor nodes, and each branch predicate must be represented appropriately. For the purposes of this paper, the *control flow graph* of a program is a directed graph with a single entry point, the start node n_s, and a single exit point, the final node n_f. Both the start node and the final node are null nodes added to the graph when necessary to accomplish this single-entry, single-exit form without loss of generality.

The procedure in Fig. 9-1 calculates the time and distance at which a starship's velocity reduces to zero on its approach to dock on the star base station. The statements in DOCKING are annotated with their associated node numbers, and Fig. 9-2 shows the control flow graph for this procedure. This procedure is used throughout the paper to demonstrate the three methods of symbolic evaluation.

A *path* in a control flow graph is a sequence of statements $(n_{i0}, n_{i1},$

n_s **procedure** DOCKING(STATION,STARSHIP,THRUST,VELOCITY,DELTAT,TIME,
DISTANCE,ERROR)

```
{                                                                        }
{    starship docking calculation (approximation) determines the time and }
{    the distance at which the starship's velocity reduces to zero on its  }
{    approach to the star base station                                     }
{                                                                        }
{    input variables:                                                     }
{      station — mass of the star base station (kg)                        }
{      starship — mass of the starship (kg)                                }
{      thrust — thrust force of the starship's engine (nt)                 }
{      velocity — initial velocity of the starship (m/s)                   }
{      deltat — change requested between iterations (a smaller value will  }
{              make the calculation more exact) (s)                        }
{      time — initial time (s)                                             }
{      distance — initial distance between the base and the starship (m)   }
{                                                                        }
{    output variables:                                                    }
{      time — final time (s)                                               }
{      distance — final distance between the base and the starship (m)     }
{      error — nonzero if any input is invalid                             }
{                                                                        }
{    intermediate variables:                                              }
{      gconst — universal gravitational constant (6.67E-11 nt-m²/kg²)       }
{      gravity — gravitational force of base station (m/s²)                 }
{      constacc — constant acceleration of starship (m/s²)                 }
{      currvel — current velocity of the starship (m/s)                    }
{      nextvel — velocity of the starship in next time interval (m/s)      }
{                                                                        }
```

real STATION,STARSHIP
real THRUST,VELOCITY
real DELTAT,TIME,DISTANCE
real GCONST,GRAVITY,CONSTACC
real CURRVEL,NEXTVEL
integer ERROR

```
{    all input values must be positive                                    }
{    set error flag if any are ≤ 0                                         }
```

```
         if (STATION ≤ 0.0 or STARSHIP ≤ 0.0 or
             THRUST ≤ 0.0 or VELOCITY ≤ 0.0 or
             DELTAT ≤ 0.0 or TIME ≤ 0.0 or DISTANCE ≤ 0.0)
             then
```
n_1
```
                 ERROR ← 1
             else
```
```
{            input values are valid, continue computation              }
{            initialize the universal gravitational constant           }
```
n_2
```
             GCONST ← 6.67*10**(−11)
```
```
{            compute the gravitational force                           }
{            first check for a zero divisor                            }
             if (DISTANCE**2 = 0.0)
                 then
```
n_3
```
                     ERROR ← 1
                 else
```

Figure 9-1

266

```
n4                          GRAVITY ←— GCONST * STATION * STARSHIP /
                                (DISTANCE**2)
         {                                                                    }
         {                  gravity and thrust are assumed constant           }
         {                  throughout the computations to follow             }
         {                  the acceleration due to the starship's            }
         {                  engine is thrust/starship                         }
         {                  (acceleration = force/mass)                       }
         {                  compute the constant acceleration of              }
         {                  the starship which is the difference              }
         {                  of these two opposing accelerations               }
n5                          CONSTACC ←— GRAVITY − THRUST / STARSHIP

         {                  current velocity is the initial velocity          }
n6                          CURRVEL ←— VELOCITY

         {                  compute the velocity in the second time           }
         {                  interval (this initializes the loop)              }
         {                  nextvel ←— vel + acceleration * deltat            }
n7                          NEXTVEL ←— CURRVEL + CONSTACC * DELTAT

         {                  determine when the velocity reduces               }
         {                  to zero by iteratively computing the              }
         {                  next velocity as a function of the                }
         {                  current velocity, the acceleration                }
         {                  (force/mass), and the change in time              }

                      repeat
n8                          DISTANCE ←— DISTANCE − CURRVEL * DELTAT
n9                          CURRVEL ←— NEXTVEL
n10                         TIME ←— TIME + DELTAT
n11                         NEXTVEL ←— CURRVEL + CONSTACC * DELTAT
                      until (NEXTVEL ≤ 0.0)
                            ERROR ←— 0
              endif
          endif
      end {DOCKING}
```

Figure 9-1 (cont.)

$\ldots, n_{it}$) such that there exists a possible transfer of control from n_{ij} to $n_{i,j+1}$ for all n_{ij}, $0 \leq j < t$. A *partial program path* T_{ku} is a path which begins with the start node; that is, $T_{ku} = (n_s, n_{k1}, n_{k2}, \ldots, n_{ku})$. Hence, for any partial program path T_{ku} with $u \geq 1$, $T_{ku} = T_{k,u-1} \frown (n_{ku})$, where $T_{k0} = (n_s)$ and $\frown$ indicates concatenation of paths. A *program path* P_H is a path that begins with the start node and ends with the final node; that is, $P_H = (n_s, n_{H1}, n_{H2}, \ldots, n_{Hv}, n_f)$. There is no guarantee that a sequence of statements representing a path is executable; some paths may be infeasible as a result of contradictory conditions governing the transfers of control along the path. The control flow graph is a representation of all possible paths through the corresponding program.

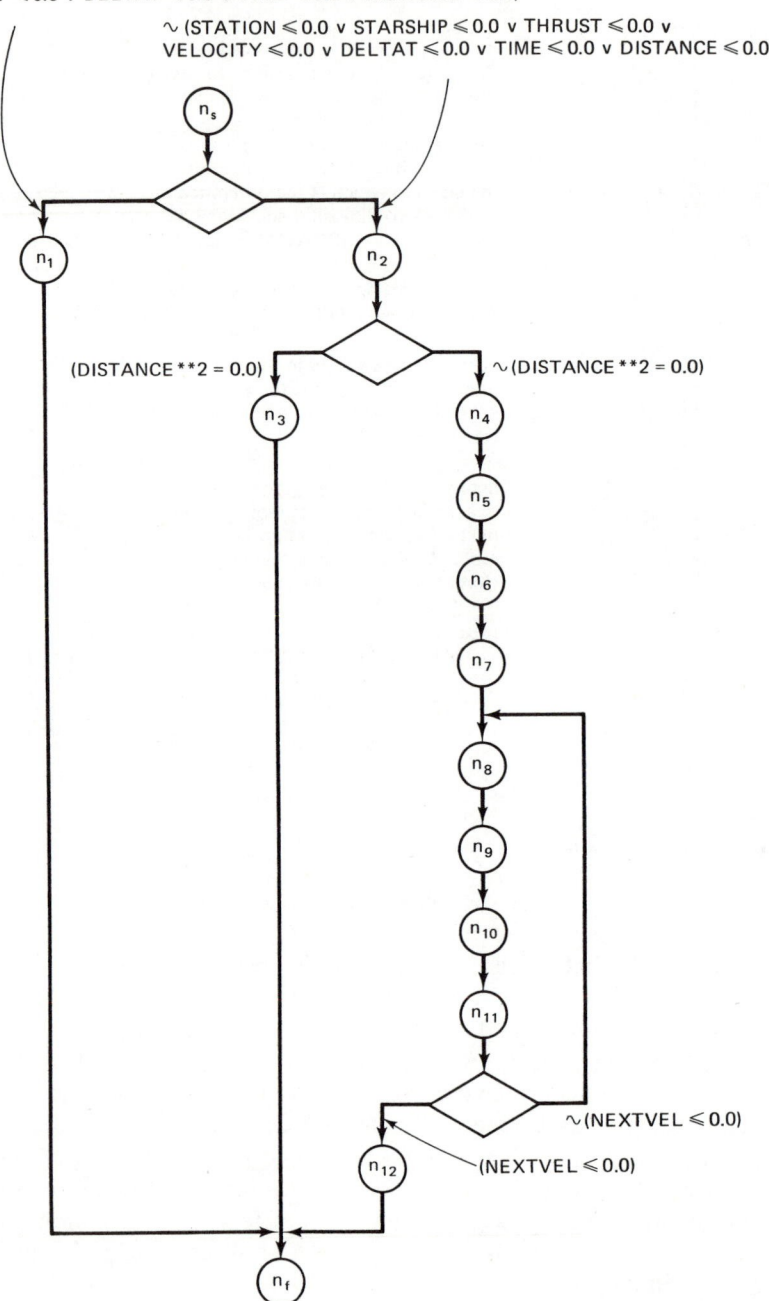

Figure 9-2

The program P specifies a set of *program paths* $\{P_1, P_2, \ldots\}$,† which are executed for disjoint subsets of the program domain. P accepts input values $(x_1, x_2, \ldots, x_M)$ and computes output values $(z_1, z_2, \ldots, z_N)$. The *domain* X of the program P is a cross product, $X = X_1 \times X_2 \times \ldots \times X_M$, where each X_I is the domain for input value x_I. An element of X is a vector x with specific input values, $x = (x_1, x_2, \ldots, x_M)$, and corresponds to a single point in the M-dimensional input space X. Likewise, the codomain Z of a program is a cross product, $Z = Z_1 \times Z_2 \times \ldots \times Z_N$, where each Z_J is the codomain for output value z_J. Thus, $P(x) \in Z$ is a vector z with specific output values, $z = (z_1, z_2, \ldots, z_N)$, and corresponds to a single point in the N-dimensional output space Z. We also refer to a vector $y = (y_1, y_2, \ldots, y_W)$ of program variables, which store the values (both intermediate and output) computed by the program, as well as the input values $(x_1, x_2, \ldots, x_M)$. For the purposes of this chapter, we assume that the program variables $y_1, y_2, \ldots, y_N$, $N \leq W$, store the output values $(z_1, z_2, \ldots, z_N)$. In addition, the simplifying assumption that each path has M input values and N output values is made without loss of generality; any program that does not satisfy this assumption can be transformed into an equivalent program that does, using Λ to represent an undefined value.

The paths of a program divide the program domain X into disjoint subdomains. Each program path P_H is executed for a *path domain* D_H^p and specifies a vector of *path functions* $(p_{H1}, p_{H2}, \ldots, p_{HN})$, where the Jth component computes z_J. Hence, for any $x \in D_H^p$, $P(x) = P_H(x) = (p_{H1}(x), p_{H2}(x), \ldots, p_{HN}(x)) \in Z$ and $p_{HJ}(x) \in Z_J$.

Symbolic evaluation can be used to generate representations for the path domains and path functions of a program. All three symbolic evaluation methods use the control flow graph to maintain a description of the program state at every point in the evaluation of the program. The state of the program includes some description of the path followed to reach the present point in the evaluation, as well as the values obtained for all program variables following the evaluation of that partial program path. The data descriptions generated in symbolic evaluation are symbolic representations of the program state. Given a partial program path, $T_{ku} = (n_s, n_{k1}, n_{k2}, \ldots, n_{ku})$, n_{ku} is the present point in the evaluation. $VAL[T_{ku}]$ represents the values of all program variables $(y_1, y_2, \ldots, y_W)$ after evaluation of the partial program path T_{ku}. $VAL[T_{ku}]$ is a vector containing an element for each program variable. Hence, $VAL[T_{ku}] = (s(y_1[T_{ku}]), s(y_2[T_{ku}]), \ldots, s(y_W[T_{ku}]))$, where $s(y_L[T_{ku}])$ denotes the symbolic value of program variable y_L, after evaluating T_{ku}, in terms of the symbolic names representing the input values. The path condition, $PC[T_{ku}]$, is the conjunct of the branch predicates evaluated along this particular partial program path. $PC[T_{ku}] = s(bp(n_s, n_{k1})[T_{k0}]) \wedge s(bp(n_{k1}, n_{k2})[T_{k1}]) \wedge \ldots \wedge s(bp(n_{k,u-1}, n_{ku})[T_{k,u-1}])$, where $s(bp(n_{k,J-1}, n_{kJ})[T_{k,J-1}])$

---

†There may be an infinite number of paths because of program loops.

denotes the symbolic value of the branch predicate when evaluated over the values of the program variables preceding traversal of the corresponding edge, that is, over $VAL[T_{k,j-1}]$. The path condition can be rewritten as $PC[T_{ku}] = PC[T_{k,u-1}] \wedge s(bp(n_{k,u-1}, n_{ku})[T_{k,u-1}])$. Finally, $STATE[T_{ku}] = (T_{ku}, VAL[T_{ku}], PC[T_{ku}])$ represents the program state following symbolic evaluation of the partial program path T_{ku}. The partial program path will not be included in the notation when the path is obvious from the context.

The symbolic evaluation of any element of the control flow graph—a statement or a transfer of control—changes the program state. Initially, the program state is defined as

$$T_{k0} = (n_s)$$
$$VAL[T_{k0}] = (\Lambda, \ldots, \Lambda)$$
$$PC[T_{k0}] = true$$
$$STATE[T_{k0}] = (T_{k0}, VAL[T_{k0}], PC[T_{k0}])$$

All variables are initialized at the start node to the undefined value Λ, with the following exceptions: variables that are initialized before execution are assigned the corresponding constant value; variables that are parameters of the initial procedure of evaluation are assigned symbolic names. Symbolic names are assigned to input variables whenever input occurs on the program path. Throughout the symbolic evaluation, all symbolic representations of variable and branch predicate values are in terms of these symbolic names that represent the input values. This is accomplished by substituting the current symbolic value of a variable into an expression wherever that variable is referenced.

When evaluating a statement, say node n_{kj}, the corresponding component of the VAL vector is updated for any variable that is assigned a new value. For instance, if the assignment statement $y_J \leftarrow y_I * y_K$ occurs, then the y_J component of the VAL vector will change from its former value $s(y_J)$ to the algebraic expression $s(y_I) * s(y_K)$. In addition, the partial path is updated, $T_{kj} = T_{k,j-1} \frown (n_{kj})$. In the evaluation of a transfer of control, say edge $(n_{kj}, n_{k,j+1})$, the path condition will be augmented by the symbolic value of the branch predicate governing traversal of this edge, that is, $PC[T_{k,j+1}] = PC[T_{kj}] \wedge s(bp(n_{kj}, n_{k,j+1})[T_{kj}])$.

Following the evaluation of a complete program path, the symbolic representation of the program state defines the path functions and path domains of a program. Given a complete path P_H, the program state after evaluation of the final node may be represented as

$$P_H = (n_s, n_{H1}, n_{H2}, \ldots, n_{Hv}, n_f)$$
$$VAL[P_H] = (s(y_1[P_H]), s(y_2[P_H]), \ldots, s(y_W[P_H]))$$
$$PC[P_H] = s(bp(n_s, n_{H1})[T_s]) \wedge \cdots \wedge s(bp(n_{Hv}, n_f)[T_{Hv}])$$
$$STATE[P_H] = (P_H, VAL[P_H], PC[P_H]).$$

The path functions $(p_{H1}, p_{H2}, \ldots, p_{HN})$, which compute the output values $(z_1, z_2, \ldots, z_N)$, are provided by $p_{HJ} = s(y_J[P_H])$. Since all symbolic representations are in terms of the symbolic input values, p_{HJ} is a symbolic computational expression of the output value z_J in terms of the input values $(x_1, x_2, \ldots, x_M)$. The path condition $PC[P_H]$ provides a system of constraints on the program's input values and defines the path domain D_H^p. The subset of elements of the program domain that will cause execution of this program path is defined by $D_H^p = \{x \in X \text{ such that } PC[P_H] \text{ is true}\}$. These path functions and path domains can be generated for any program path that can be symbolically evaluated.

Each of the three methods of symbolic evaluation maintains a slightly different representation for the program state at any point in the evaluation. Furthermore, each method generates a slight variation of the path domains and path functions as final evaluation of the program.

Symbolic execution supports a program state that most resembles the *STATE* vector defined above. This method generates output for each path that is symbolically executed. For the most part, following symbolic execution of a particular path, P_H, the output produced consists of three things: the sequence of statements forming the path, a system of constraints on the program's input variables, and a vector containing a computational expression for each output variable. The constraints are analogous to the path condition $PC[P_H]$ and define the path domain. The vector corresponds to the output variable components of the symbolic value vector $VAL[P_H]$ given by the path functions $(p_{H1}, p_{H2}, \ldots, p_{HN})$ computed along this path. After symbolic execution of a program path, therefore, output similar to that shown in Fig. 9-3 might be produced.

STATEMENTS ON THIS PATH
$n_s, n_{H1}, n_{H2}, \ldots, n_{Hv}, n_f$

SYMBOLIC REPRESENTATION OF PATH CONDITION
$s(bp(n_s, n_{H1})[T_{H0}]) \wedge s(bp(n_{H1}, n_{H2})[T_{H1}]) \wedge \ldots \wedge s(bp(n_{Hv}, n_f)[T_{Hv}])$

SYMBOLIC REPRESENTATION OF OUTPUT VARIABLES
$z_1 = p_{H1} = s(y_1[P_H])$
$z_2 = p_{H2} = s(y_2[P_H])$
.
.
.
$z_N = p_{HN} = s(y_N[P_N])$

Figure 9-3

Rather than evaluate a program on a path-by-path basis, the method of global symbolic evaluation maintains a representation of the program state at a point in the evaluation as a conditional symbolic expression. This caselike construct encompasses the symbolic values of all program variables regardless of the partial program path followed to reach this point. The output generated following global symbolic evaluation of a program reflects this representation of the program state. Suppose the program has the paths $\{P_1, P_2, \ldots, P_R\}$, then the final evaluation might have a form such as Fig. 9-4, although only the symbolic values of the output variables are shown.

$$
\begin{aligned}
\textbf{case} \\
PC[P_1]: z_1 &= p_{11} = s(y_1[P_1]) \\
z_2 &= p_{12} = s(y_2[P_1]) \\
&\quad . \\
&\quad . \\
&\quad . \\
z_N &= p_{1N} = s(y_N[P_1]) \\
\\
PC[P_R]: z_1 &= p_{R1} = s(y_1[P_R]) \\
z_2 &= p_{R2} = s(y_2[P_R]) \\
&\quad . \\
&\quad . \\
&\quad . \\
z_N &= p_{RN} = s(y_N[P_R]) \\
\textbf{endcase}
\end{aligned}
$$

Figure 9-4

On the other end of the spectrum is the method of dynamic symbolic evaluation, which performs analysis on an input-by-input basis. A particular program path is evaluated while the program is actually executed for specific input data. Given an input vector x, a path, say P_H, is executed. This method traces the statements that are executed. In addition to supplying the output values that result from the execution, dynamic symbolic evaluation provides algebraic expressions for the output values. Following dynamic symbolic evaluation, output similar to Fig. 9-5 might result, where $a(y_j[P_H])$ denotes the actual value z_j computed by the execution of the program on the data vector x.

STATEMENTS EXECUTED
$n_s, n_{H1}, \ldots, n_{Hv}, n_f$

SYMBOLIC AND ACTUAL VALUES OF OUTPUT VARIABLES
$$
\begin{aligned}
z_1 &= p_{H1} = s(y_1[P_H]) = a(y_1[P_H]) \\
z_2 &= p_{H2} = s(y_2[P_H]) = a(y_2[P_H]) \\
&\quad . \\
&\quad . \\
&\quad . \\
z_N &= p_{HN} = s(y_N[P_H]) = a(y_N[P_H])
\end{aligned}
$$

Figure 9-5

These methods of symbolic evaluation will be explained in more detail in the sections which follow.

9-3. SYMBOLIC EXECUTION

Symbolic execution analyzes distinct program paths. In general, symbolic execution is attempted on only a subset of the paths in a program since a program containing a loop may contain an infinite number of paths. Several methods for selecting a subset of program paths are discussed in Section 9-3.3. The general description of symbolic execution that follows is independent of the method of path selection; hence we assume the path is provided. Symbolic execution represents both the computations and the conditional statements on the selected path as algebraic expressions in terms of symbolic input values. This section describes symbolic execution as well as several implementation techniques and applications.

9-3.1. General Method

Symbolic execution initiates its analysis by building the control flow graph of the program. As a path through the program is evaluated or "executed," the statements on the path are evaluated as if they were straight-line code. The branch predicates encountered along the path are also evaluated; the combination of those predicates dictates the input values for which this path can be executed. When an input statement is analyzed, the input values are represented by symbolic names. Throughout the analysis, the representations of all program variables are maintained as algebraic expressions in terms of these symbolic names. These algebraic expressions are formed by the evaluation of any assignment along the path; such an assignment causes an update to the *VAL* component of the program state.

During symbolic execution of a path each branch predicate is evaluated over the symbolic values of the variables at that point on the path. The symbolic evaluation of a branch predicate results in a constraint, an equality or inequality condition, on the input data. Each constraint is then conjoined with all previously evaluated constraints for this path to form the path condition or *PC*. Not all paths in the program graph are executable. The path condition of a program path may be inconsistent, in which case no input data exists that could cause execution of the path. Symbolic execution systems create the path function and the path condition, and may determine path condition consistency.

9-3.2. Implementation Methods

Several symbolic execution systems have been developed [Boye75, ClaL76a, Howd77b, Huan75, King76, Mill75, Rama76] using either of two implementation techniques, forward expansion and backward substitution. In addition, some of these systems try to determine path condition consistency

[Boye75, ClaL76a, King76, Rama76], and again two different approaches have successfully been tried. These approaches are referred to as the *algebraic* and *axiomatic* approaches. In this section, both methods of symbolic execution and path condition consistency determination are described.

Forward expansion is the most intuitive approach to creating the algebraic expressions. Beginning with the start node, symbolic expressions are built as each statement in the path is encountered. The DOCKING procedure of Fig. 9-1 has undergone symbolic execution by forward expansion of two distinct program paths. Figure 9-6 shows how the *VAL* and *PC* evolve for an executable path, and Fig. 9-7 shows the evolution for a non-executable path.

Before either symbolic execution technique is initiated, the source code is first translated into an intermediate form of binary expressions, each containing an operator and two operands. During forward expansion, the binary expressions in each executed statement are then used to form an acyclic directed graph of the program's symbolic computations. Each variable that is assigned a value during execution of the path is actually assigned a pointer into this computational graph. The node of the graph that is pointed to by a variable can be treated as the root of a binary expression tree for this variable. Traversing the tree in inorder determines the symbolic expression for this variable. Figure 9-8 shows the graph at various stages during symbolic execution of the program path of the procedure DOCKING that was shown in Fig. 9-6.

Conditional statements can also be represented symbolically by an acyclic graph using the same form of binary expressions. The false branch of the first branch predicate is followed in the transfer from n_s to n_2, and this constraint is the *PC* for the partial program path (n_s, n_2). Figure 9-9 shows the computational graph representation for this evaluated branch predicate.

Though the computational graph appears rather complicated to follow with the eye, it is easy to build and maintain. The graph can easily be maintained in a table with three fields: one for the operator and two for the operands. The tabular representation of the computational graph in Fig. 9-8(c) is shown in Fig. 9-10 where CGi represents a pointer to the ith entry in the tabular computational graph.

A more detailed description of the forward expansion approach to symbolic execution can be found in [ClaL76a]. There is a close similarity between the described forward expansion technique and the technique of value numbering used by many optimizing compilers, which is described in [Cock70b].

The backward substitution technique [Howd75, Huan75] starts at the end of the path and develops each variable's symbolic expression by substituting the right-hand side of an assignment statement for all occurrences of the left-hand side variable. The backward substitution approach was proposed

statement	VAL	PC
n_s	TIME: time DISTANCE: distance ERROR: Λ STATION: station STARSHIP: starship THRUST: thrust VELOCITY: velocity DELTAT: deltat GCONST: Λ GRAVITY: Λ CONSTACC: Λ CURRVEL: Λ NEXTVEL: Λ	true
n_2	VAL[n_s] updated by GCONST: 6.67*10**(−11)	$PC[n_s]$ $\wedge$ $\sim$ (station $\leq$ 0.0 $\vee$ starship $\leq$ 0.0 $\vee$ thrust $\leq$ 0.0 $\vee$ velocity $\leq$ 0.0 $\vee$ deltat $\leq$ 0.0 $\vee$ time $\leq$ 0.0 $\vee$ distance $\leq$ 0.0)
n_4	VAL[n_s,n_2] updated by GRAVITY: 6.67*10**(−11) * station * starship / distance**2	$PC[n_s,n_2]$ $\wedge$ $\sim$ (distance**2 = 0.0)
n_5	VAL[n_s,n_2,n_4] updated by CONSTACC: 6.67*10**(−11) * station * starship / distance**2 − thrust / starship	$PC[n_s,n_2,n_4]$ $\wedge$ true
n_6	VAL[n_s,n_2,n_4,n_5] updated by CURRVEL: velocity	$PC[n_s,n_2,n_4,n_5]$ $\wedge$ true
n_7	VAL[n_s,n_2,n_4,n_5,n_6] updated by NEXTVEL: velocity + (6.67*10**(−11) * station * starship / distance**2 − thrust / starship) * deltat	$PC[n_s,n_2,n_4,n_5,n_6]$ $\wedge$ true

Figure 9-6

n_8	VAL$[n_s,n_2,n_4,n_5,n_6,n_7]$ updated by DISTANCE: distance $-$ velocity $*$ deltat	$PC[n_s,n_2,n_4,n_5,n_6,n_7] \wedge$ true

n_9	VAL$[n_s,n_2,n_4,n_5,n_6,n_7,n_8]$ updated by
	CURRVEL: velocity + (6.67*10**($-$11)
	        * station * starship / distance**2
	        $-$ thrust / starship) * deltat
		$PC[n_s,n_2,n_4,n_5,n_6,n_7,n_8] \wedge$
		true

n_{10}	VAL$[n_s,n_2,n_4,n_5,n_6,n_7,n_8,n_9]$ updated by TIME: time + deltat	$PC[n_s,n_2,n_4,n_5,n_6,n_7,n_8,n_9] \wedge$ true

n_{11}	VAL$[n_s,n_2,n_4,n_5,n_6,n_7,n_8,n_9,n_{10}]$ updated by
	NEXTVEL: velocity + (6.67*10**($-$11)
	        * station * starship / distance**2
	        $-$ thrust / starship) * deltat
	        + (6.67*10**($-$11) * station
	        * starship / distance**2
	        $-$ thrust / starship) * deltat
		$PC[n_s,n_2,n_4,n_5,n_6,n_7,n_8,n_9,n_{10}] \wedge$
		true

n_{12}	VAL$[n_s,n_2,n_4,n_5,n_6,n_7,n_8,n_9,n_{10},n_{11}]$ updated by ERROR: 0	$PC[n_s,n_2,n_4,n_5,n_6,n_7,n_8,n_9,n_{10},n_{11}] \wedge$ (velocity + (6.67*10**($-$11) * station * starship / distance**2 $-$ thrust / starship) * deltat + (6.67*10**($-$11) * station * starship / distance**2 $-$ thrust / starship) * deltat) ≤ 0.0

STATEMENTS ON THIS PATH
    $n_s, n_2, n_4, n_5, n_6, n_7, n_8, n_9, n_{10}, n_{11}, n_{12}, n_f$

SYMBOLIC REPRESENTATION OF PATH CONDITION
    $\sim$ (station ≤ 0.0 $\vee$ starship ≤ 0.0 $\vee$ thrust ≤ 0.0 $\vee$
    velocity ≤ 0.0 $\vee$ deltat ≤ 0.0 $\vee$ time ≤ 0.0 $\vee$ distance ≤ 0.0)
    $\wedge$ $\sim$ (distance**2 = 0.0) $\wedge$ ((velocity + (6.67*10**($-$11)
    * station * starship / distance**2 $-$ thrust / starship)
    * deltat + (6.67*10**($-$11) * station * starship / distance**2
    $-$ thrust / starship) * deltat) ≤ 0.0)

Figure 9-6 (cont.)

SIMPLIFIED SYMBOLIC REPRESENTATION OF PATH CONDITION
station > 0.0 $\wedge$ starship > 0.0 $\wedge$ thrust > 0.0 $\wedge$
velocity < 0.0 $\wedge$ deltat > 0.0 $\wedge$ time > 0.0 $\wedge$ distance > 0.0
$\wedge$ (velocity * distance**2 * starship * deltat +
13.34*10**(−11) * station * starship**2 * deltat −
2 * thrust * distance**2 * deltat) / distance**2 * starship $\leq$ 0.0

SYMBOLIC REPRESENTATION OF OUTPUT VARIABLES
TIME = time + deltat
DISTANCE = distance + velocity * deltat
ERROR = 0

Figure 9-6 (cont.)

statement	VAL	PC
		true
n_s	TIME: time DISTANCE: distance ERROR: Λ STATION: station STARSHIP: starship THRUST: thrust VELOCITY: velocity DELTAT: deltat GCONST: Λ GRAVITY: Λ CONSTACC: Λ CURRVEL: Λ NEXTVEL: Λ	$PC[n_s] \wedge$ $\sim$ (station $\leq$ 0.0 $\vee$ starship $\leq$ 0.0 $\vee$ thrust $\leq$ 0.0 $\vee$ velocity $\leq$ 0.0 $\vee$ deltat $\leq$ 0.0 $\vee$ time $\leq$ 0.0 $\vee$ distance $\leq$ 0.0)
n_2	VAL[n_s] updated by GCONST: 6.67*10**(-11)	$PC[n_s,n_2] \wedge$ distance**2 = 0.0
n_3	VAL[n_s,n_2] updated ERROR: 1	

STATEMENTS ON THIS PATH

n_s, n_2, n_3, n_f

SYMBOLIC REPRESENTATION OF PATH CONDITION

$\sim$ (station $\leq$ 0.0 $\vee$ starship $\leq$ 0.0 $\vee$ thrust $\leq$ 0.0 $\vee$
velocity $\leq$ 0.0 $\vee$ deltat $\leq$ 0.0 $\vee$ time $\leq$ 0.0 $\vee$ distance $\leq$ 0.0)
$\wedge$ distance**2 = 0.0

SIMPLIFIED SYMBOLIC REPRESENTATION OF PATH CONDITION

station > 0.0 $\wedge$ starship > 0.0 $\wedge$ thrust > 0.0 $\wedge$
velocity > 0.0 $\wedge$ deltat > 0.0 $\wedge$ time > 0.0 $\wedge$ distance > 0.0
$\wedge$ distance = 0.0

*** NONEXECUTABLE PATH ***

Figure 9-7

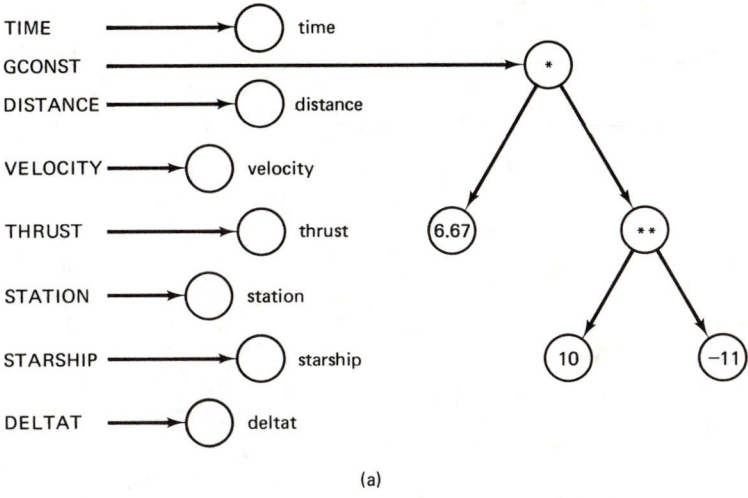

(a)

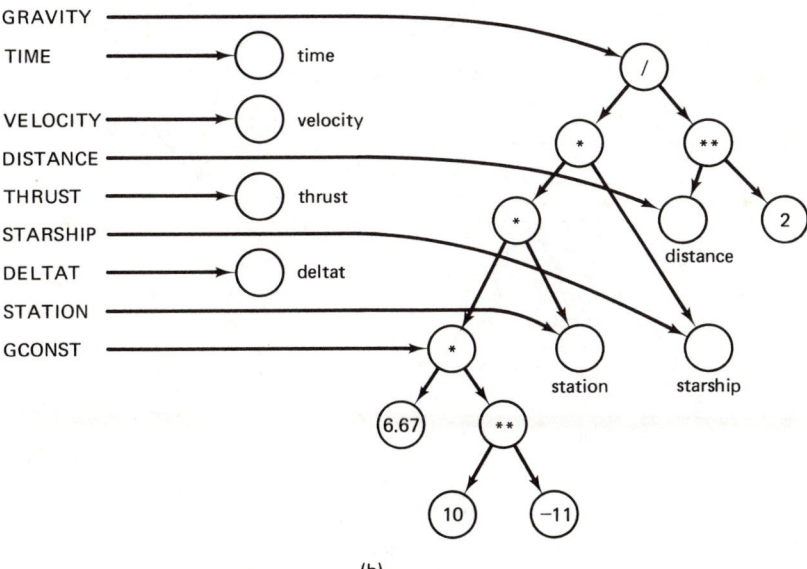

(b)

Figure 9-8

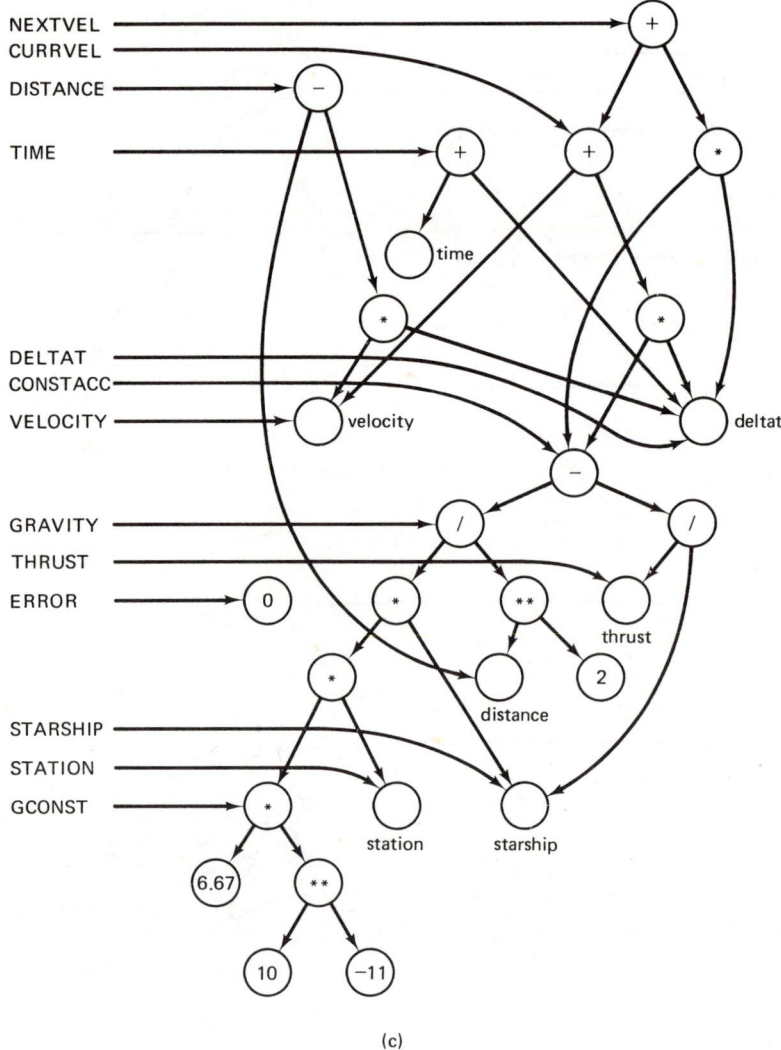

(c)

Figure 9-8 (cont.)

for systems concerned only with creating the path condition and not concerned with the symbolic expressions for intermediate or output variables. With this restriction, the backward substitution technique saves space by not maintaining extraneous expressions for the intermediate and output variables. An example of backward substitution is shown in Fig. 9-11, using the DOCKING procedure of Fig. 9-1 and again symbolically executing the program path of Fig. 9-6. An implementation technique that is just the reverse

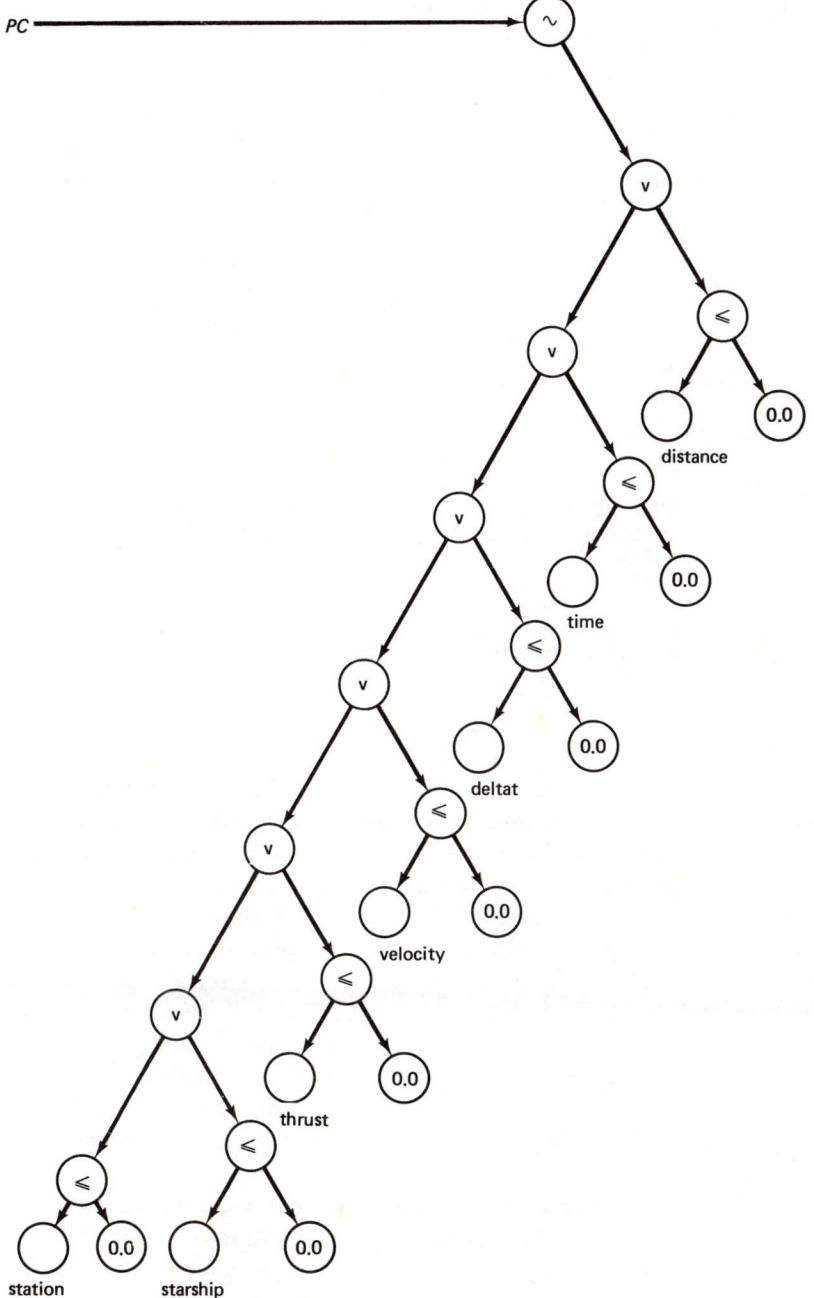

Figure 9-9

Tabular Representation

entry	operator	operand 1	operand 2
1	**	10	−11
2	*	6.67	CG1
3	*	CG2	station
4	*	CG3	starship
5	**	distance	2
6	/	CG4	CG5
7	/	thrust	starship
8	−	CG7	CG8
9	*	CG8	deltat
10	+	velocity	CG9
11	*	velocity	deltat
12	−	distance	CG11
13	+	time	deltat
14	*	CG8	deltat
15	+	CG10	CG14

Program Variables

TIME : CG13	GCONST : CG2
DISTANCE : CG12	GRAVITY : CG6
ERROR : 0	CONSTACC : CG8
STATION : station	CURRVEL : CG10
STARSHIP : starship	NEXTVEL : CG15
THRUST : thrust	
VELOCITY : velocity	
DELTAT : deltat	

Figure 9-10

of the described forward expansion technique can be used to create the symbolic expressions for backward substitution. Note that many of the statements, specifically those that do not modify variables for which values are input, can be ignored using backward substitution when only the path condition is desired. In the example of Fig. 9-11, statements 8, 10, and 12 are ignored. In a more general symbolic execution system where both the path condition and symbolic values are desired, the two approaches examine each statement and produce equivalent expressions for the *PC* and *VAL*. In systems which support early detection of nonexecutable paths, however, the forward expansion approach is more efficient. The rest of this section first describes several techniques for determining path condition consistency and then returns to the comparison between forward expansion and backward substitution.

In most cases, only a subset of the paths in a program are executable, and therefore it is desirable to determine path condition consistency. During symbolic execution it is desirable not only to recognize nonexecutable paths but to recognize the inconsistency as soon as possible. Early detection of a nonexecutable path prevents worthless, yet costly, symbolic execution of a

node or predicate	PC
n_f	true
$bp(n_{11}, n_{12})$	(nextvel) $\leq$ 0.0
n_{11}	(currvel + constacc * deltat) $\leq$ 0.0
n_9	(nextvel + constacc * deltat) $\leq$ 0.0
n_7	(currvel + constacc * deltat + constacc * deltat) $\leq$ 0.0
n_6	(velocity + constacc * deltat + constacc * deltat) $\leq$ 0.0
n_5	(velocity + (gravity − thrust / starship) * deltat + (gravity − thrust / starship) * deltat) $\leq$ 0.0
n_4	(velocity + ((gconst * station * starship / distance**2) − thrust / starship) * deltat + ((gconst * starship / distance**2) − thrust / starship) * deltat) $\leq$ 0.0
$bp(n_2, n_4)$	((velocity + ((gconst * station * starship / distance**2) − thrust / starship) * deltat + ((gconst * station * starship / distance**2) − thrust / starship) * deltat) $\leq$ 0.0) $\wedge$ $\sim$ (distance**2 = 0.0)
n_2	((velocity + ((6.67*10**(−11) * station * starship / distance**2) − thrust / starship) * deltat + ((6.67*10**(−11) * station * starship / distance**2) − thrust / starship) * deltat) $\leq$ 0.0) $\wedge$ $\sim$ (distance**2 = 0.0)
$bp(n_s, n_2)$	((velocity + ((6.67*10**(−11) * station * starship / distance**2) − thrust / starship) * deltat + ((6.67*10**(−11) * station * starship / distance**2) − thrust / starship) * deltat) $\leq$ 0.0) $\wedge$ $\sim$ (distance**2 = 0.0) $\wedge$ $\sim$ (station $\leq$ 0.0 $\vee$ starship $\leq$ 0.0 $\vee$ thrust $\leq$ 0.0 $\vee$ velocity $\leq$ 0.0 $\vee$ deltat $\leq$ 0.0 $\vee$ time $\leq$ 0.0 $\vee$ distance $\leq$ 0.0)
n_s	((velocity + ((6.67*10**(−11) * station * starship / distance**2) − thrust / starship) * deltat + ((6.67*10**(−11) * station * starship / distance**2) − thrust / starship) * deltat) $\leq$ 0.0) $\wedge$ $\sim$ (distance**2 = 0.0) $\wedge$ $\sim$ (station $\leq$ 0.0 $\vee$ starship $\leq$ 0.0 $\vee$ thrust $\leq$ 0.0 $\vee$ velocity $\leq$ 0.0 $\vee$ deltat $\leq$ 0.0 $\vee$ time $\leq$ 0.0 $\vee$ distance $\leq$ 0.0)

NOTE: The final simplified PC would be the same as the final simplified PC shown in Fig. 9-6.

Figure 9-11

nonexecutable path. Moreover, it allows an alternative edge to be selected on a partial path whenever an inconsistent branch predicate is initially encountered. Thus, the partial path that has already been symbolically executed can usually be salvaged.

Using the notation introduced in Section 9-1, whenever a partial path T_{ku} is augmented with a new node $n_{k, u+1}$, the branch predicate $s(bp(n_{ku}, n_{k, u+1})$ $[T_{ku}])$ is first simplified and then may be examined for consistency with the existing path condition $PC[T_{ku}]$. Any of several algebraic manipulation systems [Boge75, Brow73, RicD78b] can be used to simplify the PC to a canonical form, so this aspect of the implementation will not be described further. The branch predicate $s(bp(n_{ku}, n_{k, u+1})[T_{ku}])$ may either evaluate to a boolean constant (where the null branch predicate is considered to be the constant true), or it may be a symbolic expression in terms of the input variables. If the branch predicate is constant, consistency determination is immediate: $PC \wedge \text{true} = PC$ and $PC \wedge \text{false} = \text{false}$. When the branch predicate is a symbolic expression over the input values (and the PC is not the constant true), it is necessary to use a more sophisticated technique for determining path condition consistency. One approach to this problem is to use standard theorem-proving techniques. We refer to this as the axiomatic approach since it is based upon the axioms of predicate calculus. Another approach is to treat each conjunct in the PC as a constraint and to use one of several algebraic methods—such as a gradient hill-climbing algorithm [Elsp??], linear programming [Land73], or a more brute force approach [Rama76]—to solve the system of constraints. Both the axiomatic and algebraic approaches work well on the simple constraints that are generally created during symbolic execution [ClaL76b]. No method, however, can solve all arbitrary systems of constraints [Davi73]. In some instances, path consistency cannot be determined. The symbolic execution of such a path can continue, but whether or not the path can be executed is unknown.

Whenever the last node n_{ku} in the partial path T_{ku} has only one successor node, the branch predicate is null and is represented by the constant true, which is always consistent with the existing PC. When there is more than one successor node, each successor node and its respective branch predicate are considered as an alternative extension of the current path. There are three cases to be considered: (1) none of the alternative branch predicates is consistent with the PC; (2) only one of the alternative branch predicates is consistent with the PC; and (3) more than one of the alternatives are consistent with the PC. The graph shown in Fig. 9-12 demonstrates all three cases.

The first case only occurs when evaluating multiconditional predicates like those that occur for computed **go to** statements or **case** statements without an otherwise clause. This case implies a program error.

The alternative branch predicates for a set of successor nodes either all evaluate to constant boolean values, or all evaluate to symbolic expressions involving the input variables. Cases 1 and 2 can occur in either of these situations. When all the branch predicates evaluate to boolean constants, at most one of the alternatives can evaluate to true. Hence, case 3 can occur only when the branch predicates are symbolic expressions. Some symbolic execution systems will select the successor node in the first two cases and will give the user an option in selecting the path when the third case occurs.

Now to return to the comparison between forward expansion and backward substitution. Forward expansion is a more efficient technique of symbolic execution than backward substitution when PC consistency is

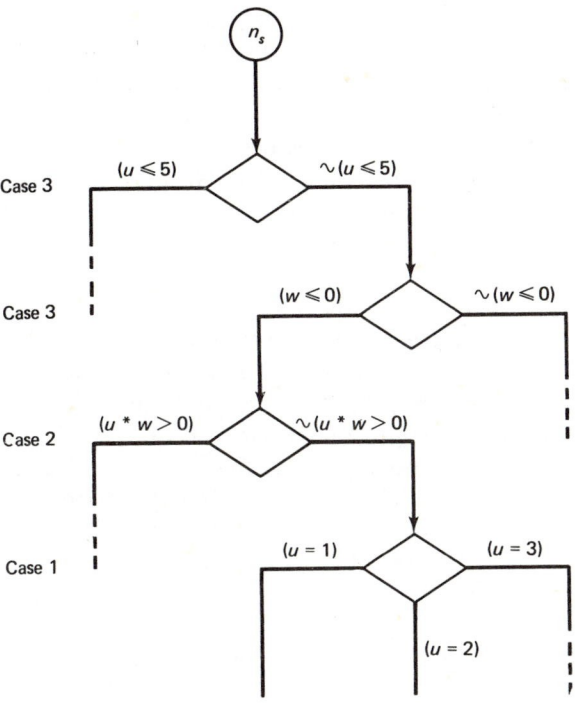

Figure 9-12

determined at each branch point. Using forward expansion, the branch predicates maintain their original form once they are created and conjoined to the *PC*. The *PC* is, therefore, only modified by the conjunction of a new, simplified constraint. In backward substitution the *PC* is likewise modified by a new, simplified constraint but, in addition, the *PC* may be modified by any assignment statement on the path that changes the value of any variable referenced in the *PC*. In other words, the *PC* that is created using forward expansion only contains expressions in terms of the input values, while that created using backward substitution may reference intermediate variables that are later modified. The additional *PC* modification during backward substitution is costly since it also requires resimplification of the modified constraints and consistency must be checked after each simplification.

9-3.3. Applications

Symbolic execution systems have several interesting applications. This section considers three applications: validation and documentation, error detection, and test data generation. The last part of this section considers methods of path selection.

The symbolic expressions that are generated for a program path can quite naturally be used for validation and documentation. The expressions often provide a concise representation of the output produced along a path. These expressions can be used to document the program or can be examined for errors. The symbolic expressions describe the path functions (p_{H1}, p_{H2}, ..., p_{HN}) for the entire path domain D_H^p. Normal execution, on the other hand, only provides particular output values ($z_1, \ldots, z_N$) for particular input values ($x_1, \ldots, x_M$). It is possible for the output data to be correct while the path functions are incorrect. To use a trivial example, assume the intended function of a program path with one input value and one output value is $2 * v + 3$ but the computed function of the path is $3 * v + 3$. If the program path is executed with $v = 0$, then the actual resulting value and intended value agree. Examination of the path function would quickly uncover the error. While not all errors would be this glaring or all symbolic expressions this short, examining the symbolic path functions is often useful in uncovering program errors [Howd76]. This is a particularly beneficial feature for examining programs for scientific applications, where it is often extremely difficult to manually compute the intended result accurately due to the complexity of the computations and domain of the input data. This method of program validation is referred to as symbolic testing.

The path functions created during symbolic execution could be evaluated for particular data values. The result would be the same as if the path had been executed. (In cases where roundoff errors, overflow, or underflow could occur, there may be discrepancies. We do not address these types of problems here.) The benefit of evaluation at this point is that the symbolic expressions for the path functions (p_{H1}, p_{H2}, ..., p_{HN}) and path domain D_H^p can be used to guide in the selection of input values. For example, boundary points of the path domain may be selected to check the correctness of the branch predicates [Whit78]. Also, if a path function is a polynomial, examination of its degree can be used in selecting the number of test data points needed to determine the correctness of this function.

Symbolic execution can also be actively applied to the detection of program errors. At appropriate points in the program, boolean conditions can be generated for certain predefined error conditions. These conditions can be evaluated and checked for consistency with the PC just as branch predicates are evaluated. Consistency implies the existence of input data in the path domain D_H^p that would cause the described error. Inconsistency implies that the error condition could not occur for any element in the input domain. This demonstrates another advantage of symbolic execution over normal program execution. Normal execution of a path may not uncover a run-time error, while symbolic execution of a path can detect the presence or guarantee the absence of some errors.

The ATTEST system [ClaL78] automatically generates constraints for certain error conditions whenever it encounters certain program constructs. For example, whenever a nonconstant divisor is encountered, a constraint is created comparing the symbolic value of the divisor to zero. This constraint is then temporarily conjoined to the *PC*. If the augmented *PC* is consistent, then input data exists that would cause a division-by-zero error; an error report is issued. If the augmented *PC* is inconsistent, then this potential run-time error could not occur for this division on this path. The division constraint is removed before symbolic execution continues.

Path verification of program assertions is another method of error detection. Instead of predefining the error conditions, user-created assertions define conditions that must be true at designated points in the program. An error exists if a condition is not true for all elements of the path domain. When an assertion is encountered during symbolic execution, the complement of the condition is evaluated and conjoined to the *PC*. The rest of the analysis is then identical to the implicit error detection described above.

Test data generation is another natural application of symbolic execution. The path condition is examined to determine a solution, that is, test data to execute the program path. Symbolic execution, like other methods of program validation, does not test the program in its natural environment. Evaluation of the path functions for particular input values return numeric results, but because the environment has been changed, these results may not always agree with those from normal execution. Errors in the hardware, operating system, compiler, or symbolic execution system may cause an erroneous result. In addition, testing a program demonstrates its actual performance characteristics. Select [Boye75] and ATTEST [ClaL78] are two symbolic execution systems that attempt to generate test data. Since an actual solution to the *PC* is desired and not just *PC* consistency, an algebraic method is used to solve the system of constraints in the *PC*. Additional work [Whit78] is being done to further refine methods of selecting data within a path domain to increase the probability of detecting errors and to insure the absence of certain error conditions.

The preceding sections assume that the paths to be analyzed by symbolic execution are provided. These paths are either chosen by the user or are selected automatically by a component of the symbolic execution system. Most symbolic execution systems support an interactive path selection facility that allows the user to "walk through" a program, statement by statement. This feature is useful for debugging since the evolution of the program's computations and path conditions can be observed. More extensive program coverage requires an automated path selection facility for choosing a set of paths based on some criterion, which is dependent on the intended application of the symbolic execution.

Three criteria that are often used for program testing are statement, branch, and path coverage. Statement coverage requires that each statement in the program occurs at least once on one of the selected paths. Testing the program on a set of paths satisfying this criterion is called *statement testing*. Likewise, branch coverage requires that each branch predicate occurs at least once on one of the selected paths, and testing such a set of paths is called *branch testing*. Path coverage requires that all paths be selected, and executing all paths is referred to as *path testing*. Branch coverage implies statement coverage, while path coverage implies branch coverage. Path coverage, in fact, implies the selection of all feasible combinations of branch predicates, which may require an infinite number of paths.

Automatically selecting a set of paths to satisfy any one of these criteria is nontrivial since nonexecutable paths must be excluded [Gabo76]. The ATTEST system [ClaL78], for example, uses a dynamic, goal-oriented method of path selection. In this system, a path is selected, statement by statement, as symbolic execution proceeds. A statement is selected based on its potential for satisfying the path selection criterion, which can be statement, branch, or path coverage. If an infeasible path is encountered, the system "backs up" (i.e., returns to the state preceding the last selected statement) and, whenever possible, selects another statement which may satisfy the selection criterion. A more complete description of path selection methods for symbolic execution systems can be found in [Wood79].

9-4. GLOBAL SYMBOLIC EVALUATION

The goal of global symbolic evaluation [Chea79] is the derivation of a global representation of the program—a representation of all program variables for all the paths rather than along a specific path through the program. In other words, global symbolic evaluation results in a closed form representation of an entire program, independent of any particular path execution. In this section, we describe the general method of global symbolic evaluation and explain the technique used in evaluating loops within a program.

9-4.1. General Method

Global symbolic evaluation, like symbolic execution, analyzes the control flow graph of the program. The nodes in the graph are numbered such that if node n_i is a predecessor of node n_j, then $i < j$. To maintain this node ordering and since loops are handled separately by loop analysis, all backward branches are disregarded. The control flow graph in Fig. 9-2 has an appropriate node numbering for global symbolic evaluation of the procedure DOCKING. The numbering of the nodes in the control flow graph provides the order in which the statements are symbolically evaluated.

As in symbolic execution, the input values are represented by symbolic names, and all program variables are represented as expressions in terms of those symbolic names throughout the analysis. The actual evaluation of a statement is performed by the same technique as that used in symbolic execution. Furthermore, the computations themselves are maintained in a form analogous to the computational graph created in symbolic execution. The two methods differ in the way in which conditional branching is analyzed. In evaluating a particular node, symbolic execution only considers the program state of the one partial program path preceding the current node, whereas global symbolic evaluation considers the program state of all immediate predecessor nodes in the control flow graph. At any node in the graph, global symbolic evaluation maintains a representation of the state that describes the conditions and computations of all partial program paths reaching that node. This results in a conditional representation, or *case*-like expression, where each component of the *case* expression represents such a path. Furthermore, a partial program path may represent a class of paths which differ by the number of iterations of any loop on the path. Loop analysis develops these classes and is explained in the next section. We therefore refer to the program state of node n_i as $STATE[n_i]$, where the state may have several PCs associated with it and each PC has a corresponding VAL. The representation of the program state for global symbolic evaluation is shown in Fig. 9-4.

To see how a node is evaluated, consider a particular node n_k, with predecessor nodes n_i and n_j (which have been previously evaluated). Control may reach n_k via either of the edges (n_i, n_k) or (n_j, n_k), and the transfer from either predecessor node occurs under the conditions of the corresponding branch predicate $bp(n_i, n_k)$ or $bp(n_j, n_k)$. Thus, when n_k is evaluated, there are two possible symbolic $STATE$s that are effective. The program state at node n_k is then a conditional symbolic expression provided by updating the $STATE$ in the context of either possible transfer to the node. In the context of the transfer from predecessor node n_i to n_k, $STATE[n_k]$ is obtained by updating the $STATE$ of node n_i in much the same way as the update is performed in symbolic execution. The branch predicate $bp(n_i, n_k)$ is conjoined to all the PCs associated with n_i, and the conjunctions are checked for consistency. If any of the augmented PCs are inconsistent, the corresponding cases are discarded from the updated $STATE$. Each remaining PC's VAL is updated in all components whose variables are modified by node n_k. The same procedure is followed for the transfer from n_j to n_k, and these two $STATE$ vectors form the conditional representation of the program state at node n_k.

9-4.2. Loop Analysis

The described representation of the state of a node in terms of all partial program paths into the node is only possible because of the form in which global symbolic evaluation represents loops. Loop analysis attempts to represent a program loop with a closed-form expression describing the effects of that loop. By doing this, paths which differ only by the number of iterations of a loop are represented by one path.

Given a loop, global symbolic evaluation develops expressions for the values of all variables modified within the body of the loop in terms of the symbolic input values and a symbolic iteration count for the loop. In addition, a conditional expression is obtained representing the actual number of iterations of the loop that will be performed for any arbitrary execution of the program, i.e., for any arbitrary assignment of input values.

Loop analysis begins by associating an iteration counter k with the loop. For each variable v whose value may change within the loop, a special symbolic value v_k is used to represent the value of the variable v at the beginning of the kth iteration of the loop. Symbolic evaluation of the loop body is then performed in much the same manner as the forward expansion technique of symbolic execution. This "execution" provides the symbolic value of the variable v at the end of the kth iteration, under the assumption of another iteration of the loop. This symbolic value is, alternatively, the variable's value at the beginning of the $(k + 1)$st iteration of the loop, v_{k+1}. The global symbolic evaluation outside the loop determines the initial value v_1 of the variable just prior to the first iteration of the loop. The symbolic expressions v_k and v_{k+1} provide a recurrence relation with the boundary value v_1. The solution to the recurrence relation, which is represented by $v(k)$, is the value of the variable v upon exit from the kth iteration of the loop.

In addition to determining this representation for the variables modified within the loop, the closed-form representation of a loop contains a conditional expression for the number of times the loop is performed. Each condition under which the loop will be exited is singled out; these are the branch predicates that control any transfer to a point outside of the loop body. Each condition is, in general, some constraint on variables modified within the loop (otherwise it would not control exit from the loop). These branch predicates can, therefore, be evaluated over the values of the modified variables at the beginning of the kth iteration, that is, over the solutions to the recurrence relations $v(k)$. This produces a symbolic representation for each exit condition as a function of the general iteration number k. The number of the iteration before which exit occurs, call it k_L, is the minimum $k, k \geq 0$, such that one of the exit conditions is true.

The loop may then be represented in its closed form by k_L, the conditional expression for the number of times the loop will be executed, and $v(k_L)$, the symbolic value of variable v after k_L iterations of the loop for each variable v modified within the loop. Figure 9-13 shows the analysis performed for the loop in the procedure DOCKING of Fig. 9-1.

Obtaining the recurrence relation $v(k)$ is not always straightforward. Complications arise in several situations. When there are simultaneous recurrence relations, several variables, which may be dependent, are modified

Variables modified within the loop
$$\text{DISTANCE}_{k+1} = \text{DISTANCE}_k - \text{CURRVEL}_k * \text{deltat}$$
$$\text{CURRVEL}_{k+1} = \text{NEXTVEL}_k$$
$$\text{TIME}_{k+1} = \text{TIME}_k + \text{deltat}$$
$$\text{NEXTVEL}_{k+1} = \text{CURRVEL}_{k+1} + (6.67*10**(-11) * \text{station} * \text{starship} / \text{distance}**2$$
$$- \text{thrust} / \text{starship}) * \text{deltat}$$

Initial values
$$\text{DISTANCE}_1 = \text{distance}$$
$$\text{CURRVEL}_1 = \text{velocity}$$
$$\text{TIME}_1 = \text{time}$$
$$\text{NEXTVEL}_1 = \text{velocity} + (6.67*10**(-11) * \text{station} * \text{starship} / \text{distance}**2$$
$$- \text{thrust} / \text{starship}) * \text{deltat}$$

Solutions to recurrence relations
$$\text{TIME}(k) = \text{time} + \sum_{i=2}^{k} \text{deltat}$$
$$\text{NEXTVEL}(k) = \text{velocity} + \sum_{i=1}^{k}[(6.67*10**(-11) * \text{station} * \text{starship} / \text{distance}**2$$
$$- \text{thrust} / \text{starship}) * \text{deltat}]$$
$$\text{CURRVEL}(k) = \text{velocity} + \sum_{i=2}^{k}[(6.67*10**(-11) * \text{station} * \text{starship} / \text{distance}**2$$
$$- \text{thrust} / \text{starship}) * \text{deltat}]$$
$$\text{DISTANCE}(k) = \text{distance} - \sum_{j=2}^{k}[(\text{velocity} + \sum_{i=2}^{j}[(6.67*10**(-11) * \text{station}$$
$$* \text{starship} / \text{distance}**2 - \text{thrust} / \text{starship}) * \text{deltat}]) * \text{deltat}]$$

Simplified solutions
$$\text{TIME}(k) = \text{time} + (k - 1) * \text{deltat}$$
$$\text{NEXTVEL}(k) = \text{velocity} + (k) * (6.67*10**(-11) * \text{station} * \text{starship}**2 * \text{deltat}$$
$$- \text{thrust} * \text{distance}**2 * \text{deltat}) / \text{distance}**2 * \text{starship}$$
$$\text{CURRVEL}(k) = \text{velocity} + (k - 1) * (6.67*10**(-11) * \text{station} * \text{starship}**2 * \text{deltat}$$
$$- \text{thrust} * \text{distance}**2 * \text{deltat}) / \text{distance}**2 * \text{starship}$$
$$\text{DISTANCE}(k) = \text{distance} - \sum_{j=2}^{k}[\text{velocity} * \text{deltat} + (j - 1) * (6.67*10**(-11) *$$
$$\text{station} * \text{starship}**2 * \text{deltat}**2 - \text{thrust} * \text{distance}**2 * \text{deltat}**2)$$
$$/ \text{distance}**2 * \text{starship}]$$

Exit condition
$$\text{NEXTVEL}(k) \leq 0.0$$

Evaluated exit condition
$$(\text{velocity} + (k) * (6.67*10**(-11) * \text{station} * \text{starship}**2 * \text{deltat}$$
$$- \text{thrust} * \text{distance}**2 * \text{deltat}) / \text{distance}**2 * \text{starship}) \leq 0.0$$

Number of iterations of loop, k_L
$$k_L = \text{minimum } k, \text{ such that } k \geq 0 \text{ and } (\text{velocity} + (k) * (6.67*10**(-11)$$
$$* \text{station} * \text{starship}**2 * \text{deltat} - \text{thrust} * \text{distance}**2 * \text{deltat}) / \text{distance}**2$$
$$* \text{starship}) \leq 0.0$$

Figure 9-13

within the loop. In particular, the dependence may be cyclic; v may depend on w, which depends on v. Problems are also caused when the recurrence relations are conditional, in which case the closed-form solution becomes quite complicated, provided it can be solved at all.

When a closed-form representation of a loop can be found by this analysis technique, it provides a more general evaluation of a loop than the technique employed by symbolic execution systems—evaluating the loop for a specific number of iterations. There is no reason, however, that this loop analysis technique could not also be incorporated into symbolic execution.

After the loop has been analyzed, the closed-form representation becomes part of the program state at the point where the loop is exited, and evaluation continues. Figure 9-14 shows the program state following global symbolic evaluation of the procedure DOCKING, where the conditions and functions have been simplified.

case

    station $\leq$ 0.0 $\vee$ starship $\leq$ 0.0 $\vee$ thrust $\leq$ 0.0 $\vee$
    velocity $\leq$ 0.0 $\vee$ deltat $\leq$ 0.0 $\vee$ time $\leq$ 0.0 $\vee$
    distance $\leq$ 0.0:
      TIME = time
      DISTANCE = distance
      ERROR = 1
      STATION = station
      STARSHIP = starship
      THRUST = thrust
      VELOCITY = velocity
      DELTAT = deltat
      GCONST = Λ
      GRAVITY = Λ
      CONSTACC = Λ
      CURRVEL = Λ
      NEXTVEL = Λ
    station > 0.0 $\wedge$ starship > 0.0 $\wedge$ thrust > 0.0 $\wedge$
    velocity > 0.0 $\wedge$ deltat > 0.0 $\wedge$ time > 0.0 $\wedge$
    distance > 0.0 :
      TIME = time + $(k_L - 1)$ * deltat
      DISTANCE = distance $- \sum_{j=2}^{k_L}$[(velocity * deltat + $(j - 1)$ * (6.67*10**(-11)
            * station * starship**2 * deltat**2 - thrust * distance**2 * deltat**2)
            / distance**2 * starship]
      ERROR = 0
      STATION = station
      STARSHIP = starship
      THRUST = thrust
      VELOCITY = velocity
      DELTAT = deltat
      GCONST = 6.67*10**(-11)
      GRAVITY = 6.67*10**(-11) * station * starship / distance**2
      CONSTACC = (6.67*10**(-11) * station * starship**2 - thrust * distance**2)
            / distance**2 * starship
      CURRVEL = velocity + $(k_L - 1)$ * (6.67*10**(-11) * station * starship**2 * deltat
            - thrust * distance**2 * deltat) / distance**2 * starship
      NEXTVEL = velocity + (k_L) * (6.67*10**(-11) * station * starship**2 * deltat
            - thrust * distance**2 * deltat) / distance**2 * starship
endcase

Figure 9-14

9-4.3. Applications

    Global symbolic evaluation has several possible applications, many of which are similar to those of symbolic execution. Test data generation could conceivably be performed by solving for the *PC*s in the **case** expression. New methods for solving a *PC* must be explored since the *PC* may contain recurrence relations as well as constraints. The closed form representation of a program could be compared with some types of program specifications to determine consistency. User-provided assertions can be checked for validity; with global symbolic evaluation, the truth of these assertions can be checked for all paths rather than a specific path. In addition, since the program state is maintained at all points in the program, assertions could be provided by the user after completion of global symbolic evaluation without requiring reevaluation of the program. Similarly, global symbolic evaluation can be used to automatically generate and check error conditions as it analyzes a program.

Global symbolic evaluation also has applications in program optimization [Town76]. As in optimizing compilers, the existence of the computational graph [Cock70b] makes common subexpression elimination and constant folding relatively straightforward. In addition, several types of loop optimizations may often be performed when the closed-form representations of loops are obtainable. Loop-invariant computations may be easily detected since they are independent of the iteration count of the loop; these may thus be moved outside of the loop. Loop fusion can sometimes be performed when the number of iterations performed by two loops can be determined to be the same, and variables manipulated in the second loop are not computed in a later iteration of the first loop. When variables modified within the loop have values that form arithmetic progressions, that is, they are incremented by the same amount each time through the loop, these computations can sometimes be moved out of the loop and replaced by expressions in terms of the iteration count. Optimizations that perform in-line substitution of a procedure may also be benefited by global symbolic evaluation, since the closed-form representation of the procedure may enable better determination of when such substitution is useful.

9-5. DYNAMIC SYMBOLIC EVALUATION

Dynamic symbolic evaluation is just one of the features provided in dynamic testing systems [Balz69, Fair75]. Using test data to determine the path, dynamic symbolic evaluation systems provide symbolic representations of the executed path's computations. This section gives a brief overview of dynamic testing systems and then describes dynamic symbolic evaluation, its implementation techniques, and its applications.

9-5.1. General Method

Dynamic testing systems monitor program behavior during execution. This is implemented by instrumenting the program, that is, by inserting calls to analysis procedures in appropriate places in the code. This is generally done by a preprocessor and may double the number of statements in the source program. The user then supplies input data to execute the instrumented program.

Dynamic testing systems may provide a profile of each execution run as well as an accumulated profile of all execution runs. Some of the types of information in a profile include the number of times each statement was executed, the number of times each edge was traversed, the minimum and maximum number of times each loop was traversed, the minimum and maximum values assigned to variables, and the paths that were executed. In addition, the system may check the validity of user assertions at run time [Fair75, Stuc73]. Unlike the assertion checking done by symbolic execution, dynamic assertion checking is done just for the supplied input data and not for the entire path domain. Either the assertion is true and thus valid for the input data, or the assertion is false and thus invalid for the program.

The dynamic symbolic evaluation component of dynamic testing systems provides a symbolic representation of the computations of each executed path. For input data that executes path P_H, $VAL[P_H]$ is provided. $VAL[P_H]$ can be represented internally as a computational graph. This computational graph would be similar to the computational graph for symbolic execution, but it would be augmented to include the value produced at each node. The computational graph can be created using the forward expansion method described in Section 9-3.2.

At the end of the path, the expression for each output variable is shown. Generally, dynamic evaluation systems display the expressions as trees instead of as mathematical expressions, though both or either form could be displayed. Using the DOCKING procedure and the same path as that in Fig. 9-6, the computational trees are shown in Fig. 9-15; Fig. 9-16 shows the output that might be produced by dynamic symbolic evaluation using the format of Fig. 9-5.

Existing dynamic symbolic evaluation systems are only concerned with the VAL component of the program state. Since the input values are known, each branch predicate evaluates to the constant value true (or a run-time error is encountered). The PC is, therefore, equal to true. It would be easy to extend dynamic symbolic evaluation to include symbolic representations of the PC. Note that the path functions are represented symbolically, though all computations evaluate to a numeric value. The PC provides valuable information by defining the path domain even though it is not necessary to check for path consistency. Examination of the PC, like examination of the VAL, may uncover program errors. An erroneous PC would imply an erroneous branch predicate or erroneous calculation affecting the branch predicate.

9-5.2. Applications

The primary application of dynamic symbolic evaluation is program debugging. When an error is uncovered in a program, dynamic symbolic evaluation provides a picture of the resulting computations. Examination

Input values

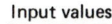

STATION = 4.0*10^{14}
STARSHIP = 100.0
THRUST = 4500.0
VELOCITY = 75.0

DELTAT = 10.0
TIME = 120530.0
DISTANCE = 2000.0

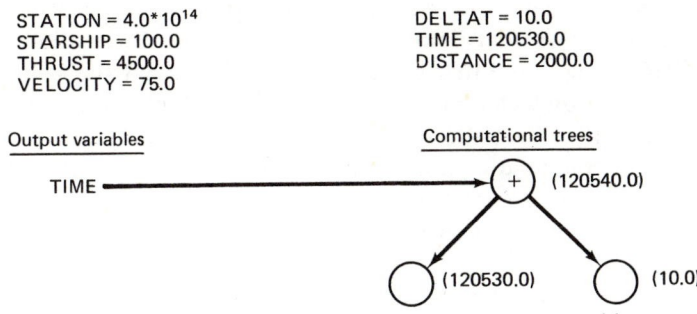

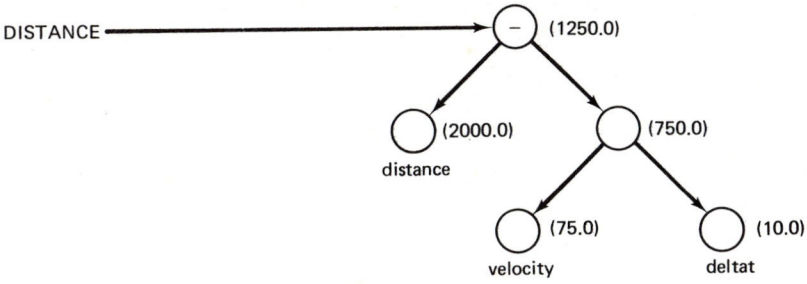

Figure 9-15

STATEMENTS EXECUTED
$n_s, n_2, n_4, n_5, n_6, n_7, n_8, n_9, n_{10}, n_{11}, n_{12}, n_f$
SYMBOLIC AND ACTUAL VALUES OF OUTPUT VARIABLES
    TIME = time + deltat = 120540.
    DISTANCE = distance − velocity * deltat = 1250.
    ERROR = 0.

Figure 9-16

of symbolic representations of the path functions and path condition often helps to isolate the cause of an error. To assist in debugging, these systems provide a capability for examining the computational graph while it is being constructed. Program execution can be followed statement-by-statement. These systems also allow the user to back up execution. In other words, the user can direct the system to execute the path backwards and thus undo the computational graph to help the user isolate the error. Experiments with ISMS [Fair75] have shown that both forward and backward execution are beneficial for debugging. Note that backward execution is not the same as the backward substitution technique described in Section 9-3.2. In backward execution, at least part of the path has already been executed and the corresponding part of the computational graph has been built. Dynamic symbolic evaluation requires an implementation method somewhat similar to forward expansion, since input data is used to determine the path, thus implying a forward analysis approach.

Dynamic symbolic evaluation can also provide an aid in the use of structured testing methods, which base the testing of a program on its internal structure. Structured testing methods select test data that cause the execution of specific computation sequences in a program. The various structured testing techniques—statement testing, branch testing and path testing—differ in the specific structure that is the goal of execution coverage. The execution profile provided by dynamic symbolic evaluation systems usually contains statement execution counts, edge traversal counts, and descriptions of the paths executed, and thus is helpful in determining when a program has been tested sufficiently based on any one of these structured testing methods.

9-6.   CONCLUSION

Symbolic evaluation has several applications for program validation and testing. Since it is a relatively new method of program analysis, there are several unsolved problems and directions for future research. Initial studies of its effectiveness have only recently been conducted. This section describes the results from one such study and sets forth several areas for future research.

9-6.1.   Effectiveness

The major use of symbolic evaluation is in the testing and analysis of programs. Howden investigated the effectiveness of several program testing and analysis techniques [Howd77a]. Included in the techniques were branch testing, path testing, and symbolic testing, each of which can be aided by symbolic evaluation. In this study, a program testing or program analysis technique is considered reliable for a particular error if the detection of the error is guaranteed by the use of the technique. For 28 errors occurring in 6 programs, the reliability of each technique was determined.

A testing strategy that involves actual execution is reliable for an error only if every test data set that satisfies the criterion of that strategy is guaranteed to reveal the error. The statistics obtained in the study indicate that the path-testing strategy was reliable for 18 of the 28 errors. Path testing involved the testing of every program path, which generally is impractical since programs may have an infinite number of paths. A strategy that approximates path testing was found to be reliable for 12 of the errors. This technique required that all program paths with two or less iterations of any loop be tested. Branch testing was guaranteed to reveal only six errors. This indicates that the detection of many of the errors is dependent on testing combinations of program branches rather than single branches. Although the statement-testing strategy was not analyzed in this study, experience has shown that this technique is, in general, less effective than the other methods of structured testing.

The analysis of the output produced by symbolic execution is referred to as symbolic testing. Symbolic testing is considered reliable for an error if the symbolic output generated for a path reveals the presence of the error in an obvious way that would catch the attention of the programmer. Symbolic testing of the set of paths chosen to approximate path testing guranteed the detection of 17 of the 28 errors.

Symbolic evaluation methods can be used to assist in all the testing techniques mentioned above. All three methods of symbolic evaluation can be used to perform symbolic testing. In addition, symbolic execution can be used to generate test data to meet the criterion of statement, branch, or path testing. Dynamic symbolic evaluation does not actively generate test data but monitors the progress towards meeting the criterion of a testing strategy. The output produced by dynamic symbolic evaluation shows the results of both symbolic and actual testing. This combination may provide more extensive error detection. Global symbolic evaluation performs symbolic testing for all program paths and also classifies paths in a way that could be used in actual testing.

Howden's study found that combining both symbolic testing and actual testing was reliable for more errors than either method used alone. It is important to note that this study only considered a method reliable for an error if it guaranteed the detection of the error for every test data set that satisfies the testing criterion. If this requirement were relaxed and data sets were intelligently selected based on the information in the symbolic output, more errors would probably be detected. Cohen and White [Whit78] have described a strategy for test data selection using the symbolic output that aids in the detection of errors in the path condition. The error analysis described in Section 9-3.3 is helpful for detecting errors in path functions.

9-6.2. Future Directions

Symbolic evaluation poses several unsolved problems and opens up several areas for future research. Two of these areas, program loop analysis and path condition consistency determination, are described above. Work is currently being done in both these areas. Another area of curent research is array element determination. A problem occurs whenever the subscript of an array depends on input values, in which case the element that is being referenced or defined in the array is unknown. Though an indeterminate array element can be represented symbolically, path condition consistency determination becomes extremely complicated when such an occurrence affects the path condition. This problem occurs frequently during both symbolic execution and global symbolic evaluation. (It cannot occur during dynamic symbolic evaluation since all values, including subscript values, are known.) Inefficient solutions exist, for in the worse case all possible subscript values can be enumerated. Though there has been some work on this problem [Rama76] and a related problem for record structures [Jone81], the results are still unsatisfactory. Efficient solutions requiring a minimal amount of backtracking are still being explored.

General problems of efficiency plague all three symbolic evaluation methods. These methods have only been implemented in experimental systems; more efficient implementations must be explored. Osterweil [Oste81] describes a method in which data flow analysis and symbolic execution can be used jointly to optimize code, particularly the instrumented code created by dynamic symbolic evaluation systems.

Osterweil also emphasizes the need for integrating analysis methods so that each will be used where it is most beneficial and so that the information gathered by one method can be used to enhance another. The coordination of data flow analysis and symbolic evaluation is an area where this integration may prove fruitful. Data flow analysis methods can be used to detect paths containing suspect sequences of events but cannot determine path feasibility. Symbolic evaluation could be used to determine feasibility of these paths. Both analysis methods are strengthened by this pairing. Data flow analysis would no longer report suspect conditions on infeasible paths, thus decreasing extraneous information, which only dilutes its effectiveness. In addition, suspect conditions on executable paths could now be reported as errors. Symbolic execution would benefit in that it would be directed to suspect paths, thus increasing its effectiveness for detecting program errors. Osterweil describes several other interesting prospects for integrating symbolic evaluation with data flow analysis.

In this paper we have focused on the analysis of the code. Future directions of program analysis will be concerned with all stages of program development. As work progresses in the areas of requirements, specifications and design, analysis methods will also progress. Symbolic evaluation methods present alternative representations and should prove useful during these earlier stages of program development. The ability to compare a specification of the intended program function with the actual implementation through the use of symbolic evaluation has been demonstrated for certain classes of specifications and programs [RicD78a]. Additional work in this area is in progress.

9-6.3. Summary

In this paper, three methods of symbolic program analysis have been described. All three methods represent a program's computations and input domains by symbolic expressions in terms of the input values, though the methods differ in their scope of representation.

Dynamic symbolic evaluation is the most restrictive method of the three. Using input data to determine a path, dynamic symbolic evaluation represents the path functions. Since input data is used to select the path, the path condition evaluates to true. Though the path condition can be described symbolically, there is no need to test it for consistency. With no simplification of the path conditions nor path condition consistency determination necessary, the implementation of dynamic symbolic evaluation is straightforward. The major application of this method is program debugging.

Symbolic execution systems are not dependent on input data to determine the path as dynamic symbolic evaluation is, but rather can analyze any specified program path. Symbolic execution systems represent the path functions and path condition. Since many program paths are not executable, symbolic execution tries to determine path condition consistency. The most efficient symbolic execution systems use a forward expansion technique of implementation and determine path condition consistency whenever a new branch predicate is conjoined to the existing path condition. In general, path condition consistency cannot always be determined. In practice, consistency can often be determined using any of several existing techniques. In addition, there is work currently being done on improving methods of solving arbitrary systems of constraints. There are several interesting applications of symbolic execution in the area of program validation including automatic error detection, test data generation, and determination of consistency with program specifications.

Global symbolic evaluation has the widest scope of analysis; it attempts to represent the total program function by a symbolic expression. Since there may be an infinite number of paths in a program, this method requires more sophisticated analysis than the mere conjunction of the symbolic expressions for each path. Instead a technique of loop analysis is used that attempts to represent each program loop in a closed form dependent on an arbitrary loop iteration count. While this approach can successfully analyze several types of loops, additional work is needed in this area. By using a closed-form representation for each loop, the computations for a set of paths and their respective domains can be represented. Each such representation is one case in the conditional program representation provided by global symbolic evaluation. Path condition consistency still must be determined for each case in this conditional representation, but now this process is even further complicated by the presence of recurrence relations describing each loop. This is another area in need of further research.

Dynamic symbolic evaluation is a well-understood process that has been implemented in two dynamic testing systems. Symbolic execution has also been successfully implemented though there are still several implementation problems to be examined, as well as several areas of research to be explored. Global symbolic evaluation is a relatively new method with prospective applications in the areas of program validation and program optimization. Its applicability in the future will most likely depend on its success in loop analysis and consistency determination.

Part IV

THEORY
OF PROGRAM FLOW
ANALYSIS

Like most aspects of computer science, flow analysis originated as a practical approach to practical problems and has only subsequently developed a rich underlying theory. The theory serves to provide foundations for the practical methods, to generalize them and demarcate their scope of validity, and to clarify their relationship to other areas.

The theory of flow analysis has drawn on model theory and formal semantics for the basic concepts of standard and nonstandard models, their properties and relationships, and tools for defining them. The theory of algorithms and concrete complexity has contributed efficient algorithms for solving flow-analytic problems. But the most prominent contributing area has been the theory of lattices and the Tarski-Knaster Fixed Point Theorem.

Flow analysis problems can generally be stated as systems of equations

$$x_1 = f_1(x_1, \ldots, x_n)$$
$$\vdots$$
$$x_n = f_n(x_1, \ldots, x_n)$$

or in vector form $\vec{x} = \vec{f}(\vec{x})$ whose solutions describe properties of a program. Often x_i represents a description of the value of a particular program variable at a particular program point. If the problem can be stated so that $\vec{x}$ ranges over a complete lattice (a set with a partial order satisfying certain properties about the existence of limits), then any solution to the system of equations is a fixed point of the function $\vec{f}$, i.e., an element $\vec{v}$ of the lattice such that $\vec{v} = \vec{f}(\vec{v})$. If $\vec{f}$ is monotone or order-preserving [i.e., $\vec{x} \leq \vec{y}$ implies $\vec{f}(\vec{x}) \leq \vec{f}(\vec{y})$], then the Tarski-Knaster Fixed Point Theorem guarantees the existence of solutions to the system of equations and, if $\vec{f}$ is continuous as well, provides a method for computing one of them, which usually happens to be the one desired.

Thus lattice theory provides the essential conceptual framework for flow analysis. In practical terms, it tells us that if one seeks to formulate a new flow-analytic problem and apply the available tools to its solution then the space of properties to be used should be a complete lattice (or at least a complete partial order), the functions used should be monotone on that lattice, and so on. If these conditions are satisfied, the standard theory and methods will apply.

The following three chapters discuss three aspects of flow analysis theory. The first, by Cousot, is of foundational importance. It develops the theory in an extremely general setting, that of deterministic discrete dynamic systems, and proves a series of theorems concerning the relationship between forward and backward flow analyses and program properties concerning correct execution, achievable values, and termination. The second chapter, by Donzeau-Gouge, demonstrates how to derive a property semantics of a programming language from a formal denotational semantics of the language. This can serve as the basis for automating the construction of flow analysis systems. The final chapter, by Jones and Muchnick, concerns the relationship between two varieties of flow analysis called the independent attribute and relational methods, their computational complexity properties, and some implications of their relative complexities.

Chapter 10

Semantic Foundations
of Program Analysis

Patrick Cousot

10-1. INTRODUCTION

In the first part we establish general mathematical techniques useful in the task of analyzing semantic properties of programs. In the second part, we describe an algorithmic and hence approximate solution to the problem of analyzing semantic properties of programs.

The term "program analysis" will be given a precise meaning, but is better introduced by the following:

Example 10-1. Consider the program:

{1}
    while $x \geq 1000$ **do**
{2}
      $x := x + y;$
{3}
    od;
{4}

where x and y are integer variables taking their values in the set I of integers included between $-b - 1$ and b where b is the greatest machine-representable integer.

By "analysis of the semantic properties" of that program we understand the determination that:

1. The execution of that program starting from the initial value $x_0 \in I$ and $y_0 \in I$ of x and y terminates without run-time error if and only if $(x_0 < 1000) \lor (y_0 < 0)$.

2. The execution of the program never terminates if and only if $(1000 \le x_0 \le b) \land (y_0 = 0)$.

3. The execution of the program leads to a run-time error (by overflow) if and only if $(x_0 \ge 1000) \land (y_0 > 0)$.

4. During any execution of the program the following assertions P_i characterize the only possible values that the variables x and y can possess at program point i:

$$P_1 = \lambda \langle x, y \rangle.[(-b - 1 \le x \le b) \land (-b - 1 \le y \le b)]$$
$$P_2 = \lambda \langle x, y \rangle.[(1000 \le x \le b) \land (-b - 1 \le y \le b)]$$
$$P_3 = \lambda \langle x, y \rangle.[(1000 + y \le x \le min(b, b + y))$$
$$\land (-b - 1 \le y \le b)]$$
$$P_4 = \lambda \langle x, y \rangle.[(-b - 1 \le x < 1000) \land (-b - 1 \le y \le b)]$$

10-2. SUMMARY

In Section 10-3 we define what we mean by flowchart programs; that is, we define their abstract syntax and operational semantics. A program defines a dynamic discrete system [Kell76, Pnue77] that is a transition relation on states. In Section 10-4 we set up general mathematical methods useful in the task of analyzing the behavior of dynamic discrete systems. In order to make this mathematically demanding section self-contained, lattice-theoretical theorems on fixed points of isotone or continuous maps are first introduced in a separate subsection. The main result of Section 10-4 shows that the predicates characterizing the descendants of the entry states, the ascendants of the exit states, the states which lead to an error, and the states which cause the system to diverge are the least or greatest solution to forward or backward fixed point equations. This result is completed by the proof that whenever a forward equation (corresponding to postconditions) is needed, a backward equation (corresponding to preconditions) can be used instead, and vice versa. Finally we show that when the set of states of the dynamic discrete system is partitioned, the forward or backward equation can be decomposed into a system of equations. Numerous examples of applications are given which provide for a very concise presentation and justification of classical [Floy67, Naur66, King69, Hoar69, Dijk76] or innovative program proving methods. Section 10-5 tailors the general mathematical techniques previously set up for analyzing the behavior of a deterministic discrete dynamic system to suit the particular case when the system is a program. Two main theorems make explicit the syntactic construction rules for obtaining the systems of semantic backward or forward equations from the text of a program. The facts that the extreme fixed points of these systems of semantic equations can lead to complete information about program behavior and that the backward and forward approaches are equivalent are illustrated on the simple introductory example.

In the second part we briefly survey our joint work with Radhia Cousot on the automatic synthesis of approximate invariant assertions for programs. Because of well-known unsolvability problems, the semantic equations which have been used in Section 10-5 for program analysis cannot be algorithmically solved. Hence we must limit ourselves to constructive methods which automatically compute aprroximate solutions. Such approximate information about the program behavior is often useful, e.g., in program verification systems, program debugging systems, optimizing compilers, etc. Approximate solutions to the semantic equations can be obtained by first simplifying these equations (Section 6.1 of [Cous79]) and next solving the simplified equations associated with the program text, using any chaotic iteration technique [Cous77b, Cous77c]. In Section 10-6.2 we show that when the exact solution to the simplified equations is obtained only after an infinite number of iteration steps, the convergence of the iterates can be sped up using an extrapolation technique based on a widening or narrowing operator [Cous77a]. A hierarchy of examples taken from [Cous77a] and [Cous78] illustrates the approximate program analysis method.

10-3. ABSTRACT SYNTAX AND OPERATIONAL SEMANTICS OF PROGRAMS

10-3.1. Abstract Syntax

Informally, programs will be abstractly represented as single-entry, single-exit directed graphs with edges labeled with instructions.

Example 10-2. The program of Example 10-2 will be represented by Fig. 10-1.

A *program graph* is a quadruple $\langle V, \epsilon, \omega, E \rangle$ where V is a finite set of vertices, $E \subseteq V \times V$ is a finite set of edges, and $\epsilon \in V, \omega \in V$ are distinct entry and exit vertices such that ϵ is of in-degree 0, ω is of out-degree 0, and every vertex lies on a path from ϵ to ω.

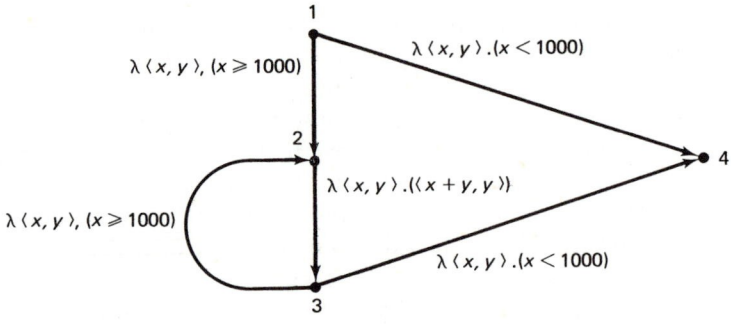

Figure 10-1

Let $\vec{v}$ be a vector of variables taking their values in a *universe U*. The set $I(U)$ of *instructions* is partitioned into a subset $I_a(U)$ of *assignments* and a subset $I_t(U)$ of *tests*. An assignment $\vec{v} := f(\vec{v})$ is represented as a partial map from U into U. A test is represented as a partial map from U into $B = \{true, false\}$.

A *program* is a triple $\langle G, U, L \rangle$ where the program graph G, the universe U, and the labeling $L \in (E \rightarrow I(U))$ are such that for every nonexit vertex n in G either n is of out-degree 1 and the edge leaving n is labeled with an assignment or n is of out-degree 2 and the edges leaving n are labeled with tests p and $\neg p$.

10-3.2. Operational Semantics

The operational semantics of a syntactically valid program π specifies the sequence of successive states of the computation defined by π.

10-3.2.1. States

The set S of *states* is the set of pairs $\langle c, m \rangle$ where $c \in V \cup \{\xi\}$ is the *control state* and $m \in U$ is the *memory state*. $\xi \notin V$ is the *error control state*.

The entry, exit, and erroneous states are respectively characterized by $v_\epsilon = \lambda\langle c, m \rangle.(c = \epsilon)$, $v_\omega = \lambda\langle c, m \rangle.(c = \omega)$ and $v_\xi = \lambda\langle c, m \rangle.(c = \xi)$.

10-3.2.2. State transition function

A program $\pi = (G, U, V)$ defines a *state transition function* $\bar{\tau} \in (S \rightarrow S)$ as follows:

1. $\bar{\tau}(\langle \xi, m \rangle) = \langle \xi, m \rangle$ (no run-time error recovery is available)

2. $\bar{\tau}(\langle \omega, m \rangle) = \langle \omega, m \rangle$

3. If $c_1 \in V$ is of out-degree 1, $\langle c_1, c_2 \rangle \in E$, $L(\langle c_1, c_2 \rangle) = f$, $f \in I_a(U)$ then if $m \in dom(f)$ then $\bar{\tau}(\langle c_1, m \rangle) = \langle c_2, f(m) \rangle$ else $\bar{\tau}(\langle c_1, m \rangle) = \langle \xi, m \rangle$.

4. If $c_1 \in V$ is of out-degree 2, $\langle c_1, c_2 \rangle \in E, \langle c_1, c_3 \rangle \in E, L(\langle c_1, c_2 \rangle) = p, L(\langle c_1, c_3 \rangle) = \neg p, p \in I_t(U)$ then if $m \notin dom(p)$ then $\bar{\tau}(\langle c_1, m \rangle) = \langle \xi, m \rangle$ else if $p(m)$ then $\bar{\tau}(\langle c_1, m \rangle) = \langle c_2, m \rangle$ else $\bar{\tau}(\langle c_1, m \rangle) = \langle c_3, m \rangle$.

The *state transition relation* $\tau \in ((S \times S) \longrightarrow B)$ defined by π is $\lambda \langle s_1, s_2 \rangle.(s_2 = \bar{\tau}(s_1))$.

10-3.2.3. Transitive closure of a binary relation

If $\alpha, \beta \in (S \times S \longrightarrow B)$ are two binary relations on S, their *product* $\alpha \circ \beta$ is defined as $\lambda \langle s_1, s_2 \rangle.[\exists s_3 \in S: \alpha(s_1, s_3) \wedge \beta(s_3, s_2)]$. For any natural number n, the *n-extension* α^n of α is defined recursively as $\alpha^0 = e\alpha = \lambda \langle s_1, s_2 \rangle.[s_1 = s_2], \alpha^{n+1} = \alpha \circ \alpha^n$. The *(reflexive) transitive closure* of α is $\alpha^* = \lambda \langle s_1, s_2 \rangle.[\exists n \geq 0: \alpha^n(s_1, s_2)]$.

10-3.2.4. Execution and output of a program

The execution of the syntactically valid program π starting from an initial state $s_1 \in S$ is said *to lead to an error* iff $[\exists s_2 \in S: \tau^*(s_1, s_2) \wedge v_\xi(s_2)]$, and to *terminate* iff $[\exists s_2 \in S: \tau^*(s_1, s_2) \wedge v_\omega(s_2)]$. Otherwise it is said to *diverge*. The *output* of the execution of a syntactically valid program π starting from an initial state $\langle \epsilon, m_1 \rangle \in S$ is defined if and only if this execution terminates with $m_2 \in U$ such that $\tau^*(\langle \epsilon, m_1 \rangle, \langle \omega, m_2 \rangle)$, and m_2 is the output.

10-4. ANALYSIS OF THE BEHAVIOR OF A DISCRETE DYNAMIC SYSTEM

In order to establish general mathematical techniques useful in analyzing semantic properties of programs, we use the model of discrete dynamic systems. The advantage is that the reasoning on a set S of states and a state transition relation τ leads to very concise notations, terse results, and brief proofs. Another benefit is that the applications of the mathematical techniques for analyzing the behavior of a dynamic discrete system are not necessarily confined within computer science.

10-4.1. Discrete Dynamic Systems

A *discrete dynamic system* is a 5-tuple $\langle S, \tau, v_\epsilon, v_\omega, v_\xi \rangle$ such that S is a nonvoid set of *states*, $\tau \in ((S \times S) \longrightarrow B)$ where $B = \{true, false\}$ is the *transition relation* holding between a state and its possible successors, $v_\epsilon \in (S \longrightarrow B)$ characterizes the *entry states*, $v_\omega \in (S \longrightarrow B)$ characterizes the *exit states*, and $v_\xi \in (S \longrightarrow B)$ characterizes the *erroneous states*. It is assumed that the entry, exit, and erroneous states are disjoint ($\forall i, j \in \{\epsilon, \omega, \xi\}, (i \neq j) \longrightarrow (\forall s \in S, \neg(v_i(s) \wedge v_j(s)))$).

The following study is devoted to *total* ($\forall s_1 \in S, \exists s_2 \in S: \tau(s_1, s_2)$) and *deterministic* ($\forall s_1, s_2, s_3 \in S, (\tau(s_1, s_2) \wedge \tau(s_1, s_3)) \Rightarrow (s_2 = s_3)$) dynamic discrete systems.

A program as defined in Section 10-3 defines a total and deterministic discrete dynamic system. Moreover the entry states are *exogenous* ($\forall s_1, s_2 \in S, \tau(s_1, s_2) \Rightarrow \neg(v_\varepsilon(s_2))$), the exit states are *stable* ($\forall s_1, s_2 \in S, (v_\omega(s_1) \wedge \tau(s_1, s_2)) \Rightarrow (s_1 = s_2)$), and the system is *without error recovery* ($\forall s_1, s_2 \in S, (v_\varepsilon(s_1) \wedge \tau(s_1, s_2)) \Rightarrow v_\varepsilon(s_2)$).

The *inverse* of $\tau \in ((S \times S) \rightarrow B)$ is $\tau^{-1} = \lambda\langle s_1, s_2\rangle.[\tau(s_2, s_1)]$. A system is *injective* if τ^{-1} is deterministic; it is *invertible* if it is injective and τ^{-1} is total. In general a program does not define an injective dynamic discrete system.

10-4.2. Fixed Point Theorems for Isotone and Continuous Operators on a Complete Lattice

This section recalls the lattice-theoretic definitions [Birk67] and theorems which are needed below.

A *partially ordered set* (*poset*) $L(\sqsubseteq)$ consists of a nonempty set L and a binary relation $\sqsubseteq$ on L which is *reflexive* ($\forall a \in L, a \sqsubseteq a$), *antisymmetric* ($\forall a, b \in L, (a \sqsubseteq b \wedge b \sqsubseteq a) \Rightarrow (a = b)$) and *transitive* ($\forall a, b, c \in L, (a \sqsubseteq b \wedge b \sqsubseteq c) \Rightarrow (a \sqsubseteq c)$). Given $H \subseteq L$, $a \in L$ is an *upper bound* of H if $b \sqsubseteq a$ for all $b \in H$. a is called the *least upper bound* of H, in symbols $\bigsqcup H$, if a is an upper bound of H and if for any upper bound b of H, $a \sqsubseteq b$. The dualized notions (that is all $\sqsubseteq$ are replaced by the inverse $\sqsupseteq$) are the ones of *lower bound* and *greatest lower bound*. $L(\sqsubseteq)$ is a *complete lattice* if the least upper bound $\bigsqcup H$ of H and the greatest lower bound $\bigsqcap H$ of H exist for all H, $H \subseteq L$. A complete lattice L has an *infimum* $\bot = \bigsqcap L$ and a *supremum* $\top = \bigsqcup L$.

An operator f on L is *strict* if $f(\bot) = \bot$, and *isotone* iff ($\forall a, b \in L, (a \sqsubseteq b) \Rightarrow (f(a) \sqsubseteq f(b))$). $a \in L$ is a *fixed point* of f iff $f(a) = a$. Tarski's Fixed Point Theorem states that the set of fixed points of an isotone operator f on a complete lattice $L(\sqsubseteq, \bot, \top, \sqcup, \sqcap)$ is a (nonempty) complete lattice with partial ordering $\sqsubseteq$. The *least fixed point* of f, in symbols $lfp(f)$, is $\bigsqcap\{x \in L: f(x) \sqsubseteq x\}$. Dually the *greatest fixed point* of f, in symbols $gfp(f)$ is $\bigsqcup\{x \in L: x \sqsubseteq f(x)\}$. An element a of L such that $a \sqsubseteq f(a)$ (respectively $f(a) \sqsubseteq a$) is called a *pre-fixed point* (*post-fixed point*) of f.

Let f be an isotone operator on the complete lattice L. The *Recursion Induction Principle* follows from Tarski's Fixed Point Theorem and states that ($\forall x \in L, (f(x) \sqsubseteq x) \Rightarrow (lfp(f) \sqsubseteq x)$). The *Dual Recursion Induction Principle* is ($\forall x \in L, (x \sqsubseteq f(x)) \Rightarrow (x \sqsubseteq gfp(f))$).

If $L(\sqsubseteq, \bot, \top, \sqcup, \sqcap)$ is a complete lattice, then the set $(M \rightarrow L)$ of total maps from the set M into L is a complete lattice $(M \rightarrow L)(\sqsubseteq', \bot', \top', \sqcup', \sqcap')$ for the *pointwise ordering* $f \sqsubseteq' g$ iff ($\forall x \in L, f(x) \sqsubseteq g(x)$). In the following the distinction between $\sqsubseteq, \bot, \top, \sqcup, \sqcap$ and $\sqsubseteq', \bot', \top', \sqcup', \sqcap'$ will be determined by the context. The set L^n of n-tuples of elements of L is a complete lattice for the *componentwise ordering* $\langle a_1, \ldots, a_n \rangle \sqsubseteq \langle b_1, \ldots, b_n \rangle$ iff $a_i \sqsubseteq b_i$ for $i = 1, \ldots, n$. The set 2^L of subsets of L is a complete lattice $2^L(\subseteq, \phi, L, \cup, \cap)$. A map $f \in (M \to L)$ will be extended to $(M^n \to L^n)$ as $\lambda \langle x_1, \ldots, x_n \rangle.[\langle f(x_1), \ldots, f(x_n) \rangle]$ and to $(2^M \to 2^L)$ as $\lambda S.\{f(x): x \in S\}$.

A sequence $x_0, x_1, \ldots, x_n, \ldots$ of elements of $L(\sqsubseteq)$ is an *increasing chain* iff $x_0 \sqsubseteq x_1 \sqsubseteq \ldots \sqsubseteq x_n \sqsubseteq \ldots$. An operator f on $L(\sqsubseteq, \bot, \top, \sqcup, \sqcap)$ is *semi-$\sqcup$-continuous* iff for any chain $C = \{x_i : i \in A\}, C \subseteq L, f(\sqcup C) = \sqcup f(C)$. Kleene's Fixed Point Theorem [Klee52] states that the least fixed point of a semi-$\sqcup$-continuous operator f on $L(\sqsubseteq, \bot, \top, \sqcup, \sqcap)$ is equal to $\sqcup\{f^i(\bot): i \geq 0\}$ where f^i is defined by recurrence as $f^0 = \lambda x.[x], f^{i+1} = \lambda x.[f(f^i(x))]$.

A poset $L(\sqsubseteq)$ is said to satisfy the *ascending chain condition* if any increasing chain terminates, that is if $x_i \in L, i = 0, 1, 2, \ldots$, and $x_0 \sqsubseteq x_1 \sqsubseteq \ldots \sqsubseteq x_n \sqsubseteq \ldots$, then for some m we have $x_m = x_{m+1} = \ldots$. An operator f on $L(\sqsubseteq, \bot, \top, \sqcup, \sqcap)$ which is semi-$\sqcup$-continuous is necessarily isotone, but the converse is not true in general. However if f is an isotone operator on a complete lattice satisfying the ascending chain condition, then f is semi-$\sqcup$-continuous. Also an operator f on a complete lattice L which is a *complete-$\sqcup$-morphism* (i.e., $\forall H \subseteq L, f(\sqcup H) = \sqcup f(H)$) is obviously semi-$\sqcup$-continuous.

Dual results hold for *decreasing chains, semi-$\sqcap$-continuous* operators, *descending chain conditions*, and *complete-$\sqcap$-morphisms*.

Suppose $L(\sqsubseteq, \bot, \top, \sqcup, \sqcap), L'(\sqsubseteq', \bot', \top', \sqcup', \sqcap')$ are complete lattices and we have the commuting diagram of isotone functions shown in Fig. 10-2, where h is strict $(h(\bot) = \bot')$ and semi-$\sqcup$-continuous. Then $h(lfp(f)) = lfp(g)$.

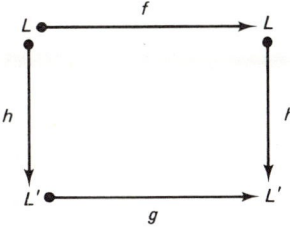

Figure 10-2

In a complete lattice $L(\sqsubseteq, \bot, \top, \sqcup, \sqcap)$, a is a *complement* of b if $a \sqcap b = \bot$ and $a \sqcup b = \top$. A *uniquely complemented complete lattice* $L(\sqsubseteq, \bot, \top, \sqcup, \sqcap, \neg)$ is a complete lattice in which every element a has a unique complement $\neg a$. Park's Theorem [Park69] states that if f is an isotone operator on a uniquely complemented complete lattice $L(\sqsubseteq, \perp, \top, \sqcup, \sqcap)$ then $\lambda x.[\neg f(\neg x)]$ is an isotone operator on L, $gfp(f) = \neg lfp(\lambda x.[\neg f(\neg x)])$.

Let $L(\sqsubseteq, \perp, \top, \sqcup, \sqcap)$ be a complete lattice, $n \geq 1$, and F a semi-$\sqcup$-continuous operator on L^n. The system of equations

$$X = F(X)$$

which can be detailed as

$$X_j = F_j(X_1, \ldots, X_n) \qquad j = 1, \ldots, n$$

has a least solution which is the least upper bound of the sequence $\{X^i : i \geq 0\}$ where $X^0 = \langle \perp, \ldots, \perp \rangle$ and $X^{i+1} = F(X^i)$, which can be detailed as:

$$X_j^{i+1} = F_j(X_1^i, \ldots, X_n^i) \qquad j = 1, \ldots, n$$

One can also use a chaotic iteration strategy and arbitrarily determine at each step which are the components of the system of equations which will evolve and in what order (as long as no component is forgotten indefinitely).

More precisely [Cous77b, Cous77c] $lfp(F)$ is the least upper bound of any chaotic iteration sequence $\{X^i : i \geq 0\}$ where $X^0 = \langle \perp, \ldots, \perp \rangle$ and

$$X_j^{i+1} = F_j(X_1^i, \ldots, X_n^i) \qquad \text{if } j \in J_i$$
$$X_j^{i+1} = X_j^i \qquad\qquad\quad \text{if } j \notin J_i$$

provided that $(\forall i \geq 0, J_i \subseteq [1, n]$ and $(\forall j \in [1, n], \exists k \geq 0 : j \in J_{i+k}))$. A dual result holds for $gfp(F)$.

10-4.3. Characterization of the Set of Descendants of the Entry States of a Discrete Dynamic System as a Least Fixed Point

Given a discrete dynamic system $(S, \tau, v_e, v_\omega, v_\xi)$, the set of *descendants of the states satisfying a condition* $\beta \in (S \longrightarrow B)$ is by definition the set characterized by

$$\lambda s_2.[\exists s_1 \in S : \beta(s_1) \wedge \tau^*(s_1, s_2) = post(\tau^*)(\beta)$$

using the notation

$$post \in (((S \times S) \longrightarrow B) \longrightarrow ((S \longrightarrow B) \longrightarrow (S \longrightarrow B)))$$
$$post = \lambda\theta.[\lambda\beta.[\lambda s_2.[\exists s_1 \in S : \beta(s_1) \wedge \theta(s_1, s_2)]]]$$

Example 10-3. Let π be a program defining a total and deterministic system $(S, \tau, v_e, v_\omega, v_\xi)$. Assume that $\phi, \Psi \in (S \longrightarrow B)$ specify what it is that π is intended to do: the execution of the program π starting with an entry state satisfying ϕ terminates and the exit state satisfies Ψ on termination of π. A *partial correctness proof* consists in showing that:

$$v_\omega \wedge post(\tau^*)(v_e \wedge \phi) \Rightarrow \Psi$$

In words, every exit state which is a descendant of an entry state satisfying ϕ must satisfy Ψ. The question of termination is not involved.

We now show that $post(\tau^*)(\beta)$ is a solution to the equation $\alpha = \beta \vee post(\tau)(\alpha)$; more precisely it is the least one for the implication $\Rightarrow$ considered as a partial ordering on $(S \longrightarrow B)$.

Theorem 10-4.

1. $((S \times S) \longrightarrow B)(\Rightarrow, \lambda(s_1, s_2).false, \lambda(s_1, s_2).true, \vee, \wedge, \neg)$ and $(S \longrightarrow B)(\Rightarrow, \lambda s.false, \lambda s.true, \vee, \wedge, \neg)$ are uniquely complemented complete lattices.

2. $\forall \theta \in ((S \times S) \longrightarrow B)$, $post(\theta)$ is a strict complete $\vee$-morphism. $\forall \beta \in (S \longrightarrow B)$, $\lambda \theta.[post(\theta)(\beta)]$ is a strict complete $\vee$-morphism.

3. $\forall \tau \in ((S \times S) \longrightarrow B)$, $\forall \beta \in (S \longrightarrow B)$,
$$post(\tau^*)(\beta) = \bigvee_{n \geq 0} post(\tau^n)(\beta) = lfp(\lambda \alpha.[\beta \vee post(\tau)(\alpha)])$$

Proof. The diagram of isotone functions shown in Fig. 10-3 is com-

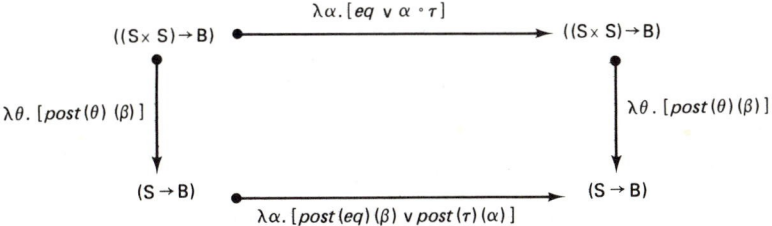

Figure 10-3

muting and $\lambda \theta.[post(\theta)(\beta)]$ is a strict complete $\vee$-morphism. Therefore

$$post(lfp(\lambda \alpha.[eq \vee \alpha \circ \tau]))(\beta) = post(\tau^*)(\beta)$$
$$= lfp(\lambda \alpha.[post(eq)(\beta) \vee post(\tau)(\alpha)])$$
$$= lfp(\lambda \alpha.[\beta \vee post(\tau)(\alpha)]).$$

Also $post(\tau^*)(\beta) = post(\bigvee_{n \geq 0} \tau^n)(\beta) = \bigvee_{n \geq 0} post(\tau^n)(\beta)$. ∎

Example 10-5. Floyd [Floy67] and Naur's [Naur66] method of inductive assertions for proving the partial correctness of π with respect to ϕ, Ψ, consists in guessing an assertion ι and showing that $(((v_\epsilon \wedge \phi) \Rightarrow \iota) \wedge (post(\tau)(\iota) \Rightarrow \iota) \wedge ((v_\omega \wedge \iota) \Rightarrow \Psi))$.

Using the recursion induction principle, from $(((v_\epsilon \wedge \phi) \Rightarrow \iota) \wedge$

$(post(\tau)(\iota) \Rightarrow \iota))$ we infer $(lfp(\lambda\alpha.[(\nu_\epsilon \wedge \phi) \vee post(\tau)(\alpha)]) \Rightarrow \iota)$. It follows from Theorem 10-4, Part 3 that $(\nu_\omega \wedge post(\tau^*)(\nu_\epsilon \wedge \phi)) \Rightarrow (\nu_\omega \wedge \iota) \Rightarrow \Psi$. The method is sound [ClaE77].

Reciprocally, if π is partially correct with respect to ϕ, Ψ, then this can be proved using the Floyd-Naur method. This completeness result follows from the fact that one can choose ι as $lfp(\lambda\alpha.[\nu_\epsilon \wedge \phi) \vee post(\tau)(\alpha)])$.

10-4.4.   Characterization of the Set of Ascendants of the Exit States of a Deterministic Discrete Dynamic System as a Least Fixed Point

In the case of a deterministic discrete dynamic system, the set of *ascendants of the states satisfying a condition* $\beta \in (S \longrightarrow B)$ is characterized by

$$\lambda s_1.[\exists s_2 \in S : \tau^*(s_1, s_2) \wedge \beta(s_2)] = pre(\tau^*)(\beta)$$

using the notation

$$pre \in (((S \times S) \longrightarrow B) \longrightarrow ((S \longrightarrow B) \longrightarrow (S \longrightarrow B)))$$
$$pre = \lambda\theta.[\lambda\beta.[\lambda s_1.[\exists s_2 \in S : \theta(s_1, s_2) \wedge \beta(s_2)]]]$$

Example 10-6.   Let π be a program defining a total and deterministic system $(S, \tau, \nu_\epsilon, \nu_\omega, \nu_\xi)$ and ϕ, $\Psi \in (S \longrightarrow B)$ be respectively entry and exit specifications. A *total correctness proof* consists in showing

$$\nu_\epsilon \wedge \phi \Rightarrow pre(\tau^*)(\nu_\omega \wedge \Psi)$$

In words, every entry state satisfying ϕ is the ascendant of an exit state satisfying Ψ. This is a proof of termination when $\Psi = \lambda s.[true]$.

Once the mathematical properties of post have been studied, similar ones can be easily derived for *pre* since $pre(\theta)(\beta) = post(\theta^{-1})(\beta)$ and $post(\theta)(\beta) = pre(\theta^{-1})(\beta)$. This point is illustrated by the proof of the following:

Theorem 10-7.

1. $\forall \theta \in ((S \times S) \longrightarrow B)$, $pre(\theta)$ is a strict complete $\vee$-morphism; $\forall \beta \in (S \longrightarrow B)$, $\lambda\theta.pre(\theta)(\beta)$ is a strict complete $\vee$-morphism.

2. $\forall \tau \in ((S \times S) \longrightarrow B)$, $\forall \beta \in (S \longrightarrow B)$,
$$pre(\tau^*)(\beta) = \bigvee_{n \geq 0} pre(\tau^n)(\beta) = lfp(\lambda\alpha.[\beta \vee pre(\tau)(\alpha)])$$

Proof. $\forall \tau, \tau_1, \ldots \in ((S \times S) \longrightarrow B)$, $(\tau_1 \circ \tau_2)^{-1} = (\tau_2^{-1} \circ \tau_1^{-1})$; $\forall n \in$ **N**, $(\tau^n)^{-1} = (\tau^{-1})^n$; $(\bigvee_i \tau_i)^{-1} = \bigvee_i (\tau_i)^{-1}$, $(\tau^*)^{-1} = (\tau^{-1})^*$. Therefore it follows from Theorem 10-4 that $\forall \theta \in ((S \times S) \longrightarrow B)$, $pre(\theta) =$

$post(\theta^{-1})$ is a strict complete $\bigvee$-morphism. $\forall \beta \in (S \longrightarrow S)$, $\lambda\theta.pre(\theta)(\beta)$ $= \lambda\theta.post(\theta^{-1})(\beta)$ is a strict complete $\bigvee$-morphism. Also

$$pre(\tau^*)(\beta) = post((\tau^*)^{-1})(\beta) = post((\tau^{-1})^*)(\beta) = \bigvee_{n \geq 0} post((\tau^{-1})^n)(\beta)$$

$$= \bigvee_{n \geq 0} post((\tau^n)^{-1})(\beta) = \bigvee_{n \geq 0} pre(\tau^n)(\beta)$$

$$= lfp(\lambda\alpha.[\beta \vee post(\tau^{-1})(\alpha)]) = lfp(\lambda\alpha.[\beta \vee pre(\tau)(\alpha)]). \quad\blacksquare$$

10-4.5. Characterization of the States of a Total Deterministic System Which Do Not Lead to an Error as a Greatest Fixed Point

The entry states which are the origins of correctly terminating or diverging execution paths of a deterministic program $\pi(S, \tau, v_\epsilon, v_\omega, v_\xi)$ are those which do not lead to a run-time error. They are characterized by $v_\epsilon \wedge \neg pre(\tau^*)(v_\xi)$.

Theorem 10-8. Let $\tau \in ((S \times S) \longrightarrow B)$ be total and deterministic.

$$\forall \beta \in (S \longrightarrow B), \quad \neg pre(\tau^*)(\beta) = gfp(\lambda\alpha.[\neg\beta \wedge pre(\tau)(\alpha)])$$

Proof. $\neg pre(\tau^*)(\beta) = \neg lfp(\lambda\alpha.[\beta \vee pre(\tau)(\alpha)]) = \neg lfp(\neg\lambda\alpha.[\neg\beta \wedge pre(\tau)(\neg(\neg\alpha))])$. According to Park's Fixed Point Theorem, this is equal to $gfp(\lambda\alpha.[\neg\beta \wedge \neg pre(\tau)(\neg\alpha)])$. Let $\bar\tau \in (S \longrightarrow S)$ be such that $(\forall s_1, s_2 \in S, (\tau(s_1, s_2) \leftrightarrow (\bar\tau(s_1) = s_2)))$. We have $\neg pre(\tau)(\neg\alpha) = \lambda s_1.[\neg\neg\alpha(\bar\tau(s_1))] = \lambda s_1.[\alpha(\bar\tau(s_1))] = pre(\tau)(\alpha)$. $\quad\blacksquare$

10-4.6. Analysis of the Behavior of a Total Deterministic Discrete Dynamic System

Given a total deterministic system $\pi(S, \tau, v_\epsilon, v_\sigma, v_\xi)$ we have established that the analysis of the behavior of this system can be carried out by solving fixed point equations as follows:

Theorem 10-9.

1. The set of descendants of the entry states satisfying an entry condition $\phi \in (S \longrightarrow B)$ is characterized by:

$$post(\tau^*)(v_\epsilon \wedge \phi) = lfp(\lambda\alpha.[(v_\epsilon \wedge \phi) \vee post(\tau)(\alpha)])$$

2. The set of ascendants of the exit states satisfying an exit condition $\Psi \in (S \longrightarrow B)$ is characterized by:

$$pre(\tau^*)(v_\omega \wedge \Psi) = lfp(\lambda\alpha.[(v_\omega \wedge \Psi) \vee pre(\tau)(\alpha)])$$

3. The set of states leading to an error is characterized by:

$$pre(\tau^*)(v_\xi) = lfp(\lambda\alpha.[v_\xi \vee pre(\tau)(\alpha)])$$

4. The set of states which do not lead to an error (i.e., cause the system either to properly terminate or to diverge) is characterized by:

$$\neg pre(\tau^*)(v_\xi) = gfp(\lambda\alpha.[\neg v_\xi \wedge pre(\tau)(\alpha)])$$

5. The set of states which cause the system to diverge is characterized by:

$$\neg pre(\tau^*)(v_\omega \vee v_\xi) = gfp(\lambda\alpha.[\neg v_\omega \wedge \neg v_\xi \wedge pre(\tau)(\alpha)])$$

Example 10-10. The proof that a program $\pi(S, \tau, v_\epsilon, v_\sigma, v_\xi)$ does not terminate for the entry states satisfying a condition $\delta \in (S \longrightarrow B)$ consists in proving that $v_\epsilon \wedge \delta \Rightarrow \neg pre(\tau^*)(v_\omega \vee v_\xi)$. It follows from Theorem 10-9(5) and the Dual Recursion Induction Principle that this can be done by guessing an assertion $\iota \in (S \longrightarrow B)$ and proving that $(((v_\epsilon \wedge \delta) \Rightarrow \iota) \wedge (\iota \Rightarrow \neg v_\omega \wedge \neg v_\xi \wedge pre(\tau)(\iota)))$.

10-4.7. Relationships Between *pre* and *post*

Theorem 10-11. Let $\theta \in ((S \times S) \longrightarrow B)$. $\forall \beta, \gamma \in (S \longrightarrow B)$,

1. $pre(\theta)(\beta) = post(\theta^{-1})(\beta), post(\theta)(\beta) = pre(\theta^{-1})(\beta)$
2. If θ is deterministic, then:

$$post(\theta)(pre(\theta)(\beta)) = (\beta \wedge post(\theta)(true)) \Rightarrow \beta$$

3. If θ is total, then:

$$\beta \Rightarrow pre(\theta)(post(\theta)(\beta))$$

4. If θ is total and deterministic, then:

$$(\beta \Rightarrow pre(\theta)(\gamma)) \text{ iff } (post(\theta)(\beta) \Rightarrow \gamma)$$
$$post(\theta)(\beta) = \bigwedge\{\gamma \in (S \longrightarrow B): \beta \Rightarrow pre(\theta)(\gamma)\}$$
$$pre(\theta)(\beta) = \bigvee\{\gamma \in (S \longrightarrow B): post(\theta)(\gamma) \Rightarrow \beta\}$$

Proof.

1. $pre(\theta)(\beta) = \lambda s_1.[\exists s_2 : \theta(s_1, s_2) \wedge \beta(s_2)] = \lambda s_1.[\exists s_2 : \beta(s_2) \wedge \theta^{-1}(s_2, s_1)] = post(\theta^{-1})(\beta). \ post(\theta)(\beta) = post((\theta^{-1})^{-1})(\beta) = pre(\theta^{-1})(\beta)$.

2. If θ is deterministic, then there exists $\bar\theta \in (S \longrightarrow S)$ such that $\theta(s_1, s_2) \Longleftrightarrow s_2 = \bar\theta(s_1)$. Therefore $post(\theta)(pre(\theta)(\beta)) = \lambda s_3.[\exists s_1 : (\exists s_2 : s_2 = \bar\theta(s_1) \wedge \beta(s_2)) \wedge s_3 = \bar\theta(s_1)] = \lambda s_3.[\exists s_1 : \beta(\bar\theta(s_1)) \wedge s_3 = \bar\theta(s_1)] = post(\theta)(true) \wedge \beta$.

3. If θ is total, then $\forall s_3 \in S, \beta(s_3) \Rightarrow (\beta(s_3) \wedge (\exists s_2 : \theta(s_3, s_2))) \Rightarrow (\exists s_2 : \theta(s_3, s_2) \wedge (\exists s_1 : \theta(s_1, s_2) \wedge \beta(s_1))) = pre(\theta)(post(\theta)(\beta))(s_3)$.

4. If $(\beta \Rightarrow pre(\theta)(\gamma))$, then by isotony $post(\theta)(\beta) \Rightarrow post(\theta)$
    $(pre(\theta)(\gamma)) \Rightarrow \gamma$. If $(post(\theta)(\beta) \Rightarrow \gamma)$, then by isotony $\beta \Rightarrow$
    $pre(\theta)(post(\theta)(\beta)) \Rightarrow pre(\theta)(\gamma)$. $post(\theta)(\beta) = \bigwedge\{\gamma: post(\theta)(\beta)$
    $\Rightarrow \gamma\} = \bigwedge\{\gamma: \beta \Rightarrow pre(\theta)(\gamma)\}$. $pre(\theta)(\beta) = \bigvee\{\gamma: \gamma \Rightarrow pre(\theta)(\beta)\}$
    $= \bigvee\{\gamma: post(\theta)(\gamma) \Rightarrow \beta\}$. ∎

Example 10-12. According to Theorem 10-11.4, Floyd-Naur's method for proving the partial correctness of π with respect to ϕ, Ψ which consists in guessing an assertion ι and showing that $(((v_\epsilon \wedge \phi) \Rightarrow \iota) \wedge (post(\tau)(\iota) \Rightarrow \iota)$ $\wedge ((v_\omega \wedge \iota) \Rightarrow \Psi))$ is equivalent to Hoare's method [Hoar69], which consists of guessing an assertion ι and showing that $(((v_\epsilon \wedge \phi) \wedge (\iota \Rightarrow pre(\tau)(\iota)) \wedge ((v_\omega \wedge \iota) \Rightarrow \Psi))$.

We have seen that the analysis of a system consists of solving "forward" fixpoint equations of the form $\alpha = \beta \; \mathbb{X} \; post(\tau)(\alpha)$ or "backward" fixpoint equations of the form $\alpha = \beta \; \mathbb{X} \; pre(\tau)(\alpha)$ (where $\beta \in (S \rightarrow B)$ and $\mathbb{X}$ is either $\vee$ or $\wedge$). In fact whenever a forward equation is needed, a backward equation can be used instead, and vice versa.

Theorem 10-13.

$$\forall \theta \in ((S \times S) \rightarrow B), \forall \beta \in (S \rightarrow B),$$
$$post(\theta)(\beta) = \lambda\bar{s}.[\exists s_1 \in S: \beta(s_1) \wedge pre(\theta)(\lambda s.[s = \bar{s}])(s_1)]$$
$$pre(\theta)(\beta) = \lambda\bar{s}.[\exists s_2 \in S: post(\theta)(\lambda s.[s = \bar{s}])(s_2) \wedge \beta(s_2)]$$

Proof. $post(\theta)(\beta) = \lambda\bar{s}.[\exists s_1 \in S: \beta(s_1) \wedge \theta(s_1, \bar{s})] = \lambda\bar{s}.[\exists s_1 \in S: \beta(s_1) \wedge (\exists s \in S: (s = \bar{s}) \wedge \theta(s_1, s))] = \lambda\bar{s}.[\exists s_1 \in S: \beta(s_1) \wedge pre(\theta)$ $(\lambda s.[s = \bar{s}])(s_1)]$. ∎

Example 10-14. A total correctness proof of a program π with respect to ϕ, Ψ consists in showing that $((v_\epsilon \wedge \phi) \Rightarrow pre(\tau^*)(v_\omega \wedge \Psi))$, that is to say $((v_\epsilon \wedge \phi) \Rightarrow lfp(\lambda\alpha.[(v_\omega \wedge \Psi) \vee pre(\tau)(\alpha)]))$. Equivalently, using $post$, one can show that: $\forall \bar{s} \in S$, $(v_\epsilon(\bar{s}) \wedge \phi(\bar{s})) \Rightarrow (\exists s_2 \in S: v_\omega(s_2) \wedge \Psi(s_2) \wedge lfp(\lambda\alpha. [\lambda s.(s = \bar{s}) \vee post(\tau)(\alpha)])(s_2))$ More generally we have:

$$post(\tau^*)(\beta) = \lambda\bar{s}.[\exists s_1 \in S: \beta(s_1) \wedge lfp(\lambda\alpha.[\lambda s.(s = \bar{s}) \vee pre(\tau)(\alpha)])(s_1)]$$
$$pre(\tau^*)(\beta) = \lambda\bar{s}.[\exists s_2 \in S: \beta(s_2) \wedge lfp(\lambda\alpha.[\lambda s.(s = \bar{s}) \vee post(\tau)(\alpha)])(s_2)]$$

10-4.8. Partitioned Dynamic Discrete Systems

A dynamic discrete system $(S, \tau, v_\epsilon, v_\sigma, v_\xi)$ is said to be *partitioned* if there exist $n \geq 1$, $U_1, \ldots, U_n, \iota_1, \ldots, \iota_n$ such that $\forall i \in [1, n]$, ι_i is a partial one-to-one map from S onto U_i and $\{\iota_i^{-1}(U_i): i \in [1, n]\}$ is a partition of S, (therefore $S = \bigcup_{i=1}^{n} \iota_i^{-1}(U_i)$ and every $s \in S$ is an element of exactly one $\iota_i^{-1}(U_i)$).

When studying the behavior of a partitioned system, the equations $\alpha = \beta \; \text{\Large⋉} \; post(\tau)(\alpha)$ or $\alpha = \beta \; \text{\Large⋉} \; pre(\tau)(\alpha)$ can be replaced by systems of equations defined as follows. Let us define: $\forall i \in [1, n]$, $\sigma_i \in ((S \to B) \to (U_i \to B))$, $\sigma_i = \lambda \beta.[\beta \circ \iota_i^{-1}]$, $\sigma_i^{-1} = \lambda \beta.[\lambda s.[s \in \iota_i^{-1}(U_i) \wedge \beta(\iota_i(s))]]$, $\sigma \in ((S \to B) \to (\prod_{i=1}^{n} (U_i \to B))$, $\sigma = \lambda \beta.(\prod_{i=1}^{n} \sigma_i(\beta)) = \lambda \beta.\langle \sigma_1(\beta), \ldots, \sigma_n(\beta) \rangle$. σ is a strict isomorphism from $(S \to B)$ onto $\prod_{i=1}^{n} (U_i \to B)$. Its inverse is $\sigma^{-1} = \lambda \langle \beta_1, \ldots, \beta_n \rangle.\left[\bigvee_{i=1}^{n} \sigma_i^{-1}(\beta_i) \right]$.

For any isotone operator f on $(S \to B)$, the diagram in Fig. 10-4 commutes, so that the sets of pre-fixed points, fixed points and post-fixed

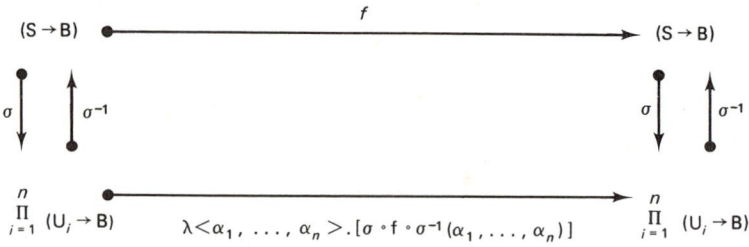

Figure 10-4

points of f coincide (up to the isomorphism σ) with the pre-solutions, solutions and post-solutions to the *direct decomposition* of $\alpha = f(\alpha)$ on $\prod_{i=1}^{n} (U_i \to B)$ which is the system of equations:

$$\alpha_1 = \sigma_1 \circ f \circ \sigma^{-1}(\alpha_1, \ldots, \alpha_n)$$
$$\vdots$$
$$\alpha_n = \sigma_n \circ f \circ \sigma^{-1}(\alpha_1, \ldots, \alpha_n)$$

In particular when $f = \lambda \alpha.[\beta \; \text{\Large⋉} \; post(\tau)(\alpha)]$ or $f = \lambda \alpha.[\beta \; \text{\Large⋉} \; pre(\tau)(\alpha)]$, we have the following:

Theorem 10-15. $\forall i \in [1, n]$, $\sigma_i \circ \lambda \alpha.[\beta \; \text{\Large⋉} \; post(\tau)(\alpha)] \circ \sigma^{-1}$ is equal to

$$\lambda \langle \alpha_1, \ldots, \alpha_n \rangle.\left[\sigma_i(\beta) \; \text{\Large⋉} \; \left(\bigvee_{j \in pred_\tau (i)} post(\tau_{ji})(\alpha_j) \right) \right]$$

whereas $\sigma_i \circ \lambda \alpha.[\beta \; \text{\Large⋉} \; pre(\tau)(\alpha)] \circ \sigma^{-1}$ is equal to

$$\lambda \langle \alpha_1, \ldots, \alpha_n \rangle.\left[\sigma_i(\beta) \; \text{\Large⋉} \; \left(\bigvee_{j \in succ_\tau (i)} pre(\tau_{ij})(\alpha_j) \right) \right]$$

where

$$\tau_{ij} \in ((U_i \times U_j) \rightarrow B), \tau_{ij} = \lambda \langle s_1, s_2 \rangle . [\tau(\iota_i^{-1}(s_1), \iota_j^{-1}(s_2))]$$

$$pred_\tau = \lambda i . \{ j \in [1, n]: (\exists s_1 \in U_j, \exists s_2 \in U_i: \tau_{ji}(s_1, s_2)) \}$$

$$succ_\tau = \lambda i . \{ j \in [1, n]: (\exists s_1 \in U_j, \exists s_2 \in U_i: \tau_{ij}(s_1, s_2)) \}$$

Proof.

$$\sigma_i(\beta \text{ \Finv } post(\tau)(\sigma^{-1}(\alpha_1, \ldots, \alpha_n))) = \sigma_i(\beta) \text{ \Finv } \sigma_i\left(post(\tau)\left(\bigvee_{j=1}^{n} \sigma_j^{-1}(\alpha_j) \right) \right)$$

$$= \sigma_i(\beta) \text{ \Finv } \bigvee_{j=1}^{n} (post(\tau)(\sigma_j^{-1}(\alpha_j)) \circ \iota_i^{-1}).$$

Moreover

$$post(\tau)(\sigma_j^{-1}(\alpha_j)) \circ \iota_i^{-1} = \lambda s_2 . [\exists s_1 \in S: \sigma_j^{-1}(\alpha_j)(s_1) \wedge \tau(s_1, \iota_i^{-1}(s_2))]$$

$$= \lambda s_2 . [\exists s_1 \in U_j: \alpha_j(s_1) \wedge \tau(\iota_j^{-1}(s_1), \iota_i^{-1}(s_2))]$$

$$= \lambda s_2 . [\exists s_1 \in U_j: \alpha_j(s_1) \wedge \tau_{ji}(s_1, s_2)]$$

$$= post(\tau_{ji})(\alpha_j).$$

Therefore $\bigvee_{j=1}^{n} (post(\tau)(\sigma_j^{-1}(\alpha_j)) \circ \iota_i^{-1}) = \bigvee_{j \in pred_\tau(i)} post(\tau_{ji})(\alpha_j)$ since

$(j \notin pred_\tau(i))$ implies $\forall s_1, s_2, \neg \tau_{ji}(s_1, s_2)$. Also $pre(\tau) = post(\tau^{-1})$,
$(\tau_{ij})^{-1} = \tau_{ji}$ and $succ_\tau = pred_{\tau^{-1}}$. ∎

10-5. SEMANTIC ANALYSIS OF PROGRAMS

The fixed point approach to the analysis of the behavior of total deterministic discrete dynamic systems is now applied to the case of programs as defined in Section 10-3.

A program $\langle G, U, L \rangle$ where $G = \langle V, \epsilon, \omega, E \rangle$ and $V = [1, n] - \{\xi\}$ defines a partitioned discrete dynamic system $\langle \tau, S, \nu_\epsilon, \nu_\omega, \nu_\xi \rangle$ where $S = ([1, n] \times U)$, $\forall i \in [1, n], U_i = U, \iota_i = \lambda \langle c, m \rangle . m, \iota_i^{-1} = \lambda m . \langle i, m \rangle$. Hence two states $\langle c_1, m_1 \rangle$ and $\langle c_2, m_2 \rangle$ are in the same block of the partition iff $c_1 = c_2$, that is, iff both states correspond to the same program point or are both erroneous.

10-5.1. System of Forward Semantic Equations Associated with a Program and an Entry Specification

The system of forward semantic equations $P = F_\pi(\phi)(P)$ associated with a program π and an entry specification $\phi \in (U \rightarrow B)$ is the direct decomposition of $\alpha = (\nu_\epsilon \wedge \sigma_\epsilon^{-1}(\phi)) \vee post(\tau)(\alpha)$ on $(U \rightarrow B)^n$; that is,

$$P_i = \sigma_i(\nu_\epsilon \wedge \sigma_\epsilon^{-1}(\phi)) \vee \left(\bigvee_{j \in pred_\tau(i)} post(\tau_{ji})(P_j) \right) \qquad i = 1, \ldots, n$$

From the abstract syntax and operational semantics of programs we derive a set of construction rules for obtaining this system of equations from the program text:

1. If i is the program entry point, $i = \epsilon$ and $pred_\tau(\epsilon) = \phi$; therefore $P_\epsilon = \sigma_\epsilon(v_\epsilon \wedge \sigma_\epsilon^{-1}(\phi)) = \sigma_\epsilon(\lambda\langle c, m \rangle.((c = \epsilon) \wedge \phi(m))) = \phi$. Otherwise $i \neq \epsilon$, in which case $\sigma_i(v_\epsilon \wedge \sigma_\epsilon^{-1}(\phi)) = \lambda m.\textit{false}$ and

    $$P_i = \bigvee_{j \in pred_\tau(i)} post(\tau_{ji})(P_j)$$
    $$= \bigvee_{j \in pred_\tau(i)} \lambda m_2.[\exists\, m_1 \in U: P_j(m_1) \wedge (\bar{\tau}(\langle j, m_1 \rangle) = \langle i, m_2 \rangle)]$$

    When $i \neq \epsilon$ and $i \neq \xi$, notice that $pred_\tau(i)$ is contained in the set of origins of the edges entering i, that is, the set $pred_\pi(i)$ of predecessors of the vertex i in the program graph G of π. The expression $\lambda m_2.[\exists\, m_1 \in U: P_j(m_1) \wedge (\bar{\tau}(\langle j, m_1 \rangle) = \langle i, m_2 \rangle)]$ depends on the instruction $L(\langle j, i \rangle)$ labeling the edge $\langle j, i \rangle$.

2. If $\langle j, i \rangle$ is labeled with an assignment $\vec{v} = f(\vec{v})$, then

    $$\lambda m_2.[\exists\, m_1 \in U: P_j(m_1) \wedge (\bar{\tau}(\langle j, m_1 \rangle) = \langle i, m_2 \rangle)]$$
    $$= \lambda m_2.[\exists\, m_1 \in U: P_j(m_1) \wedge m_1 \in dom(f) \wedge (m_2 = f(m_1))]$$

3. If $\langle j, i \rangle$ is labeled with a test p, then

    $$\lambda m_2.[\exists\, m_1 \in U: P_j(m_1) \wedge (\tau(\langle j, m_1 \rangle) = \langle i, m_2 \rangle)]$$
    $$= \lambda m_2.[\exists\, m_1 \in U: P_j(m_1) \wedge (m_1 \in dom(p)) \wedge p(m_1)$$
    $$\wedge (m_1 = m_2)]$$
    $$= \lambda m_2.[P_j(m_2) \wedge (m_2 \in dom(p)) \wedge p(m_2)]$$

4. If $i = \xi$, then

    $$P_\xi = \bigvee_{j \in pred_\tau(\xi)} \lambda m_2.[\exists\, m_1 \in U: P_j(m_1) \wedge (\bar{\tau}(\langle j, m_1 \rangle) = \langle \xi, m_2 \rangle)]$$
    $$= P_\xi \vee \bigvee_{j \in at(\pi)} \lambda m_2.[P_j(m_2) \wedge (m_2 \notin dom(expr(j)))]$$

    where $at(\pi)$ is the set of program points j preceding an assignment $\vec{v} = f(\vec{v})$ or a test $p(\vec{v})$ and $expr(j)$ is the corresponding f or p.

The above analysis can be summarized by the following.

Definition 10-16. The *system of forward semantic equations* $P = F_\pi(\phi)(P)$ *associated with a program* π *and an entry specification* $\phi \in (U \longrightarrow B)$ *is*

$$P_\epsilon = \phi$$
$$P_i = \bigvee_{j \in pred_\pi(i)} post(L(\langle j, i \rangle))(P_j) \qquad i \in ([1, n] - \{\epsilon, \xi\})$$
$$P_\xi = \Big(\bigvee_{j \in at(\pi)} \lambda m.[P_j(m) \wedge m \notin dom(expr(j))] \Big) \vee P_\xi$$

where $\forall f \in I_a(U)$, $post(f) = \lambda P.[\lambda m.[\exists m' \in U: P(m') \wedge m' \in dom(f) \wedge m = f(m')]]$; $\forall p \in I_t(U)$, $post(p) = \lambda P.[\lambda m.[P(m) \wedge m \in dom(p) \wedge p(m)]]$; $at(\pi)$ is the set of program points j preceding an assignment $\vec{v} = f(\vec{v})$ or a test $p(\vec{v})$ and $expr(j)$ is the corresponding f or p.

Theorem 10-17. The system of forward semantic equations $P = F_\pi(\phi)(P)$ associated with a program π and an entry specification $\phi \in (U \to B)$ is the direct decomposition of $\alpha = (v_\epsilon \wedge \sigma_\epsilon^{-1}(\phi)) \vee post(\tau)(\alpha)$ on $(U \to B)^n$.

10-5.2. System of Backward Semantic Equations Associated with a Program and an Exit Specification

As above the abstract syntax and operational semantics of programs can be used in order to derive sets of construction rules for associating with any program π the systems of equations which are the direct decomposition of backward equations of type $\alpha = \beta \ \mathbb{X} \ pre(\tau)(\alpha)$ on $(U \to B)^n$; that is,

$$P_i = \sigma_i(\beta) \ \mathbb{X} \bigvee_{j \in succ_\tau(i)} \lambda m_1.[\exists m_2 \in U: (\bar{\tau}(\langle m_1, i \rangle) = \langle m_2, j \rangle) \wedge P_j(m_2)]$$

$$i = 1, \dots, n$$

The result of this study can be summarized by the following.

Definition 10-18. The *system of backward semantic equations* $P = B_\pi(\Psi)(P)$ *associated with a program* π *and an exit specification* $\Psi \in (U \to B)$ is

$$P_i = \bigvee_{j \in succ_\pi(i)} pre(L(\langle i, j \rangle))(P_j) \qquad i \in ([1, n] - \{\omega, \xi\})$$

$$P_\sigma = \Psi$$

where $\forall f \in I_a(U)$, $pre(f) = \lambda P.[\lambda m.[m \in dom(f) \wedge P(f(m))]]$; $\forall p \in I_t(U)$, $pre(p) = \lambda P.[\lambda m.[m \in dom(f) \wedge p(m) \wedge P(m)]]$; and $succ_\pi(i)$ is the set of successors of the vertex i in the program graph of π.

Theorem 10-19.

1. The direct decomposition $P = B(P)$ of $\alpha = (v_\omega \wedge \sigma_\omega^{-1}(\Psi)) \vee pre(\tau)(\alpha)$ on $(U \to B)^n$ is

$$P_i = B_\pi(\Psi)_i(P) \vee error(i) \qquad \text{for } i \in ([1, n] - \{\xi, \omega\})$$

$$P_\omega = \Psi \vee P_\omega$$

$$P_\xi = P_\xi$$

where $error(i) = \lambda m \in U.[P_\xi(m) \wedge i \in at(\pi) \wedge m \notin dom(expr(i))]$; $\forall i \in ([1, n] - \{\xi\})$, $lfp(B)_i = lfp(B_\pi(\Psi))_i$; and $lfp(B)_\xi = \lambda m.[false]$.

2. The direct decomposition $P = B(P)$ of $\alpha = \neg v_\xi \wedge pre(\tau)(\alpha)$ on $(U \longrightarrow B)^n$ is

$$P_i = B_\pi(\lambda m.[true])_i(P) \qquad \text{for } i \in ([1, n] - \{\omega, \xi\})$$

$$P_\omega = P_\omega$$

$$P_\xi = \lambda m.[false]$$

$\forall i \in ([1, n] - \{\xi\})$, $gfp(B)_i = gfp(B_\pi(\lambda m.[true]))_i$, and $gfp(B)_\xi = \lambda m.[false]$.

3. The direct decomposition $P = B(P)$ of $\alpha = v_\xi \vee pre(\tau)(\alpha)$ on $(U \longrightarrow B)^n$ is

$$P_i = B_\pi(\lambda m.[false])_i(P) \vee error(i) \quad \text{for } i \in ([1, n] - \{\omega, \xi\})$$

$$P_\omega = P_\omega$$

$$P_\xi = \lambda m.[true]$$

The least solution to the above system of equations is equal to the least solution to

$$P_i = B_\pi(\lambda m.[false])_i(Q) \vee \lambda m.[m \notin dom(expr(i))]$$
$$\text{for } i \in ([1, n] - \{\omega, \xi\})$$

$$P_\omega = \lambda m.[false]$$

$$P_\xi = \lambda m.[true]$$

where Q_i stands for P_i when $i \in ([1, n] - \{\omega, \xi\})$, Q_ω stands for $\lambda m.[false]$ and Q_ξ stands for $\lambda m.[true]$.

4. The direct decomposition of $\alpha = \neg v_\omega \wedge \neg v_\xi \wedge pre(\tau)(\alpha)$ on $(U \longrightarrow B)^n$ is

$$P_i = B_\pi(\lambda m.[false])_i(P) \qquad \text{for } i \in ([1, n] - \{\xi\})$$

$$P_\xi = \lambda m.[false]$$

5. The direct decomposition of $\alpha = \lambda s.[s = \bar{s}] \vee pre(\tau)(\alpha)$ on $(U \longrightarrow B)^n$ is

$$P_i = \lambda m.[\langle i, m \rangle = \bar{s}] \vee B_\pi(\lambda m.[false])_i(P) \vee error(i)$$
$$\text{for } i \in ([1, n] - \{\omega, \xi\})$$

$$P_\omega = \lambda m.[\langle \sigma, m \rangle = \bar{s}] \vee P_\omega$$

$$P_\xi = \lambda m.[\langle \xi, m \rangle = \bar{s}] \vee P_\xi$$

10-5.3. Analysis of the Behavior of a Program

In order to illustrate the application of Theorem 10-9 to the analysis of the behavior of a program, we choose the introductory example program π:

$\{1\}$

    while $x \geq 1000$ **do**

$\{2\}$

        $x := x + y;$

$\{3\}$

    od;

$\{4\}$

It is assumed that the domain of values of the variables x and y is $I = \{n \in \mathbf{Z}: -b - 1 \leq n \leq b\}$ where b is the greatest and $-b - 1$ the least machine-representable integer.

10-5.3.1. *Forward semantic analysis*

    The system $P = F_\pi(\phi)(P)$ (where $F_\pi(\phi) \in ((I^2 \longrightarrow B)^5 \longrightarrow (I^2 \longrightarrow B)^5)$) of forward semantic equations associated with the above program π and an entry specification $\phi \in (I^2 \longrightarrow B)$ is the following:

$$P_1 = \phi$$
$$P_2 = \lambda\langle x, y\rangle.[(P_1 \lor P_3)(x, y) \land (x \in I) \land (x \geq 1000)]$$
$$P_3 = \lambda\langle x, y\rangle.[\exists\, x' \in I: P_2(x', y) \land ((x' + y) \in I) \land (x = x' + y)]$$
$$P_4 = \lambda\langle x, y\rangle.[(P_1 \lor P_3)(x, y) \land (x \in I) \land (x < 1000)]$$
$$P_\xi = \lambda\langle x, y\rangle.[((P_1 \lor P_3)(x, y) \land (x \notin I)) \lor (P_2(x, y) \land ((x + y) \notin I))]$$

    The *set of entry states which are ascendants of the exit states* (i.e., cause the program to terminate properly) is characterized by:

$$\sigma_\epsilon(v_\epsilon \land pre(\tau^*)(v_\omega))$$
$$= \sigma_\epsilon(\lambda\bar{s}.[\exists\, s_2 \in S: v_\omega(s_2) \land post(\tau^*)(\lambda s.[s = \bar{s}])(s_2)])$$

                      (Theorem 10-13)

$$= \lambda\bar{m}.[\exists\, s_2 \in S: v_\omega(s_2) \land post(\tau^*)(\lambda s.[s = \langle\epsilon, \bar{m}\rangle])(s_2)]$$
$$= \lambda\bar{m}.[\exists\, s_2 \in S: v_\omega(s_2) \land lfp(\lambda\alpha.[(v_\epsilon \land \sigma_\epsilon^{-1}(\lambda m.[m = \bar{m}]))$$
$$\lor post(\tau)(\alpha)])(s_2)] \quad \text{(Theorem 10-4(3))}$$
$$= \lambda\bar{m}.[\exists\, s_2 \in S: v_\omega(s_2) \land \sigma^{-1}(lfp(F_\pi(\lambda m.[m = \bar{m}])))(s_2)]$$

                      (Theorem 10-17)

$$= \lambda\bar{m}.\left[\exists\, s_2 \in S: v_\omega(s_2) \land \left(\bigvee_{i=1}^{n} lfp(F_\pi(\lambda m.[m = \bar{m}]))_i(\iota_i(s_2))\right)\right]$$
$$= \lambda\bar{m}.\left[\bigvee_{i=1}^{n}(\exists\, m_2 \in U_i: v_\omega(\iota_i^{-1}(m_2)) \land lfp(F_\pi(\lambda m.[m = \bar{m}]))_i(m_2))\right]$$
$$= \lambda\bar{m}.[\exists\, m_2 \in U_\omega: lfp(F_\pi(\lambda m.[m = \bar{m}]))_\omega(m_2)]$$

The least fixed point P^∞ of $F_\pi(\lambda\langle x, y\rangle.[(x = \bar{x}) \wedge (y = \bar{y})])$ is computed iteratively using a chaotic iteration sequence as follows:

$$P_i^0 = \lambda\langle x, y\rangle.[false] \qquad i = 1, \ldots, 4, \xi$$

$$P_1^1 = \lambda\langle x, y\rangle.[(x = \bar{x}) \wedge (y = \bar{y})] \qquad \text{where } \langle \bar{x}, \bar{y}\rangle \in I^2$$

$$P_2^1 = \lambda\langle x, y\rangle.[(P_1^1 \vee P_3^0)(x, y) \wedge (x \in I) \wedge (x \geq 1000)]$$

$$= \lambda\langle x, y\rangle.[(\bar{x} \in I \wedge 1000 \leq \bar{x}) \wedge (x = \bar{x}) \wedge (y = \bar{y})]$$

$$P_3^1 = \lambda\langle x, y\rangle.[\exists\, x' \in I: P_2^1(x', y) \wedge ((x' + y) \in I) \wedge (x = x' + y)]$$

$$= \lambda\langle x, y\rangle.[(\bar{x} \in I \wedge (\bar{x} + \bar{y}) \in I \wedge 1000 \leq \bar{x}) \wedge (x = \bar{x} + \bar{y}) \wedge (y = \bar{y})]$$

$$P_2^2 = \lambda\langle x, y\rangle.[(P_1^1 \vee P_3^1)(x, y) \wedge (x \in I) \wedge (x \geq 1000)]$$

$$= \lambda\langle x, y\rangle.[((\bar{x} \in I \wedge 1000 \leq \bar{x}) \wedge (x = \bar{x}) \wedge (y = \bar{y}))$$

$$\vee ((\bar{x} \in I \wedge (\bar{x} + \bar{y}) \in I \wedge 1000 \leq \bar{x} \wedge 1000 \leq (\bar{x} + \bar{y}))$$

$$\wedge (x = \bar{x} + \bar{y}) \wedge (y = \bar{y}))]$$

Assume as induction hypothesis that

$$P_2^k = \lambda\langle x, y\rangle.[\exists\, j \in [0, k-1]: \bigwedge_{i=0}^{j} ((\bar{x} + i\bar{y}) \in I \wedge 1000 \leq (\bar{x} + i\bar{y}))$$

$$\wedge (x = \bar{x} + j\bar{y}) \wedge (y = \bar{y})]$$

then

$$P_3^k = \lambda\langle x, y\rangle.[\exists\, x' \in I: P_2^k(x', y) \wedge ((x' + y) \in I) \wedge (x = x' + y)]$$

$$= \lambda\langle x, y\rangle.[\exists\, j \in [1, k]: \bigwedge_{i=0}^{j-1} ((\bar{x} + i\bar{y}) \in I \wedge 1000 \leq (\bar{x} + i\bar{y}))$$

$$\wedge ((\bar{x} + j\bar{y}) \in I) \wedge (x = \bar{x} + j\bar{y}) \wedge (y = \bar{y})]$$

$$P_2^{k+1} = \lambda\langle x, y\rangle.[(P_1^1 \vee P_3^k)(x, y) \wedge (x \in I) \wedge (x \geq 1000)$$

$$= \lambda\langle x, y\rangle.[\exists\, j \in [0, k]: \bigwedge_{i=0}^{j} ((\bar{x} + i\bar{y}) \in I \wedge 1000 \leq (\bar{x} + i\bar{y}))$$

$$\wedge (x = \bar{x} + j\bar{y}) \wedge (y = \bar{y})]$$

proving by induction on k that P_2^k is of the form assumed in the induction hypothesis. Then passing to the limit,

$$P_2^\omega = \bigvee_{k\geq 0} P_2^k$$

$$= \lambda\langle x, y\rangle.[\exists\, j \geq 0: \left[\bigwedge_{i=0}^{j} ((\bar{x} + i\bar{y}) \in I \wedge 1000 \leq (\bar{x} + i\bar{y}))\right.$$

$$\left. \wedge (x = \bar{x} + j\bar{y}) \wedge (y = \bar{y})\right]$$

$$= \lambda\langle x, y\rangle.[\exists\, j \geq 0: (1000 \leq min(\bar{x}, x)) \wedge (max(\bar{x}, x) \leq b)$$

$$\wedge (x = \bar{x} + j\bar{y}) \wedge (y = \bar{y})]$$

(It is worth noting that the use of the symbolic entry condition $\lambda\langle x, y\rangle.[(x = \bar{x}) \wedge (y = \bar{y})]$ and of the above iteration strategy corresponds to a symbolic execution of the program loop [Hant76] with the difference that all possible execution paths are considered simultaneously and the induction step as well as the passage to the limit deal with infinite paths.) The remaining components of $lfp(F_\pi(\lambda\langle x, y\rangle.[(x = \bar{x}) \wedge (y = \bar{y})]))$ are:

$$P_1^\omega = \lambda\langle x, y\rangle.[(x = \bar{x}) \wedge (y = \bar{y})]$$

$$P_3^\omega = \lambda\langle x, y\rangle.[\exists\, x' \in I: P_2^\omega(x', y) \wedge ((x' + y) \in I) \wedge (x = x' + y)]$$

$$= \lambda\langle x, y\rangle.[\exists\, j \geq 1: (1000 \leq min(\bar{x}, x - \bar{y})) \wedge (max(\bar{x}, x) \leq b)$$
$$\wedge (x = \bar{x} + j\bar{y}) \wedge (y = \bar{y})]$$

$$P_4^\omega = \lambda\langle x, y\rangle.[(P_1^\omega \vee P_3^\omega)(x, y) \wedge (x \in I) \wedge (x < 1000)]$$

$$= \lambda\langle x, y\rangle.[((\bar{x} < 1000) \wedge (x = \bar{x}) \wedge (x = \bar{y}))$$
$$\vee ((\bar{x} \geq 1000) \wedge (\bar{y} < 0)$$
$$\wedge (x = \bar{x} + (((\bar{x} - 1000)\, div\, |\bar{y}|) + 1)\bar{y}) \wedge (y = \bar{y}))]$$

$$P_\xi^\omega = \lambda\langle x, y\rangle.[((P_1^\omega \vee P_3^\omega)(x, y) \wedge (x \notin I)) \vee (P_2^\omega(x, y) \wedge ((x + y) \notin I))]$$
$$\vee P_\xi^0$$

$$= \lambda\langle x, y\rangle.[(\bar{x} \geq 1000) \wedge (\bar{y} > 0) \wedge (x = \bar{x} + ((b - \bar{x})div\, \bar{y})\bar{y})$$
$$\wedge (y = \bar{y})]$$

The *set of entry states which cause the program to terminate properly* is characterized by

$$\lambda\langle \bar{x}, \bar{y}\rangle.[\exists\, x_2, y_2 \in I: P_4^\omega(x_2, y_2)] = \lambda\langle x, y\rangle.[(\bar{x} < 1000) \vee (\bar{y} < 0)]$$

The *set of entry states leading to a run-time error* is characterized by

$$\sigma_\epsilon(v_\epsilon \wedge pre(\tau^*)(v_\xi)) = \lambda\bar{m}.[\exists\, m_2 \in U_\xi: lfp(F_\pi(\lambda m.[m = \bar{m}]))_\xi(m_2)]$$

that is,

$$\lambda\langle \bar{x}, \bar{y}\rangle.[\exists\, x_2, y_2 \in I: P_\xi^\omega(x_2, y_2)] = \lambda\langle \bar{x}, \bar{y}\rangle.[(\bar{x} \geq 1000) \wedge (\bar{y} > 0)]$$

The *set of entry states which cause the program to diverge* is characterized by

$$\sigma_\epsilon(v_\epsilon \wedge \neg pre(\tau^*)(v_\omega \vee v_\xi))$$

$$= \lambda\bar{m}.\neg\left[\bigvee_{i=1}^{n}(\exists\, m_2 \in U_i: (v_\omega \vee v_\xi)(\langle i, m_2\rangle)\right.$$

$$\left.\wedge lfp(F_\pi(\lambda m.[m = \bar{m}]))_i(m_2))\right]$$

$$= \lambda\bar{m}.[\neg(\exists\, m_2 \in U_\omega: lfp(F_\pi(\lambda m.[m = \bar{m}]))_\omega(m_2))$$

$$\wedge \neg(\exists\, m_2 \in U_\xi: lfp(F_\pi(\lambda m.[m = \bar{m}]))_\xi(m_2))]$$

that is,

$$\lambda\langle\bar{x},\bar{y}\rangle.[\neg(\exists x_2, y_2 \in I: P^\omega_4(x_2, y_2)) \wedge \neg(\exists x_2, y_2 \in I: P^\omega_\xi(x_2, y_2))]$$
$$= \lambda\langle\bar{x},\bar{y}\rangle.[(\bar{x} \geq 1000) \wedge (y = 0)]$$

The *set of descendants of the entry states satisfying the entry condition* $\phi \in (I^2 \rightarrow B)$ is characterized by $post(\tau^*)(v_\epsilon \wedge \sigma^{-1}_\epsilon(\phi))$; that is (Theorem 10-9 and Theorem 10-17) up to the isomorphism σ by $Q^\omega = lfp(F_\pi(\phi))$:

$$Q^\omega_1 = \phi$$

$$Q^\omega_2 = \lambda\langle x, y\rangle.[\exists j \geq 0: \phi(x - jy, y) \wedge (1000 \leq min(x - jy, x))$$
$$\wedge (max(x - jy, x) \leq b)]$$

$$Q^\omega_3 = \lambda\langle x, y\rangle.[\exists j \geq 1: \phi(x - jy, y) \wedge (1000 \leq min(x - jy, x - y))$$
$$\wedge (max(x - jy, x) \leq b)]$$

$$Q^\omega_4 = \lambda\langle x, y\rangle.[(\phi(x, y) \wedge (x < 1000)) \vee ((y < 0) \wedge (\exists j \geq 1: \phi(x - jy, y)$$
$$\wedge (x - jy \leq b) \wedge (x < 1000 \leq x - y)))]$$

$$Q^\omega_\xi = \lambda\langle x, y\rangle.[(y > 0) \wedge (\exists j \geq 0: \phi(x - jy, y)$$
$$\wedge (1000 \leq x - jy < x \leq b < x + y))]$$

Equivalently Q^ω can be obtained from P^ω as follows:

$$\sigma_i(post(\tau^*)(v_\epsilon \wedge \sigma^{-1}_\epsilon(\phi)))$$
$$= \sigma_i(\lambda s_2.[\exists \bar{s}: v_\epsilon(\bar{s}) \wedge \sigma^{-1}_\epsilon(\phi)(\bar{s}) \wedge post(\tau^*)(\lambda s.[s = \bar{s}])(s_2)])$$
$$= \lambda m_2.[\exists \bar{m}: \phi(\bar{m}) \wedge post(\tau^*)(\lambda s.[s = \langle \epsilon, \bar{m}\rangle])(\langle i, m_2\rangle)]$$
$$= \lambda m_2.[\exists \bar{m}: \phi(\bar{m}) \wedge \sigma^{-1}(lfp(F_\pi(\lambda m.[m = \bar{m}])))(\langle i, m_2\rangle)]$$
$$= \lambda m_2.[\exists \bar{m}: \phi(\bar{m}) \wedge lfp(F_\pi(\lambda m.[m = \bar{m}]))_i(m_2)]$$

Therefore at each program point i the set of descendants of the entry states satisfying the entry condition $\phi \in (I^2 \rightarrow B)$ is characterized by

$$Q^\omega_i = \lambda\langle x, y\rangle.[\exists \bar{x}, \bar{y} \in I^2: \phi(\bar{x}, \bar{y}) \wedge P^\omega_i(x, y)]$$

For example:

$$Q^\omega_\xi = \lambda(x, y).[\exists \bar{x}, \bar{y} \in I^2: \phi(\bar{x}, \bar{y}) \wedge (\bar{x} \geq 1000) \wedge (\bar{y} > 0)$$
$$\wedge (x = \bar{x} + ((b - \bar{x}) div \bar{y})\bar{y}) \wedge (y = \bar{y})]$$
$$= \lambda(x, y).[\exists \bar{x} \in I: (\exists j: \phi(x - jy, y) \wedge (x - jy \geq 1000)$$
$$\wedge (y > 0) \wedge (x = \bar{x} + jy) \wedge j = (b - \bar{x}) div y]$$
$$= \lambda(x, y).[(y > 0) \wedge (\exists j \geq 0: \phi(x - jy, y)$$
$$\wedge (1000 \leq x - jy < x \leq b) \wedge (j = j + (b - x) div y))]$$
$$= \lambda(x, y).[(y > 0) \wedge (\exists j \geq 0: \phi(x - jy, y)$$
$$\wedge (1000 \leq x - jy < x \leq b < x + y))]$$

We now recommence the semantic analysis of this program, but this time using backward equations.

10-5.3.2. Backward semantic analysis

The system $P = B_\pi(\Psi)(P)$ (where $B_\pi(\Psi) \in ((I^2 \to B)^4 \to (I^2 \to B)^4))$ of backward semantic equations associated with the example program π and an exit specification $\Psi \in (I^2 \to B)$ is the following:

$$P_1 = \lambda\langle x, y\rangle.[((x \in I) \wedge (x \geq 1000) \wedge P_2(x, y)) \vee ((x \in I)$$
$$\wedge (x < 1000) \wedge P_4(x, y))]$$

$$P_2 = \lambda\langle x, y\rangle.[((x + y) \in I) \wedge P_3(x + y, y)]$$
$$P_3 = \lambda\langle x, y\rangle.[((x \in I) \wedge (x \geq 1000) \wedge P_2(x, y)) \vee ((x \in I)$$
$$\wedge (x < 1000) \wedge P_4(x, y))]$$

$$P_4 = \Psi$$

The *set of entry states which are ascendants of the exit states* (i.e., cause the program to terminate properly) is characterized by

$$\sigma_\epsilon(v_\epsilon \wedge pre(\tau^*)(v_\omega))$$
$$= \sigma_\epsilon(v_\epsilon \wedge lfp(\lambda\alpha.[v_\omega \vee pre(\tau)(\alpha)])) \qquad \text{[Theorem 10-9(2)]}$$
$$= \sigma_\epsilon(v_\epsilon \wedge \sigma^{-1}(lfp(B_\pi(\lambda m.[true])))) \qquad \text{[Theorem 10-19(1)]}$$
$$= \sigma_\epsilon\big(\bigvee_{i \in [1, n]} \lambda s.[v_\epsilon(s) \wedge s \in \iota_i^{-1}(U) \wedge lfp(B_\pi(\lambda m.[true]))_i(\iota_i(s))]\big)$$
$$= \sigma_\epsilon(lfp(B_\pi(\lambda m.[true]))_\epsilon \circ \iota_\epsilon)$$
$$= lfp(B_\pi(\lambda m.[true]))_\epsilon$$

The least fixed point P^ω of the above system of equations where $\Psi = \lambda\langle x, y\rangle.[true]$ is

$$P_1^\omega = \lambda\langle x, y\rangle.[(x < 1000) \vee (y < 0)]$$
$$P_2^\omega = \lambda\langle x, y\rangle.[((x + y) \in I) \wedge ((x + y < 1000) \vee (y < 0))]$$
$$P_3^\omega = \lambda\langle x, y\rangle.[(x < 1000) \vee (y < 0)]$$
$$P_4^\omega = \lambda\langle x, y\rangle.[true]$$

The *set of entry states which do not lead to a run-time error* (i.e., cause the program to properly terminate or diverge) is characterized by

$$\sigma_\epsilon(v_\epsilon \wedge \neg pre(\tau^*)(v_\xi))$$
$$= \sigma_\epsilon(v_\epsilon \wedge gfp(\lambda\alpha.[\neg v_\xi \wedge pre(\tau)(\alpha)])) \qquad \text{[Theorem 10-9(3)]}$$
$$= \sigma_\epsilon(v_\epsilon \wedge \sigma^{-1}(gfp(B_\pi(\lambda m.[true])))) \qquad \text{[Theorem 10-19(2)]}$$
$$= gfp(B_\pi(\lambda m.[true]))_\epsilon$$

The greatest fixed point Q^ω of the above system of equations where Ψ $= \lambda\langle x, y\rangle.[true]$ can be computed iteratively starting from $Q_i^0 = \lambda\langle x, y\rangle.[true]$, $i = 1, \ldots, 4$, inventing the general term of a chaotic iteration sequence, and passing to the limit:

$$Q_1^\omega = \lambda\langle x, y\rangle.[(y \leq 0) \vee (x < 1000)]$$

$$Q_2^\omega = \lambda\langle x, y\rangle.[((x + y \leq 0) \vee (x + y < 1000)) \wedge ((x + y) \in I)]$$

$$Q_3^\omega = \lambda\langle x, y\rangle.[(y \leq 0) \vee (x < 1000)]$$

$$Q_4^\omega = \lambda\langle x, y\rangle.[true]$$

The *set of entry states leading to a run-time error* is characterized by $\lambda\langle x, y\rangle \in I^2.[\neg Q_1^\omega(x, y)] = \lambda\langle x, y\rangle \in I^2.[(y > 0) \wedge (x \geq 1000)]$.

Equivalently, the set of ascendants of the run-time error states is characterized by $pre(\tau^*)(v_\xi)$, which, according to Theorem 10-9(3) and Theorem 10-19(3), is equal (up to the isomorphism σ) to the least solution R^ω to

$$P_1 = \lambda\langle x, y\rangle.[(x \geq 1000) \wedge P_2(x, y)]$$

$$P_2 = \lambda\langle x, y\rangle.[(((x + y) \in I) \in P_3(x + y, y)) \vee ((x + y) \notin I)]$$

$$P_3 = \lambda\langle x, y\rangle.[(x \geq 1000) \wedge P_2(x, y)]$$

$$P_4 = \lambda\langle x, y\rangle.[false]$$

$$P_\xi = \lambda\langle x, y\rangle.[true]$$

that is, $R_1^\omega = R_3^\omega = \lambda\langle x, y\rangle.[(x \geq 1000) \wedge (y > 0)]$, $R_2^\omega = \lambda\langle x, y\rangle.[((x + y) \geq 0 \wedge (y > 0)) \vee ((x + y) \notin I)]$, $R_4^\omega = \lambda\langle x, y\rangle.[false]$, $R_\xi^\omega = \lambda\langle x, y\rangle.[true]$.

The *set of entry states which cause the program to diverge* is characterized by $\lambda\langle x, y\rangle.[Q_1^\omega(x, y) \wedge \neg P_1^\omega(x, y)] = \lambda\langle x, y\rangle.[(x \geq 1000) \wedge (y = 0)]$.

Equivalently, the states which cause the program to diverge can be characterized by $\neg pre(\tau^*)(v_\xi \vee v_\sigma) = gfp(\lambda\alpha.[\neg v_\sigma \wedge \neg v_\xi \wedge pre(\tau)(\alpha)])$, which, according to Theorem 10-19(4) is equal (up to the isomorphism σ) to $D^\omega = gfp(B_\pi(\lambda\langle x, v\rangle.[false]))$, that is, $D_1^\omega = D_2^\omega = D_3^\omega = \lambda\langle x, y\rangle.[(x \geq 1000) \wedge (y = 0)]$ and $D_4^\omega = D_\xi^\omega = \lambda\langle x, y\rangle.[false]$.

The *set of descendants of the input states satisfying an entry condition* $\phi \in (I^2 \rightarrow B)$ is characterized by

$post(\tau^*)(v_\epsilon \wedge \sigma_\epsilon^{-1})\phi))$

$\quad = \lambda\bar{s}.[\exists s_1 \in S: v_\epsilon(s_1) \wedge \sigma_\epsilon^{-1}(\phi)(s_1) \wedge lfp(\lambda\alpha.[\lambda s.[s = \bar{s}]$

$$\vee pre(\tau)(\alpha)])(s_1)]$$

$\quad = \lambda\bar{s}.[\exists m_\epsilon \in U_\epsilon: \phi(m_\epsilon) \wedge \sigma^{-1}(lfp(\sigma \circ \lambda\alpha.[\lambda s.[s = \bar{s}]$

$$\vee pre(\tau(\alpha)] \circ \sigma^{-1}))(\langle\epsilon, m_\epsilon\rangle)]$$

$\quad = \lambda\bar{s}.[\exists m_\epsilon \in U_\epsilon: \phi(m_\epsilon) \wedge lfp(\sigma \circ \lambda\alpha.[\lambda s.[s = \bar{s}] \vee pre(\tau)(\alpha)] \circ \sigma^{-1})_\epsilon(m_\epsilon)]$

According to Theorem 10-19(5), the direct decomposition of $\lambda\alpha.[\lambda s.[s = \bar{s}] \vee pre(\tau)(\alpha)]$ is the following when τ is defined by our example program.

$$P_1 = \lambda\langle x, y\rangle.[(\langle 1, \langle x, y\rangle\rangle = \bar{s}) \lor (x \in I \land x \geq 1000 \land P_2(x, y))$$
$$\lor (x \in I \land x \leq 1000 \land P_4(x, y)) \lor (P_\xi(x, y) \land x \notin I)]$$

$$P_2 = \lambda\langle x, y\rangle.[(\langle 2, \langle x, y\rangle\rangle = \bar{s}) \lor (x + y \in I \land P_3(x + y, y))$$
$$\lor (P_\xi(x, y) \land x + y \notin I)]$$

$$P_3 = \lambda\langle x, y\rangle.[(\langle 3, \langle x, y\rangle\rangle = \bar{s}) \lor (x \in I \land x \geq 1000 \land P_2(x, y))$$
$$\lor (x \in I \land x < 1000 \land P_4(x, y)) \lor (P_\xi(x, y) \land x \notin I)]$$

$$P_4 = \lambda\langle x, y\rangle.[(\langle 4, \langle x, y\rangle\rangle = \bar{s}) \lor P_4(x, y)]$$

$$P_\xi = \lambda\langle x, y\rangle.[(\langle \xi, \langle x, y\rangle\rangle = \bar{s}) \lor P_\xi(x, y)]$$

If $P^\infty(\bar{s})$ denotes $lfp(\sigma \circ \lambda\alpha.[\lambda s.[s = \bar{s}] \lor pre(\tau)(\alpha)] \circ \sigma^{-1})$, we determine that

$$P_1^\infty(\bar{s}) = \lambda\langle x, y\rangle.[(\langle 1, \langle x, y\rangle\rangle = \bar{s})$$
$$\lor (\exists j \geq 0 : (\forall i \in [0, j], 1000 \leq x + iy \leq b)$$
$$\land (\langle 2, \langle x + jy, y\rangle\rangle = \bar{s}))$$
$$\lor (\exists j \geq 1 : (\forall i \in [0, j - 1], 1000 \leq x + iy \leq b)$$
$$\land (x + jy \in I) \land (\langle 3, \langle x + jy, y\rangle\rangle = \bar{s}))$$
$$\lor (\exists j \geq 0 : (\forall i \in [0, j - 1], 1000 \leq x + iy \leq b)$$
$$\land (x + jy \in I) \land (x + jy < 1000) \land (\langle 4, \langle x + jy, y\rangle\rangle = \bar{s}))$$
$$\lor (\exists j \geq 1 : (\forall i \in [0, j - 1], 1000 \leq x + jy \leq b)$$
$$\land (x + jy \notin I) \land (\langle \xi, \langle x + (j - 1)y, y\rangle\rangle = \bar{s}))]$$

At program point i, the set of descendants of the input states satisfying ϕ is

$$\sigma_i(\lambda\bar{s}.[\exists m_\epsilon \in U_\epsilon : \phi(m_\epsilon) \land P_\epsilon^\infty(\bar{s})(m_\epsilon)]) = \lambda m.[\exists m_\epsilon \in U_\epsilon : \phi(m_\epsilon)$$
$$\land P_\epsilon^\infty(\langle i, m\rangle)(m_\epsilon)]$$

For our example

$$\lambda\langle x, y\rangle.[\exists \langle x_\epsilon, y_\epsilon\rangle \in I^2 : \phi(x_\epsilon, y_\epsilon) \land P_1^\infty(\langle i, \langle x, y\rangle\rangle)(\langle x_\epsilon, y_\epsilon\rangle)]$$

when $i = 2$, this is equal to

$$\lambda\langle x, y\rangle.[\exists \langle x_\epsilon, y_\epsilon\rangle \in I^2 : \phi(x_\epsilon, y_\epsilon) \land (\exists j \geq 0 : \forall i \in [0, j],$$
$$1000 \leq x_\epsilon + iy_\epsilon \leq b) \land (\langle 2, \langle x_\epsilon + jy_\epsilon, y_\epsilon\rangle\rangle = \langle 2, \langle x, y\rangle\rangle))]$$
$$= \lambda\langle x, y\rangle.[\exists j \geq 0 : \phi(x - jy, y) \land 1000 \leq min(x - jy, x)$$
$$\land (max(x - jy, x) \leq b)]$$

10-5.3.3. Forward versus backward semantic analysis of programs

In the literature on program verification, backward program analysis is often preferred to forward analysis (e.g., [Dijk76]). Theorem 10-19(1)–(2) clearly shows that the two approaches are not strictly equivalent, but this point of view is complemented by Theorem 10-13 and Section 10-5.3, which show that, using symbolic variables, one approach can serve as a substitute for the other.

10-6. APPROXIMATE ANALYSIS OF PROGRAMS

Although the above approach to solving semantic fixed point equations can lead to complete information about program behavior, it is essentially mathematically ideal since it is well known that decision problems connected with programs such as termination are algorithmically unsolvable. The trouble is that fixed points are obtained as limits of infinitely long iteration sequences and that machines are unable (and humans, as well, for nontrivial examples) to guess a suitable induction hypothesis to be used in the induction step which avoids the need to compute all terms of the iteration sequence. Hence we must limit ourselves to constructive methods which automatically compute *approximate* solutions to the semantic equations. Such approximate information is often useful. For example in program verification systems, a total correctness proof (Examples 10-6, 10-14) can be approximated by a partial correctness proof (Examples 10-3, 10-5, 10-12). Optimizing compilers only need a conservative approximate analysis of programs, since whenever insufficient information is available no optimization will take place. For example if an array index cannot be proved to be within the array bounds, a run-time check can be generated. In the same way, a large part of the debugging process can be automated to detect some but not all programming errors.

An example of approximate information about the behavior of a program $\pi(S, \tau, v_\epsilon, v_\omega, v_\xi)$ is given by a predicate $P \in (S \longrightarrow B)$ characterizing a superset of the descendants of the entry states satisfying an input specification ϕ, that is, such that $post(\tau^*)(v_\epsilon \wedge \phi) \Rightarrow P$. P gives a partial answer to the termination problem since if $P \wedge v_\sigma$ is false, then π surely always diverges, whereas if $P \wedge v_\sigma$ is not false, then one cannot conclude whether π terminates or not. Also P can be used for a partial correctness proof (Example 10-3). It follows from Theorem 10-9(1) that P must be an upper approximation of the least solution to the equation $\alpha = (v_\epsilon \wedge \phi) \vee post(\tau)(\alpha)$, that is, such that $lfp(\lambda\alpha.[v_\epsilon \wedge \phi) \vee post(\tau)(\alpha)]) \Rightarrow P$.

Another example of approximate information about the behavior of a program $\pi(S, \tau, v_\epsilon, v_\omega, v_\xi)$ is given by a predicate $Q \in (S \longrightarrow B)$ which is a lower approximation of the greatest solution to the equation $\alpha = \neg v_\omega \wedge \neg v_\xi \wedge pre(\tau)(\alpha)$, that is, (Theorem 10-9(5)) such that $Q \Rightarrow \neg pre(\tau^*)$ $(v_\omega \wedge v_\xi)$. The approximation is that Q characterizes only a subset of the states which cause π to diverge.

Hence an approximate program analysis can be automated by effectively computing a lower or upper approximation of the least or greatest solution to the fixed point equations $x = f(x)$ on $(S \longrightarrow B)$ considered in Theorem 10-9. Our approach consists in solving a simplified equation $x = f'(x)$ on a complete lattice L which is a simpler and computer-representable image of $(S \longrightarrow B)$. A solution to the simplified equation $x = f'(x)$ will be computed iteratively using an extrapolation technique in order to accelerate the convergence when necessary. We will consider only the upper approximation of least fixed points since the other cases are duals to it.

10-6.1. Considering Simplified Equations

Assume we have to compute an upper approximation of the least fixed point $lfp(f)$ of an isotone operator f on a complete lattice $L(\sqsubseteq, \bot, \top, \sqcap, \sqcup)$. We will consider a simplified and computer-representable image $\bar{L}$ of L and solve a less complex equation $x = \bar{f}(x)$ on $\bar{L}$. [Cous79] justifies the fact that the following connection must be established between L and $\bar{L}$.

Definition 10-20. Let $L(\sqsubseteq, \bot, \top, \sqcup, \sqcap)$ and $\bar{L}(\sqsubseteq, \bot, \top, \sqcup, \sqcap)$ be complete lattices. $\bar{L}$ is *an upper approximation* of L iff there exists a one-to-one complete $\sqcap$-morphism γ from $\bar{L}$ onto L.

Example 10-21. Let π be a program over n integer variables $X_1, \ldots, X_n$. Assume that at each program point i we have to determine the signs of the variables $X_1, \ldots, X_n$. This consists in finding out Q_i such that $lfp(F_\pi(\phi))_i \Rightarrow Q_i$ where Q_i belongs to the subset $L_1' \subseteq L_1 = (I^n \rightarrow B)$ of predicates of the form $\lambda\langle X_1, \ldots, X_n\rangle.\left[\bigwedge_{j=1}^{n} P_j(X_j)\right]$, where P_j belongs to the subset $L_2' = \{\lambda X.[false], \lambda X.[X = 0], \lambda X.[-b - 1 \le X \le 0], \lambda X.[0 \le X \le b], \lambda X.[true]\}$ of $L_2 = (I \rightarrow B)$. We can define an upper approximation $\bar{L}_2$ of L_2 as shown in Fig. 10-5.

$$\bar{L}_2 = $$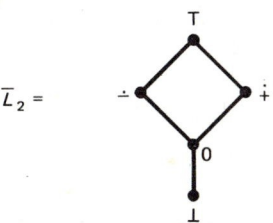

Figure 10-5

where $\gamma_2 \in (\bar{L}_2 \rightarrow L_2)$ is defined by

$$\gamma_2 = \lambda s.[\textbf{case } s \textbf{ in}$$
$$\bot \rightarrow \lambda X.[false]$$
$$\dot{-} \rightarrow \lambda X.[-b - 1 \le X \le 0]$$
$$0 \rightarrow \lambda X.[X = 0]$$
$$+ \rightarrow \lambda X.[0 \le X \le b]$$
$$\top \rightarrow \lambda X.[true]$$
$$\textbf{esac]}$$

The upper approximation $\bar{L}_1$ of L_1 can be defined as

$$\bar{L}_1 = \{\langle s_1, \ldots, s_n\rangle : (\forall j \in [1, n], s_j \in \bar{L}_2 - \{\bot\})\} \cup \{\langle \bot, \ldots, \bot\rangle\}$$

and $\gamma_1 \in (\bar{L}_1 \to L_1)$ is such that

$$\gamma_1 = \lambda\langle s_1, \ldots, s_n\rangle.\left[\lambda\langle X_1, \ldots, X_n\rangle.\left[\bigwedge_{j=1}^{n} \gamma_2(s_j)(X_j)\right]\right]$$

Intuitively, γ gives the meaning $\gamma(\bar{x})$ of the elements $\bar{x}$ of $\bar{L}$. γ is assumed to be one-to-one so that no two distinct elements of $\bar{L}$ can have the same meaning. The hypothesis that γ is a complete $\sqcap$-morphism implies that for all $x \in L$ the set $\{\bar{y} \in \bar{L} : x \sqsubseteq \gamma(\bar{y})\}$ of upper approximations of x in $\bar{L}$ has a least element, namely $\alpha(x) = \sqcap\{\bar{y} \in \bar{L} : x \sqsubseteq \gamma(\bar{y})\}$. The close relationship between α and γ is described by the following:

Theorem 10-22. Let $\alpha \in (L \to \bar{L})$ be $\lambda x.\sqcap\{\bar{y} \in \bar{L} : x \sqsubseteq \gamma(\bar{y})\}$. α is a complete $\sqcup$-morphism from L onto $\bar{L}$. $\alpha \circ \gamma = \lambda\bar{x}.[\alpha(\gamma(\bar{x}))]$ is the identity function on $\bar{L}$. $\gamma \circ \alpha$ is an isotone, idempotent ($\gamma \circ \alpha \circ \gamma \circ \alpha = \gamma \circ \alpha$) and extensive ($\forall x \in L, x \sqsubseteq \gamma \circ \alpha(x)$) operator on L. Moreover $\gamma = \lambda\bar{y}.\sqcup\{x \in L : \alpha(x) \sqsubseteq \bar{y}\}$.

Example 10-23.　Coming back to Example 10-21, we have:

$$\alpha_2 = \lambda P \in (I \to B).[\textbf{if}\quad P = \lambda X.[\textit{false}]\ \textbf{then}\ \bot$$
$$\textbf{elsif}\ P \Rightarrow \lambda X.[X = 0]\ \textbf{then}\ 0$$
$$\textbf{elsif}\ P \Rightarrow \lambda X.[X \leq 0]\ \textbf{then}\ \dot{-}$$
$$\textbf{elsif}\ P \Rightarrow \lambda X.[X \geq 0]\ \textbf{then}\ \dot{+}$$
$$\textbf{else}\ \top\ \textbf{fi}]$$

$$\alpha_1 = \lambda P \in (I^n \to B).\left[\prod_{j=1}^{n} \alpha_2(\lambda X.[\exists \langle X_1, \ldots, X_{j-1}, X_{j+1}, \ldots, X_n\rangle \in I^{n-1} :\right.$$

$$P(X_1, \ldots, X_{j-1}, X, X_{j+1}, \ldots, X_n)])\Big]$$

For example,

$$\alpha_1(\lambda\langle x, y\rangle.[(x \geq 1) \wedge (x + y = 2) \wedge even(y)])$$
$$= \langle\alpha_2(\lambda x.[(1 \leq x \leq b) \wedge even(x)]), \alpha_2(\lambda y.[(-b + 2 \leq y \leq 1)$$
$$\wedge\ even(y)])\rangle$$

$$= \langle\dot{+}, \dot{-}\rangle$$

An upper approximation of the least fixed point $lfp(f)$ of an isotone operator f on the complete lattice L can be defined using an approximate image $\bar{f}$ of f on $(\bar{L} \to \bar{L})$ as follows:

Definition 10-24. Let $\bar{L}(\sqsubseteq, \bot, \top, \sqcup, \sqcap)$ be an upper approximation of $L(\sqsubseteq, \bot, \top, \sqcup, \sqcap)$ and f be an isotone operator on L. $\bar{f}$ is an *upper approximation* of f on $\bar{L}$ iff $\bar{f}$ is an isotone operator on $\bar{L}$ such that $(\forall \bar{x} \in \bar{L}, \alpha(f(\gamma(\bar{x}))) \sqsubseteq \bar{f}(\bar{x}))$.

Theorem 10-25. If $\bar{f}$ is an upper approximation of f on $\bar{L}$, then $lfp(f) \sqsubseteq \gamma(lfp(\bar{f}))$ and $gfp(f) \sqsubseteq \gamma(gfp(\bar{f}))$.

Once an application-dependent upper approximation has been chosen (Definition 10-20) and knowing the construction rules for associating a system of semantic equations with a program (Theorems 10-17 and 10-19), one can determine the construction rules for associating a system of approximate equations with a program.

Example 10-26. Let us determine the construction rules of the approximate equations corresponding to Example 10-21. For simplicity we consider only the forward rule for the assignment $x := x + 1$ in a program with a single variable x. The exact rule is Definition 10-16.

$$P_i = \bigvee_{j \in pred_\pi(i)} post(\lambda x.[x+1])(P_j) \qquad \text{where } P_i, P_j \in (I \to B)$$

The approximate rule is Definition 10-24.

$$P_i = \alpha_2 \left(\bigvee_{j \in pred_\pi(i)} post(\lambda x.[x+1])(\gamma_2(P_j)) \right) \qquad \text{where } P_i, P_j \in \bar{L}_2$$

$$= \bigsqcup_{j \in pred_\pi(i)} \alpha_2(post(\lambda x.[x+1])(\gamma_2(P_j))) \qquad \text{(Theorem 10-22)}$$

It remains to analyze:

$$\alpha_2(post(\lambda x.[x+1])(\gamma_2(P_j)))$$
$$= \alpha_2(\lambda x.[\exists\, x' \in I: \gamma_2(P_j)(x') \wedge x' \in dom(\lambda x.[x+1]) \wedge x = x'+1])$$
$$= \alpha_2(\lambda x.[\gamma_2(P_j)(x-1) \wedge (-b-1 \le x \le b-1)])$$

According to the possible values of P_j we can distinguish the following cases:

$$\alpha_2(post(\lambda x.[x+1])(\gamma_2(\bot))) = \alpha_2(\lambda x.[false]) = \bot$$
$$\alpha_2(post(\lambda x.[x+1])\ (\gamma_2(0))) = \alpha_2(\lambda x.[x=1]) = +$$
$$\alpha_2(post(\lambda x.[x+1])(\gamma_2(\dot{-}))) = \alpha_2(\lambda x.[-b \le x \le 1]) = \top$$
$$\alpha_2(post(\lambda x.[x+1])(\gamma_2(\dot{+}))) = \alpha_2(\lambda x.[1 \le x \le b-1]) = +$$
$$\alpha_2(post(\lambda x.[x+1])(\gamma_2(\top))) = \alpha_2(\lambda x.[-b \le x \le b-1]) = \top$$

More generally the approximate forward assignment rule consists, given the signs of the variables before the assignment, in applying the rules of signs to the right-hand-side expression ($+ + + = +, + + \dot{-} = \top$, $\dot{-} - + = \dot{-}, \dot{-} * \dot{-} = +, \ldots$) and assigning the result to the left-hand-side variable. The signs of the other variables are left unchanged.

We can now write a program, which, given a program text π, constructs the associated system of approximate equations $x = \bar{f}(x)$. Whenever $\bar{L}$ satisfies the ascending chain condition, we can write a program for computing the least fixed point $lfp(\bar{f})$ of any isotone operator $\bar{f}$ on $\bar{L}$. Starting from the infimum of $\bar{L}$, the algorithm can proceed iteratively using any efficient chaotic strategy until the iterates stabilize.

Example 10-27.   The system of approximate equations associated with the introductory example program

> {1}
>> **while** $x \geq 1000$ **do**
>
> {2}
>> $x := x + y;$
>
> {3}
>> **od**;
>
> {4}

is the following:

$$\langle x_1, y_1 \rangle = \phi$$
$$\langle x_2, y_2 \rangle = smash(\langle if\ (x_1 \sqcup x_3) \sqsubseteq \dot{-}\ then\ \perp\ else + fi, y_1 \sqcup y_3 \rangle)$$
$$\langle x_3, y_3 \rangle = smash(\langle x_2 + y_2, y_2 \rangle)$$
$$\langle x_4, y_4 \rangle = smash(\langle x_1 \sqcup x_3, y_1 \sqcup y_3 \rangle)$$
$$\langle x_\xi, y_\xi \rangle = if\ (x_2 \sqsubseteq 0) \vee (y_2 \sqsubseteq 0) \vee ((x_2 = +) \wedge (y_2 = \dot{-})) \vee ((x_2 = \dot{-})$$
$$\wedge\ (y_2 = +))\ then\ \langle \perp, \perp \rangle\ else\ \langle x_2, y_2 \rangle fi$$

where $smash(\langle x, y \rangle) = if\ (x = \perp)\ or\ (y = \perp)\ then\ \langle \perp, \perp \rangle\ else\ \langle x, y \rangle fi$. Taking $\phi = \langle +, \dot{-} \rangle$, a chaotic iterative resolution corresponding to a symbolic execution of the program is the following:

$$\langle x_i^0, y_i^0 \rangle = \langle \perp, \perp \rangle \qquad i = 1, \ldots, 4, \xi$$
$$\langle x_1^1, y_1^1 \rangle = \phi = \langle +, \dot{-} \rangle$$
$$\langle x_2^1, y_2^1 \rangle = smash(\langle if\ (x_1^1 \sqcup x_3^0) \sqsubseteq \dot{-}\ then\ \perp\ else + fi, y_1^1 \sqcup y_3^0 \rangle) = \langle +, \dot{-} \rangle$$
$$\langle x_3^1, y_3^1 \rangle = smash(\langle x_2^1 + y_2^1, y_2^1 \rangle) = \langle \top, \dot{-} \rangle$$
$$\langle x_2^2, y_2^2 \rangle = smash(\langle if\ (x_1^1 \sqcup x_3^1) \sqsubseteq \dot{-}\ then\ \perp\ else + fi, y_1^1 \sqcup y_3^1 \rangle) = \langle +, \dot{-} \rangle$$

Stabilizing around the loop, the remaining components are

$$\langle x_4^2, y_4^2 \rangle = smash(\langle x_1^1 \sqcup x_3^1, y_1^1 \sqcup y_3^1 \rangle) = \langle \top, \dot{-} \rangle$$
$$\langle x_\xi^2, y_\xi^2 \rangle = if\ (x_2^2 \sqsubseteq 0) \vee (y_2^2 \sqsubseteq 0) \vee ((x_2^2 = +) \wedge (y_2^2 = \dot{-}))$$
$$\vee\ ((x_2^2 = \dot{-}) \wedge (y_2^2 = +))\ then\ \langle \perp, \perp \rangle\ else\ \langle x_2, y_2 \rangle fi$$
$$= \langle \perp, \perp \rangle$$

The results are approximate but not useless since, e.g., they prove that no overflow can occur when the entry specification $(x \geq 0 \wedge y \leq 0)$ is true.

10-6.2. Speeding Up the Convergence of Chaotic Iterations Using Extrapolation Techniques

When $\bar{L}$ does not satisfy the ascending chain condition, infinitely many steps may be necessary in order to ensure the convergence of a chaotic version of the iterates $\bigsqcup_{i \geq 0} \bar{f}^i(\perp)$ to the least fixed point $lfp(\bar{f})$. It may also be the case that the number of iterations required is not infinite but so large as to be unacceptable in practice.

Example 10-28. In order to analyze programs over n integer variables $X_1, \ldots, X_n$ let us consider:

1. The complete lattice $\bar{L}_2 = \{\perp\} \cup \{[l, u]: -b - 1 \leq l \leq u \leq b\}$ where $\perp$ is the infimum and $([l_1, u_1] \sqsubseteq [l_2, u_2])$ iff $(l_2 \leq l_1 \leq u_1 \leq u_2)$. The meaning of the elements of $\bar{L}_2$ is given by $\gamma_2(\perp) = \lambda X.[false]$ and $\gamma_2([l, u]) = \lambda X.[l \leq X \leq u]$.

2. The complete lattice $\bar{L}_1 = \{\langle i_1, \ldots, i_n \rangle: (\forall j \in [1, n], i_j \in (\bar{L}_2 - \{\perp\}))\} \cup \{\langle \perp, \ldots, \perp \rangle\}$ with $\gamma_1 = \lambda \langle i_1, \ldots, i_n \rangle.[\lambda \langle X_1, \ldots, X_n \rangle.[\bigwedge_{j=1}^{n} \gamma_2(i_j)(X_j)]]$.

3. The resolution of the equation $x = [0, 0] \sqcup (x + 1)$ on $\bar{L}_2$ where $\perp + 1 = \perp$ and $[l, u] + 1 = [l + 1, min(u + 1, b)]$ involves a very large number of iterates $x^0 = \perp, x^1 = [0, 0], x^2 = [0, 1], x^3 = [0, 2], \ldots, x^{b+1} = [0, b], x^{b+2} = [0, b]$.

However, using the notion of extrapolation [Cous77a], we are able to speed up the convergence of the iteration and obtain a close approximation to the least fixed point in a finite number of steps.

Definition 10-29. A *widening operator* $\nabla \in (\mathbf{N} \rightarrow (\bar{L} \times \bar{L} \rightarrow \bar{L}))$ is such that:

1. $\forall j > 0, \forall x, y \in \bar{L}, x \sqcup y \sqsubseteq x \nabla(j) y$

2. For any ascending chain $y^0 \sqsubseteq y^1 \sqsubseteq \ldots \sqsubseteq y^n \sqsubseteq \ldots$ of elements of $\bar{L}$, the ascending chain $x^0 = y^0, x^1 = x^0 \nabla(1) y^1, \ldots, x^n = x^{n-1} \nabla(n) y^n, \ldots$ is eventually stable; i.e., there exists a $k \geq 0$ such that for $i \geq k, x^i = x^k$. x^k is called the limit of the chain.

A widening operator will be used to extrapolate each iterate until a post-fixed point is reached, in which case an upper approximation of the least fixed point has been found.

Theorem 10-30. Let $\bar{f}$ be an isotone operator on $\bar{L}(\sqsubseteq, \bot, \top, \sqcup, \sqcap)$ and ∇ be a widening operator. The limit u of the sequence

$$x^0 = d$$
$$x^{n+1} = x^n \, \nabla(n+1) \, \bar{f}(x^n) \qquad \text{if } \neg(\bar{f}(x^n) \sqsubseteq x^n)$$
$$x^{n+1} = x^n \qquad\qquad\qquad \text{if } \bar{f}(x^n) \sqsubseteq x^n$$

can be computed in a finite number of steps. Moreover $lfp(\bar{f}) \sqsubseteq u$ and $\bar{f}(u) \sqsubseteq u$.

Example 10-31. When $\bar{L}$ satisfies the ascending chain condition, one can choose $\forall j > 0, \nabla(j) = \sqcup$, in which case $x^k = lfp(\bar{f})$. However the widening operator may be necessary when the convergence of the iterates must be speeded up as in Example 10-28. Although the above definition allows a different extrapolation to be applied at each step, the widening operator will most often be independent of j. For Example 10-28, one can choose for all $j > 0$:

$$\forall x \in \bar{L}_2, \bot \, \nabla_2(j) \, x = x \, \nabla_2(j) \, \bot = x$$
$$[l_1, u_1] \, \nabla_2(j) \, [l_2, u_2]$$
$$= [\textit{if } 0 \le l_2 < l_1 \textit{ then } 0 \textit{ elsif } l_2 < l_1 \textit{ then } -b - 1 \textit{ else } l_1 \textit{ fi},$$
$$\textit{if } u_1 < u_2 \le 0 \textit{ then } 0 \textit{ elsif } u_1 < u_2 \textit{ then } b \textit{ else } u_1 \textit{ fi}]$$

A widening ∇_1 on $\bar{L}_1$ is obtained by applying ∇_2 componentwise:

$$\langle i_1, \ldots, i_n \rangle \, \nabla_1(j) \, \langle i'_1, \ldots, i'_n \rangle = \langle i_1 \, \nabla_2(j) \, i'_1, \ldots, i_n \, \nabla_2(j) \, i'_n \rangle$$

With regard to systems of equations it is not necessary to use a widening for each component. Considering the program graph as defined in Section 10-3.1 (or the reversed graph for backward equations), the widening operation need only be used for the components corresponding to loop head nodes. A set S of loop head nodes is a minimal set of vertices such that any oriented cycle in the graph contains an element of S. In general such a set is not unique, and an arbitrary choice may be made (but when the graph is reducible, interval headers [Alle70] should be preferred).

Example 10-32. The loop head nodes of the program graph in Fig. 10-6 are marked $\odot$.

Example 10-33. When considering the approximation defined in Example 10-28, the system of simplified forward equations corresponding to the program $\odot$.

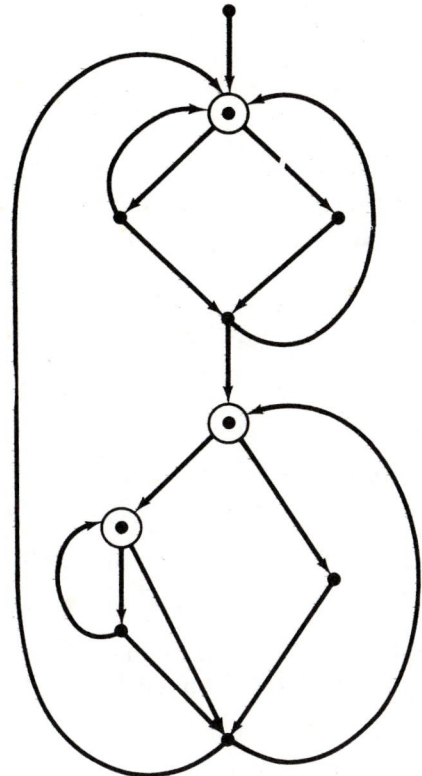

Figure 10-6

{1}

  while $(10 \leq x) \wedge (x \leq 100)$ **do**

{2}

   $x := x + y;$

{3}

  od;

{4}

is the following:

$$\begin{cases} \langle x_1, y_1 \rangle = \phi \\ \langle x_2, y_2 \rangle = smash(\langle ((x_1 \sqcup x_3) \sqcap [10, 100]), (y_1 \sqcup y_3) \rangle) \\ \langle x_3, y_3 \rangle = smash(\langle x_2 + y_2, y_2 \rangle) \\ \langle x_4, y_4 \rangle = smash(\langle ((x_1 \sqcup x_3) \sqcap (-b - 1, 9]), (y_1 \sqcup y_3) \rangle) \\ \langle x_\xi, y_\xi \rangle = \textit{if } \langle x_2, y_2 \rangle = \langle \bot, \bot \rangle \textit{ then } \langle \bot, \bot \rangle \textit{ else underflow}(x_2, y_2) \\ \qquad\qquad\qquad\qquad\qquad\qquad\qquad\qquad \sqcup \textit{ overflow}(x_2, y_2)\textit{ fi} \end{cases}$$

where

$$\forall x \in \bar{L}_2, \bot \sqcup x = x \sqcup \bot = x,$$
$$\bot \sqcap x = x \sqcap \bot = \bot,$$
$$\bot + x = x + \bot = \bot,$$

$$[l_1, u_1] \sqcup [l_2, u_2] = [min(l_1, l_2), max(u_1, u_2)]$$

$$[l_1, u_1] \sqcap [l_2, u_2] = if \; max(l_1, l_2) \leq min(u_1, u_2) \; then \; [max(l_1, l_2), \; min(u_1, u_2)]$$
$$else \; \bot \; fi$$

$$[l_1, u_1] + [l_2, u_2] = [l_1 + l_2, u_1 + u_2] \sqcap [-b - 1, b]$$

$$overflow([l_1, u_1], [l_2, u_2]) = if \; (u_1 \geq 1) \wedge (u_2 \geq 1) \; then \; \langle ([l_1, u_1]$$
$$\sqcap [b - u_2 + 1, b]), ([l_2, u_2] \sqcap [b - u_1 + 1, b]) \rangle \; else \; \langle \bot, \bot \rangle \; fi$$

$$underflow([l_1, u_1], [l_2, u_2]) = if \; (l_1 \leq -1) \wedge (l_2 \leq -1) \; then \; \langle ([l_1, u_1]$$
$$\sqcap [-b - 1, -b - 2 - l_2]), ([l_2, u_2]$$
$$\sqcap [-b - 1, -b - 2 - l_1]) \rangle \; else \; \langle \bot, \bot \rangle \; fi$$

$$smash(\langle x, y \rangle) = if \; (x = \bot) \vee (y = \bot) \; then \; \langle \bot, \bot \rangle \; else \; \langle x, y \rangle fi$$

Taking $\phi = \langle [9, 11], [-1, +1] \rangle$ the resolution uses the widening operators of Example 10-31 for the loop head node 2:

$$\langle x_i^0, y_i^0 \rangle = \langle \bot, \bot \rangle \qquad i = 1, \ldots, 4, \xi$$

$$\langle x_1^1, y_1^1 \rangle = \phi = \langle [9, 11], [-1, 1] \rangle$$

$$\langle x_2^1, y_2^1 \rangle = \langle x_2^0, y_2^0 \rangle \nabla_1(1) \; smash(\langle (x_1^1 \sqcup x_3^0) \sqcap [10, 100], (y_1^1 \sqcup y_3^0) \rangle)$$
$$= \langle \bot \nabla_2(1) [10, 11], \bot \nabla_2(1) [-1, 1] \rangle = \langle [10, 11], [-1, 1] \rangle$$

$$\langle x_3^1, y_3^1 \rangle = smash(\langle x_2^1 + y_2^1, y_2^1 \rangle) = \langle [9, 12], [-1, 1] \rangle$$

$$\langle x_2^2, y_2^2 \rangle = \langle x_2^1, y_2^1 \rangle \nabla_1(2) \; smash(\langle (x_1^1 \sqcup x_3^1) \sqcap [10, 100], (y_1^1 \sqcup y_3^1) \rangle)$$
$$= \langle [10, 11) \nabla_2(2) [10, 12], [-1, 1] \nabla_2(2) [-1, 1] \rangle = \langle [10, b], [-1, 1] \rangle$$

The effect of the widening is to extrapolate to zero or infinity ($-b - 1$ or b) the bounds which are not stable around the loop.

$$\langle x_3^2, y_3^2 \rangle = smash(\langle x_2^2 + y_2^2, y_2^1 \rangle) = \langle [9, b], [-1, +1] \rangle$$

According to the definition of the approximate iteration sequence in Theorem 10-30, we have

$$\langle x_2^3, y_2^3 \rangle = \langle x_2^2, y_2^2 \rangle = \langle [10, b], [-1, 1] \rangle$$

since $\langle [10, 100], [-1, 1] \rangle = smash(\langle (x_1^1 \sqcup x_3^2) \sqcap [10, 100], (y_1^1 \sqcup y_3^2) \rangle)$ $\sqsubseteq \langle x_2^2, y_2^2 \rangle$. The remaining components are:

$$\langle x_4^3, y_4^3 \rangle = smash(\langle\langle((x_1^1 \sqcup x_3^3) \sqcap [-b - 1, 9]), (y_1^1 \sqcup y_3^3)\rangle\rangle)$$
$$= \langle [9, 9], [-1, +1]\rangle$$
$$\langle x_\xi^3, y_\xi^3 \rangle = if \langle x_2^3, y_2^3 \rangle = \langle \bot, \bot \rangle \ then \ \langle \bot, \bot \rangle \ else \ underflow(x_2^3, y_2^3)$$
$$\sqcup \ overflow(x_2^3, y_2^3) \ fi$$
$$= \langle \bot, \bot \rangle \sqcup \langle [b, b], [1, 1] \rangle = \langle [b, b], [1, 1] \rangle$$

The approximate result is

$$\langle x_1^1, y_1^1 \rangle = \langle [9, 11], [-1, 1] \rangle$$
$$\langle x_2^3, y_2^3 \rangle = \langle [10, b], [-1, 1] \rangle$$
$$\langle x_3^3, y_3^3 \rangle = \langle [9, b], [-1, 1] \rangle$$
$$\langle x_4^3, y_4^3 \rangle = \langle [9, 9], [-1, 1] \rangle$$
$$\langle x_\xi^3, y_\xi^3 \rangle = \langle [b, b], [1, 1] \rangle$$

Any upper approximation u of the least fixed point $lfp(\bar{f})$ of an isotone operator $\bar{f}$ on a complete lattice $\bar{L}(\sqsubseteq, \bot, \top, \sqcup, \sqcap)$ can be improved by any term of the decreasing chain $x^0 = u, \ldots, x^{n+1} = x^n \sqcap \bar{f}(x^n), \ldots$. (We have $lfp(\bar{f}) \sqsubseteq u = x^0$. If by induction hypothesis $lfp(\bar{f}) \sqsubseteq x^n$, then by the fixed point property and isotony $lfp(\bar{f}) = \bar{f}(lfp(\bar{f})) \sqsubseteq \bar{f}(x^n)$, so that $lfp(\bar{f}) \sqsubseteq x^n \sqcap \bar{f}(x^n) = x^{n+1}$, proving by recurrence that for all $k \geq 0$, $lfp(\bar{f}) \sqsubseteq x^k$.)

Yet notice that when u is already a fixed point no improvement is possible. In general the chain is strictly decreasing, and when $\bar{L}$ does not satisfy the descending chain condition, it may not stabilize. However one can stop the iteration process after any number of steps or use the following extrapolation technique.

Definition 10-34. A *narrowing operator* $\Delta \in (\mathbf{N} \longrightarrow ((\bar{L} \times \bar{L}) \longrightarrow \bar{L}))$ is such that:

1. $\forall j > 0, (\forall x, y \in \bar{L}^2 : y \sqsubseteq x), y \sqsubseteq x \Delta(j) y \sqsubseteq x$
2. For any descending chain $y^0 \sqsupseteq y^1 \sqsupseteq \ldots \sqsupseteq y^n \sqsupseteq \ldots$ of elements of $\bar{L}$, the descending chain $x^0 = y^0, \ldots, x^n = x^{n-1} \Delta(n) y^n, \ldots$ is eventually stable.

Example 10-35. Coming back to Example 10-28, one can choose for all $j > 0$:

$$\forall x \in \bar{L}_2, \bot \Delta_2(j) x = x \Delta_2(j) \bot = \bot$$
$$[l_1, u_1] \Delta_2(j) [l_2, u_2] = [if \ (l_1 = b - 1) \lor (l_1 = 0) \ then \ l_2 \ else \ min(l_1, l_2) \ fi,$$
$$if \ (u_1 = b) \lor (u_1 = 0) \ then \ u_2 \ else \ max(u_1, u_2) \ fi]$$

This narrowing operator attempts to improve the zero or infinite bounds $(-b - 1$ and $b)$ which might have been too imprecisely extrapolated by the widening operator.

> **Theorem 10-36.** Let $u \in \bar{L}$ be such that $(lfp(\bar{f}) \sqsubseteq u)$ and $(\bar{f}(u) \sqsubseteq u)$. The decreasing chain $x^0 = u, \ldots, x^n = x^{n-1} \Delta(n) \bar{f}(x^{n-1}), \ldots$ is eventually stable. Moreover $\forall k \geq 0, lfp(\bar{f}) \sqsubseteq x^k$.

Example 10-37.   This is a continuation of Example 10-33.

$$\langle x_2^4, y_2^4 \rangle = \langle x_2^3, y_2^3 \rangle \Delta_1(1) \, smash(\langle ((x_1^1 \sqcup x_3^2) \sqcap [10, 100], (y_1^1 \sqcup y_3^2) \rangle)$$
$$= \langle [10, b] \Delta_2(1) \, [10, 100], [-1, 1] \Delta_2(1) \, [-1, 1] \rangle$$
$$= \langle [10, 100], [-1, 1] \rangle$$
$$\langle x_3^4, y_3^4 \rangle = smash(\langle x_2^4 + y_2^4, y_2^4 \rangle) = \langle [9, 101], [-1, 1] \rangle$$
$$\langle x_2^4, y_2^5 \rangle = \langle x_2^4, y_2^4 \rangle \Delta_1(2) \, smash(\langle ((x_1^1 \sqcup x_3^4) \sqcap [10, 100], (y_1^1 \sqcup y_3^2) \rangle)$$
$$= \langle [10, 100] \Delta_2(2) \, [10, 100], [-1, 1] \Delta_2(2) \, [-1, 1] \rangle$$
$$= \langle [10, 100], [-1, 1] \rangle = \langle x_2^4, y_2^4 \rangle$$

Stabilization around the loop has been achieved. The components depending on $\langle x_2^5, y_2^5 \rangle$ remain to be evaluated. The final result is

$$\langle x_1^1, y_1^1 \rangle = \langle [9, 11], [-1, 1] \rangle$$
$$\langle x_2^5, y_2^5 \rangle = \langle [10, 100], [-1, 1] \rangle$$
$$\langle x_3^4, y_3^4 \rangle = \langle [9, 101], [-1, 1] \rangle$$
$$\langle x_4^5, y_4^5 \rangle = \langle [9, 9], [-1, 1] \rangle$$
$$\langle x_\xi^5, y_\xi^5 \rangle = \langle \bot, \bot \rangle$$

10-6.3.   Hierarchy of Approximate Program Analyses

Let us give three examples of approximate analysis of the same program.

Given an array R of integers whose elements are sorted in increasing order, the following procedure searches for a given argument k and returns the position m such that $R(m) = k$. When the search is unsuccessful, $m = lb(R) - 1$ where $lb(R)$ and $ub(R)$ are respectively the least and greatest indices of R.

```
type table = array [1, 100] of integer;
procedure binary-search (var R: table; value k: integer;
                                           result m: integer) =
    var bi, bs: integer;
    begin
    bi := lb(R); bs := ub(R);
```

{1}
      while $bi \leq bs$ **do**

{2}
         $m := (bi + bs)$ **div** 2;

{3}
         if $k = R(m)$ **then**
           $bi := bs + 1$;

{4}
         elsif $k < R(m)$ **then**
           $bs := m - 1$;

{5}
         else
           $bi := m + 1$;

{6}
         fi;

{7}
      od;

{8}
      if $R(m) \neq k$ **then** $m := lb(R) - 1$ **fi**;

{9}
    end;

The approximation considered in Examples 10-21, 10-23, 10-26, and 10-27 can be briefly sketched using a geometrical analogy. A predicate P over two numerical variables x and y, whose characteristic set $\bar{P}$ is shown in Fig. 10-7(a), is approximated from above by the predicate characterizing the quadrant of the plane containing all the points of $\bar{P}$, as shown in Fig. 10-7(b). If, contrary to Example 10-21, we make a distinction between predicates such as $\lambda x.[x \geq 0]$ and $\lambda x.[x > 0]$ and if we are only concerned by the behavior

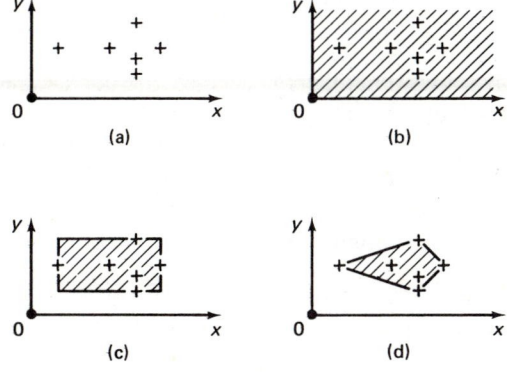

Figure 10-7

of the variables bi, bs, and m then the corresponding approximate analysis of the procedure *binary-search* is the following:

$$P_1 = (bi > 0) \wedge (bs > 0)$$
$$P_2 = (bi > 0) \wedge (bs > 0)$$
$$P_3 = (bi > 0) \wedge (bs > 0) \wedge (m > 0)$$
$$P_4 = (bi > 0) \wedge (bs > 0) \wedge (m > 0)$$
$$P_5 = (bi > 0) \wedge (bs \geq 0) \wedge (m > 0)$$
$$P_6 = (bi > 0) \wedge (bs > 0) \wedge (m > 0)$$
$$P_7 = (bi > 0) \wedge (bs \geq 0) \wedge (m > 0)$$
$$P_8 = (bi > 0) \wedge (bs \geq 0)$$
$$P_9 = (bi > 0) \wedge (bs \geq 0)$$

The approximation considered at Examples 10-28, 10-31, 10-33, 10-35, and 10-37 is more precise and consists of approximating the characteristic set of P by the smallest rectangle including it and whose sides run parallel with the axes, as shown in Fig. 10-7(c).

The corresponding analysis of the procedure *binary-search* is the following:

$$P_1 = (bi = 1) \wedge (bs = 100)$$
$$P_2 = (1 \leq bi \leq 100) \wedge (1 \leq bs \leq 100)$$
$$P_3 = (1 \leq bi \leq 100) \wedge (1 \leq bs \leq 100) \wedge (1 \leq m \leq 100)$$
$$P_4 = (2 \leq bi \leq 101) \wedge (1 \leq bs \leq 100) \wedge (1 \leq m \leq 100)$$
$$P_5 = (1 \leq bi \leq 100) \wedge (0 \leq bs \leq 99) \wedge (1 \leq m \leq 100)$$
$$P_6 = (2 \leq bi \leq 101) \wedge (1 \leq bs \leq 100) \wedge (1 \leq m \leq 100)$$
$$P_7 = (1 \leq bi \leq 101) \wedge (0 \leq bs \leq 100) \wedge (1 \leq m \leq 100)$$
$$P_8 = (1 \leq bi \leq 101) \wedge (0 \leq bs \leq 100) \wedge (1 \leq m \leq 100)$$
$$P_9 = (1 \leq bi \leq 101) \wedge (0 \leq bs \leq 100) \wedge (0 \leq m \leq 100)$$

This analysis shows that all array accesses are correct, neither underflow nor overflow can occur, the integer division by 2 can be implemented by a logical right shift, bi and bs should have been declared bi: $1 .. 101$; bs: $0 .. 100$, and the result m returned by the procedure is always included between the bounds 0 and 100.

Some programming languages allow a declaration such as:

type table: **array[1,n] of integer**;

where n is a symbolic constant the value of which is known only at run time. In such a case a more precise program analysis might be necessary in order to discover relationships between bi, bs, m, and n. For example [Cous78], it can be useful to look for linear equality or inequality relationships between the numerical variables of the program. This consists in approximating the characteristic set of a predicate P by the convex-hull of this set, as shown in Fig. 10-7(d).

The corresponding analysis of the procedure *binary-search* is now:

$$P_1 = (bi = 1) \wedge (bs = n)$$

$$P_2 = (1 \leq bi \leq bs \leq n)$$

$$P_3 = (1 \leq bi \leq bs \leq n) \wedge (2m \leq bi + bs \leq 2m + 1)$$

$$\text{(hence } 1 \leq m \leq n \text{ since } m \text{ is integer)}$$

$$P_4 = (1 \leq bs \leq n) \wedge (bs \leq 2m \leq 2bs) \wedge (bi = bs + 1)$$

$$P_5 = (1 \leq bi \leq n) \wedge (2bi - 1 \leq 2m \leq bi + n) \wedge (m = bs + 1)$$

$$P_6 = (1 \leq bs \leq n) \wedge (bs \leq 2m \leq 2bs) \wedge (bi = m + 1)$$

$$P_7 = (m \leq bs + 1) \wedge (3bi \leq 2bs + n + 3) \wedge (3bi \leq 2bs + 2m + 3)$$
$$\wedge (2bi \leq 2bs + 3) \wedge (bs + m + 1 \leq bi + n)$$
$$\wedge (bi + m \leq bs + n + 1) \wedge (1 \leq n) \wedge (bs \leq n) \wedge (bs \leq 2m)$$
$$\wedge (bs + 4 \leq 3bi + m) \wedge (1 \leq 2m) \wedge (bs + 1 \leq bi + m)$$

$$P_8 = (1 \leq bi) \wedge (bs \leq n) \wedge (bs \leq bi - 1)$$

Notice that at program point $\{8\}$ nothing is known about m. Contrary to the previous analysis, it may be the case that $n < 1$, in which case m is not initialized.

10-7. BIBLIOGRAPHIC NOTES

References [Schae73, Aho77 (chapter 14), Hech77] are introductions to program flow analysis which put emphasis on the boolean techniques (which historically appeared first). This bibliography is devoted to program analysis methods which do not make the hypothesis that the information to be gathered about programs can be naturally represented as boolean vectors.

Nonboolean program analysis techniques can be traced back to [Naur66] and [Sint72]; [Kild73, Wegb75] introduced iterative algorithms using a lattice satisfying the ascending chain condition in order to represent the information to be gathered about programs. The fixed point theory of approximate program analysis is discussed by [Kam77, Cous77a]. The problem of using iterative algorithms with lattices not satisfying the ascending chain condition is treated by [Cous77a]. [Tarj76] presents an efficient (but not general) implementation of iterative algorithms which extends [Kenn75b, Aho76]. Noniterative program analysis methods include [Grah76, ReiJ77, ReiJ78, Rose77a, Rose78a, Tarj75b]. Boolean techniques for interprocedural analysis of recursive programs are proposed by [Spil72, Alle74, Lome75, Rose79, Bart77a], whereas [Cous77a, Shar80] handle more ambitious analyses related to program verification.

Automatic methods for program analysis have numerous applications including type determination [Jone76, Kapl78a, Tene74b], gathering information for automatic data structure selection in very-high-level languages [Schw75b, Schw75c], detection of induction variables and strength reduction [Fong75, Fong76] or discovery of generalized common subexpressions [Fong77] for set-theoretic languages, determination of affine equality relationships among variables of a program [Karr76], detection of programming errors [Fosd76, Gill77], static array bound checking [Cous77a, Cous78, Germ78, Harr77a, Suzu77, Wels77], determination of linear [Cous78] or nonlinear [Berm76] invariant assertions, synthesis of resource invariants for concurrent programs [ClaE79], and so on.

ACKNOWLEDGMENT

I owe a deep debt to C. Pair whose argumented advice to study program analysis techniques using the model of discrete dynamic systems was very helpful. I wish to thank Radhia Cousot for her collaboration.

Chapter 11

Denotational Definition
of Properties
# of Program Computations

Veronique Donzeau-Gouge

INTRODUCTION

Syntactic transformations of a program may be done if properties which characterize its behavior have been defined and associated with elements of the program. For instance let us assume that the expression $x + 2$ in a program prog is replaced by the constant 5. This transformation is valid if the initial program prog and the modified one prog' are strongly equivalent. This can be proved if a property associated with the identifier x specifies that its value is equal to 3 for each computation of prog.

Properties of program computations can be defined by nonstandard interpretations [Cous77a, Sint72, Wegb75], i.e., by interpretations defined on domains suitably constructed to model the desired properties. This notion of nonstandard interpretation exists also in arithmetic: "casting out nines" can be understood as a nonstandard interpretation of multiplication which gives information about its correctness. In physics, calculation of the dimensions of a formula gives its units. The properties defined for a program by nonstandard interpretations must be satisfied by any computation described by the standard interpretation of the program. To verify this coherence, we must define and prove relations between these interpretations. For instance the relation between casting out nines and multiplication uses properties of the modulo operation.

These comparisons of interpretations may be done more easily if mathematical descriptions of the interpretations are used. Using the work of Scott and Strachey, we can define an interpretation as a function from input to output domains, where a domain is a partially ordered set in which the partial ordering models the notion of approximation in sequences of computations. An undefined element is included so that only total functions need be considered; completeness properties ensure the existence of limits for sequences of computed objects.

This denotational semantics gives an abstract definition of each property which is independent of any algorithms used to compute the property. Using this abstraction, we prove a congruence between nonstandard and standard interpretations.

Properties of the behavior of program computations have often been studied in the literature as "flow analysis problems"; this work concerns classical flow analysis. We consider data flow analyses used to compute properties of the values of expressions:

(a) *Constant propagation.* An occurrence of an expression is a constant if for each computation of the program the value of this occurrence is a known constant. The problem is to find such occurrences and the associated constant values.

(b) *Determination of common subexpressions.* The problem is to associate with each occurrence of an expression the set of expressions which have the same value in all computations as the one considered. This problem includes the determination of available expressions (an expression is available if its value has been previously computed and, since the last evaluation of the expression, no identifier appearing in the expression has had its value changed).

(c) *Scalar propagation.* The same problem as the previous one, restricted to the set of identifiers which have, in all computations, the same value as the expression at the occurrence considered.

(d) *Determination of invariant expressions.* An expression is invariant in a computation if its value remains constant during the computation: the goal is to determine the expressions which are invariant in all computations.

We use a simple Algol-like language to illustrate this study. A larger language could be managed by similar methods, but the proof would be longer and more tedious. The definitions of the different denotational interpretations of this simple language have been checked using the SIS system of Mosses [Moss78]. The concrete and abstract syntaxes of the simple language are written in GRAM. The language DSL is used to write the semantic functions.

We expect the reader to have a good understanding of denotational semantics [Tenn 67] and of its basic concepts of currying and continuation. A knowledge of the SIS system and of the syntax of the GRAM and DSL languages is useful but not necessary; these languages are very similar respectively to Backus-Naur Form and the notations usual in denotational semantics.

The plan of this study is as follows:

1. Introduction to some basic concepts used in denotational semantics
2. Specification of the concrete and abstract syntax of the simple language
3. Presentation of the notion of occurrence, a formalization of the notion of program point
4. Formal definition, including occurrences of the standard semantics of the simple language
5. Definition of the domains and equations used in a denotational definition of properties associated with expressions
6. Proof of coherence of the nonstandard interpretation and the standard one
7. Applications to some classical data flow analysis problems

11-1. DENOTATIONAL SEMANTICS

Based on the work of Scott and Strachey, this approach to semantics associates with each program a total function defined from input data to answers. A *domain* is a partially ordered set $\langle D, \sqsubseteq \rangle$ with an element $\perp$ and a binary operation $\sqcup$ such that [Scot77]:

1. $\perp \sqsubseteq d, \forall d \in D$.
2. $d_1, d_2, d_3 \in D$ and $d_1, d_2 \sqsubseteq d_3$ imply $d_1 \sqcup d_2$ is defined.
3. $d_1 \sqsubseteq d_1 \sqcup d_2$ and $d_2 \sqsubseteq d_1 \sqcup d_2$.
4. $d_1, d_2 \sqsubseteq d_3$ imply $d_1 \sqcup d_2 \sqsubseteq d_3$.

The existence of the limit of a sequence of elements is ensured by the notion of completeness: a domain D is *complete* if whenever S is a directed subset of D, that is,

$$S \neq \varnothing \quad \text{and} \quad \forall s_1, s_2 \in S \; \exists s_3 \in S \; s_1 \sqsubseteq s_3 \text{ and } s_2 \sqsubseteq s_3$$

then there exists $\bigsqcup S \in D$ such that:

1. $s \sqsubseteq \bigsqcup S, \; \forall s \in S.$
2. $\forall d \in D \, (\forall s \, s \sqsubseteq d)$ implies $\bigsqcup s \sqsubseteq d.$

Operations can be defined on domains. It is proved in [Scot77] that if D and D' are domains, so are:

1. The product $\langle D, D' \rangle = \{\langle d, d' \rangle | d \in D, d' \in D'\}$
2. The sum $D \, / \, D' = \{\langle 1, d \rangle | d \in D\} \cup \{\langle 2, d' \rangle | d' \in D'\} \cup \{\perp\}$
3. $D \rightarrow D'$, the domain of continuous functions from D to D'
4. D^*, the domain of finite sequences of elements of D:

$$D^* = \langle \, \rangle \, / \, \langle D, D^* \rangle$$

We say that s is an upper bound of S iff:

$$\forall s' \quad s' \in S \text{ implies } s' \sqsubseteq s$$

Two elements $d_1, d_2 \in D$ are *compatible* if $\{d_1, d_2\}$ has an upper bound.

The denotational semantics of a programming language associates with each syntactic construct a function which models its meaning in terms of the meanings of its components. In fact, a semantic function is associated with each syntactic domain defined by the abstract syntax of the programming language.

11-2. SYNTAX OF A SIMPLE LANGUAGE

To illustrate this study we define a simple Algol-like language. The semantics is defined on the abstract syntax of the language: it maps trees to denotations. Thus it is necessary to specify the correspondence between the concrete strings defined by the syntactic rules and the abstract syntax trees. We give in Figure 11-1 a formal definition of the syntax of the simple language, together with a corresponding abstract syntax. The reader may refer to [Moss78] for the details of the notations. Using this definition, a concrete program written in this simple language can be translated to its abstract representation.

The intuitive meaning of each production should be clear. When an expression of the form "**valof**" stm-train "**end**" is encountered, the statement part is executed until a form "**resultis**" exp is encountered. Then control passes out of the smallest "**valof**" expression containing this command. The value of exp is taken as the value of the original expression. The remaining expressions are more familiar.

The lexical part of the simple language specification does not require

```
GRAM "simple"
!****************************************
 SYNTAX                                 !*
!****************************************

program ::= "begin" stm-train "end" ;

! [Statements]
!-------------
stm-train  ::= statement+-";" ;

statement ::= asgt-stm  : asgt-stm /
              cond-stm : cond-stm /
              loop-stm : loop-stm /
              transput-stm : transput-stm /
              result-stm : result-stm ;

result-stm ::= "resultis" exp ;

asgt-stm  ::= id ":=" exp ;

cond-stm  ::= "if" exp "then" stm-train "fi" /
              "if" exp "then" stm-train "else" stm-train "fi" ;

loop-stm  ::= "while" exp "do" stm-train "end" ;

transput-stm ::= "input" id /
                 "output" exp mode ;

mode       ::= "int" : "int" /
               "bool" : "bool" ;

! [Expressions]
!-------------
exp        ::= factor :factor /
               exp add-op factor ;

factor     ::= primary :primary /
               factor mult-op primary ;

primary    ::= id : id                     /
               constant : constant         /
               "(" exp ")" : exp           /
               "(" compare ")" : compare /
               "valof" stm-train "end" ;

compare    ::= exp rel-op exp ;

! [Constants and Identifiers]
!-----------------
add-op === "+" / "or" ;
mult-op === "*" / "and" ;
rel-op === "=" / "#" ;
```

Figure 11-1

```
id          ::= ident ;

constant    ::= bool /
                num ;

bool        ::= "true" : TT /
                "false" : FF ;

num         ::= "NUM" n : n ;

ident       ::= "ID" q : q ;

!***********
 DOMAINS !*
!***********
mult-op,add-op,rel-op : Op ;

stm-train,statement : Stm ;

exp,factor,primary,compare : Exp ;


!*****************************************
 LEXIS                                   !*
!*****************************************

program     ::= word+ : (CONC word+) ;
word        ::= layoutchar+  : ⟨ ⟩              /
                identifier   : ⟨OUT "ID", identifier  ⟩ /
                numeral      : ⟨OUT "NUM", numeral⟩ ;

layoutchar === " "/ CC"C" / CC"L" ;

identifier  ::= letter+ : (QUOTE letter+) ;

letter   === "A" ... "Z" ;

numeral  ::= digit+ : (NUMBER digit+) ;

digit    === "0" ... "9" ;

END
```

Fig. 11-1 (cont.)

any particular comment. Some GRAM notations need to be described; the reader may refer to [Moss78] for more details:

1. A production has a nonterminal to the left of "::=" and a list of alternatives separated by "/" to the right; it is terminated by a ";".
2. The iterator "item 1 +— item 2" allows one or more occurrences of item 1, separated by occurrences of item 2.

11-3. OCCURRENCES

In order to define properties associated with elements of programs, we must be able to name those elements. In a standard denotational definition, each semantic function follows the structure of the syntactic domain on which it is defined—the function which defines an interpretation of a program follows the syntactic structure of the program—but it doesn't allow the elements of this structure to be named. In order to do this, we formalize the intuitive notion of an access path.

11-3.1. Notion of Occurrence

A program can be viewed abstractly as a labeled tree. The set of rules that define the abstract syntax of the language describes the set of well-formed trees. Each node is an operator of fixed arity, so that for example the following program is denoted by Figure 11-2.

```
begin
    I := J ≤ 5;
    if I then J := 0
        else J := 10
    fi
end
```

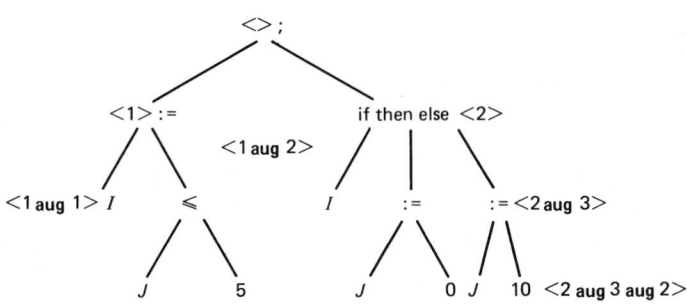

Figure 11-2

Let N^* be the set of finite sequences of positive integers, $\langle\rangle$ the empty sequence on N^*, and **aug** the right concatenation of sequences. We call the elements of N^* "occurrences" and use "occ" as a metavariable defined on N^*.

Using occurrences, we can access and name all subtrees of a tree, i.e., each element of a program. For each tree t, let $\mathrm{Occ}(t)$ be the set of occurrences of t. If occ belongs to $\mathrm{Occ}(t)$, "t at occ" denotes the subtree of t at occ. In the example, "t at $\langle 2\ \mathbf{aug}\ 3\rangle$" is the subtree which denotes "$J := 10$".

11-3.2. Occurrences and Denotational Semantics

Introducing occurrences to semantic functions allows us to attach meanings to specific elements of a given program. Semantic functions are now defined by:

run: Prog $\longrightarrow$ Occ $\longrightarrow$ Semantic domains

locate: Id $\longrightarrow$ Occ $\longrightarrow$ Semantic domains

evaluate: Exp $\longrightarrow$ Occ $\longrightarrow$ Semantic domains

execute: Stm $\longrightarrow$ Occ $\longrightarrow$ Semantic domains

The computation of the occurrences follows the syntactic structure of the program; thus it follows the recursive structure of the semantic functions and appears explicitly in the equations. For instance the equation associated with a sequence of statements might become:

execute[[stm 1; stm 2]]

$\qquad$ = **lam** occ. execute[[stm 1]] occ **aug** 1; execute[[stm 2]] occ **aug** 2

This can be paraphrased as "the semantics of a sequence of statements 'stm1; stm2' is a function of an occurrence occ which applies the semantic function execute to the first statement of the sequence and to the current occurrence occ concatenated with 1, then applies the function execute to the second element of the sequence and to the current occurrence concatenated with 2."

11-4. DENOTATIONAL SEMANTICS OF THE SIMPLE LANGUAGE

The formal semantics of the language is presented in Figures 11-3 and 11-4. It is written in DSL [Moss78] and structured into two parts:

1. An abstract machine in which basic functions are defined (Figure 11-4)
2. A function "semant" parameterized by the abstract machine, which associates to every abstract program a function from an input stream to an output stream (Figure 11-3)

11-4.1. The Function Semant

The syntactic and semantic domains are self-explanatory. Note that the "**valof**" expressions can be nested and the matching of "**resultis**" statements with "**valof**" expressions is done textually. Hence we make environments equal to expression continuations: Env = Eval-cont.

Continuation domains are defined as usual. A value can be a location value (in this simple language it can only be an identifier) or a storable value (here a boolean or an integer). The domains of answers, states, and inputs are defined in the abstract machine. Statements and expressions are to be understood in terms of semantic evaluations: a function maps the syntactic

DSL "SIMPLE semantics"
DOMAINS

! SYNTACTIC VARIABLES AND DOMAINS
! ************************************

```
prog : Prog = ["begin" Stm "end"] ;
stm : Stm =    [Stm+]
           / [ Id ":=" Exp ]
           / ["if" Exp "then" Stm "fi"]
           / ["if" Exp "then" Stm "else" Stm "fi"]
           / ["while" Exp "do" Stm "end"]
           / ["input" Id ]
           / ["output" Exp Mode]
           / ["resultis" Exp ]
           ;
mode : Mode = "int" / "bool" ;

exp : Exp =     [ Exp Op Exp ]
           / ["valof" Stm "end"]
           / Id
           / [Num]
           / [Bool]
           ;
id    : Id = [Ident] ;
ident : Ident = Q ;
num : Num = N ;
bool : Bool = T ;
op    : Op   = "+" / "*" / "or" / "and" / "=" / "#" ;
```

!SEMANTIC VARIABLES AND DOMAINS
!************************************

```
answ : Answ ;                                    !Answers
occ  : Occ = N* ;                                !Occurrences
env  : Env = Eval-cont ;                         !Environments
exec-cont : Exec-cont = State -> Input* -> Answ; !Command continuations
value : Value = R-value / L-value ;
r-value : R-value = N / T ;                      !Storable values
l-value : L-value = Ident ;
eval-cont : Eval-cont = Value -> Exec-cont;      !Expression continuations
state : State ;                                  !States
input : Input ;                                  !Inputs
```

!TYPES OF SEMANTIC FUNCTIONS
!********************************

```
run := Prog -> Exec-cont;
execute := Stm -> Occ -> Env -> Exec-cont -> Exec-cont;
execute-list := Stm* -> Occ -> Env -> Exec-cont -> Exec-cont;
evaluate := Exp -> Occ -> Env -> Eval-cont -> Exec-cont;
locate := Id -> Occ -> Env -> Eval-cont -> Exec-cont;
no-action := Exec-cont -> Exec-cont;
```

IN

LAM prog.

Figure 11-3

```
!PRIMITIVES
!************

LAM <
        init-state : State,
        maxint    : N,
        wrong     : (Q -> Exec-cont),
        update    : ((Ident,R-value) -> Exec-cont -> Exec-cont),
        content   : (Ident -> Eval-cont -> Exec-cont),
        write     : ((R-value,Mode) -> Exec-cont -> Exec-cont),
        read      : (Ident -> Eval-cont -> Exec-cont),
        op-val    : ((R-value,R-value,Op) -> Eval-cont -> Exec-cont)
    >.


!FUNCTION DEFINITIONS
!***********************

LET no-action : (Exec-cont -> Exec-cont) = LAM exec-cont. exec-cont
                                                    !Identity on continuations
ALSO init-env : Env = LAM value. init-exec-cont     !Empty environment
ALSO init-exec-cont : Exec-cont = LAM state. LAM input*. <>   !Null continuation
ALSO init-occ : Occ = <>                            !Initial occurrence

DEF
        !PROGRAM
        !**********

        run ["begin" stm "end"] : Exec-cont =
                excute(stm)(init-occ)init-env;
                init-exec-cont
        WITH
        !EXPRESSIONS
        !*************

        evaluate (exp)(occ)env;eval-cont : Exec-cont =
                CASE exp
                /[ident] ->
                        content(ident);
                        eval-cont
                /[num] ->
                        LET exec-cont=eval-cont(num)
                        IN exec-cont
                /[bool] ->
                        LET exec-cont=eval-cont(bool)
                        IN exec-cont

                /[exp 1 op exp2] ->
                        evaluate(exp1)(occ AUG 1)env; LAM r-value1.
                        evaluate(exp2)(occ AUG 2)env; LAM r-value2.
                        op-val(r-value1,r-value2,op);
                        eval-cont

                /["valof" stm "end"] ->
                        LET env' = eval-cont
                        IN execute(stm)(occ AUG 1)env';
                        wrong"resultis missing"
                ESAC
```

Figure 11-3 (cont.)

```
WITH
!IDENTIFIERS
!************

locate(id)(occ)env;eval-cont:Exec-cont =

          LET [ident] = id IN
            eval-cont(ident)
WITH
!STATEMENTS
!*************

execute(stm)(occ)env;exec-cont : Exec-cont =
          CASE stm
          /[stm+] -> execute-list(stm+)(occ)env;
                    exec-cont

          /["if" exp "then" stm1 "fi"] ->
                    evaluate(exp)(occ AUG 1)env; LAM t.
                    (t -> execute(stm1)(occ AUG 2)env , no-action) ;
                    exec-cont

          /["if" exp "then" stm1 "else" stm2 "fi"] ->
                    evaluate(exp)(occ AUG 1)env; LAM t.
                    (t -> execute(stm1)(occ AUG 2)env ,
                    execute(stm2)(occ AUG 3)env) ;
                    exec-cont

          /["while" exp "do" stm "end"] ->
                    DEF exec-cont' =
                       evaluate(exp)(occ AUG 1)env; LAM t.
                       (t -> execute(stm)(occ AUG 2)env;exec-cont', exec-cont)
                    IN exec-cont'

          /["input" id ] ->
                    locate(id)(occ AUG 1)env; LAM ident. read(ident) ;
                    LAM r-value. update(ident,r-value) ;
                    exec-cont

          /["output" exp mode] ->
                    evaluate(exp)(occ AUG 1)env; LAM r-value.
                    write(r-value,mode) ;
                    exec-cont

          /[id ":=" exp] ->
                    locate(id)(occ AUG 1)env; LAM ident.
                    evaluate(exp)(occ AUG 2)env; LAM r-value.
                    update(ident,r-value) ;
                    exec-cont

          /["resultis" exp] ->
                    LET eval-cont = env
                    IN evaluate(exp)(occ AUG 1)(env) ;
                       eval-cont
          ESAC
          WITH
          !auxiliary functions for statements
          !- - - - - - - - - - - - - - - - - -
```

Figure 11-3 (cont.)

```
execute-list(stm*)(occ)env;exec-cont : Exec-cont =
CASE stm*
/stm1 PRE stm2* ->
          execute(stm1)(occ AUG 1)env;
          execute-list(stm2*)(occ AUG 2)env;
          exec-cont
/<> ->    exec-cont
ESAC
IN
run (prog) (init-state) : (Input* -> Answ)
```

Figure 11-3 (cont.)

domains into semantic domains. Thus evaluate is such that:

$$\text{evaluate} := \text{Exp} \longrightarrow \text{Occ} \longrightarrow \text{Env} \longrightarrow \text{Eval-cont} \longrightarrow \text{Exec-cont}$$

Its application to a syntactic expression, an occurrence, and the current environment maps into a transformation from expression continuations to command continuations. Both the evaluation of the expression and its side effects are incorporated in this transformation. The function locate is similarly defined:

$$\text{locate} := \text{Id} \longrightarrow \text{Occ} \longrightarrow \text{Env} \longrightarrow \text{Eval-cont} \longrightarrow \text{Exec-cont}$$

The function execute has functionality:

$$\text{execute} := \text{Stm} \longrightarrow \text{Occ} \longrightarrow \text{Env} \longrightarrow \text{Exec-cont} \longrightarrow \text{Exec-cont}$$

A program is denoted by:

$$\text{run} := \text{Prog} \longrightarrow \text{Exec-cont}$$

11-4.1.1. Programs

The list of statements which compose a program is interpreted with the initial environment and with the null continuation.

11-4.1.2. Statements

The interpretation of a list of statements is defined by the auxiliary function "execute-list" applied to the current occurrence, current environment, and current continuation. The execution of a **while** statement is described with a recursively defined continuation exec-cont'. The semantic definition of the conditional is familiar. Input and output statements use in their definitions the "read" and "write" functions described in the machine.

The assignment statement first evaluates the location value of its left-hand side, then evaluates the right-hand-side expression in the current environment, updates the left value with the right value, and carries on by executing the current continuation. The execution of a **"resultis"** statement evaluates the expression in the current environment with the continuation included in the environment as the new continuation.

```
DSL "machine"

DOMAINS

!SEMANTIC VARIABLES AND DOMAINS
!************************************
input     : Input = N / T ;                              !Inputs
answ      : Answ = Q* ;                                  !Answers
mode      : Mode = "int" / "bool" ;                      !For input/output
r-value   : R-value = N / T ;                            !Storable values
state     : State = Ident -> R-value ;                   !States
exec-cont : Exec-cont = State -> (Input* -> Answ) ;      !Statement continuations
eval-cont : Eval-cont = Value -> Exec-cont ;             !Expression continuations

!TYPES OF FUNCTIONS
!*********************
init-state  := State ;                                   !Initial state
maxint      := N ;                                       !Maximal integer
wrong       := Q -> Exec-cont ;
update      := <Ident,R-value> -> Exec-cont -> Exec-cont ;
content     := Ident -> Eval-cont -> Exec-cont ;
write       := <R-value,Mode> -> Exec-cont -> Exec-cont ;
read        := Ident -> Eval-cont -> Exec-cont ;
op-val      := <R-value,R-value,Op> -> Eval-cont -> Exec-cont ;


IN
!DESCRIPTION OF FUNCTIONS
!****************************

LET      maxint : N = 10000

ALSO     wrong(q)(state)(input*) : Answ =
                  <QUOTE<"ERROR : ",q>>

!State handling
!--------
ALSO     initial-state : State =
                  LAM ident. ?

ALSO     update(ident,r-value)(exec-cont)(state) : (Input* -> Answ) =
                  LET state' = state \ ident <- r-value
                  IN exec-cont(state')

LET      content(ident)(eval-cont)(state) : (Input* -> Answ) =
                  LET r-value = state(ident)
                  IN eval-cont(r-value)(state)

!Input-output
!-------
ALSO     write(r-value,mode)(exec-cont)(state)(input*) : Answ =
                  LET q = CASE mode
                          /"int" ->       LET NUMBER q'* = r-value
                                          IN QUOTE q'*
                          /"bool" ->      (r-value -> "true","false")
                          ESAC
                  IN <q> CAT (exec-cont(state)(input*))

ALSO     read(ident)(eval-cont)(state)(input*) : Answ =
                  CASE input*
```

Figure 11-4

```
                    /input 1 PRE input2* ->
                            eval-cont(input1)(state)(input2*)
                    /<> -> wrong "end of file" (state)(<>)
                    ESAC
ALSO    op-val(r-value1,r-value2,op)(eval-cont)(state) : (Input* -> Answ) =
                    CASE op
                    /"+" ->
                            LET n= r-value1 PLUS r-value2
                            IN n LE maxint -> eval-cont(n), wrong"overflow"
                    /"*" ->
                            LET n= r-value1 MULT r-value2
                            IN n LE maxint -> eval-cont(n), wrong"overflow"
                    /"or" ->
                            LET t= r-value1 OR r-value2
                            IN eval-cont(t)
                    /"and" ->
                            LET t= r-value1 AND r-value2
                            IN eval-cont(t)
                    /"=" ->
                            r-value1 EQ r-value2 -> eval-cont(TT),
                                                    eval-cont(FF)
                    /"#" ->
                            r-value1 NE r-value2 -> eval-cont(TT),
                                                    eval-cont(FF)
                    ESAC
IN <initial-state,maxint,wrong,update,content,write,read,op-val>
END
```

Figure 11-4 (cont.)

11-4.1.3. *Expressions*

The "**valof**" expression saves the current continuation in the environment and interprets the statement part. If no "**resultis**" statement has been encountered when the end of the expression is reached, the current continuation is replaced by the constant function "wrong", which writes an error message and stops execution.

11-4.2. The Abstract Machine

In this part, the low-level functions used in the denotational definition are described. They model state handling and input-output transactions. As in [Donz78a], input and output are slightly asymmetrical, in that LAMB constants are read and strings of characters are output.

11-5. DENOTATIONAL DEFINITION
OF PROPERTIES ASSOCIATED
WITH THE ELEMENTS OF A PROGRAM

Using the notion of occurrence, we can now define properties associated with the elements of a program. These properties are defined by nonstandard interpretations. The denotational definitions of these interpretations give mathematical specifications of the various algorithms used to compute such properties.

11-5.1. Domains and Functions Involved in the Denotational Definition of the Properties

The result of a nonstandard interpretation associates properties with elements that are indexed by occurrences. Let Prop be the domain of properties and Answ be the domain of answers. Answ is defined by

$$\text{Answ: Occ} \longrightarrow \text{Prop}$$

Properties are associated with elements which belong to a common syntactic domain. Let us call this domain Elem; it will be specified for each application. In each of our examples Elem is the same as Exp. Let R-value be the domain of basic values of the nonstandard interpretation. The properties are defined from the basic values by the function:

$$\text{prop-def} := R\text{-value} \longrightarrow \text{State} \longrightarrow \text{Prop}$$

which will be specified in the description of each application.

For example in the problem of constant propagation:

Elem is the syntactic domain Exp

R-value is the domain N / T

Prop is the domain R-value $/ \{\text{var}\}$

A state associates to each element a basic value, so the domain State is defined by Elem $\longrightarrow R$-value. A continuation function applied to a state and an input stream defines a final answer:

$$\text{Continuation: State} \longrightarrow \text{Input*} \longrightarrow \text{Answ.}$$

Let "continue" be a meta-variable defined on the domain of continuations. The function "update" modifies the current state:

$$\text{update} := \langle \text{Elem}, R\text{-value} \rangle \longrightarrow \text{Continuation} \longrightarrow \text{Continuation}$$

It is defined by:

$$\text{update(elem, } r\text{-value); continue: Continuation} =$$
$$\textbf{lam state.}$$
$$\textbf{let } \text{state}' = \text{state} \setminus \text{elem} \longleftarrow r\text{-value}$$
$$\textbf{in } \text{continue(state}')$$

In an answer the property associated with an occurrence must be compatible with the current property defined from the current computed value, each time control reaches this occurrence. This condition can be expressed by the function

$$\text{attach} := \langle \text{Occ, } R\text{-value} \rangle \longrightarrow \text{Continuation} \longrightarrow \text{Continuation}$$

defined by

> attach(occ, *r*-value); continue: Continuation =
> **lam** state. **lam** input*.
>   **let** prop = prop-def(*r*-value)
>   **let** answ = continue(state)(input*)
>   **let** prop' = answ(occ)
>   **let** prop" = compatible(prop, prop')
>   **in** answ \ occ ⟵ prop".

A current property prop is obtained from the current *r*-value by the function prop-def. Each new approximation to the final answer associates with the current occurrence occ a property prop" which is compatible with the current property prop and with the property prop' associated with occ in the current answer.

If prop and prop' are compatible in the domain Prop, the result of the function "compatible" is the least upper bound of prop and prop' in Prop; if not its result is an element of Prop not compatible with prop or prop'. The definition of the "compatible" function depends on the definition of the domain Prop. It corresponds to the lattice operation used in classical flow analysis [Kild73, Kam76, Hech77].

Properties associated with elements are defined by a semantic function:

definition-of-properties := Elem ⟶ Occ ⟶ Env ⟶
                                    Continuation ⟶ Continuation

described by

> definition-of-properties(elem)(occ)(env); continue: Continuation =
>   **let** *r*-value be the current value of elem
>   **in** attach(occ, *r*-value);
>   update(elem, *r*-value);
>   continue.

The function "definition-of-properties" applied to the element elem at the occurrence occ with the environment env may be paraphrased by

> it evaluates the current value: *r*-value;
>
> this value is used to
>
> —define a new approximation to the final answer by the function attach
>
> —modify the current state by the function update;
>
> then it applies the current continuation.

In this kind of nonstandard interpretation the value of a boolean expression may not be a boolean constant. The alternatives of a conditional statement are interpreted in parallel, and the final answer is the one which is compatible with the answers resulting from these parallel interpretations. This operation is defined by the function

$$\text{joint} := \langle \text{Continuation,Continuation} \rangle \longrightarrow \text{Continuation}$$

described by

$$\text{joint(continue',continue'')}: \text{Continuation} =$$
$$\textbf{lam} \text{ state. } \textbf{lam} \text{ input*. } \textbf{lam} \text{ occ.}$$
$$\textbf{let} \text{ answ'} = \text{continue'(state)(input*)}$$
$$\textbf{let} \text{ answ''} = \text{continue''(state)(input*)}$$
$$\textbf{in} \text{ compatible(answ'(occ),answ''(occ))}$$

11-5.2. Application

We give in Figure 11-5 a denotational definition of properties for the simple language used in this study. The syntactic variables and domains used are those given in Figure 11-3.

In this application, properties are associated with expressions; hence the semantic domain L-value is equal to the syntactic domain Exp, the domain Prop is introduced, and Answ is modified to $\text{Occ} \longrightarrow \text{Prop}$.

```
DSL "SIMPLE properties"
DOMAINS

! SYNTACTIC VARIABLES AND DOMAINS
!****************************************

prog : Prog    = ["begin" Stm "end"] ;
stm  : Stm     = [ Stm+ ]
                 / [ Id ":=" Exp ]
                 / ["if" Exp "then" Stm "fi"]
                 / ["if" Exp "then" Stm "else" Stm "fi"]
                 / ["while" Exp "do" Stm "end"]
                 / ["input" Id ]
                 / ["output" Exp Mode]
                 / ["resultis" Exp ]
                 ;

mode : Mode = "int" / "bool" ;

exp  : Exp     = [ Exp Op Exp ]
                 / ["valof" Stm "end"]
                 / Id
                 / [Num]
                 / [Bool]
                 ;
id      : Id = [Ident] ;
ident : Ident = Q ;
num   : Num = N ;
bool  : Bool = T ;
op      : Op   = "+" / "*" / "or" / "and" / "=" / "#" ;
```

Figure 11-5

```
!SEMANTIC VARIABLES AND DOMAINS
!**************************************
prop  : Prop;
answ  : Answ = Occ -> Prop ;                              !Answers
occ   : Occ = N* ;                                        !Occurrences
env   : Env = Eval-cont ;                                 !Environments
exec-cont : Exec-cont = State -> Input* -> Answ;          !Command continuations
value : Value = R-value / L-value ;
r-value  : R-value ;
l-value : L-value = Exp ;
eval-cont : Eval-cont = Value -> Exec-cont;               !Expressions continuations
state : State = Exp -> R-value ;                          !States
input : Input ;                                           !Inputs

!TYPES OF SEMANTIC FUNCTIONS
!********************************

run := Prog -> Exec-cont;
execute := Stm -> Occ -> Env -> Exec-cont -> Exec-cont;
execute-list := Stm* -> Occ -> Env -> Exec-cont -> Exec-cont ;
evaluate := Exp -> Occ -> Env -> Eval-cont -> Exec-cont ;
locate := Id -> Occ -> Env -> Eval-cont -> Exec-cont ;
no-action := Exec-cont -> Exec-cont ;
joint := <Exec-cont,Exec-cont> -> Exec-cont ;
attach := <Occ,R-value> -> Exec-cont -> Exec-cont ;
update := <Exp,State> -> Exec-cont -> Exec-cont ;
content := L-value -> Eval-cont -> Exec-cont ;
wrong := Exec-cont ;


IN

LAM prog.

!PRIMITIVES
!***********

LAM <
        init-prop    : (Prop),
        read         : (Ident -> Eval-cont -> Exec-cont),
        compatible : ((Prop,Prop) -> Prop),
        prop-def   : (R-value -> State -> Prop),
        op-val       : ((R-value,R-value,Op) -> R-value)
    >.

!FUNCTION DEFINITIONS
!***********************


LET init-answ  : Answ = LAM occ. init-prop
ALSO init-state  : State = LAM exp. ?
ALSO init-env : Env = LAM value. init-exec-cont              !Empty environment
ALSO init-exec-cont : Exec-cont = LAM state. LAM input*. init-answ   !Null continuati

ALSO init-occ : Occ = <>                                     !Initial occurrences

ALSO wrong : Exec-cont = init-exec-cont
DEF
        !PROGRAM
        !**********
```

Figure 11-5 (cont.)

```
run ["begin" stm "end"] : Exec-cont =
          execute(stm)(init-occ)init-env ;
          init-exec-cont
WITH
!EXPRESSIONS
!*************

evaluate (exp)(occ)env ;eval-cont : Exec-cont =
          CASE exp
          /[ident]  ->
                     content(ident) ;LAM r-value.
                     attach(occ,r-value) ;
                     update(exp,r-value) ;
                     eval-cont(r-value)

          /[num]  ->
                     attach(occ,num) ;
                     update(exp,num) ;
                     eval-cont(num)
          /[bool]  ->
                     attach(occ,bool) ;
                     update(exp,bool) ;
                     eval-cont(bool)

          /[exp1 op exp2]  ->
                     evaluate(exp1)(occ AUG 1)env; LAM r-value1.
                     evaluate(exp2)(occ AUG 2)env; LAM r-value2.
                     LET r-value=op-val(r-value1,r-value2,op)
                     IN        attach(occ,r-value) ;
                               update(exp,r-value) ;
                               eval-cont(r-value)

          /["valof"  stm "end"]  ->
                     LET env'=
                       LAM r-value.
                               attach(occ,r-value) ;
                               update(exp,r-value) ;
                               eval-cont(r-value)
                     IN        execute(stm)(occ AUG 1)env' ;
                               wrong
          ESAC
WITH
  !Auxiliary functions for defining properties
  !-----------------------
attach(occ,r-value) ;exec-cont : Exec-cont =
          LAM state. LAM input*.
          LET answ=exec-cont(state)(input*)
          ALSO prop = prop-def(r-value)(state)
          IN
                     answ\occ <- compatible(prop,answ(occ))
WITH
joint(exec-cont1,exec-cont2) : Exec-cont =
          LAM state. LAM input*.
          LET answ1 = exec-cont1(state)(input*)
          LET answ2 = exec-cont2(state)(input*)
          IN
                     LAM occ.
                     compatible(answ1(occ),answ2(occ))
```

Figure 11-5 (cont.)

```
WITH
update(exp,r-value) ;exec-cont: Exec-cont =
        LAM state.
        LET state' = state\exp < - r-value
        IN exec-cont(state')
WITH
content(exp) ;eval-cont: Exec-cont =
        LAM state.
        LET r-value = state(exp)
        IN eval-cont(r-value)(state)
WITH
!IDENTIFIERS
!************

locate(id)(occ)env ;eval-cont :Exec-cont =

        LET [ident] = id IN
          eval-cont(ident)
WITH
!STATEMENTS
!************

execute(stm)(occ)env ;exec-cont : Exec-cont =
        CASE stm
        /[stm+] -> execute-list(stm+)(occ)env ;
                   exec-cont

        /["if" exp "then" stm1 "fi"] ->
                   evaluate(exp)(occ AUG 1)env ; LAM t.
                   joint    (execute(stm1)(occ AUG 2)(env) ;exec-cont,
                            exec-cont)

        /["if" exp "then" stm1 "else" stm2 "fi"] ->
                   evaluate(exp)(occ AUG 1)env ; LAM t.
                   joint    (execute(stm1)(occ AUG 2)(env) ;exec-cont,
                                        execute(stm2)(occ AUG 3)(env) ;exec-cont)

        /["while" exp "do" stm "end"] ->
                   DEF exec-cont'=
                      evaluate(exp)(occ AUG 1)env ; LAM t.
                      joint (execute(stm)(occ AUG 2)(env) ;exec-cont',
                            exec-cont)
                   IN exec-cont'

        /["input" id ] ->
                   locate(id)(occ AUG 1)env ; LAM ident.
                   read(ident) ;LAM r-value.
                   update(ident,r-value) ;
                   exec-cont

        /["output" exp mode] ->
                   evaluate(exp)(occ AUG 1)env ; LAM r-value.
                   exec-cont

        /[id ":=" exp] ->
                   locate(id)(occ AUG 1)env ; LAM ident.
                   evaluate(exp)(occ AUG 2)env ; LAM r-value.
                   update(ident,r-value) ;
                   exec-cont
```

Figure 11-5 (cont.)

```
          /["resultis" exp] ->
                    LET eval-cont = env
                    IN evaluate(exp)(occ AUG 1)(env);
                        eval-cont
          ESAC
WITH
!auxiliary functions for statements
!-------------------

execute-list(stm*)(occ)env; exec-cont : Exec-cont =
CASE stm*
/stm1 PRE stm2* ->
          execute(stm1)(occ AUG 1)env;
          execute-list(stm2*)(occ AUG 2)env;
          exec-cont
/<> ->    exec-cont
ESAC
IN
run (prog) (init-state) : (Input* -> Answ)
END
```

Figure 11-5 (cont.)

The function "evaluate" of type

$$\text{Exp} \to \text{Occ} \to \text{Env} \to \text{Eval-cont}$$

can be paraphrased by

1. Compute the current value "r-value" of the current expression using the current state.

2. Define a new approximation to the final answer (function "attach").

3. Modify the current state (function "update").

4. Apply the current continuation.

The function execute is modified in the definition of the conditional and iterative statements, which use the function joint. The functions locate and run are not changed from the standard interpretation. This nonstandard interpretation is parameterized by the domains of properties and values and by the basic functions defined on those domains. Their specifications entirely define the desired properties associated with expressions.

11-6. CONGRUENCE BETWEEN THE USUAL INTERPRETATION AND THE DENOTATIONAL DEFINITION OF PROPERTIES

To establish a connection between the usual semantics and the nonstandard one, we must define relations between the two sets of functions. The properties associated with syntactic elements characterize the behavior of semantic objects used in the standard interpretation. These objects can be states or continuations, depending on the properties we are interested in.

11-6.1.   Extension of the Standard Interpretation

We can explicitly express this behavior by "tracing" the computation in the domain of answers. The trace is a list of pairs $\langle occ, object \rangle$; and the extended domain of answers including the trace is defined by Answ: $\langle Occ, Object \rangle *$.

The functions which define this extended standard interpretation are the usual semantic functions modified according to the following pattern:

semantic-function(elem)(occ)(env); continue: Continuation =
lam state.
   let object be the current semantic object
      in lam input*. $\langle occ,object \rangle$ **pre** continue(state)(input*)

The write function is the identity on continuations.

11-6.2.   Relations Between Domains

We express the relations by predicates defined from pairs $\langle$Nonstandard domain, Standard-domain$\rangle$ into T' where T' is the complete lattice having "and" as its join operation, "true" as its least element, and "false" as its only other element. Each predicate applied to $\langle \perp, \perp \rangle$ is made equal to "true". The exact nature of the predicates will be stated precisely in the application.

Predicates are defined on the semantic functions; their definitions are of the form†

P-Elem(property-definition(elem), semantic-definition(elem)) =
   (*P-Env*(env-1, env-2) **and** *P-Cont*(continue-1, continue-2)) $\longrightarrow$
      P-Cont(property-definition(elem)(occ)(env-1); continue-1,
         semantic-definition(elem)(occ)(env-2); continue-2)

The standard and nonstandard interpretations are congruent if for each syntactic domain Elem, the predicate *P-Elem* is true. The proof of *P-Elem* is by structural induction on the abstract constructs which belong to Elem.

11-6.3.   Existence of the Predicates

For more complex languages, including, for example, functions with local declarations, the predicates are on recursively defined domains. In such cases their existence is not obvious; however, they can be constructed as

†$a \longrightarrow b$ denotes: **if** a is true **then** b **else** false.

limits of predicates defined on retracts. Milne describes such techniques in [Miln76].

11-6.4. Application

A property associated with an expression at the occurrence occ is characterized by (1) the set of current states each time the control reaches this occurrence or (2) the set of current values this expression can take at this occurrence.

Hence the semantic objects we are interested in are states or values depending on the property with which we are concerned.

As we are required to compare pairs of functions (one from each definition scheme) which may both be called by the same name, we will, in a systematic way, add the suffix -1 (respectively -2) to the names belonging to the nonstandard interpretations (respectively, extended standard one). Thus let us assume the existence of the following predicates, defined on the basic domains:

$$P\text{-}Prop := \langle \text{Prop}, \langle \text{Occ}, \text{State-2} \rangle \rangle \longrightarrow T'$$
$$P\text{-}Value := \langle \text{Value-1}, \text{Value-2} \rangle \longrightarrow T'$$
$$P\text{-}Input := \langle \text{Input*-1}, \text{Input*-2} \rangle \longrightarrow T'$$

Their exact nature will be precisely stated for each property definition in the next section. In the following, free variables (such as input-2) are universally quantified. We define

$$P\text{-}Answ := \langle \text{Answ-1}, \text{Answ-2} \rangle \longrightarrow T'$$

by

$P\text{-}Answ$(answ-1, answ-2) = true if $P\text{-}Prop$(answ-1(occ), $\langle$occ, state-2$\rangle$) is true for every $\langle$occ, state-2$\rangle$ in answ-2;

and

$$P\text{-}State := \langle \text{state-1}, \text{state-2} \rangle \longrightarrow T'$$

by

$P\text{-}State$(state-1, state-2) = true if $P\text{-}Value$ (state-1(ident), state-2(ident)) is true for every ident in Ident.

We define

$$P\text{-}Cont := \langle \text{Continuation-1}, \text{Continuation-2} \rangle \longrightarrow T'$$

by

$P\text{-}Cont$(continue-1, continue-2) =
$\quad$($P\text{-}State$(state-1, state-2) **and** $P\text{-}Input$(input*-1, input*-2)) $\longrightarrow$
$\quad\quad P\text{-}Answ$(continue-1(state-1)(input*-1),
$\quad\quad\quad$ continue-2(state-2)(input*-2))

In the same way, we define

$$P\text{-}Eval\text{-}cont := \langle \text{Eval-cont-1, Eval-cont-2} \rangle \rightarrow T'$$

by

$P\text{-}Eval\text{-}cont$(eval-cont-1, eval-cont-2) =
         ($P\text{-}Value$(value-1, value-2) **and** $PState$(state-1, state-2) **and**
         $P\text{-}Input$(input*-1, input*-2)) $\rightarrow$
                 $P\text{-}Answ$(eval-cont-1(value-1)(state-1)(input*-1),
                        eval-cont-2(value-2)(state-2)(input*-2))

We use this predicate to define $P\text{-}Env := P\text{-}Eval\text{-}cont$. For each application we must prove

Property 1.   For all exp which belong to Exp,

     $P\text{-}Exp$(evaluate-1(exp), evaluate-2(exp)) is true,
where
     $P\text{-}Exp$(evaluate-1(exp), evaluate-2(exp)) =
         ($P\text{-}Env$(env-1, env-2) **and** $P\text{-}Eval\text{-}cont$(eval-cont-1, eval-
         cont-2)) $\rightarrow$
             $P\text{-}Cont$(evaluate-1(exp)(occ)(env-1)(eval-cont-1),
                 evaluate-2(exp)(occ)(env-2)(eval-cont-2))

To be able to prove this property we express relations based on the domains and functions which parameterize the function defined in Figure 11-5. These relations will be specified for each application.

Relation 1.

     ($P\text{-}Value$(value'-1, value'-2) **and** $P\text{-}Value$(value''-1, value''-2))
     implies
         $P\text{-}Value$(value-1, value-2)

where value = op-val(value', value'', op)

Relation 2.

     $P\text{-}Prop$(prop, $\langle$occ, object$\rangle$) implies $P\text{-}Prop$(prop', $\langle$occ, object$\rangle$)

where prop' is any element of Prop which is compatible with prop

Relation 3.

     ($P\text{-}State$(state-1, state-2) **and** $P\text{-}Value$(value-1, value-2)) implies
         $P\text{-}Prop$(prop, $\langle$occ, object$\rangle$)

where prop = prop-def(value-1)(state-1)

Some technical lemmata are needed to prove Property 1.

Lemma 1.

> *P-Eval-cont*(eval-cont-1, eval-cont-2) implies
> > *P-Cont*(content(ident)(eval-cont-1), content(ident)(eval-cont-2))

Proof. Assume that

> *P-State*(state-1, state-2) is equal to "true". Then
> *P-Value*(state-1(ident), state-2(ident))

is "true" by the definition of *P-State*. The result is obtained using the hypothesis and the definition of the function content. ∎

Lemma 2.

> (*P-Value*(value-1, value-2) **and** *P-Cont*(continue-1, eval-cont-2
> (value-2))) implies
> > *P-Cont*(update(exp, value-1)(continue-1), eval-cont-2(value-2))

Proof obvious.

Lemma 3.

> (*P-Value*(value-1, value-2) **and** *P-Cont*(continue-1, eval-cont-2
> (value-2))) implies
> > *P-Cont*(attach(occ, value-1)(continue-1),
> > > **lam** state. **lam** input*. ⟨occ, object⟩ **pre**
> > > eval-cont-2(value-2)(state)(input*))

Proof. *P-State*(state-1, state-2) and *P-Input*(input*-1, input*-2) are true from the hypothesis. Let answ-1 = continue-1(state-1)(input*-1) and answ-2 = eval-cont-2(value-2)(state-2)(input*-2). Then *P-Answ*(answ-1, answ-2) is true from its definition. Let answ'-1 = answ-1 \ occ ⟶ compatible(answ-1(occ), prop) where prop = prop-def(value-1)(state-1). The result is obtained using Relations 2 and 3. ∎

Lemma 4.

> (*P-Cont*(continue'-1, continue'-2) **and** *P-Cont*(continue''-1,
> continue''-2)) implies
> > **let** continue-2 = joint(continue'-2, continue''-2)
> > > **in** (*P-Cont*(continue'-1, continue-2) and
> > > *P-Cont*(continue''-1, continue-2))

The proof is obvious using the definitions of *P-Cont* and Relation 2.

Proof of Property 1.   Assuming the relations defined above are verfied, we can now prove Property 1. The proof uses a structural induction on the domain Exp.

> / id →
> evaluate-1(id)(occ)(env-1); eval-cont-1: Exec-cont-1 =
>   content(id; **lam** value-1.
>   attach(occ, value-1);
>   update(exp, value-1);
>   eval-cont-1(value-1)

and

> evaluate-2(id)(occ)(env-2); eval-cont-2: Exec-cont-2 =
>   content (id); **lam** value-2. **lam** state-2. **lam** input*.
>   ⟨occ, object⟩ **pre** eval-cont-2 (value-2)

Using Lemma 1, the result is obtained if

1. *P-Cont*(attach(occ, value-1)(cont-1), cont-2) is true where

    > cont-1 = update(exp, value-1)(eval-cont-1(value-1))
    > cont-2 = **lam** state-2. ⟨occ, object⟩
    >   **pre** eval-cont-2(value-2)(state-2)

Using Lemma 3, (1) is proved if

2. (*P-Cont*(cont-1, eval-cont-2(value-2)) **and** *P-Value*(value-1, value-2)) is true.

From the hypothesis *P-State*(state-1, state-2) is true. Hence we know from the definition of the function content that *P-Value*(value-1, value-2) is true. To prove (2) we have only to show that *P-Cont*(cont-1, eval-cont-2(value-2)) is true. This is done using Lemma 2 and the hypothesis.

> / num, / bool
>   the proof uses the same arguments as in the previous case.

> / **"valof"** stm
>   the result is obtained using the same reasoning as in the first case
>   and the induction hypothesis on *P-Stm*.

/ exp1 op exp2
  evaluate-1(exp1 op exp2)(occ)(env-1); eval-cont-1: Exec-cont =
  evaluate-1(exp1)(occ **aug** 1)(env-1); **lam** value'-1.
  evaluate-1(exp2)(occ **aug** 2)(env-1); **lam** value''-1.
    let value-1 = value-def(value'-1, value''-1, op)
      in attach(occ, value-1);
        update(exp, value-1);
        eval-cont-1(value-1).

  evaluate-2(exp1 op exp2)(occ)(env-2); eval-cont-2: Exec-cont =
  evaluate-2(exp1)(occ **aug** 1)(env-2); **lam** value'-2.
  evaluate-2(exp2)(occ **aug** 2)(env-2); **lam** value''-2.
    let value-2 = value-def(value'-2, value''-2, op)
      in eval-cont-2(value-2).

By hypothesis *P-State*(state-1, state-2) is true. The induction hypothesis is: *P-Exp*(evaluate-1(exp), evaluate-2(exp)) = true. Using the induction hypothesis, the result is obtained if we show that:

1. *P-Eval-cont*(eval-cont'-1, eval-cont'-2) is true, where eval-cont'-1 is the continuation of the function evaluate-1(exp1)(occ)(env-1) in evaluate-1(exp1 op exp2) and eval-cont'-2 is the continuation of evaluate-2(exp1)(occ)(env2) in evaluate-2(exp1 op exp2). In other words (1) is true if:

2. [(*P-State*(state'-1, state'-2) **and** *P-Value*(value'-1, value'-2)) → *P-Answ*(answ'-1, answ'-2)] is true,
  where
      answ'-1 = evaluate-1(exp2)(occ **aug** 2)
                 (env-1)(eval-cont''-1)(state'-1)
      answ'-2 = evaluate-2(exp2)(occ **aug** 2)
                 (env-2)(eval-cont''-2)(state'-2)
  By the induction hypothesis *P-Exp*(evaluate-1(exp2), evaluate-2(exp2)) is true. Thus (2) is true if

3. *P-Eval-cont*(eval-cont''-1, eval-cont''-2) is true, where eval-cont''-1 is the current continuation of evaluate-1(exp2)(occ **aug** 2)(env-1) in evaluate-1(exp1 op exp2) and eval-cont''-2 is the symmetric current continuation in evaluate-2(exp1 op exp2). The predicate (3) is true if

4. [(*P-State*(state''-1, state''-2) **and** *P-Value*(value''-1, value''-2)) → *P-Answ*(answ''-1, answ''-2)] is true,
  where
      answ''-1 = eval-cont''-1(value''-1)
      answ''-2 = eval-cont''-2(value''-2)

Assume the left part of (4). From Relation 1 we know that *P-Value*(value-1, value-2) is true; using the same arguments as in the first case, we can show that (4) is true; thus the result is proved. ■

Property 2. *P-Id*(locate-1(id), locate-2(id)) is true.

Trivially true from the definitions of locate-1 and locate-2.

Property 3. *P-Stm*(execute-1(stm), execute-2(stm)) is true.

The proof uses a structural induction on the domain Stm and a computational induction for the while loop. The result is easily obtained using Property 1, Property 2, and Lemma 4.

Property 4. *P-Input*(input-1, input-2) implies *P-Prog*(run-1(prog), run-2(prog))

Proof. Assume *P-Input*(input-1, input-2) is true. *P-Env*(init-env-1, init-env-2) is true; thus it is enough to show that
     P-Cont(execute-1(stm)(init-occ **aug** 2) init-env-1(init-cont-1),
               execute-2(stm)(init-occ **aug** 2) init-env-2(init-cont-2))
          is true.
Using Property 3, it is enough to show that *P-Cont*(init-cont-1, init-cont-2) is true. This is done using the definitions of *P-Cont* and the initial continuation. ■

11-7. SOME CLASSICAL DATA FLOW ANALYSES

In this section we give a denotational definition of some classical data flow analyses which compute properties of expressions. Each definition is obtained by stating the basic domains and functions which parameterize the definition given in Fig. 11-5. For each application, basic predicates are defined and the relations based on the domains and functions are proved. The coherence between the usual interpretation and the denotational definition of the properties is shown using Property 4.

11-7.1. Constant Propagation

An expression is a constant at an occurrence occ if, in any computation, the value of this expression at occ is constant. The aim is to discover in any program the occurrences of expressions which are known constants.

11-7.1.1. Basic domains and functions

The domain of values is formed from the basic domain including integer and boolean values plus the element *var*. The domain of properties is the domain of values. A state associates to each expression a value. Thus if occ is an occurrence of an expression in a program prog, answ is the result of this nonstandard interpretation applied to prog:

$$
\text{answ(occ)} = \begin{cases} n & \text{if the expression at occ in prog is a constant} \\ & \text{whose value is } n \\ var & \text{if this expression is not known to have a} \\ & \text{constant value} \\ \text{undefined } (= ?) & \text{if this expression has never been evaluated} \end{cases}
$$

The semantic definition described in Fig. 11-5 parameterized by the domains and functions described in Fig. 11-6 entirely defines the property. The function prop-def is the identity on Value. The compatibility function is defined on the flat domain Value whose structure is

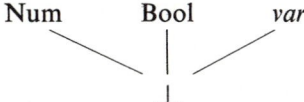

The read function associates to an identifier the value "*var*", and the write function is the identity.

11-7.1.2. Definition of the basic predicates

In this application the semantic objects are values. We define:

P-Value(value-1, value-2) by (value-1 **eq** "*var*") **or** (value-1 **eq** value-2);
P-Prop(prop, ⟨occ, value-2⟩) by *P-Value*(prop, value-2);
P-Input(input*-1, input*-2) is always true, since input*-1 equals *var* and *P-Value*(var, input-2) is true.

11-7.1.3. Proof of the relations defined on the basic domains

Relation 1.

(*P-Value*(value'-1, value'-2) **and** *P-Value*(value''-1, value''-2)) implies
    P-Value(value-1, value-2)
    where value-1 = op-val-1(value'-1, value''-1, op)
          value-2 = op-val-2(value'-2, value''-2, op)

Proof. The proof is obvious and uses the definitions of the op-val functions and the predicate *P-Value*. ∎

```
DSL "constant-propagation"
DOMAINS
!SEMANTIC VARIABLES AND DOMAINS
!************************************

state      : State = Exp -> R-value;
r-value    : R-value = N / T /"var";
prop       : Prop = R-value;
exec-cont  : Exec-cont = State -> Input* -> Answ;
answ       : Answ;
input      : Input;
eval-cont  : Eval-cont = R-value -> Exec-cont;

!TYPES OF FUNCTIONS
!**********************

init-prop   := Prop;
wrong       := Exec-cont;
read        := Ident -> Eval-cont -> Exec-cont;
compatible  := <Prop,Prop> -> Prop;
prop-def    := R-value -> State -> Prop;
op-val      := <R-value,R-value,Op> -> R-value;

IN
!DESCRIPTION OF FUNCTIONS
!*****************************

LET     init-prop : Prop = ?

ALSO    read(ident); eval-cont: Exec-cont =
            eval-cont("var")

ALSO    compatible(prop1,prop2) : Prop =
            prop1 IS prop2 -> prop1, "var"

ALSO prop-def(r-value)(state) : Prop =
            r-value

ALSO op-val(r-value1,r-value2,op) : R-value =
            (r-value1 IS "var") OR (r-value2 IS "var") -> "var",
            CASE op
            /"+"      -> r-value1 PLUS r-value2
            /"*"      -> r-value1 MULT r-value2
            /"="      -> r-value1 EQ r-value2
            /"#"      -> r-value1 NE r-value2
            /"or"     -> r-value1 OR r-value2
            /"and"    -> r-value1 AND r-value2
            ESAC
IN <init-prop,read,compatible,prop-def,op-val>
END
```

Figure 11-6

Relation 2. If *P-Prop*(prop, $\langle$occ, value-2$\rangle$) is true, then for any prop′ compatible with prop, *P-Prop*(prop′, $\langle$occ, value-2$\rangle$) is true.

Proof. Let value-1 = prop and value′-1 = prop′. We have to show that *P-Value*(value′-1, value′-2) is true. If value′-1 is equal to value-1, then the result is true (by hypothesis). If value′-1 is equal to *var*, then the result is obtained using the definition of *P-Value*. ∎

Relation 3.

(P-$State$(state-1, state-2) **and** P-$Value$(value-1, value-2)) implies
  P-$Prop$(prop, $\langle$occ, value-2$\rangle$) where prop $=$ prop-def(value-1)
(state-1)

Proof. The proof is obvious. ■

11-7.1.4. Coherence problem

In this application P-$Input$(input*-1, input*-2) is trivially true, so from Property 4 we know that P-$Prog$(run-1(prog), run-2(prog)) is true.

11-7.2. Determination of Common Subexpressions

This application detects redundant calculations of expressions. The calculation of an expression is redundant at an occurrence occ if, in every computation, its value has already been evaluated.

Example. (from [Kild73])
$$r := a + b; \ldots r + x; \ldots (a + b) + x;$$
Assume that r, a, b, and x are not modified. Then the second occurrence of r is redudant as well as the second occurrence of $(a + b)$ and the expression $(a + b) + x$.

11-7.2.1. Domains and Functions

The result of this nonstandard interpretation applied to a program associates with an occurrence occ of an expression exp the set of those expressions of the program that have already been evaluated and have the same value at occ as exp. This set is defined by a predicate from Exp to T' and thus
$$\text{Prop} = \text{Exp} \longrightarrow T'$$

Let answ be the result of this nonstandard interpretation applied to a program prog: If there is an exp$'$ such that answ(occ)(exp$'$) is true, then exp and exp$'$ have the same value at occ and the calculation of exp is redundant; otherwise the calculation of exp at occ is not redundant.

The basic values of this interpretation are symbolic terms:

1. To each constant we associate a symbolic constant identified with the syntactic element.
2. To each read variable we associate a symbolic value (which is different for each read performed. This symbolic value is identified with a syntactic identifier and thus the domain of input values is Input $=$ Ident).

3. To each operator op we associate the symbolic operator "op" which defines from symbolic terms "t_1", "t_2" the term "t_1 op t_2".

In fact this domain of symbolic terms is equal to the domain Exp restricted to

$$[id] / [num] / [bool] / [exp_1 \text{ op } exp_2]$$

Thus a state associates to each expression a symbolic term:

$$\text{State} := \text{Exp} \longrightarrow \text{Exp}.$$

This nonstandard interpretation is entirely defined by the functions described in Figure 11-5 parameterized by the basic domains and functions given in Figure 11-7. Comments on the basic functions:

1. The write function is the identity.
2. The read function associates to an identifier a symbolic value taken from the input stream.
3. The operation compatible defined on Prop is the logical operator **and** (that is, interesection of sets).
4. The prop-def function builds the set of expressions which have the same value as its argument.

11-7.2.2. *Definition of the basic predicates*

Associated with each usual interpretation we can build a valuation function v from the symbolic input stream of the nonstandard interpretation to the input stream of the standard one:

$$v(\text{input-2 pre input*-1}) = \text{input-2 pre } v(\text{input*-1})$$

Thus if id belongs to input*-1, $v(id)$ is defined as above. We extend this function to terms in the following way:

$$v: \text{Value-1} \longrightarrow \text{Value-2}$$

by

$$v(\text{num}) = \text{num}$$

$$v(\text{bool}) = \text{bool}$$

$$v(\text{term 1 op term 2}) = v(\text{term1}) \text{ op } v(\text{term2})$$

We define *P-Value*(value-1, value-2) by $v(\text{value-1}) = \text{value-2}$.

In this application the semantic objects considered are states.

We define *P-Prop*(prop, $\langle occ, state-2 \rangle$) as follows for any prog, any occ in Occ(prog), any exp'' and any input-2:

        let exp' = prog at occ
          in prop(exp'') $\longrightarrow$ (value''-2 **eq** value'-2)

```
DSL "common subexpressions"
DOMAINS

!SEMANTIC VARIABLES AND DOMAINS
!**************************************

r-value    : R-value = Exp;
state      : State   = Exp -> R-value;
prop       : Prop    = Exp -> T;
exec-cont  : Exec-cont = State -> Input* -> Answ;
answ       : Answ;
eval-cont  : Eval-cont = R-value -> Exec-cont;
input      : Input   = Q;

!TYPES OF FUNCTIONS
!**********************

init-prop   := Prop;
read        := Ident -> Eval-cont -> Exec-cont;
compatible  := <Prop,Prop> -> Prop;
prop-def    := R-value -> State -> Prop;
op-val      := <R-value,R-value,Op> -> R-value;
wrong       := Exec-cont;

IN
!DESCRIPTION OF FUNCTIONS
!*****************************

LET    init-prop : Prop = LAM exp. FF

ALSO read(ident) ;eval-cont : Exec-cont =
            LAM state.
            LAM input*.
            CASE input*
            /input1 PRE input2* ->
                    LET exp = [input1]
                    IN eval-cont(exp)(state)(input2*)
            /<>     -> wrong(state)(input*)
            ESAC

ALSO      compatible(prop1,prop2) : Prop =
                    LAM exp.
                    prop1(exp) AND prop2(exp)

ALSO      prop-def(r-value)(state) : Prop =
                    LAM exp.
                    state(exp) IS r-value -> TT,FF

ALSO      op-val(r-value1,r-value2,op) : R-value =
                    CASE op
                    /"+" ->    [r-value1 "+" r-value2]
                    /"*" ->    [r-value1 "*" r-value2]
                    /"=" ->    [r-value1 "=" r-value2]
                    /"#" ->    [r-value1 "#" r-value2]
                    /"or" ->   [r-value1 "or" r-value2]
                    /"and" ->  [r-value1 "and" r-value2]
                    ESAC

IN <init-prop,read,compatible,prop-def,op-val>
END
```

Figure 11-7

where†

QN(value'-2) = evaluate-2(exp')(occ)(env-2)
    (**lam** value. **lam** state. QN(value))(state-2)(input*-2)

QN(value''-2) = evaluate-2(exp'')(occ)(env-2)
    (**lam** value. **lam** state. QN(value))(state-2)(input*-2)

11-7.2.3. Proof of the relations defined on the basic domains

Relation 1.
(P-*Value*(value'-1, value'-2) **and** P-*Value*(value''-1, value''-2)) implies
    P-*Value*(value-1, value-2)
where value = op-val(value', value'', op)

The proof is obvious from the definition of the valuation function v, the definition of P-*Value*, and the definitions of the op-val functions.

Relation 2. If P-*Prop*(prop, ⟨occ, state-2⟩) is true then for any prop' such that prop and prop' are compatible: P-*Prop*(prop', ⟨occ, state-2⟩) is true.

The proof is obvious since in this application the "compatible" operation is the intersection (i.e., **and**) operation on T'.

Lemma 8. P-*State*(state-1, state-2) implies

$$P\text{-}Value(\text{state-1}(\exp), \text{value-2}),$$

where

QN(value-2) = evaluate-2(exp)(occ)(env)
    (**lam** value. **lam** state. QN(value))(state-2)(input*-2)

The proof is by structural induction on exp.

Relation 3. For any prog, for any occ in Occ(prog)
(P-*State*(state-1, state-2) **and** P-*Value*(value-1, value-2)) implies
    P-*Prop*(prop, ⟨occ, state-2⟩) where
prop = prop-def(value-1)(state-1)
QN(value) = evaluate-2(prog at occ)(occ)(env)
    (**lam** value. **lam** state. QN(value))(state-2)(input*-2)

Proof. Let exp = prog at occ. From the definition of the function prop-def we know that for any exp':

$$\text{if prop}(\exp') = \text{true then state-1}(\exp') = \text{value-1}.$$

†QN stands for the SIS function **lam** value. QUOTE(NUMBER(value))

From Lemma 8 we know that $v(\text{state-1}(\text{exp}')) = \text{value}'\text{-2}$ where

$$\text{value}'\text{-2} = \text{evaluate-2}(\text{exp}')(\text{occ})(\text{env})$$
$$(\textbf{lam value. lam state. } QN(\text{value}))(\text{state-2})(\text{input*-2})$$

Using the definition of *P-Value*, we can write $v(\text{state-1}(\text{exp})) = \text{value-2}$; hence

$$v(\text{state-1}(\text{exp}')) = \text{value-2}, \ v(\text{value-1}) = \text{value-2} \text{ and}$$
$$\text{value}'\text{-2} = \text{value-2}. \quad \blacksquare$$

11-7.3. Determination of Invariant Expressions

An expression is invariant at an occurrence occ in a program prog if its value is the same each time control reaches occ. We want to determine the expressions that are invariant in any usual interpretation. This property can be defined by an interpretation similar to the one used for the constant propagation problem defined with a basic value domain of symbolic terms.

11-7.3.1. Domains and functions

The domain of values is equal to the domain of symbolic terms, that is Exp plus the element *var*, so Value = Exp / *var*. A state associates a value with each expression. If occ is an occurrence, answ is the result of this non-standard interpretation:

$$\text{answ(occ)} = \begin{cases} \text{exp if the expression at occ is invariant and exp} \\ \quad \text{is its symbolic value} \\ \textit{var} \text{ otherwise} \end{cases}$$

If answ(occ) is undefined, then this expression has never been evaluated. This interpretation is entirely defined by Figs. 11-5 and 11-8. An input is identified with a syntactic identifier. The write function is the identity. The read function associates with an identifier a symbolic value taken from the input stream. The function compatible is defined on the flat domain.

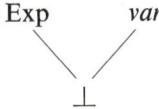

11-7.3.2. Definition of the predicates used

As in the previous application, we build a valuation function v from the symbolic inputs to the standard ones. Using this function, we define

$$P\text{-}Value(\text{value-1}, \text{value-2}) = (v(\text{value-1}) \textbf{ eq } \text{value-2}) \textbf{ or } (\text{value-1} \textbf{ eq } \textit{var})$$

```
DSL "invariant expressions"
DOMAINS
!SEMANTIC VARIABLES AND DOMAINS
!***************************************

state     : State    = Exp -> R-value;
r-value   : R-value = Exp / "var";
prop      : Prop     = R-value;
exec-cont : Exec-cont = State -> Input* -> Answ;
answ      : Answ;
input     : Input    = Q;
eval-cont : Eval-cont = R-value -> Exec-cont;

!TYPES OF FUNCTIONS
!**********************

init-prop   := Prop;
read        := Ident -> Eval-cont -> Exec-cont;
compatible  := <Prop,Prop> -> Prop;
prop-def    := R-value -> State -> Prop;
op-val      := <R-value,R-value,Op> -> R-value;
wrong       := Exec-cont;

!DEFINITIONS OF FUNCTIONS
!*****************************

LET init-prop: Prop  = ?
ALSO read(ident); eval-cont: Exec-cont =
        LAM state.
         LAM input*.
         CASE input*
         /input1 PRE input2* ->
                   LET exp = [input1]
                   IN eval-cont(exp)(state)(input2*)
         /<> ->    wrong(state)(input*)
         ESAC

ALSO  compatible(prop1,prop2) : Prop =
                   prop1 IS prop2 -> prop1,["var"]
ALSO  prop-def(r-value)(state) : Prop =
                   r-value
ALSO  op-val(r-value1,r-value2,op) : R-value =
                   (r-value1 IS ["var"]) OR (r-value2 IS ["var"]) -> ["var"],
                  CASE op
                  /"+" ->    [r-value1 "+" r-value2]
                  /"*" ->    [r-value1 "*" r-value2]
                  /"=" ->    [r-value1 "=" r-value2]
                  /"#" ->    [r-value1 "#" r-value2]
                  /"or" ->   [r-value1 "or" r-value2]
                  /"and" ->  [r-value1 "and" r-value2]
                  ESAC

IN
<init-prop,read,compatible,prop-def,op-val>
END
```

Figure 11-8

In this application, semantic objects are values. We define *P-Prop*(prop, $\langle$occ, value-2$\rangle$) = *P-Value*(prop, value-2).

P-Input is true from the definition of v.

11-7.3.3. Proof of the basic relations

Relation 1.
(*P-Value*(value'-1, value'-2) **and** *P-Value*(value''-1, value''-2)) implies
    P-Value(value-1, value-2)
where value = op-val(value', value'', op)

The proof is obvious from the definitions of v, *P-Value* and the function op-val.

Relation 2. If *P-Prop*(prop, $\langle$occ, value-2$\rangle$) is true, then for any prop' compatible with prop *P-Prop*(prop', $\langle$occ, value-2$\rangle$) is true.

The proof of this relation is the same as for the constant propagation problem.

Relation 3. For any prog, for any occ such that occ $\in$ Occ(prog), *P-State*(state-1, state-2) and *P-Value*(value-1, value-2) implies
    P-Prop(prop, $\langle$occ, value-2$\rangle$) where prop = prop-def(value-1, state-1)

The proof uses the definition of the function v and follows the same reasoning as in the constant propagation problem.

11-7.3.4. Coherence problem

As *P-Input*(input-1, input-2) is true, this problem is solved using Property 4. Hence *P-Prog*(run-1(prog), run-2(prog)) is true.

ACKNOWLEDGMENTS

I thank R. Burstall and R. Tennent for their interest in this study and for their useful comments, P. Mosses for his help in using his SIS system, and B. Lang, G. Kahn, and G. Huet for their continuing support.

Chapter 12

Complexity of Flow Analysis, Inductive Assertion Synthesis and a Language Due to Dijkstra[†]

Neil D. Jones
Steven S. Muchnick

12-1. INTRODUCTION

A number of researchers have developed methods for static analysis of programs, usually to extract execution-time properties for optimization purposes [Aho77, Cous78, Hech77, Jone76, Jone81, Schw75b, Schw75c, Wegb75], but also notably for verification [Cous77c] and software reliability [Fosd76]. In this chapter we show that two different methods are in use, one a significant generalization of the other, and that the two methods have significantly different intrinsic computational complexities. As an outgrowth of our observations we show that a feature of the programming language used by Dijkstra in [Dijk76] makes it unsuitable for compile-time type checking, thus suggesting that flow analysis is applicable to the design of programming languages, as well as to their implementation. We also show that program verification by the method of inductive assertions [Floy67, Mann74, Wegb77] is very likely to lead to assertions whose lengths and proofs are not polynomially bounded in the size of the program being verified, even for very simple

†The research reported here was partially supported by the National Science Foundation under grant MCS76–80269.

programs. This last observation casts further doubt on the practicality and relevance of mechanized verification of arbitrary programs [DeMi77, Wegb77]

Let P be a program in a simple language with assignments and conditional branches, and with variables $X_1, \ldots, X_n$. We annotate a flowchart representation of P with program points $I_1, \ldots, I_m$, one for each arc. Let D be a finite lattice whose elements are properties which the value of a variable may satisfy at a program point. For example, we might have $D = $ Powerset ($\{integer, real, boolean\}$) with the partial order given by subset inclusion.

The first flow analysis method, which we shall call the *independent attribute method*, associates with each program point I a function $f_I: \{X_1, \ldots, X_n\} \longrightarrow D$. Usually $f_I(X_i)$ describes some of the attributes that X_i may have whenever execution reaches point I; e.g., $f_I(X_i) = \{real, boolean\}$ might signify that X_i may have a real value or a boolean value at point I. The analysis process begins by constructing a system of simultaneous equations of the form $f_{I_i}(X_i) = g_{i_j}(f_{I_1}(X_1), \ldots, f_{I_m}(X_n))$, either in fact or in effect. In most cases the $g_{i_j}(\ )$ are monotonic (and hence continuous since the lattice is finite), and so the system may be solved by fixed-point iteration or by more efficient special-purpose adaptations of fixed-point iteration, such as use-definition chains [Aho77, Hech77, Jone81, Tene74b]. For example, for the program in Fig. 12-1 we have the independent attribute flow equations

$$F_0(X) = \{integer, real, boolean\} \qquad F_0(Y) = \{integer, real, boolean\}$$
$$F_1(X) = F_0(X) \qquad\qquad\qquad F_1(Y) = F_0(Y)$$
$$F_2(X) = F_0(X) \qquad\qquad\qquad F_2(Y) = F_0(Y)$$
$$F_3(X) = F_1(X) \qquad\qquad\qquad F_3(Y) = \{integer\}$$
$$F_4(X) = F_2(X) \qquad\qquad\qquad F_4(Y) = \{real\}$$
$$F_5(X) = F_3(Y) \cup F_4(Y) \qquad\quad F_5(Y) = F_3(Y) \cup F_4(Y)$$

and the solution

$$F_0(X) = \{integer, real, boolean\} \qquad F_0(Y) = \{integer, real, boolean\}$$
$$F_1(X) = \{integer, real, boolean\} \qquad F_1(Y) = \{integer, real, boolean\}$$
$$F_2(X) = \{integer, real, boolean\} \qquad F_2(Y) = \{integer, real, boolean\}$$
$$F_3(X) = \{integer, real, boolean\} \qquad F_3(Y) = \{integer\}$$
$$F_4(X) = \{integer, real, boolean\} \qquad F_4(Y) = \{real\}$$
$$F_5(X) = \{integer, real\} \qquad\qquad\quad F_5(Y) = \{integer, real\}$$

The second flow analysis method, which we shall call the *relational method*, generalizes the independent attribute method. It associates with each program point I a relation (or predicate) $f_I \subseteq D^n$ with the interpretation that

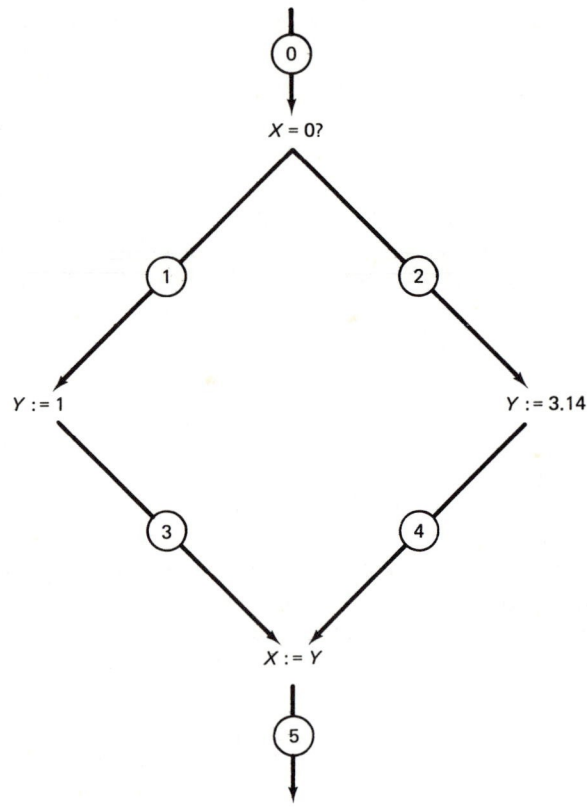

Figure 12-1

f_I is a set of n-tuples describing relationships among the values of $X_1, \ldots, X_n$ at program point I. We obtain the following equations for Fig. 12-1.

$$F_0 = \{\langle\{integer, real, boolean\}, \{integer, real, boolean\}\rangle\}$$
$$F_1 = F_0$$
$$F_2 = F_0$$
$$F_3 = \{\langle p, \{integer\}\rangle \mid \exists\, q\, \langle p, q\rangle \in F_1\}$$
$$F_4 = \{\langle p, \{real\}\rangle \mid \exists\, q\, \langle p, q\rangle \in F_2\}$$
$$F_5 = \{\langle q, q\rangle \mid \exists\, p\, \langle p, q\rangle \in F_3 \cup F_4\}$$

and the solution is

$$F_0 = \{\langle\{integer, real, boolean\}, \{integer, real, boolean\}\rangle\}$$
$$F_1 = \{\langle\{integer, real, boolean\}, \{integer, real, boolean\}\rangle\}$$
$$F_2 = \{\langle\{integer, real, boolean\}, \{integer, real, boolean\}\rangle\}$$

$$F_3 = \{\langle\{integer, real, boolean\}, \{integer\}\rangle\}$$
$$F_4 = \{\langle\{integer, real, boolean\}, \{real\}\rangle\}$$
$$F_5 = \{\langle\{integer\}, \{integer\}\rangle, \langle\{real\}, \{real\}\rangle\}$$

This clearly shows that X and Y must have the same type at point 5.

Note that the independent attribute method may be viewed as a special case of the relational method by use of cartesian products; for example, $F_5(X)$ and $F_5(Y)$ would naturally correspond to

$$F_5' = \{\langle\{integer, real\}, \{integer, real\}\rangle\}$$

or more generally

$$F_I = \{\langle F_I(X_1), F_I(X_2), \ldots, F_I(X_n)\rangle\}$$

Further, the independent attribute method is easily seen to be insufficient for some important types of program analysis, such as memory sharing [Jone78†, Kapl78b, Schw75a, Schw75b], determining linear relationships among variables [Cous78], and generation of invariants for verification [Cous77c, Wegb77].

Another instance in which the power of the relational method is required is to do compile-time data type analysis in the language used by Dijkstra in [Dijk76]. We shall show that, for this reason, type incorrectness of programs in Dijkstra's language is an $\mathfrak{NP}$-complete problem [Aho74]. This property would seem sufficient to make the language unsuitable for compile-time type checking, since it is very likely that any deterministic algorithm for an $\mathfrak{NP}$-complete problem will require exponential time.

In the final section of this chapter we consider a class of very simple programs which may be verified by relational flow analysis of a type very similar to that used in analyzing Dijkstra's language. We show that the existence of short (polynomially length-bounded) inductive assertions or short proofs of invariance for such programs is highly unlikely because of the resulting computational complexity consequences.

12-2. COMPLEXITY OF THE INDEPENDENT ATTRIBUTE METHOD

We consider now the complexity of independent attribute flow analysis as a function of program length, assuming a fixed finite lattice D. With m

---

†Actually the basic relational model presented here is insufficient to represent the k-limited graph model of memory sharing, as well. Rather, k-limited graphs can be thought of as carriers of sets of relations, where the set of relations grows exponentially with the number of variables.

program points and n variables we have mn equations of the form

$$f_{I_i}(X_i) = g_{i_j}(f_{I_1}(X_1), \ldots, f_{I_m}(X_n))$$

Assuming the g_{i_j} are monotone, the least fixpoint of this system of simultaneous equations can be found by forming an $m \times n$ matrix A^0 with all elements set to a first approximation value $\bot \in D$ and then iterating

$$A_{ij}^{k+1} = g_{i_j}(A_{11}^k, \ldots, A_{mn}^k)$$

for $k = 0, 1, 2, \ldots$ until a value of k is reached such that $A^k = A^{k+1}$. It is easily seen that such a k is bounded by mnd, where d is the cardinality of D. If the original program had length p, then $n \leq p$ and typically† $m \leq p$ so a solution may be obtained in time p^2d, a polynomial in the length of the program.

Consequently the independent attribute method has complexity lying in $\mathcal{P}$. In fact, it is possible to show that there are simple programming languages whose type correctness may be determined by the independent attribute method, and such that determination of type correctness is log-space complete for $\mathcal{P}$. This may be done by a simple reduction from the circuit value problem of Ladner [Ladn75].

In [Kapl78b] Kaplan discusses a model for analysis of memory sharing based on the use of binary relations, an intermediate step between the independent attribute method and the full relational method. This results in an $n \times n$ matrix of values for each program point and hence raises the time complexity from p^2d to p^3d, assuming unit time for the $g_{i_j}(\ )$ operations.

12-3. TYPE CORRECTNESS IN DIJKSTRA'S LANGUAGE

This section and the following ones concern two instances of relational flow analysis methods and their computational complexities.

Dijkstra's language in [Dijk76] uses syntactical methods to ensure that every variable has been initialized before its first use. This is done by explicit initialization statements which must be so arranged that any execution path will pass through exactly one initialization for each variable. Ensuring that variables are properly initialized, by this or some other means, is certainly desirable and should substantially aid program reliability.

A complication arises, however, from a further feature: Dijkstra allows the type of a variable to be specified in the initialization statement.

---

†Actually it is possible that m be as large as p^2, such as in an ALGOL 60 program containing a **switch** declaration and many **go tos** using it, but this is highly atypical. Certainly, for well-structured programs $m \leq p$.

Thus different execution paths may lead to different types for a variable, as shown by the following example:

begin glovar Y_1, Y_2; **virvar** X_1, X_2;
   if $Y_1 = 0 \longrightarrow X_1$ **vir** *int* := 0; X_2 **vir** *int* := 0
   ☐ $Y_1 \neq 0 \longrightarrow X_1$ **vir** *bool* := *true*;
     if $Y_2 = 0 \longrightarrow X_2$ **vir** *int* := 0
     ☐ $Y_2 \neq 0 \longrightarrow X_2$ **vir** *bool* := *true*
     fi
  fi

.
.
.

Clearly in the portion of the program following the above excerpt there are three possible combinations of types for X_1 and X_2, depending on the execution path taken through the initializations, and a compiler would need to keep track of the possible relationships between the types of the two variables.

In Dijkstra's own words [Dijk76],

> At each activation of the block, one out of a set of primitive initializing statements will be executed. As far as I am concerned they could initialize variables of different types, something no one can object to as long as the same functions and operations are defined on time. Whether such a freedom of choice for the type of a private variable is a useful thing or not is something that seems hard to discuss at this stage; at any rate it seems unwise to choose now a notational convention that does not leave the option open.

We now show that for any propositional formula $\mathfrak{F}$ in conjunctive normal form we can construct in polynomial time a program $P_\mathfrak{F}$ in Dijkstra's language which has a type inconsistency if and only if $\mathfrak{F}$ is satisfiable. Consequently a (deterministic) polynomial-time algorithm for determining type consistency is very unlikely since it would imply the existence of a polynomial-time algorithm for satisfiability, which in turn would imply $\mathscr{P} = \mathfrak{NP}$.

Note that it is easy to show that type inconsistency is determinable in $\mathfrak{NP}$: one simply guesses the path through the initializations which will result in an error and then checks that set of type assignments against the remainder of the program, as in [Ledg72]. Thus the construction just mentioned will establish $\mathfrak{NP}$-completeness of type inconsistency for Dijkstra's language.

We shall illustrate the construction of $P_\mathfrak{F}$ from $\mathfrak{F}$ by an example; the extension to the general case should be evident. Let $\mathfrak{F} = (x_1 \lor x_2) \land (x_1 \lor \bar{x}_2) \land (\bar{x}_1 \lor \bar{x}_2)$. For this $\mathfrak{F}$ we construct the program $P_\mathfrak{F}$ which follows:

```
begin privar X₁, X₂, Y₁, Y₂, S;
  Y₁ vir int := input; Y₂ vir int := input; S vir real := 0;
  if Y₁ = 0 → X₁ vir int := 0
  [] Y₁ ≠ 0 → X₁ vir real := 0
  fi
  if Y₂ = 0 → X₂ vir int := 0
  [] Y₂ ≠ 0 → X₂ vir real := 0
  fi
  S := ISREAL((X₁ orop X₂) andop (X₁ orop (notop X₂)) andop
      ((notop X₁) orop (notop X₂)))
end
```

The operator symbols *orop, andop, notop,* and the procedure ISREAL are assumed to compute functions whose result types are related to their argument types as follows:

orop	*int*	*real*		*andop*	*int*	*real*		*notop*			*ISREAL*	
int	*int*	*int*		*int*	*int*	*real*		*int*	*real*		*int*	$\top$
real	*int*	*real*		*real*	*real*	*real*		*real*	*int*		*real*	*real*

where $\top$ indicates a type error. If we interpret *int* as *true* and *real* as *false*, then *orop, andop, notop,* behave like $\lor$, $\land$, $\neg$, respectively, and it is easy to see that the assignment to S contains a type error if and only if its argument can evaluate to something of type *int* ($\equiv$ *true*). Effectively the **if** statements assign truth values to X_1 and X_2 during execution, and the argument to ISREAL will have type *int* just in case the resulting truth values of X_1 and X_2 satisfy $\mathfrak{F}$. Thus $\mathfrak{F}$ is satisfiable if and only if $P_{\mathfrak{F}}$ has a type error.

The execution of $P_{\mathfrak{F}}$ can be mimicked by an appropriate relational flow analysis system. An appropriate lattice is

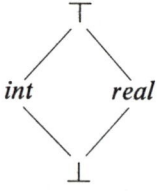

where $\bot$ signifies unknown type and $\top$ a type error. Adapting the notation used in the second part of [Jone81], we write, for example, $F(3) = \{\langle real, int, real\rangle, \langle int, int, real\rangle\}$ to indicate that at program point 3 either X_1 has type *real* and X_2 has type *int* and S has type *real*, or X_1 has type *int* and X_2 has type *int* and S has type *real* (we ignore Y_1 and Y_2). Also, we write, for example, $F(4) = F(2)\{X_1 \leftarrow real\}$ to indicate that $F(4)$ is $F(2)$ with the X_1 components in its tuples replaced by *real*.

To analyze the program we first rewrite it as the flowchart in Fig. 12-2 so as to introduce program points. The resulting system of forward flow equations is:

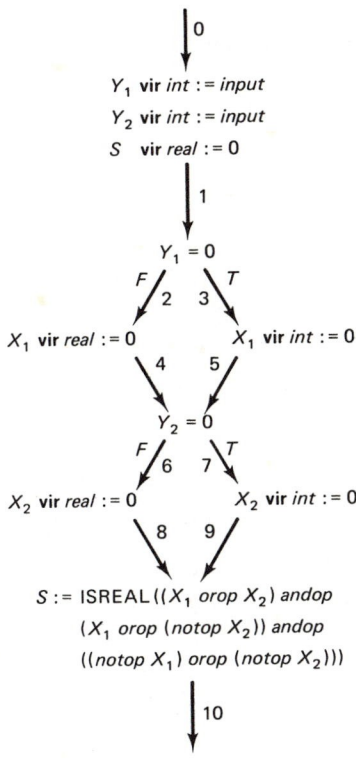

Figure 12-2

$$F(0) = \{\langle \perp, \perp, \perp \rangle\}$$
$$F(1) = F(0)\{S \leftarrow real\}$$
$$F(2) = F(1)$$
$$F(3) = F(1)$$
$$F(4) = F(2)\{X_1 \leftarrow real\}$$
$$F(5) = F(3)\{X_1 \leftarrow int\}$$
$$F(6) = F(4) \cup F(5)$$
$$F(7) = F(4) \cup F(5)$$
$$F(8) = F(6)\{X_2 \leftarrow real\}$$
$$F(9) = F(7)\{X_2 \leftarrow int\}$$

$$F(10) = (F(8) \cup F(9))$$

$$\{S \leftarrow \text{type(ISREAL}((X_1 \ orop \ X_2)$$
$$andop \ (X_1 \ orop \ notop \ X_2)$$
$$andop \ (notop \ X_1 \ orop \ notop \ X_2)))\}$$

The solution to the above equations is:

$F(0) = \{\langle \perp, \perp, \perp \rangle\}$

$F(1) = \{\langle \perp, \perp, real \rangle\}$

$F(2) = \{\langle \perp, \perp, real \rangle\}$

$F(3) = \{\langle \perp, \perp, real \rangle\}$

$F(4) = \{\langle real, \perp, real \rangle\}$

$F(5) = \{\langle int, \perp, real \rangle\}$

$F(6) = \{\langle real, \perp, real \rangle, \langle int, \perp, real \rangle\}$

$F(7) = \{\langle real, \perp, real \rangle, \langle int, \perp, real \rangle\}$

$F(8) = \{\langle real, real, real \rangle, \langle int, real, real \rangle\}$

$F(9) = \{\langle real, int, real \rangle, \langle int, int, real \rangle\}$

$F(10) = \{\langle real, real, real \rangle, \langle int, real, \top \rangle, \langle real, int, real \rangle, \langle int, int, real \rangle\}$

and the presence of the tuple $\langle int, real, \top \rangle$ in $F(10)$ indicates the type error.

Generalization of the methods used in the above example clearly establishes the theorem:

Theorem.   Determining type inconsistency for Dijkstra's language is $\mathfrak{NP}$-complete.

12-4.   AN EVEN HARDER FLOW ANALYSIS PROBLEM

The language of Dijkstra and our analysis of it in the preceding section have two simple characteristics which, with a slight addition, will prove to be of further interest. These characteristics are:

1. Solving the relational flow analysis equations can be thought of as symbolic execution of programs written in a language with statements of the following forms:

   (a) $X := B_i(Y_1, \ldots, Y_n)$ (assignment of some set of functions)

   (b) $S_1; S_2$ (sequencing)

(c)   **if** $true \rightarrow S_1$ (uninterpreted branching)
   $\Box$ $true \rightarrow S_2$
   fi

2. The attribute domain includes two values which can be identified as *true* and *false*, and the functions B_i in item (1) can be interpreted as boolean functions on these values.

Thus the symbolic execution becomes, in effect, parallel execution on the (symbolic) domain $\{true, false\}$. Note that viewing data flow analysis as symbolic execution is clearly seen in [Sint72, Cous77c, Jone81, Wegb75].

Now suppose the flow analysis method is capable of propagating relational information around loops and differentially through the branches of a conditional. These capabilities are present in the analysis methods of [Cous77c, Jone81] and are routinely used in verification [Ledg72, Wegb75]. In this case we can show that the complexity of the analysis is (presumably) increased from $\mathcal{NP}$ to $\mathcal{PSPACE}$. Further, this is true for single-loop programs in which the **if** statement is deterministic.

Rather than embed our construction in a specific language, let us simply state that we wish to be able to simulate faithfully by flow analysis, statements of the following forms:

1. $X := B_i(Y_1, \ldots, Y_n)$
2. $S_1; S_2$
3.   **while** X **do** S **od**
4.   **if** E **then** S_1 **else** S_2 **fi**

Here the variables are boolean, the B_i denote boolean functions, and E is a boolean-valued expression. We use exactly one **while** in each program. Note that the **if** is inessential since it can be expressed by (1) and (2), but is included for the sake of clarity.

It is known [Stoc76] that the following problem is $\mathcal{PSPACE}$-hard:

Given a quantified boolean formula $\mathcal{F}$ without free variables
To decide whether $\mathcal{F}$ is true.

We show how to construct from $\mathcal{F}$ a program $P_{\mathcal{F}}$ such that $\mathcal{F}$ is true just in case the variable Y_1 has value *true* at the end of executing $P_{\mathcal{F}}$. Suppose, for example, that $\mathcal{F}$ has the form $Q_1 X_1\, Q_2 X_2\, Q_3 X_3\, Q_4 X_4\, \mathcal{G}$ where $\mathcal{G}$ is strictly propositional and each Q_i is either $\forall$ or $\exists$. The program simply evaluates $\mathcal{F}$ by varying $X_1, \ldots, X_4$ over $\{true, false\}^4$ and uses Y_i to accumulate the value of $Q_i X_i \ldots Q_4 X_4\, \mathcal{G}$. More specifically, let Q_1 and Q_3 be $\forall$ and Q_2

and Q_4 be $\exists$. Then $P_{\mathfrak{F}}$ is as follows:

```
LOOPING := true;
X₁, X₂, X₃, X₄ := false, false, false, false;
Y₁, Y₂, Y₃, Y₄ := true, false, true, false;
while LOOPING
do
    Y₄ := Y₄ ∨ 𝒢(X₁, X₂, X₃, X₄);
    if ~X₄ then X₄ := true
    else Y₃ := Y₃ ∧ Y₄; Y₄ := false; X₄ := false;
      if ~X₃ then X₃ := true
      else Y₂ := Y₂ ∨ Y₃; Y₃ := true; X₃ := false;
        if ~X₂ then X₂ := true
        else Y₁ := Y₁ ∧ Y₂; Y₂ := false; X₂ := false;
          if ~X₁ then X₁ := true
          else LOOPING := false
          fi
        fi
      fi
    fi
od
```

The generalization of the construction to an arbitrary quantified boolean formula should be evident. We have thus proved the following:

Lemma. There is a polynomial-time algorithm which, given a quantified formula $\mathfrak{F}$ of boolean algebra without free variables, will construct a program $P_{\mathfrak{F}}$ such that $\mathfrak{F}$ is true just in case the final value of Y_1 is *true*.

Since execution of $P_{\mathfrak{F}}$ is sufficient to determine the truth of $\mathfrak{F}$, any flow analysis method powerful enough to, in effect, execute such a program as it analyzes it is $\mathcal{PSPACE}$-hard and thus is very likely in the worst case to require exponential time in the size of the program.

12-5. LENGTH OF INDUCTIVE ASSERTIONS AND PROOFS IN PROGRAM VERIFICATION

We now derive some implications for program verification of the construction in the preceding section. Wegbreit [Wegb77] has studied the problem of the time which construction of inductive assertions contributes to program verification. Using his terminological style, let $\{T\}$ denote the set of triples $\langle \Phi, P, \Psi \rangle$ where P is the program corresponding to some quantified boolean formula $\mathcal{F}$ (by our construction), the input assertion Φ is *"true"*, and the output assertion Ψ is *"$Y_1 = true$"*. Such a triple is called *consistent* just in case the truth of Φ before execution of P results in Ψ's being true after execution of P whenever P terminates. Clearly $\langle \Phi, P, \Psi \rangle \in \{T\}$ is consistent if and only if $\mathcal{F}$ is true. The class $\{T\}$ has the following properties:

1. Programs in $\{T\}$ are very simple. They each have only a single loop; all terminate and manipulate only boolean values. One would reasonably expect a verifier to be able to handle them.

2. The consistency problem for $\{T\}$ is $\mathcal{PSPACE}$-hard.

3. Consistency can be established by the method of inductive assertions. In particular let $\vec{\xi}$ be the vector of variables in P and $\vec{v}_1, \ldots, \vec{v}_m$ be all the vectors of values which $\vec{\xi}$ can assume at the beginning of the body of the loop during execution of P. Then $\vec{\xi} = \vec{v}_1 \lor \cdots \lor \vec{\xi} = \vec{v}_m$ would be a suitable though very long inductive assertion for the single loop in P.

4. As we shall show, it is very unlikely that consistency of triples in $\{T\}$ can be established by either: (a) short propositional inductive assertions or (b) inductive assertions of any sort which have short proofs of invariance. "Short" is to be interpreted here as "bounded in length by a polynomial function of the length of the program."

5. Consequently arbitrary programs in $\{T\}$ are unlikely to be verified by any practical mechanical means at all.

The first result in item (4) is established by the following:

Theorem. Suppose consistency of triples in $\{T\}$ could be established by inductive assertions with invariance proofs which are polynomially bounded in length. Then $\mathcal{NP} = \mathcal{PSPACE}$.

Proof. Let $L \subseteq \Sigma^*$ be any set of strings in $\mathcal{PSPACE}$ and let $x \in \Sigma^*$ be any string. The question "is $x \in L$?" can be answered by the following process:

1. Construct a quantified boolean formula $\mathcal{F}$ by the method of Meyer and Stockmeyer [Meye73] such that $x \in L$ iff $\mathcal{F}$ is true and $|\mathcal{F}|$ is bounded by a polynomial in $|x|$.

2. From $\mathcal{F}$ construct the triple $\langle \Phi, P, \Psi \rangle$ as above, so that $x \in L$ if and only if $\langle \Phi, P, \Psi \rangle$ is consistent.

3. Nondeterministically guess an inductive assertion I and an alleged proof that I is invariant and that $I \land \sim\text{LOOPING} \Rightarrow \Psi$.

4. Check whether the alleged proof is in fact a proof and answer "$x \in L$" just in case it is.

If the premise of the theorem is satisfied, then step (3) can be done in time polynomial in $|x|$. All the remaining steps can be done in polynomial time, and so the entire process can be performed nondeterministically in polynomial time. Hence if the premise is true, $L \in \mathcal{NP}$; since L was arbitrarily chosen in $\mathcal{PSPACE}$, it follows that $\mathcal{NP} = \mathcal{PSPACE}$. ∎

Since it is widely believed that $\mathcal{NP}$ is properly contained in $\mathcal{PSPACE}$, this theorem provides circumstantial evidence that verification requires long proofs, even for relatively simple programs.

The polynomial time hierarchy [Stoc76] is a sequence $\Sigma_0^p \subseteq \Sigma_1^p \subseteq \Sigma_2^p \subseteq \ldots$ of subclasses of $\mathcal{PSPACE}$ such that $\Sigma_0^p = \mathcal{P}$ and Σ_{k+1}^p is the class of sets accepted in polynomial time by nondeterministic Turing machines with oracles for sets in Σ_k^p. Clearly $\Sigma_1^p = \mathcal{NP}$. It is widely suspected that $\Sigma_k^p \subsetneq \Sigma_{k+1}^p$ for $k = 0, 1, 2, \ldots$, but this has not been proved. Note that for $k = 0$ this is the $\mathcal{P} = \mathcal{NP}$ question.

We next show that if verification can be done with short assertions then the polynomial-time hierarchy collapses at $k = 2$, i.e., that $\Sigma_2^p = \Sigma_3^p = \ldots = \mathcal{PSPACE}$:

Theorem. Suppose consistency of triples in $\{T\}$ can be established with propositional inductive assertions whose lengths are polynomially bounded in the lengths of the programs. Then $\Sigma_2^p = \mathcal{PSPACE}$.

Proof. Let $L \subseteq \Sigma^*$ be in $\mathcal{PSPACE}$ and $x \in \Sigma^*$. Assuming the premise of the theorem, we can decide whether $x \in L$ as follows:

1. Construct $\mathcal{F}$ and $\langle \Phi, P, \Psi \rangle$ as in the proof of the preceding theorem, so that $x \in L$ if and only if $\langle \Phi, P, \Psi \rangle$ is consistent.

2. Nondeterministically guess a propositional inductive assertion I of length polynomially bounded in $|x|$.

3. Let $\rho(\vec{\xi}, \vec{\eta})$ be the predicate such that if $\vec{\xi}$ records the values of the variables in P as the body of the **while** loop is entered, then $\vec{\eta}$ records their values after the body has been executed once. Note that $\rho(\ )$ can be written as a propositional formula with length polynomially bounded in $|x|$.

4. Let $\vec{\xi}_0$ be the vector of values of P's variables just prior to entering the **while** loop. Determine whether it is true that
$$I(\vec{\xi}_0) \wedge \forall \vec{\xi} \, \forall \vec{\eta} [(I(\vec{\xi}) \wedge \rho(\vec{\xi}, \vec{\eta}) \Rightarrow I(\vec{\eta})) \wedge (I(\vec{\xi}) \wedge \sim \text{LOOPING} \Rightarrow \Psi(\vec{\xi}))].$$

5. Answer $x \in L$ just in case the above is true.

The first through third steps can clearly be done in nondeterministic polynomial time. Step (4) requires us to determine whether a formula is a tautology, which can be done by showing its negation to be unsatisfiable. This can be done in polynomial time by appealing to an oracle for $\mathfrak{NP} = \Sigma_1^p$, and hence the whole process can be done in Σ_2^p. L was arbitrary in $\mathcal{PSPACE}$, so $\Sigma_2^p = \mathcal{PSPACE}$. ∎

Note, finally, that the existence of short invariance proofs would require the existence of short inductive assertions (since the assertions would occur in the proofs), though the assertions might not be propositional in form.

Bibliography

Aho72   AHO, ALFRED V., RAVI SETHI, and JEFFREY D. ULLMAN, "Code Optimization and Finite Church-Rosser Systems," in *Design and Optimization of Compilers*, ed. Randall Rustin. Englewood Cliffs, NJ: Prentice-Hall, 1972.

Aho73   AHO, ALFRED V., and JEFFREY D. ULLMAN, *The Theory of Parsing, Translation, and Compiling: Volume I*. Englewood Cliffs, NJ: Prentice-Hall, 1973.

Aho74   AHO, ALFRED V., JOHN HOPCROFT, and JEFFREY D. ULLMAN, *The Design and Analysis of Computer Algorithms*. Reading, MA: Addison-Wesley, 1974.

Aho76   AHO, ALFRED V., and JEFFREY D. ULLMAN, "Node Listings for Reducible Flow Graphs," *J. Comput. Syst. Sci.*, 13, no. 3 (December 1976), 286–299.

Aho77   AHO, ALFRED V., and JEFFREY D. ULLMAN, *Principles of Compiler Design*. Reading, MA: Addison-Wesley, 1977.

Alfo77   ALFORD, M. W., "A Requirements Engineering Methodology for Real-Time Processing Requirements," *IEEE Trans. Software Eng.*, SE-3, no. 1 (January 1977), 60–69.

Alle69   ALLEN, FRANCES E., "Program Optimization," in *Annual Review of Automatic Programming*, 5, 239–307. Elmsford, NY: Pergamon, 1969.

Alle70   ———, "Control Flow Analysis," *SIGPLAN Notices*, 5, no. 7 (July 1970), 1–19.

Alle71   ———, "A Basis for Program Optimization," *Information Processing 71*, Proc. IFIP Congress 71, Ljubljana, Yugoslavia (August 1971), ed. C. V. Freiman, pp. 385–390. Amsterdam: North-Holland, 1972.

Alle72a ALLEN, FRANCES E., and JOHN COCKE, "A Catalogue of Optimizing Transformations," in *Design and Optimization of Compilers*, ed. Randall Rustin. Englewood Cliffs, NJ: Prentice-Hall, 1972.

Alle72b ———, "Graph Theoretic Constructs for Program Control Flow Analysis," Research Report RC3923 (July 1972), T. J. Watson Research Center, Yorktown Heights, NY.

Alle74 ALLEN, FRANCES E., "Interprocedural Data Flow Analysis," *Information Processing 74*, Proc. IFIP Congress 74, Stockholm, Sweden (August 1974), ed. J. L. Rosenfield, pp. 398–408. Amsterdam: North-Holland, 1974.

Alle76 ALLEN, FRANCES E., and JOHN COCKE, "A Program Data Flow Analysis Procedure," *Commun. ACM*, 19, no. 3 (March 1976), 137–147.

Alle77 ALLEN, FRANCES E., *et al.*, "The Experimental Compiling System Project," IBM Research Report RC-6718 (1977), T. J. Watson Research Center, Yorktown Heights, NY.

Alle81 ALLEN, FRANCES E., JOHN COCKE, and KENNETH KENNEDY, "Reduction of Operator Strength," this volume.

Ashc71 ASHCROFT, EDWARD, and ZOHAR MANNA, "The Translation of 'goto' Programs to 'while' Programs," *Information Processing 71*, Proc. IFIP Congress 71, Ljubljana, Yugoslavia (August 1971), ed. C. V. Freiman, pp. 250–255. Amsterdam: North-Holland, 1972.

Babi78a BABICH, W. A., and M. JAZAYERI, "The Method of Attributes for Data Flow Analysis: Part I. Exhaustive Analysis," *Acta Inf.*, 10 (1978), 245–264.

Babi78b ———, "The Method of Attributes for Data Flow Analysis: Part II. Demand Analysis," *Acta Inf.*, 10, fasc. 3 (1978), 265–272.

Bake78 BAKER, HENRY G., JR., "List Processing in Real Time on a Serial Computer," *Commun. ACM*, 21, no. 4 (April 1978), 280–294.

Balz69 BALZER, R. M., "EXDAMS: Extendable Debugging and Monitoring System," *Proc. AFIPS 1969 Spring Joint Computer Conference*, Boston, MA, 34, pp. 567–580. Montvale, NJ: AFIPS Press, 1969.

Bann79 BANNING, J., "An Efficient Way to Find the Side Effects of Procedure Calls and Aliases of Variables," *Proc. 6th Ann. ACM Symp. on Principles of Programming Languages*, San Antonio, TX (January 1979), pp. 29–41.

Bart77a BARTH, JEFFREY M., "An Interprocedural Data Flow Analysis Algorithm," *Conf. Rec. 4th ACM Symp. on Principles of Programming Languages*, Los Angeles, CA (January 1977), pp. 119–131.

Bart77b ———, "Shifting Garbage Collector Overhead to Compile Time," *Commun. ACM*, 20, no. 7 (July 1977), 513–518.

Bart78 ———, "A Practical Interprocedural Data Flow Analysis Algorithm," *Commun. ACM*, 21, no. 9 (September 1978), 724–736.

Beat72 BEATTY, J. C., "An Axiomatic Approach to Code Optimization for Expressions," *J. ACM*, 19, no. 4 (October 1972), 613–640.

Beat74 ———, "Register Assignment Algorithm for Generation of Highly Optimized Object Code," *IBM J. Res. Dev.*, 18, no. 1 (January 1974), 20–39.

Bell77 BELL, T. E., D. C. BIXLER, and M. E. DYER, "An Extendable Approach to Computer-Aided Software Requirements Engineering," *IEEE Trans. Software Eng.*, SE-3, no. 1 (January 1977), 49–59.

Berm76   BERMAN, LEONARD, and GEORGE MARKOWSKY, "Linear and Non-linear Approximate Invariants," IBM RC7241 (February 1976), T. J. Watson Research Center, Yorktown Heights, NY.

Birk67   BIRKHOFF, G., *Lattice Theory* (3rd ed.), Vol. 25. Providence, RI: AMS Colloquium Publications, 1967.

Blac77   BLACK, R. K. E., "Effects of Modern Programming Practice on Software Development Costs," *Proceedings Fall Compcon 77* (September 1977), pp. 250–253.

Boge75   BOGEN, R., *MACSYMA Reference Manual*, The Mathlab Group, Project MAC, Massachusetts Institute of Technology, 1975.

Böhm66   BÖHM, C., and G. JACOPINI, "Flow Diagrams, Turing Machines and Languages with Only Two Formation Rules," *Commun ACM*, 9, no. 5 (May 1966), 366–371.

Boll79   BOLLACKER, L. A., "Detecting Unexecutable Paths Through Program Flow Graphs," unpublished Master's thesis, Department of Computer Science, University of Colorado, Boulder, CO, 1979.

Boye75   BOYER, R. S., B. ELSPAS, and K. N. LEVITT, "SELECT—A Formal System for Testing and Debugging Programs by Symbolic Execution," *Proc. Int. Conf. Reliable Software*, Los Angeles, CA (April 1975), pp. 234–244.

Brai69   BRAINERD, W. S., "Tree Generating Regular Systems," *Inf. Control*, 14, no. 2 (February 1969), 217–231.

BroA78   BROWN, ALLEN L., JR., personal communication (August 1978).

BroJ78   BROWN, J. R., "Programming Practices for Increased Software Quality," in *Software Quality Management*. New York: Petrocelli Books, 1978.

BroW73   BROWN, W. S., *Altran User Manual 1* (1973), Bell Telephone Laboratory.

Büch64   BÜCHI, J. R., "Regular Canonical Systems," *Archiv. F. Math. Logik und Grund.*, 6, nos. 3–4 (April 1964), 91–111.

Cart77   CARTER, J. L., "A Case Study of a New Code Generation Technique for Compilers," *Commun. ACM*, 20, no. 12 (December 1977), 914–920.

Chaz69   CHAZAN, D., and W. MIRANKER, "Chaotic Relaxation," *Linear Algebra and Its Applications*, 2, no. 2 (April 1969), 199–222.

Chea78   CHEATHAM, THOMAS E., JR., and D. WASHINGTON, "Program Loop Analysis by Solving First Order Recurrence Relations," TR-13-78, Harvard University Center for Research in Computing Technology, 1978.

Chea79   CHEATHAM, THOMAS E., JR., G. H. HALLOWAY, and J. A. TOWNLEY, "Symbolic Evaluation and the Analysis of Programs," to appear in *IEEE Trans. Software Eng.*

ClaE77   CLARKE, E. M., JR., "Program Invariants as Fixed Points," *Proc. 18th Ann. Symp. on Foundations of Computer Science*, Providence, RI (October–November 1977), pp. 18–29.

ClaE79   ———, "Synthesis of Resource Invariants for Concurrent Programs," *Conf. Rec. 6th ACM Symp. on Principles of Programming Languages*, San Antonio, TX (January 1979), pp. 211–221.

ClaL76a CLARKE, LORI A., "A System to Generate Test Data and Symbolically Execute Programs," *IEEE Trans. Software Eng.*, SE-2, no. 3 (September 1976), 215–222.

ClaL76b ———, "Test Data Generation and Symbolic Execution of Programs as an Aid to Program Validation," thesis, Department of Computer Science, University of Colorado, 1976.

ClaL78 ———, "Automatic Test Data Selection Techniques," *Infotech State of the Art Report on Software Testing* (September 1978).

ClaS77 CLARK, S. W., and C. C. GREEN, "An Empirical Study of List Structure in LISP," *Commun. ACM*, 20, no. 2 (February 1977), 78–87.

Cock69 COCKE, JOHN, and R. E. MILLER, "Some Analysis Techniques for Optimizing Computer Programs," *Proc. 2nd Int. Conf. on System Sciences*, Hawaii, 1969, pp. 143–146.

Cock70a COCKE, JOHN, "Global Common Subexpressions Elimination," *SIGPLAN Notices*, 5, no. 7 (July 1970), 20–24.

Cock70b COCKE, JOHN, and J. T. SCHWARTZ, *Programming Languages and Their Compilers; Preliminary Notes*. New York: Courant Institute of Mathematical Sciences, New York University, 1970.

Cock76 COCKE, JOHN, and K. KENNEDY, "Profitability Computations on Program Flow Graphs," *Comput. Math. Appl.*, 2, no. 2 (1976), 145–159.

Cock77 ———, "An Algorithm for Reduction of Operator Strength," *Commun. ACM*, 20, no. 11 (November 1977), 850–856.

Cock78 COCKE, JOHN, and PETER W. MARKSTEIN, "Strength Reduction for Division and Modulo with Application to Accessing a Multilevel Store," IBM Research Report RC7013 (March 1978), T. J. Watson Research Center, Yorktown Heights, NY.

Cous77a COUSOT, PATRICK, and RADHIA COUSOT, "Abstract Interpretation: A Unified Lattice Model for Static Analysis of Programs by Construction or Approximation of Fixpoints," *Conf. Rec. of 4th ACM Symp. on Principles of Programming Languages*, Los Angeles, CA (January 1977), pp. 238–252.

Cous77b COUSOT, PATRICK, "Asynchronous Iterative Methods for Solving a Fixed Point System of Monotone Equations in a Complete Lattice," Rapport de Recherche No. 88 (September 1977), Laboratoire d'Informatique, Grenoble, France.

Cous77c COUSOT, PATRICK, and RADHIA COUSOT, "Automatic Synthesis of Optimal Invariant Assertions: Mathematical Foundations," *Proc. ACM Symp. on Artificial Intelligence and Programming Languages*, Rochester, NY, *SIGPLAN Notices*, 12, no. 8 (August 1977), 1–12.

Cous77d ———, "Constructive Versions of Tarski's Fixed Point Theorems," *Pacific J. Math*, 82, no. 1 (May 1979), 43–57.

Cous77e ———, "Static Determination of Dynamic Properties of Recursive Procedures," *IFIP Working Conf. on Programming Concepts*, St. Andrews, N.B., Canada (August 1977), ed. Erich J. Neuhold. New York: North-Holland, 1978, pp. 237–277.

Cous77f ———, "Static Determination of Dynamic Properties of Generalized Type Unions," *SIGPLAN Notices*, 12, no. 3 (March 1977), 77–94.

Cous78 COUSOT, PATRICK, and N. HALBWACHS, "Automatic Discovery of Linear Restraints Among Variables of a Program," *Conf. Rec. 5th ACM Symp. on Principles of Programming Languages*, Tucson, AZ (January 1978), pp. 84–97.

Cous79   COUSOT, PATRICK, and RADHIA COUSOT, "Systematic Design of Program Analysis Frameworks," *Conf. Rec. 6th ACM Symp. on Principles of Programming Languages*, San Antonio, TX (January 1979), pp. 269–282.

Davi73   DAVIS, M., "Hilbert's Tenth Problem is Unsolvable," *Am. Math. Mon.*, 80, no. 3 (March 1973), 233–269.

DeBa75   DE BAKKER, J. W., and L. G. L. T. MEERTENS, "On the Completeness of the Inductive Assertion Method," *J. Comput. Syst. Sci.*, 11, no. 3 (December 1975), 323–357.

DeMi77   DE MILLO, RICHARD A., RICHARD J. LIPTON, and ALAN J. PERLIS, "Social Processes and Proofs of Theorems and Programs," *Conf. Rec. 4th ACM Symp. on Principles of Programming Languages*, Los Angeles, CA (January 1977), pp. 206–214.

DeRe74   DE REMER, F. L., "Transformational Grammars," in *Compiler Construction: An Advanced Course*, Lecture Notes in Computer Science 21, eds. F. L. Bauer and J. Eickel. New York: Springer-Verlag, 1974, pp. 121–145.

Dewa77   DEWAR, ROBERT B. K., A. GRAND, S. C. LIU, E. SCHONBERG, and J. T. SCHWARTZ, "Programming by Refinement as Exemplified by the SETL Representation Sublanguage," draft, Department of Computer Science, New York University, 1977.

Dijk76   DIJKSTRA, EDSGER W., *A Discipline of Programming*. Englewood Cliffs, NJ: Prentice-Hall, 1976.

Donz78a   DONZEAU-GOUGE, VERONIQUE, GILLES KAHN, and BERNARD LANG, "A Complete Machine-checked Definition of a Simple Programming Language Using Denotational Semantics," Research Report No. 330 (1978), IRIA Laboria, Rocquencourt, France.

Donz78b   DONZEAU-GOUGE, VERONIQUE, "Utilisation de la Sémantique Dénotationnelle pour la Description d'Interprétations Non-standard: Application à la Validation et à l'Optimisation des Programmes," 3rd *Int. Symp. on Programming*, Dunod, Paris (1978).

Earl74   EARLEY, J., "High Level Iterators and a Method of Automatically Designing Data Structure Representation," Research Report ERL-M416 (February 1974), Computer Science Division, University of California, Berkeley.

Earn72   EARNEST, C., K. BALKE, and J. ANDERSON, "Analysis of Graphs by Ordering of Nodes," *J. ACM*, 19, no. 1 (January 1972), 23–42.

Earn74   EARNEST, C., "Some Topics in Code Optimization," *J. ACM*, 21, no. 1 (January 1974), 76–102.

Elsp72   ELSPAS, B., K. N. LEVITT, R. J. WALDINGER, and A. WAKSMAN, "An Assessment of Techniques for Proving Program Correctness," *ACM Comput. Surv.*, 4, no. 2 (June 1972), 97–147.

Elsp??   ELSPAS, B., M. GREEN, A. KORSAK, and P. WONG, "Solving Non Linear Inequalities Associated with Computer Program Paths," preliminary draft, Stanford Research Institute, Menlo Park, CA.

Enge75   ENGELFRIET, JOOST, "Tree Automata and Tree Grammars," DAIMI Report FN-10 (April 1975), Department of Computer Science, University of Aarhus, Denmark.

Fair75   FAIRLEY, RICHARD E., "An Experimental Program Testing Facility," *Proc. 1st Nat. Conf. on Software Engineering* (1975), pp. 47–55.

Farr75   FARROW, R., K. KENNEDY, and L. ZUCCONI, "Graph Grammars and Global Program Flow Analysis," *Proc. 17th Ann. IEEE Symp. on Foundations of Computer Science*, Houston, TX (November 1975).

Floy67   FLOYD, R. W., "Assigning Meanings to Programs," *Proc. Symp. in Applied Mathematics of the AMS*, ed. J. T. Schwartz, Providence, RI (1967), 19–32.

Fong75   FONG, AMELIA C., J. KAM, and JEFFREY D. ULLMAN, "Application of Lattice Algebra to Loop Optimization," *Conf. Rec. 2nd ACM Symp. on Principles of Programming Languages*, Palo Alto, CA (January 1975), pp. 1–9.

Fong76   FONG, AMELIA C., and JEFFREY D. ULLMAN, "Induction Variables in Very High Level Languages," *Conf. Rec. 3rd ACM Symp. on Principles of Programming Languages*, Atlanta, GA (January 1976), pp. 104–112.

Fong77   FONG, AMELIA C., "Generalized Common Subexpressions in Very High Level Languages," *Conf. Rec. 4th ACM Symp. on Principles of Programming Languages*, Los Angeles, CA (January 1977), pp. 48–57.

Fosd76   FOSDICK, L. D., and L. J. OSTERWEIL, "Data Flow Analysis in Software Reliability," *Comput. Surv.*, 8, no. 3 (September 1976), 305–330.

Gabo76   GABOW, H. N., S. N. MAHESHWARI, and L. J. OSTERWEIL, "On Two Problems in the Generation of Program Test Paths," *IEEE Trans. Software Eng.*, SE-2, no. 3 (September 1976), 227–231.

Gall78   GALLIER, J. H., "Semantics and Correctness of Nondeterministic Flowchart Programs with Recursive Procedures," *5th Int. Colloquium on Automata, Languages & Programming*, Udine, Italy (1978).

Ganz74   GANZINGER, HARALD, "Modifizierte Attributierte Grammatiken," Report No. 7420 (1974), Abt. Mathematik, Technische Universität München.

Ganz76   ——, "MUGl-Manual," Report No. 7608 (1976), Institut für Informatik, Technische Universität München.

Ganz77   GANZINGER, HARALD, KNUT RIPKEN, and REINHARD WILHELM, "Automatic Generation of Optimizing Multipass Compilers," *Information Processing 77*, Proc. IFIP Congress 77, Toronto (August 1977), ed. B. Gilchrist, pp. 535–540. New York: North-Holland, 1977.

Germ78   GERMAN, S., "Automating Proofs of the Absence of Common Runtime Errors," *Conf. Rec. 5th ACM Symp. on Principles of Programming Languages*, Tucson, AZ (January 1978), pp. 105–118.

Gieg78   GIEGERICH, R., and R. WILHELM, "Attribute Evaluation," *in State of the Art and Future Trends in Compilation*. Rocquencourt, France: IRIA, 1978.

Gieg79   GIEGERICH, R., "Introduction to the Compiler Generating System MUG2," Technical Report (1979), Institüt für Informatik, Technische Universität München.

Gill77   GILLETT, W. D., "Iterative Global Flow Techniques for Detecting Program Anomalies," Ph.D. thesis UIUCDCS-R-77-868, (January 1977), University of Illinois at Urbana-Champaign.

Gins66   GINSBURG, SEYMOUR, *The Mathematical Theory of Context-Free Languages*. New York: McGraw-Hill, 1966.

Gold72   GOLDSTINE, HERMAN HEINE, *The Computer from Pascal to Von Neumann*. Princeton, NJ: Princeton University Press, 1972.

Goto74   GOTO, EIICHI, *Monocopy & Associative Algorithms in an Extended LISP.*
              Tokyo, Japan: University of Tokyo, May 1974.

Grah76   GRAHAM, S. L., and M. WEGMAN, "A Fast and Usually Linear Algorithm
              for Global Flow Analysis," *J. ACM*, 23, no. 1 (January 1976), 172–202.

Grei75   GREIBACH, SHEILA A., *Theory of Program Structures: Schemes, Semantics,
              Verification*, Lecture Notes in Computer Science 36. New York: Springer-
              Verlag, 1975.

Gris70   GRISHMAN, R., "The Debugging System AIDS," in *AFIPS 1970 Spring
              Joint Computer Conference*, Atlantic City, NJ, AFIPS Conf. Proceedings
              36, pp. 59–64. Montvale, NJ: AFIPS Press, 1970.

Hant76   HANTLER, S. L., and J. C. KING, "An Introduction to Proving the Correct-
              ness of Programs," *Comp. Surv.*, 8, no. 3 (September 1976), 331–353.

Hare76   HAREL, DAVID, AMIR PNUELI, and J. STAVE, "Completeness Issues for
              Inductive Assertions and Hoare's Method," Computer Science Technical
              Report (1976), Tel Aviv University.

Harr77a   HARRISON, WILLIAM H., "Compiler Analysis of the Value Ranges for
              Variables," *IEEE Trans. Software Eng.*, SE-3, no. 3 (May 1977), 243–250.

Harr77b   ——, "A New Strategy for Code Generation—The General Purpose
              Optimizing Compiler," *Conf. Rec. 4th ACM Symp. on Principles of Pro-
              gramming Languages*, Los Angeles, CA (January 1977), pp. 29–37.

Hart71   HARTMANIS, J., and J. E. HOPCROFT, "An Overview of the Theory of Com-
              putational Complexity," *ACM*, 18, no. 3 (July 1971), 444–475.

Hech72   HECHT, MATTHEW S., and J. D. ULLMAN, "Flow Graph Reducibility,"
              SIAM J. Comput., 1, no. 2 (June 1972), 188–202.

Hech74   ——, "Characterizations of Reducible Flow Graphs," *J. ACM*, 21, no. 3
              (July 1974), 367–375.

Hech75   ——, "A Simple Algorithm for Global Data Flow Analysis Problems,"
              SIAM J. Comput., 4, no. 4 (December 1975), 519–532.

Hech77   HECHT, MATTHEW S., *Flow Analysis of Computer Programs*. New York:
              Elsevier North-Holland, 1977.

Hewi75   HEWITT, C., and B. SMITH, "Towards a Programming Apprentice," *Proc.
              of IEEE Trans. Software Eng.*, SE-1, no. 1 (March 1975), 26–45.

Hoar69   HOARE, C. A. R., "An Axiomatic Basis for Computer Programming,"
              Commun. ACM, 12, no. 10 (October 1969), 576–583.

Hoar77   ——, "Recursive Data Structures," *Int. J. Comput. Inf. Sci.*, 4, no. 2
              (June 1975), 105–132.

Holl78   HOLLEY, HOWARD, personal communication, November 1978.

Howd75   HOWDEN, WILLIAM E., "Methodology for the Generation of Program Test
              Data," *IEEE Trans. Comput.* (May 1975), pp. 554–559.

Howd76   ——, "Reliability of the Path Analysis Testing Strategy," *IEEE Trans.
              Software Eng.*, SE-2, no. 3 (September 1976), 208–215.

Howd77a   ——, "Symbolic Evaluation—Design Techniques, Cost and Effectiveness,"
              National Technical Inf. Service PB268517 (1977).

Howd77b   ——, "Symbolic Testing and the DISSECT Symbolic Evaluation System"
              IEEE Trans. Software Eng., SE-3, no. 4 (July 1977), 266–278.

Howd78   ———, "DISSECT—A Symbolic Evaluation and Program Testing System," *IEEE Trans. Software Eng.*, SE-4, no. 1 (January 1978), 70–73.

Huan75   HUANG, J. C., "An Approach to Program Testing," *ACM Comput. Surv.*, 7, no. 3 (September 1975), 113–128.

Huet77   HUET, G., "Confluent Reductions: Abstract Properties and Applications to Term Rewriting Systems," *Proc. 18th Ann. IEEE Symp. on Foundations of Computer Science*, Providence, RI (October 1977), pp. 30–45.

Jaza75a   JAZAYERI, MEHDI, W. F. OGDEN, and W. C. ROUNDS, "The Intrinsically Exponential Complexity of the Circularity Problem for Attribute Grammars," *Commun. ACM*, 18, no. 12 (December 1975), 697–706.

Jaza75b   JAZAYERI, MEHDI, "Live Variable Analysis, Attribute Grammars, and Program Optimization," draft (March 1975), Department of Computer Science, University of North Carolina, Chapel Hill, NC.

Jone76   JONES, NEIL D., and STEVEN S. MUCHNICK, "Binding Time Optimization in Programming Languages: Some Thoughts Toward the Design of an Ideal Language," *Conf. Rec. 3rd ACM Symp. on Principles of Programming Languages*, Altanta, GA (January 1976), pp. 77–94.

Jone81   JONES, NEIL D., and STEVEN MUCHNICK, "Flow Analysis and Optimization of LISP-like Structures," this volume, chap. 4.

Kam76   KAM, J. B., and JEFFREY D. ULLMAN, "Global Data Flow Analysis and Iterative Algorithms," *J. ACM*, 23, no. 1 (January 1976), 158–171.

Kam77   ———, "Monotone Data Flow Analysis Frameworks," *Acta Inf.*, 7, fasc. 3 (1977), 305–317.

Kapl78a   KAPLAN, M. A., and JEFFREY D. ULLMAN, "A General Scheme for the Automatic Inference of Variable Types," *Conf. Rec. 5th ACM Symp. on Principles of Programming Languages*, Tucson, AZ (January 1978), pp. 60–75.

Kapl78b   KAPLAN, M. A., "Relational Data Flow Analysis," TR-243 (April 1978), Department of Electrical Engineering and Computer Science, Princeton University.

Karr76   KARR, M., "Affine Relationships Among Variables of a Program," *Acta Inf.*, 6, fasc. 2 (April 1976), 133–151.

Kell76   KELLER, R. M., "Formal Verification of Parallel Programs," *Commun. ACM*, 19, no. 7 (July 1976), 371–384.

Kenn71a   KENNEDY, KENNETH W., "A Global Flow Analysis Algorithm," *Int. J. of Comput. Math.*, sec. A, vol. 3 (December 1971), 5–15.

Kenn71b   KENNEDY, KENNETH W., and P. OWENS, "An Algorithm for Use-Definition Chaining," *SETL Newsletter 37* (October 1971), Courant Institute of Mathematical Sciences, New York University.

Kenn73a   KENNEDY, KENNETH W., "Global Dead Computation Elimination," *SETL Newsletter 111* (August 1973), Courant Institute of Mathematical Sciences, New York University.

Kenn73b   ———, "Variable Subsumption with Constant Folding," *SETL Newsletter 112* (August 1973), Courant Institute of Mathematical Sciences, New York University.

Kenn74   ———, "An Algorithm to Compute Compacted Use-Definition Chains," *SETL Newsletter 122* (February 1974), Courant Institute of Mathematical Sciences, New York University.

Kenn75a   KENNEDY, KENNETH W., and J. T. SCHWARTZ, "An Introduction to the Set
           Theoretic Language SETL," *Comput. Math. Appl.*, 1, no. 1 (1975), 97–119.

Kenn75b   KENNEDY, KENNETH W., "Node Listing Applied to Data Flow Analysis,"
           Conf. Rec. 2nd ACM Symp. on Principles of Programming Languages,
           Palo Alto, CA (January 1975), pp. 10–21.

Kenn75c   ——, "Use-definition Chains with Applications," Technical Report 476-
           093-9 (April 1975), Department of Mathematical Sciences, Rice University,
           Houston, TX.

Kenn76   ——, "A Comparison of Two Algorithms for Global Data Flow Analysis,"
           SIAM J. Comput., 5, no. 1 (March 1976), 158–180.

Kenn77   KENNEDY, KENNETH W., and LINDA ZUCCONI, "Applications of a Graph
           Grammar for Program Control Flow Analysis," *Conf. Rec. 4th ACM
           Symp. on Principles of Programming Languages*, Los Angeles, CA (January
           1977), pp. 72–85.

Kenn78   ——, "Basic Block Optimization in MODEL," Draft Report (1978), Los
           Alamos Scientific Laboratory, Los Alamos, NM.

Kenn81   KENNEDY, KENNETH W., "A Survey of Compiler Optimization," this volume,
           chap. 1.

Kild73   KILDALL, G. A., "A Unified Approach to Global Program Optimization,"
           Conf. Rec. ACM Symp. on Principles of Programming Languages, Boston,
           MA (October 1973), pp. 194–206.

King69   KING, J., "A Program Verifier," Ph.D. thesis, Department of Computer
           Science, Carnegie-Mellon University, Pittsburgh, PA, 1969.

King76   KING, J., "Symbolic Execution and Program Testing," *Commun. ACM*, 19,
           no. 7 (July 1976), 385–394.

Klee52   KLEENE, STEPHEN COLE, *Introduction to Metamathematics.* New York:
           D. Van Nostrand, 1952.

Knut68   KNUTH, DONALD E., "Semantics of Context-free Languages," *Mathematical
           Syst. Theory*, 2, no. 2 (June 1968), 127–145.

Knut71   ——, "An Empirical Study of FORTRAN Programs," *Software Pract.
           Exper.*, 1, no. 2 (April–June 1971), 105–133.

Knut74   ——, "Structured Programming with 'GO TO' Statements," *Comput.
           Surv.*, 6, no. 4 (December 1974), 261–302.

Ladn75   LADNER, RICHARD E., "The Circuit Value Problem is Log Space Complete
           for P," *SIGACT News*, 7, no. 1 (January 1975), 18–20.

Land73   LAND, A. H., and S. POWELL, *FORTRAN Codes for Mathematical Pro-
           gramming.* New York: Wiley, 1973.

Ledg72   LEDGARD, HENRY F., "A Model for Type Checking—with an Application to
           ALGOL 60," *Commun. ACM*, 15, no. 11 (November 1972), 956–966.

Lisk77   LISKOV, B. H., A. SNYDER, R. ATKINSON, and C. SCHAFFERT, "Abstraction
           Mechanisms in CLU," *Commun. ACM*, 20, no. 8 (August 1977), 564–576.

Lome75   LOMET, D. B., "Data Flow Analysis in the Presence of Procedure Calls,"
           IBM Research Report RC-5728 (1975), T. J. Watson Research Center,
           Yorktown Heights, NY.

Lond75   LONDON, R. L., "A View of Program Verification," *1975 Int. Conf. on
           Reliable Software*, Los Angeles, CA (April 1975), pp. 534–545.

Love77   LOVEMAN, D. B., "Program Improvement by Source-to-Source Transformation," *J. ACM*, 24, no. 1 (January 1977), 121–145.

Lowr69   LOWRY, E. S., and C. W. MEDLOCK, "Object Code Optimization," *Commun. ACM*, 12, no. 1 (January 1969), 13–22.

Mann74   MANNA, ZOHAR, *Mathematical Theory of Computation*, New York: McGraw-Hill, 1974.

Mark75   MARKOWSKY, G., and R. E. TARJAN, "Lower Bounds on the Lengths of Node Sequences in Directed Graphs," IBM Research Report RC-5477 (July 1975), Thomas J. Watson Research Center, Yorktown Heights, NY.

Meye73   MEYER, ALBERT, and L. J. STOCKMEYER, "Word Problems Requiring Exponential Time," *Conf. Rec. 5th Annual ACM Symp. on Theory of Computing*, Austin, TX (April–May 1973), pp. 1–9.

Mill74   MILLER, E. F., JR., "RXVP, Fortran Automated Verification System," Program Validation Project (October 1974), General Research Corp., Santa Barbara, CA.

Mill75   MILLER, E. F., JR., and R. A. MELTON, "Automated Generation of Test Case Datasets," *Proc. Int. Conf. Reliable Software*, Los Angeles, CA (April 1975), pp. 51–58.

Miln76   MILNE, ROBERT, and CHRISTOPHER STRACHEY, *A Theory of Programming Language Semantics*. London: Chapman and Hall, 1976.

Mira77   MIRANKER, W. L., "Parallel Methods for Solving Equations," IBM Research Report RC-654 (May 1977), Mathematical Sciences Department, T. J. Watson Research Center, Yorktown Heights, NY.

More74   MOREL, ETIENNE, and CLAUDE RENVOISE, "Design and Implementation of a Global Optimizer," thesis, Université de Paris VI, June 1974.

More79   ——, "Global Optimization by Suppression of Partial Redundancies," *Commun. ACM*, 22, no. 2 (February 1979), 96–103.

Moss74   MOSSES, P. D., "The Mathematical Semantics of ALGOL 60," Technical Monograph PRG-12 (January 1974), Programming Research Group, Oxford University Computing Laboratory.

Moss78   ——, "SIS: A Compiler-generator System Using Denotational Semantics," DIAMI (1978), University of Aarhus, Aarhus, Denmark.

Naur65   NAUR, P., "Checking of Operand Types in ALGOL Compilers," *BIT*, 5 (1965), 151–163.

Naur66   ——, "Proof of Algorithms by Generalized Snapshots," *BIT*, 6 (1966), 310–316.

Neel75   NEEL, D., and M. AMIRCHAHY, "Removal of Invariant Statements from Nested-Loops in a Single Effective Compiler Pass," *SIGPLAN Notices*, 10, no. 3 (March 1975), 87–96.

Oste76   OSTERWEIL, L. J., and L. D. FOSDICK, "DAVE—A Validation, Error Detection and Documentation System for FORTRAN Programs," *Software Pract. Exper.*, 6, no. 4 (September 1976), 473–486.

Oste77   OSTERWEIL, L. J., "The Detection of Unexecutable Program Paths Through Static Data Flow Analysis," *Proceedings COMPSAC 77* (1977), pp. 406–413.

Oste81   ——, "Using Data Flow Tools in Software Engineering," this volume, chap. 8.

Paig77   PAIGE, BOB, and J. T. SCHWARTZ, "Expression Continuity and the Formal Differentiation of Algorithms," *Conf. Rec. 4th ACM Symp. on Principles of Programming Languages*, Los Angeles, CA (January 1977), pp. 58–71.

Park69   PARK, DAVID, "Fixpoint Induction and Proofs of Program Properties," in *Machine Intelligence 5*, ed. Bernard Meltzer and Donald Michie. New York: American Elsevier, 1969, pp. 59–78.

Parn74   PARNAS, D. L., "On the Criteria to be Used in Decomposing Systems into Modules," *Commun. ACM*, 15, no. 12 (December 1972), 1053–1058.

Pnue77   PNUELI, A., "The Temporal Logic of Programs," *Proc. 18th Ann. Symp. on Foundations of Computer Science*, Providence, RI (October–November 1977), pp. 46–57.

Rama75   RAMAMOORTHY, C. V., and S.-B. F. Ho, "Testing Large Software With Automated Software Evaluation Systems," *IEEE Trans. Software Eng.*, SE-1, no. 1 (March 1975), 46–58.

Rama76   RAMAMOORTHY, C. V., S.-B. F. Ho, and W. T. CHEN, "On Automated Generation of Program Test Data," *IEEE Trans. Software Eng.*, SE-2, no. 4 (December 1976), 293–300.

ReiD75   REIFER, D. J., "Automated Aids for Reliable Software," *Proc. 1975 Int. Conf. on Reliable Software*, Los Angeles, CA (April 1975), pp. 131–142.

ReiJ77   REIF, JOHN H., and HARRY R. LEWIS, "Symbolic Evaluation and the Global Value Graph," *Conf. Rec. 4th ACM Symp. on Principles of Programming Languages*, Los Angeles, CA (January 1977), pp. 104–118.

ReiJ78   REIF, JOHN H., "Symbolic Program Analysis in Almost Linear Time," *Conf. Rec. 5th ACM Symp. on Principles of Programming Languages*, Tucson, AZ (January 1978), pp. 76–83.

Reyn68   REYNOLDS, JOHN C., "Automatic Computation of Data Set Definitions," *Proc. of IFIP Congress 68* (August 1968), pp. B69–B73.

RicC76   RICH, CHARLES, and HOWARD E. SHROBE, *Initial Report on A LISP Programmer's Apprentice*, Technical Report AI-TR-354 (December 1976), Artificial Intelligence Laboratory, Massachusetts Institute of Technology.

RicD78a   RICHARDSON, D. J., "Theoretical Considerations in Testing Programs by Demonstrating Consistency with Specifications," Workshop on Software Testing and Test Documentation, Florida (December 1978), pp. 19–56.

RicD78b   RICHARDSON, D. J., L. A. CLARKE, and D. L. BENNETT, "SYMPLR, SYmbolic Multivariate Polynomial Linearization and Reduction," TR-78-16 (1978), Department of Computer and Information Science, University of Massachusetts.

Ripk75   RIPKEN, KNUT, "Generating an Intermediate-code Generator in a Compiler-Writing System," *4th Int. Comput. Symp.*, Antibes, France (June 1975), ed. E. Gelenbe and D. Potier, pp. 121–127. Amsterdam: North-Holland, 1975.

Rose73   ROSEN, BARRY K., "Tree-Manipulating Systems and Church-Rosser Theorems," *J. ACM*, 20, no. 1 (1973), 160–187.

Rose77a   ———, "Applications of High Level Control Flow," *Conf. Rec. 4th ACM Symp. on Principles of Programming Languages*, Los Angeles, CA (January 1977), pp. 38–47.

Rose77b   ———, "Arcs in Graphs Are Not Pairs of Nodes," *SIGACT News*, 9, no. 3 (Fall 1977), 25–27.

Rose77c   ———, "High Level Data Flow Analysis," *Commun. ACM*, 20, no. 10 (October 1977), 712–724.

Rose78a   ———, "Monoids for Rapid Data Flow Analysis," *Proc. 5th ACM Symp. on Principles of Programming Languages*, Tucson, AZ (January 1978), pp. 47–59.

Rose78b   ———, "Monoids for Rapid Data Flow Analysis," IBM Research Report RC-7032 (1978), Yorktown Heights. (For a condensation of an earlier version of this work see Rose78a.)

Rose79   ———, "Data Flow Analysis for Procedural Languages," *J. ACM*, 26, no. 2 (April 1979), 322–344.

Ross77   Ross, D. T., and K. E. Schoman, Jr., "Structured Analysis for Requirements Definition," *IEEE Trans. Software Eng.*, SE-3, no. 1 (January 1977), 6–15.

Scha73   Schaefer, Marvin, *A Mathematical Theory of Global Program Optimization*. Englewood Cliffs, NJ: Prentice-Hall, 1973.

Schn73   Schneck, P. B., and E. Angel, "A FORTRAN to FORTRAN optimising compiler," *Comput. J.*, 16, no. 4 (November 1973), 322–330.

Schn75   Schneck, P. B., "Movement of Implicit Parallel and Vector Expressions out of Program Loops," *SIGPLAN Notices*, 10, no. 3 (March 1975), 103–106.

Schw67   Schwartz, Jacob T., "Reduction in Strength (or Babbage's Difference Engine in Modern Dress)," IBM (1967), Menlo Park, CA.

Schw74a   ———, "Automatic and Semiautomatic Optimization of SETL," *SIGPLAN Notices*, 9, no. 4 (April 1974), 43–49.

Schw74b   ———, "On Earley's Method of Iterator Inversion," *SETL Newsletter 138* (1974), Courant Institute of Mathematical Sciences, New York University.

Schw75a   ———, "Automatic Data Structure Choice in a Language of Very High Level," *Commun. ACM*, 18, no. 12 (December 1975), 722–728.

Schw75b   ———, "Optimization of Very High Level Languages I: Value Transmission and its Corollaries," *J. Comput. Languages*, 1 (1975), 161–194.

Schw75c   ———, "Optimization of Very High Level Languages II: Deducing Relationships of Inclusion and Membership," *J. Comput. Languages*, 1 (1975), 197–218.

Schw75d   ———, *On Programming: An Interim Report on the SETL Project*, 2nd ed.. New York: Courant Institute of Mathematical Sciences, New York University, 1975.

Scot77   Scott, Dana, "Course Notes," Séminaire Avancé de Sémantique (September 1977), Sophia-Antipolis, France.

Seth70   Sethi, Ravi, and J. D. Ullman, "The Generation of Optimal Code for Arithmetic Expressions," *J. ACM*, 17, no. 4 (October 1970), 715–728.

Seth74   Sethi, Ravi, "Testing for the Church-Rosser Property," *J. ACM*, 21, no. 4 (October 1974), 671–679; "Errata," *J. ACM*, 22, no. 3 (July 1975), 424.

Shar77   Sharir, M., "Interprocedural Data Flow Analysis," *SETL Newsletter 187* (1977), Courant Institute of Mathematical Sciences, New York University.

Shar78a   ———, "A Few Cautionary Remarks on the Convergence of Iterative Data-Flow Analysis Algorithms," *SETL Newsletter 208* (1978), Courant Institute of Mathematical Sciences, New York University.

Shar78b   SHARIR, M., and A. PNEULI, "Two Approaches to Interprocedural Data Flow
            Analysis," Technical Report No. 002 (September 1978), Courant Institute
            of Mathematical Sciences, New York University.

Shar81   ———, "Two Approaches to Interprocedural Data Flow Analysis," this
            volume, chap. 7.

Sint72   SINTZOFF, M., "Calculating Properties of Programs by Valuations on
            Specific Models," *Proc. ACM Conf. on Proving Assertions about Programs*,
            New Mexico (1972), pp. 203–207.

Spil72   SPILLMAN, THOMAS C., "Exposing Side-Effects in a PL/I Optimizing Com-
            piler," *Information Processing 71*, Proc. IFIP Congress 71, Ljubljana,
            Yugoslavia (August 1971), ed. C. V. Freiman, 376–381. Amsterdam:
            North-Holland, 1972.

Stan76   STANDISH, T. A., et. al., "The Irvine Program Transformation Catalogue,"
            Department of Information and Computer Science, University of Cali-
            fornia at Irvine, January 1976.

Stee76   STEELE, GUY LEWIS, JR., "LAMBDA: The Ultimate *Declarative*," AI Memo
            379 (November 1976), Artificial Intelligence Laboratory, MIT.

Step78   STEPHENS, S. A., and L. L. TRIPP, "A Requirements Expression and Valida-
            tion Tool," *Proc. 3rd Int. Conf. on Software Engineering*, Atlanta (May 1978).

Stoc76   STOCKMEYER, L. J., "The Polynomial-Time Hierarchy," *Theor. Comput.
            Sci.*, 3, no. 1 (October 1976), 1–22.

Stoy77   STORY, JOSEPH E., *Denotational Semantics: The Scott-Strachey Approach to
            Programming Language Theory*. Cambridge, MA: MIT Press, 1977.

Stuc73   STUCKI L. G., "Automatic Generation of Self-Metric Software," *Rec. 1973
            IEEE Symp. Software Reliability*, pp. 94–100.

Stuc75   STUCKI, L. G., and G. L. FOSHEE, "New Assertion Concepts for Self-Metric
            Software Validation," *Proc. 1975 Int. Conf. Reliable Software*, Los Angeles,
            CA (April 1975), pp. 59–71.

Suzu77   SUZUKI, NORIHISA, and KIYOSHI ISHIHATA, "Implementation of Array Bound
            Checker," *Conf. Rec. of 4th ACM Symp. on Principles of Programming
            Languages*, Los Angeles, CA (January 1977), pp. 132–143.

Tarj75a   TARJAN, ROBERT ENDRE, "Applications of Path Compression on Balanced
            Trees," Technical Report STAN-75-512 (1975), Computer Science Depart-
            ment, Stanford University, Stanford, CA.

Tarj75b   ———, "Solving Path Problems on Directed Graphs," Technical Report
            STAN-CS-75-528 (November 1975), Computer Science Department,
            Stanford University, Stanford, CA.

Tarj76   ———, "Iterative Algorithms for Global Flow Analysis," in *Algorithms and
            Complexity, New Directions and Recent Results*, ed. J. F. Traub. New
            York: Academic Press, 1976, pp. 11–101.

Tars55   TARSKI, A., "A Lattice Theoretical Fixpoint Theorem and Its Applications,"
            Pac. J. Math., 5, no. 2 (June 1955), 285–309.

Tayl79   TAYLOR, R. N., and LEON J. OSTERWEIL, "Anomaly Detection in Concurrent
            Software by Static Data Flow Analysis," Technical Report #CU-CS-
            152-79 (April 1979), Univ. of Colorado at Boulder, Department of
            Computer Sciences.

Teic77   TEICHROEW, D., and E. A. HERSHEY III, "PSL/PSA: A Computer-Aided Technique for Structured Documentation and Analysis of Information Processing Systems," *IEEE Trans. Software Eng.*, SE-3, no. 1 (January 1977), 41–48.

Tene74a   TENENBAUM, AARON, "Automatic Type Analysis in a Very High Level Language," Ph.D. thesis, Computer Science Department, New York University, October 1974.

Tene74b   ———, "Type Determination for Very High Level Languages," Report NSO-3 (October 1974), Computer Science Department, New York University.

Tenn76   TENNENT, ROBERT D., "The Denotational Semantics of Programming Languages," *Commun. ACM*, 19, no. 8 (August 1976), 437–453.

Tenn77   ———, "A Denotational Definition of the Programming Language PASCAL," Technical Report 77–47, Department of Computing and Information Science, Queen's University, Kingston, Ontario, Canada, July 1977.

That73   THATCHER, JAMES W., "Tree Automata: An Informal Survey," in *Currents in the Theory of Computing*, ed. Alfred Aho. Englewood Cliffs, NJ: Prentice-Hall, 1973, pp. 143–172.

Town76   TOWNLEY, JUDY A., "The Harvard Program Manipulation System," Technical Report TR-23-76, Center for Research in Computing Technology, Harvard University.

Ullm73   ULLMAN, JEFFREY D., "Fast Algorithms for the Elimination of Common Subexpressions," *Acta Inf.*, 2, fasc. 3 (July 1973), 191–213.

Ullm75   ———, "A Survey of Data Flow Analysis Techniques," *Proc. 2nd USA-Japan Comp. Conf.*, Tokyo, Japan (August 1975).

Wegb75   WEGBREIT, BEN, "Property Extraction in Well-founded Property Sets," *IEEE Trans. Software Eng.*, SE-1, no. 3 (September 1975), 270–285.

Wegb77   ———, "Complexity of Synthesizing Inductive Assertions," *J. ACM*, 24, no. 3 (July 1977), 504–512.

Wels77   WELSH, J., "Economic Range Checking in PASCAL," Department of Computer Science, Queen's University, Belfast, Northern Ireland, October 1977.

Whit78   WHITE, L. J., and E. I. COHEN, "A Domain Strategy for Computer Program Testing," Workshop on Software Testing and Test Documentation, Florida (December 1978), pp. 335–354.

Wilh74   WILHELM, REINHARD, "Codeoptimierung Mittels Attributierter Transformations-grammatiken," in *Lecture Notes in Computer Science 26*. New York: Springer-Verlag, 1974, pp. 257–266.

Wilh76   WILHELM, R., K. RIPKEN, J. CIESINGER, H. GANZINGER, W. LAHNER, and R. D. NOLLMANN, "Design Evaluation of the Compiler Generating System MUG1" *Proc. 2nd Int. Conf. on Software Engineering*, San Francisco (October 1976), pp. 571–576.

Wood79   WOODS, J. L., "Path Selection for Symbolic Execution Systems," Ph.D. thesis, University of Massachusetts, August 1979.

Wulf71   WULF, W. A., D. B. RUSSELL, and A. N. HABERMANN, "BLISS: A Language for Systems Programming," *Commun. ACM*, 14, no. 12 (December 1971), 780–790.

Wulf75   WULF, W., R. K. JOHNSON, C. B. WEINSTOCK, S. O. HOBBS, and C. M. GESCHKE, *The Design of an Optimizing Compiler*. New York: Elsevier North-Holland, 1975.

Subject Index

Name Index